MODESTY Blaise
YELLOWSTONE BOOTY

Also featuring IDAHO GEORGE
and THE GOLDEN FROG

PETER O'DONNELL
ENRIC BADIA ROMERO
JOHN BURNS

TITAN ✦ BOOKS

Modesty Blaise: Yellowstone Booty

ISBN-10: 1 84576 419 6
ISBN-13: 9781845764197

Published by Titan Books,
a division of Titan Publishing Group Ltd.
144 Southwark St
London SE1 0UP

A CIP catalogue record for this title is available from the British Library.

This edition first published: May 2008
10 9 8 7 6 5 4 3 2 1

Printed in Italy.

Also available from Titan Books:
Modesty Blaise: The Gabriel Set-Up (ISBN-13: 9781840236583)
Modesty Blaise: Mister Sun (ISBN-13: 9781840237214)
Modesty Blaise: Top Traitor (ISBN-13: 9781840236842)
Modesty Blaise: The Black Pearl (ISBN-13: 9781840238426)
Modesty Blaise: Bad Suki (ISBN-13: 9781840238648)
Modesty Blaise: The Hell-Makers (ISBN-13: 9781840238655)
Modesty Blaise: The Green-Eyed Monster (ISBN-13: 9781840238662)
Modesty Blaise: The Puppet Master (ISBN-13: 9781840238679)
Modesty Blaise: The Gallows Bird (ISBN-13: 9781840238686)
Modesty Blaise: Cry Wolf (ISBN-13: 9781840238693)
Modesty Blaise: The Inca Trail (ISBN-13: 9781845764173)
Modesty Blaise: Death Trap (ISBN-13: 9781845764180)

Grateful thanks to Peter O'Donnell, Lawrence Blackmore, William Gardiner and Geoff Malyon for their help and support in the production of this book.

'The Art of John Burns' © Lawrence Blackmore 2008.

What did you think of this book? We love to hear from our readers. Please email us at: readerfeedback@titanemail.com, or write to us at the above address.

To receive advance information, news, competitions and exclusive Titan offers online, please register as a member by clicking the "sign up" button on our website: **www.titanbooks.com**

Much of the comic strip material used by Titan in this edition is exceedingly rare. As such, we hope that readers appreciate that the quality of the materials can be variable.

THE ART OF JOHN BURNS

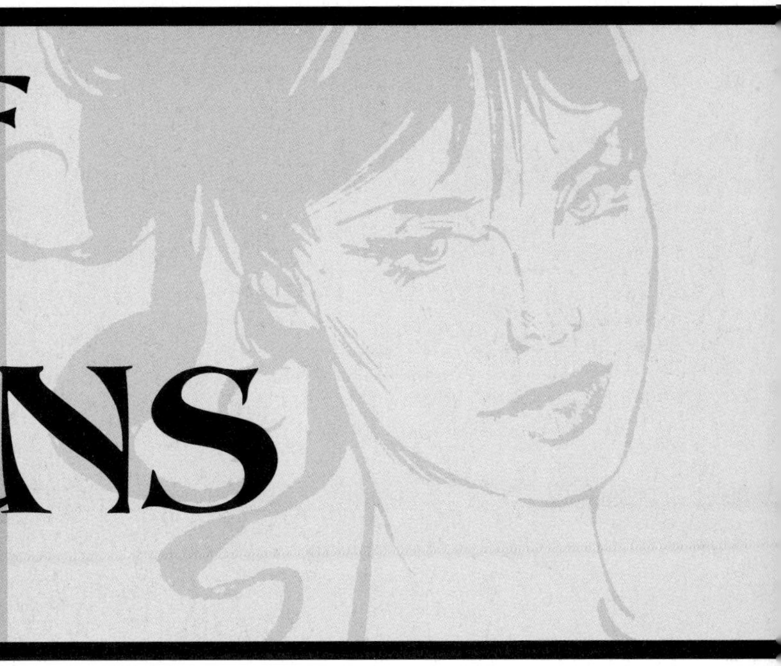

By Lawrence Blackmore

Of over ten-thousand *Modesty Blaise* strips that were drawn by her five artists, John Burns illustrated only 272. Nevertheless his visual impact and influence on the perception of Modesty following her syndication must be considered alongside her visual creator, Jim Holdaway and the most prolific of her artists, Enric Badia Romero.

Burns had illustrated Peter O'Donnell's first novel, 'Modesty Blaise' for the Viaduct Publications Bestsellers series in 1983 and when Titan Books decided to launch *Modesty* in its Great British Newspaper Strips series in 1985, it was to Burns they turned for the covers. Modesty and Willie had been seen before in colour on the covers of the novels published by Souvenir Press, but only three of these had been drawn by Jim Holdaway. For the covers of the Titan editions Modesty and Willie were shown in a larger format, in a full colour action shot and with a new logo. Burns drew all eight of the covers and provided a visual continuity which set a standard others have been unable to match.

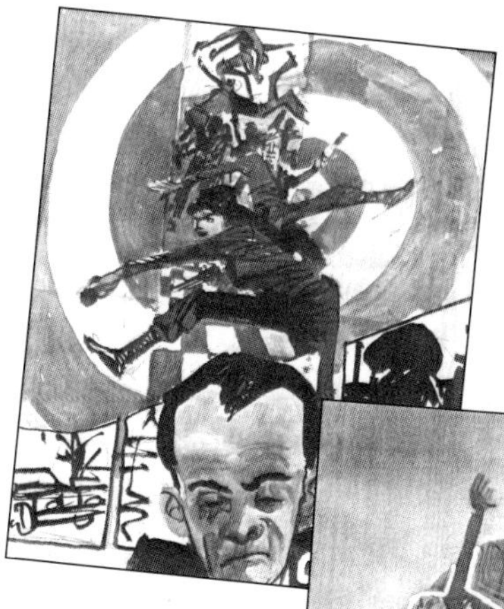

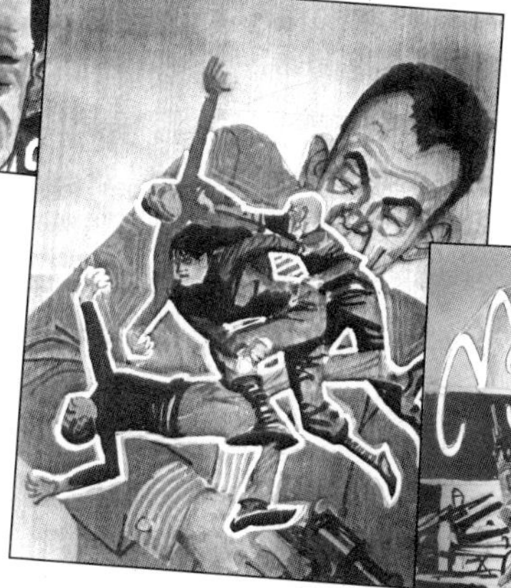

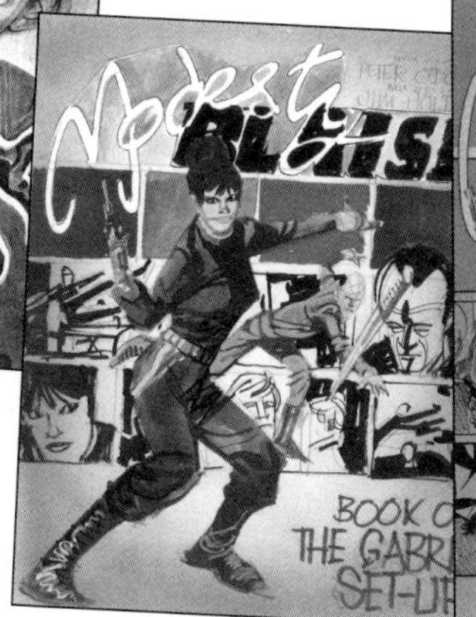

Modesty
BLAISE
BOOK ONE
THE GABRIEL SET-UP

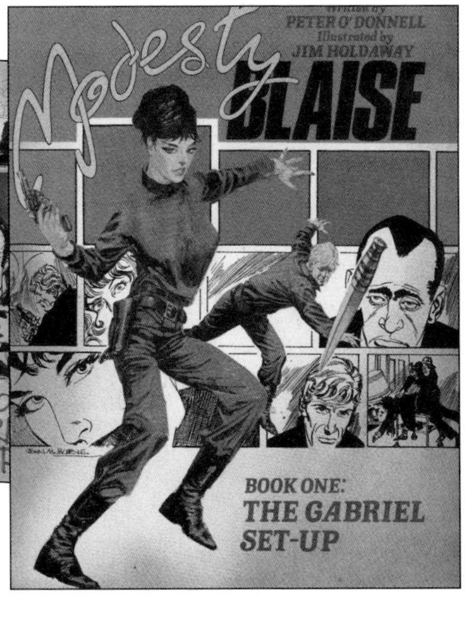

Written by
PETER O'DONNELL
Illustrated by
JIM HOLDAWAY
Modesty
BLAISE
BOOK ONE:
THE GABRIEL
SET-UP

Left: Three previously unseen preliminary paintings by Burns. These developed into the final cover used for Titan's very first *Modesty Blaise* book in 1985.

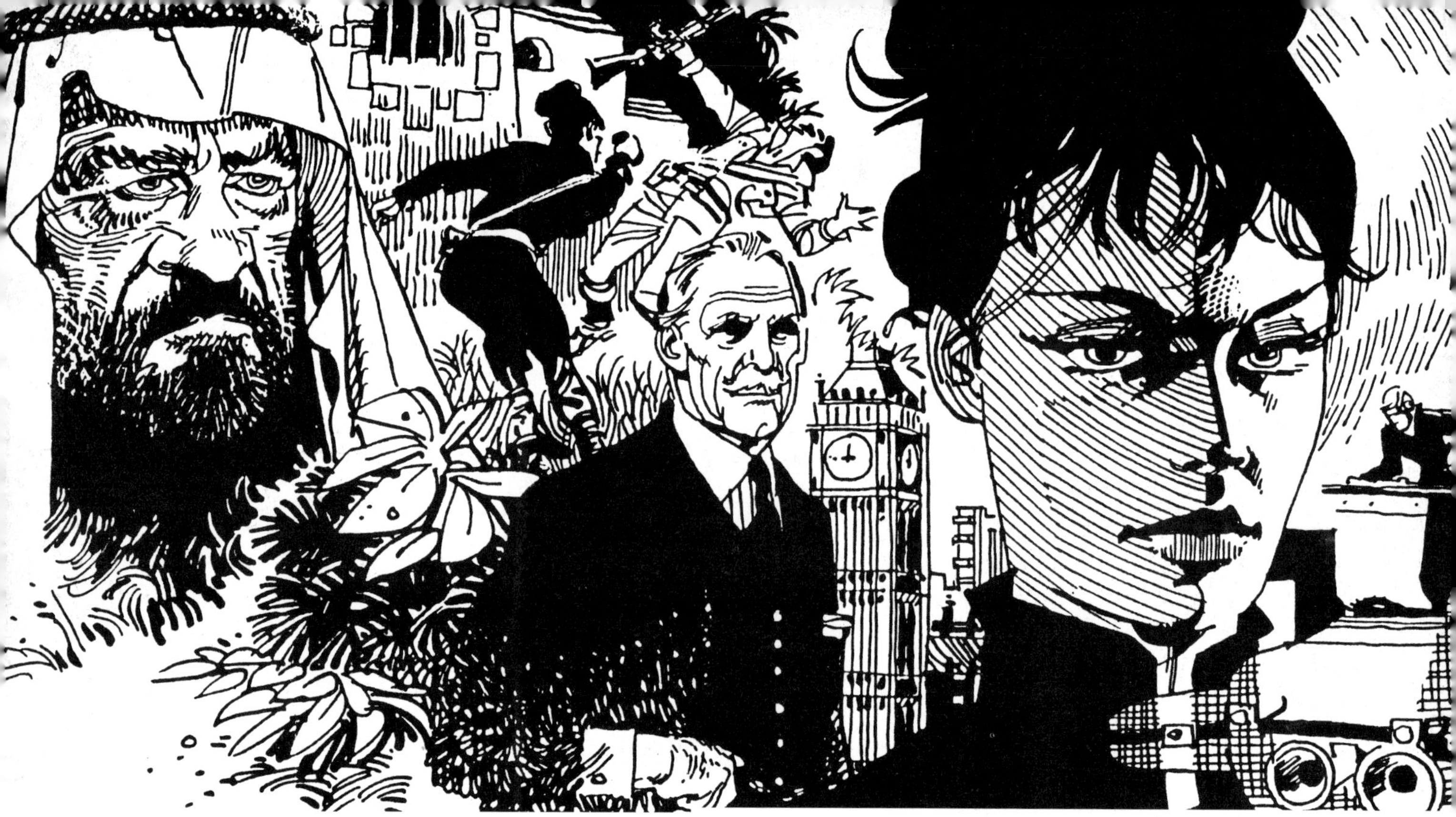

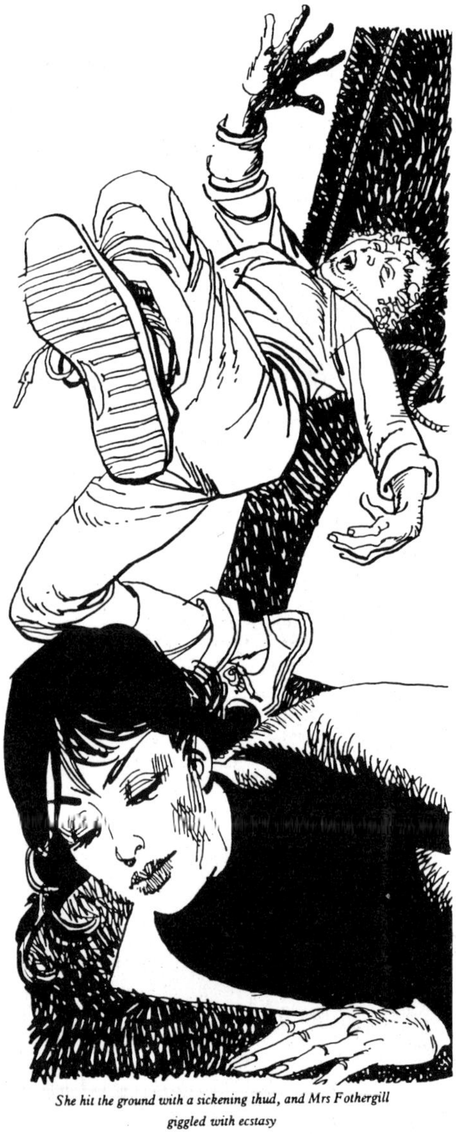

She hit the ground with a sickening thud, and Mrs Fothergill giggled with ecstasy

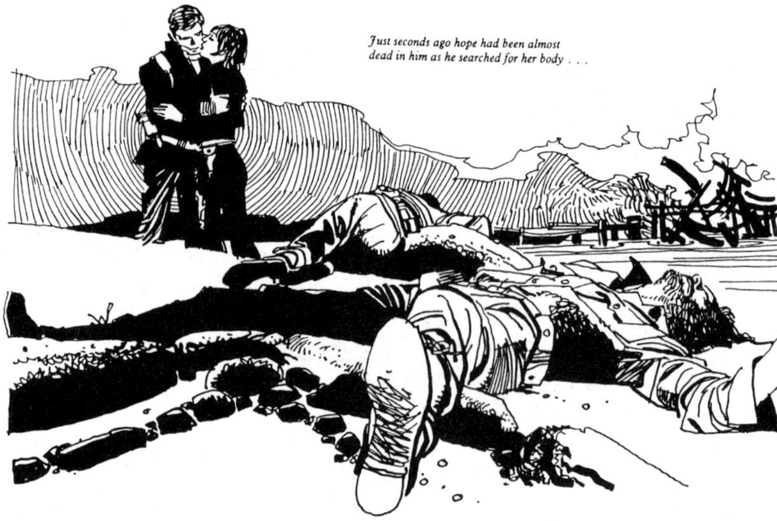

Just seconds ago hope had been almost dead in him as he searched for her body . . .

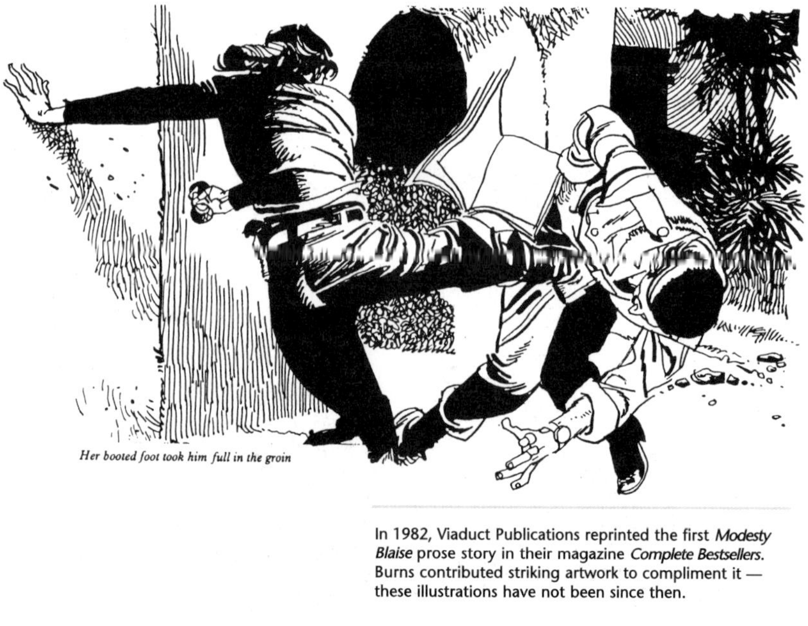

Her booted foot took him full in the groin

In 1982, Viaduct Publications reprinted the first *Modesty Blaise* prose story in their magazine *Complete Bestsellers*. Burns contributed striking artwork to compliment it — these illustrations have not been since then.

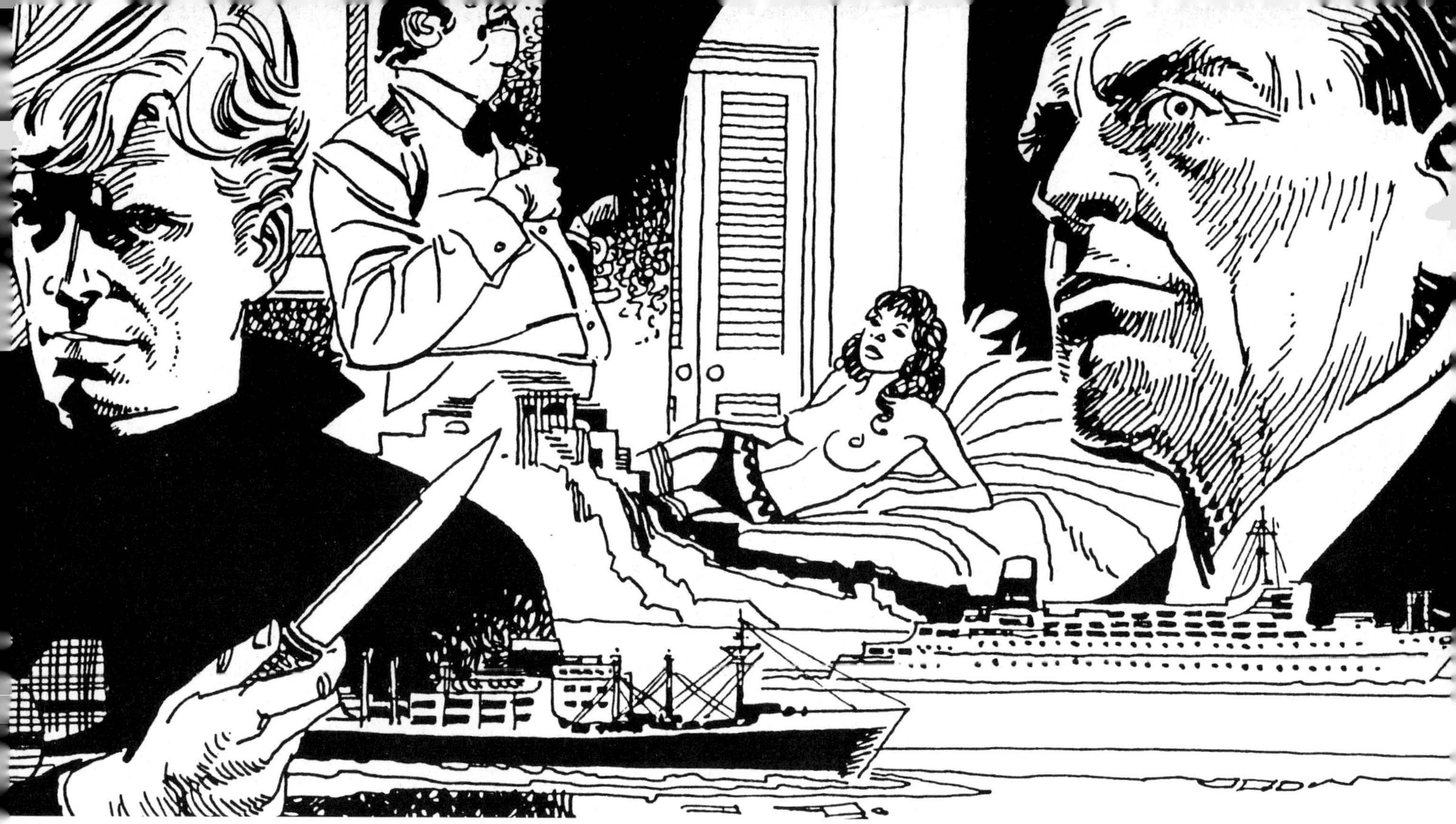

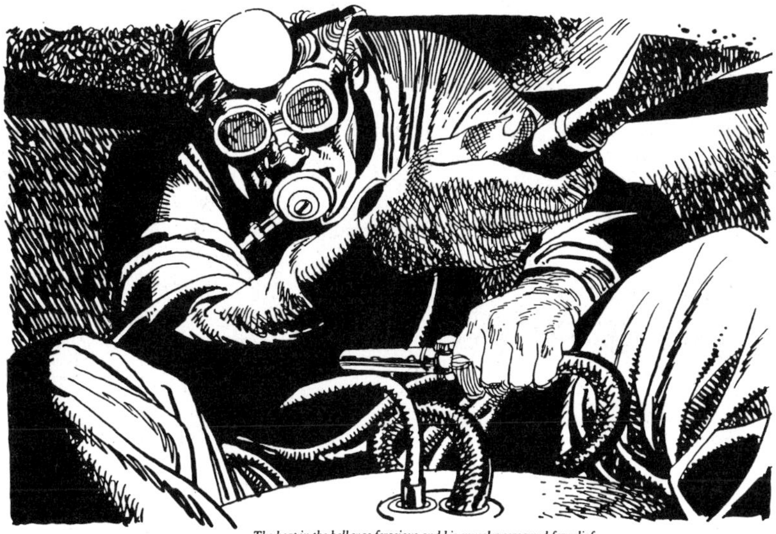

The heat in the bell was ferocious and his muscles screamed for relief

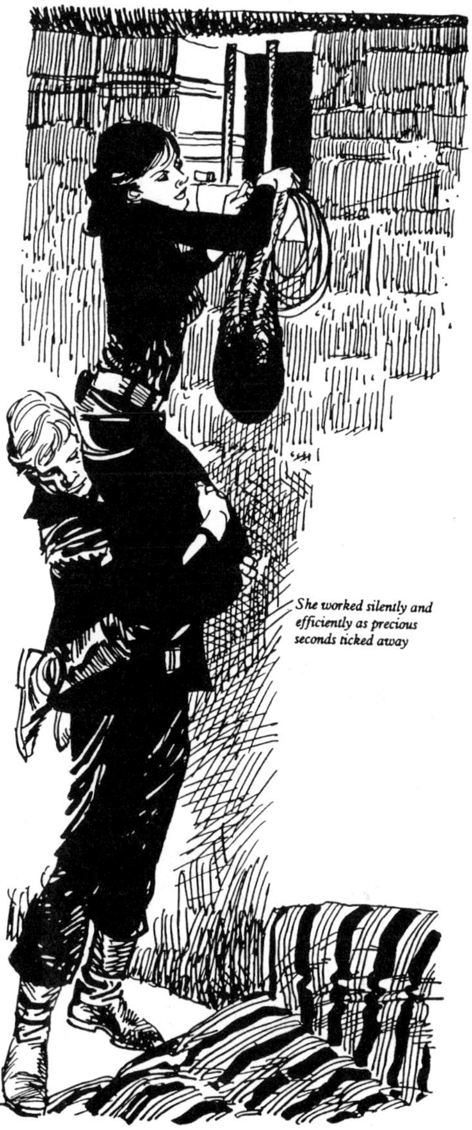

She worked silently and efficiently as precious seconds ticked away

The caper had begun, and to Willie she was no longer a woman

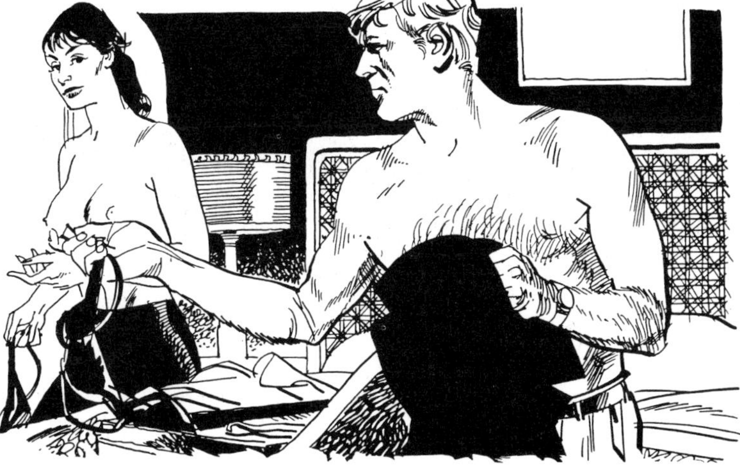

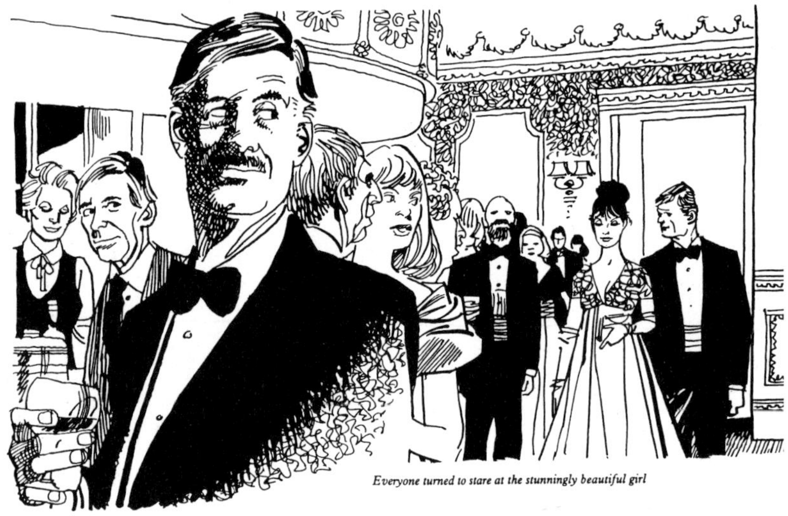

Everyone turned to stare at the stunningly beautiful girl

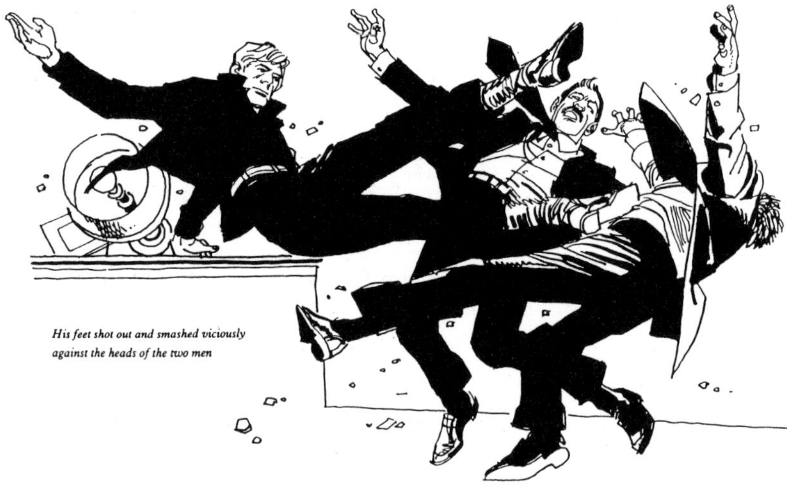

His feet shot out and smashed viciously against the heads of the two men

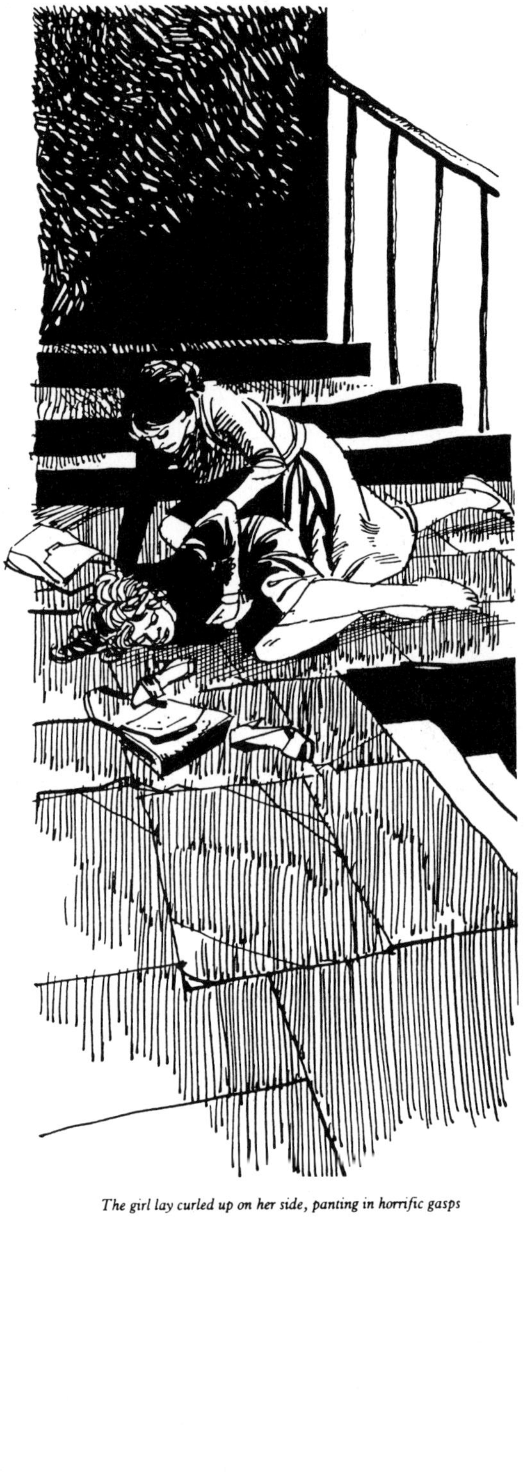

The girl lay curled up on her side, panting in horrific gasps

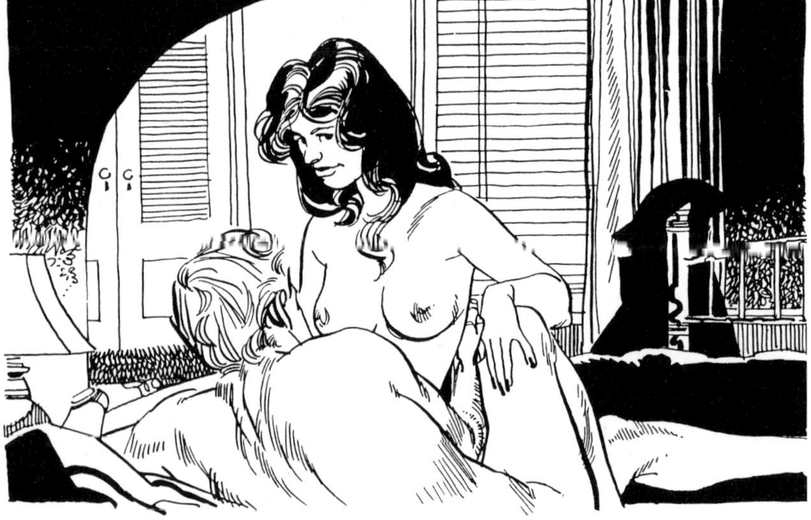

A shadow crossed her face. 'Believe me, Willie, he will do bad things against you.'

IDAHO GEORGE

When the editor asked me to write introductions for the three stories in this edition of *Modesty Blaise* I was surprised to find that one of the stories was called 'Idaho George'. Since I wrote close on a hundred of Modesty's capers in strip form I don't remember every plot, but the title usually triggers a vague memory. Not so with 'Idaho George'. It rang no bell for me and I found this baffling.

'Idaho George' — not much of a title, is it? Nothing intriguing about it. Nothing to make you eager to read on. The other two stories at least have a touch of colour in their titles, but this is just a name. Here's a character called Idaho — so what? So when I started to read the story I was happy to find Anastasia pictured in the early strips, for then I was reminded of how much I enjoyed creating her and members of her gang, like Big Nosey, Strangler (her butler), Meat-hook Charlie and the other specialists you'll meet on the way.

You'll also be meeting Idaho George himself when he performs a miracle on television. I still can't imagine why I used his name for the title — it's one of those silly memory failures that keep nagging at you but doesn't really matter. At least George is quite lively in the story, and Romero makes a great character of him as you'll see. I particularly like the close-up in strip #4403.

Life is full of coincidences so I wasn't greatly surprised when another miracle occurred. This one is performed by Modesty when she returns from the dead, much to the annoyance of the ungodly, who put her down in no uncertain manner. You'll perhaps find quite a bit of comedy in this story, but since it springs mainly from Anastasia and her henchmen, its pretty black humour. And no joke for Modesty.

Well, that's all for now (Thinks: I really must stop fretting about why I used his stupid name for the title!).

PETER O'DONNELL

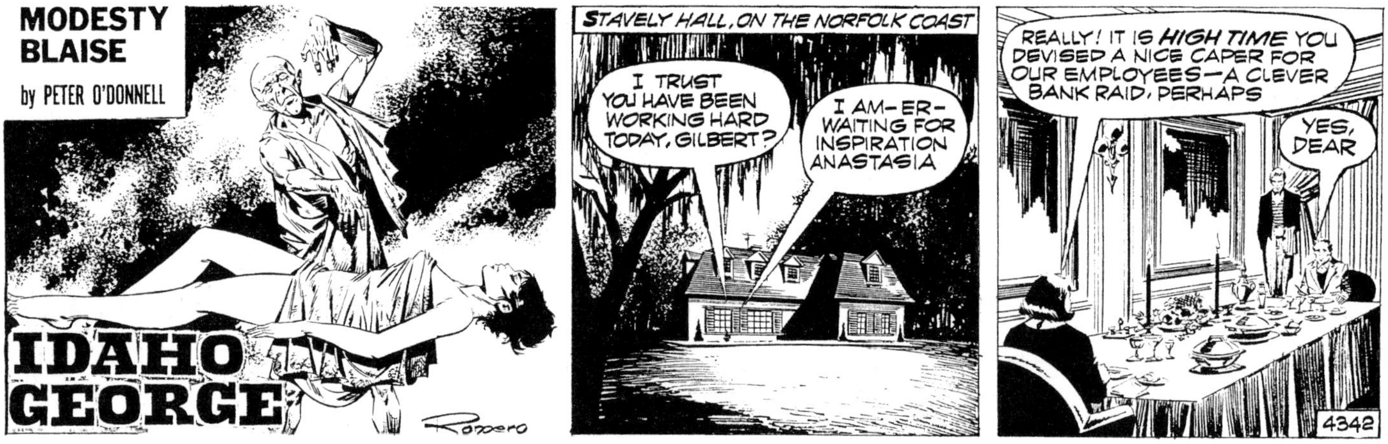
MODESTY BLAISE
by PETER O'DONNELL
IDAHO GEORGE
STAVELY HALL, ON THE NORFOLK COAST
I TRUST YOU HAVE BEEN WORKING HARD TODAY, GILBERT?
I AM—ER—WAITING FOR INSPIRATION ANASTASIA
REALLY! IT IS HIGH TIME YOU DEVISED A NICE CAPER FOR OUR EMPLOYEES—A CLEVER BANK RAID, PERHAPS
YES, DEAR
4342

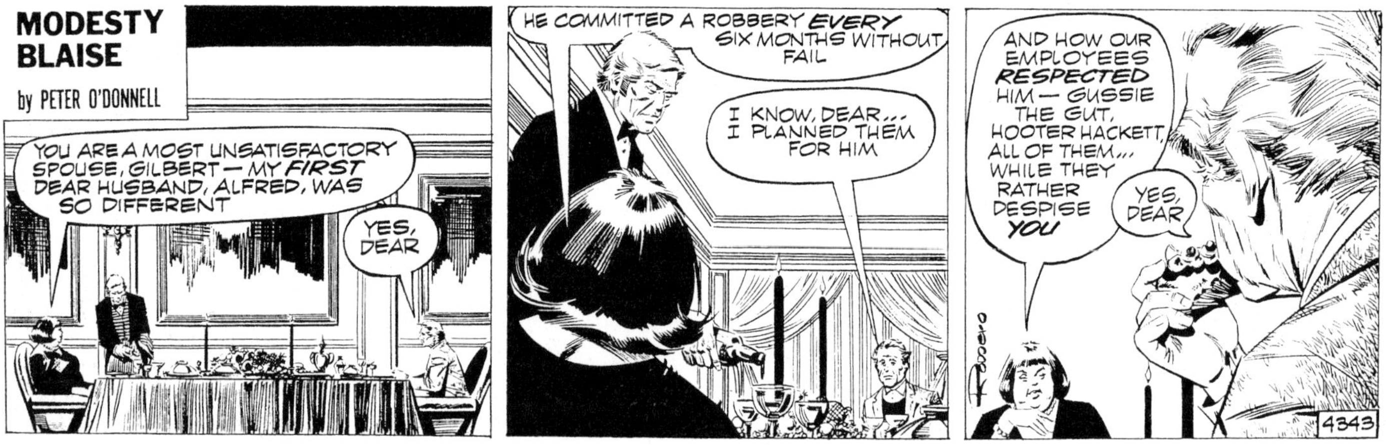
MODESTY BLAISE
by PETER O'DONNELL
YOU ARE A MOST UNSATISFACTORY SPOUSE, GILBERT—MY FIRST DEAR HUSBAND, ALFRED, WAS SO DIFFERENT
YES, DEAR
HE COMMITTED A ROBBERY EVERY SIX MONTHS WITHOUT FAIL
I KNOW, DEAR... I PLANNED THEM FOR HIM
AND HOW OUR EMPLOYEES RESPECTED HIM—GUSSIE THE GUT, HOOTER HACKETT, ALL OF THEM... WHILE THEY RATHER DESPISE YOU
YES, DEAR
4343

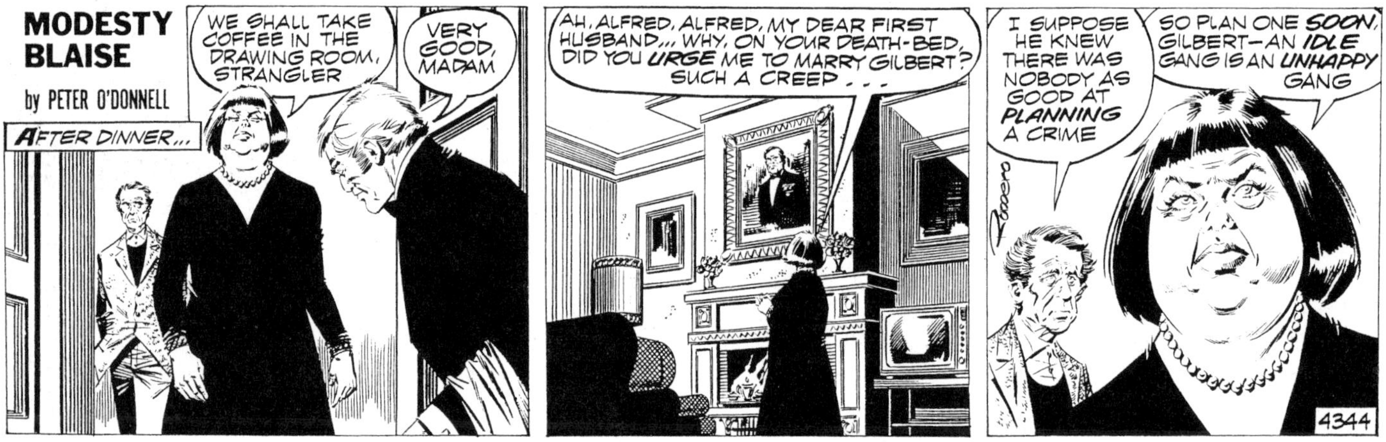
MODESTY BLAISE
by PETER O'DONNELL
AFTER DINNER...
WE SHALL TAKE COFFEE IN THE DRAWING ROOM, STRANGLER
VERY GOOD, MADAM
AH, ALFRED, ALFRED, MY DEAR FIRST HUSBAND... WHY, ON YOUR DEATH-BED, DID YOU URGE ME TO MARRY GILBERT? SUCH A CREEP . . .
I SUPPOSE HE KNEW THERE WAS NOBODY AS GOOD AT PLANNING A CRIME
SO PLAN ONE SOON, GILBERT—AN IDLE GANG IS AN UNHAPPY GANG
4344

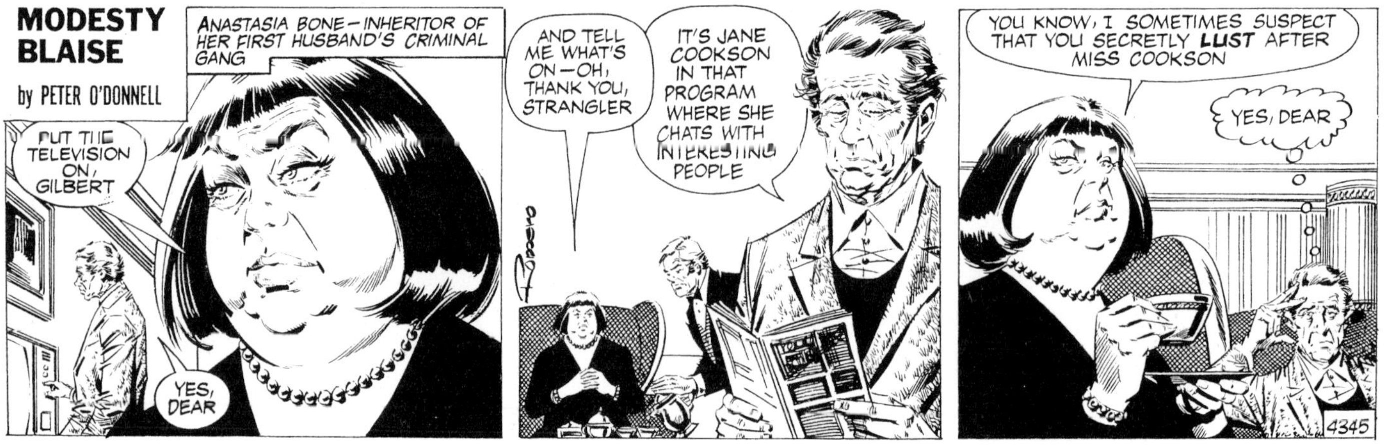
MODESTY BLAISE
by PETER O'DONNELL
ANASTASIA BONE—INHERITOR OF HER FIRST HUSBAND'S CRIMINAL GANG
PUT THE TELEVISION ON, GILBERT
YES, DEAR
AND TELL ME WHAT'S ON—OH, THANK YOU, STRANGLER
IT'S JANE COOKSON IN THAT PROGRAM WHERE SHE CHATS WITH INTERESTING PEOPLE
YOU KNOW, I SOMETIMES SUSPECT THAT YOU SECRETLY LUST AFTER MISS COOKSON
YES, DEAR
4345

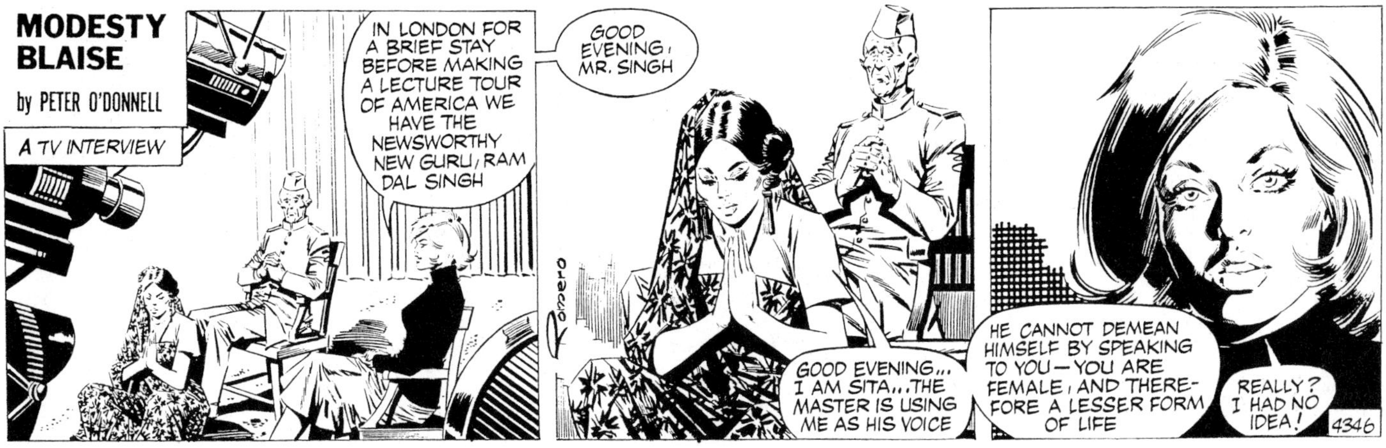
MODESTY BLAISE
by PETER O'DONNELL
A TV INTERVIEW
IN LONDON FOR A BRIEF STAY BEFORE MAKING A LECTURE TOUR OF AMERICA WE HAVE THE NEWSWORTHY NEW GURU, RAM DAL SINGH
GOOD EVENING, MR. SINGH
GOOD EVENING... I AM SITA...THE MASTER IS USING ME AS HIS VOICE
HE CANNOT DEMEAN HIMSELF BY SPEAKING TO YOU—YOU ARE FEMALE, AND THEREFORE A LESSER FORM OF LIFE
REALLY? I HAD NO IDEA!
4346

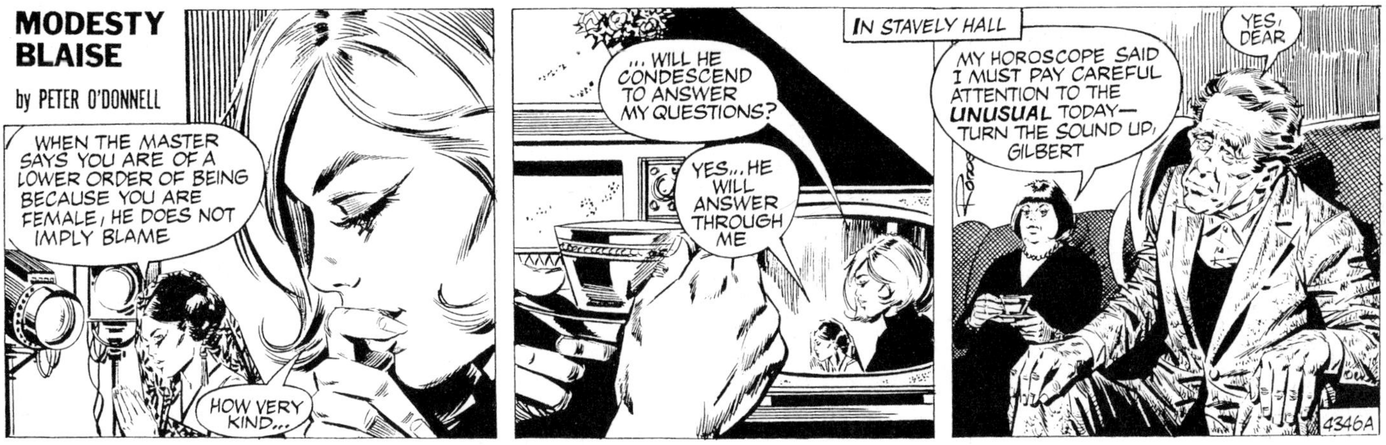
MODESTY BLAISE
by PETER O'DONNELL
WHEN THE MASTER SAYS YOU ARE OF A LOWER ORDER OF BEING BECAUSE YOU ARE FEMALE, HE DOES NOT IMPLY BLAME
HOW VERY KIND...
IN STAVELY HALL
...WILL HE CONDESCEND TO ANSWER MY QUESTIONS?
YES...HE WILL ANSWER THROUGH ME
MY HOROSCOPE SAID I MUST PAY CAREFUL ATTENTION TO THE UNUSUAL TODAY—TURN THE SOUND UP, GILBERT
YES, DEAR
4346A

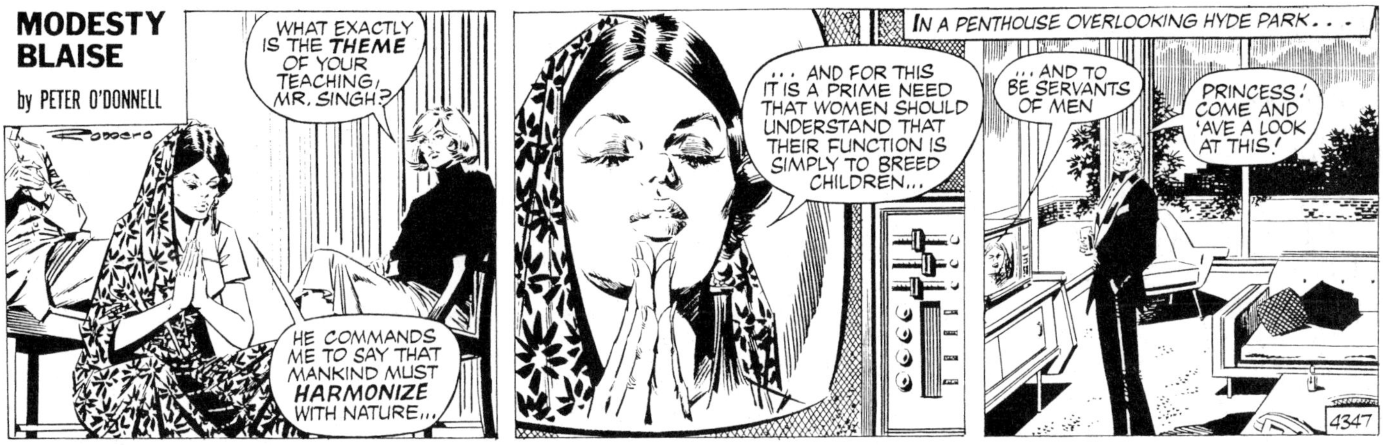
MODESTY BLAISE
by PETER O'DONNELL
WHAT EXACTLY IS THE THEME OF YOUR TEACHING, MR. SINGH?
HE COMMANDS ME TO SAY THAT MANKIND MUST HARMONIZE WITH NATURE...
IN A PENTHOUSE OVERLOOKING HYDE PARK...
...AND FOR THIS IT IS A PRIME NEED THAT WOMEN SHOULD UNDERSTAND THAT THEIR FUNCTION IS SIMPLY TO BREED CHILDREN...
...AND TO BE SERVANTS OF MEN
PRINCESS! COME AND 'AVE A LOOK AT THIS!
4347

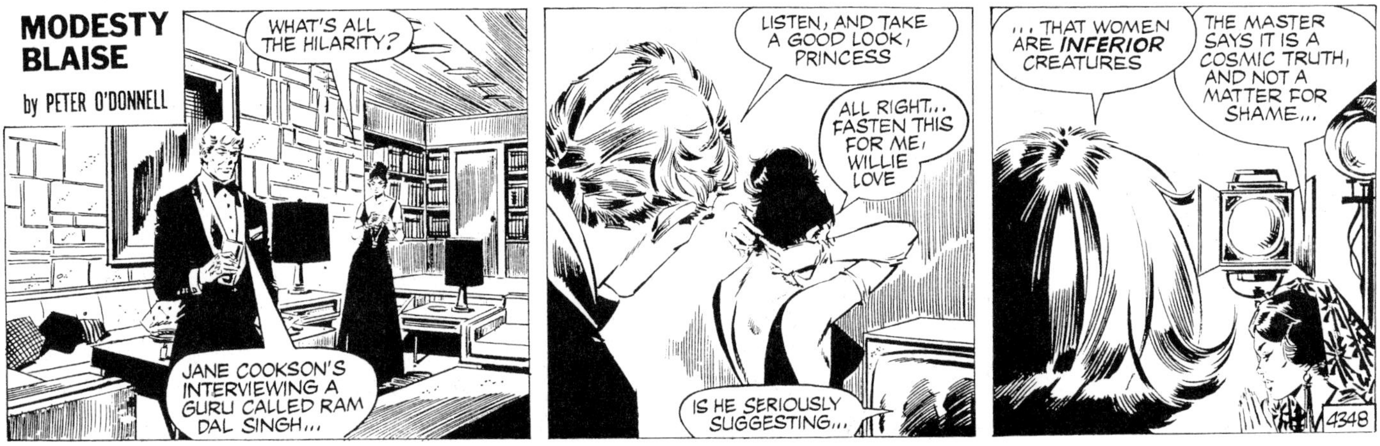
MODESTY BLAISE
by PETER O'DONNELL
WHAT'S ALL THE HILARITY?
JANE COOKSON'S INTERVIEWING A GURU CALLED RAM DAL SINGH...
LISTEN, AND TAKE A GOOD LOOK, PRINCESS
ALL RIGHT... FASTEN THIS FOR ME, WILLIE LOVE
IS HE SERIOUSLY SUGGESTING...
...THAT WOMEN ARE INFERIOR CREATURES
THE MASTER SAYS IT IS A COSMIC TRUTH, AND NOT A MATTER FOR SHAME...
4348

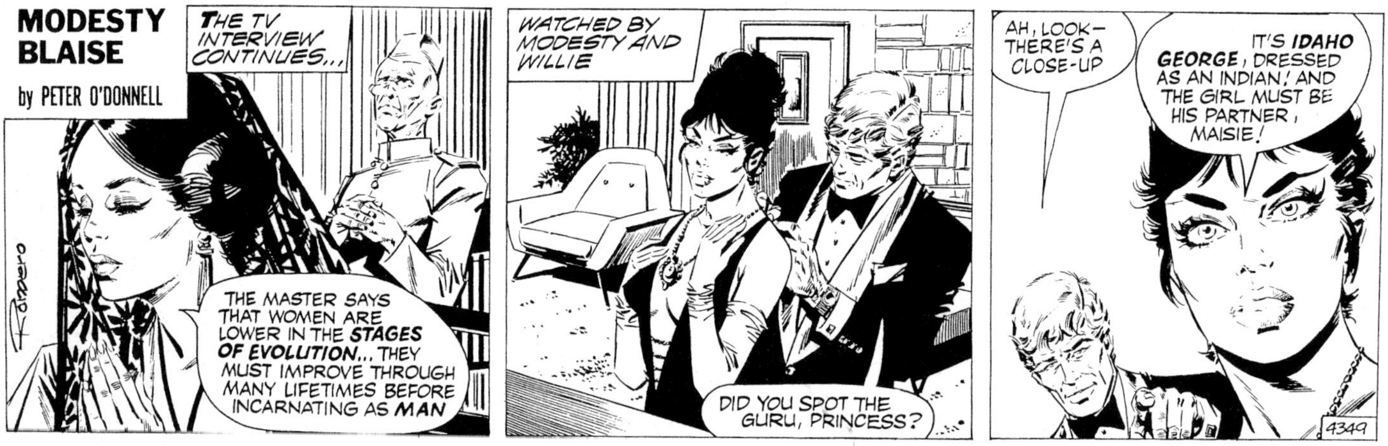
MODESTY BLAISE
by PETER O'DONNELL
THE TV INTERVIEW CONTINUES...
THE MASTER SAYS THAT WOMEN ARE LOWER IN THE **STAGES OF EVOLUTION**... THEY MUST IMPROVE THROUGH MANY LIFETIMES BEFORE INCARNATING AS **MAN**
WATCHED BY MODESTY AND WILLIE
DID YOU SPOT THE GURU, PRINCESS?
AH, LOOK— THERE'S A CLOSE-UP
IT'S **IDAHO GEORGE**, DRESSED AS AN INDIAN! AND THE GIRL MUST BE HIS PARTNER, MAISIE!
4349

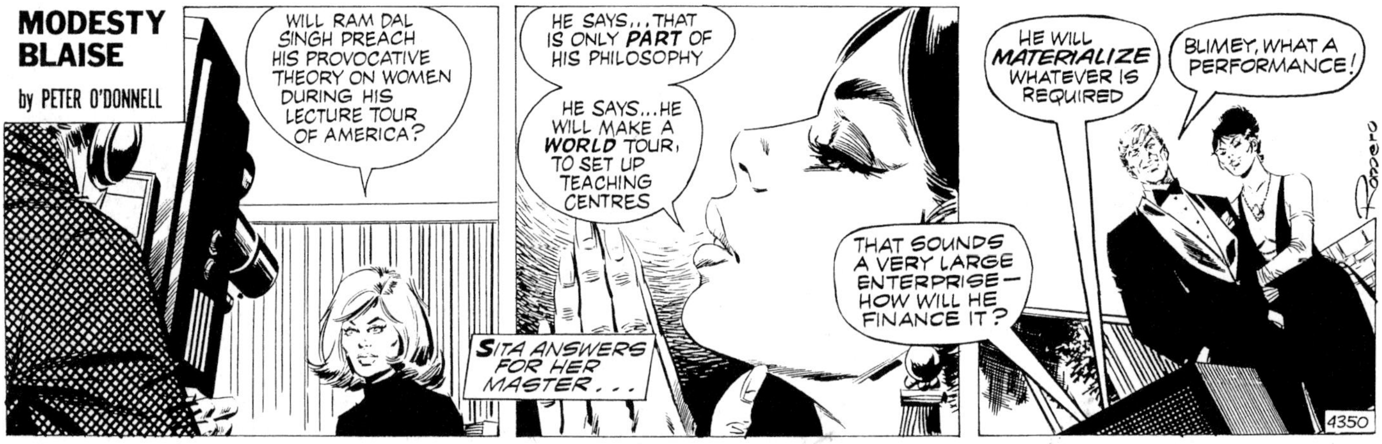
MODESTY BLAISE
by PETER O'DONNELL
WILL RAM DAL SINGH PREACH HIS PROVOCATIVE THEORY ON WOMEN DURING HIS LECTURE TOUR OF AMERICA?
HE SAYS... THAT IS ONLY **PART** OF HIS PHILOSOPHY
HE SAYS... HE WILL MAKE A **WORLD** TOUR, TO SET UP TEACHING CENTRES
SITA ANSWERS FOR HER MASTER...
THAT SOUNDS A VERY LARGE ENTERPRISE— HOW WILL HE FINANCE IT?
HE WILL **MATERIALIZE** WHATEVER IS REQUIRED
BLIMEY, WHAT A PERFORMANCE!
4350

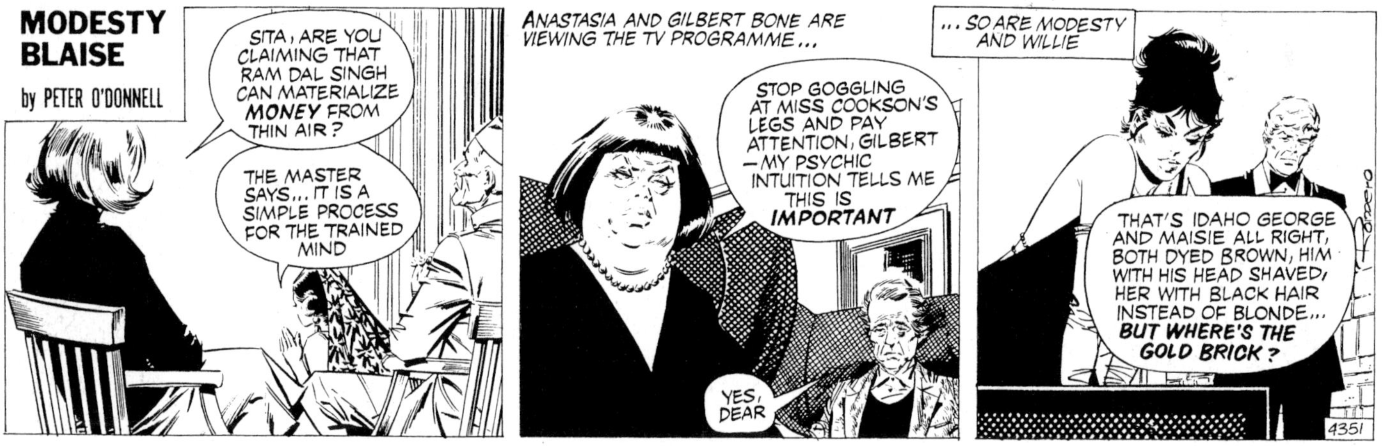
MODESTY BLAISE
by PETER O'DONNELL
SITA, ARE YOU CLAIMING THAT RAM DAL SINGH CAN MATERIALIZE **MONEY** FROM THIN AIR?
THE MASTER SAYS... IT IS A SIMPLE PROCESS FOR THE TRAINED MIND
ANASTASIA AND GILBERT BONE ARE VIEWING THE TV PROGRAMME...
STOP GOGGLING AT MISS COOKSON'S LEGS AND PAY ATTENTION, GILBERT —MY PSYCHIC INTUITION TELLS ME THIS IS **IMPORTANT**
YES, DEAR
... SO ARE MODESTY AND WILLIE
THAT'S IDAHO GEORGE AND MAISIE ALL RIGHT, BOTH DYED BROWN, HIM WITH HIS HEAD SHAVED, HER WITH BLACK HAIR INSTEAD OF BLONDE... **BUT WHERE'S THE GOLD BRICK?**
4351

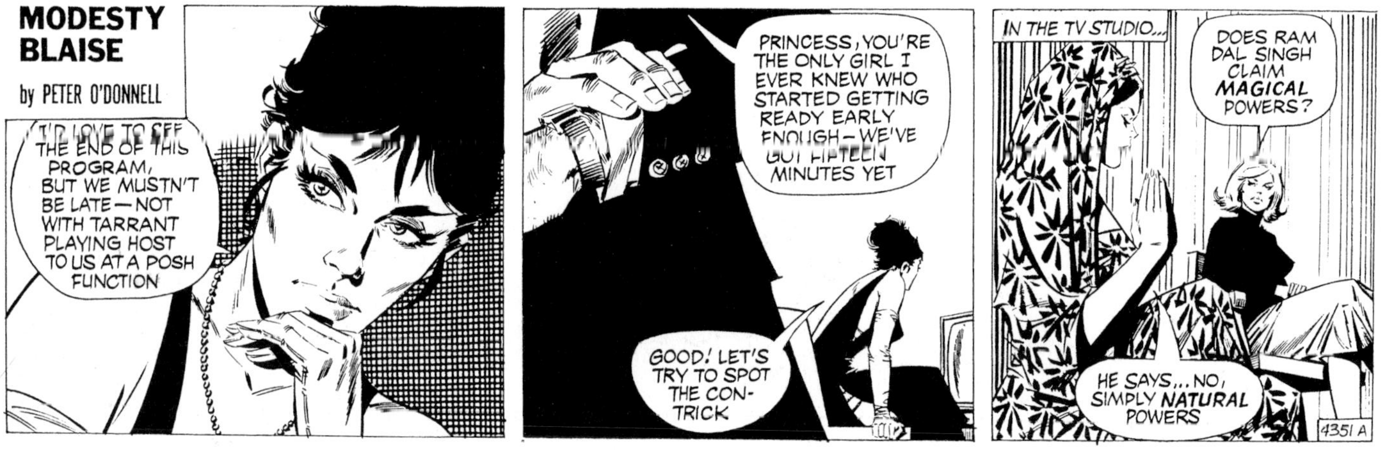
MODESTY BLAISE
by PETER O'DONNELL
I'D LOVE TO SEE THE END OF THIS PROGRAM, BUT WE MUSTN'T BE LATE—NOT WITH TARRANT PLAYING HOST TO US AT A POSH FUNCTION
PRINCESS, YOU'RE THE ONLY GIRL I EVER KNEW WHO STARTED GETTING READY EARLY ENOUGH—WE'VE GOT FIFTEEN MINUTES YET
GOOD! LET'S TRY TO SPOT THE CON-TRICK
IN THE TV STUDIO...
DOES RAM DAL SINGH CLAIM **MAGICAL** POWERS?
HE SAYS... NO, SIMPLY **NATURAL** POWERS
4351 A

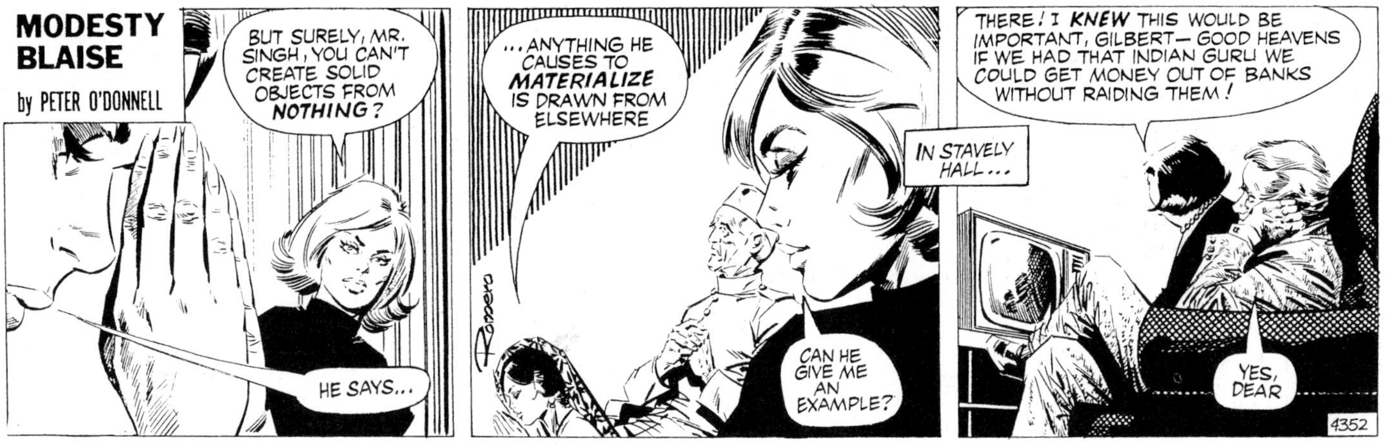
MODESTY BLAISE
by PETER O'DONNELL
BUT SURELY, MR. SINGH, YOU CAN'T CREATE SOLID OBJECTS FROM NOTHING?
HE SAYS...
...ANYTHING HE CAUSES TO MATERIALIZE IS DRAWN FROM ELSEWHERE
CAN HE GIVE ME AN EXAMPLE?
IN STAVELY HALL...
THERE! I KNEW THIS WOULD BE IMPORTANT, GILBERT— GOOD HEAVENS IF WE HAD THAT INDIAN GURU WE COULD GET MONEY OUT OF BANKS WITHOUT RAIDING THEM!
YES, DEAR
4352

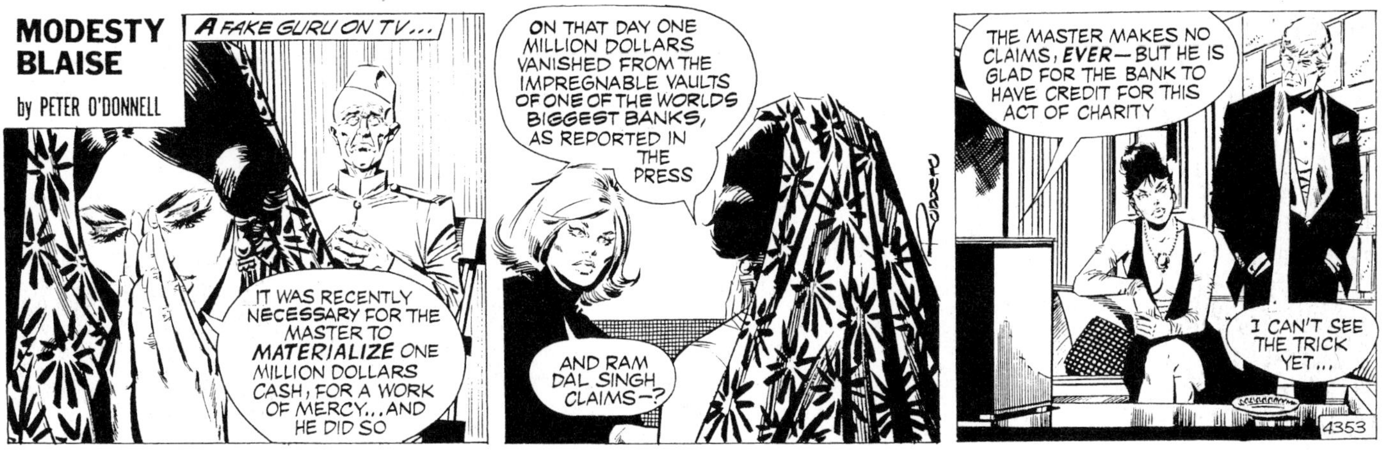
MODESTY BLAISE
by PETER O'DONNELL
A FAKE GURU ON TV...
IT WAS RECENTLY NECESSARY FOR THE MASTER TO MATERIALIZE ONE MILLION DOLLARS CASH, FOR A WORK OF MERCY...AND HE DID SO
AND RAM DAL SINGH CLAIMS—?
ON THAT DAY ONE MILLION DOLLARS VANISHED FROM THE IMPREGNABLE VAULTS OF ONE OF THE WORLDS BIGGEST BANKS, AS REPORTED IN THE PRESS
THE MASTER MAKES NO CLAIMS; EVER— BUT HE IS GLAD FOR THE BANK TO HAVE CREDIT FOR THIS ACT OF CHARITY
I CAN'T SEE THE TRICK YET...
4353

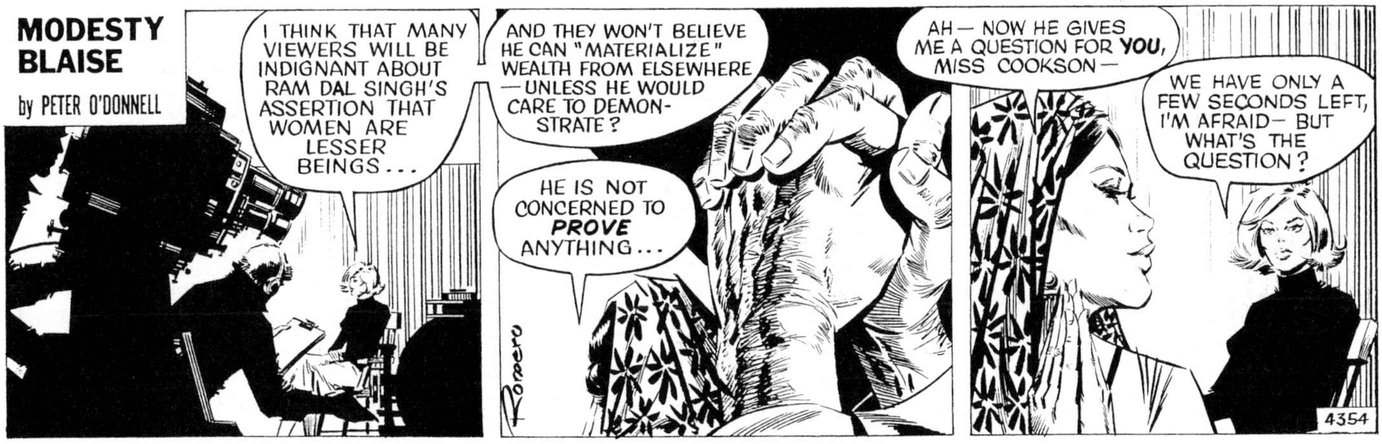
MODESTY BLAISE
by PETER O'DONNELL
I THINK THAT MANY VIEWERS WILL BE INDIGNANT ABOUT RAM DAL SINGH'S ASSERTION THAT WOMEN ARE LESSER BEINGS...
AND THEY WON'T BELIEVE HE CAN "MATERIALIZE" WEALTH FROM ELSEWHERE —UNLESS HE WOULD CARE TO DEMON-STRATE?
HE IS NOT CONCERNED TO PROVE ANYTHING...
AH— NOW HE GIVES ME A QUESTION FOR YOU, MISS COOKSON—
WE HAVE ONLY A FEW SECONDS LEFT, I'M AFRAID— BUT WHAT'S THE QUESTION?
4354

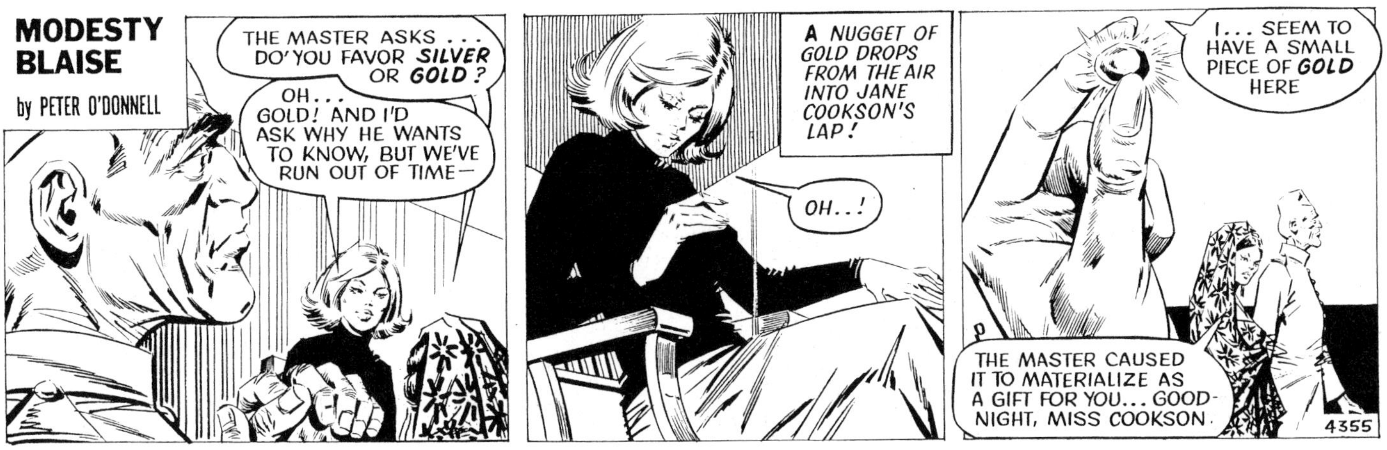
MODESTY BLAISE
by PETER O'DONNELL
THE MASTER ASKS... DO YOU FAVOR SILVER OR GOLD?
OH... GOLD! AND I'D ASK WHY HE WANTS TO KNOW, BUT WE'VE RUN OUT OF TIME—
A NUGGET OF GOLD DROPS FROM THE AIR INTO JANE COOKSON'S LAP!
OH...!
I... SEEM TO HAVE A SMALL PIECE OF GOLD HERE
THE MASTER CAUSED IT TO MATERIALIZE AS A GIFT FOR YOU... GOOD-NIGHT, MISS COOKSON.
4355

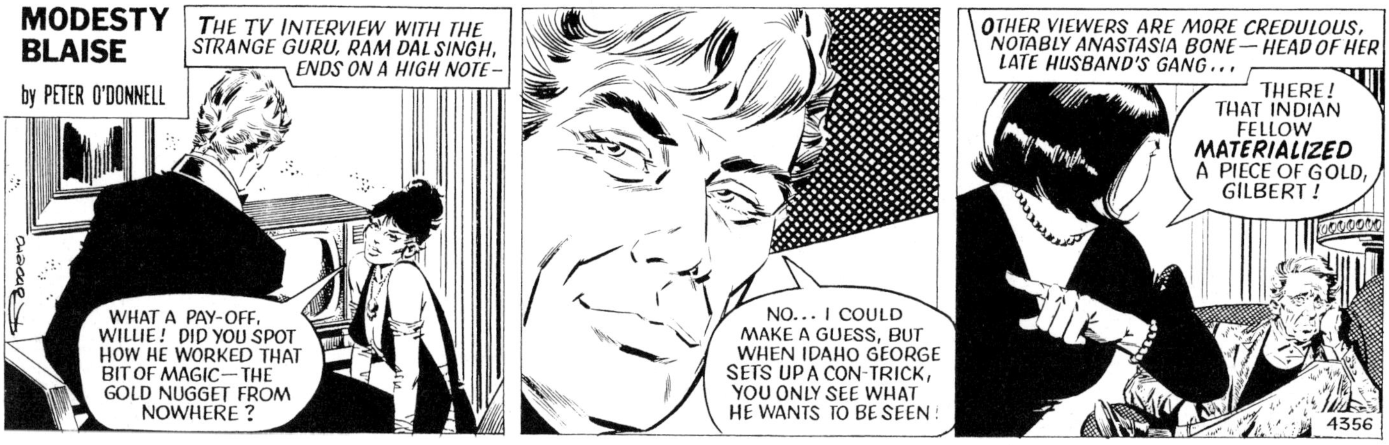

MODESTY BLAISE
by PETER O'DONNELL
THE TV INTERVIEW WITH THE STRANGE GURU, RAM DAL SINGH, ENDS ON A HIGH NOTE—
WHAT A PAY-OFF, WILLIE! DID YOU SPOT HOW HE WORKED THAT BIT OF MAGIC—THE GOLD NUGGET FROM NOWHERE?
NO... I COULD MAKE A GUESS, BUT WHEN IDAHO GEORGE SETS UP A CON-TRICK, YOU ONLY SEE WHAT HE WANTS TO BE SEEN!
OTHER VIEWERS ARE MORE CREDULOUS, NOTABLY ANASTASIA BONE—HEAD OF HER LATE HUSBAND'S GANG...
THERE! THAT INDIAN FELLOW MATERIALIZED A PIECE OF GOLD, GILBERT!
4356

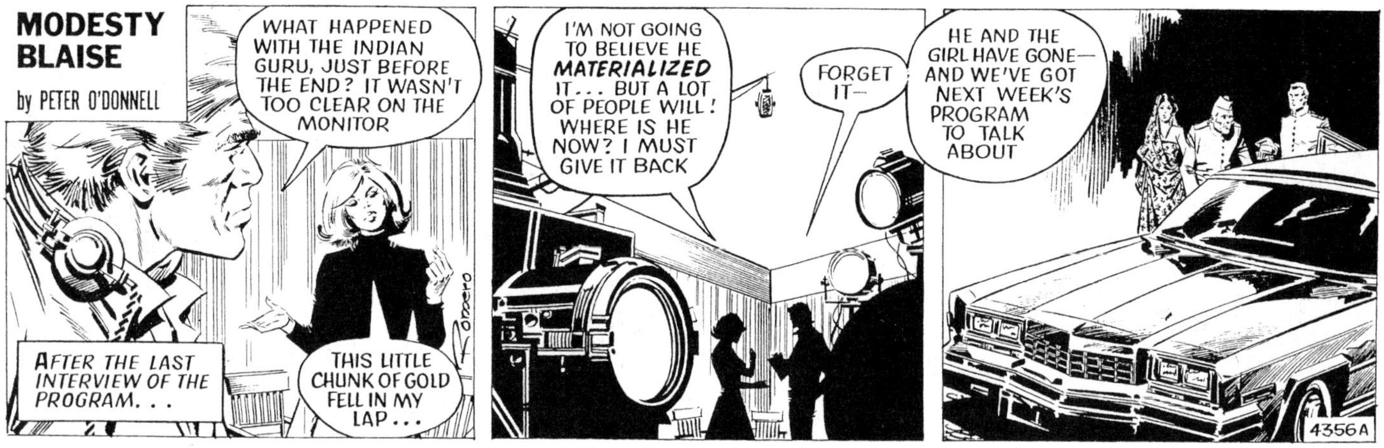

MODESTY BLAISE
by PETER O'DONNELL
WHAT HAPPENED WITH THE INDIAN GURU, JUST BEFORE THE END? IT WASN'T TOO CLEAR ON THE MONITOR
AFTER THE LAST INTERVIEW OF THE PROGRAM...
THIS LITTLE CHUNK OF GOLD FELL IN MY LAP...
I'M NOT GOING TO BELIEVE HE MATERIALIZED IT... BUT A LOT OF PEOPLE WILL! WHERE IS HE NOW? I MUST GIVE IT BACK
FORGET IT—
HE AND THE GIRL HAVE GONE—AND WE'VE GOT NEXT WEEK'S PROGRAM TO TALK ABOUT
4356A

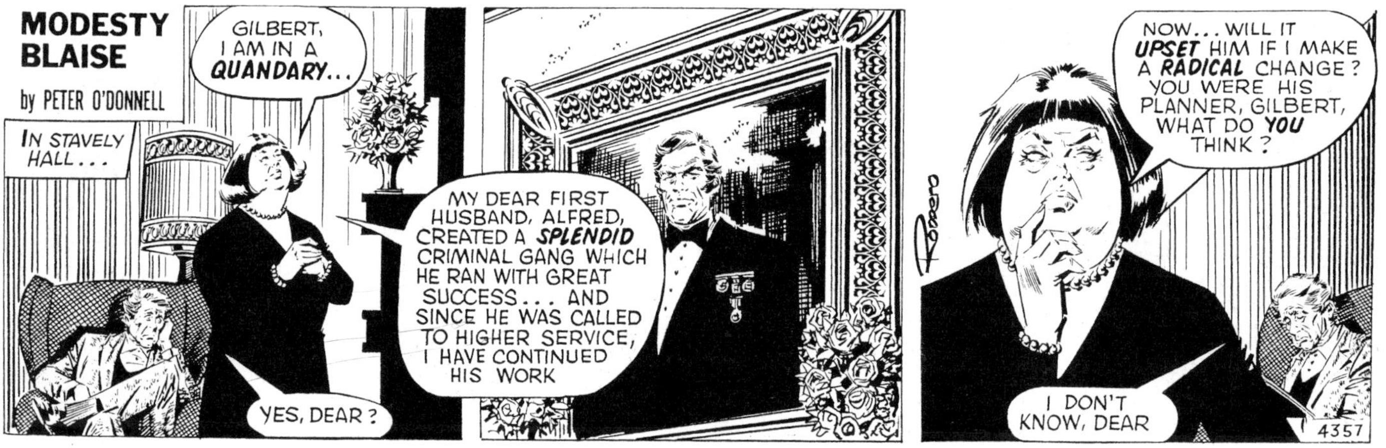

MODESTY BLAISE
by PETER O'DONNELL
IN STAVELY HALL...
GILBERT, I AM IN A QUANDARY...
YES, DEAR?
MY DEAR FIRST HUSBAND, ALFRED, CREATED A SPLENDID CRIMINAL GANG WHICH HE RAN WITH GREAT SUCCESS... AND SINCE HE WAS CALLED TO HIGHER SERVICE, I HAVE CONTINUED HIS WORK
NOW... WILL IT UPSET HIM IF I MAKE A RADICAL CHANGE? YOU WERE HIS PLANNER, GILBERT, WHAT DO YOU THINK?
I DON'T KNOW, DEAR
4357

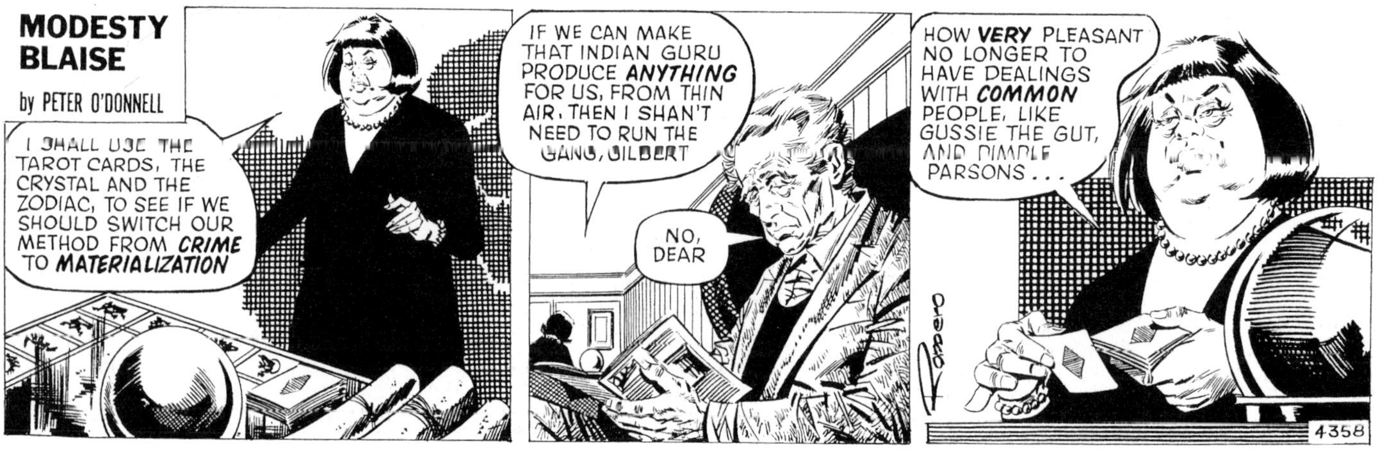

MODESTY BLAISE
by PETER O'DONNELL
I SHALL USE THE TAROT CARDS, THE CRYSTAL AND THE ZODIAC, TO SEE IF WE SHOULD SWITCH OUR METHOD FROM CRIME TO MATERIALIZATION
IF WE CAN MAKE THAT INDIAN GURU PRODUCE ANYTHING FOR US, FROM THIN AIR, THEN I SHAN'T NEED TO RUN THE GANG, GILBERT
NO, DEAR
HOW VERY PLEASANT NO LONGER TO HAVE DEALINGS WITH COMMON PEOPLE, LIKE GUSSIE THE GUT, AND PIMPLE PARSONS...
4358

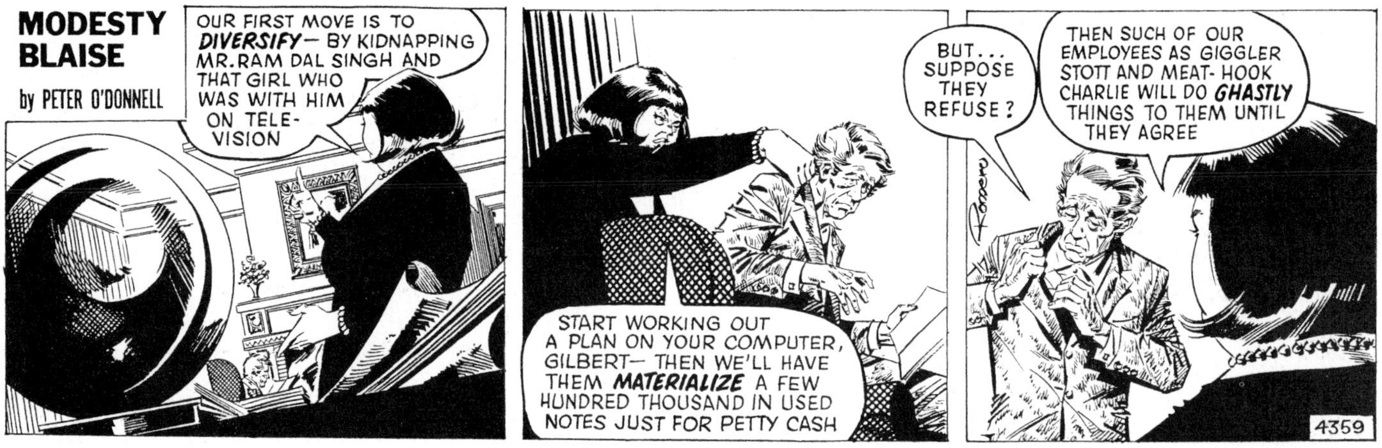
MODESTY BLAISE
by PETER O'DONNELL
OUR FIRST MOVE IS TO DIVERSIFY— BY KIDNAPPING MR. RAM DAL SINGH AND THAT GIRL WHO WAS WITH HIM ON TELE-VISION
START WORKING OUT A PLAN ON YOUR COMPUTER, GILBERT— THEN WE'LL HAVE THEM MATERIALIZE A FEW HUNDRED THOUSAND IN USED NOTES JUST FOR PETTY CASH
BUT... SUPPOSE THEY REFUSE?
THEN SUCH OF OUR EMPLOYEES AS GIGGLER STOTT AND MEAT-HOOK CHARLIE WILL DO GHASTLY THINGS TO THEM UNTIL THEY AGREE
4359

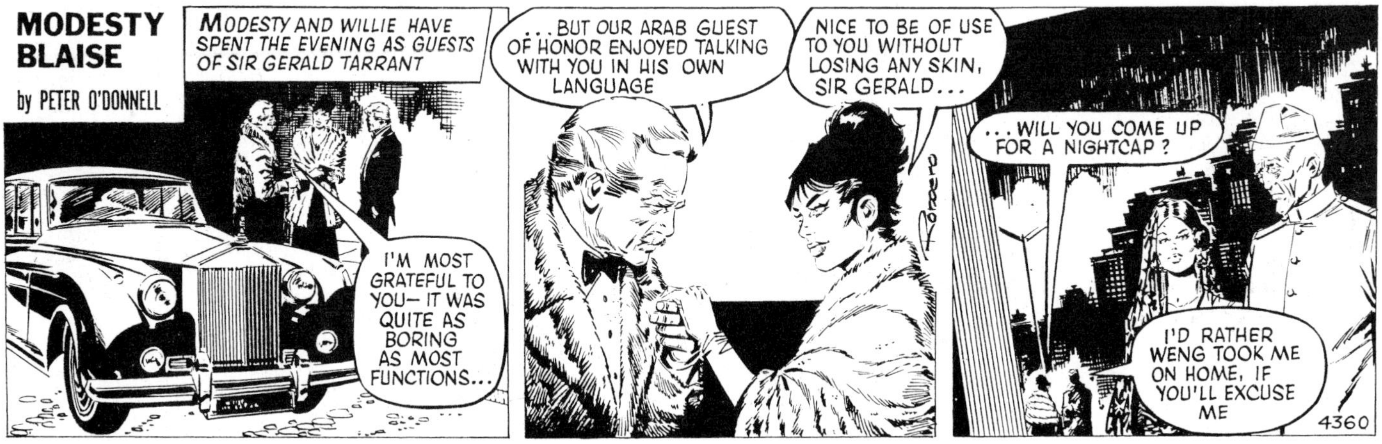
MODESTY BLAISE
by PETER O'DONNELL
MODESTY AND WILLIE HAVE SPENT THE EVENING AS GUESTS OF SIR GERALD TARRANT
I'M MOST GRATEFUL TO YOU— IT WAS QUITE AS BORING AS MOST FUNCTIONS...
...BUT OUR ARAB GUEST OF HONOR ENJOYED TALKING WITH YOU IN HIS OWN LANGUAGE
NICE TO BE OF USE TO YOU WITHOUT LOSING ANY SKIN, SIR GERALD...
...WILL YOU COME UP FOR A NIGHTCAP?
I'D RATHER WENG TOOK ME ON HOME, IF YOU'LL EXCUSE ME
4360

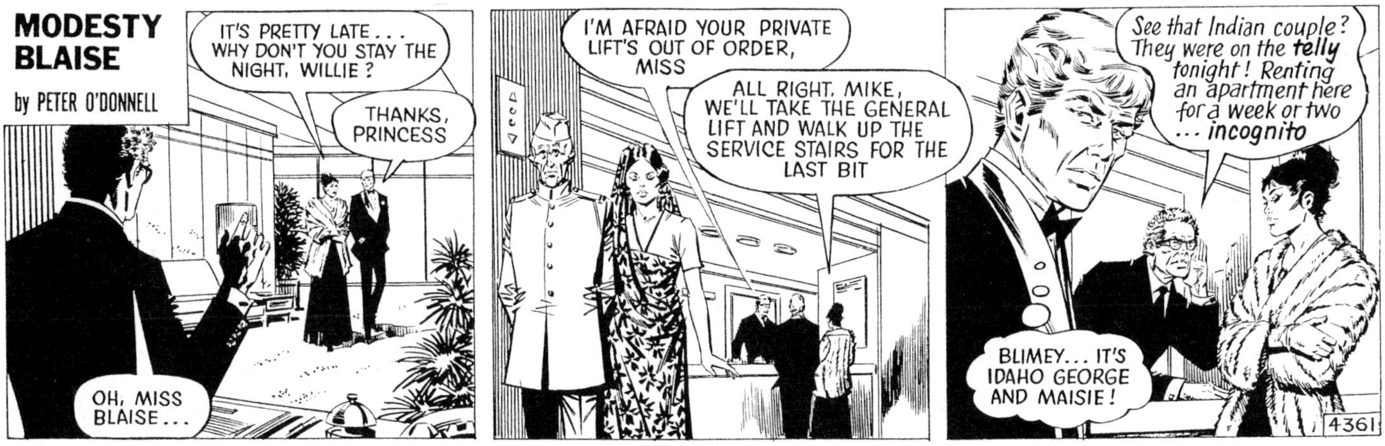
MODESTY BLAISE
by PETER O'DONNELL
IT'S PRETTY LATE... WHY DON'T YOU STAY THE NIGHT, WILLIE?
THANKS, PRINCESS
OH, MISS BLAISE...
I'M AFRAID YOUR PRIVATE LIFT'S OUT OF ORDER, MISS
ALL RIGHT, MIKE, WE'LL TAKE THE GENERAL LIFT AND WALK UP THE SERVICE STAIRS FOR THE LAST BIT
See that Indian couple? They were on the telly tonight! Renting an apartment here for a week or two ... incognito
BLIMEY... IT'S IDAHO GEORGE AND MAISIE!
4361

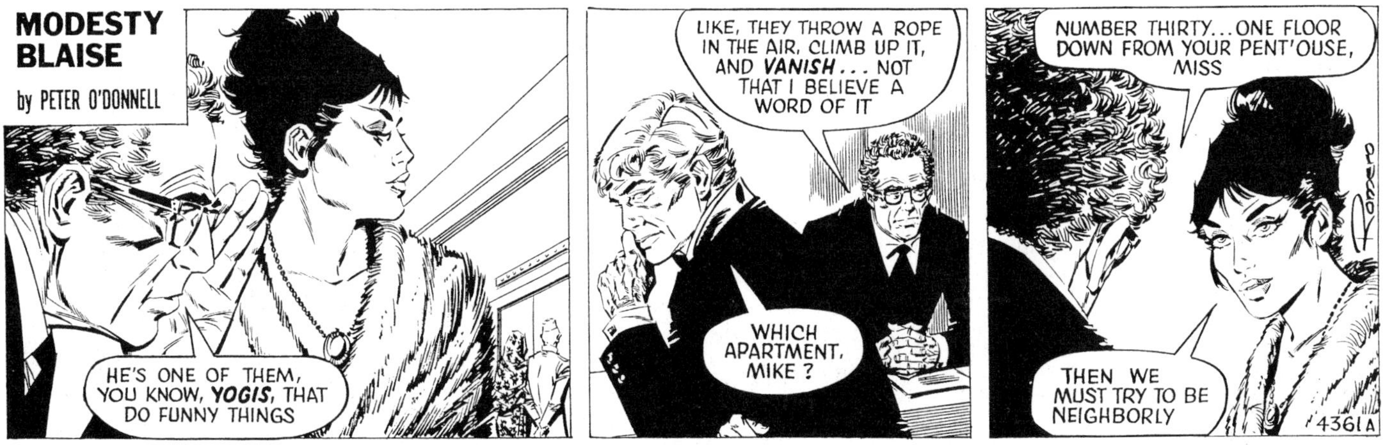
MODESTY BLAISE
by PETER O'DONNELL
HE'S ONE OF THEM, YOU KNOW, YOGIS, THAT DO FUNNY THINGS
LIKE, THEY THROW A ROPE IN THE AIR, CLIMB UP IT, AND VANISH... NOT THAT I BELIEVE A WORD OF IT
WHICH APARTMENT, MIKE?
NUMBER THIRTY... ONE FLOOR DOWN FROM YOUR PENT'OUSE, MISS
THEN WE MUST TRY TO BE NEIGHBORLY
4361A

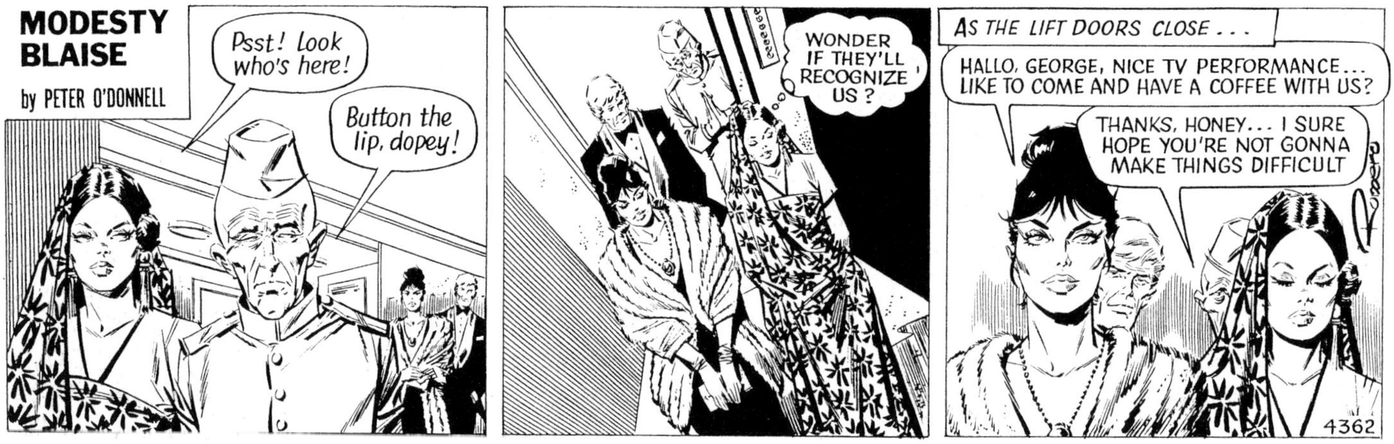
MODESTY BLAISE
by PETER O'DONNELL
Psst! Look who's here!
Button the lip, dopey!
WONDER IF THEY'LL RECOGNIZE US?
AS THE LIFT DOORS CLOSE...
HALLO, GEORGE, NICE TV PERFORMANCE... LIKE TO COME AND HAVE A COFFEE WITH US?
THANKS, HONEY... I SURE HOPE YOU'RE NOT GONNA MAKE THINGS DIFFICULT
4362

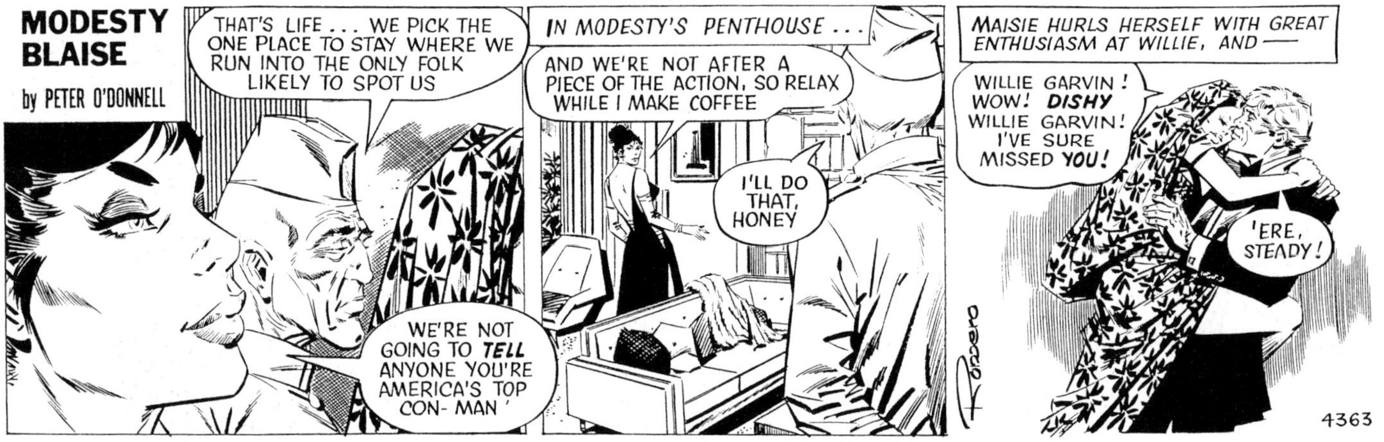
MODESTY BLAISE
by PETER O'DONNELL
THAT'S LIFE... WE PICK THE ONE PLACE TO STAY WHERE WE RUN INTO THE ONLY FOLK LIKELY TO SPOT US
WE'RE NOT GOING TO TELL ANYONE YOU'RE AMERICA'S TOP CON-MAN
IN MODESTY'S PENTHOUSE...
AND WE'RE NOT AFTER A PIECE OF THE ACTION, SO RELAX WHILE I MAKE COFFEE
I'LL DO THAT, HONEY
MAISIE HURLS HERSELF WITH GREAT ENTHUSIASM AT WILLIE, AND—
WILLIE GARVIN! WOW! DISHY WILLIE GARVIN! I'VE SURE MISSED YOU!
'ERE, STEADY!
4363

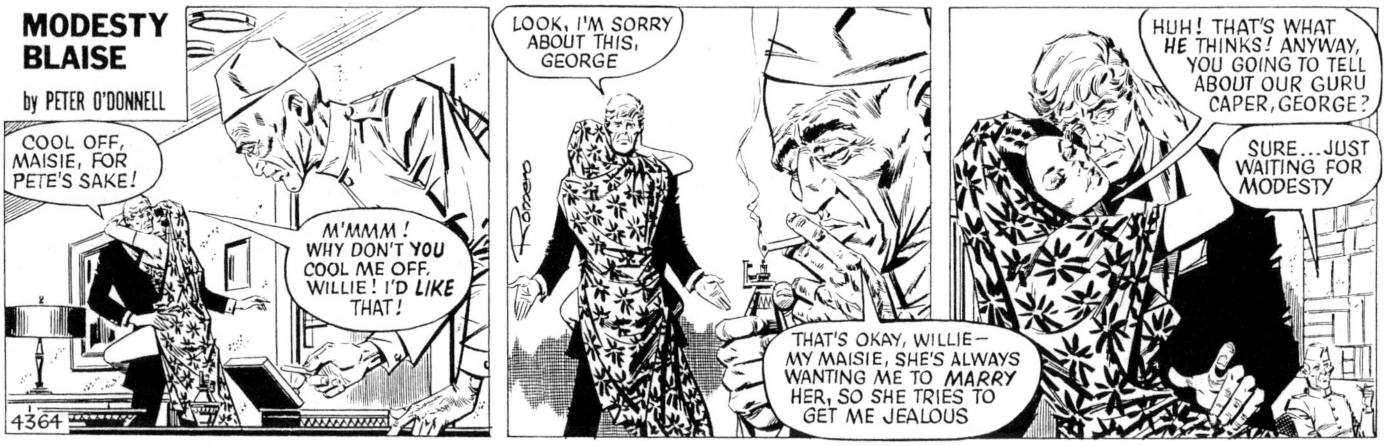
MODESTY BLAISE
by PETER O'DONNELL
COOL OFF, MAISIE, FOR PETE'S SAKE!
M'MMM! WHY DON'T YOU COOL ME OFF, WILLIE! I'D LIKE THAT!
4364
LOOK, I'M SORRY ABOUT THIS, GEORGE
THAT'S OKAY, WILLIE— MY MAISIE, SHE'S ALWAYS WANTING ME TO MARRY HER, SO SHE TRIES TO GET ME JEALOUS
HUH! THAT'S WHAT HE THINKS! ANYWAY, YOU GOING TO TELL ABOUT OUR GURU CAPER, GEORGE?
SURE... JUST WAITING FOR MODESTY

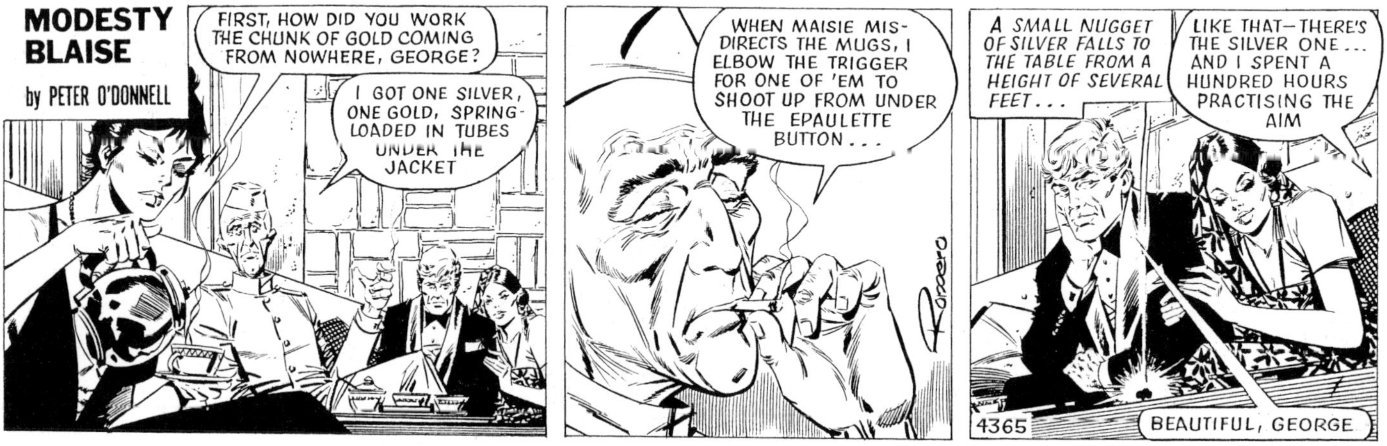
MODESTY BLAISE
by PETER O'DONNELL
FIRST, HOW DID YOU WORK THE CHUNK OF GOLD COMING FROM NOWHERE, GEORGE?
I GOT ONE SILVER, ONE GOLD, SPRING-LOADED IN TUBES UNDER THE JACKET
WHEN MAISIE MIS-DIRECTS THE MUGS, I ELBOW THE TRIGGER FOR ONE OF 'EM TO SHOOT UP FROM UNDER THE EPAULETTE BUTTON...
A SMALL NUGGET OF SILVER FALLS TO THE TABLE FROM A HEIGHT OF SEVERAL FEET...
LIKE THAT—THERE'S THE SILVER ONE... AND I SPENT A HUNDRED HOURS PRACTISING THE AIM
4365
BEAUTIFUL, GEORGE

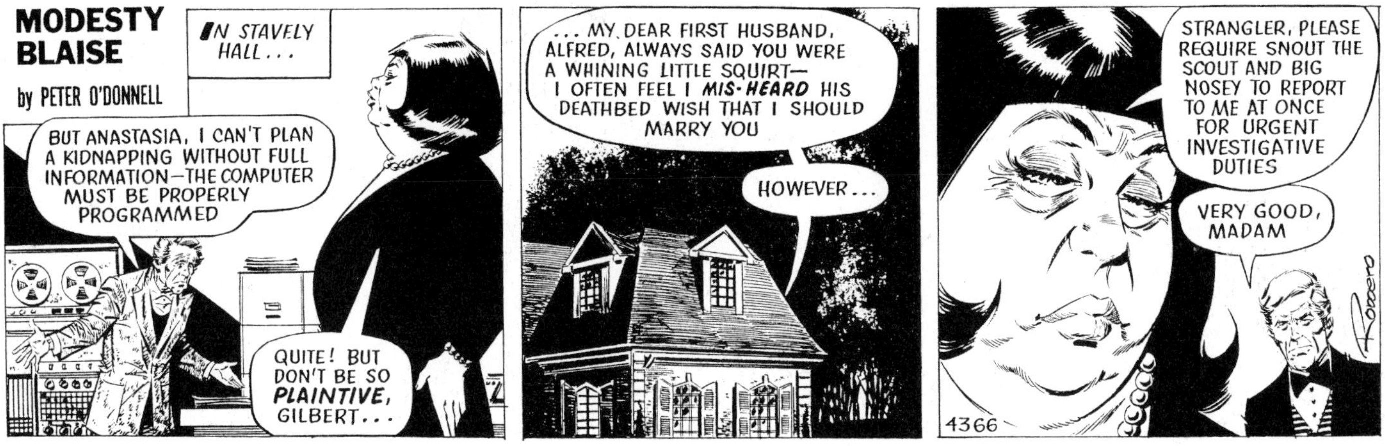
MODESTY BLAISE
by PETER O'DONNELL
IN STAVELY HALL...
BUT ANASTASIA, I CAN'T PLAN A KIDNAPPING WITHOUT FULL INFORMATION—THE COMPUTER MUST BE PROPERLY PROGRAMMED
QUITE! BUT DON'T BE SO **PLAINTIVE**, GILBERT...
... MY DEAR FIRST HUSBAND, ALFRED, ALWAYS SAID YOU WERE A WHINING LITTLE SQUIRT— I OFTEN FEEL I **MIS-HEARD** HIS DEATHBED WISH THAT I SHOULD MARRY YOU
HOWEVER...
STRANGLER, PLEASE REQUIRE SNOUT THE SCOUT AND BIG NOSEY TO REPORT TO ME AT ONCE FOR URGENT INVESTIGATIVE DUTIES
VERY GOOD, MADAM
Romero
4366

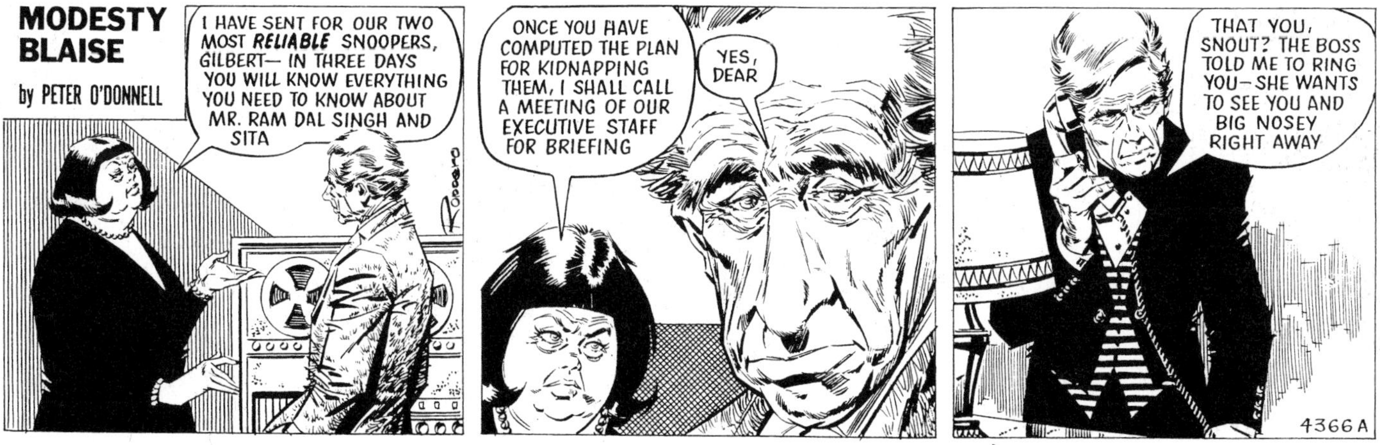
MODESTY BLAISE
by PETER O'DONNELL
I HAVE SENT FOR OUR TWO MOST **RELIABLE** SNOOPERS, GILBERT— IN THREE DAYS YOU WILL KNOW EVERYTHING YOU NEED TO KNOW ABOUT MR. RAM DAL SINGH AND SITA
Romero
ONCE YOU HAVE COMPUTED THE PLAN FOR KIDNAPPING THEM, I SHALL CALL A MEETING OF OUR EXECUTIVE STAFF FOR BRIEFING
YES, DEAR
THAT YOU, SNOUT? THE BOSS TOLD ME TO RING YOU—SHE WANTS TO SEE YOU AND BIG NOSEY RIGHT AWAY
4366 A

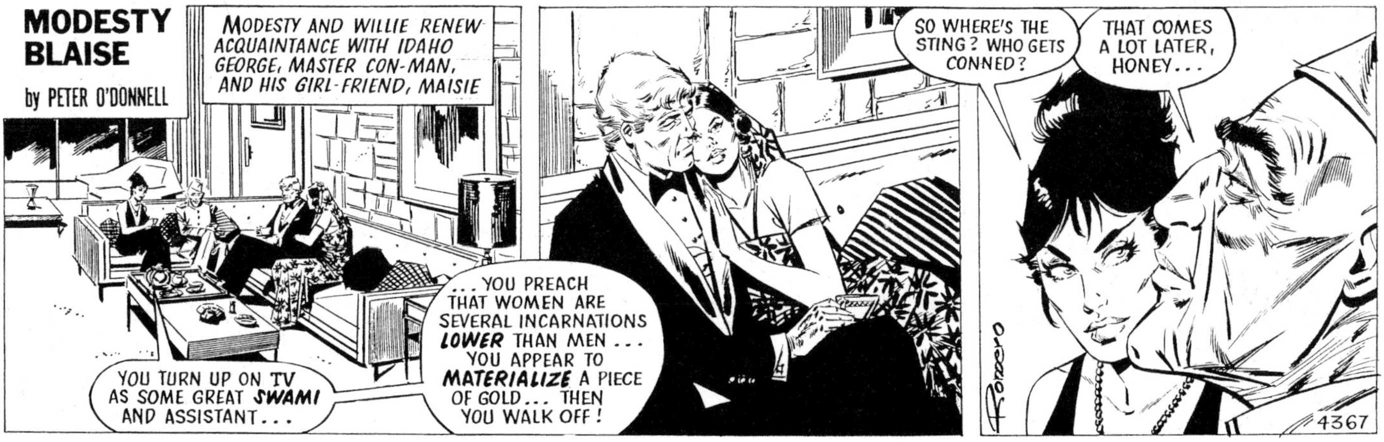
MODESTY BLAISE
by PETER O'DONNELL
MODESTY AND WILLIE RENEW ACQUAINTANCE WITH IDAHO GEORGE, MASTER CON-MAN, AND HIS GIRL-FRIEND, MAISIE
YOU TURN UP ON TV AS SOME GREAT **SWAMI** AND ASSISTANT...
... YOU PREACH THAT WOMEN ARE SEVERAL INCARNATIONS **LOWER** THAN MEN ... YOU APPEAR TO **MATERIALIZE** A PIECE OF GOLD... THEN YOU WALK OFF!
SO WHERE'S THE STING? WHO GETS CONNED?
THAT COMES A LOT LATER, HONEY...
Romero
4367

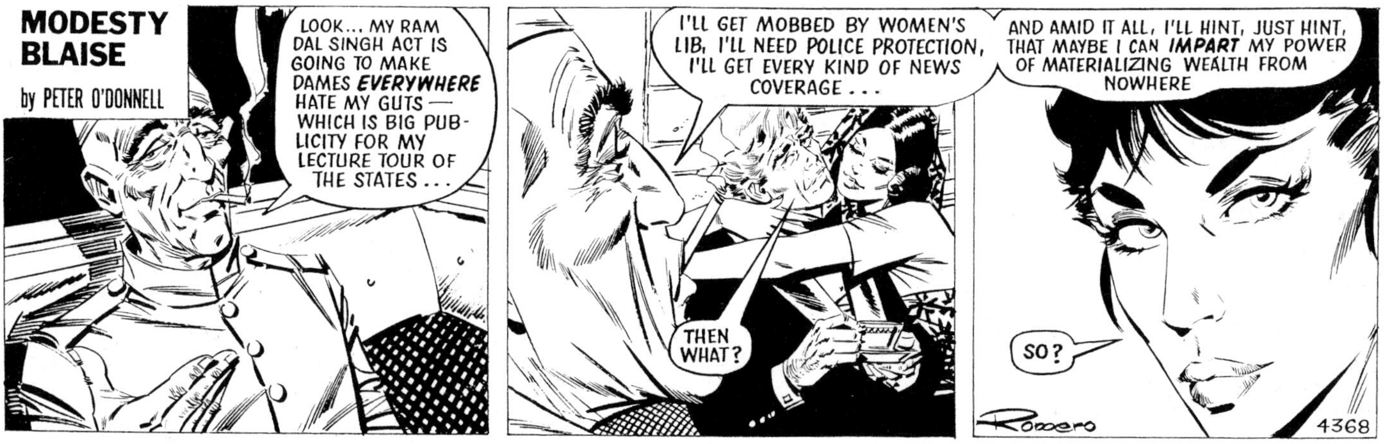
MODESTY BLAISE
by PETER O'DONNELL
LOOK... MY RAM DAL SINGH ACT IS GOING TO MAKE DAMES **EVERYWHERE** HATE MY GUTS — WHICH IS BIG PUBLICITY FOR MY LECTURE TOUR OF THE STATES...
I'LL GET MOBBED BY WOMEN'S LIB, I'LL NEED POLICE PROTECTION, I'LL GET EVERY KIND OF NEWS COVERAGE...
THEN WHAT?
AND AMID IT ALL, I'LL HINT, JUST HINT, THAT MAYBE I CAN **IMPART** MY POWER OF MATERIALIZING WEALTH FROM NOWHERE
SO?
Romero
4368

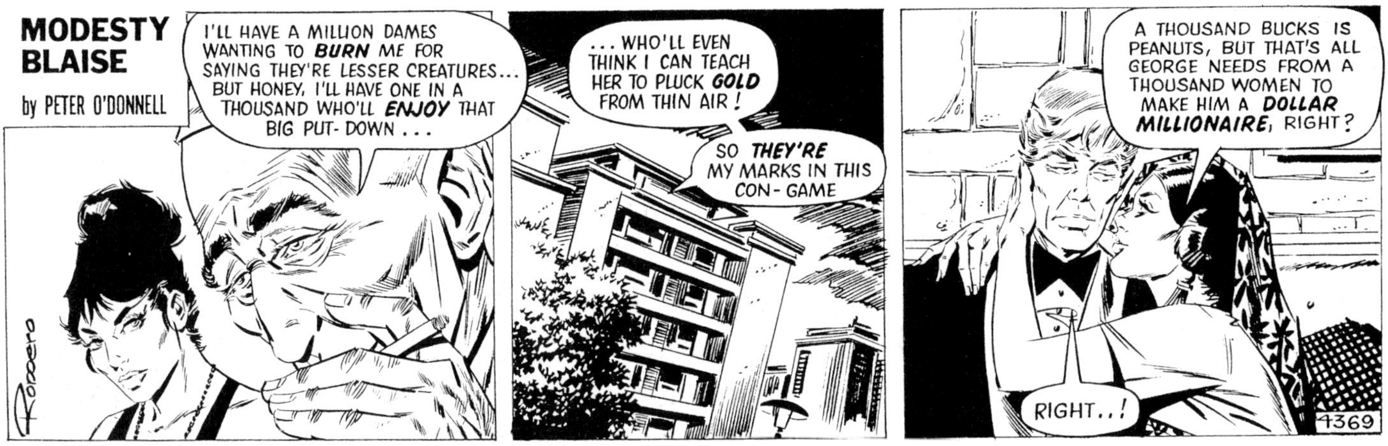
MODESTY BLAISE
by PETER O'DONNELL
I'LL HAVE A MILLION DAMES WANTING TO BURN ME FOR SAYING THEY'RE LESSER CREATURES... BUT HONEY, I'LL HAVE ONE IN A THOUSAND WHO'LL ENJOY THAT BIG PUT-DOWN ...
... WHO'LL EVEN THINK I CAN TEACH HER TO PLUCK GOLD FROM THIN AIR !
SO THEY'RE MY MARKS IN THIS CON-GAME
A THOUSAND BUCKS IS PEANUTS, BUT THAT'S ALL GEORGE NEEDS FROM A THOUSAND WOMEN TO MAKE HIM A DOLLAR MILLIONAIRE, RIGHT?
RIGHT..!
4369

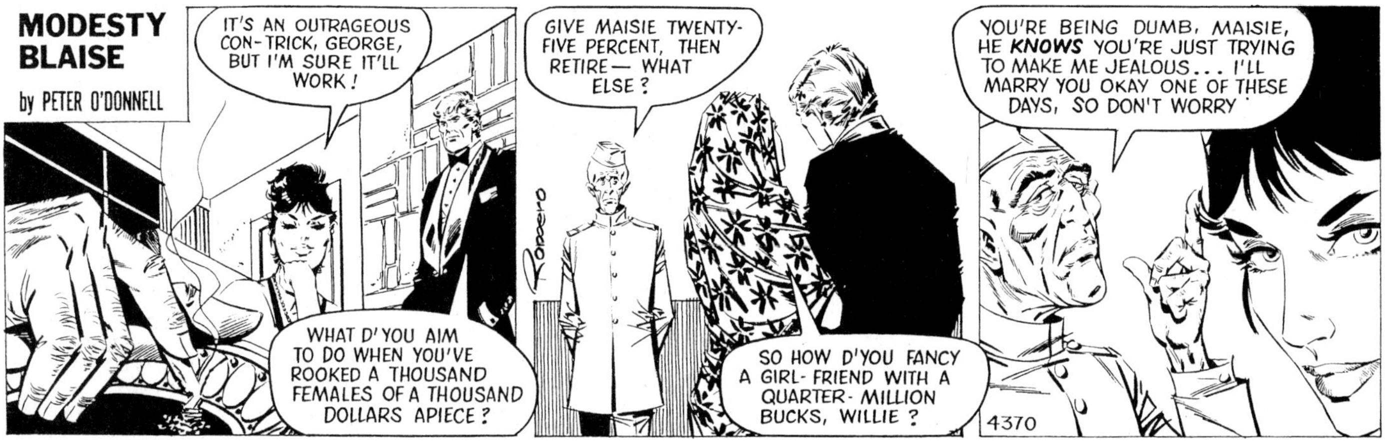
MODESTY BLAISE
by PETER O'DONNELL
IT'S AN OUTRAGEOUS CON-TRICK, GEORGE, BUT I'M SURE IT'LL WORK!
WHAT D'YOU AIM TO DO WHEN YOU'VE ROOKED A THOUSAND FEMALES OF A THOUSAND DOLLARS APIECE?
GIVE MAISIE TWENTY-FIVE PERCENT, THEN RETIRE— WHAT ELSE?
SO HOW D'YOU FANCY A GIRL-FRIEND WITH A QUARTER-MILLION BUCKS, WILLIE?
YOU'RE BEING DUMB, MAISIE, HE KNOWS YOU'RE JUST TRYING TO MAKE ME JEALOUS... I'LL MARRY YOU OKAY ONE OF THESE DAYS, SO DON'T WORRY
4370

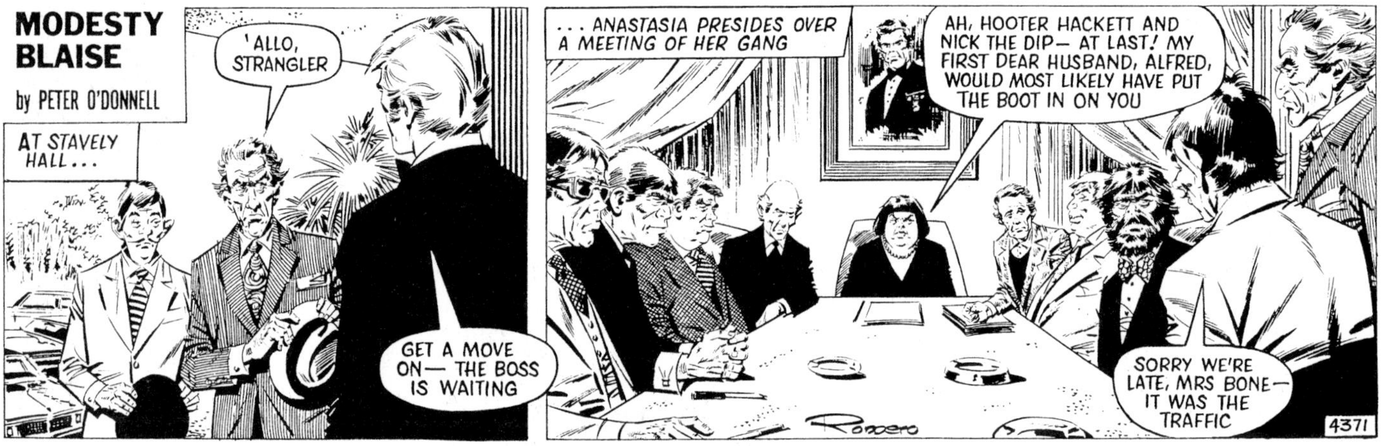
MODESTY BLAISE
by PETER O'DONNELL
AT STAVELY HALL...
'ALLO, STRANGLER
GET A MOVE ON— THE BOSS IS WAITING
... ANASTASIA PRESIDES OVER A MEETING OF HER GANG
AH, HOOTER HACKETT AND NICK THE DIP— AT LAST! MY FIRST DEAR HUSBAND, ALFRED, WOULD MOST LIKELY HAVE PUT THE BOOT IN ON YOU
SORRY WE'RE LATE, MRS BONE— IT WAS THE TRAFFIC
4371

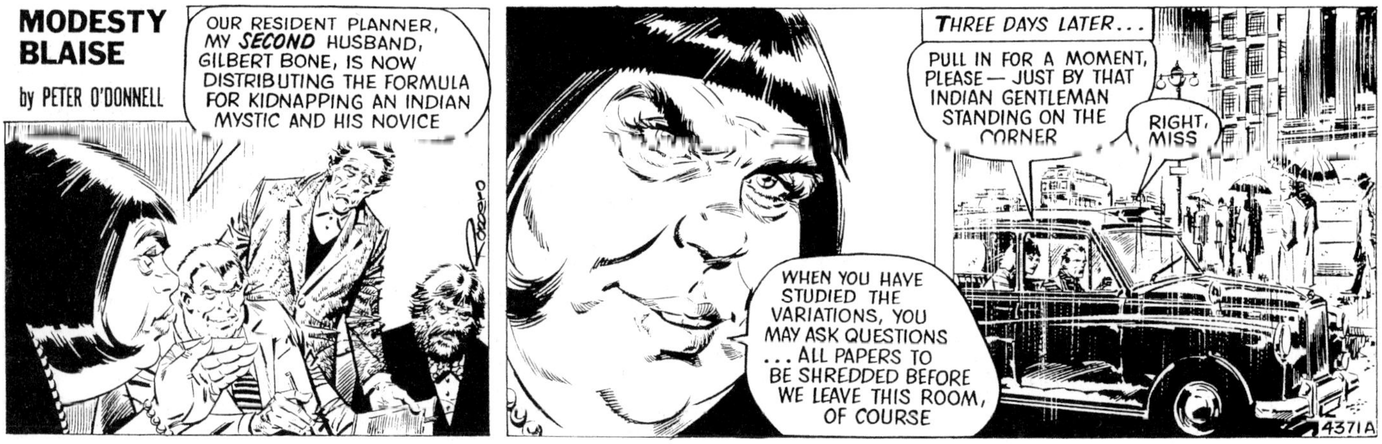
MODESTY BLAISE
by PETER O'DONNELL
OUR RESIDENT PLANNER, MY SECOND HUSBAND, GILBERT BONE, IS NOW DISTRIBUTING THE FORMULA FOR KIDNAPPING AN INDIAN MYSTIC AND HIS NOVICE
WHEN YOU HAVE STUDIED THE VARIATIONS, YOU MAY ASK QUESTIONS ... ALL PAPERS TO BE SHREDDED BEFORE WE LEAVE THIS ROOM, OF COURSE
THREE DAYS LATER...
PULL IN FOR A MOMENT, PLEASE— JUST BY THAT INDIAN GENTLEMAN STANDING ON THE CORNER
RIGHT, MISS
4371A

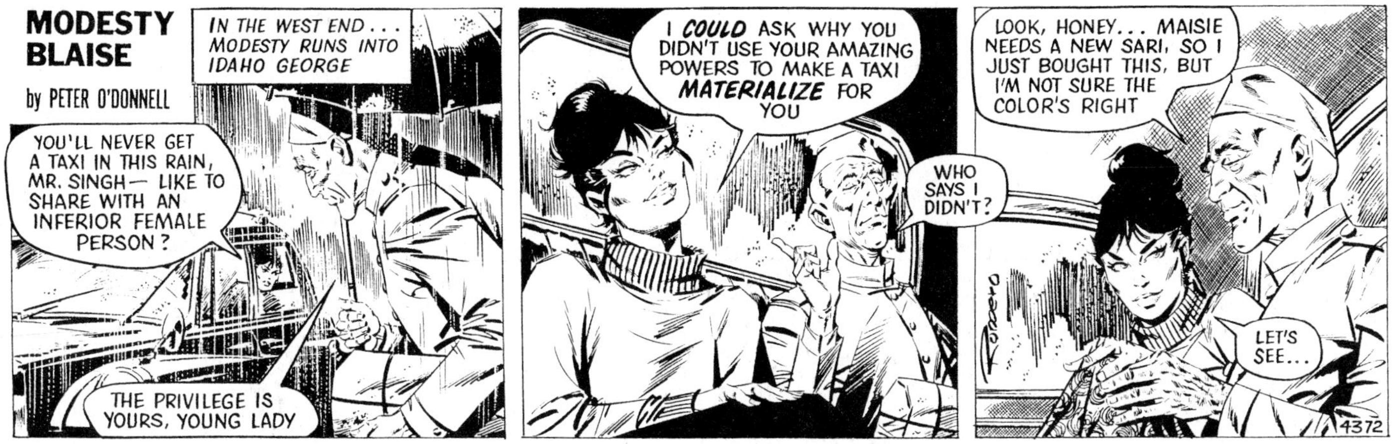
MODESTY BLAISE
by PETER O'DONNELL
IN THE WEST END... MODESTY RUNS INTO IDAHO GEORGE
YOU'LL NEVER GET A TAXI IN THIS RAIN, MR. SINGH— LIKE TO SHARE WITH AN INFERIOR FEMALE PERSON?
THE PRIVILEGE IS YOURS, YOUNG LADY
I COULD ASK WHY YOU DIDN'T USE YOUR AMAZING POWERS TO MAKE A TAXI MATERIALIZE FOR YOU
WHO SAYS I DIDN'T?
LOOK, HONEY... MAISIE NEEDS A NEW SARI, SO I JUST BOUGHT THIS, BUT I'M NOT SURE THE COLOR'S RIGHT
LET'S SEE...
4372

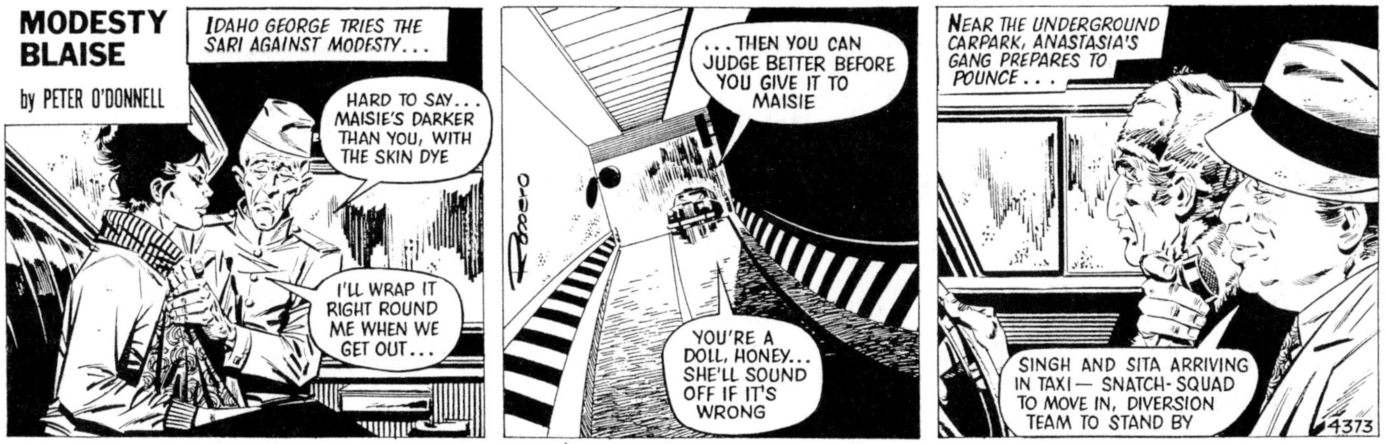
MODESTY BLAISE
by PETER O'DONNELL
IDAHO GEORGE TRIES THE SARI AGAINST MODESTY...
HARD TO SAY... MAISIE'S DARKER THAN YOU, WITH THE SKIN DYE
I'LL WRAP IT RIGHT ROUND ME WHEN WE GET OUT...
...THEN YOU CAN JUDGE BETTER BEFORE YOU GIVE IT TO MAISIE
YOU'RE A DOLL, HONEY... SHE'LL SOUND OFF IF IT'S WRONG
NEAR THE UNDERGROUND CARPARK, ANASTASIA'S GANG PREPARES TO POUNCE...
SINGH AND SITA ARRIVING IN TAXI— SNATCH-SQUAD TO MOVE IN, DIVERSION TEAM TO STAND BY
4373

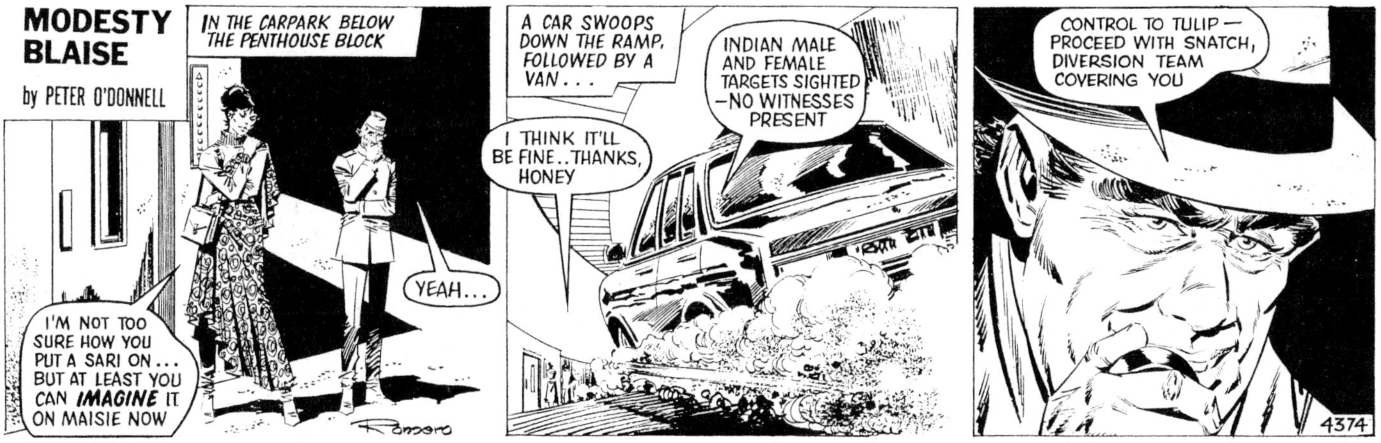
MODESTY BLAISE
by PETER O'DONNELL
IN THE CARPARK BELOW THE PENTHOUSE BLOCK
I'M NOT TOO SURE HOW YOU PUT A SARI ON... BUT AT LEAST YOU CAN IMAGINE IT ON MAISIE NOW
YEAH...
A CAR SWOOPS DOWN THE RAMP, FOLLOWED BY A VAN...
I THINK IT'LL BE FINE.. THANKS, HONEY
INDIAN MALE AND FEMALE TARGETS SIGHTED —NO WITNESSES PRESENT
CONTROL TO TULIP— PROCEED WITH SNATCH, DIVERSION TEAM COVERING YOU
4374

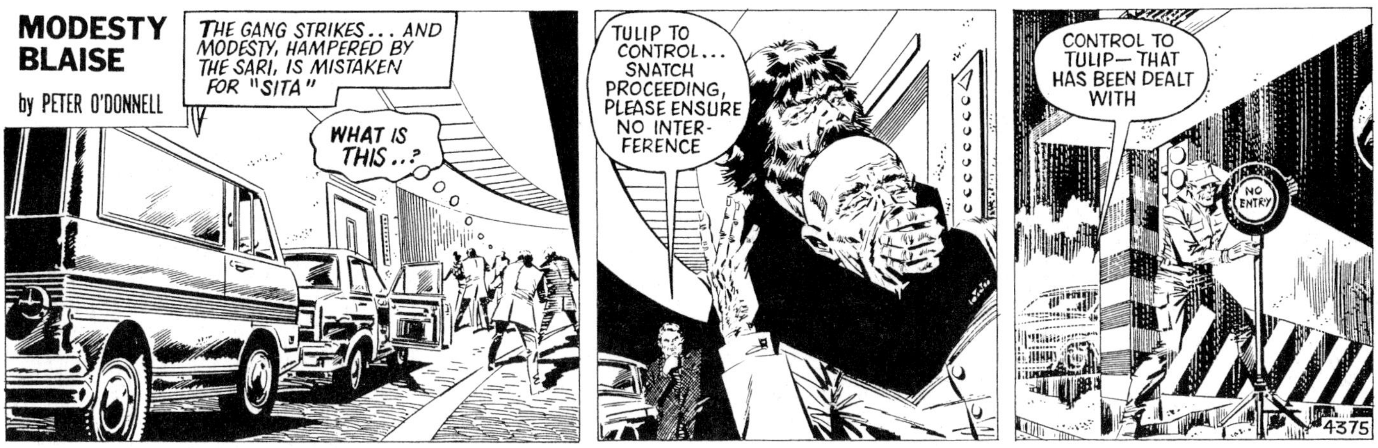
MODESTY BLAISE
by PETER O'DONNELL
THE GANG STRIKES... AND MODESTY, HAMPERED BY THE SARI, IS MISTAKEN FOR "SITA"
WHAT IS THIS..?
TULIP TO CONTROL... SNATCH PROCEEDING, PLEASE ENSURE NO INTER-FERENCE
CONTROL TO TULIP— THAT HAS BEEN DEALT WITH
NO ENTRY
4375

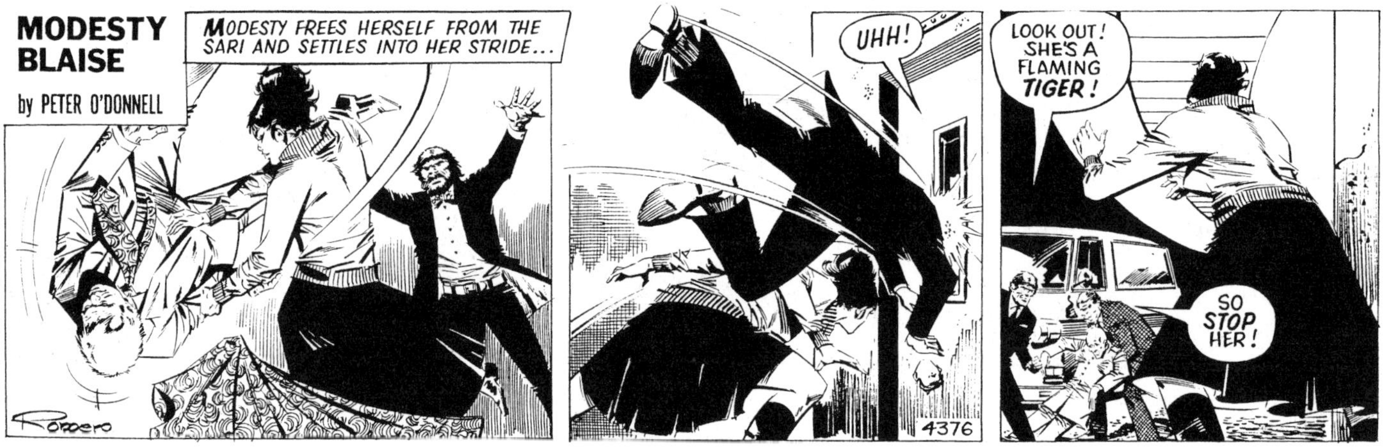
MODESTY BLAISE
by PETER O'DONNELL
MODESTY FREES HERSELF FROM THE SARI AND SETTLES INTO HER STRIDE...
UHH!
LOOK OUT! SHE'S A FLAMING TIGER!
SO STOP HER!
4376

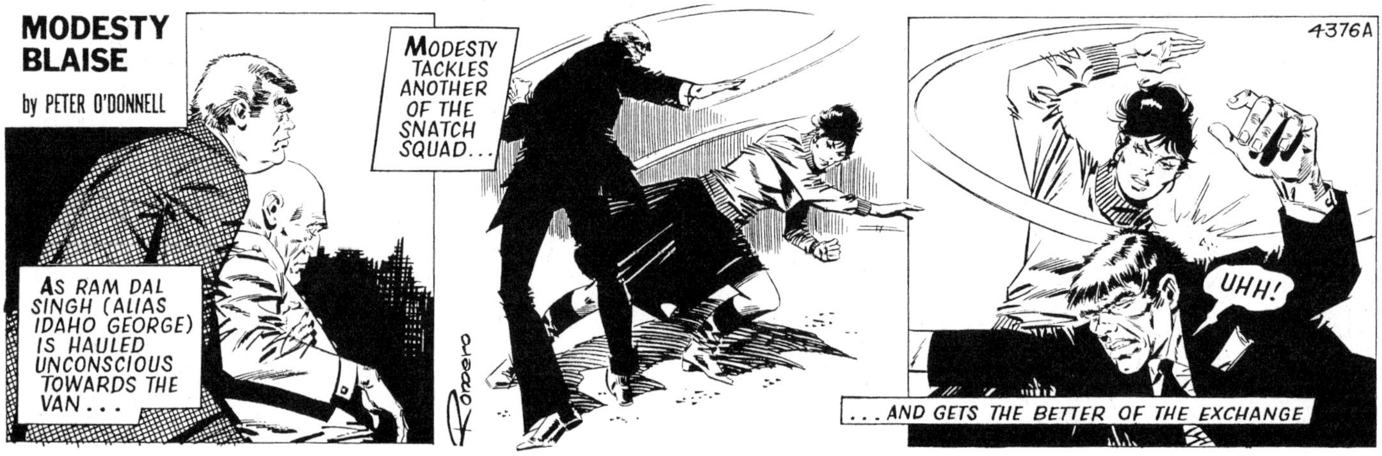
MODESTY BLAISE
by PETER O'DONNELL
AS RAM DAL SINGH (ALIAS IDAHO GEORGE) IS HAULED UNCONSCIOUS TOWARDS THE VAN...
MODESTY TACKLES ANOTHER OF THE SNATCH SQUAD...
4376A
UHH!
...AND GETS THE BETTER OF THE EXCHANGE

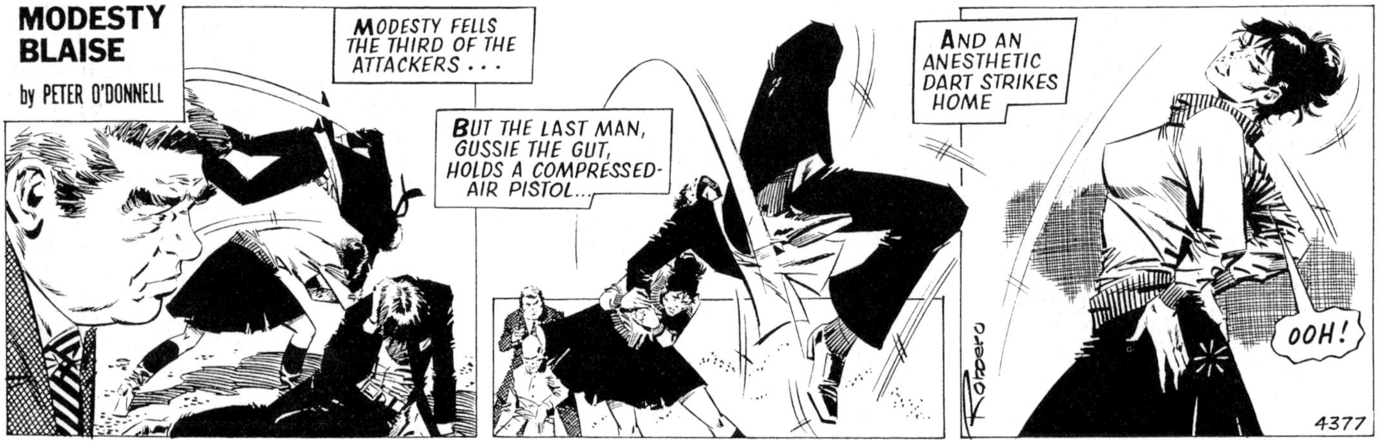
MODESTY BLAISE
by PETER O'DONNELL
MODESTY FELLS THE THIRD OF THE ATTACKERS...
BUT THE LAST MAN, GUSSIE THE GUT, HOLDS A COMPRESSED-AIR PISTOL...
AND AN ANESTHETIC DART STRIKES HOME
OOH!
4377

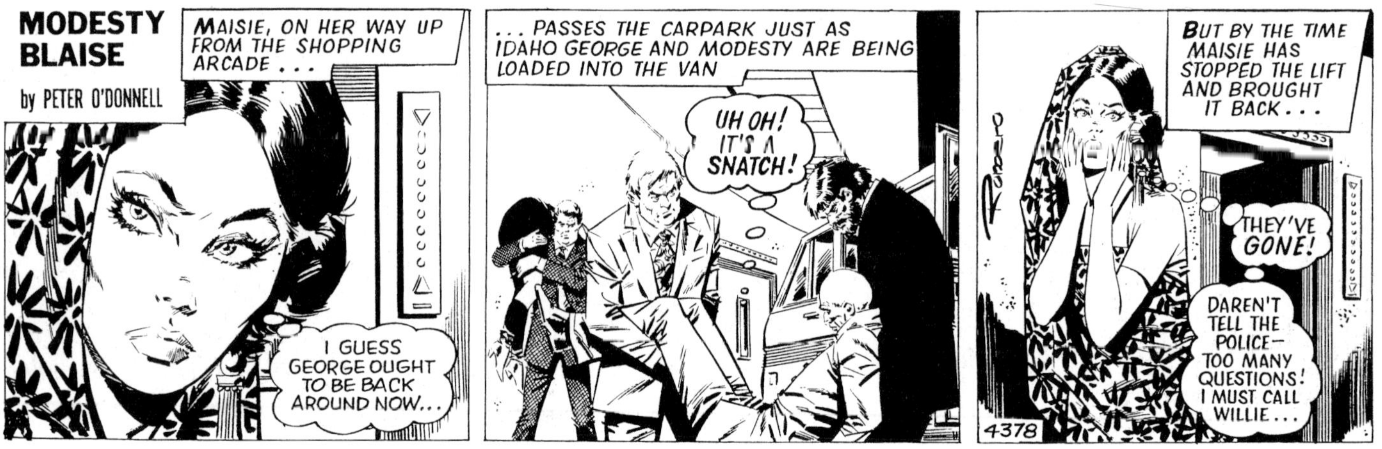
MODESTY BLAISE
by PETER O'DONNELL
MAISIE, ON HER WAY UP FROM THE SHOPPING ARCADE...
I GUESS GEORGE OUGHT TO BE BACK AROUND NOW...
...PASSES THE CARPARK JUST AS IDAHO GEORGE AND MODESTY ARE BEING LOADED INTO THE VAN
UH OH! IT'S A SNATCH!
BUT BY THE TIME MAISIE HAS STOPPED THE LIFT AND BROUGHT IT BACK...
THEY'VE GONE!
DAREN'T TELL THE POLICE—TOO MANY QUESTIONS! I MUST CALL WILLIE...
4378

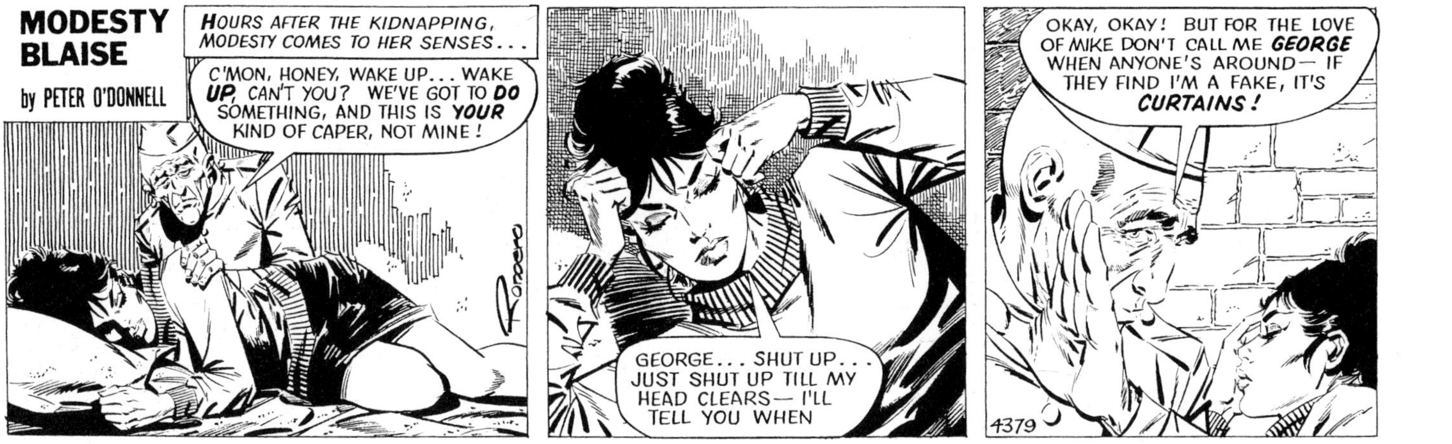
MODESTY BLAISE
by PETER O'DONNELL
HOURS AFTER THE KIDNAPPING, MODESTY COMES TO HER SENSES...
C'MON, HONEY, WAKE UP... WAKE UP, CAN'T YOU? WE'VE GOT TO DO SOMETHING, AND THIS IS YOUR KIND OF CAPER, NOT MINE!
GEORGE... SHUT UP... JUST SHUT UP TILL MY HEAD CLEARS— I'LL TELL YOU WHEN
OKAY, OKAY! BUT FOR THE LOVE OF MIKE DON'T CALL ME GEORGE WHEN ANYONE'S AROUND— IF THEY FIND I'M A FAKE, IT'S CURTAINS!
4379

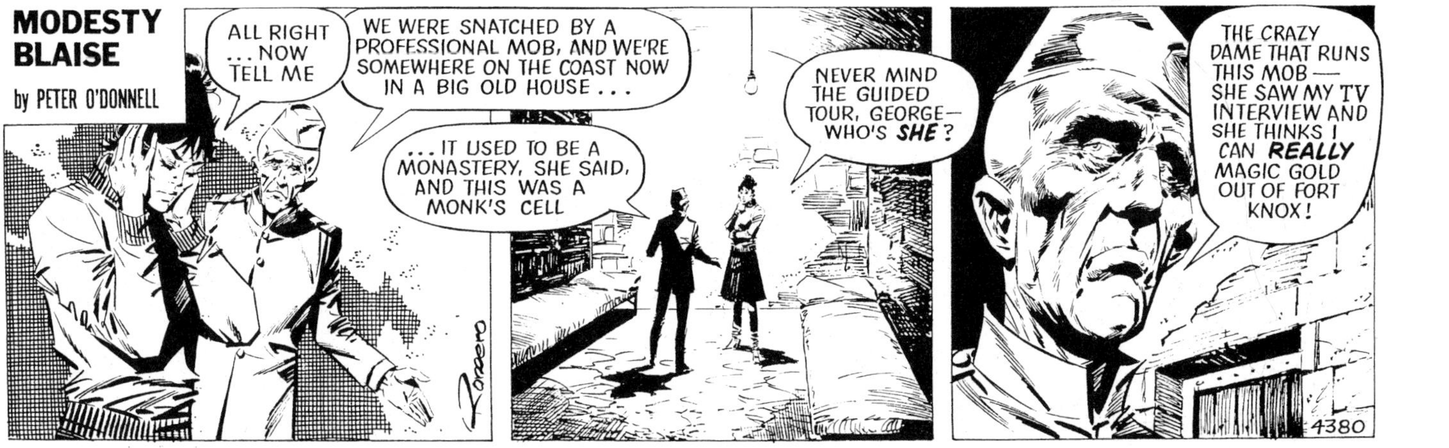
MODESTY BLAISE
by PETER O'DONNELL
ALL RIGHT ... NOW TELL ME
WE WERE SNATCHED BY A PROFESSIONAL MOB, AND WE'RE SOMEWHERE ON THE COAST NOW IN A BIG OLD HOUSE...
...IT USED TO BE A MONASTERY, SHE SAID, AND THIS WAS A MONK'S CELL
NEVER MIND THE GUIDED TOUR, GEORGE— WHO'S SHE?
THE CRAZY DAME THAT RUNS THIS MOB— SHE SAW MY TV INTERVIEW AND SHE THINKS I CAN REALLY MAGIC GOLD OUT OF FORT KNOX!
4380

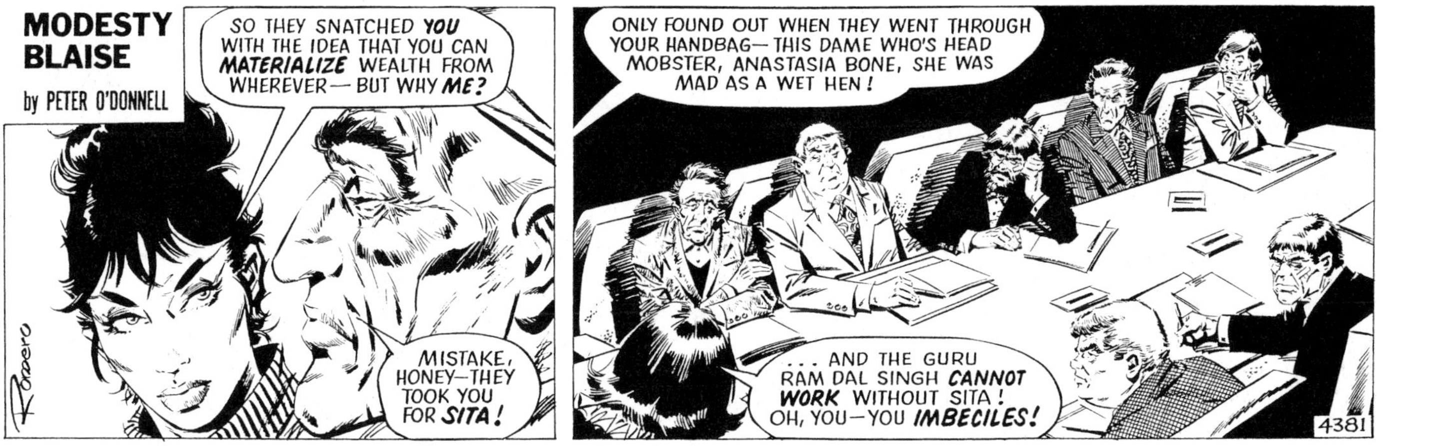
MODESTY BLAISE
by PETER O'DONNELL
SO THEY SNATCHED YOU WITH THE IDEA THAT YOU CAN MATERIALIZE WEALTH FROM WHEREVER— BUT WHY ME?
MISTAKE, HONEY—THEY TOOK YOU FOR SITA!
ONLY FOUND OUT WHEN THEY WENT THROUGH YOUR HANDBAG— THIS DAME WHO'S HEAD MOBSTER, ANASTASIA BONE, SHE WAS MAD AS A WET HEN!
...AND THE GURU RAM DAL SINGH CANNOT WORK WITHOUT SITA! OH, YOU—YOU IMBECILES!
4381

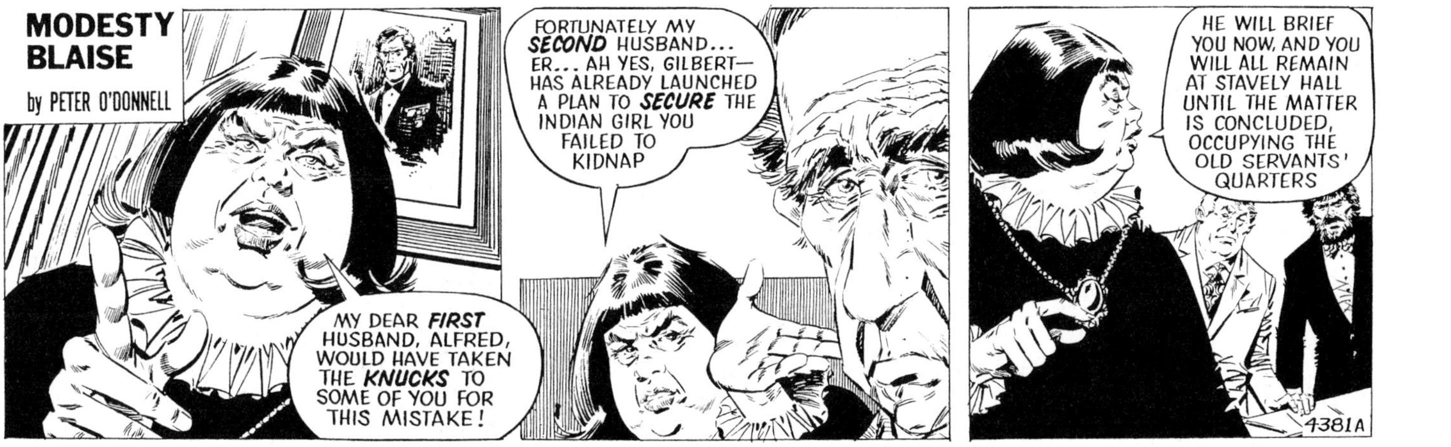
MODESTY BLAISE
by PETER O'DONNELL
MY DEAR FIRST HUSBAND, ALFRED, WOULD HAVE TAKEN THE KNUCKS TO SOME OF YOU FOR THIS MISTAKE!
FORTUNATELY MY SECOND HUSBAND... ER... AH YES, GILBERT— HAS ALREADY LAUNCHED A PLAN TO SECURE THE INDIAN GIRL YOU FAILED TO KIDNAP
HE WILL BRIEF YOU NOW, AND YOU WILL ALL REMAIN AT STAVELY HALL UNTIL THE MATTER IS CONCLUDED, OCCUPYING THE OLD SERVANTS' QUARTERS
4381A

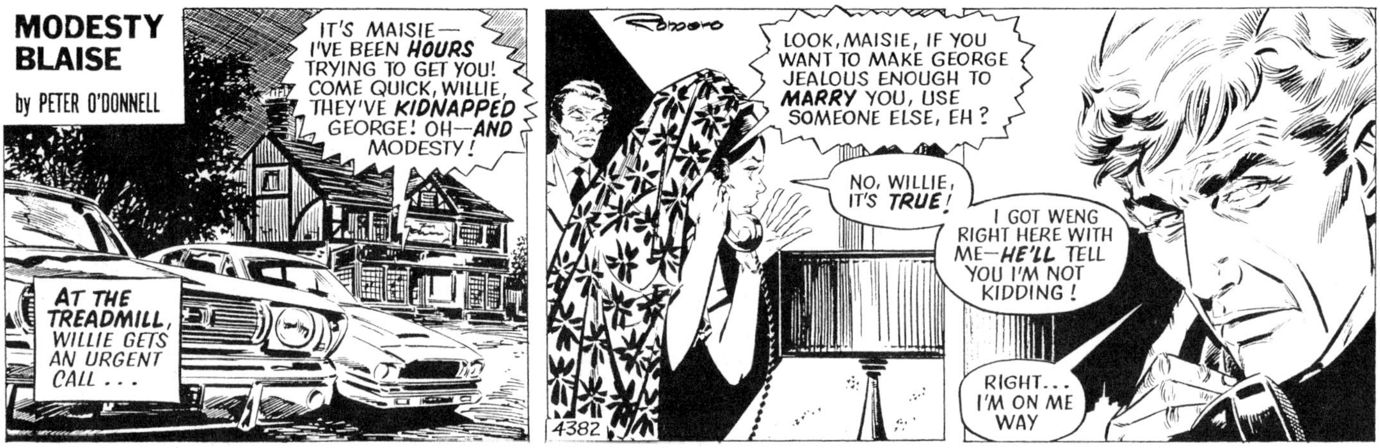
MODESTY BLAISE
by PETER O'DONNELL
IT'S MAISIE— I'VE BEEN HOURS TRYING TO GET YOU! COME QUICK, WILLIE, THEY'VE KIDNAPPED GEORGE! OH—AND MODESTY!
AT THE TREADMILL, WILLIE GETS AN URGENT CALL...
LOOK, MAISIE, IF YOU WANT TO MAKE GEORGE JEALOUS ENOUGH TO MARRY YOU, USE SOMEONE ELSE, EH?
NO, WILLIE, IT'S TRUE!
I GOT WENG RIGHT HERE WITH ME—HE'LL TELL YOU I'M NOT KIDDING!
RIGHT... I'M ON ME WAY
4382

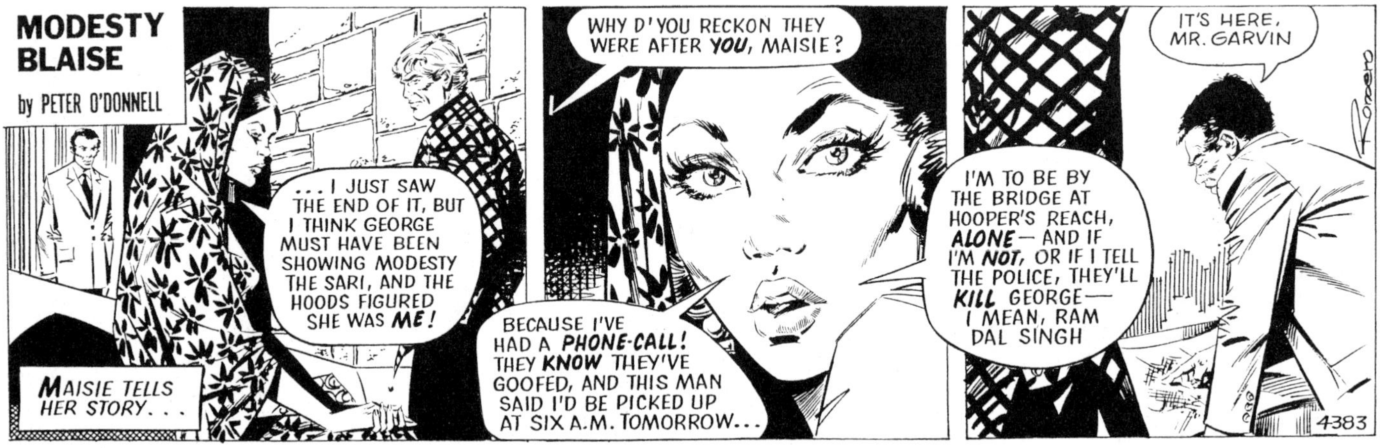
MODESTY BLAISE
by PETER O'DONNELL
MAISIE TELLS HER STORY...
...I JUST SAW THE END OF IT, BUT I THINK GEORGE MUST HAVE BEEN SHOWING MODESTY THE SARI, AND THE HOODS FIGURED SHE WAS ME!
WHY D'YOU RECKON THEY WERE AFTER YOU, MAISIE?
BECAUSE I'VE HAD A PHONE-CALL! THEY KNOW THEY'VE GOOFED, AND THIS MAN SAID I'D BE PICKED UP AT SIX A.M. TOMORROW...
IT'S HERE, MR. GARVIN
I'M TO BE BY THE BRIDGE AT HOOPER'S REACH, ALONE—AND IF I'M NOT, OR IF I TELL THE POLICE, THEY'LL KILL GEORGE— I MEAN, RAM DAL SINGH
4383

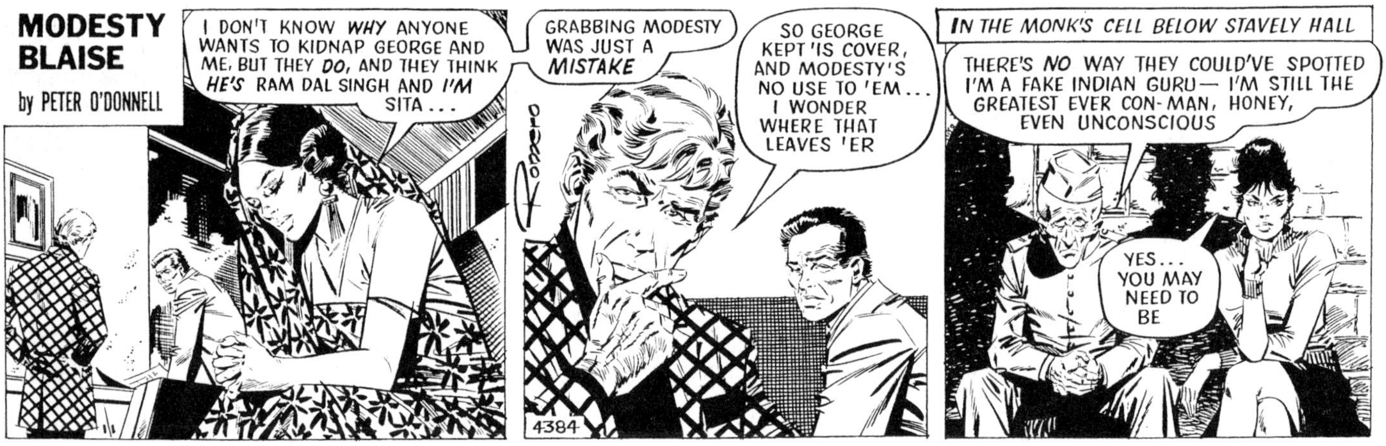
MODESTY BLAISE
by PETER O'DONNELL
I DON'T KNOW WHY ANYONE WANTS TO KIDNAP GEORGE AND ME, BUT THEY DO, AND THEY THINK HE'S RAM DAL SINGH AND I'M SITA...
GRABBING MODESTY WAS JUST A MISTAKE
SO GEORGE KEPT 'IS COVER, AND MODESTY'S NO USE TO 'EM... I WONDER WHERE THAT LEAVES 'ER
4384
IN THE MONK'S CELL BELOW STAVELY HALL
THERE'S NO WAY THEY COULD'VE SPOTTED I'M A FAKE INDIAN GURU— I'M STILL THE GREATEST EVER CON-MAN, HONEY, EVEN UNCONSCIOUS
YES... YOU MAY NEED TO BE

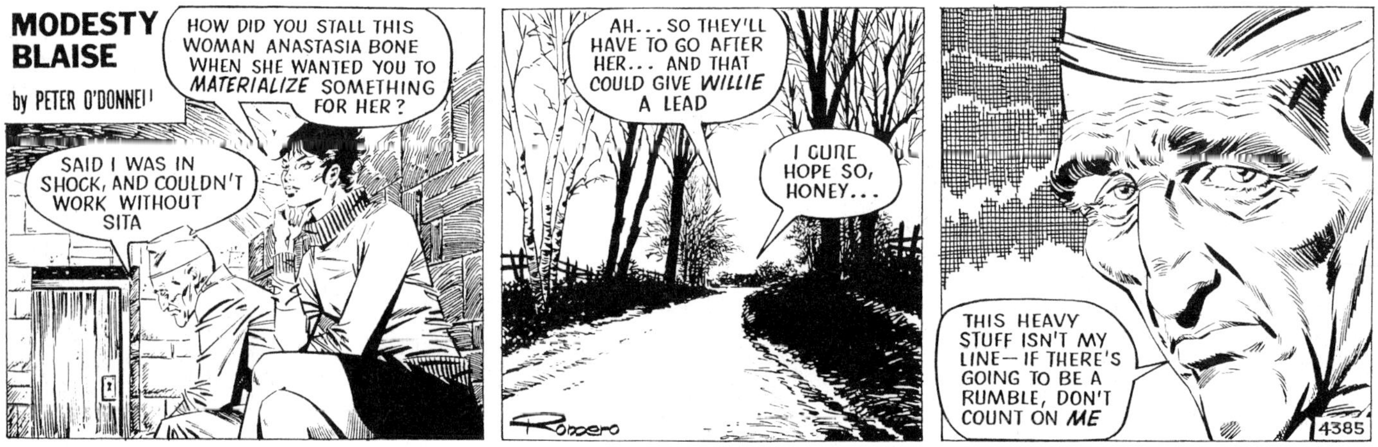
MODESTY BLAISE
by PETER O'DONNELL
HOW DID YOU STALL THIS WOMAN ANASTASIA BONE WHEN SHE WANTED YOU TO MATERIALIZE SOMETHING FOR HER?
SAID I WAS IN SHOCK, AND COULDN'T WORK WITHOUT SITA
AH... SO THEY'LL HAVE TO GO AFTER HER... AND THAT COULD GIVE WILLIE A LEAD
I SURE HOPE SO, HONEY...
THIS HEAVY STUFF ISN'T MY LINE— IF THERE'S GOING TO BE A RUMBLE, DON'T COUNT ON ME
4385

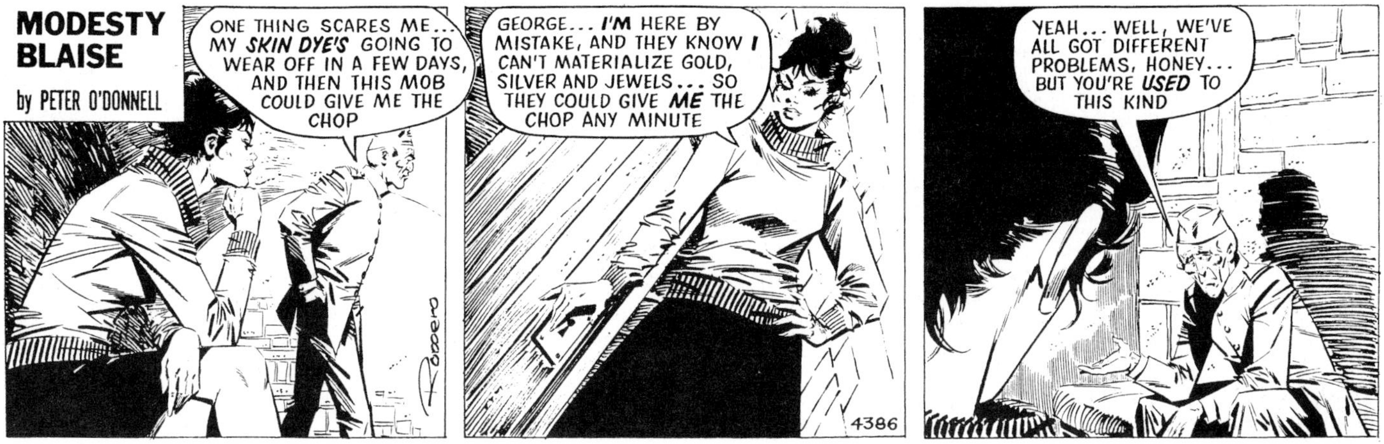
MODESTY BLAISE
by PETER O'DONNELL
ONE THING SCARES ME... MY SKIN DYE'S GOING TO WEAR OFF IN A FEW DAYS, AND THEN THIS MOB COULD GIVE ME THE CHOP
GEORGE... I'M HERE BY MISTAKE, AND THEY KNOW I CAN'T MATERIALIZE GOLD, SILVER AND JEWELS... SO THEY COULD GIVE ME THE CHOP ANY MINUTE
YEAH... WELL, WE'VE ALL GOT DIFFERENT PROBLEMS, HONEY... BUT YOU'RE USED TO THIS KIND
Romero
4386

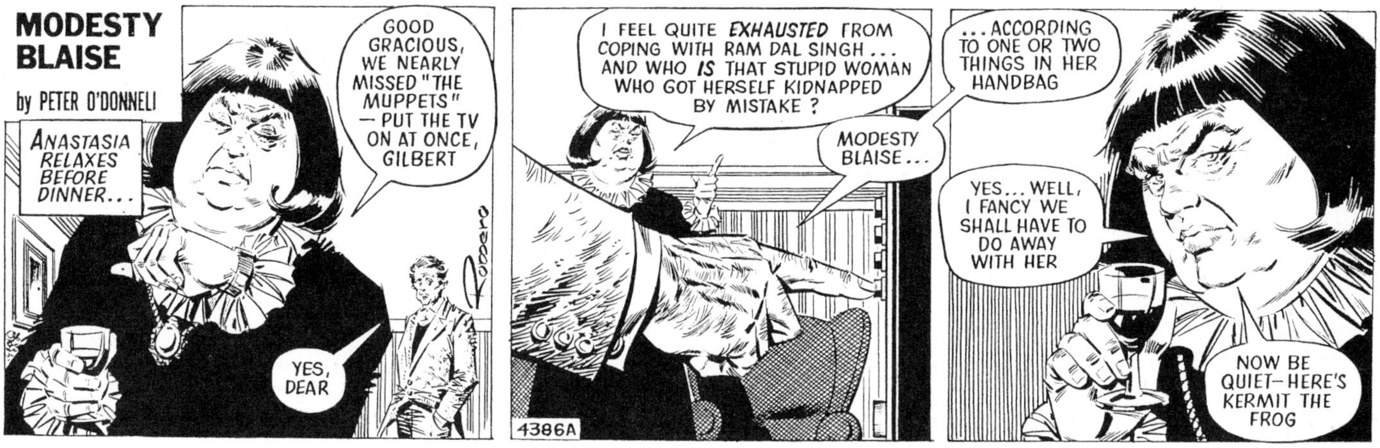
MODESTY BLAISE
by PETER O'DONNELL
ANASTASIA RELAXES BEFORE DINNER...
GOOD GRACIOUS, WE NEARLY MISSED "THE MUPPETS" — PUT THE TV ON AT ONCE, GILBERT
YES, DEAR
Romero
4386A
I FEEL QUITE EXHAUSTED FROM COPING WITH RAM DAL SINGH... AND WHO IS THAT STUPID WOMAN WHO GOT HERSELF KIDNAPPED BY MISTAKE?
MODESTY BLAISE...
...ACCORDING TO ONE OR TWO THINGS IN HER HANDBAG
YES... WELL, I FANCY WE SHALL HAVE TO DO AWAY WITH HER
NOW BE QUIET—HERE'S KERMIT THE FROG

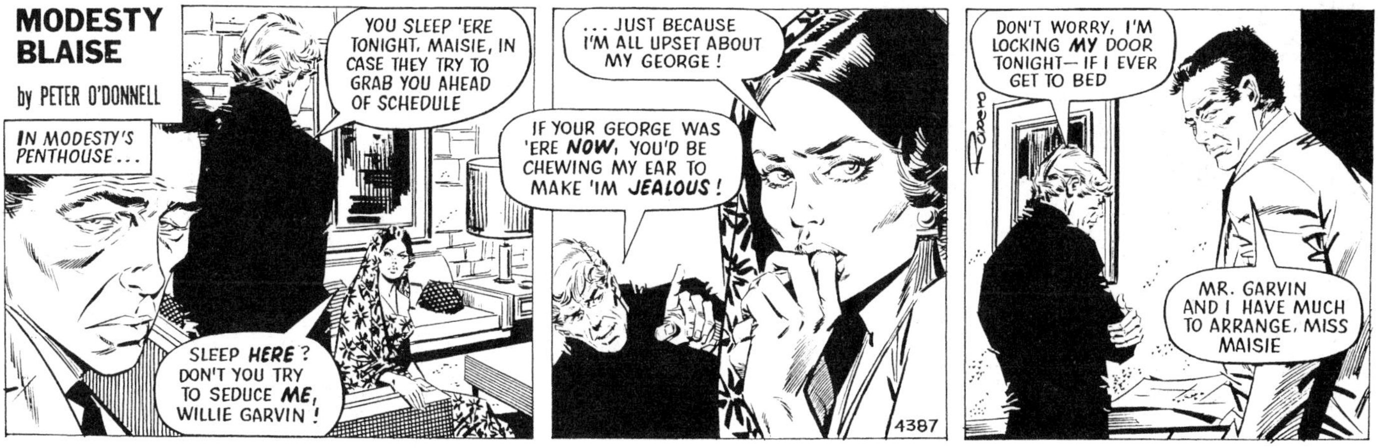
MODESTY BLAISE
by PETER O'DONNELL
IN MODESTY'S PENTHOUSE...
YOU SLEEP 'ERE TONIGHT, MAISIE, IN CASE THEY TRY TO GRAB YOU AHEAD OF SCHEDULE
SLEEP HERE? DON'T YOU TRY TO SEDUCE ME, WILLIE GARVIN!
... JUST BECAUSE I'M ALL UPSET ABOUT MY GEORGE!
IF YOUR GEORGE WAS 'ERE NOW, YOU'D BE CHEWING MY EAR TO MAKE 'IM JEALOUS!
4387
DON'T WORRY, I'M LOCKING MY DOOR TONIGHT— IF I EVER GET TO BED
Romero
MR. GARVIN AND I HAVE MUCH TO ARRANGE, MISS MAISIE

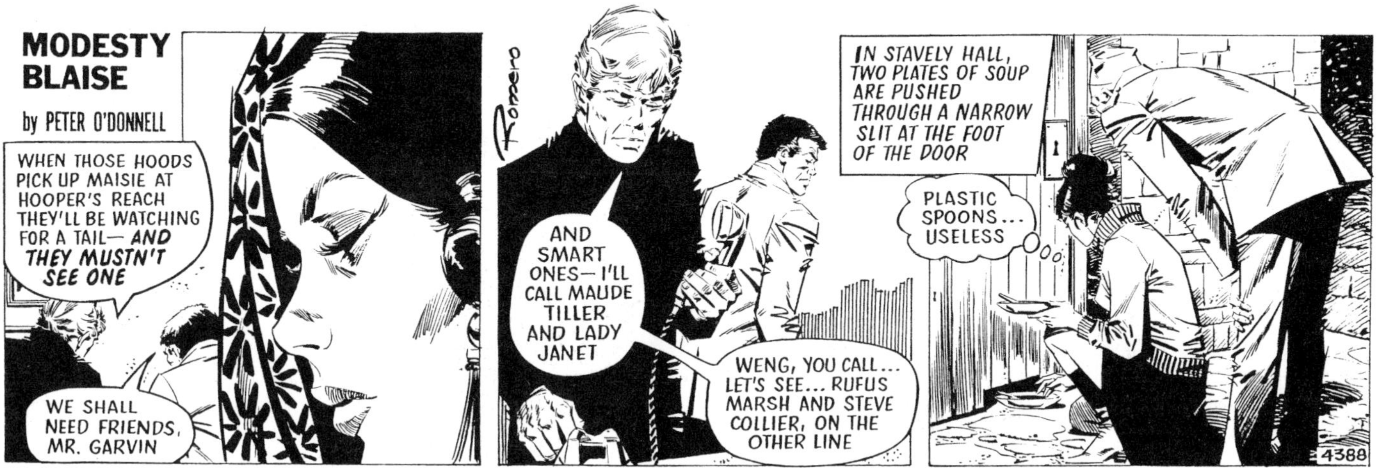
MODESTY BLAISE
by PETER O'DONNELL
WHEN THOSE HOODS PICK UP MAISIE AT HOOPER'S REACH THEY'LL BE WATCHING FOR A TAIL— AND THEY MUSTN'T SEE ONE
WE SHALL NEED FRIENDS, MR. GARVIN
Romero
AND SMART ONES— I'LL CALL MAUDE TILLER AND LADY JANET
WENG, YOU CALL... LET'S SEE... RUFUS MARSH AND STEVE COLLIER, ON THE OTHER LINE
IN STAVELY HALL, TWO PLATES OF SOUP ARE PUSHED THROUGH A NARROW SLIT AT THE FOOT OF THE DOOR
PLASTIC SPOONS... USELESS
4388

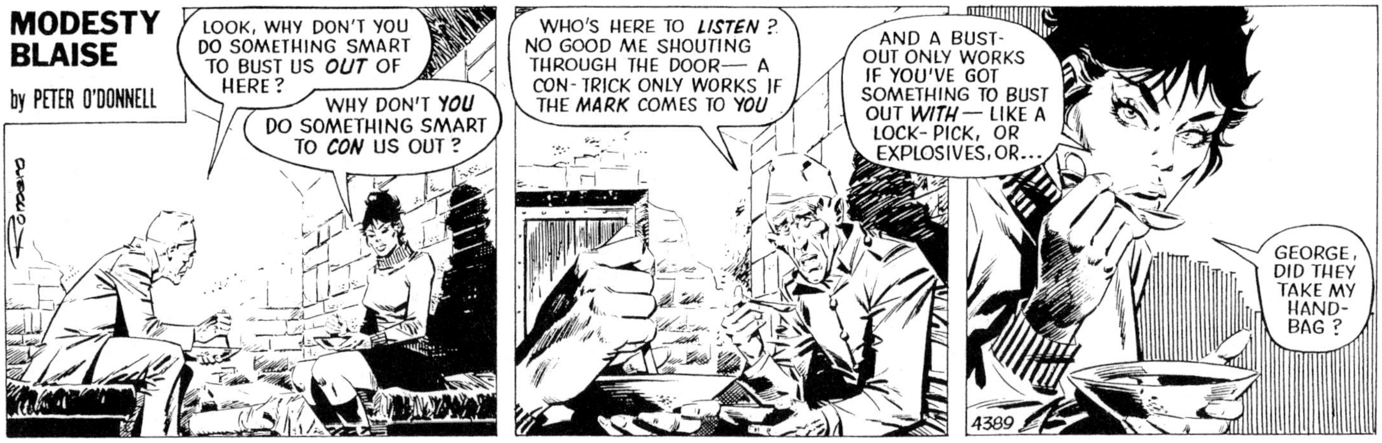
MODESTY BLAISE
by PETER O'DONNELL
LOOK, WHY DON'T YOU DO SOMETHING SMART TO BUST US OUT OF HERE?
WHY DON'T YOU DO SOMETHING SMART TO CON US OUT?
WHO'S HERE TO LISTEN? NO GOOD ME SHOUTING THROUGH THE DOOR— A CON-TRICK ONLY WORKS IF THE MARK COMES TO YOU
AND A BUST-OUT ONLY WORKS IF YOU'VE GOT SOMETHING TO BUST OUT WITH— LIKE A LOCK-PICK, OR EXPLOSIVES, OR...
GEORGE, DID THEY TAKE MY HAND-BAG?
4389

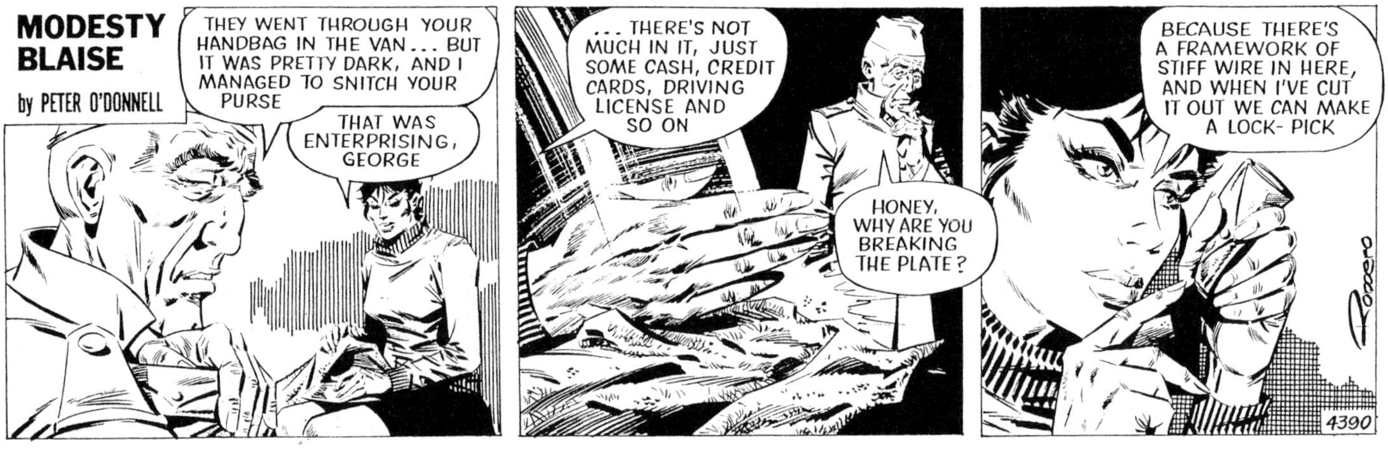
MODESTY BLAISE
by PETER O'DONNELL
THEY WENT THROUGH YOUR HANDBAG IN THE VAN... BUT IT WAS PRETTY DARK, AND I MANAGED TO SNITCH YOUR PURSE
THAT WAS ENTERPRISING, GEORGE
... THERE'S NOT MUCH IN IT, JUST SOME CASH, CREDIT CARDS, DRIVING LICENSE AND SO ON
HONEY, WHY ARE YOU BREAKING THE PLATE?
BECAUSE THERE'S A FRAMEWORK OF STIFF WIRE IN HERE, AND WHEN I'VE CUT IT OUT WE CAN MAKE A LOCK-PICK
4390

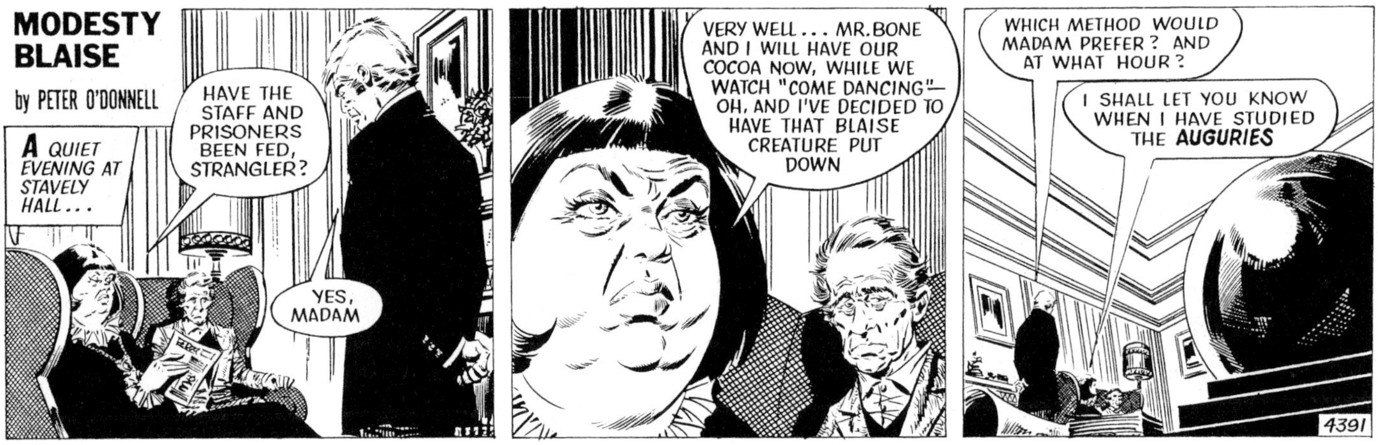
MODESTY BLAISE
by PETER O'DONNELL
A QUIET EVENING AT STAVELY HALL...
HAVE THE STAFF AND PRISONERS BEEN FED, STRANGLER?
YES, MADAM
VERY WELL... MR. BONE AND I WILL HAVE OUR COCOA NOW, WHILE WE WATCH "COME DANCING"— OH, AND I'VE DECIDED TO HAVE THAT BLAISE CREATURE PUT DOWN
WHICH METHOD WOULD MADAM PREFER? AND AT WHAT HOUR?
I SHALL LET YOU KNOW WHEN I HAVE STUDIED THE AUGURIES
4391

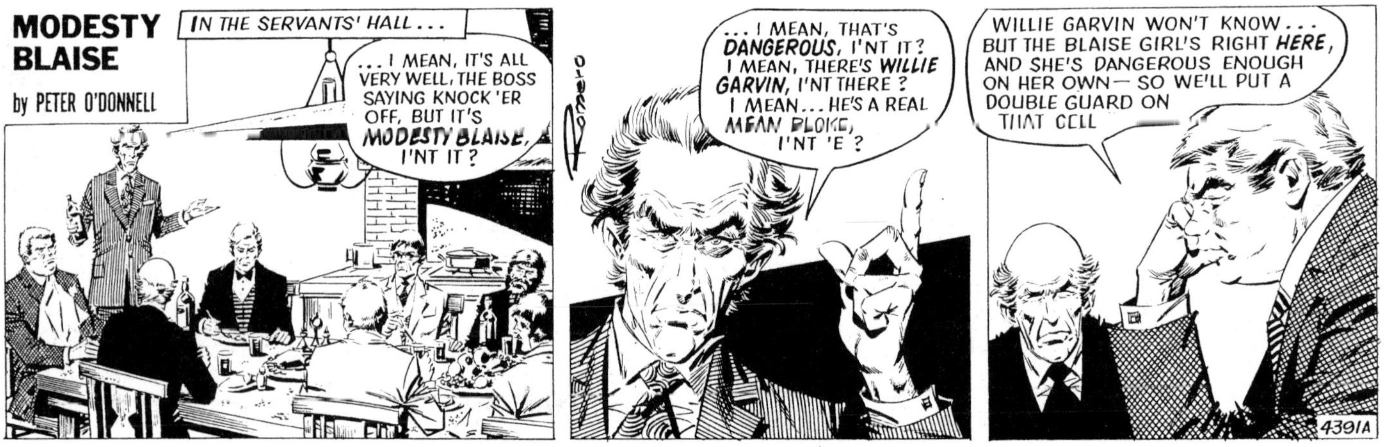
MODESTY BLAISE
by PETER O'DONNELL
IN THE SERVANTS' HALL...
... I MEAN, IT'S ALL VERY WELL, THE BOSS SAYING KNOCK 'ER OFF, BUT IT'S MODESTY BLAISE, I'NT IT?
... I MEAN, THAT'S DANGEROUS, I'NT IT? I MEAN, THERE'S WILLIE GARVIN, I'NT THERE? I MEAN... HE'S A REAL MEAN BLOKE, I'NT 'E?
WILLIE GARVIN WON'T KNOW... BUT THE BLAISE GIRL'S RIGHT HERE, AND SHE'S DANGEROUS ENOUGH ON HER OWN— SO WE'LL PUT A DOUBLE GUARD ON THAT CELL
4391A

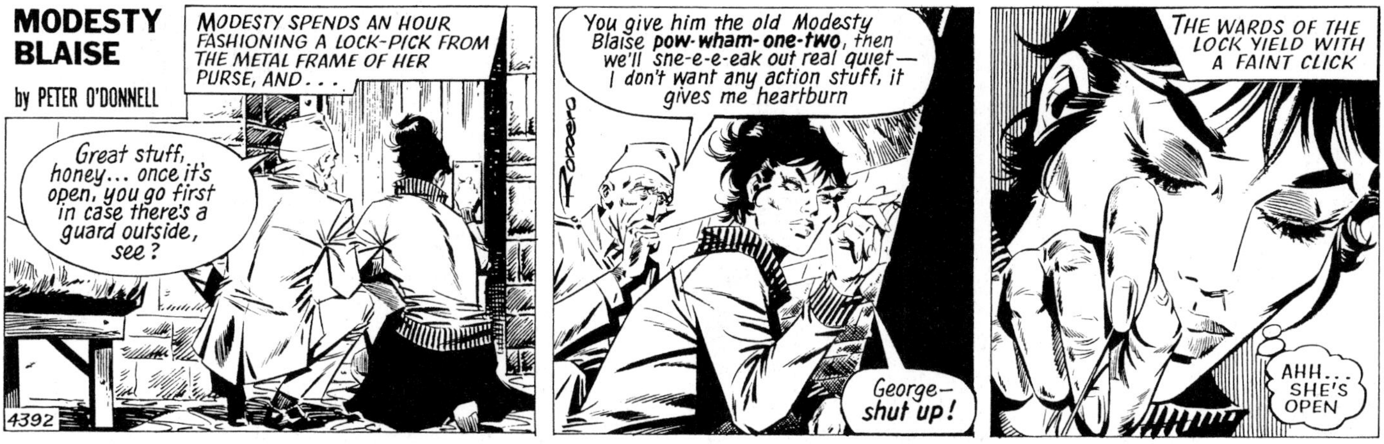
MODESTY BLAISE
by PETER O'DONNELL
MODESTY SPENDS AN HOUR FASHIONING A LOCK-PICK FROM THE METAL FRAME OF HER PURSE, AND . . .
Great stuff, honey... once it's open, you go first in case there's a guard outside, see?
You give him the old Modesty Blaise pow-wham-one-two, then we'll sne-e-eak out real quiet— I don't want any action stuff, it gives me heartburn
George— shut up!
THE WARDS OF THE LOCK YIELD WITH A FAINT CLICK
AHH... SHE'S OPEN
4392

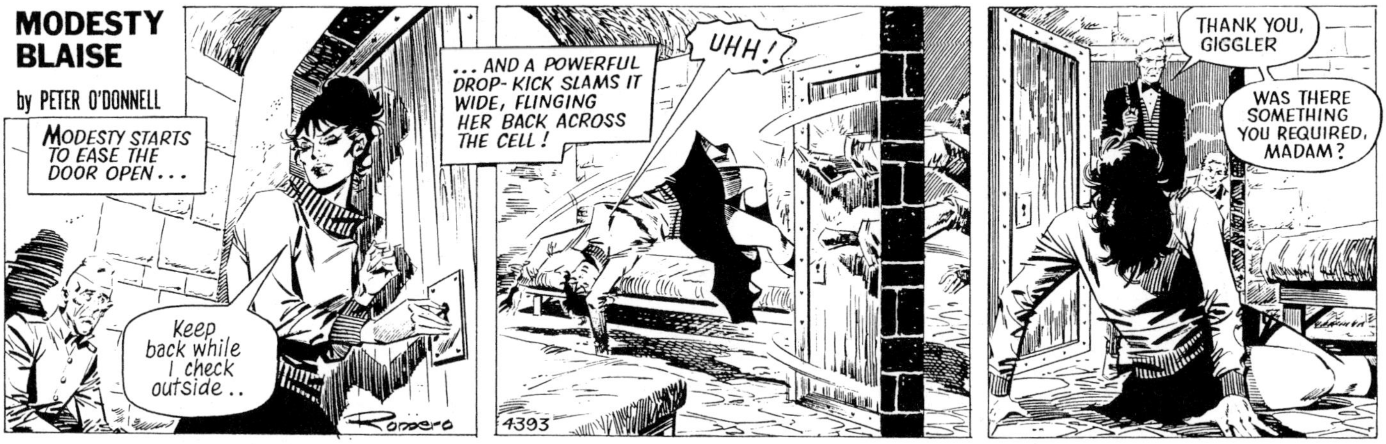
MODESTY BLAISE
by PETER O'DONNELL
MODESTY STARTS TO EASE THE DOOR OPEN...
Keep back while I check outside..
... AND A POWERFUL DROP-KICK SLAMS IT WIDE, FLINGING HER BACK ACROSS THE CELL!
UHH!
THANK YOU, GIGGLER
WAS THERE SOMETHING YOU REQUIRED, MADAM?
4393

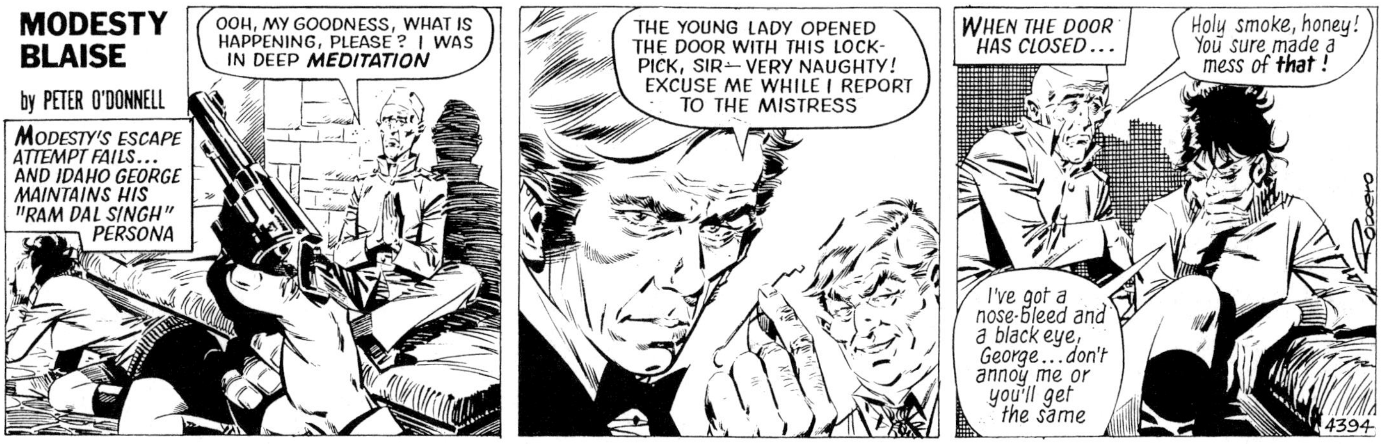
MODESTY BLAISE
by PETER O'DONNELL
MODESTY'S ESCAPE ATTEMPT FAILS... AND IDAHO GEORGE MAINTAINS HIS "RAM DAL SINGH" PERSONA
OOH, MY GOODNESS, WHAT IS HAPPENING, PLEASE? I WAS IN DEEP MEDITATION
THE YOUNG LADY OPENED THE DOOR WITH THIS LOCK-PICK, SIR— VERY NAUGHTY! EXCUSE ME WHILE I REPORT TO THE MISTRESS
WHEN THE DOOR HAS CLOSED...
Holy smoke, honey! You sure made a mess of that!
I've got a nose-bleed and a black eye, George... don't annoy me or you'll get the same
4394

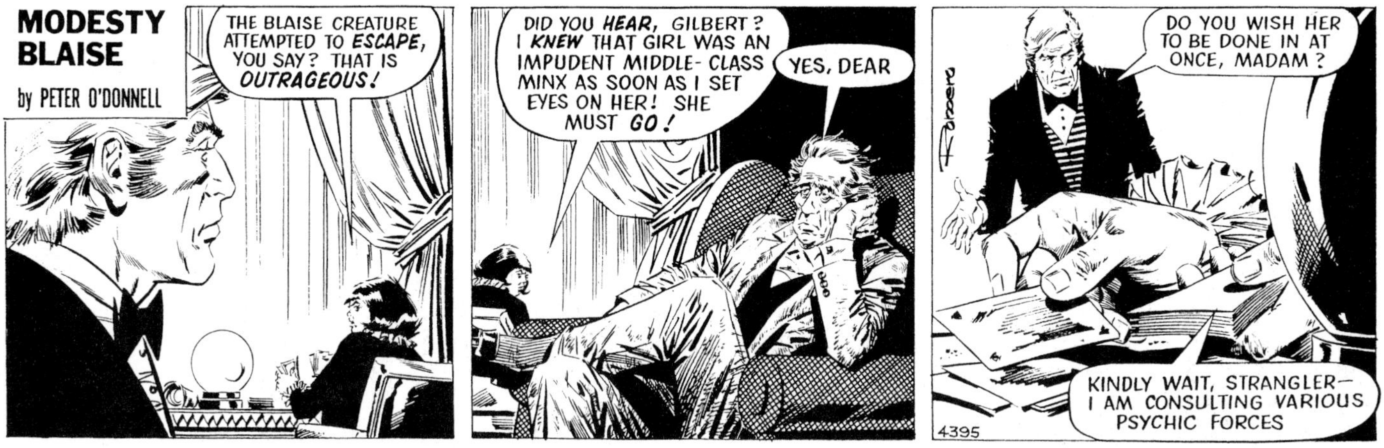
MODESTY BLAISE
by PETER O'DONNELL
THE BLAISE CREATURE ATTEMPTED TO ESCAPE, YOU SAY? THAT IS OUTRAGEOUS!
DID YOU HEAR, GILBERT? I KNEW THAT GIRL WAS AN IMPUDENT MIDDLE-CLASS MINX AS SOON AS I SET EYES ON HER! SHE MUST GO!
YES, DEAR
DO YOU WISH HER TO BE DONE IN AT ONCE, MADAM?
KINDLY WAIT, STRANGLER— I AM CONSULTING VARIOUS PSYCHIC FORCES
4395

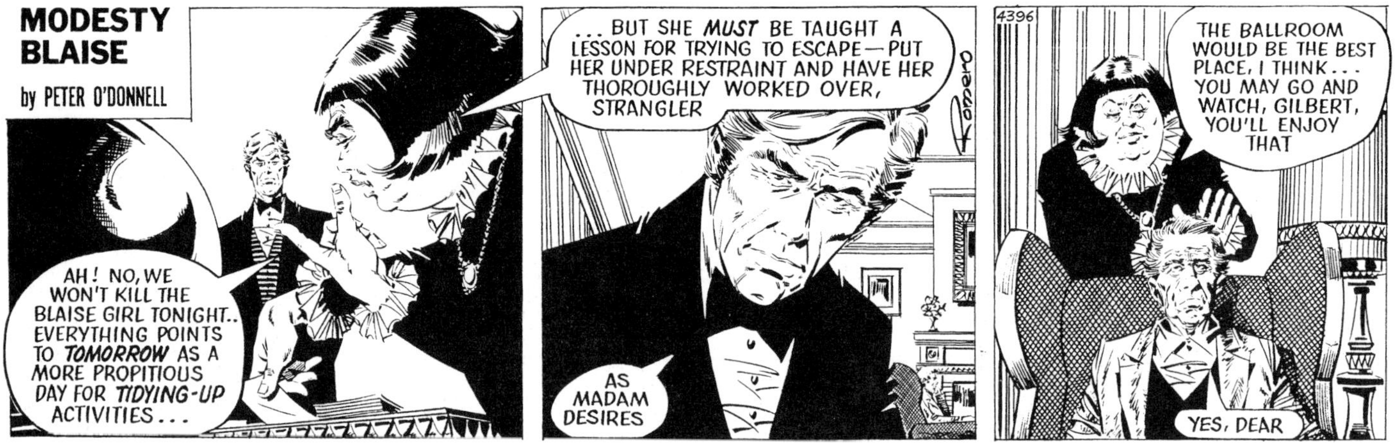
MODESTY BLAISE
by PETER O'DONNELL
AH! NO, WE WON'T KILL THE BLAISE GIRL TONIGHT.. EVERYTHING POINTS TO *TOMORROW* AS A MORE PROPITIOUS DAY FOR *TIDYING-UP* ACTIVITIES...
... BUT SHE *MUST* BE TAUGHT A LESSON FOR TRYING TO ESCAPE—PUT HER UNDER RESTRAINT AND HAVE HER THOROUGHLY WORKED OVER, STRANGLER
AS MADAM DESIRES
4396
THE BALLROOM WOULD BE THE BEST PLACE, I THINK... YOU MAY GO AND WATCH, GILBERT, YOU'LL ENJOY THAT
YES, DEAR

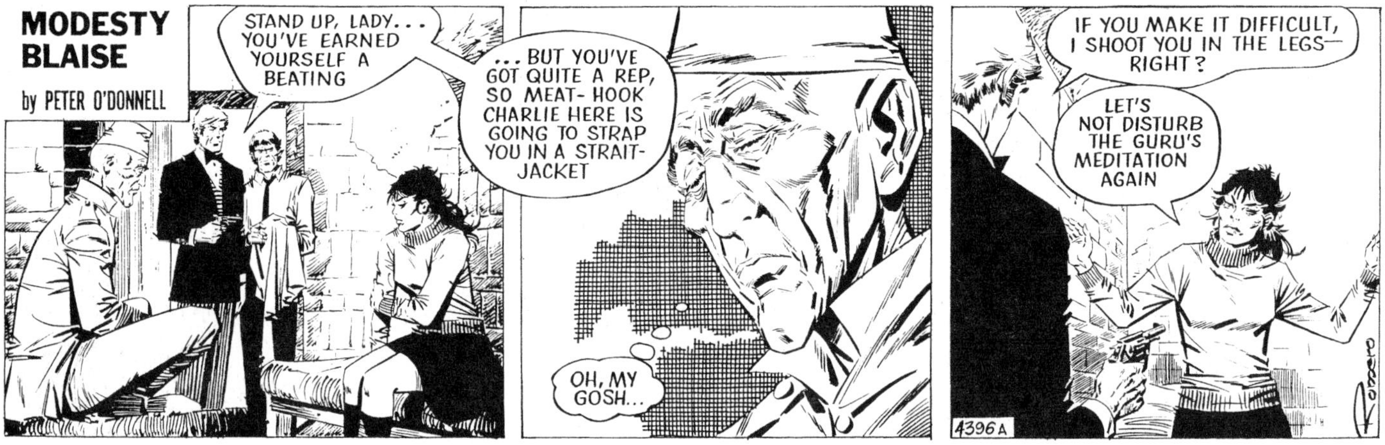
MODESTY BLAISE
by PETER O'DONNELL
STAND UP, LADY... YOU'VE EARNED YOURSELF A BEATING
... BUT YOU'VE GOT QUITE A REP, SO MEAT-HOOK CHARLIE HERE IS GOING TO STRAP YOU IN A STRAIT-JACKET
OH, MY GOSH...
4396A
IF YOU MAKE IT DIFFICULT, I SHOOT YOU IN THE LEGS—RIGHT?
LET'S NOT DISTURB THE GURU'S MEDITATION AGAIN

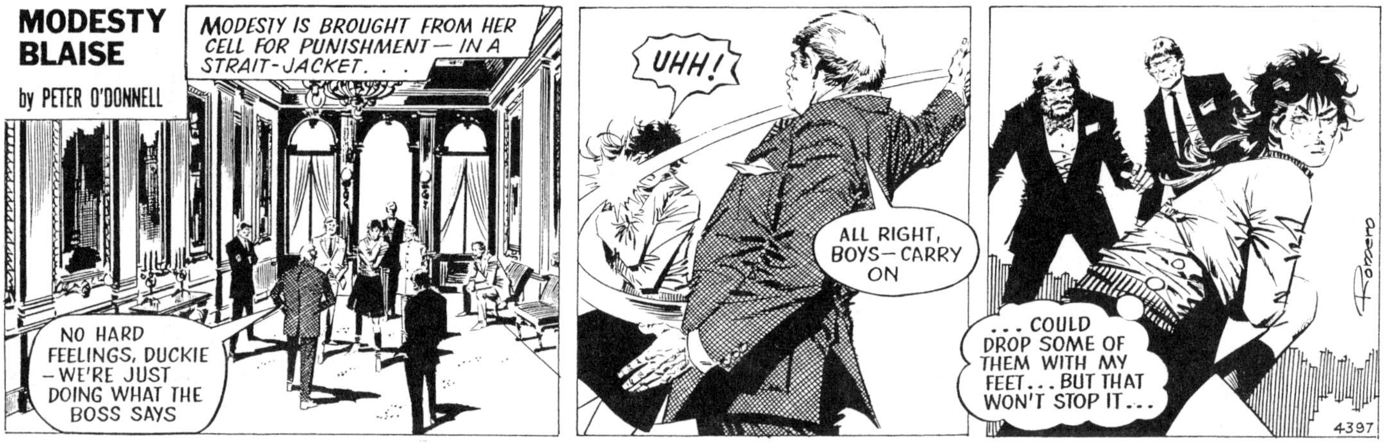
MODESTY BLAISE
by PETER O'DONNELL
MODESTY IS BROUGHT FROM HER CELL FOR PUNISHMENT—IN A STRAIT-JACKET...
NO HARD FEELINGS, DUCKIE—WE'RE JUST DOING WHAT THE BOSS SAYS
UHH!
ALL RIGHT, BOYS—CARRY ON
... COULD DROP SOME OF THEM WITH MY FEET... BUT THAT WON'T STOP IT...
4397

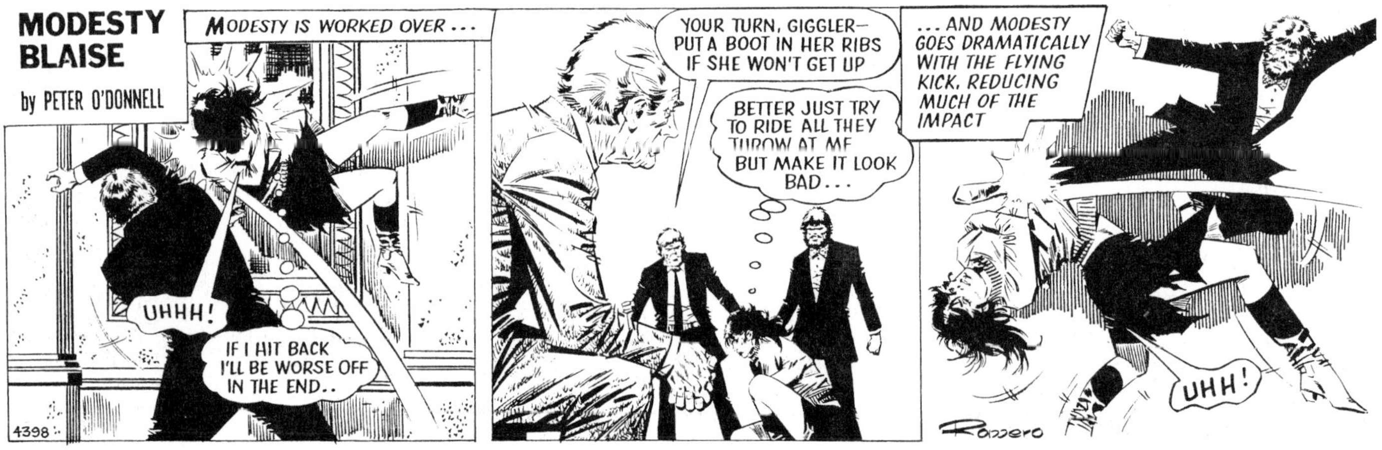
MODESTY BLAISE
by PETER O'DONNELL
MODESTY IS WORKED OVER...
UHHH!
IF I HIT BACK I'LL BE WORSE OFF IN THE END..
4398
YOUR TURN, GIGGLER—PUT A BOOT IN HER RIBS IF SHE WON'T GET UP
BETTER JUST TRY TO RIDE ALL THEY THROW AT ME BUT MAKE IT LOOK BAD...
... AND MODESTY GOES DRAMATICALLY WITH THE FLYING KICK, REDUCING MUCH OF THE IMPACT
UHH!

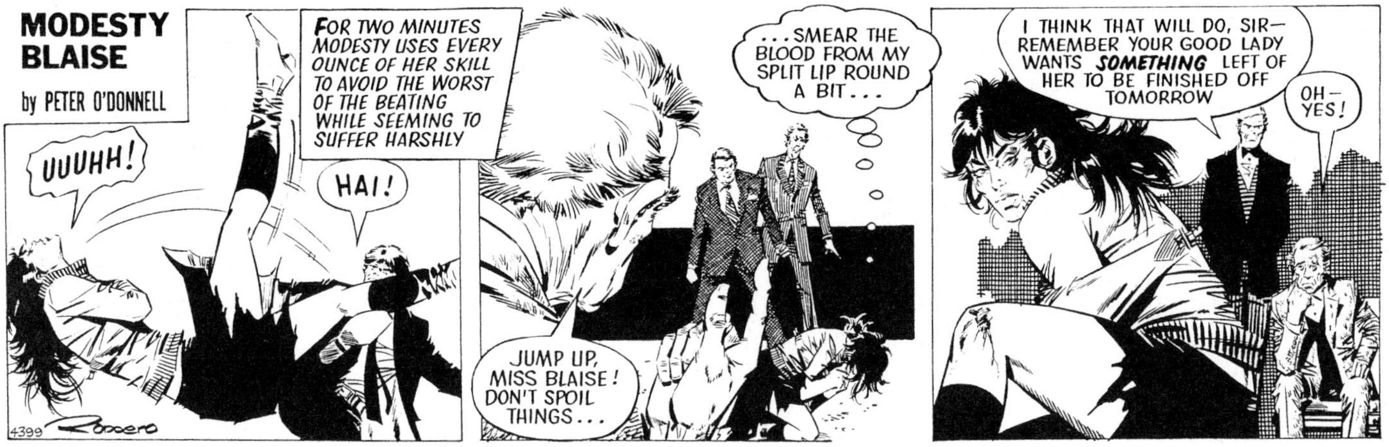
MODESTY BLAISE
by PETER O'DONNELL
FOR TWO MINUTES MODESTY USES EVERY OUNCE OF HER SKILL TO AVOID THE WORST OF THE BEATING WHILE SEEMING TO SUFFER HARSHLY
UUUHH!
HAI!
...SMEAR THE BLOOD FROM MY SPLIT LIP ROUND A BIT...
JUMP UP, MISS BLAISE! DON'T SPOIL THINGS...
I THINK THAT WILL DO, SIR— REMEMBER YOUR GOOD LADY WANTS SOMETHING LEFT OF HER TO BE FINISHED OFF TOMORROW
OH— YES!
4399
Romero

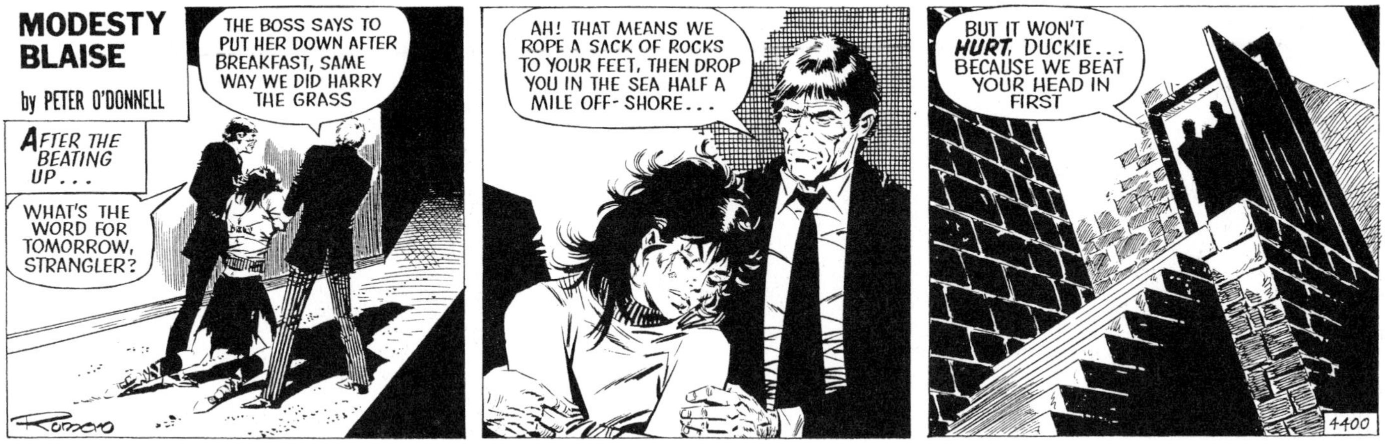
MODESTY BLAISE
by PETER O'DONNELL
AFTER THE BEATING UP...
THE BOSS SAYS TO PUT HER DOWN AFTER BREAKFAST, SAME WAY WE DID HARRY THE GRASS
WHAT'S THE WORD FOR TOMORROW, STRANGLER?
AH! THAT MEANS WE ROPE A SACK OF ROCKS TO YOUR FEET, THEN DROP YOU IN THE SEA HALF A MILE OFF-SHORE...
BUT IT WON'T HURT, DUCKIE... BECAUSE WE BEAT YOUR HEAD IN FIRST
Romero
4400

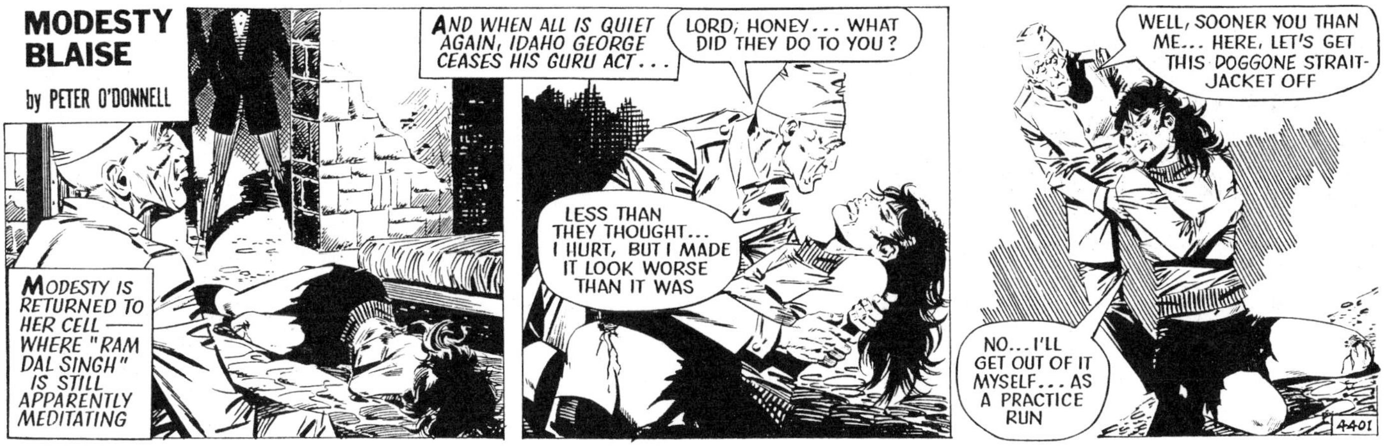
MODESTY BLAISE
by PETER O'DONNELL
MODESTY IS RETURNED TO HER CELL — WHERE "RAM DAL SINGH" IS STILL APPARENTLY MEDITATING
AND WHEN ALL IS QUIET AGAIN, IDAHO GEORGE CEASES HIS GURU ACT...
LORD; HONEY... WHAT DID THEY DO TO YOU?
LESS THAN THEY THOUGHT... I HURT, BUT I MADE IT LOOK WORSE THAN IT WAS
WELL, SOONER YOU THAN ME... HERE, LET'S GET THIS DOGGONE STRAIT-JACKET OFF
NO... I'LL GET OUT OF IT MYSELF... AS A PRACTICE RUN
4401

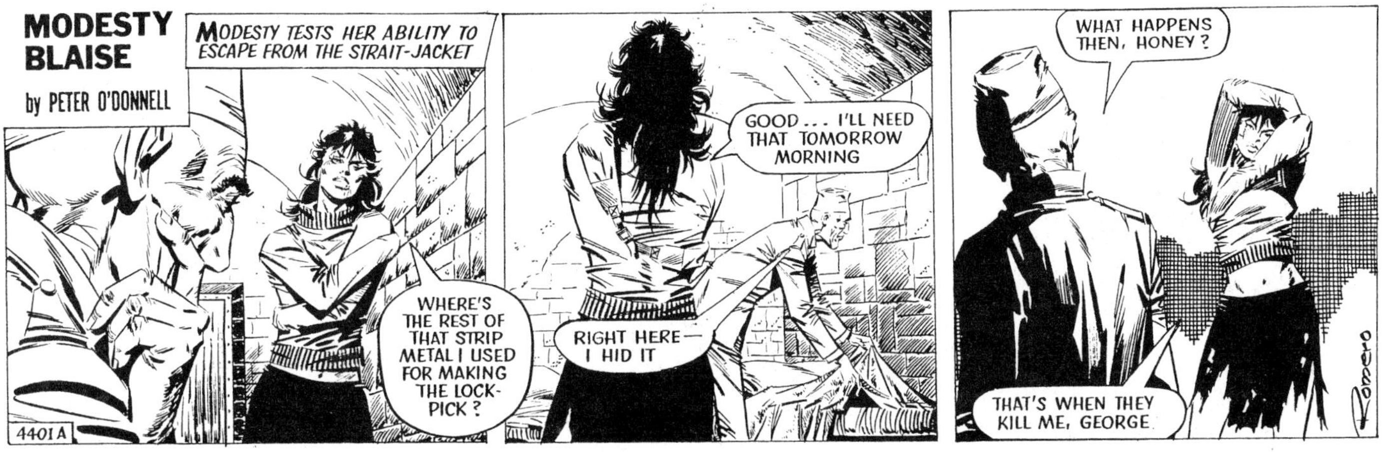
MODESTY BLAISE
by PETER O'DONNELL
MODESTY TESTS HER ABILITY TO ESCAPE FROM THE STRAIT-JACKET
WHERE'S THE REST OF THAT STRIP METAL I USED FOR MAKING THE LOCK-PICK?
RIGHT HERE— I HID IT
GOOD... I'LL NEED THAT TOMORROW MORNING
WHAT HAPPENS THEN, HONEY?
THAT'S WHEN THEY KILL ME, GEORGE
Romero
4401A

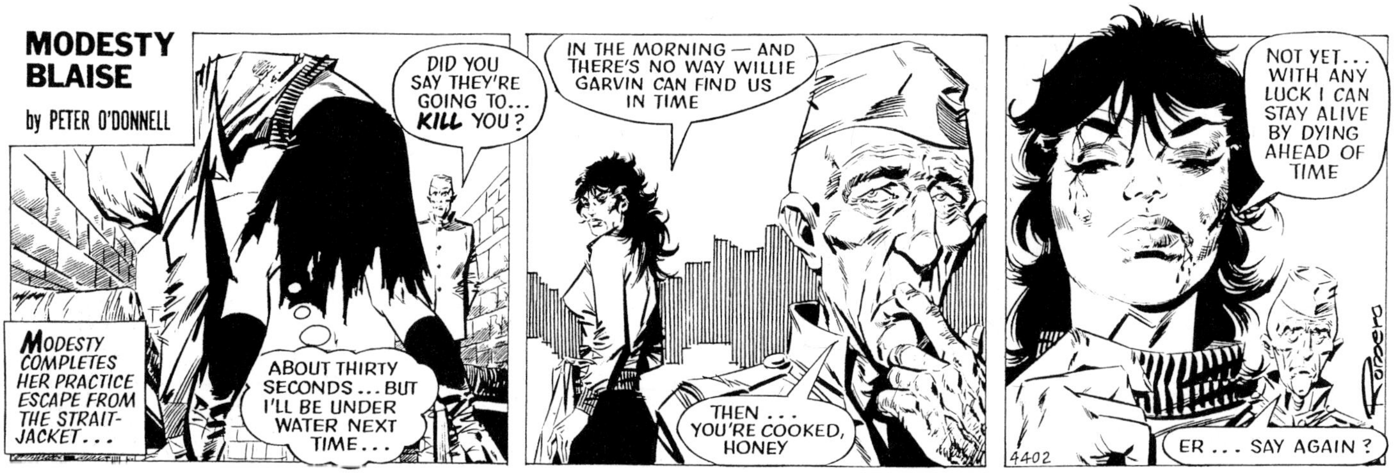
MODESTY BLAISE
by PETER O'DONNELL
MODESTY COMPLETES HER PRACTICE ESCAPE FROM THE STRAIT-JACKET...
DID YOU SAY THEY'RE GOING TO... KILL YOU?
ABOUT THIRTY SECONDS... BUT I'LL BE UNDER WATER NEXT TIME...
IN THE MORNING — AND THERE'S NO WAY WILLIE GARVIN CAN FIND US IN TIME
THEN... YOU'RE COOKED, HONEY
NOT YET... WITH ANY LUCK I CAN STAY ALIVE BY DYING AHEAD OF TIME
ER... SAY AGAIN?
Romero
4402

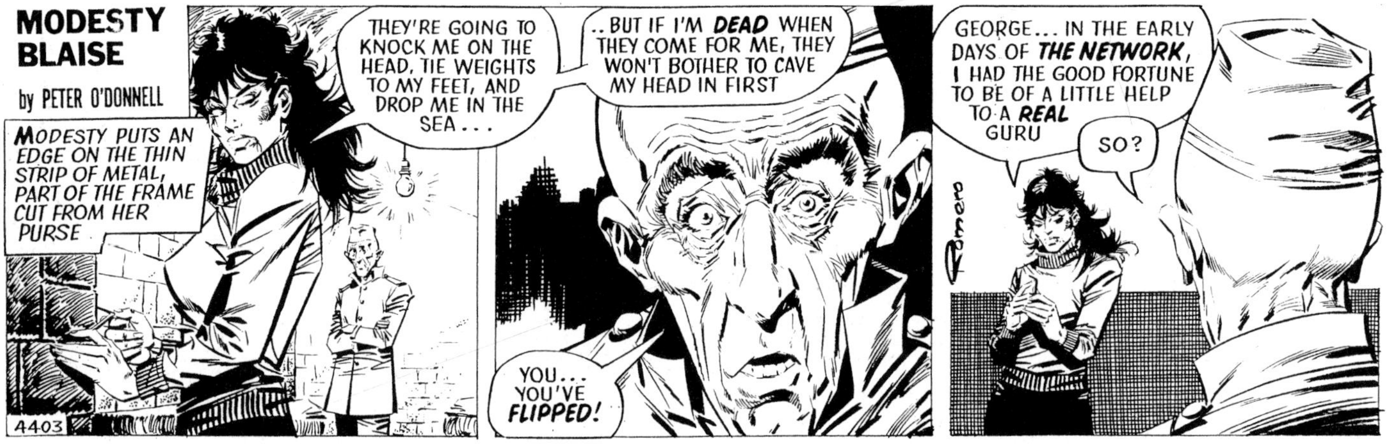
MODESTY BLAISE
by PETER O'DONNELL
MODESTY PUTS AN EDGE ON THE THIN STRIP OF METAL, PART OF THE FRAME CUT FROM HER PURSE
THEY'RE GOING TO KNOCK ME ON THE HEAD, TIE WEIGHTS TO MY FEET, AND DROP ME IN THE SEA...
4403
..BUT IF I'M DEAD WHEN THEY COME FOR ME, THEY WON'T BOTHER TO CAVE MY HEAD IN FIRST
YOU... YOU'VE FLIPPED!
GEORGE... IN THE EARLY DAYS OF THE NETWORK, I HAD THE GOOD FORTUNE TO BE OF A LITTLE HELP TO A REAL GURU
SO?
Romero

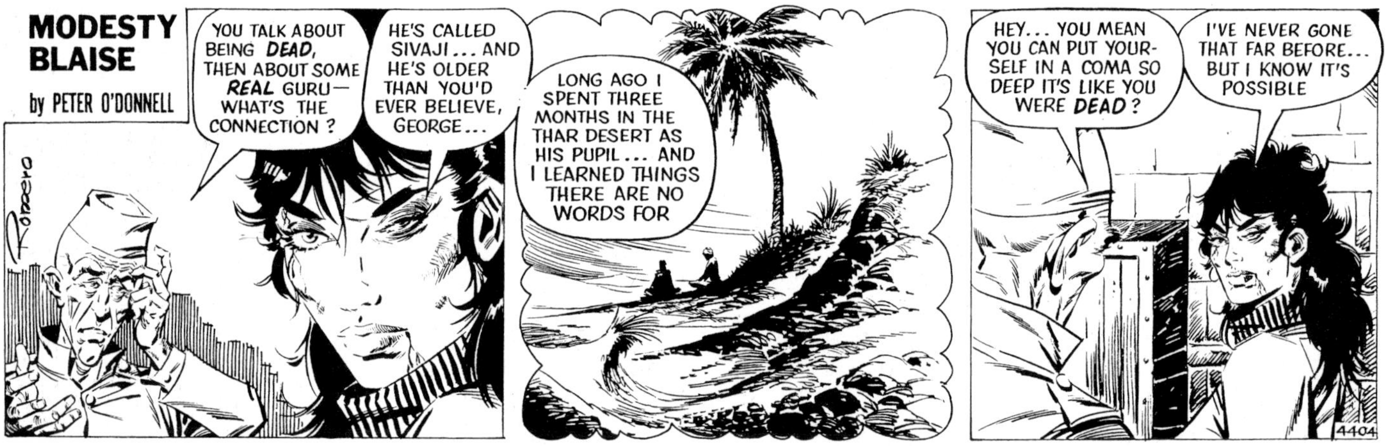
MODESTY BLAISE
by PETER O'DONNELL
YOU TALK ABOUT BEING DEAD, THEN ABOUT SOME REAL GURU— WHAT'S THE CONNECTION?
HE'S CALLED SIVAJI... AND HE'S OLDER THAN YOU'D EVER BELIEVE, GEORGE...
Romero
LONG AGO I SPENT THREE MONTHS IN THE THAR DESERT AS HIS PUPIL... AND I LEARNED THINGS THERE ARE NO WORDS FOR
HEY... YOU MEAN YOU CAN PUT YOURSELF IN A COMA SO DEEP IT'S LIKE YOU WERE DEAD?
I'VE NEVER GONE THAT FAR BEFORE... BUT I KNOW IT'S POSSIBLE
4404

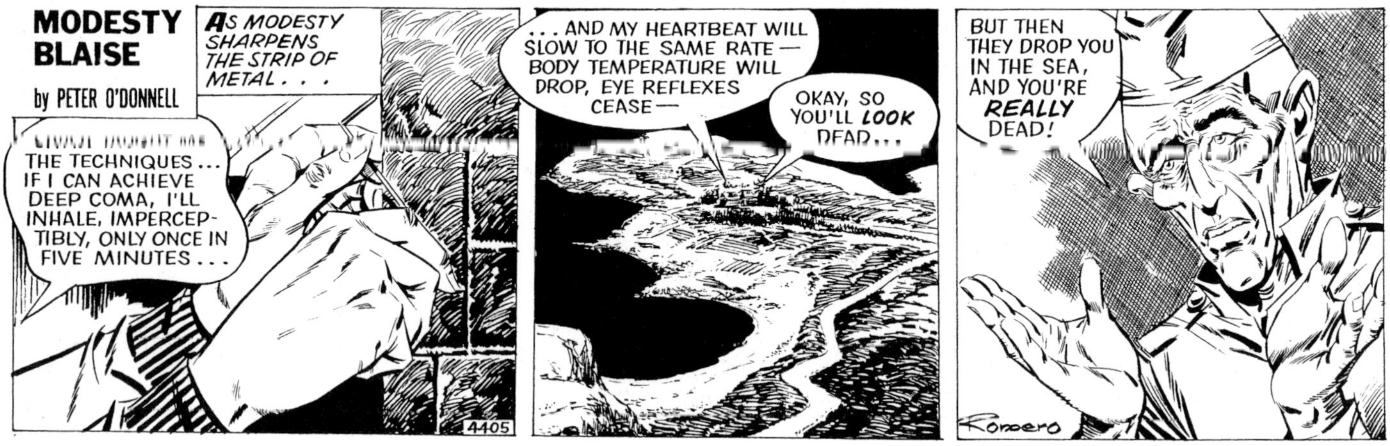
MODESTY BLAISE
by PETER O'DONNELL
AS MODESTY SHARPENS THE STRIP OF METAL...
THE TECHNIQUES... IF I CAN ACHIEVE DEEP COMA, I'LL INHALE, IMPERCEPTIBLY, ONLY ONCE IN FIVE MINUTES...
...AND MY HEARTBEAT WILL SLOW TO THE SAME RATE — BODY TEMPERATURE WILL DROP, EYE REFLEXES CEASE—
OKAY, SO YOU'LL LOOK DEAD...
4405
BUT THEN THEY DROP YOU IN THE SEA, AND YOU'RE REALLY DEAD!
Romero

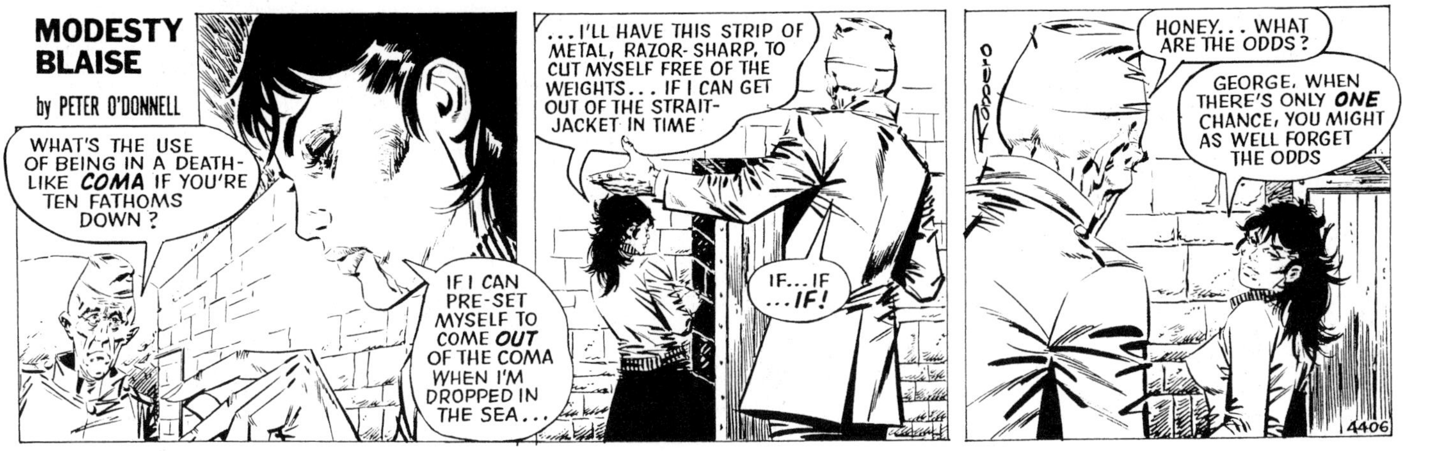
MODESTY BLAISE
by PETER O'DONNELL
WHAT'S THE USE OF BEING IN A DEATH-LIKE COMA IF YOU'RE TEN FATHOMS DOWN?
IF I CAN PRE-SET MYSELF TO COME OUT OF THE COMA WHEN I'M DROPPED IN THE SEA...
...I'LL HAVE THIS STRIP OF METAL, RAZOR-SHARP, TO CUT MYSELF FREE OF THE WEIGHTS... IF I CAN GET OUT OF THE STRAIT-JACKET IN TIME
IF... IF ...IF!
HONEY... WHAT ARE THE ODDS?
GEORGE, WHEN THERE'S ONLY ONE CHANCE, YOU MIGHT AS WELL FORGET THE ODDS
4406

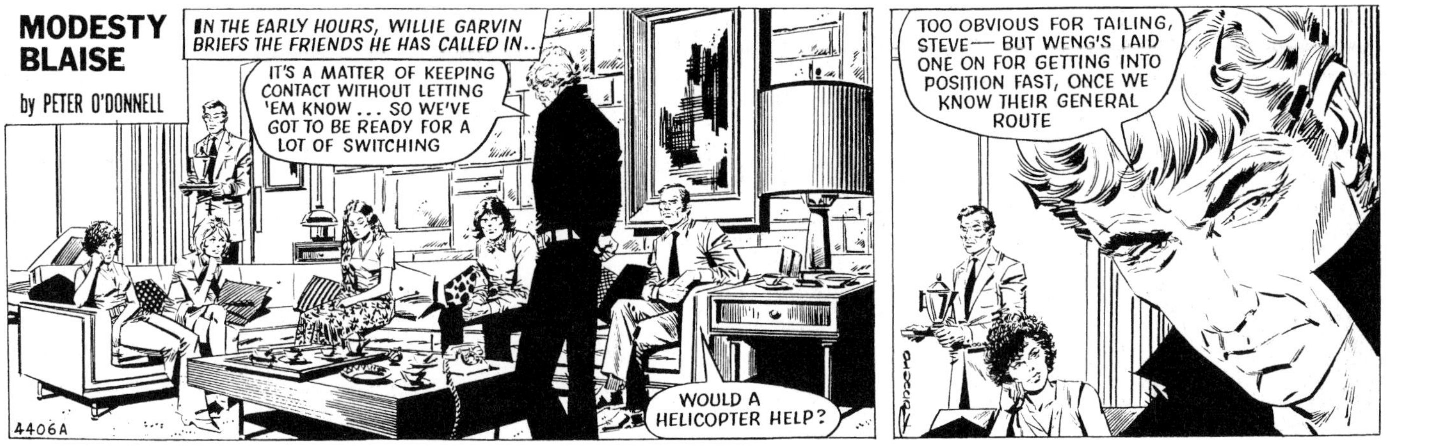
MODESTY BLAISE
by PETER O'DONNELL
IN THE EARLY HOURS, WILLIE GARVIN BRIEFS THE FRIENDS HE HAS CALLED IN..
IT'S A MATTER OF KEEPING CONTACT WITHOUT LETTING 'EM KNOW ... SO WE'VE GOT TO BE READY FOR A LOT OF SWITCHING
WOULD A HELICOPTER HELP?
4406A
TOO OBVIOUS FOR TAILING, STEVE— BUT WENG'S LAID ONE ON FOR GETTING INTO POSITION FAST, ONCE WE KNOW THEIR GENERAL ROUTE

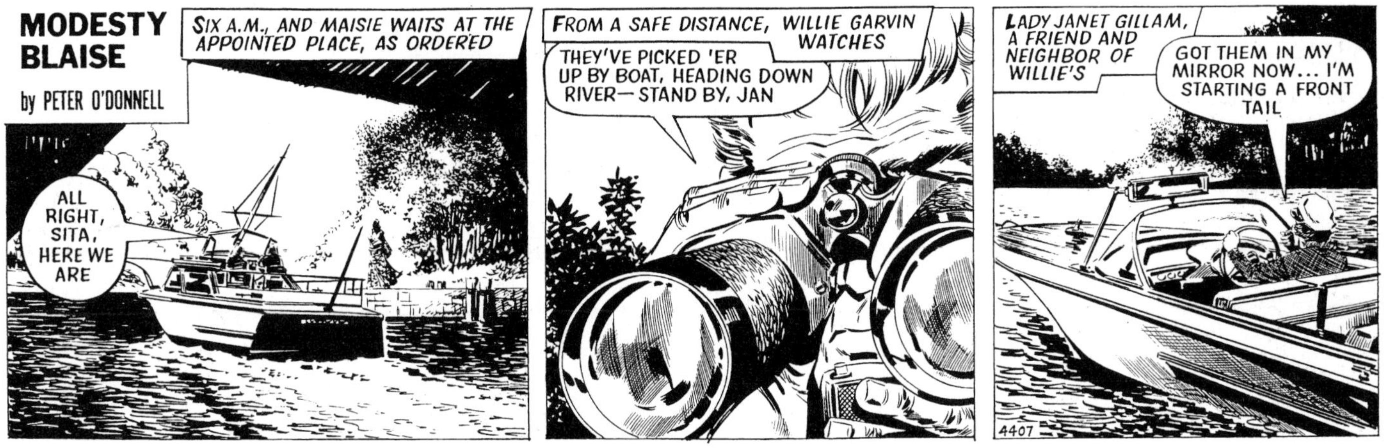
MODESTY BLAISE
by PETER O'DONNELL
SIX A.M., AND MAISIE WAITS AT THE APPOINTED PLACE, AS ORDERED
ALL RIGHT, SITA, HERE WE ARE
FROM A SAFE DISTANCE, WILLIE GARVIN WATCHES
THEY'VE PICKED 'ER UP BY BOAT, HEADING DOWN RIVER— STAND BY, JAN
LADY JANET GILLAM, A FRIEND AND NEIGHBOR OF WILLIE'S
GOT THEM IN MY MIRROR NOW... I'M STARTING A FRONT TAIL
4407

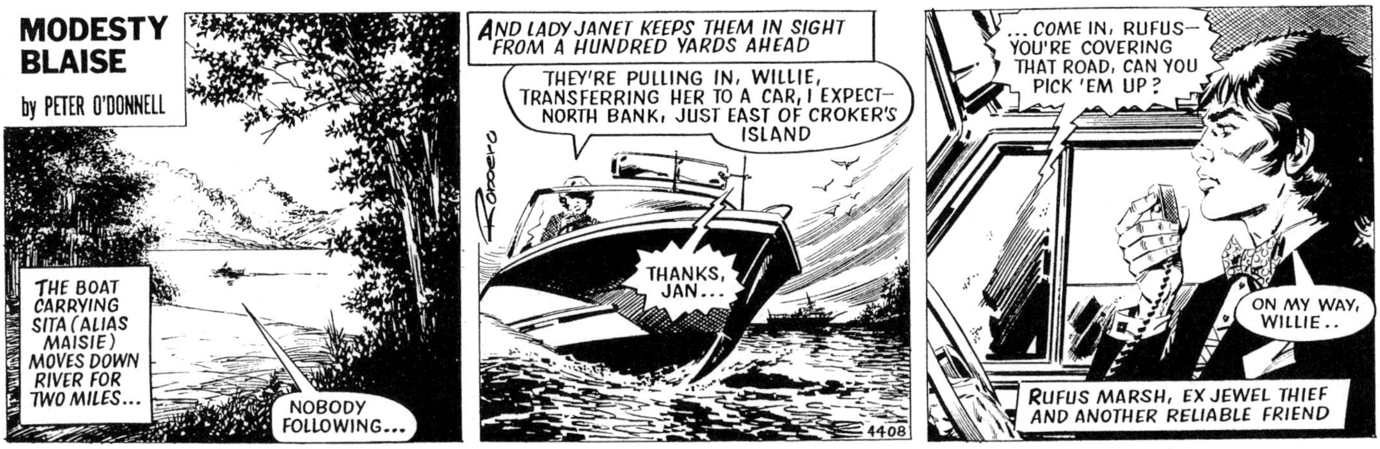
MODESTY BLAISE
by PETER O'DONNELL
THE BOAT CARRYING SITA (ALIAS MAISIE) MOVES DOWN RIVER FOR TWO MILES...
NOBODY FOLLOWING...
AND LADY JANET KEEPS THEM IN SIGHT FROM A HUNDRED YARDS AHEAD
THEY'RE PULLING IN, WILLIE, TRANSFERRING HER TO A CAR, I EXPECT- NORTH BANK, JUST EAST OF CROKER'S ISLAND
THANKS, JAN...
4408
...COME IN, RUFUS— YOU'RE COVERING THAT ROAD, CAN YOU PICK 'EM UP?
ON MY WAY, WILLIE..
RUFUS MARSH, EX JEWEL THIEF AND ANOTHER RELIABLE FRIEND

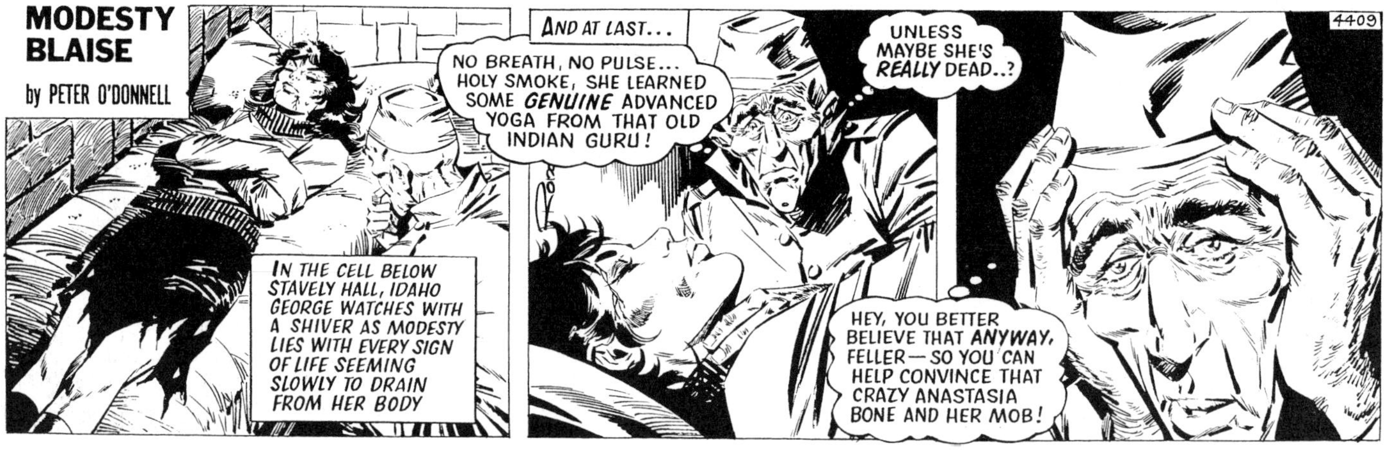
MODESTY BLAISE
by PETER O'DONNELL
4409
IN THE CELL BELOW STAVELY HALL, IDAHO GEORGE WATCHES WITH A SHIVER AS MODESTY LIES WITH EVERY SIGN OF LIFE SEEMING SLOWLY TO DRAIN FROM HER BODY
AND AT LAST...
NO BREATH, NO PULSE... HOLY SMOKE, SHE LEARNED SOME GENUINE ADVANCED YOGA FROM THAT OLD INDIAN GURU!
UNLESS MAYBE SHE'S REALLY DEAD..?
HEY, YOU BETTER BELIEVE THAT ANYWAY, FELLER—SO YOU CAN HELP CONVINCE THAT CRAZY ANASTASIA BONE AND HER MOB!

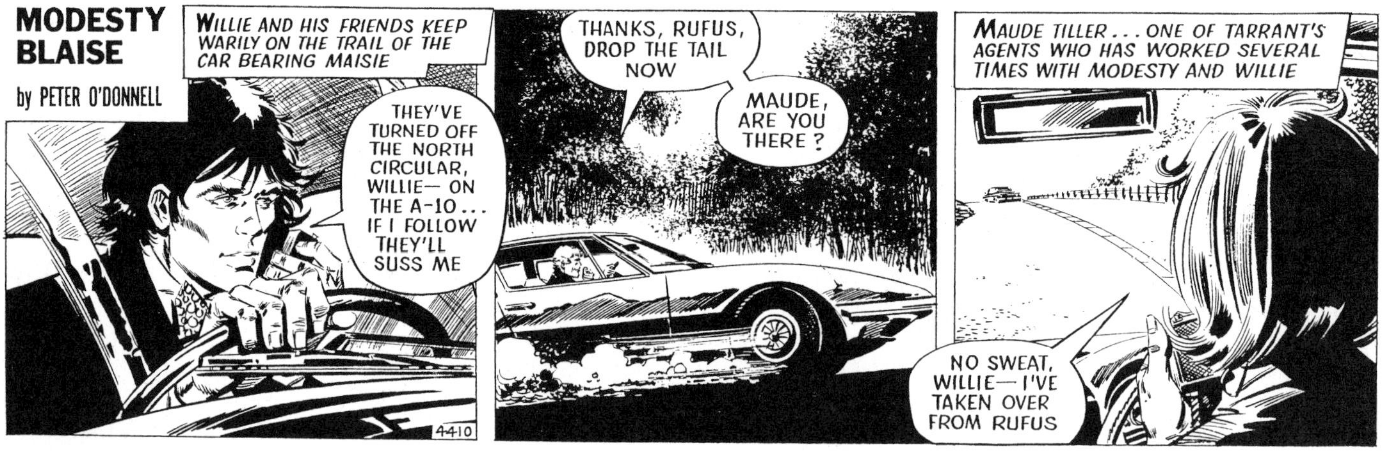
MODESTY BLAISE
by PETER O'DONNELL
WILLIE AND HIS FRIENDS KEEP WARILY ON THE TRAIL OF THE CAR BEARING MAISIE
THEY'VE TURNED OFF THE NORTH CIRCULAR, WILLIE— ON THE A-10... IF I FOLLOW THEY'LL SUSS ME
4410
THANKS, RUFUS, DROP THE TAIL NOW
MAUDE, ARE YOU THERE?
MAUDE TILLER... ONE OF TARRANT'S AGENTS WHO HAS WORKED SEVERAL TIMES WITH MODESTY AND WILLIE
NO SWEAT, WILLIE— I'VE TAKEN OVER FROM RUFUS

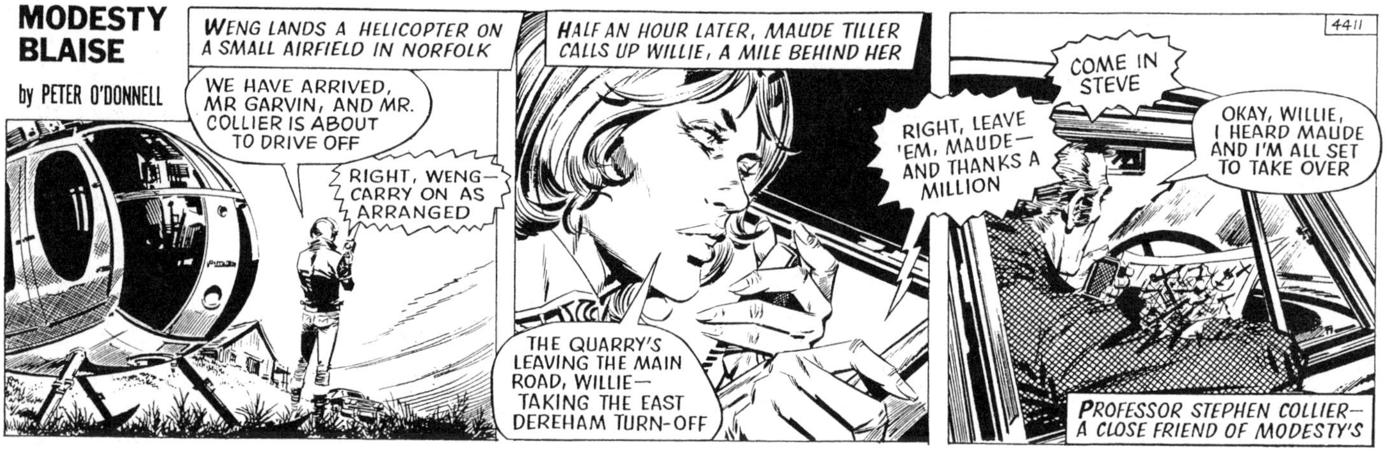
MODESTY BLAISE
by PETER O'DONNELL
WENG LANDS A HELICOPTER ON A SMALL AIRFIELD IN NORFOLK
WE HAVE ARRIVED, MR GARVIN, AND MR. COLLIER IS ABOUT TO DRIVE OFF
RIGHT, WENG— CARRY ON AS ARRANGED
HALF AN HOUR LATER, MAUDE TILLER CALLS UP WILLIE, A MILE BEHIND HER
THE QUARRY'S LEAVING THE MAIN ROAD, WILLIE— TAKING THE EAST DEREHAM TURN-OFF
RIGHT, LEAVE 'EM, MAUDE— AND THANKS A MILLION
4411
COME IN STEVE
OKAY, WILLIE, I HEARD MAUDE AND I'M ALL SET TO TAKE OVER
PROFESSOR STEPHEN COLLIER— A CLOSE FRIEND OF MODESTY'S

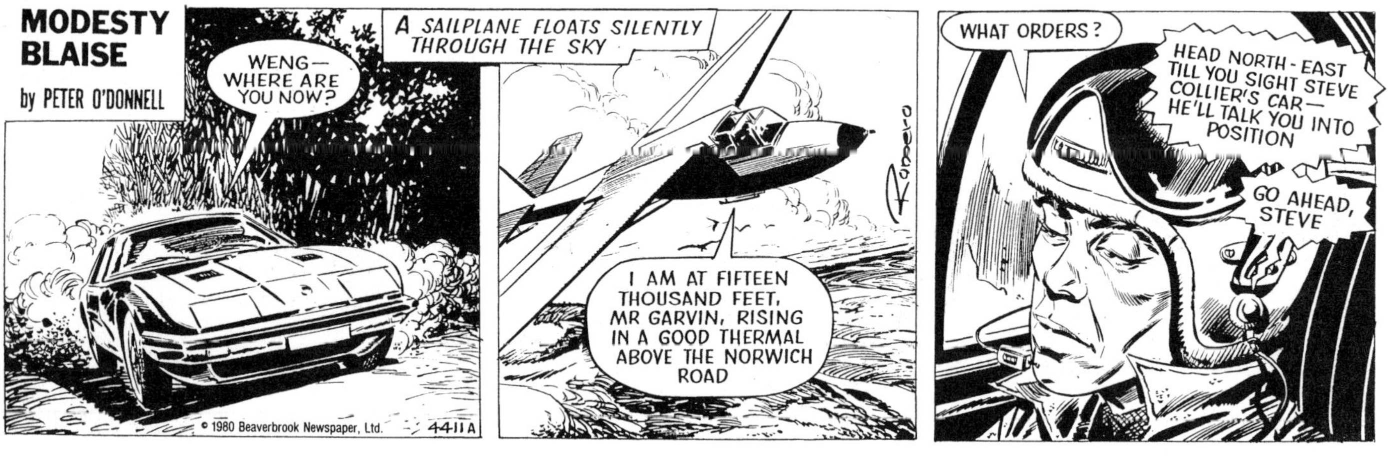
MODESTY BLAISE
by PETER O'DONNELL
WENG— WHERE ARE YOU NOW?
© 1980 Beaverbrook Newspaper, Ltd.
4411 A
A SAILPLANE FLOATS SILENTLY THROUGH THE SKY
I AM AT FIFTEEN THOUSAND FEET, MR GARVIN, RISING IN A GOOD THERMAL ABOVE THE NORWICH ROAD
WHAT ORDERS?
HEAD NORTH-EAST TILL YOU SIGHT STEVE COLLIER'S CAR— HE'LL TALK YOU INTO POSITION
GO AHEAD, STEVE

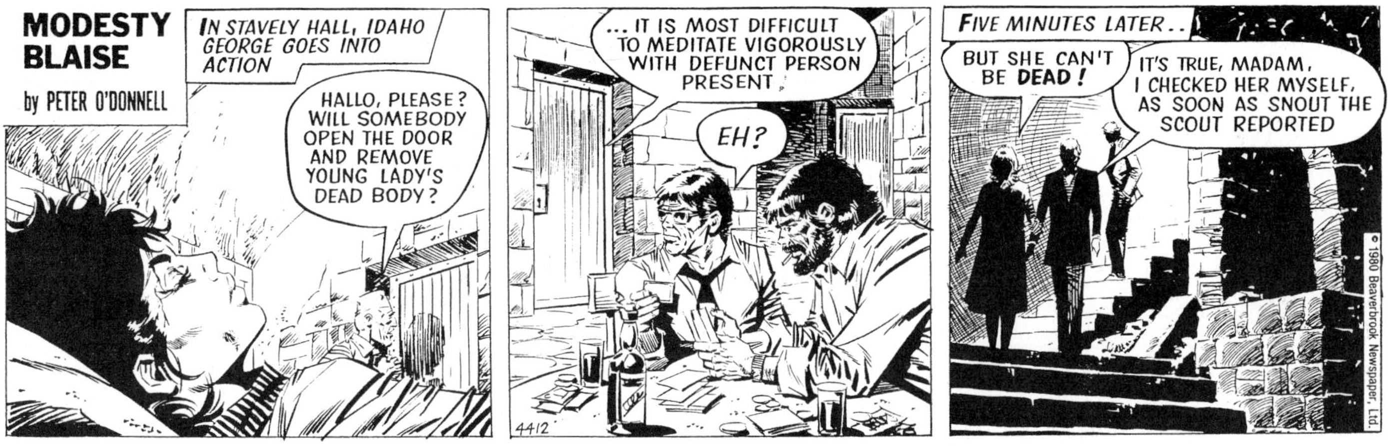
MODESTY BLAISE
by PETER O'DONNELL
IN STAVELY HALL, IDAHO GEORGE GOES INTO ACTION
HALLO, PLEASE? WILL SOMEBODY OPEN THE DOOR AND REMOVE YOUNG LADY'S DEAD BODY?
... IT IS MOST DIFFICULT TO MEDITATE VIGOROUSLY WITH DEFUNCT PERSON PRESENT
EH?
4412
FIVE MINUTES LATER..
BUT SHE CAN'T BE DEAD!
IT'S TRUE, MADAM, I CHECKED HER MYSELF, AS SOON AS SNOUT THE SCOUT REPORTED
© 1980 Beaverbrook Newspaper, Ltd.

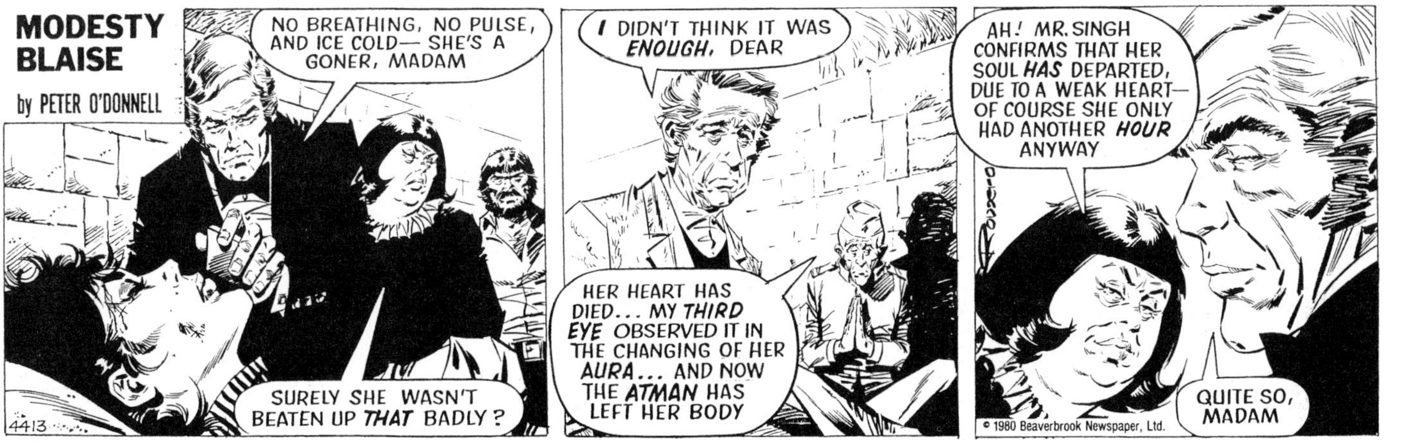
MODESTY BLAISE
by PETER O'DONNELL
NO BREATHING, NO PULSE, AND ICE COLD— SHE'S A GONER, MADAM
SURELY SHE WASN'T BEATEN UP THAT BADLY?
4413
I DIDN'T THINK IT WAS ENOUGH, DEAR
HER HEART HAS DIED... MY THIRD EYE OBSERVED IT IN THE CHANGING OF HER AURA... AND NOW THE ATMAN HAS LEFT HER BODY
AH! MR. SINGH CONFIRMS THAT HER SOUL HAS DEPARTED, DUE TO A WEAK HEART— OF COURSE SHE ONLY HAD ANOTHER HOUR ANYWAY
QUITE SO, MADAM
© 1980 Beaverbrook Newspaper, Ltd.

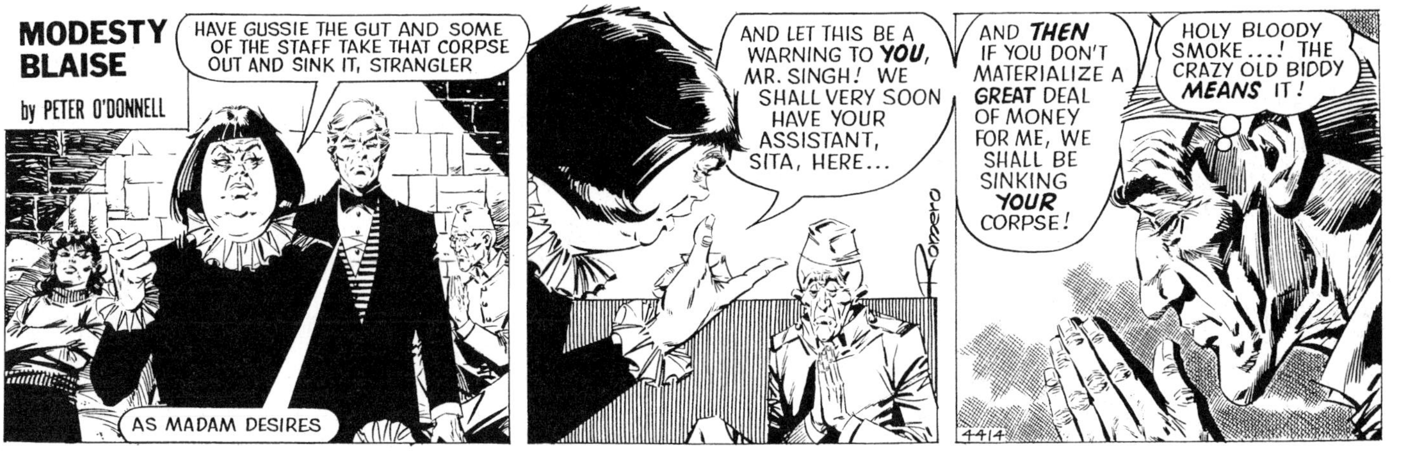
MODESTY BLAISE
by PETER O'DONNELL
HAVE GUSSIE THE GUT AND SOME OF THE STAFF TAKE THAT CORPSE OUT AND SINK IT, STRANGLER
AS MADAM DESIRES
AND LET THIS BE A WARNING TO YOU, MR. SINGH! WE SHALL VERY SOON HAVE YOUR ASSISTANT, SITA, HERE...
AND THEN IF YOU DON'T MATERIALIZE A GREAT DEAL OF MONEY FOR ME, WE SHALL BE SINKING YOUR CORPSE!
HOLY BLOODY SMOKE...! THE CRAZY OLD BIDDY MEANS IT!
4414

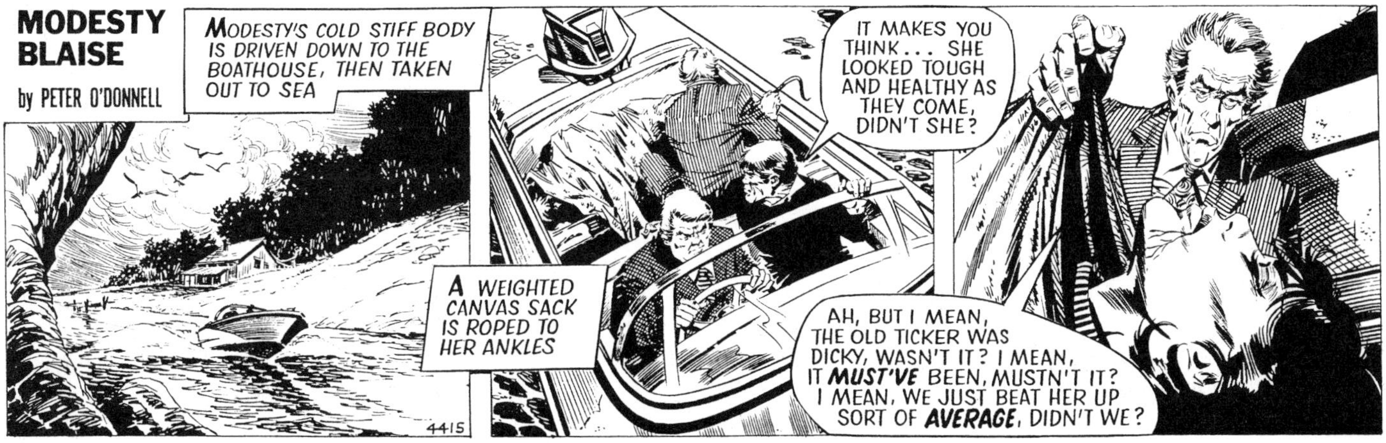
MODESTY BLAISE
by PETER O'DONNELL
MODESTY'S COLD STIFF BODY IS DRIVEN DOWN TO THE BOATHOUSE, THEN TAKEN OUT TO SEA
4415
A WEIGHTED CANVAS SACK IS ROPED TO HER ANKLES
IT MAKES YOU THINK... SHE LOOKED TOUGH AND HEALTHY AS THEY COME, DIDN'T SHE?
AH, BUT I MEAN, THE OLD TICKER WAS DICKY, WASN'T IT? I MEAN, IT MUST'VE BEEN, MUSTN'T IT? I MEAN, WE JUST BEAT HER UP SORT OF AVERAGE, DIDN'T WE?

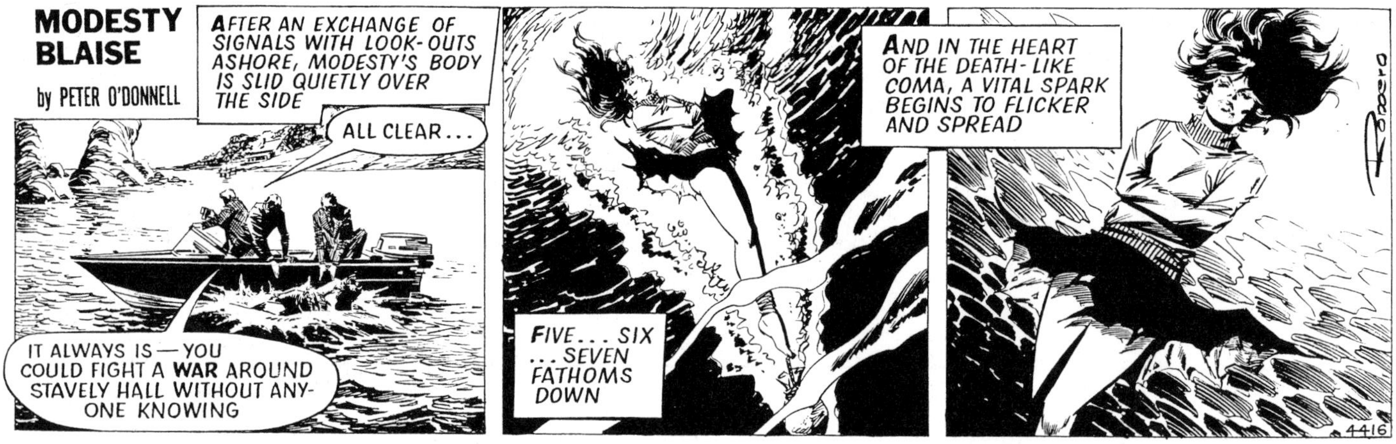
MODESTY BLAISE
by PETER O'DONNELL
AFTER AN EXCHANGE OF SIGNALS WITH LOOK-OUTS ASHORE, MODESTY'S BODY IS SLID QUIETLY OVER THE SIDE
ALL CLEAR . . .
IT ALWAYS IS — YOU COULD FIGHT A **WAR** AROUND STAVELY HALL WITHOUT ANY-ONE KNOWING
FIVE . . . SIX . . . SEVEN FATHOMS DOWN
AND IN THE HEART OF THE DEATH-LIKE COMA, A VITAL SPARK BEGINS TO FLICKER AND SPREAD
Romero
4416

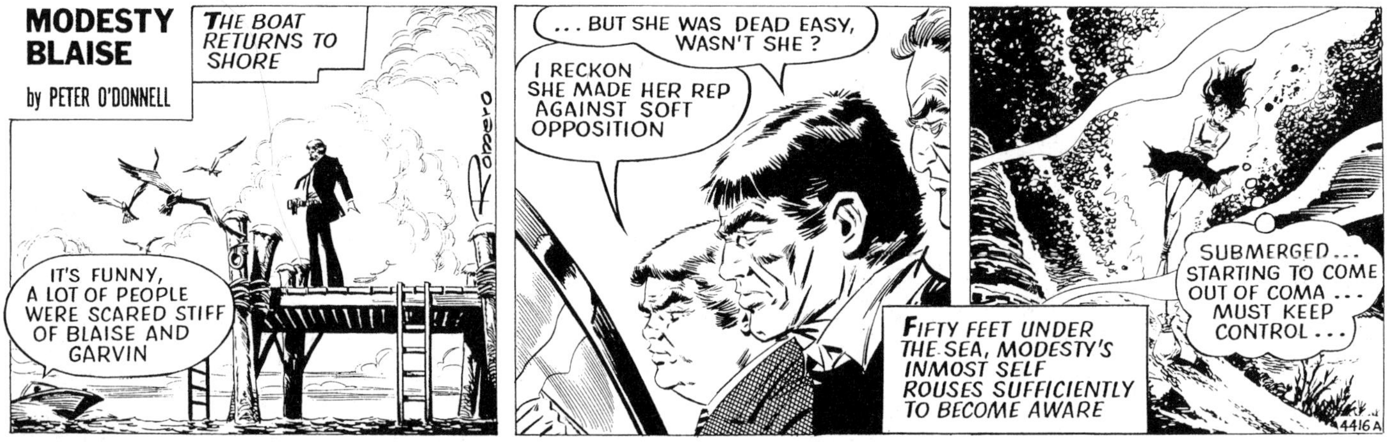
MODESTY BLAISE
by PETER O'DONNELL
THE BOAT RETURNS TO SHORE
Romero
IT'S FUNNY, A LOT OF PEOPLE WERE SCARED STIFF OF BLAISE AND GARVIN
. . . BUT SHE WAS DEAD EASY, WASN'T SHE ?
I RECKON SHE MADE HER REP AGAINST SOFT OPPOSITION
FIFTY FEET UNDER THE SEA, MODESTY'S INMOST SELF ROUSES SUFFICIENTLY TO BECOME AWARE
SUBMERGED . . . STARTING TO COME OUT OF COMA . . . MUST KEEP CONTROL . . .
4416 A

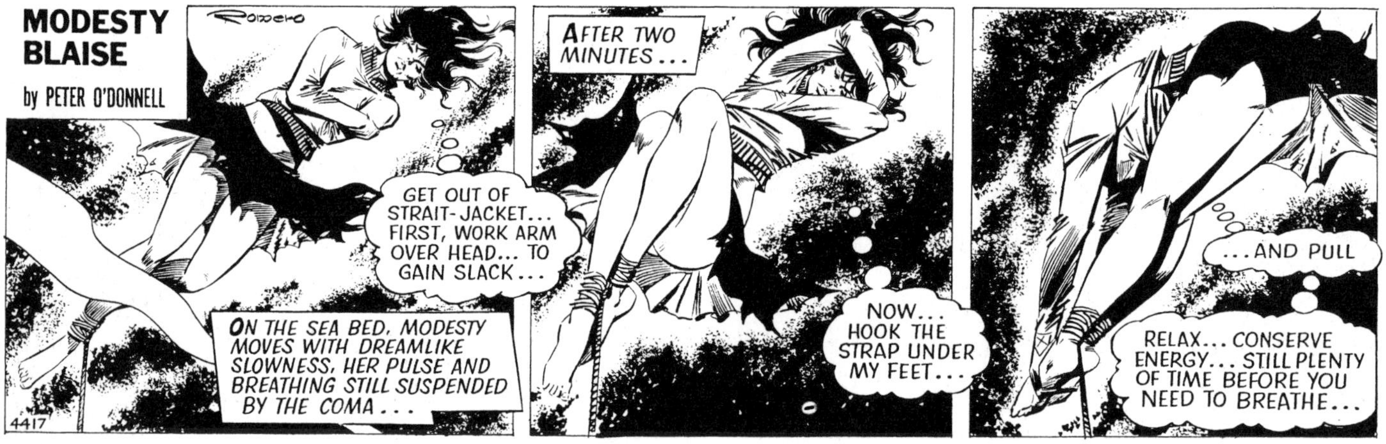
MODESTY BLAISE
by PETER O'DONNELL
Romero
GET OUT OF STRAIT-JACKET . . . FIRST, WORK ARM OVER HEAD . . . TO GAIN SLACK . . .
ON THE SEA BED, MODESTY MOVES WITH DREAMLIKE SLOWNESS, HER PULSE AND BREATHING STILL SUSPENDED BY THE COMA . . .
AFTER TWO MINUTES . . .
NOW . . . HOOK THE STRAP UNDER MY FEET . . .
. . . AND PULL
RELAX . . . CONSERVE ENERGY . . . STILL PLENTY OF TIME BEFORE YOU NEED TO BREATHE . . .
4417

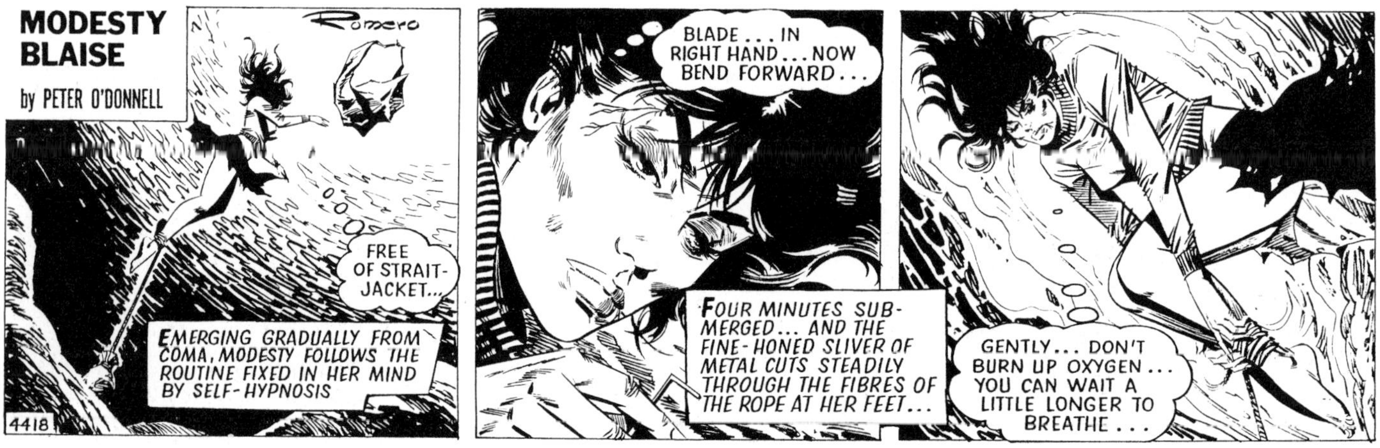
MODESTY BLAISE
by PETER O'DONNELL
Romero
FREE OF STRAIT-JACKET . . .
EMERGING GRADUALLY FROM COMA, MODESTY FOLLOWS THE ROUTINE FIXED IN HER MIND BY SELF-HYPNOSIS
BLADE . . . IN RIGHT HAND . . . NOW BEND FORWARD . . .
FOUR MINUTES SUB-MERGED . . . AND THE FINE-HONED SLIVER OF METAL CUTS STEADILY THROUGH THE FIBRES OF THE ROPE AT HER FEET . . .
GENTLY . . . DON'T BURN UP OXYGEN . . . YOU CAN WAIT A LITTLE LONGER TO BREATHE . . .
4418

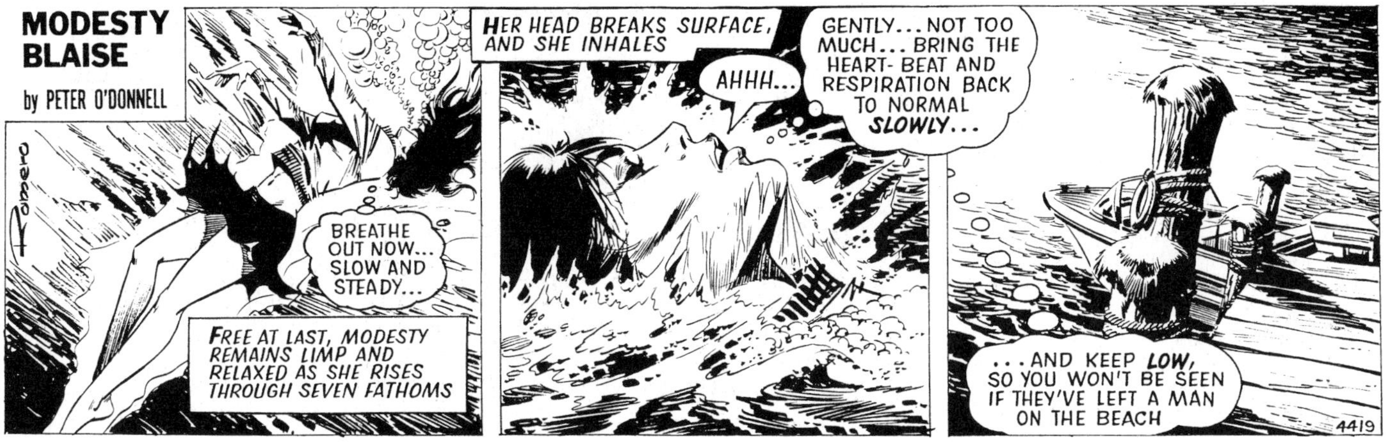
MODESTY BLAISE
by PETER O'DONNELL
Romero
FREE AT LAST, MODESTY REMAINS LIMP AND RELAXED AS SHE RISES THROUGH SEVEN FATHOMS
BREATHE OUT NOW... SLOW AND STEADY...
HER HEAD BREAKS SURFACE, AND SHE INHALES
AHHH...
GENTLY... NOT TOO MUCH... BRING THE HEART-BEAT AND RESPIRATION BACK TO NORMAL SLOWLY...
...AND KEEP LOW, SO YOU WON'T BE SEEN IF THEY'VE LEFT A MAN ON THE BEACH
4419

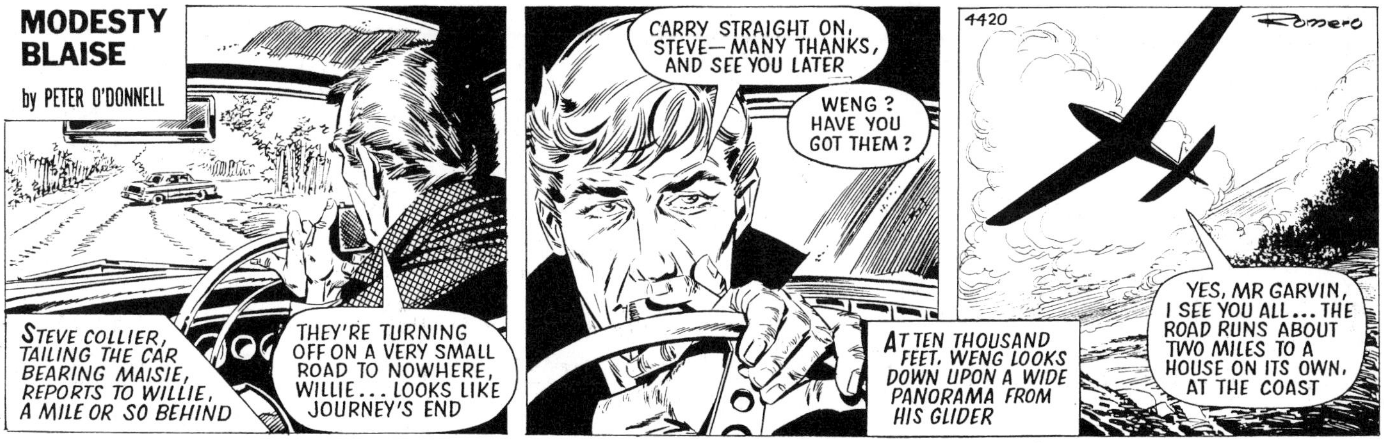
MODESTY BLAISE
by PETER O'DONNELL
STEVE COLLIER, TAILING THE CAR BEARING MAISIE, REPORTS TO WILLIE, A MILE OR SO BEHIND
THEY'RE TURNING OFF ON A VERY SMALL ROAD TO NOWHERE, WILLIE... LOOKS LIKE JOURNEY'S END
CARRY STRAIGHT ON, STEVE— MANY THANKS, AND SEE YOU LATER
WENG ? HAVE YOU GOT THEM ?
4420
Romero
AT TEN THOUSAND FEET, WENG LOOKS DOWN UPON A WIDE PANORAMA FROM HIS GLIDER
YES, MR GARVIN, I SEE YOU ALL... THE ROAD RUNS ABOUT TWO MILES TO A HOUSE ON ITS OWN, AT THE COAST

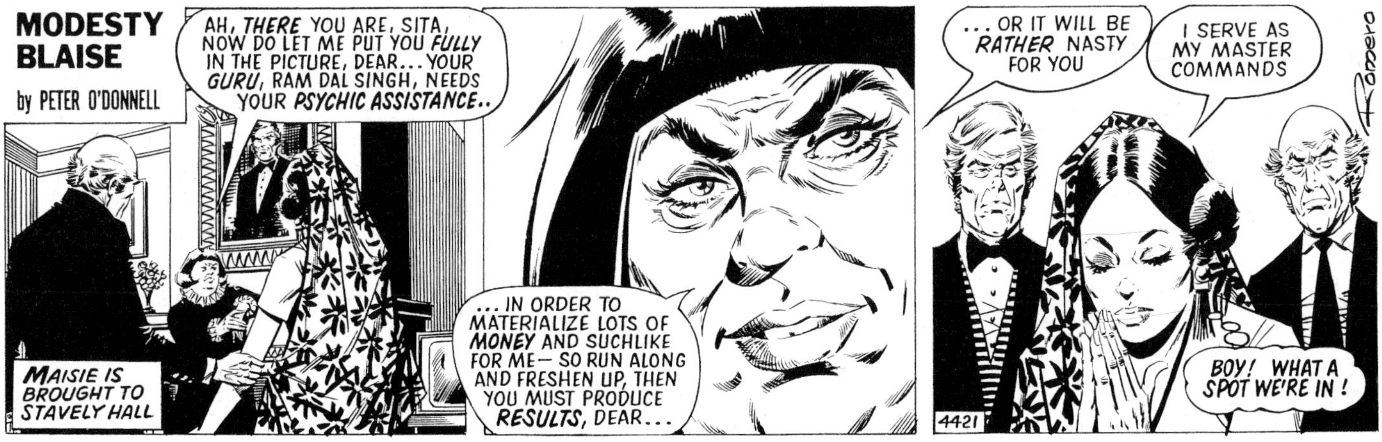
MODESTY BLAISE
by PETER O'DONNELL
MAISIE IS BROUGHT TO STAVELY HALL
AH, THERE YOU ARE, SITA, NOW DO LET ME PUT YOU FULLY IN THE PICTURE, DEAR... YOUR GURU, RAM DAL SINGH, NEEDS YOUR PSYCHIC ASSISTANCE..
...IN ORDER TO MATERIALIZE LOTS OF MONEY AND SUCHLIKE FOR ME— SO RUN ALONG AND FRESHEN UP, THEN YOU MUST PRODUCE RESULTS, DEAR...
...OR IT WILL BE RATHER NASTY FOR YOU
I SERVE AS MY MASTER COMMANDS
Romero
BOY! WHAT A SPOT WE'RE IN!
4421

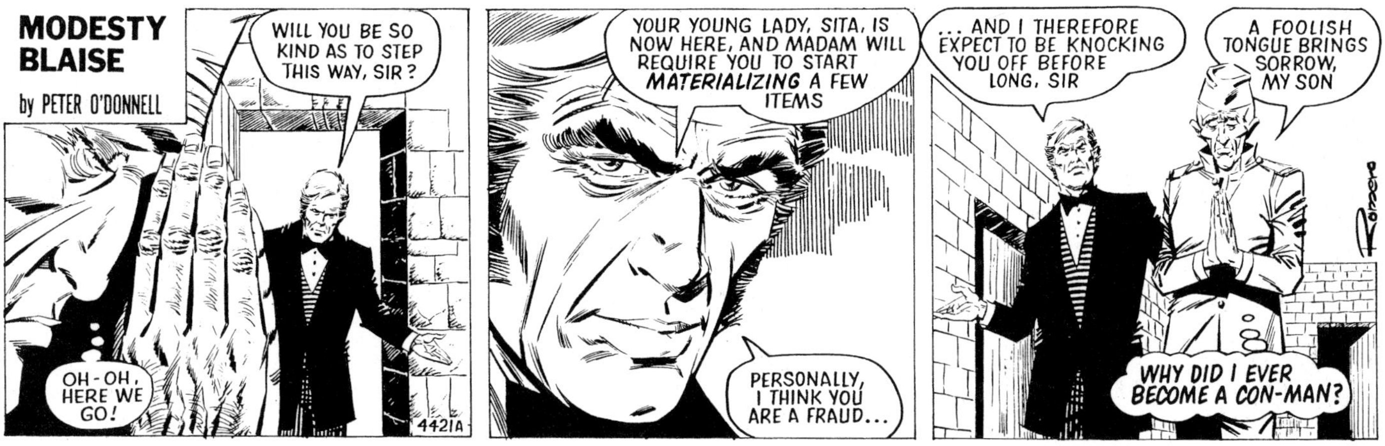
MODESTY BLAISE
by PETER O'DONNELL
WILL YOU BE SO KIND AS TO STEP THIS WAY, SIR?
OH-OH, HERE WE GO!
4421A
YOUR YOUNG LADY, SITA, IS NOW HERE, AND MADAM WILL REQUIRE YOU TO START MATERIALIZING A FEW ITEMS
PERSONALLY, I THINK YOU ARE A FRAUD...
...AND I THEREFORE EXPECT TO BE KNOCKING YOU OFF BEFORE LONG, SIR
A FOOLISH TONGUE BRINGS SORROW, MY SON
Romero
WHY DID I EVER BECOME A CON-MAN?

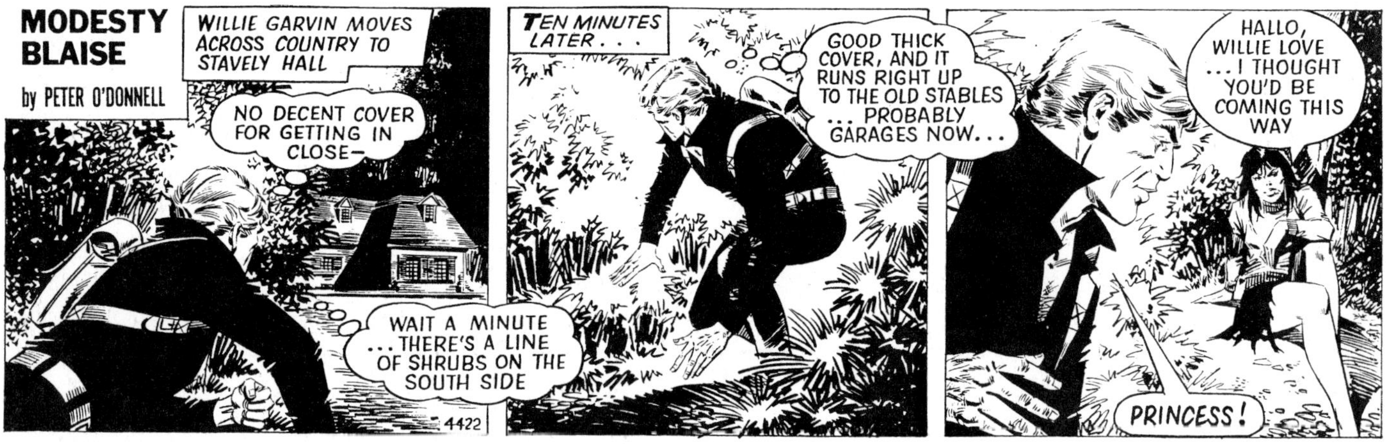
MODESTY BLAISE
by PETER O'DONNELL
WILLIE GARVIN MOVES ACROSS COUNTRY TO STAVELY HALL
NO DECENT COVER FOR GETTING IN CLOSE—
WAIT A MINUTE ...THERE'S A LINE OF SHRUBS ON THE SOUTH SIDE
4422
TEN MINUTES LATER . . .
GOOD THICK COVER, AND IT RUNS RIGHT UP TO THE OLD STABLES ... PROBABLY GARAGES NOW...
HALLO, WILLIE LOVE ...I THOUGHT YOU'D BE COMING THIS WAY
PRINCESS!

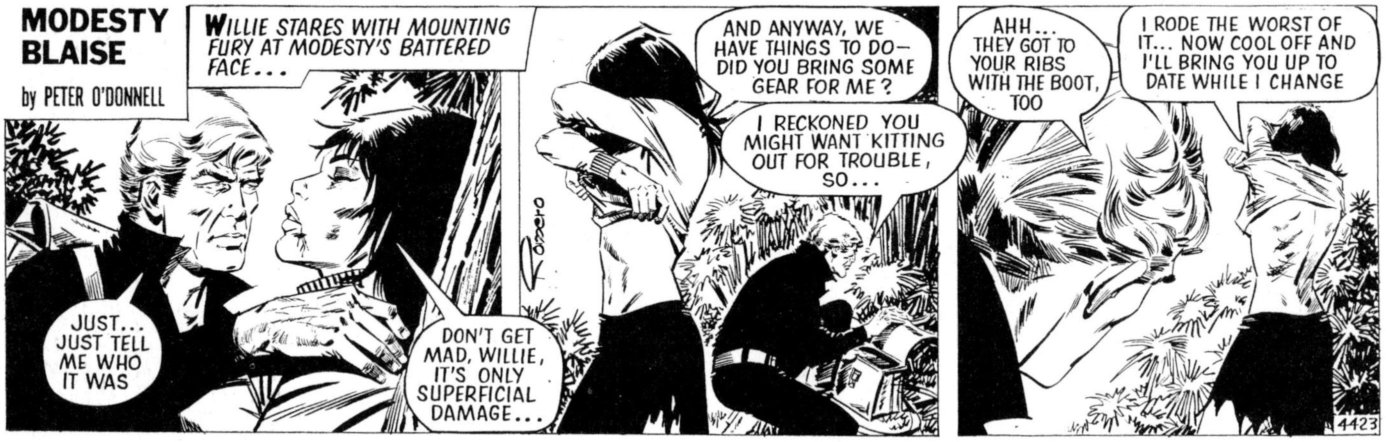
MODESTY BLAISE
by PETER O'DONNELL
WILLIE STARES WITH MOUNTING FURY AT MODESTY'S BATTERED FACE...
JUST... JUST TELL ME WHO IT WAS
DON'T GET MAD, WILLIE, IT'S ONLY SUPERFICIAL DAMAGE...
AND ANYWAY, WE HAVE THINGS TO DO— DID YOU BRING SOME GEAR FOR ME?
I RECKONED YOU MIGHT WANT KITTING OUT FOR TROUBLE, SO...
AHH... THEY GOT TO YOUR RIBS WITH THE BOOT, TOO
I RODE THE WORST OF IT... NOW COOL OFF AND I'LL BRING YOU UP TO DATE WHILE I CHANGE
4423

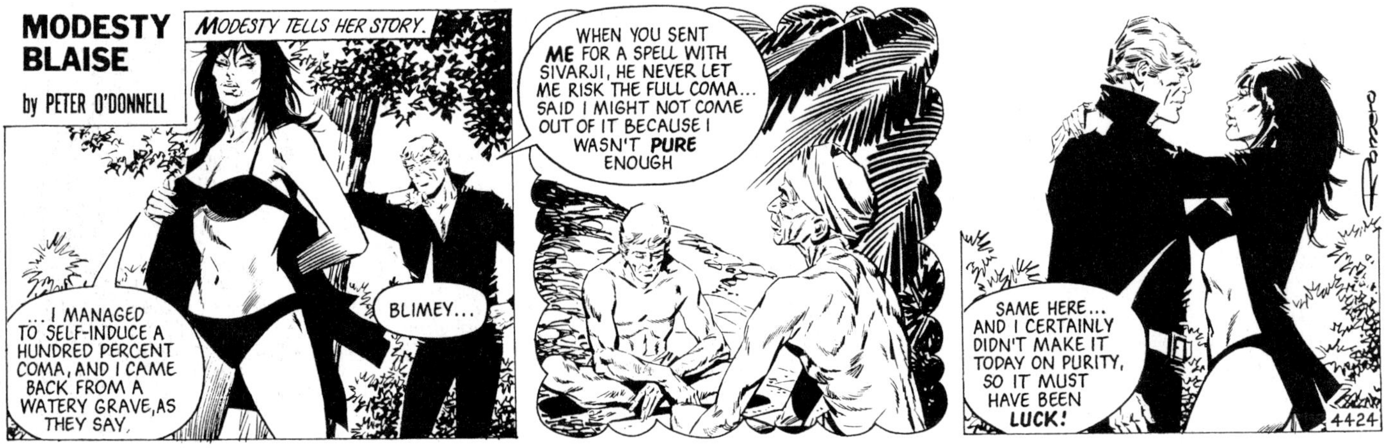
MODESTY BLAISE
by PETER O'DONNELL
MODESTY TELLS HER STORY.
...I MANAGED TO SELF-INDUCE A HUNDRED PERCENT COMA, AND I CAME BACK FROM A WATERY GRAVE, AS THEY SAY,
BLIMEY...
WHEN YOU SENT ME FOR A SPELL WITH SIVARJI, HE NEVER LET ME RISK THE FULL COMA... SAID I MIGHT NOT COME OUT OF IT BECAUSE I WASN'T PURE ENOUGH
SAME HERE... AND I CERTAINLY DIDN'T MAKE IT TODAY ON PURITY, SO IT MUST HAVE BEEN LUCK!
4424

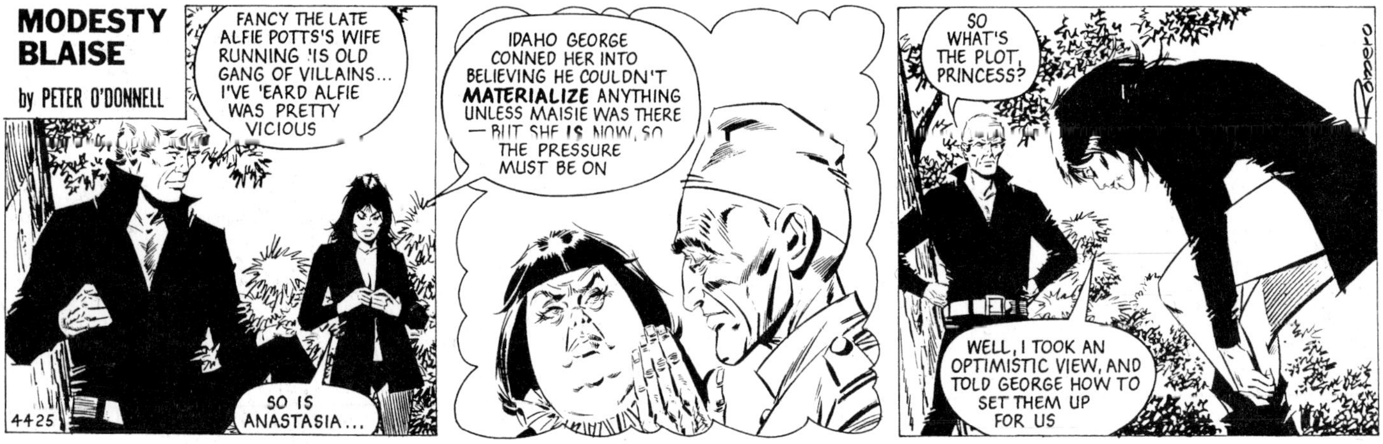
MODESTY BLAISE
by PETER O'DONNELL
FANCY THE LATE ALFIE POTTS'S WIFE RUNNING 'IS OLD GANG OF VILLAINS... I'VE 'EARD ALFIE WAS PRETTY VICIOUS
SO IS ANASTASIA...
4425
IDAHO GEORGE CONNED HER INTO BELIEVING HE COULDN'T MATERIALIZE ANYTHING UNLESS MAISIE WAS THERE — BUT SHE IS NOW, SO THE PRESSURE MUST BE ON
SO WHAT'S THE PLOT, PRINCESS?
WELL, I TOOK AN OPTIMISTIC VIEW, AND TOLD GEORGE HOW TO SET THEM UP FOR US

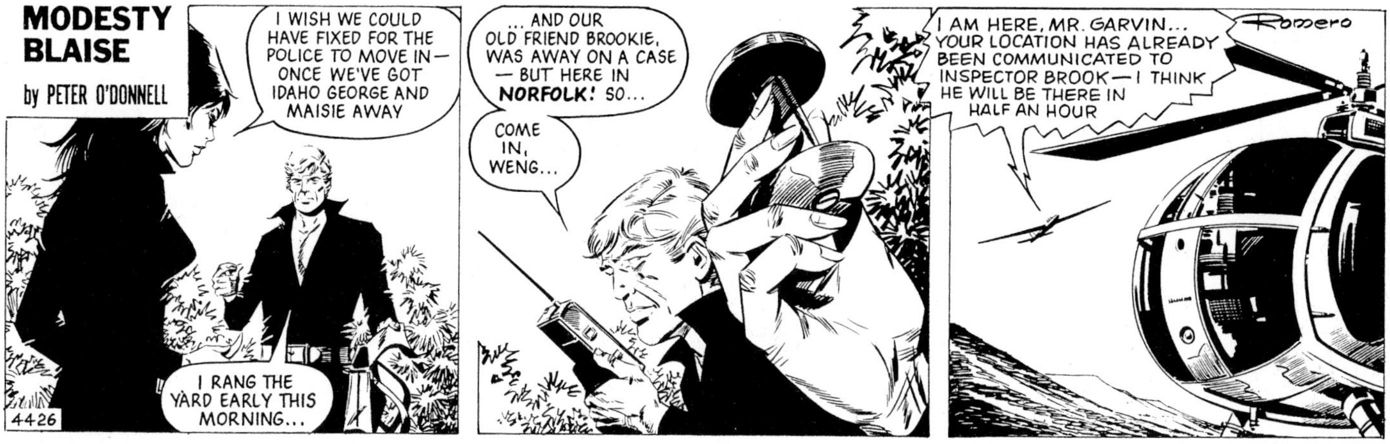
MODESTY BLAISE
by PETER O'DONNELL
I WISH WE COULD HAVE FIXED FOR THE POLICE TO MOVE IN— ONCE WE'VE GOT IDAHO GEORGE AND MAISIE AWAY
I RANG THE YARD EARLY THIS MORNING...
... AND OUR OLD FRIEND BROOKIE, WAS AWAY ON A CASE — BUT HERE IN NORFOLK! SO...
COME IN, WENG...
I AM HERE, MR. GARVIN... YOUR LOCATION HAS ALREADY BEEN COMMUNICATED TO INSPECTOR BROOK— I THINK HE WILL BE THERE IN HALF AN HOUR
Romero
4426

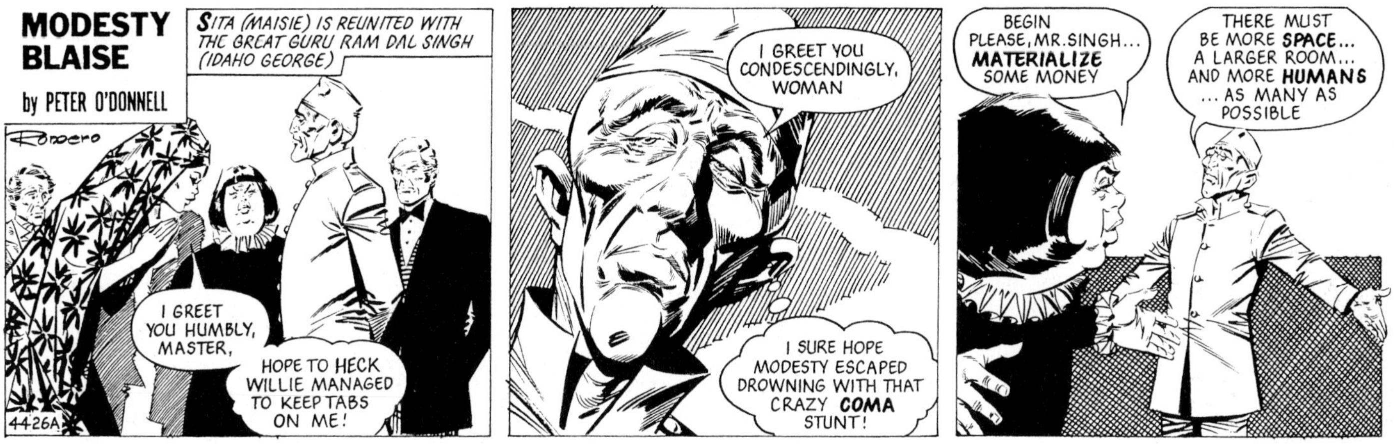
MODESTY BLAISE
by PETER O'DONNELL
SITA (MAISIE) IS REUNITED WITH THE GREAT GURU RAM DAL SINGH (IDAHO GEORGE)
Romero
I GREET YOU HUMBLY, MASTER,
HOPE TO HECK WILLIE MANAGED TO KEEP TABS ON ME!
I GREET YOU CONDESCENDINGLY, WOMAN
I SURE HOPE MODESTY ESCAPED DROWNING WITH THAT CRAZY COMA STUNT!
BEGIN PLEASE, MR. SINGH... MATERIALIZE SOME MONEY
THERE MUST BE MORE SPACE... A LARGER ROOM... AND MORE HUMANS ... AS MANY AS POSSIBLE
4426A

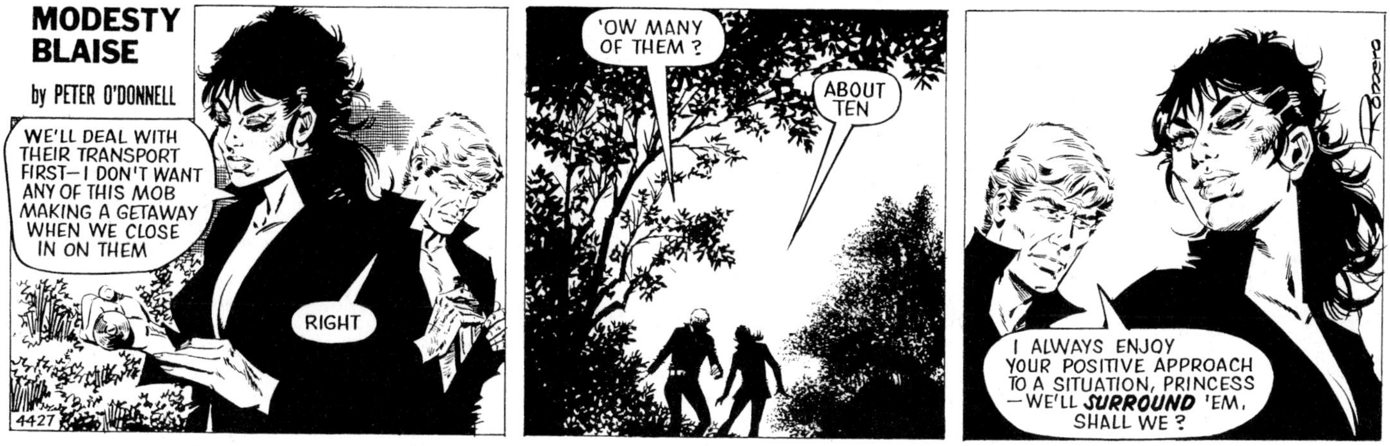
MODESTY BLAISE
by PETER O'DONNELL
WE'LL DEAL WITH THEIR TRANSPORT FIRST— I DON'T WANT ANY OF THIS MOB MAKING A GETAWAY WHEN WE CLOSE IN ON THEM
RIGHT
'OW MANY OF THEM ?
ABOUT TEN
Romero
I ALWAYS ENJOY YOUR POSITIVE APPROACH TO A SITUATION, PRINCESS —WE'LL SURROUND 'EM, SHALL WE ?
4427

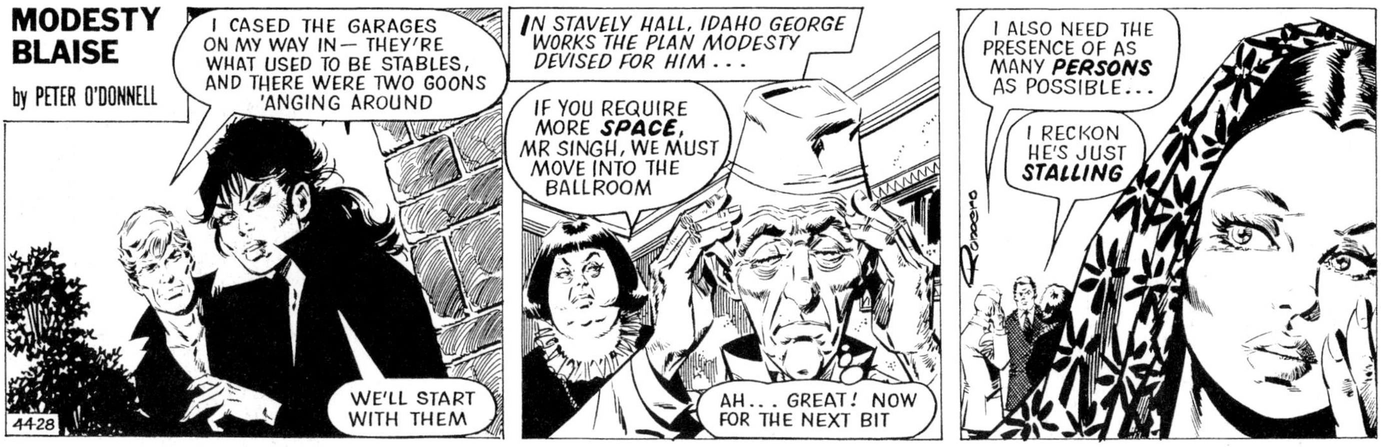
MODESTY BLAISE
by PETER O'DONNELL
I CASED THE GARAGES ON MY WAY IN— THEY'RE WHAT USED TO BE STABLES, AND THERE WERE TWO GOONS 'ANGING AROUND
WE'LL START WITH THEM
IN STAVELY HALL, IDAHO GEORGE WORKS THE PLAN MODESTY DEVISED FOR HIM . . .
IF YOU REQUIRE MORE SPACE, MR SINGH, WE MUST MOVE INTO THE BALLROOM
AH... GREAT! NOW FOR THE NEXT BIT
I ALSO NEED THE PRESENCE OF AS MANY PERSONS AS POSSIBLE...
I RECKON HE'S JUST STALLING
Romero
4428

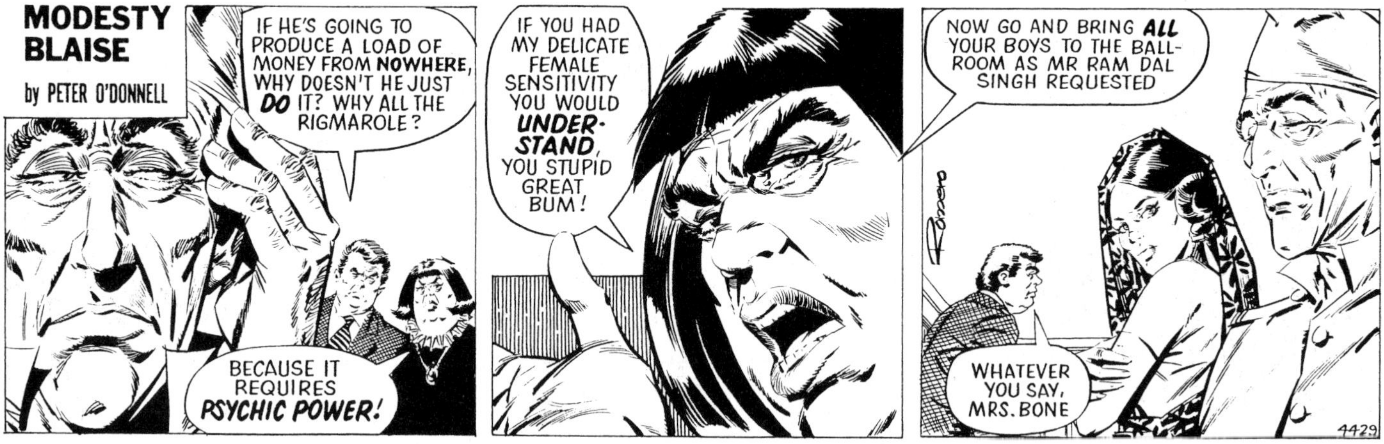
MODESTY BLAISE
by PETER O'DONNELL
IF HE'S GOING TO PRODUCE A LOAD OF MONEY FROM NOWHERE, WHY DOESN'T HE JUST DO IT? WHY ALL THE RIGMAROLE?
BECAUSE IT REQUIRES PSYCHIC POWER!
IF YOU HAD MY DELICATE FEMALE SENSITIVITY YOU WOULD UNDER-STAND, YOU STUPID GREAT BUM!
NOW GO AND BRING ALL YOUR BOYS TO THE BALL-ROOM AS MR RAM DAL SINGH REQUESTED
WHATEVER YOU SAY, MRS. BONE
4429

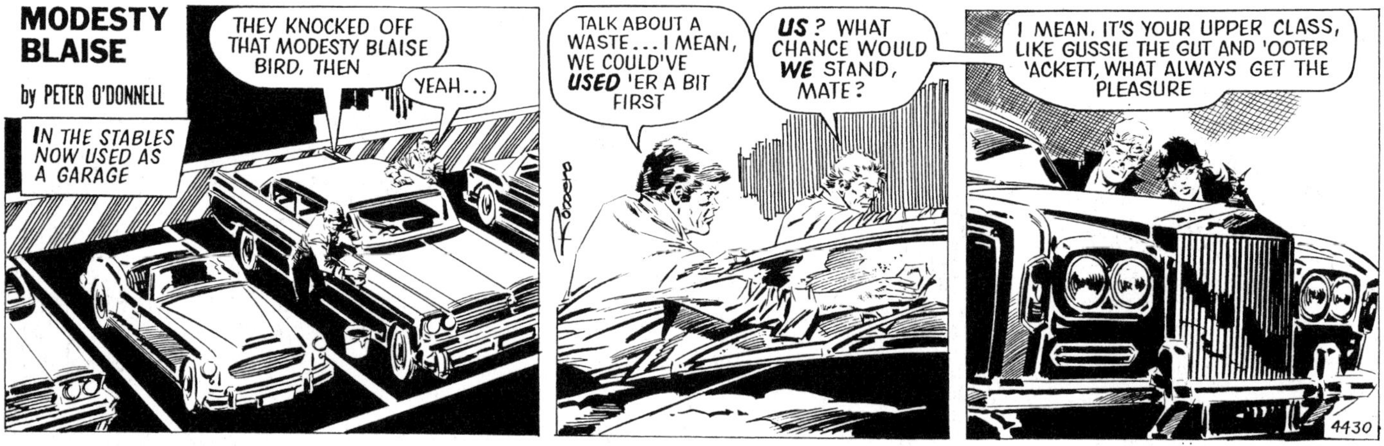
MODESTY BLAISE
by PETER O'DONNELL
IN THE STABLES NOW USED AS A GARAGE
THEY KNOCKED OFF THAT MODESTY BLAISE BIRD, THEN
YEAH...
TALK ABOUT A WASTE... I MEAN, WE COULD'VE USED 'ER A BIT FIRST
US? WHAT CHANCE WOULD WE STAND, MATE?
I MEAN, IT'S YOUR UPPER CLASS, LIKE GUSSIE THE GUT AND 'OOTER 'ACKETT, WHAT ALWAYS GET THE PLEASURE
4430

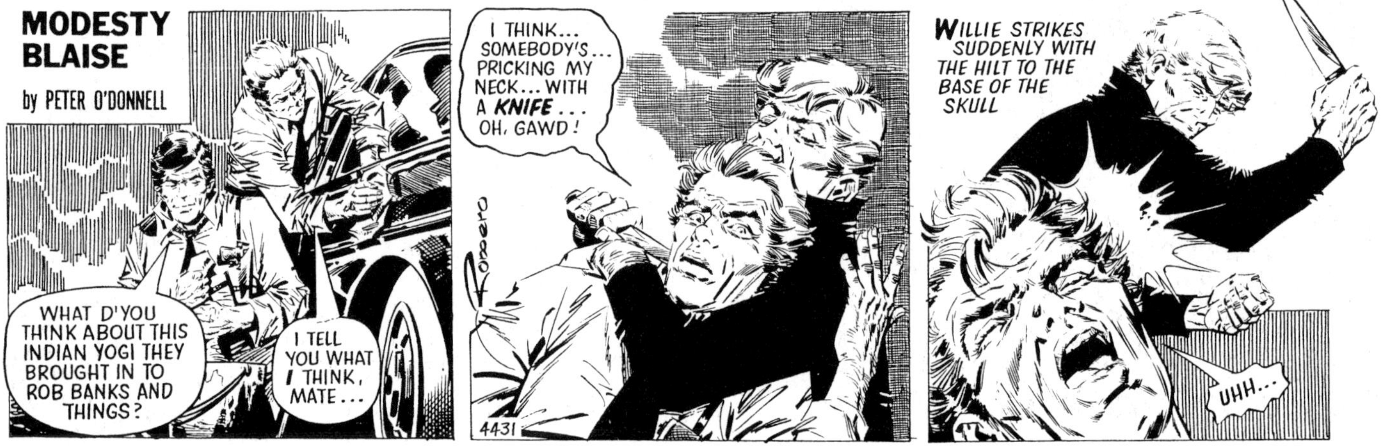
MODESTY BLAISE
by PETER O'DONNELL
WHAT D'YOU THINK ABOUT THIS INDIAN YOGI THEY BROUGHT IN TO ROB BANKS AND THINGS?
I TELL YOU WHAT I THINK, MATE...
I THINK... SOMEBODY'S... PRICKING MY NECK... WITH A KNIFE... OH, GAWD!
4431
WILLIE STRIKES SUDDENLY WITH THE HILT TO THE BASE OF THE SKULL
UHH...

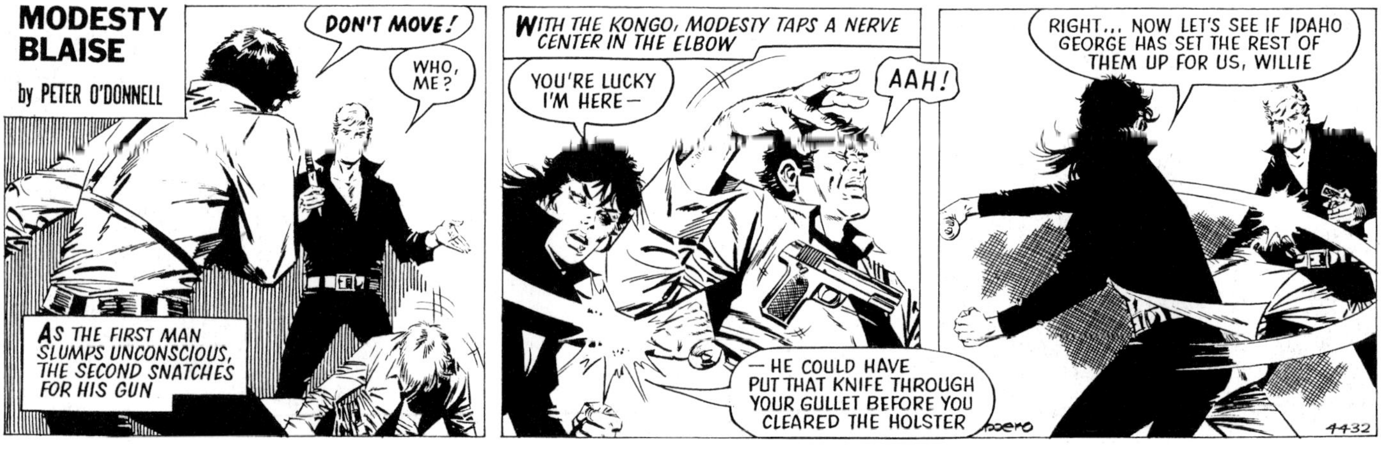
MODESTY BLAISE
by PETER O'DONNELL
DON'T MOVE!
WHO, ME?
AS THE FIRST MAN SLUMPS UNCONSCIOUS, THE SECOND SNATCHES FOR HIS GUN
WITH THE KONGO, MODESTY TAPS A NERVE CENTER IN THE ELBOW
YOU'RE LUCKY I'M HERE—
AAH!
—HE COULD HAVE PUT THAT KNIFE THROUGH YOUR GULLET BEFORE YOU CLEARED THE HOLSTER
RIGHT... NOW LET'S SEE IF IDAHO GEORGE HAS SET THE REST OF THEM UP FOR US, WILLIE
4432

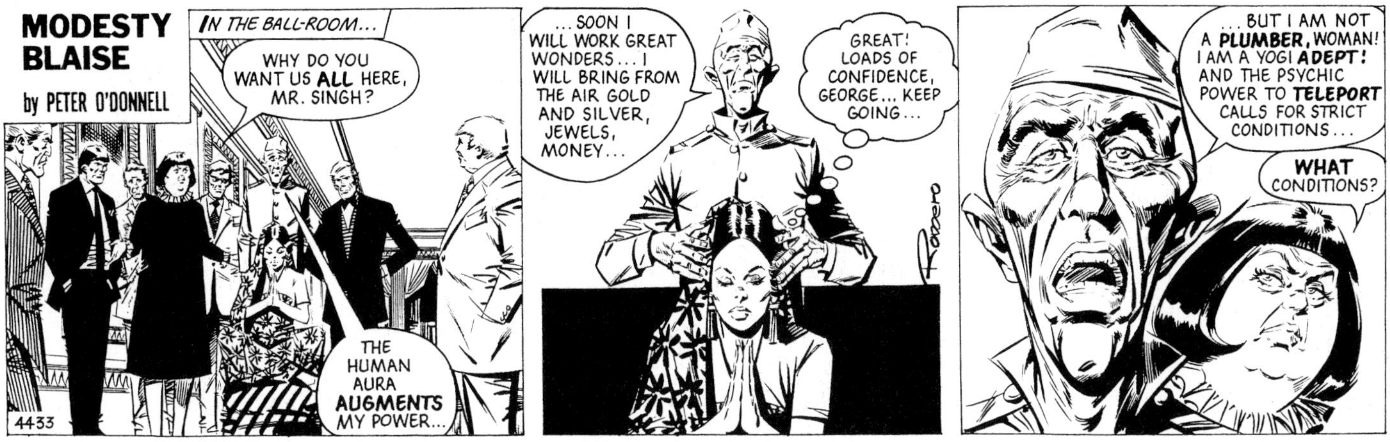
MODESTY BLAISE
by PETER O'DONNELL
IN THE BALL-ROOM...
WHY DO YOU WANT US ALL HERE, MR. SINGH?
THE HUMAN AURA AUGMENTS MY POWER...
4433
...SOON I WILL WORK GREAT WONDERS... I WILL BRING FROM THE AIR GOLD AND SILVER, JEWELS, MONEY...
GREAT! LOADS OF CONFIDENCE, GEORGE... KEEP GOING...
...BUT I AM NOT A PLUMBER, WOMAN! I AM A YOGI ADEPT! AND THE PSYCHIC POWER TO TELEPORT CALLS FOR STRICT CONDITIONS...
WHAT CONDITIONS?

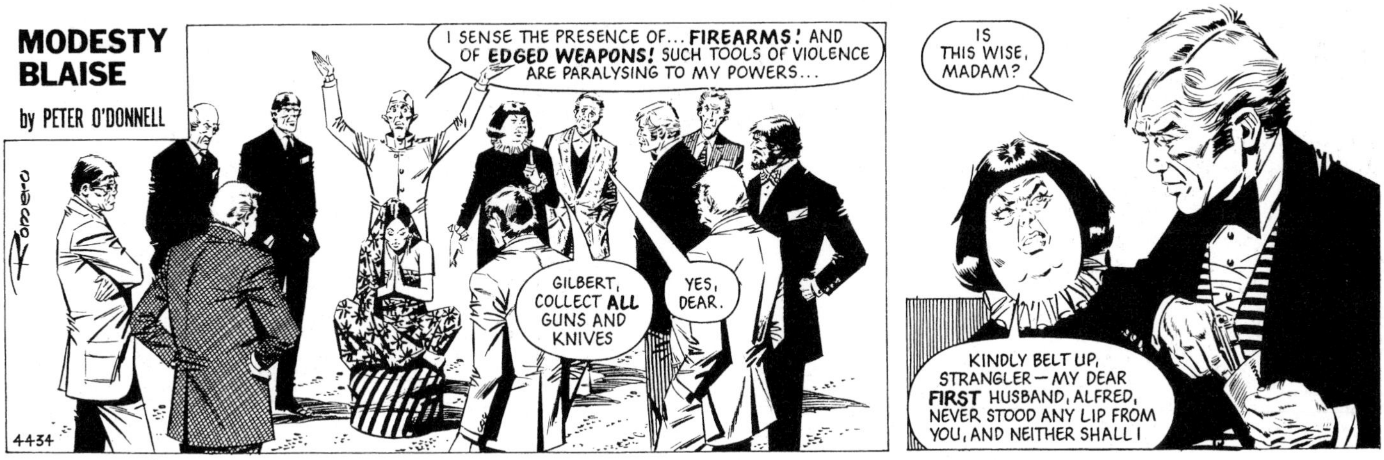
MODESTY BLAISE
by PETER O'DONNELL
I SENSE THE PRESENCE OF... FIREARMS! AND OF EDGED WEAPONS! SUCH TOOLS OF VIOLENCE ARE PARALYSING TO MY POWERS...
GILBERT, COLLECT ALL GUNS AND KNIVES
YES, DEAR.
4434
IS THIS WISE, MADAM?
KINDLY BELT UP, STRANGLER—MY DEAR FIRST HUSBAND, ALFRED, NEVER STOOD ANY LIP FROM YOU, AND NEITHER SHALL I

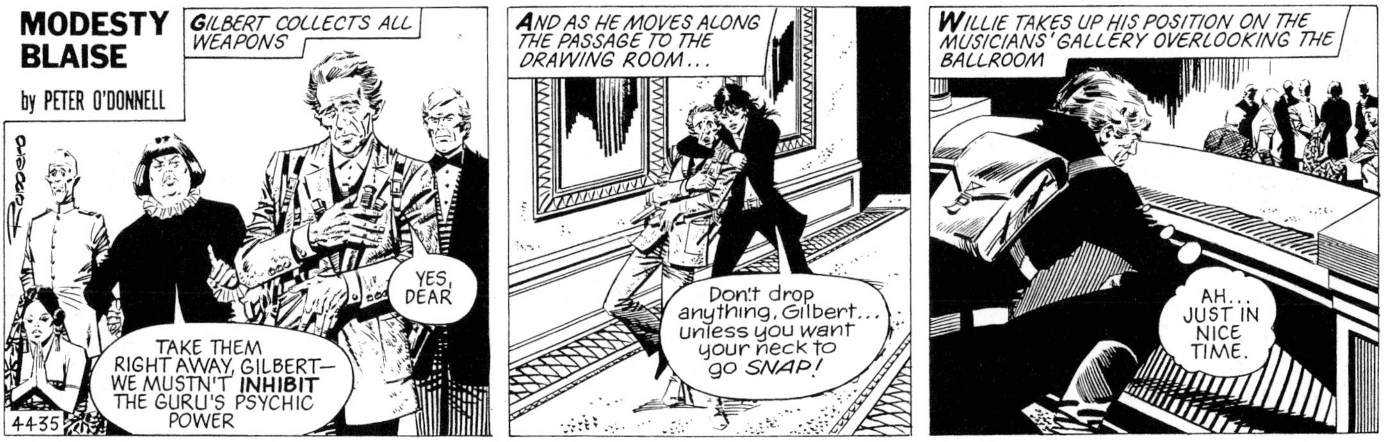
MODESTY BLAISE
by PETER O'DONNELL
GILBERT COLLECTS ALL WEAPONS
YES, DEAR
TAKE THEM RIGHT AWAY, GILBERT—WE MUSTN'T INHIBIT THE GURU'S PSYCHIC POWER
4435
AND AS HE MOVES ALONG THE PASSAGE TO THE DRAWING ROOM...
Don't drop anything, Gilbert... unless you want your neck to go SNAP!
WILLIE TAKES UP HIS POSITION ON THE MUSICIANS' GALLERY OVERLOOKING THE BALLROOM
AH... JUST IN NICE TIME.

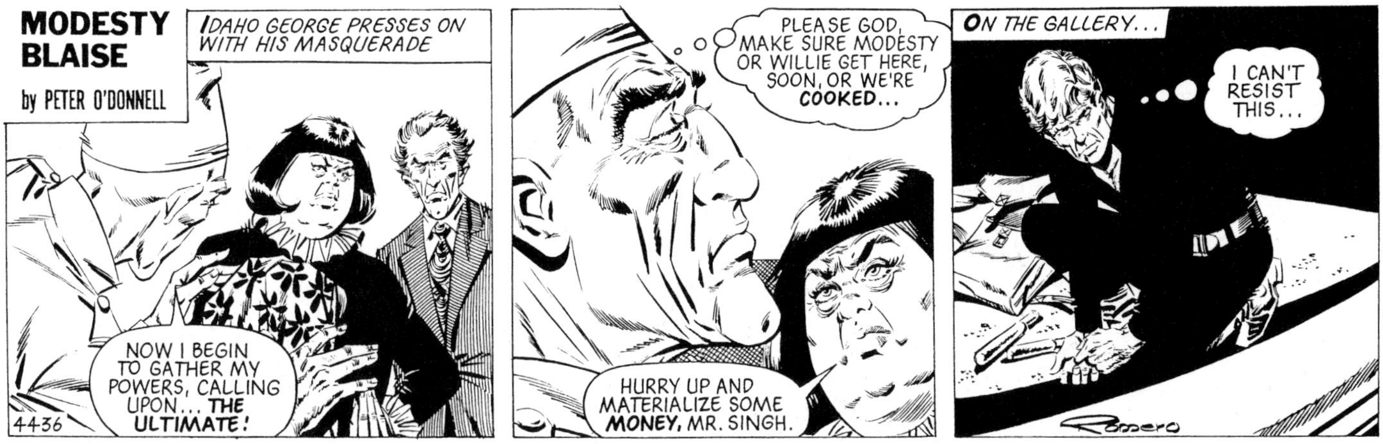
MODESTY BLAISE
by PETER O'DONNELL
IDAHO GEORGE PRESSES ON WITH HIS MASQUERADE
NOW I BEGIN TO GATHER MY POWERS, CALLING UPON... THE ULTIMATE!
4436
PLEASE GOD, MAKE SURE MODESTY OR WILLIE GET HERE SOON, OR WE'RE COOKED...
HURRY UP AND MATERIALIZE SOME MONEY, MR. SINGH.
ON THE GALLERY...
I CAN'T RESIST THIS...

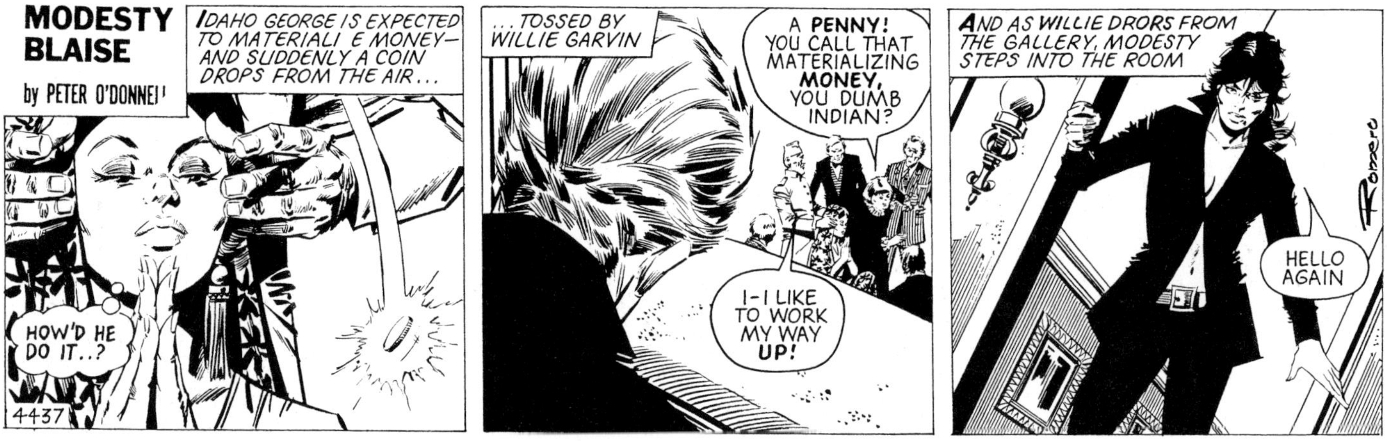

MODESTY BLAISE
by PETER O'DONNE
IDAHO GEORGE IS EXPECTED TO MATERIALI E MONEY— AND SUDDENLY A COIN DROPS FROM THE AIR...
HOW'D HE DO IT..?
4437
...TOSSED BY WILLIE GARVIN
A PENNY! YOU CALL THAT MATERIALIZING MONEY, YOU DUMB INDIAN?
I-I LIKE TO WORK MY WAY UP!
AND AS WILLIE DRORS FROM THE GALLERY, MODESTY STEPS INTO THE ROOM
HELLO AGAIN
Romero

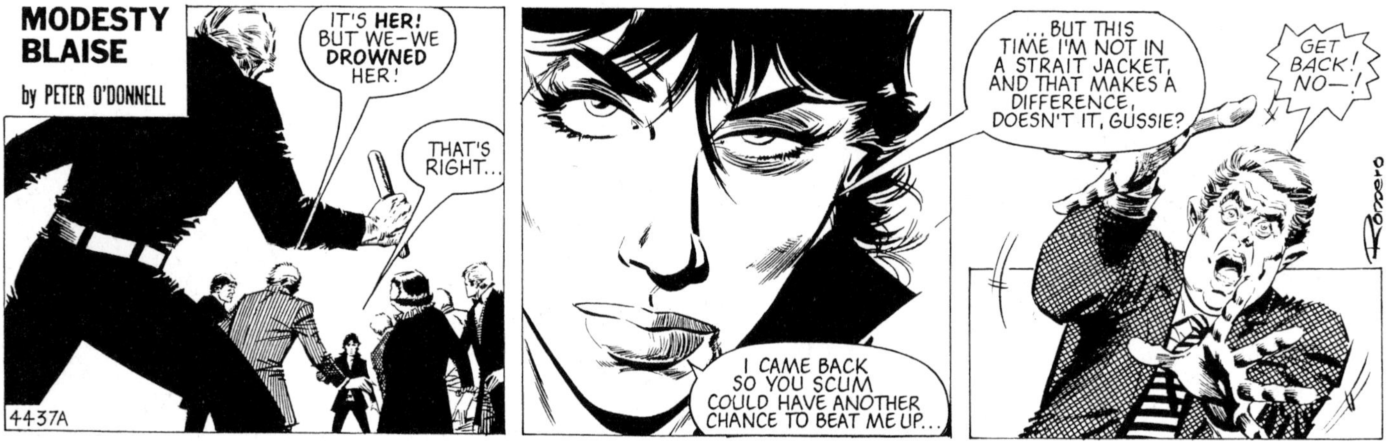

MODESTY BLAISE
by PETER O'DONNELL
IT'S HER! BUT WE–WE DROWNED HER!
THAT'S RIGHT...
4437A
I CAME BACK SO YOU SCUM COULD HAVE ANOTHER CHANCE TO BEAT ME UP...
...BUT THIS TIME I'M NOT IN A STRAIT JACKET, AND THAT MAKES A DIFFERENCE, DOESN'T IT, GUSSIE?
GET BACK! NO—!
Romero

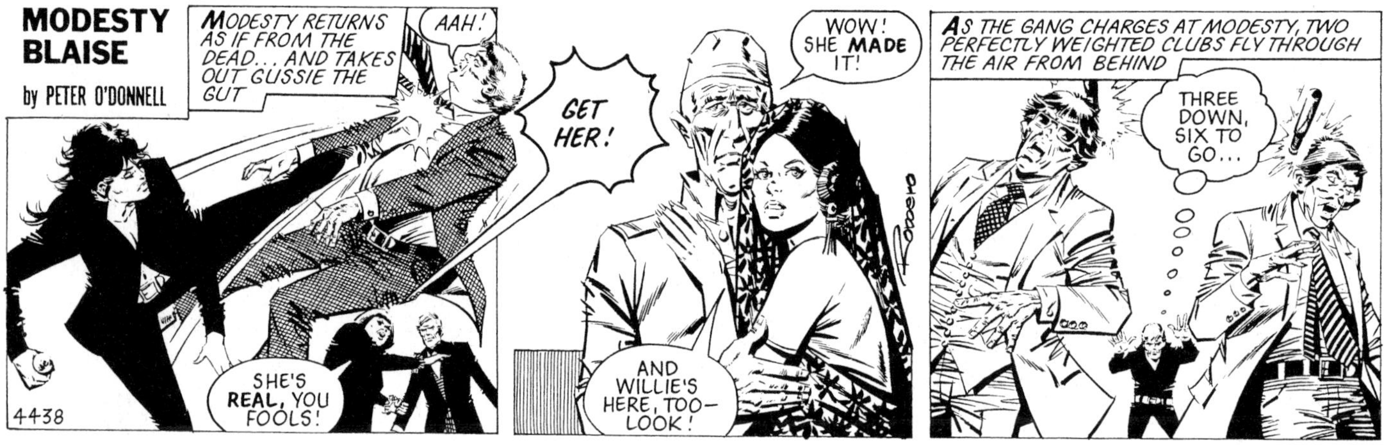

MODESTY BLAISE
by PETER O'DONNELL
MODESTY RETURNS AS IF FROM THE DEAD... AND TAKES OUT GUSSIE THE GUT
AAH!
GET HER!
SHE'S REAL, YOU FOOLS!
4438
WOW! SHE MADE IT!
AND WILLIE'S HERE, TOO— LOOK!
Romero
AS THE GANG CHARGES AT MODESTY, TWO PERFECTLY WEIGHTED CLUBS FLY THROUGH THE AIR FROM BEHIND
THREE DOWN, SIX TO GO...

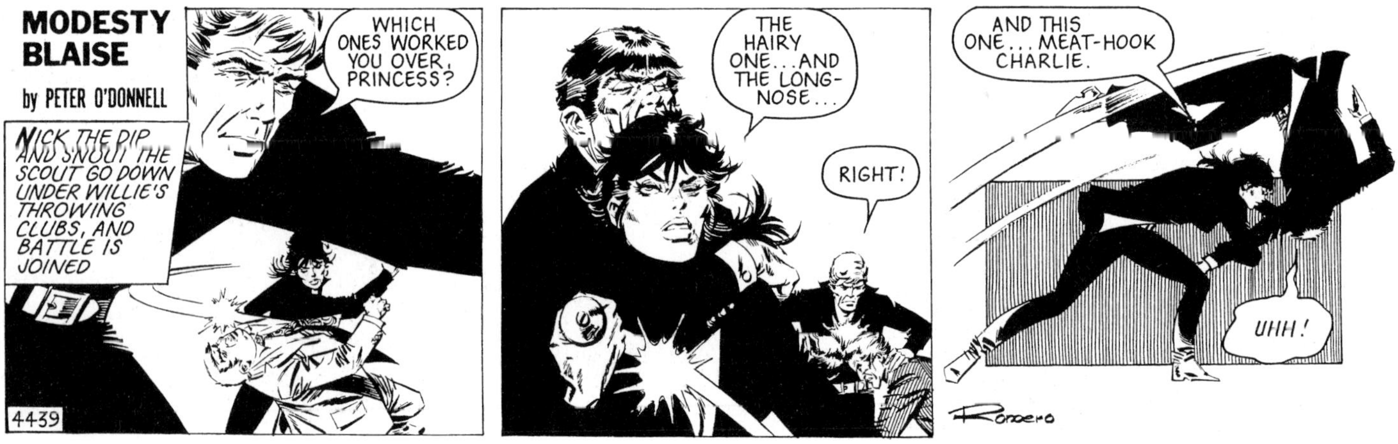

MODESTY BLAISE
by PETER O'DONNELL
WHICH ONES WORKED YOU OVER, PRINCESS?
NICK THE DIP AND SNOUT THE SCOUT GO DOWN UNDER WILLIE'S THROWING CLUBS, AND BATTLE IS JOINED
4439
THE HAIRY ONE...AND THE LONG-NOSE...
RIGHT!
AND THIS ONE... MEAT-HOOK CHARLIE.
UHH!
Romero

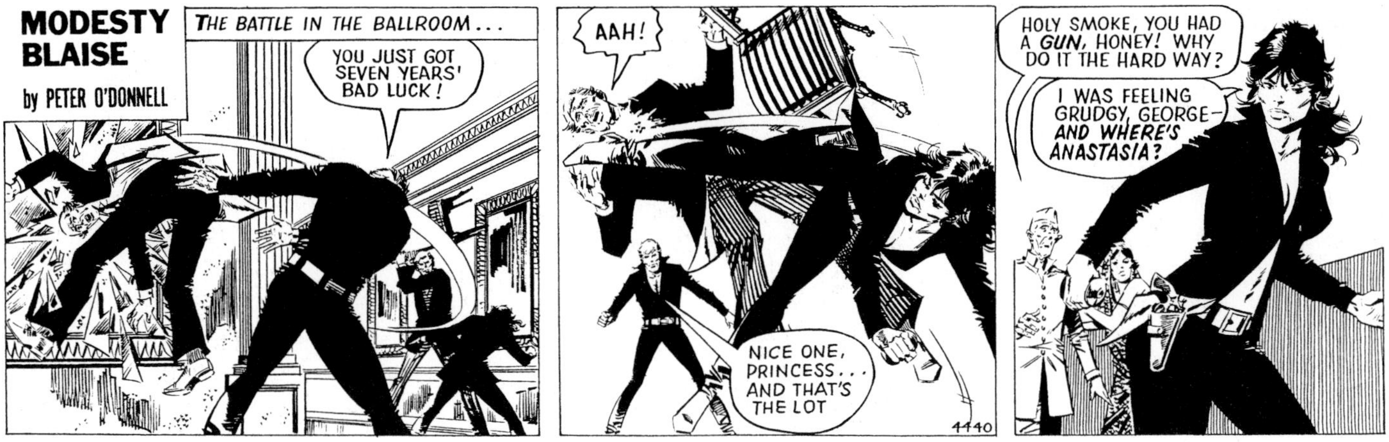
MODESTY BLAISE
by PETER O'DONNELL
THE BATTLE IN THE BALLROOM...
YOU JUST GOT SEVEN YEARS' BAD LUCK!
AAH!
NICE ONE, PRINCESS... AND THAT'S THE LOT
4440
HOLY SMOKE, YOU HAD A GUN, HONEY! WHY DO IT THE HARD WAY?
I WAS FEELING GRUDGY, GEORGE— AND WHERE'S ANASTASIA?

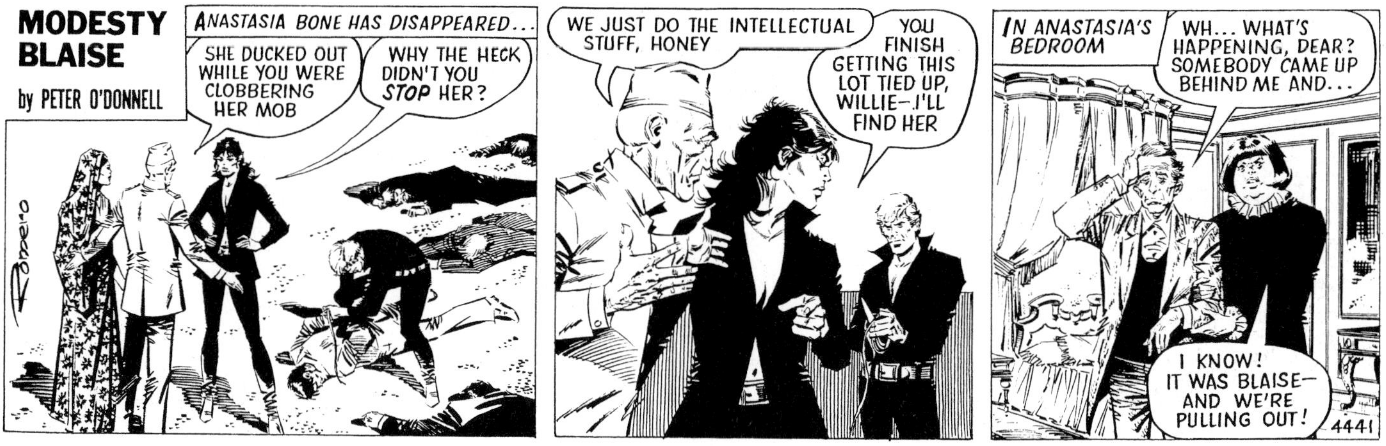
MODESTY BLAISE
by PETER O'DONNELL
ANASTASIA BONE HAS DISAPPEARED...
SHE DUCKED OUT WHILE YOU WERE CLOBBERING HER MOB
WHY THE HECK DIDN'T YOU STOP HER?
Romero
WE JUST DO THE INTELLECTUAL STUFF, HONEY
YOU FINISH GETTING THIS LOT TIED UP, WILLIE—I'LL FIND HER
IN ANASTASIA'S BEDROOM
WH... WHAT'S HAPPENING, DEAR? SOMEBODY CAME UP BEHIND ME AND...
I KNOW! IT WAS BLAISE— AND WE'RE PULLING OUT!
4441

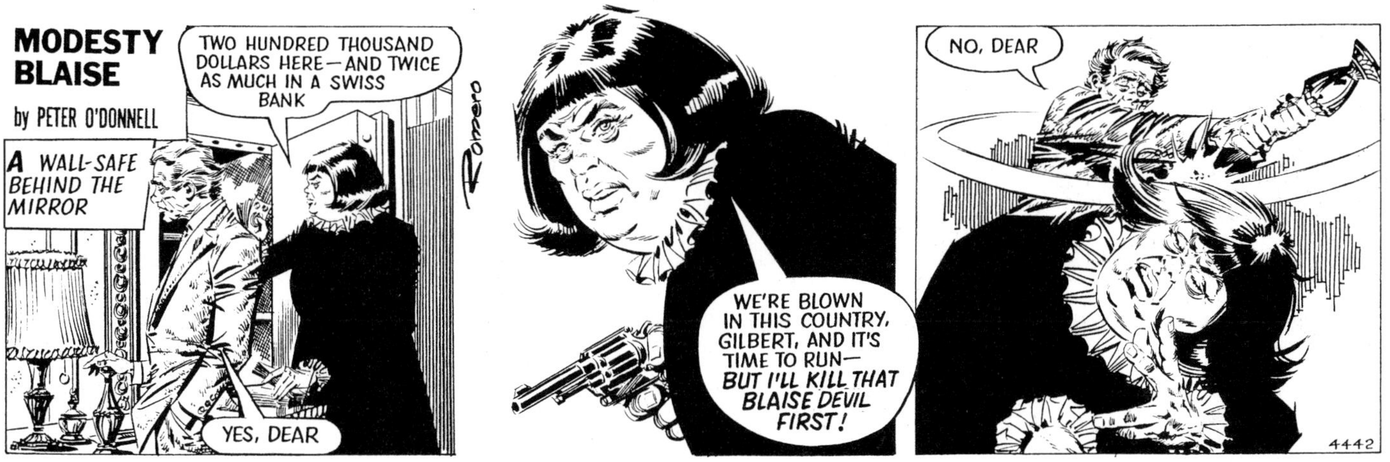
MODESTY BLAISE
by PETER O'DONNELL
TWO HUNDRED THOUSAND DOLLARS HERE—AND TWICE AS MUCH IN A SWISS BANK
A WALL-SAFE BEHIND THE MIRROR
YES, DEAR
Romero
WE'RE BLOWN IN THIS COUNTRY, GILBERT, AND IT'S TIME TO RUN— BUT I'LL KILL THAT BLAISE DEVIL FIRST!
NO, DEAR
4442

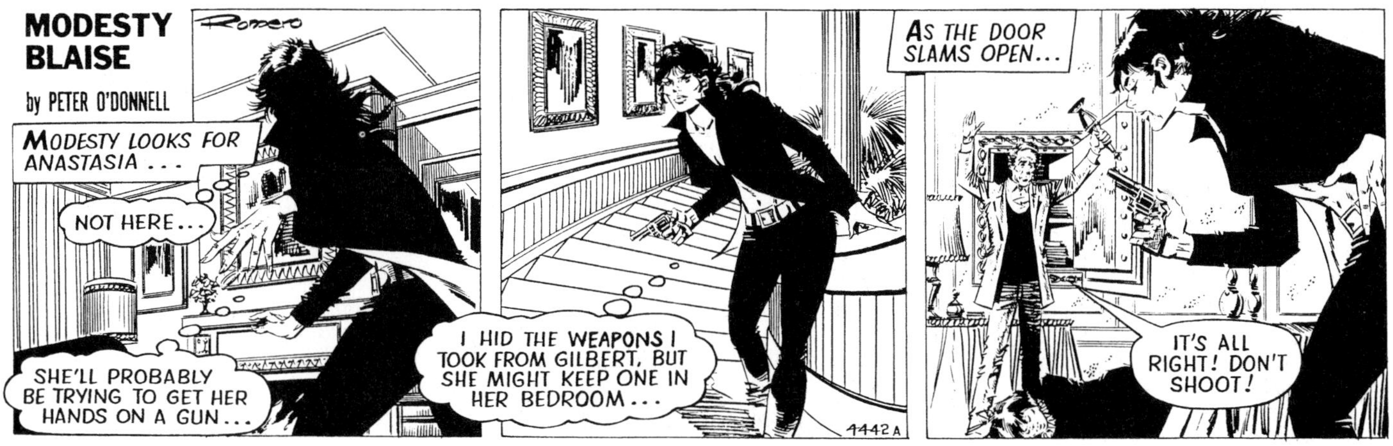
MODESTY BLAISE
by PETER O'DONNELL
Romero
MODESTY LOOKS FOR ANASTASIA...
NOT HERE...
SHE'LL PROBABLY BE TRYING TO GET HER HANDS ON A GUN...
I HID THE WEAPONS I TOOK FROM GILBERT, BUT SHE MIGHT KEEP ONE IN HER BEDROOM...
4442A
AS THE DOOR SLAMS OPEN...
IT'S ALL RIGHT! DON'T SHOOT!

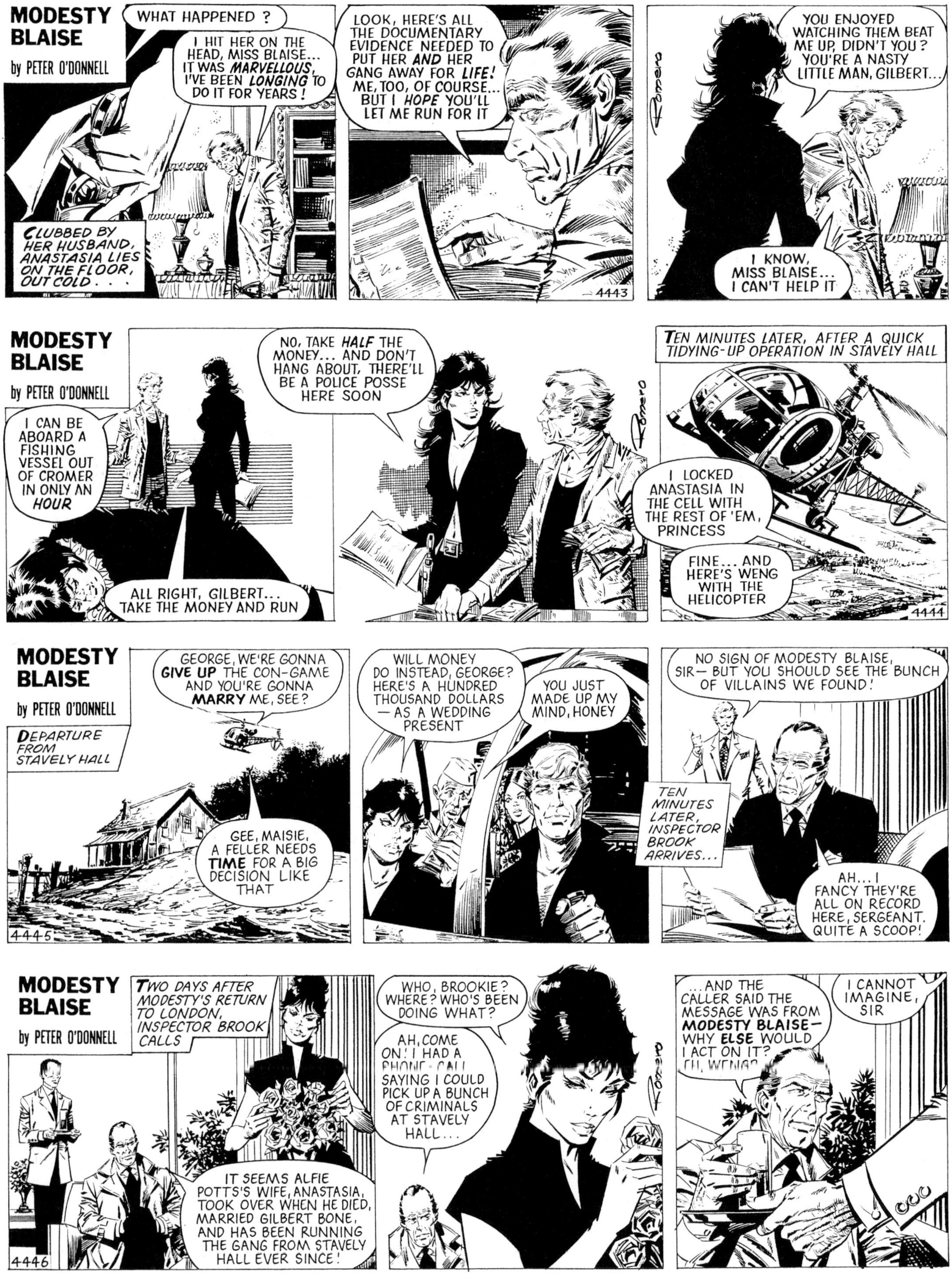
MODESTY BLAISE
by PETER O'DONNELL
WHAT HAPPENED ?
I HIT HER ON THE HEAD, MISS BLAISE... IT WAS MARVELLOUS, I'VE BEEN LONGING TO DO IT FOR YEARS!
CLUBBED BY HER HUSBAND, ANASTASIA LIES ON THE FLOOR, OUT COLD . . .
LOOK, HERE'S ALL THE DOCUMENTARY EVIDENCE NEEDED TO PUT HER AND HER GANG AWAY FOR LIFE! ME, TOO, OF COURSE... BUT I HOPE YOU'LL LET ME RUN FOR IT
4443
YOU ENJOYED WATCHING THEM BEAT ME UP, DIDN'T YOU? YOU'RE A NASTY LITTLE MAN, GILBERT...
I KNOW, MISS BLAISE... I CAN'T HELP IT
Romero
MODESTY BLAISE
by PETER O'DONNELL
I CAN BE ABOARD A FISHING VESSEL OUT OF CROMER IN ONLY AN HOUR
ALL RIGHT, GILBERT... TAKE THE MONEY AND RUN
NO, TAKE HALF THE MONEY... AND DON'T HANG ABOUT, THERE'LL BE A POLICE POSSE HERE SOON
Romero
TEN MINUTES LATER, AFTER A QUICK TIDYING-UP OPERATION IN STAVELY HALL
I LOCKED ANASTASIA IN THE CELL WITH THE REST OF 'EM, PRINCESS
FINE... AND HERE'S WENG WITH THE HELICOPTER
4444
MODESTY BLAISE
by PETER O'DONNELL
DEPARTURE FROM STAVELY HALL
GEORGE, WE'RE GONNA GIVE UP THE CON-GAME AND YOU'RE GONNA MARRY ME, SEE?
GEE, MAISIE, A FELLER NEEDS TIME FOR A BIG DECISION LIKE THAT
4445
WILL MONEY DO INSTEAD, GEORGE? HERE'S A HUNDRED THOUSAND DOLLARS — AS A WEDDING PRESENT
YOU JUST MADE UP MY MIND, HONEY
NO SIGN OF MODESTY BLAISE, SIR — BUT YOU SHOULD SEE THE BUNCH OF VILLAINS WE FOUND!
TEN MINUTES LATER, INSPECTOR BROOK ARRIVES...
AH... I FANCY THEY'RE ALL ON RECORD HERE, SERGEANT. QUITE A SCOOP!
MODESTY BLAISE
by PETER O'DONNELL
TWO DAYS AFTER MODESTY'S RETURN TO LONDON, INSPECTOR BROOK CALLS
IT SEEMS ALFIE POTTS'S WIFE, ANASTASIA, TOOK OVER WHEN HE DIED, MARRIED GILBERT BONE, AND HAS BEEN RUNNING THE GANG FROM STAVELY HALL EVER SINCE!
4446
WHO, BROOKIE? WHERE? WHO'S BEEN DOING WHAT?
AH, COME ON! I HAD A PHONE-CALL SAYING I COULD PICK UP A BUNCH OF CRIMINALS AT STAVELY HALL...
Romero
...AND THE CALLER SAID THE MESSAGE WAS FROM MODESTY BLAISE — WHY ELSE WOULD I ACT ON IT?
I CANNOT IMAGINE, SIR

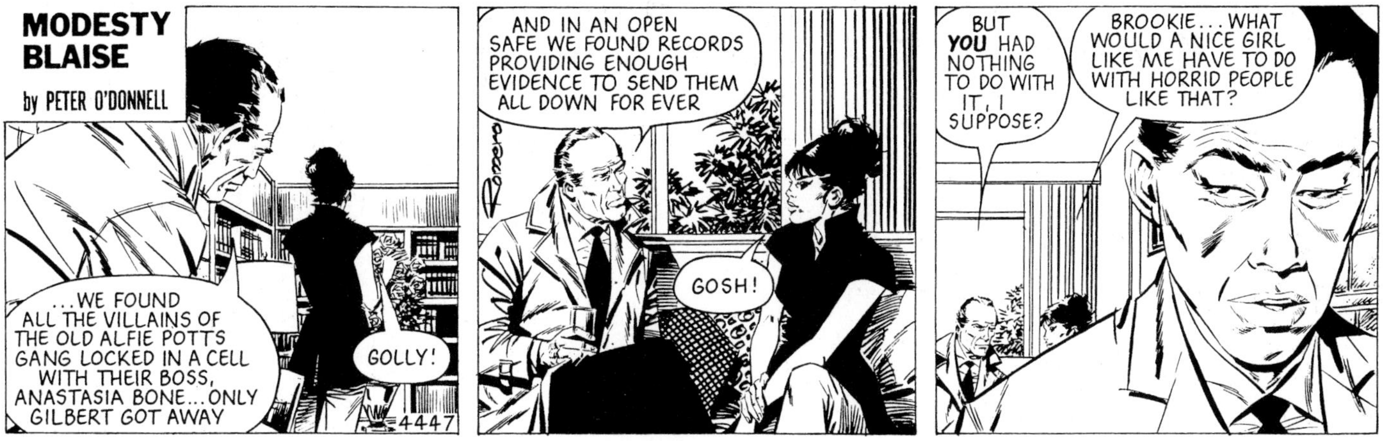
MODESTY BLAISE
by PETER O'DONNELL
...WE FOUND ALL THE VILLAINS OF THE OLD ALFIE POTTS GANG LOCKED IN A CELL WITH THEIR BOSS, ANASTASIA BONE...ONLY GILBERT GOT AWAY
GOLLY!
4447
AND IN AN OPEN SAFE WE FOUND RECORDS PROVIDING ENOUGH EVIDENCE TO SEND THEM ALL DOWN FOR EVER
GOSH!
BUT YOU HAD NOTHING TO DO WITH IT, I SUPPOSE?
BROOKIE...WHAT WOULD A NICE GIRL LIKE ME HAVE TO DO WITH HORRID PEOPLE LIKE THAT?

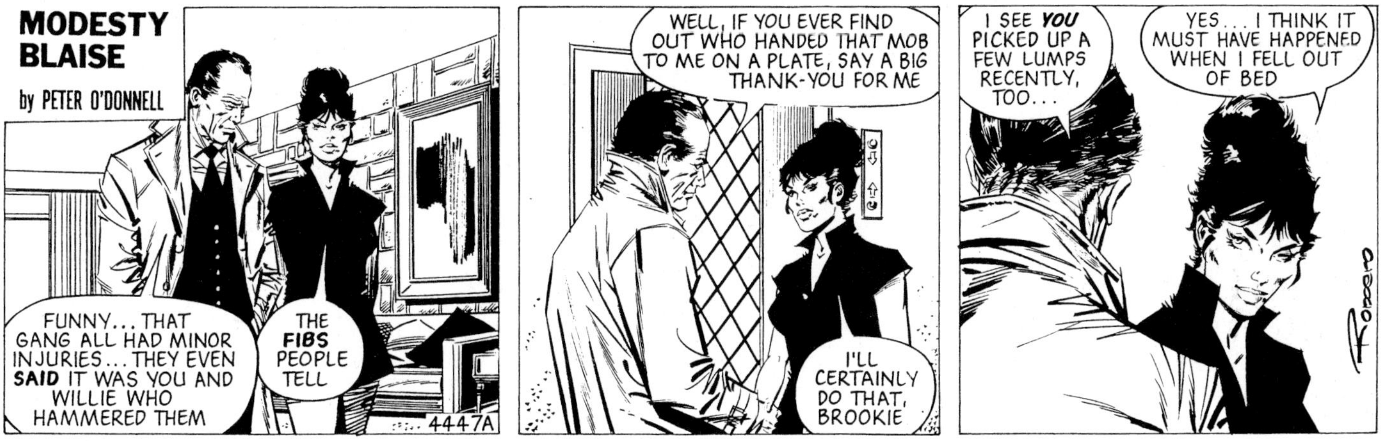
MODESTY BLAISE
by PETER O'DONNELL
FUNNY...THAT GANG ALL HAD MINOR INJURIES...THEY EVEN SAID IT WAS YOU AND WILLIE WHO HAMMERED THEM
THE FIBS PEOPLE TELL
4447A
WELL, IF YOU EVER FIND OUT WHO HANDED THAT MOB TO ME ON A PLATE, SAY A BIG THANK-YOU FOR ME
I'LL CERTAINLY DO THAT, BROOKIE
I SEE YOU PICKED UP A FEW LUMPS RECENTLY, TOO...
YES...I THINK IT MUST HAVE HAPPENED WHEN I FELL OUT OF BED

THE GOLDEN FROG

In the early days of The Network, before Modesty and Willie met, they had each trained under Saragam at his School of Combat in Cambodia. I've referred to Saragam by name a number of times both in the strip stories and the novels because he is acknowledged to be the world's greatest master in the art of combat, but in this story, 'The Golden Frog', he appears for the first time in the flesh as it were, and plays a leading role.

In the world where various forms of unarmed combat compete, Saragam is regarded as the supreme master, for his skills go far beyond the physical. To him combat is a true art form, never to be misused, and demanding honour of the highest nature from its disciples.

I see from my records that I wrote this story in 1978, which would be after the Khmer Rouge had seized control of Cambodia and were busy killing off any dangerous opposition to their rule. If you had a little education you were considered dangerous, and even wearing glasses was enough to put you in that category. Saragam's son and his wife were among the slaughtered, but Saragam escaped across the border into Thailand with his grand-daughter.

Modesty and Willie regard Saragam with awe, marvelling at the way his powers extend beyond physical boundaries. From this I have taken licence in the finalé of the story to show him using these powers. Could they possibly exist? Mass hypnosis or something of that order — the enemy rendered harmless by his subconscious certainty that his blade will be turned aside?

If I'd used this idea in one of the novels there'd be plenty of room to argue the point, but here I've just run out of space so I'll leave it to you.

PETER O'DONNELL

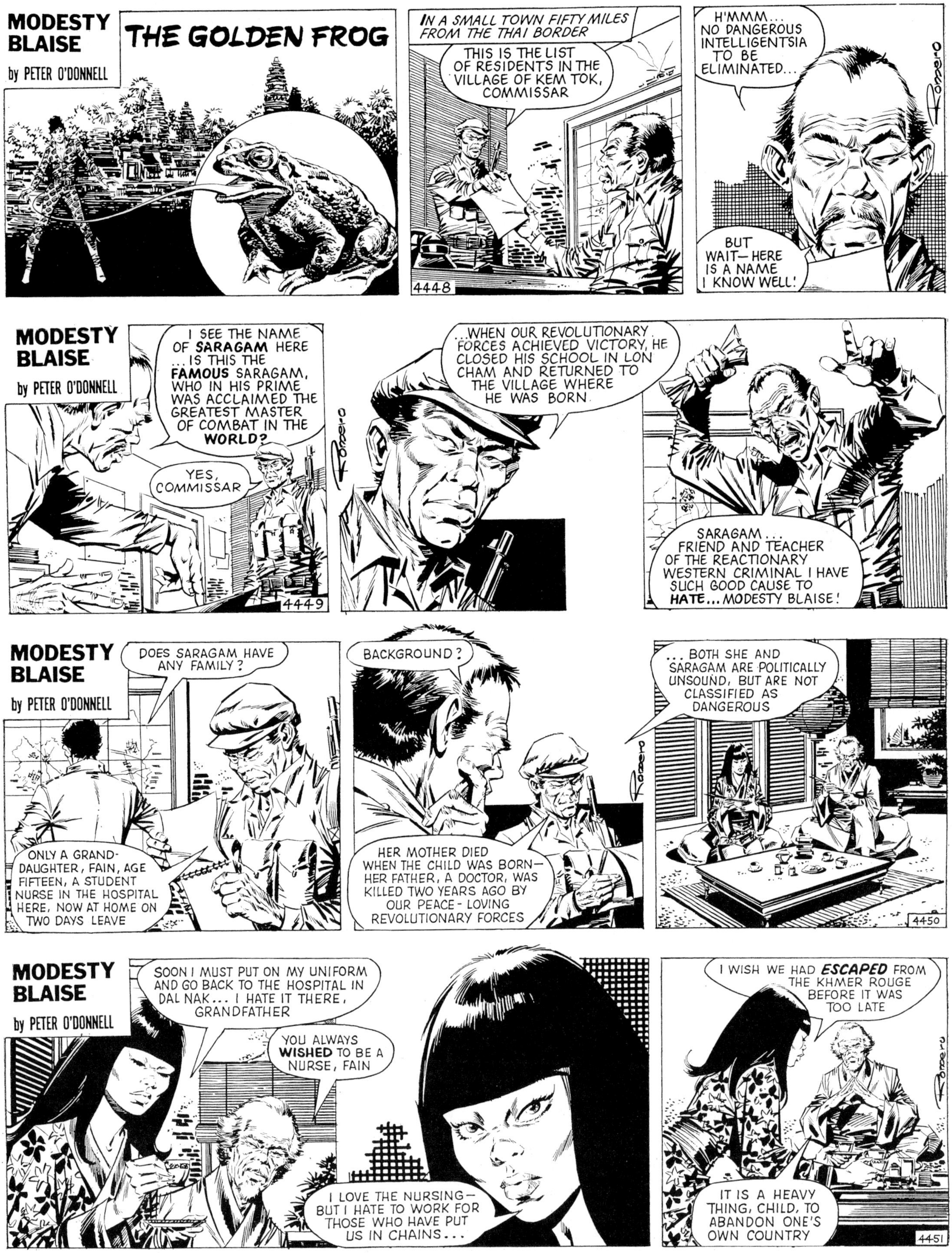

MODESTY BLAISE
by PETER O'DONNELL
THE GOLDEN FROG
IN A SMALL TOWN FIFTY MILES FROM THE THAI BORDER
THIS IS THE LIST OF RESIDENTS IN THE VILLAGE OF KEM TOK, COMMISSAR
4448
H'MMM... NO DANGEROUS INTELLIGENTSIA TO BE ELIMINATED...
BUT WAIT— HERE IS A NAME I KNOW WELL!
MODESTY BLAISE
by PETER O'DONNELL
I SEE THE NAME OF SARAGAM HERE ...IS THIS THE FAMOUS SARAGAM, WHO IN HIS PRIME WAS ACCLAIMED THE GREATEST MASTER OF COMBAT IN THE WORLD?
YES, COMMISSAR
4449
...WHEN OUR REVOLUTIONARY FORCES ACHIEVED VICTORY, HE CLOSED HIS SCHOOL IN LON CHAM AND RETURNED TO THE VILLAGE WHERE HE WAS BORN
SARAGAM... FRIEND AND TEACHER OF THE REACTIONARY WESTERN CRIMINAL I HAVE SUCH GOOD CAUSE TO HATE... MODESTY BLAISE!
MODESTY BLAISE
by PETER O'DONNELL
DOES SARAGAM HAVE ANY FAMILY?
ONLY A GRAND-DAUGHTER, FAIN, AGE FIFTEEN, A STUDENT NURSE IN THE HOSPITAL HERE, NOW AT HOME ON TWO DAYS LEAVE
BACKGROUND?
HER MOTHER DIED WHEN THE CHILD WAS BORN— HER FATHER, A DOCTOR, WAS KILLED TWO YEARS AGO BY OUR PEACE-LOVING REVOLUTIONARY FORCES
...BOTH SHE AND SARAGAM ARE POLITICALLY UNSOUND, BUT ARE NOT CLASSIFIED AS DANGEROUS
4450
MODESTY BLAISE
by PETER O'DONNELL
SOON I MUST PUT ON MY UNIFORM AND GO BACK TO THE HOSPITAL IN DAL NAK... I HATE IT THERE, GRANDFATHER
YOU ALWAYS WISHED TO BE A NURSE, FAIN
I LOVE THE NURSING— BUT I HATE TO WORK FOR THOSE WHO HAVE PUT US IN CHAINS...
I WISH WE HAD ESCAPED FROM THE KHMER ROUGE BEFORE IT WAS TOO LATE
IT IS A HEAVY THING, CHILD, TO ABANDON ONE'S OWN COUNTRY
4451

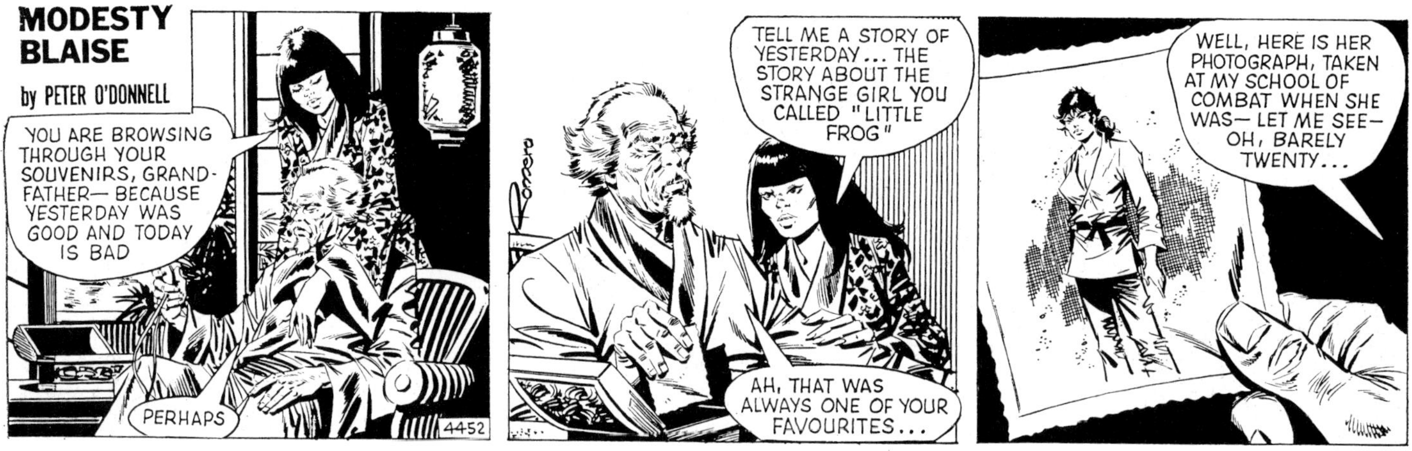
MODESTY BLAISE
by PETER O'DONNELL
YOU ARE BROWSING THROUGH YOUR SOUVENIRS, GRAND-FATHER— BECAUSE YESTERDAY WAS GOOD AND TODAY IS BAD
PERHAPS
TELL ME A STORY OF YESTERDAY... THE STORY ABOUT THE STRANGE GIRL YOU CALLED "LITTLE FROG"
AH, THAT WAS ALWAYS ONE OF YOUR FAVOURITES...
WELL, HERE IS HER PHOTOGRAPH, TAKEN AT MY SCHOOL OF COMBAT WHEN SHE WAS— LET ME SEE— OH, BARELY TWENTY...
4452

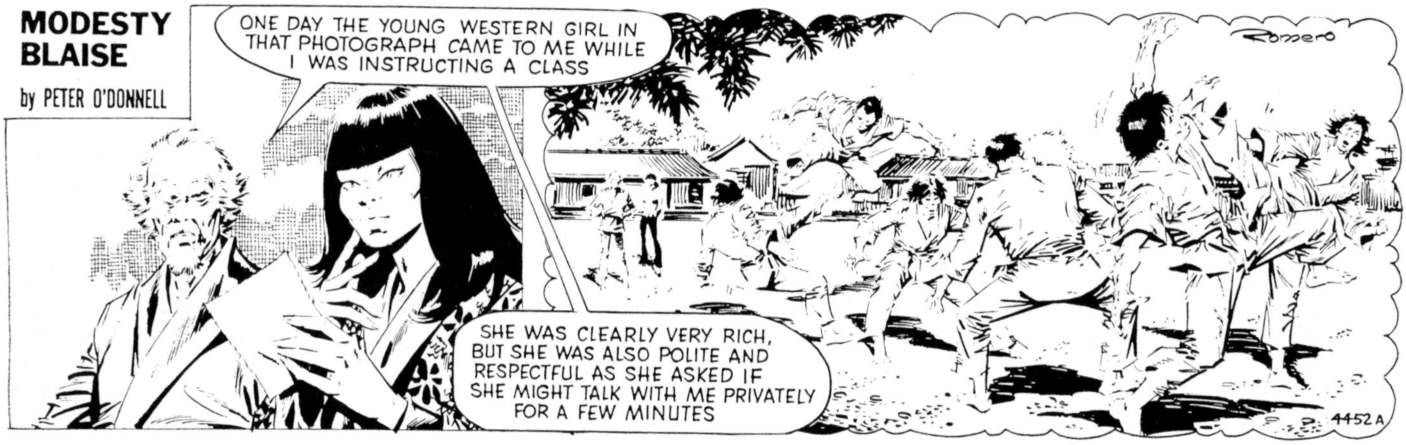
MODESTY BLAISE
by PETER O'DONNELL
ONE DAY THE YOUNG WESTERN GIRL IN THAT PHOTOGRAPH CAME TO ME WHILE I WAS INSTRUCTING A CLASS
SHE WAS CLEARLY VERY RICH, BUT SHE WAS ALSO POLITE AND RESPECTFUL AS SHE ASKED IF SHE MIGHT TALK WITH ME PRIVATELY FOR A FEW MINUTES
4452 A

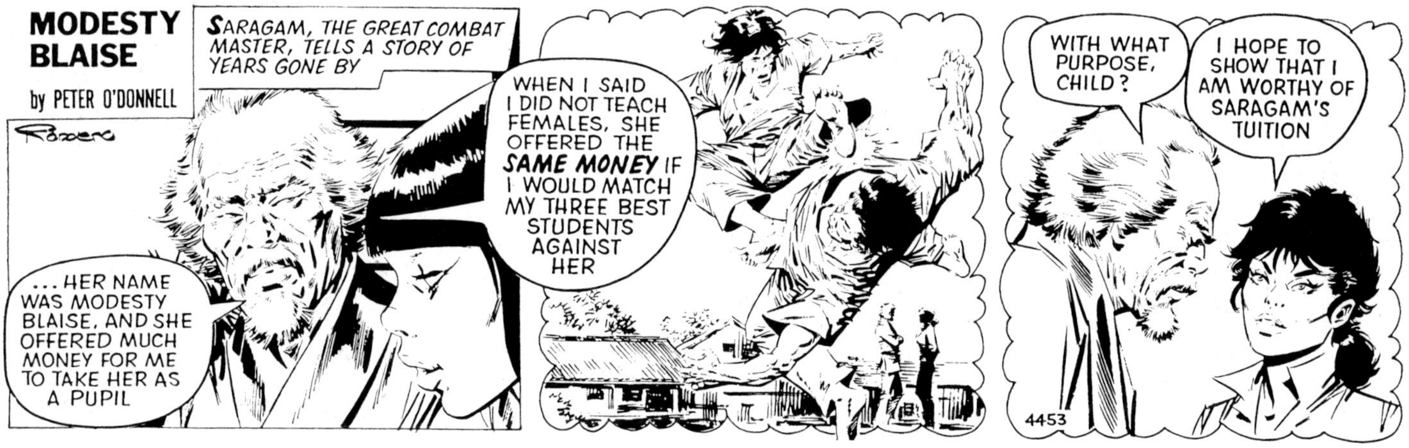
MODESTY BLAISE
by PETER O'DONNELL
SARAGAM, THE GREAT COMBAT MASTER, TELLS A STORY OF YEARS GONE BY
...HER NAME WAS MODESTY BLAISE, AND SHE OFFERED MUCH MONEY FOR ME TO TAKE HER AS A PUPIL
WHEN I SAID I DID NOT TEACH FEMALES, SHE OFFERED THE SAME MONEY IF I WOULD MATCH MY THREE BEST STUDENTS AGAINST HER
WITH WHAT PURPOSE, CHILD?
I HOPE TO SHOW THAT I AM WORTHY OF SARAGAM'S TUITION
4453

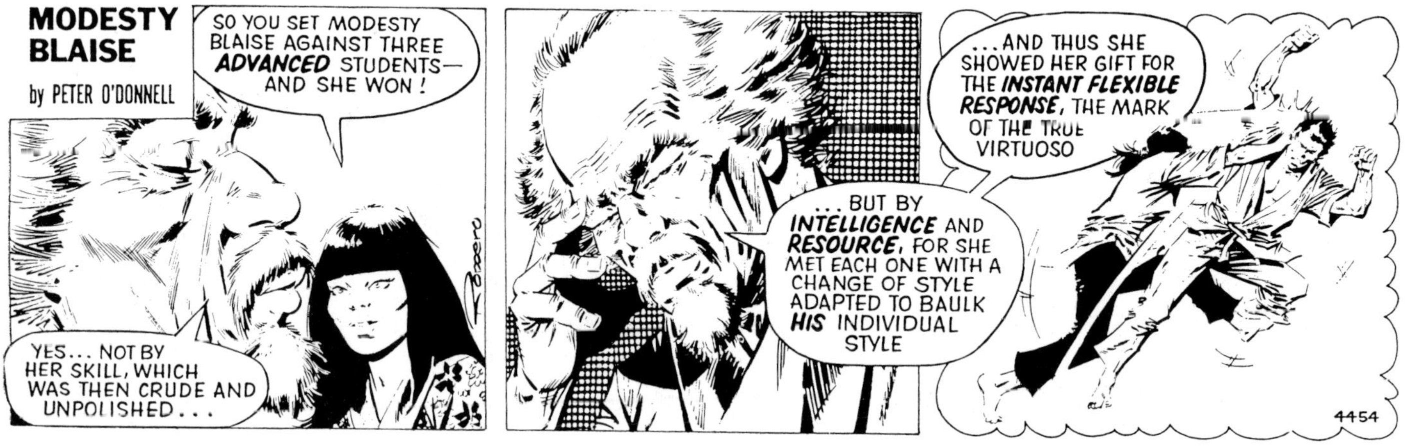
MODESTY BLAISE
by PETER O'DONNELL
SO YOU SET MODESTY BLAISE AGAINST THREE ADVANCED STUDENTS— AND SHE WON!
YES... NOT BY HER SKILL, WHICH WAS THEN CRUDE AND UNPOLISHED...
...BUT BY INTELLIGENCE AND RESOURCE, FOR SHE MET EACH ONE WITH A CHANGE OF STYLE ADAPTED TO BAULK HIS INDIVIDUAL STYLE
...AND THUS SHE SHOWED HER GIFT FOR THE INSTANT FLEXIBLE RESPONSE, THE MARK OF THE TRUE VIRTUOSO
4454

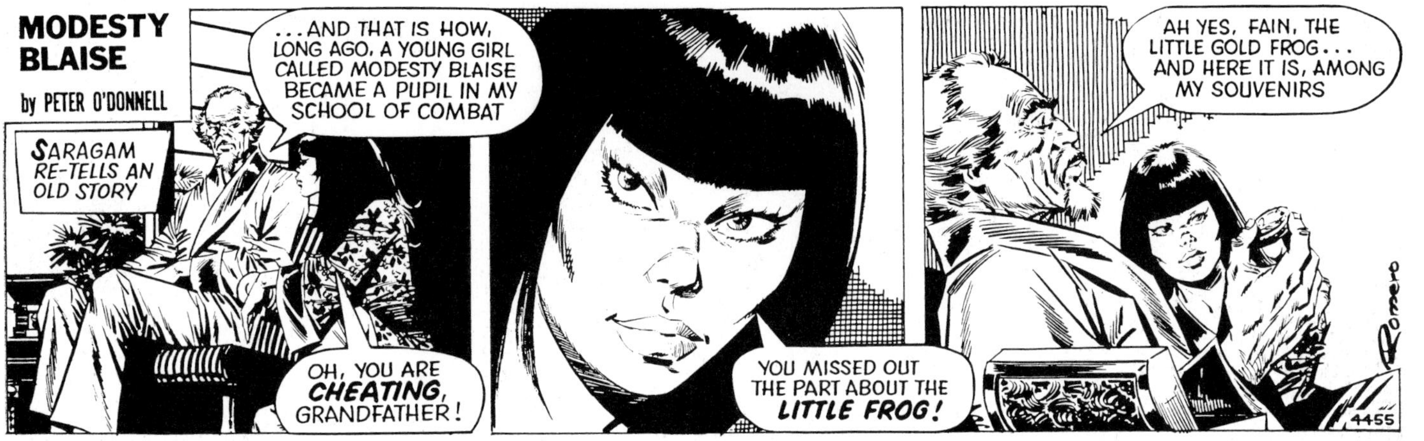
MODESTY BLAISE
by PETER O'DONNELL
SARAGAM RE-TELLS AN OLD STORY
...AND THAT IS HOW, LONG AGO, A YOUNG GIRL CALLED MODESTY BLAISE BECAME A PUPIL IN MY SCHOOL OF COMBAT
OH, YOU ARE CHEATING, GRANDFATHER!
YOU MISSED OUT THE PART ABOUT THE LITTLE FROG!
AH YES, FAIN, THE LITTLE GOLD FROG... AND HERE IT IS, AMONG MY SOUVENIRS
4455

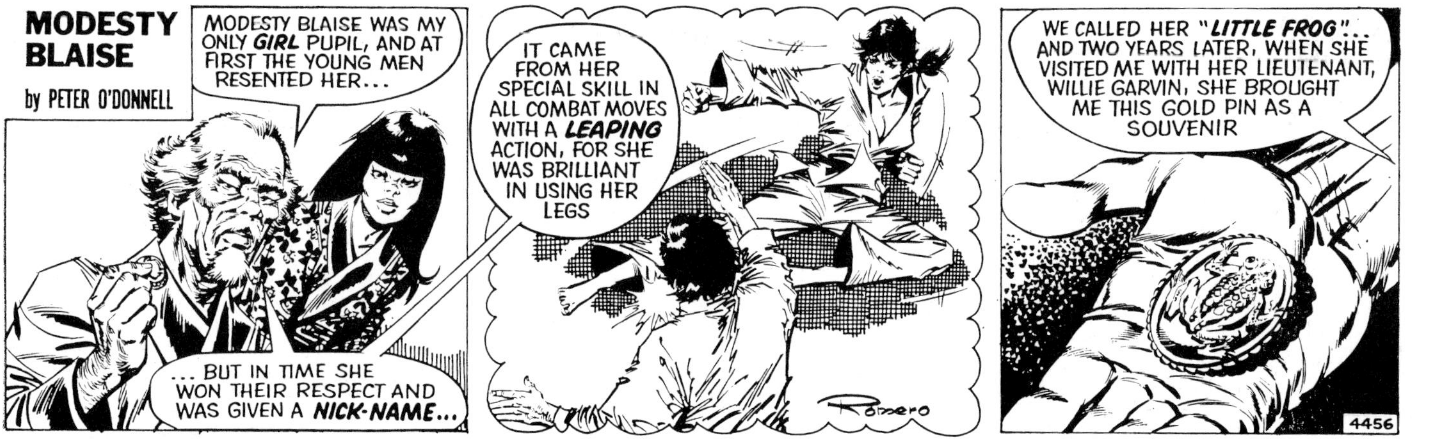
MODESTY BLAISE
by PETER O'DONNELL
MODESTY BLAISE WAS MY ONLY GIRL PUPIL, AND AT FIRST THE YOUNG MEN RESENTED HER...
... BUT IN TIME SHE WON THEIR RESPECT AND WAS GIVEN A NICK-NAME...
IT CAME FROM HER SPECIAL SKILL IN ALL COMBAT MOVES WITH A LEAPING ACTION, FOR SHE WAS BRILLIANT IN USING HER LEGS
WE CALLED HER "LITTLE FROG"... AND TWO YEARS LATER, WHEN SHE VISITED ME WITH HER LIEUTENANT, WILLIE GARVIN, SHE BROUGHT ME THIS GOLD PIN AS A SOUVENIR
4456

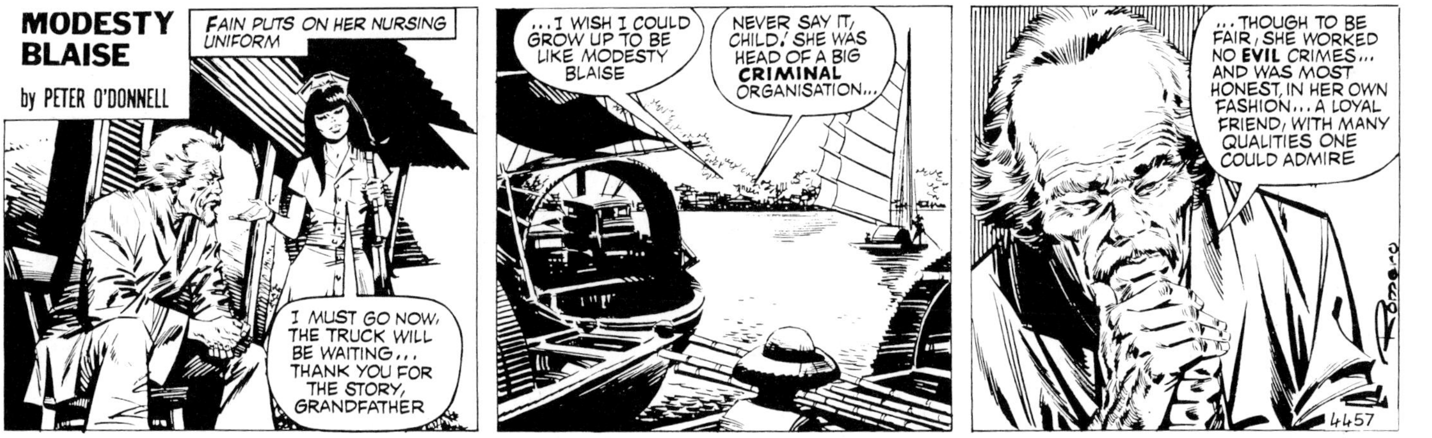
MODESTY BLAISE
by PETER O'DONNELL
FAIN PUTS ON HER NURSING UNIFORM
I MUST GO NOW, THE TRUCK WILL BE WAITING... THANK YOU FOR THE STORY, GRANDFATHER
...I WISH I COULD GROW UP TO BE LIKE MODESTY BLAISE
NEVER SAY IT, CHILD! SHE WAS HEAD OF A BIG CRIMINAL ORGANISATION...
...THOUGH TO BE FAIR, SHE WORKED NO EVIL CRIMES... AND WAS MOST HONEST, IN HER OWN FASHION... A LOYAL FRIEND, WITH MANY QUALITIES ONE COULD ADMIRE
4457

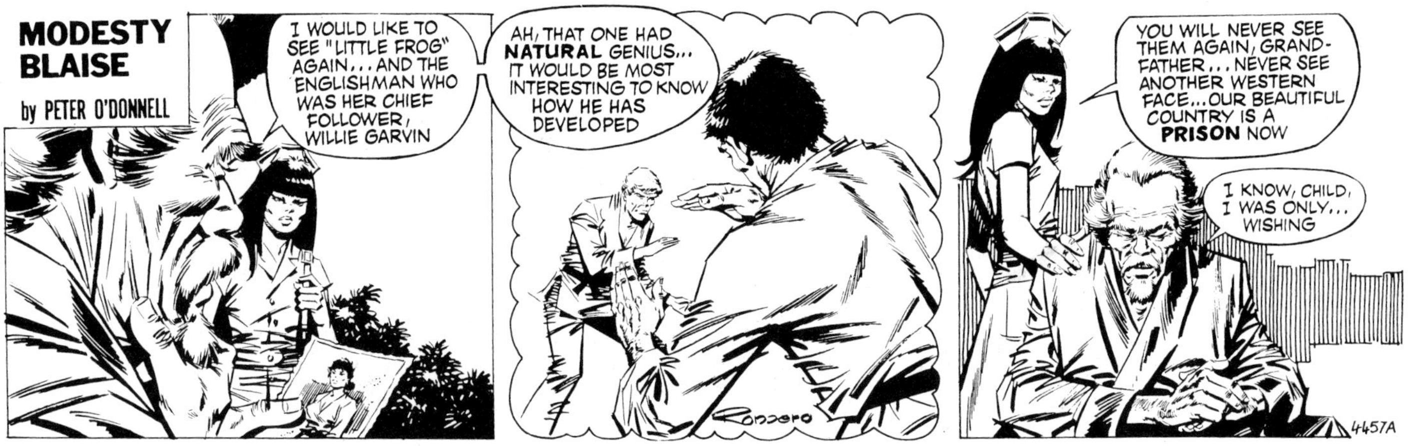
MODESTY BLAISE
by PETER O'DONNELL
I WOULD LIKE TO SEE "LITTLE FROG" AGAIN... AND THE ENGLISHMAN WHO WAS HER CHIEF FOLLOWER, WILLIE GARVIN
AH, THAT ONE HAD NATURAL GENIUS... IT WOULD BE MOST INTERESTING TO KNOW HOW HE HAS DEVELOPED
YOU WILL NEVER SEE THEM AGAIN, GRAND-FATHER... NEVER SEE ANOTHER WESTERN FACE... OUR BEAUTIFUL COUNTRY IS A PRISON NOW
I KNOW, CHILD, I WAS ONLY... WISHING
4457A

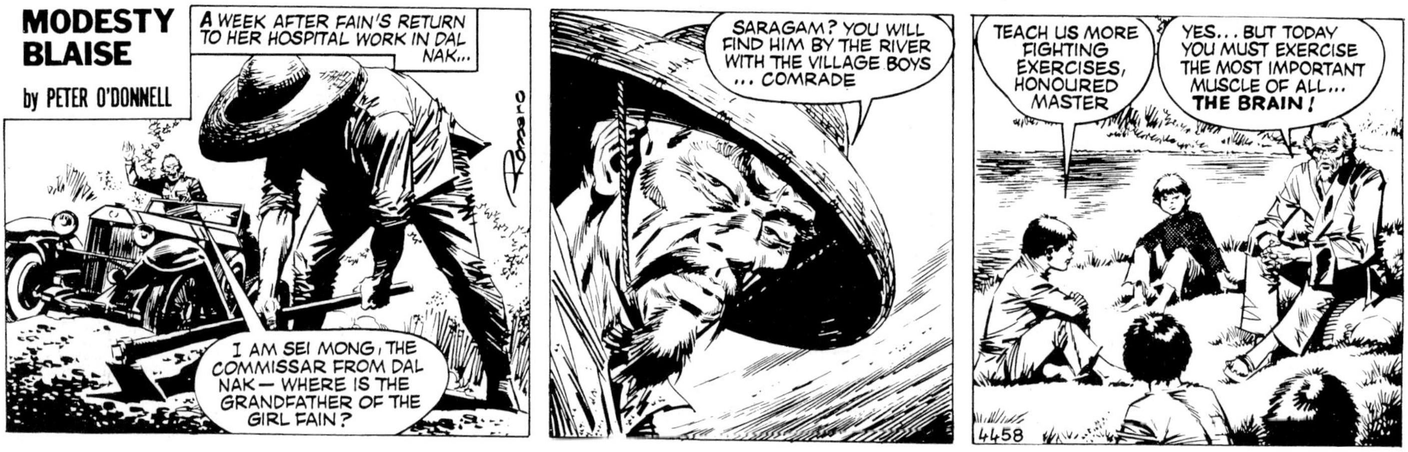
MODESTY BLAISE
by PETER O'DONNELL
A WEEK AFTER FAIN'S RETURN TO HER HOSPITAL WORK IN DAL NAK...
I AM SEI MONG, THE COMMISSAR FROM DAL NAK — WHERE IS THE GRANDFATHER OF THE GIRL FAIN?
SARAGAM? YOU WILL FIND HIM BY THE RIVER WITH THE VILLAGE BOYS ... COMRADE
TEACH US MORE FIGHTING EXERCISES, HONOURED MASTER
YES... BUT TODAY YOU MUST EXERCISE THE MOST IMPORTANT MUSCLE OF ALL... **THE BRAIN!**
4458

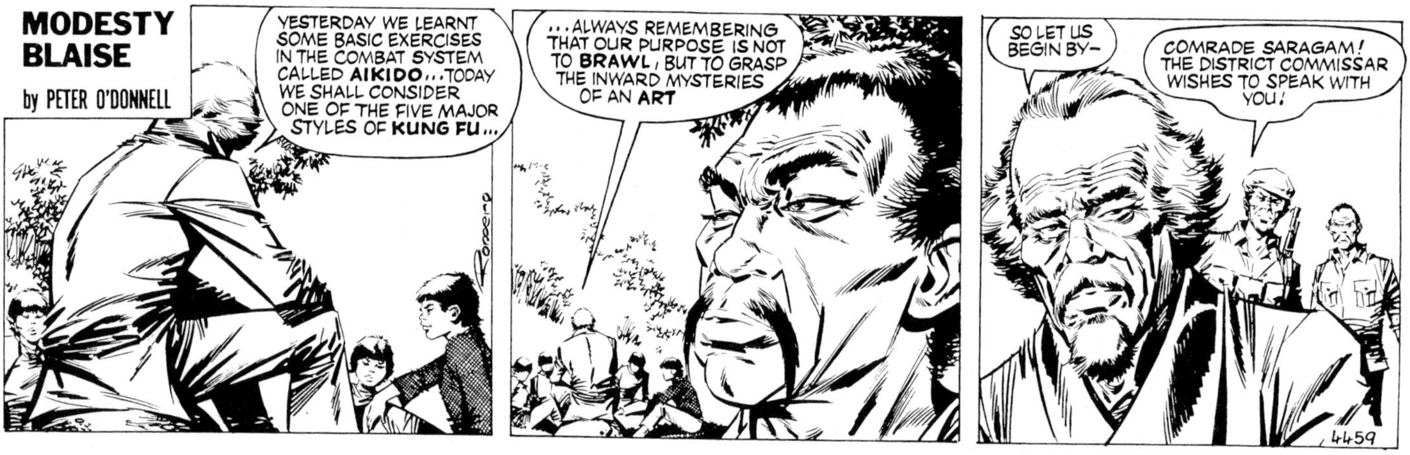
MODESTY BLAISE
by PETER O'DONNELL
YESTERDAY WE LEARNT SOME BASIC EXERCISES IN THE COMBAT SYSTEM CALLED **AIKIDO**... TODAY WE SHALL CONSIDER ONE OF THE FIVE MAJOR STYLES OF **KUNG FU**...
...ALWAYS REMEMBERING THAT OUR PURPOSE IS NOT TO **BRAWL**, BUT TO GRASP THE INWARD MYSTERIES OF AN **ART**
SO LET US BEGIN BY—
COMRADE SARAGAM! THE DISTRICT COMMISSAR WISHES TO SPEAK WITH YOU!
4459

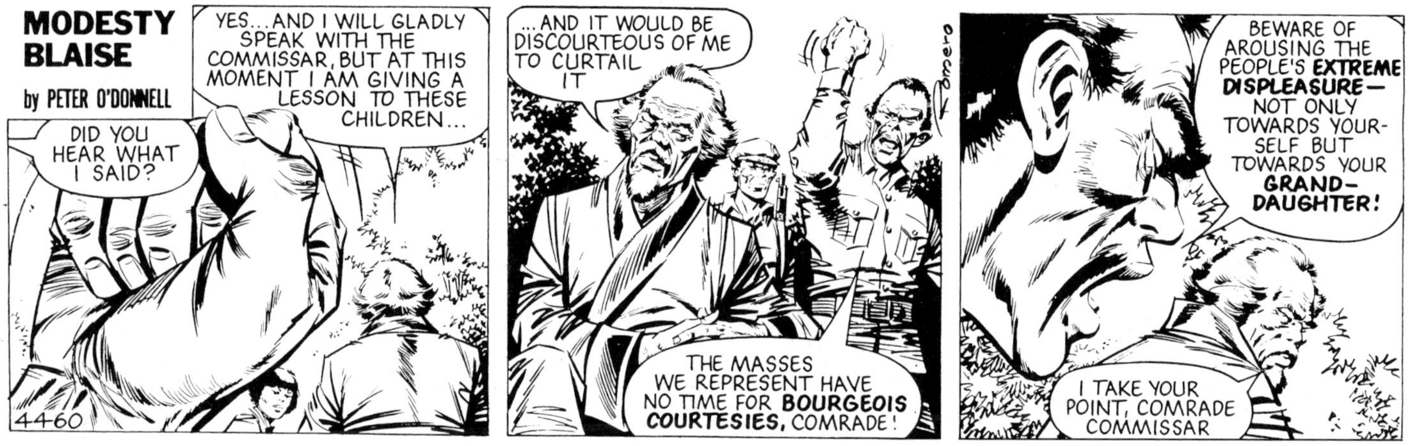
MODESTY BLAISE
by PETER O'DONNELL
YES... AND I WILL GLADLY SPEAK WITH THE COMMISSAR, BUT AT THIS MOMENT I AM GIVING A LESSON TO THESE CHILDREN...
DID YOU HEAR WHAT I SAID?
...AND IT WOULD BE DISCOURTEOUS OF ME TO CURTAIL IT
THE MASSES WE REPRESENT HAVE NO TIME FOR **BOURGEOIS COURTESIES**, COMRADE!
BEWARE OF AROUSING THE PEOPLE'S **EXTREME DISPLEASURE**— NOT ONLY TOWARDS YOURSELF BUT TOWARDS YOUR **GRAND-DAUGHTER!**
I TAKE YOUR POINT, COMRADE COMMISSAR
4460

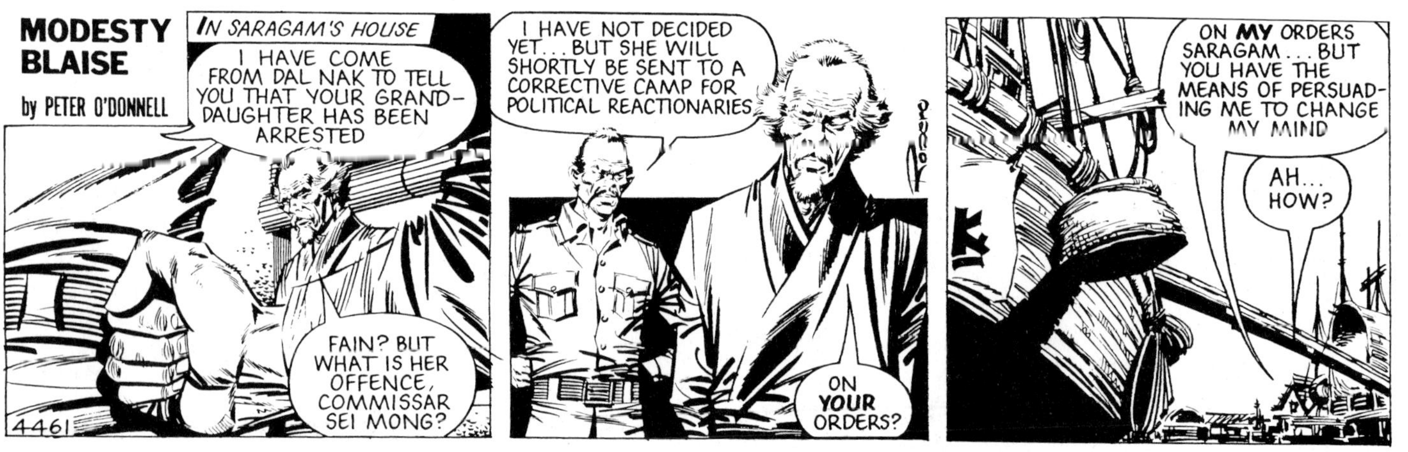
MODESTY BLAISE
by PETER O'DONNELL
IN SARAGAM'S HOUSE
I HAVE COME FROM DAL NAK TO TELL YOU THAT YOUR GRAND-DAUGHTER HAS BEEN ARRESTED
FAIN? BUT WHAT IS HER OFFENCE, COMMISSAR SEI MONG?
I HAVE NOT DECIDED YET... BUT SHE WILL SHORTLY BE SENT TO A CORRECTIVE CAMP FOR POLITICAL REACTIONARIES
ON **YOUR** ORDERS?
ON **MY** ORDERS SARAGAM... BUT YOU HAVE THE MEANS OF PERSUADING ME TO CHANGE MY MIND
AH... HOW?
4461

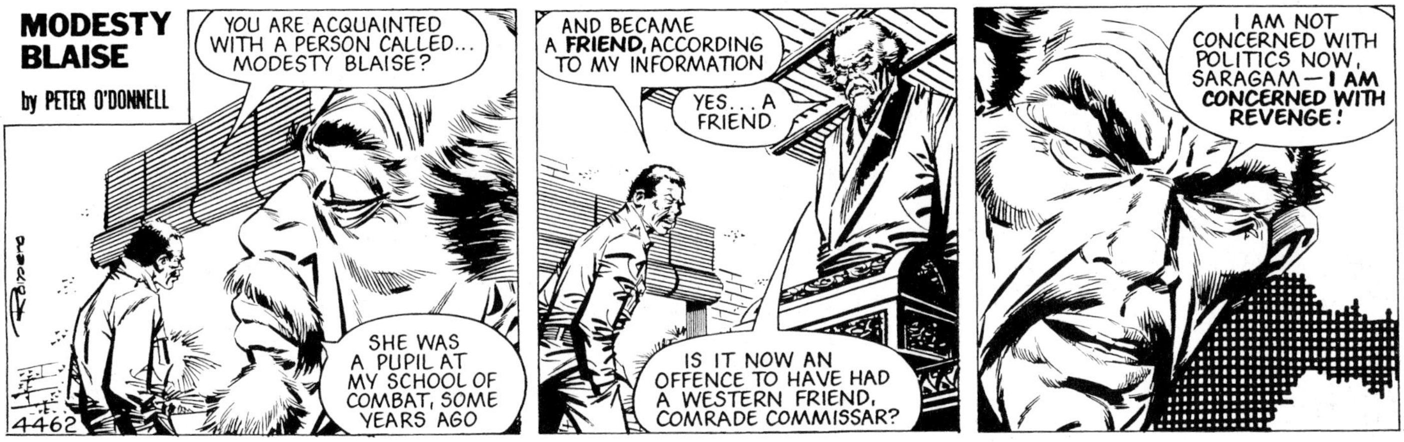
MODESTY BLAISE
by PETER O'DONNELL
YOU ARE ACQUAINTED WITH A PERSON CALLED... MODESTY BLAISE?
SHE WAS A PUPIL AT MY SCHOOL OF COMBAT, SOME YEARS AGO
4462
AND BECAME A **FRIEND**, ACCORDING TO MY INFORMATION
YES... A FRIEND.
IS IT NOW AN OFFENCE TO HAVE HAD A WESTERN FRIEND, COMRADE COMMISSAR?
I AM NOT CONCERNED WITH POLITICS NOW, SARAGAM — **I AM CONCERNED WITH REVENGE!**

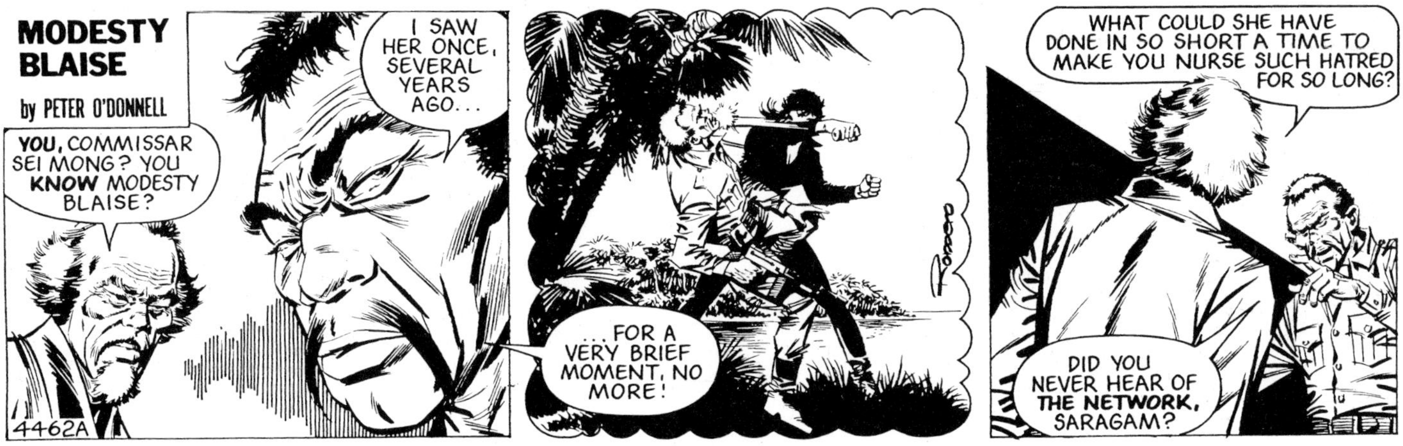
MODESTY BLAISE
by PETER O'DONNELL
YOU, COMMISSAR SEI MONG? YOU **KNOW** MODESTY BLAISE?
I SAW HER ONCE, SEVERAL YEARS AGO...
4462A
...FOR A VERY BRIEF MOMENT, NO MORE!
WHAT COULD SHE HAVE DONE IN SO SHORT A TIME TO MAKE YOU NURSE SUCH HATRED FOR SO LONG?
DID YOU NEVER HEAR OF **THE NETWORK,** SARAGAM?

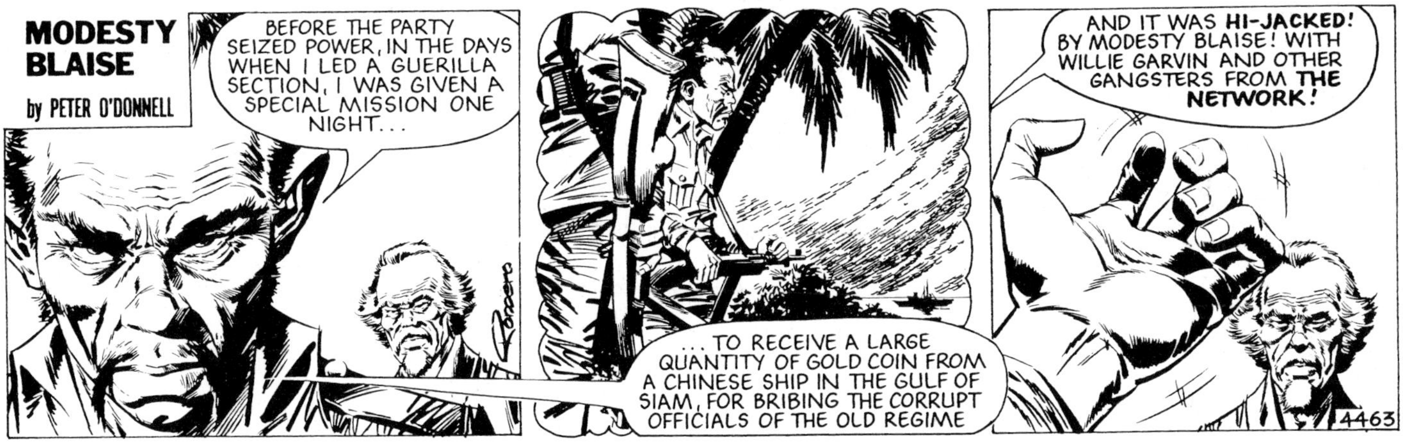
MODESTY BLAISE
by PETER O'DONNELL
BEFORE THE PARTY SEIZED POWER, IN THE DAYS WHEN I LED A GUERILLA SECTION, I WAS GIVEN A SPECIAL MISSION ONE NIGHT...
...TO RECEIVE A LARGE QUANTITY OF GOLD COIN FROM A CHINESE SHIP IN THE GULF OF SIAM, FOR BRIBING THE CORRUPT OFFICIALS OF THE OLD REGIME
AND IT WAS **HI-JACKED!** BY MODESTY BLAISE! WITH WILLIE GARVIN AND OTHER GANGSTERS FROM **THE NETWORK!**
4463

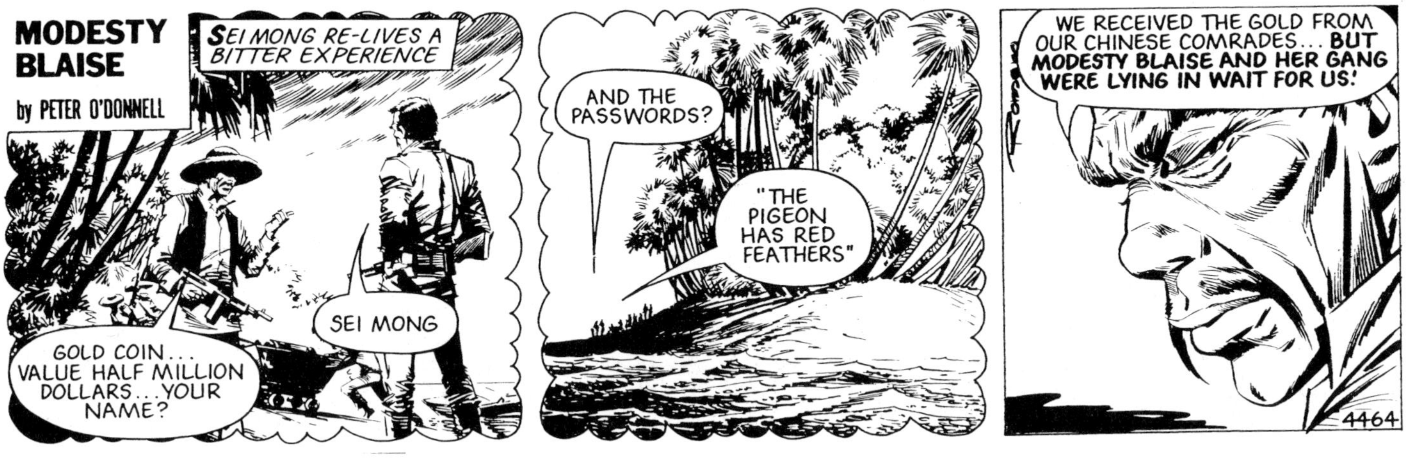
MODESTY BLAISE
by PETER O'DONNELL
SEI MONG RE-LIVES A BITTER EXPERIENCE
GOLD COIN... VALUE HALF MILLION DOLLARS... YOUR NAME?
SEI MONG
AND THE PASSWORDS?
"THE PIGEON HAS RED FEATHERS"
WE RECEIVED THE GOLD FROM OUR CHINESE COMRADES... **BUT MODESTY BLAISE AND HER GANG WERE LYING IN WAIT FOR US!**
4464

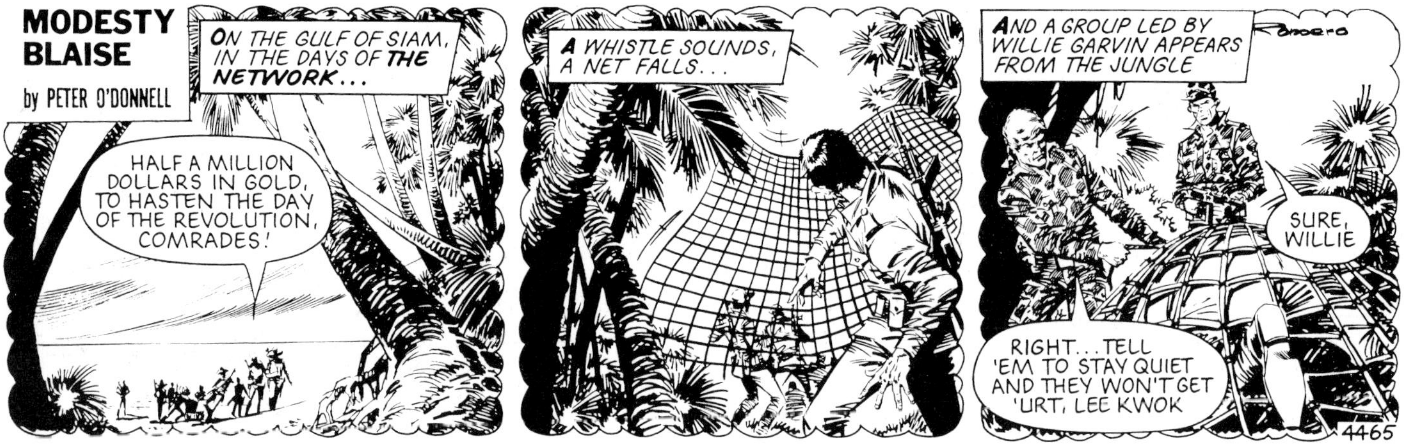
MODESTY BLAISE
by PETER O'DONNELL
ON THE GULF OF SIAM, IN THE DAYS OF THE NETWORK...
HALF A MILLION DOLLARS IN GOLD, TO HASTEN THE DAY OF THE REVOLUTION, COMRADES!
A WHISTLE SOUNDS, A NET FALLS...
AND A GROUP LED BY WILLIE GARVIN APPEARS FROM THE JUNGLE
Romero
RIGHT...TELL 'EM TO STAY QUIET AND THEY WON'T GET 'URT, LEE KWOK
SURE, WILLIE
4465

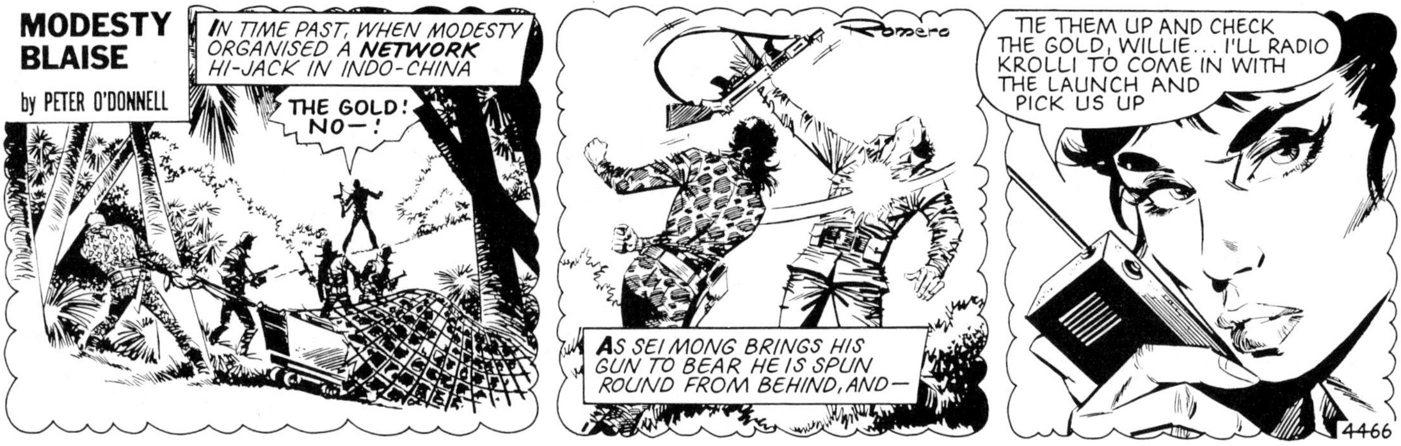
MODESTY BLAISE
by PETER O'DONNELL
IN TIME PAST, WHEN MODESTY ORGANISED A NETWORK HI-JACK IN INDO-CHINA
THE GOLD! NO—!
Romero
AS SEI MONG BRINGS HIS GUN TO BEAR HE IS SPUN ROUND FROM BEHIND, AND—
TIE THEM UP AND CHECK THE GOLD, WILLIE... I'LL RADIO KROLLI TO COME IN WITH THE LAUNCH AND PICK US UP
4466

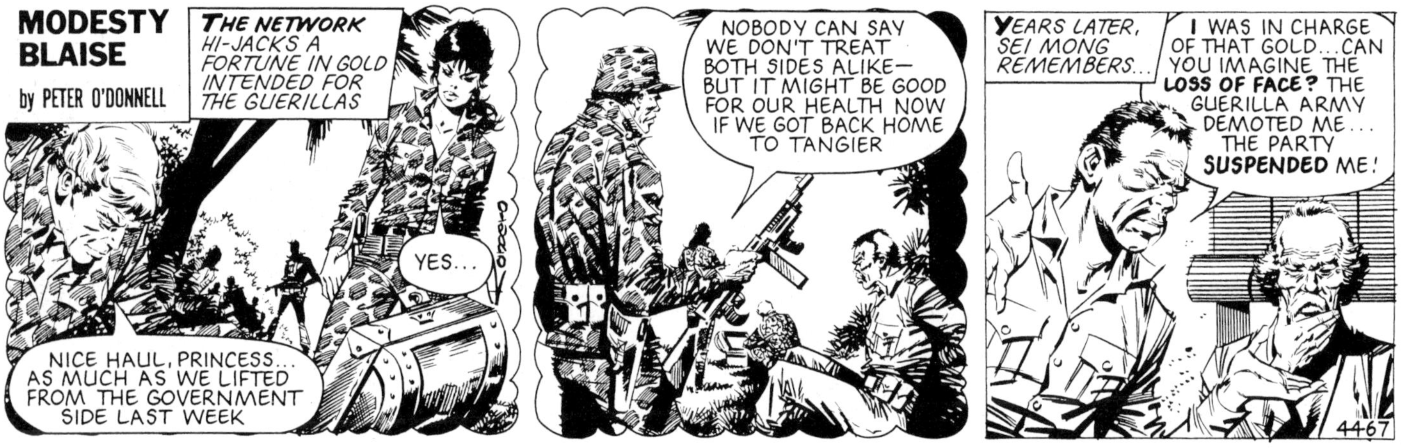
MODESTY BLAISE
by PETER O'DONNELL
THE NETWORK HI-JACKS A FORTUNE IN GOLD INTENDED FOR THE GUERILLAS
NICE HAUL, PRINCESS... AS MUCH AS WE LIFTED FROM THE GOVERNMENT SIDE LAST WEEK
YES...
Romero
NOBODY CAN SAY WE DON'T TREAT BOTH SIDES ALIKE— BUT IT MIGHT BE GOOD FOR OUR HEALTH NOW IF WE GOT BACK HOME TO TANGIER
YEARS LATER, SEI MONG REMEMBERS...
I WAS IN CHARGE OF THAT GOLD...CAN YOU IMAGINE THE LOSS OF FACE? THE GUERILLA ARMY DEMOTED ME... THE PARTY SUSPENDED ME!
4467

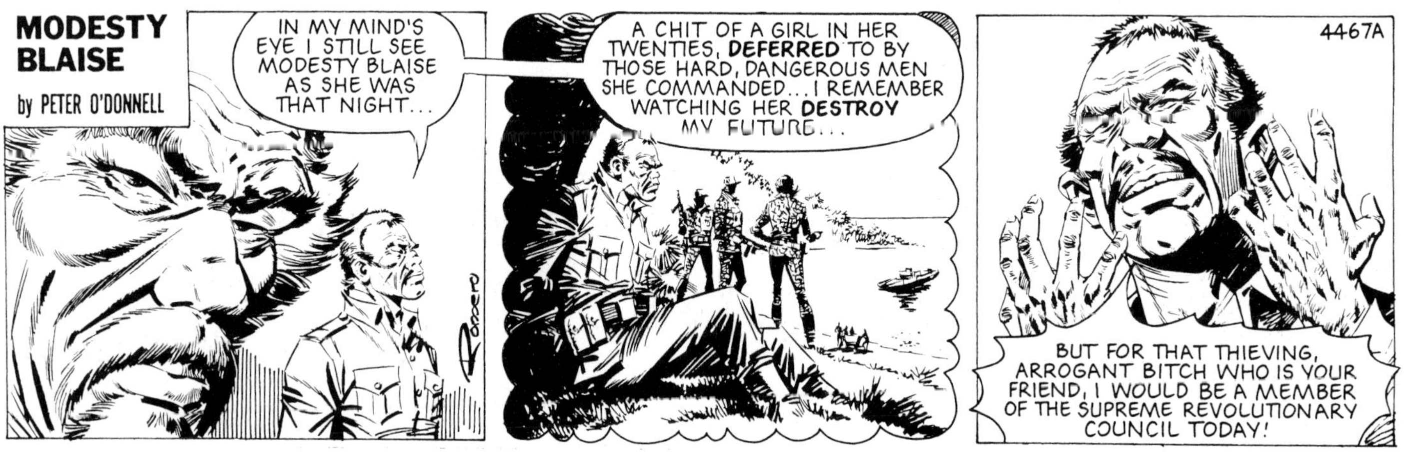
MODESTY BLAISE
by PETER O'DONNELL
IN MY MIND'S EYE I STILL SEE MODESTY BLAISE AS SHE WAS THAT NIGHT...
Romero
A CHIT OF A GIRL IN HER TWENTIES, DEFERRED TO BY THOSE HARD, DANGEROUS MEN SHE COMMANDED... I REMEMBER WATCHING HER DESTROY MY FUTURE...
4467A
BUT FOR THAT THIEVING, ARROGANT BITCH WHO IS YOUR FRIEND, I WOULD BE A MEMBER OF THE SUPREME REVOLUTIONARY COUNCIL TODAY!

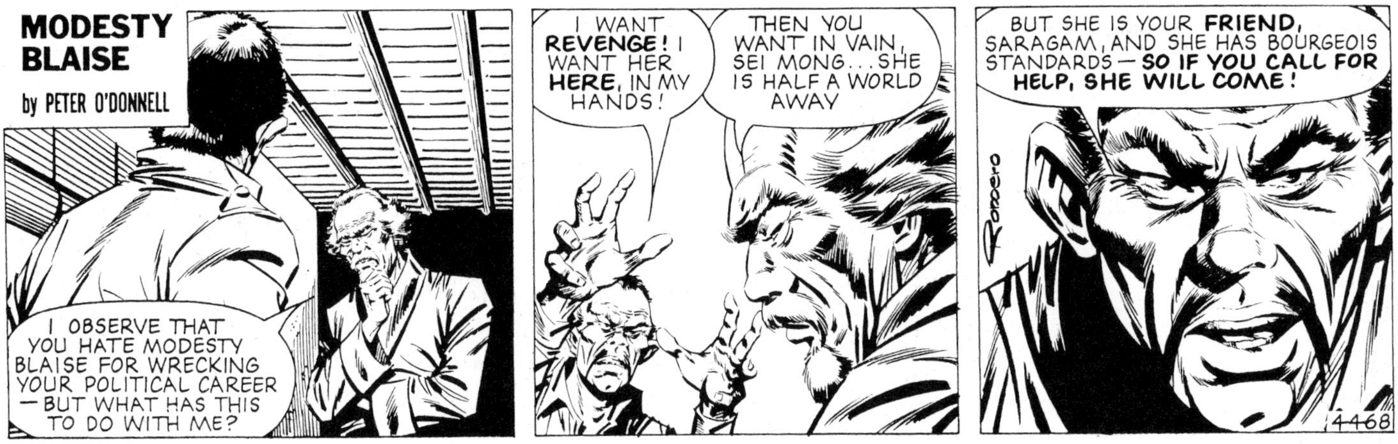
MODESTY BLAISE
by PETER O'DONNELL
I OBSERVE THAT YOU HATE MODESTY BLAISE FOR WRECKING YOUR POLITICAL CAREER — BUT WHAT HAS THIS TO DO WITH ME?
I WANT REVENGE! I WANT HER HERE, IN MY HANDS!
THEN YOU WANT IN VAIN, SEI MONG... SHE IS HALF A WORLD AWAY
BUT SHE IS YOUR FRIEND, SARAGAM, AND SHE HAS BOURGEOIS STANDARDS — SO IF YOU CALL FOR HELP, SHE WILL COME!
4468

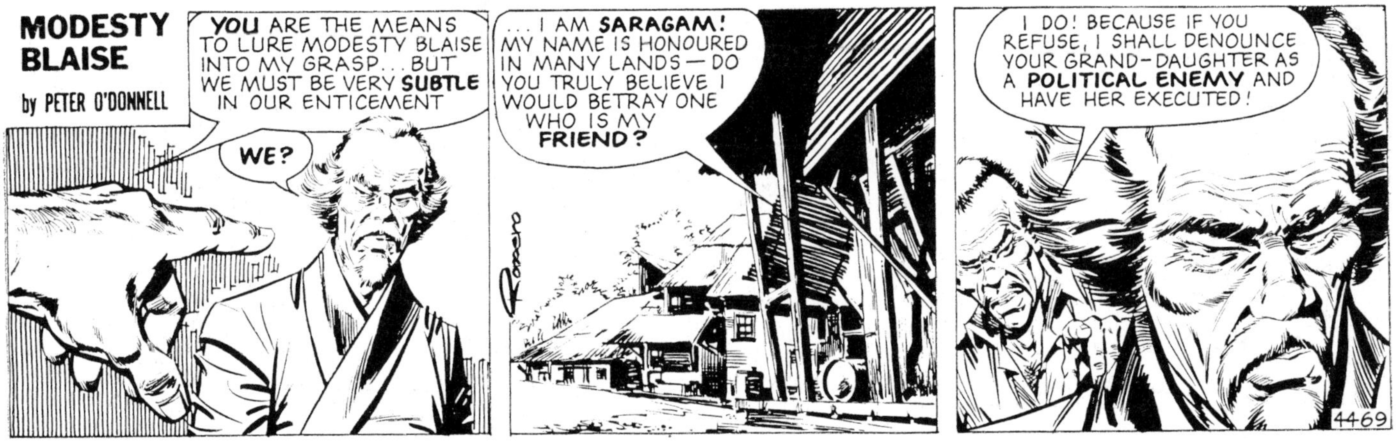
MODESTY BLAISE
by PETER O'DONNELL
YOU ARE THE MEANS TO LURE MODESTY BLAISE INTO MY GRASP... BUT WE MUST BE VERY SUBTLE IN OUR ENTICEMENT
WE?
... I AM SARAGAM! MY NAME IS HONOURED IN MANY LANDS — DO YOU TRULY BELIEVE I WOULD BETRAY ONE WHO IS MY FRIEND?
I DO! BECAUSE IF YOU REFUSE, I SHALL DENOUNCE YOUR GRAND-DAUGHTER AS A POLITICAL ENEMY AND HAVE HER EXECUTED!
4469

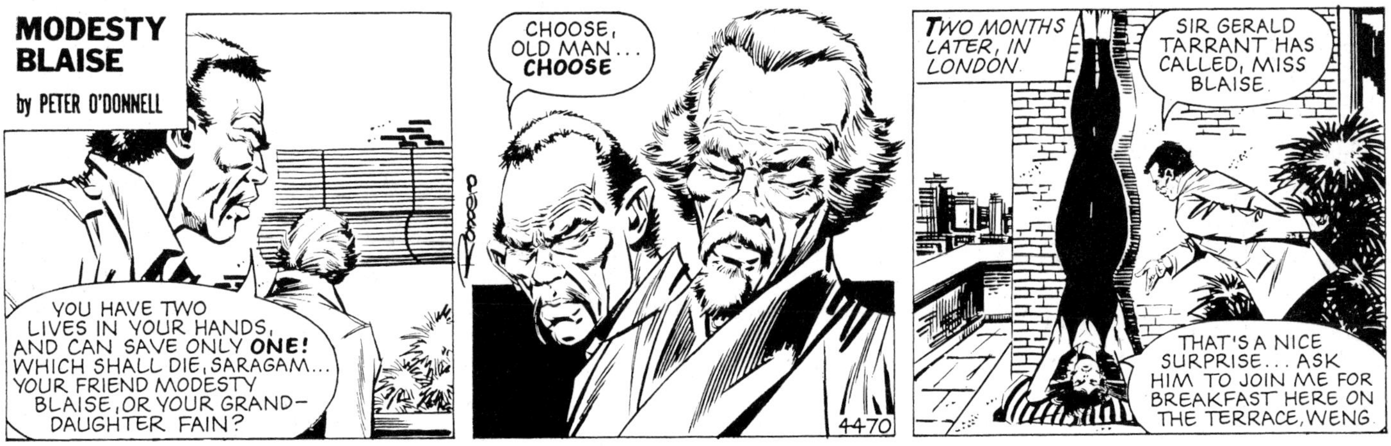
MODESTY BLAISE
by PETER O'DONNELL
YOU HAVE TWO LIVES IN YOUR HANDS, AND CAN SAVE ONLY ONE! WHICH SHALL DIE, SARAGAM... YOUR FRIEND MODESTY BLAISE, OR YOUR GRAND-DAUGHTER FAIN?
CHOOSE, OLD MAN... CHOOSE
4470
TWO MONTHS LATER, IN LONDON
SIR GERALD TARRANT HAS CALLED, MISS BLAISE
THAT'S A NICE SURPRISE... ASK HIM TO JOIN ME FOR BREAKFAST HERE ON THE TERRACE, WENG

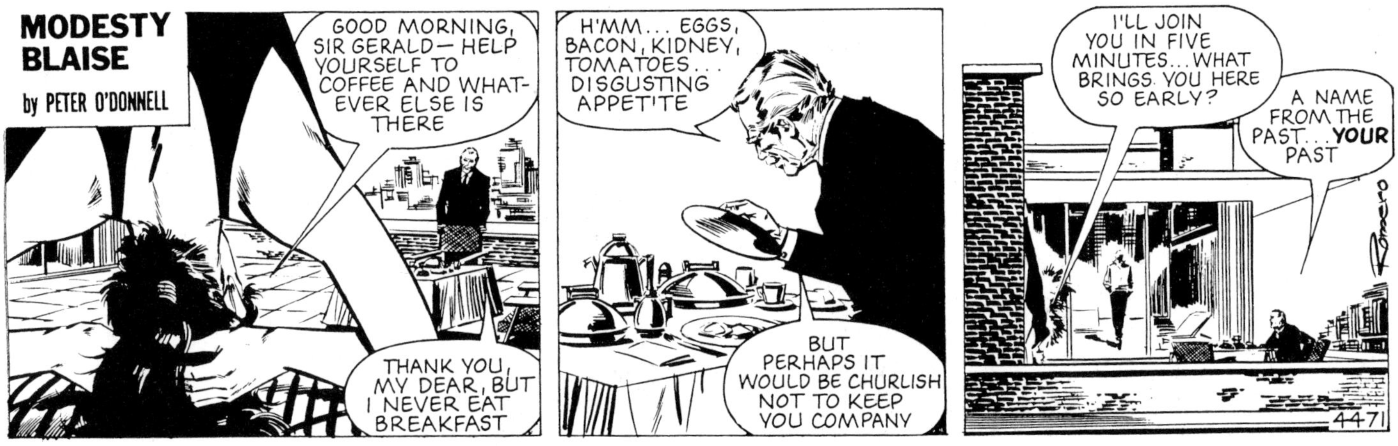
MODESTY BLAISE
by PETER O'DONNELL
GOOD MORNING, SIR GERALD — HELP YOURSELF TO COFFEE AND WHATEVER ELSE IS THERE
THANK YOU, MY DEAR, BUT I NEVER EAT BREAKFAST
H'MM... EGGS, BACON, KIDNEY, TOMATOES... DISGUSTING APPETITE
BUT PERHAPS IT WOULD BE CHURLISH NOT TO KEEP YOU COMPANY
I'LL JOIN YOU IN FIVE MINUTES... WHAT BRINGS YOU HERE SO EARLY?
A NAME FROM THE PAST... YOUR PAST
4471

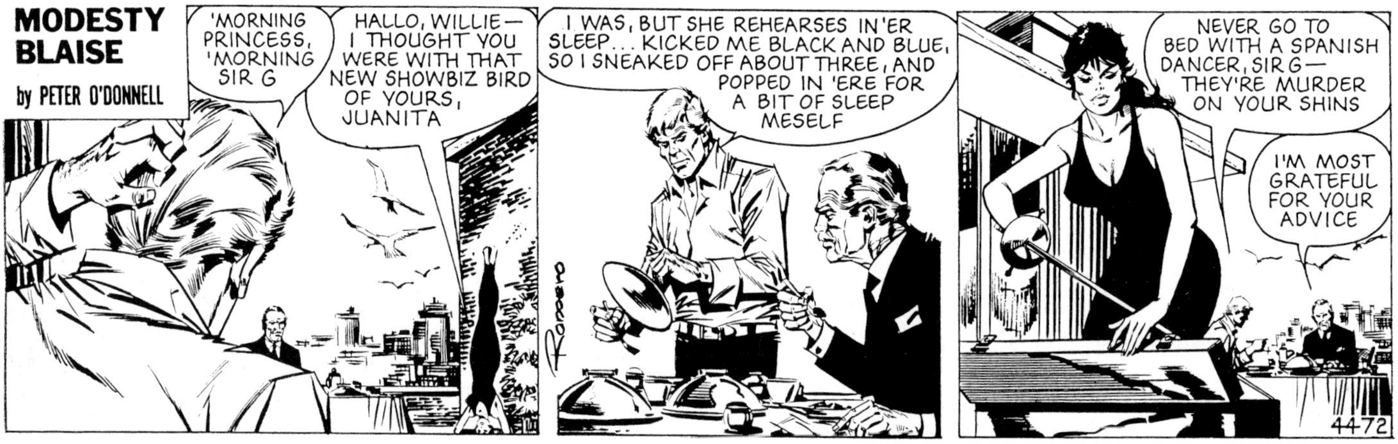
MODESTY BLAISE
by PETER O'DONNELL
'MORNING PRINCESS, 'MORNING SIR G
HALLO, WILLIE — I THOUGHT YOU WERE WITH THAT NEW SHOWBIZ BIRD OF YOURS, JUANITA
I WAS, BUT SHE REHEARSES IN 'ER SLEEP... KICKED ME BLACK AND BLUE, SO I SNEAKED OFF ABOUT THREE, AND POPPED IN 'ERE FOR A BIT OF SLEEP MESELF
NEVER GO TO BED WITH A SPANISH DANCER, SIR G — THEY'RE MURDER ON YOUR SHINS
I'M MOST GRATEFUL FOR YOUR ADVICE
4472

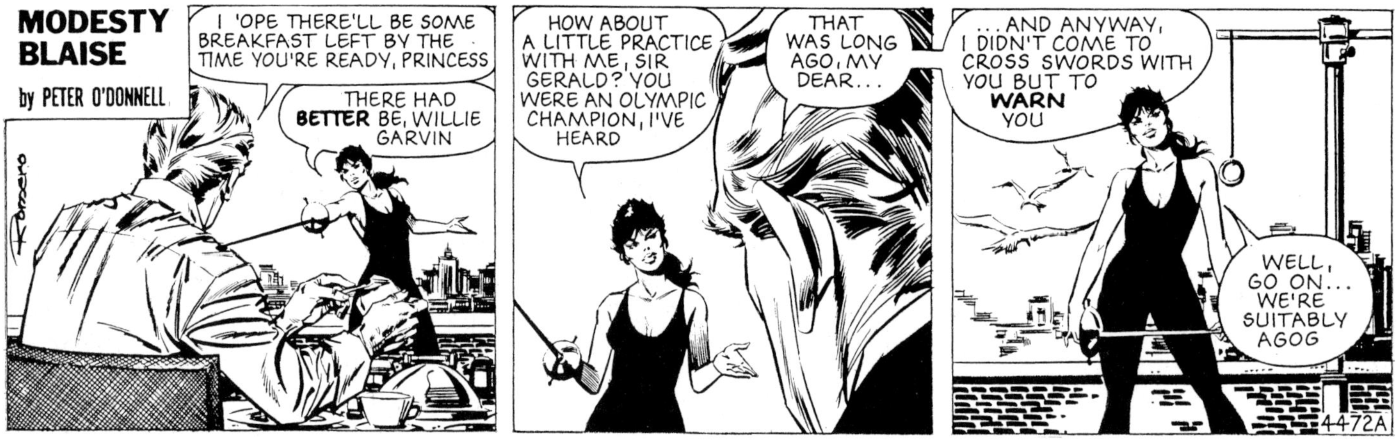
MODESTY BLAISE
by PETER O'DONNELL
I 'OPE THERE'LL BE SOME BREAKFAST LEFT BY THE TIME YOU'RE READY, PRINCESS
THERE HAD **BETTER** BE, WILLIE GARVIN
HOW ABOUT A LITTLE PRACTICE WITH ME, SIR GERALD? YOU WERE AN OLYMPIC CHAMPION, I'VE HEARD
THAT WAS LONG AGO, MY DEAR...
...AND ANYWAY, I DIDN'T COME TO CROSS SWORDS WITH YOU BUT TO **WARN** YOU
WELL, GO ON... WE'RE SUITABLY AGOG
4472A

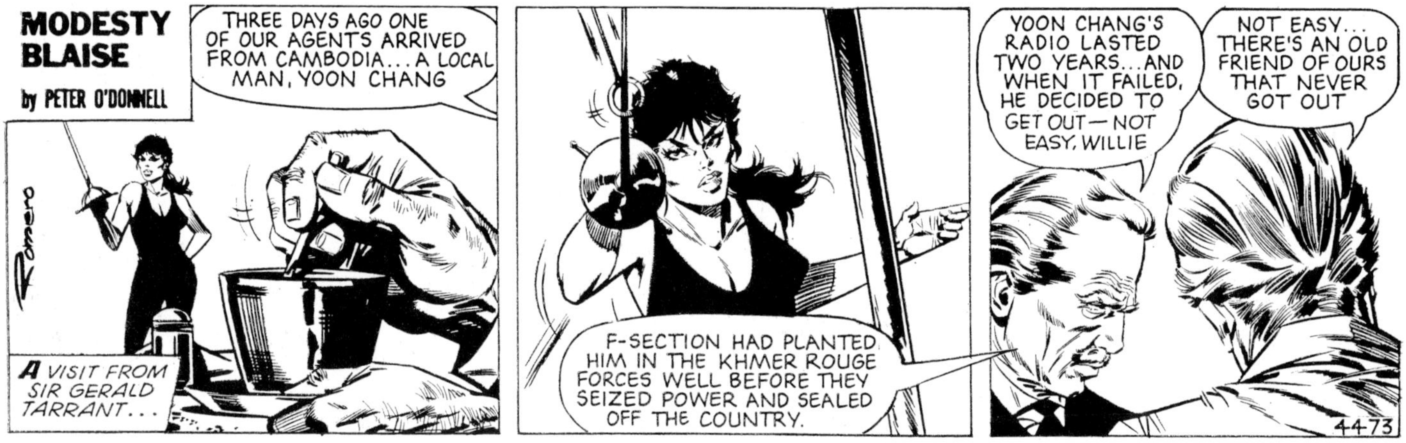
MODESTY BLAISE
by PETER O'DONNELL
THREE DAYS AGO ONE OF OUR AGENTS ARRIVED FROM CAMBODIA... A LOCAL MAN, YOON CHANG
A VISIT FROM SIR GERALD TARRANT...
F-SECTION HAD PLANTED HIM IN THE KHMER ROUGE FORCES WELL BEFORE THEY SEIZED POWER AND SEALED OFF THE COUNTRY.
YOON CHANG'S RADIO LASTED TWO YEARS... AND WHEN IT FAILED, HE DECIDED TO GET OUT — NOT EASY, WILLIE
NOT EASY... THERE'S AN OLD FRIEND OF OURS THAT NEVER GOT OUT
4473

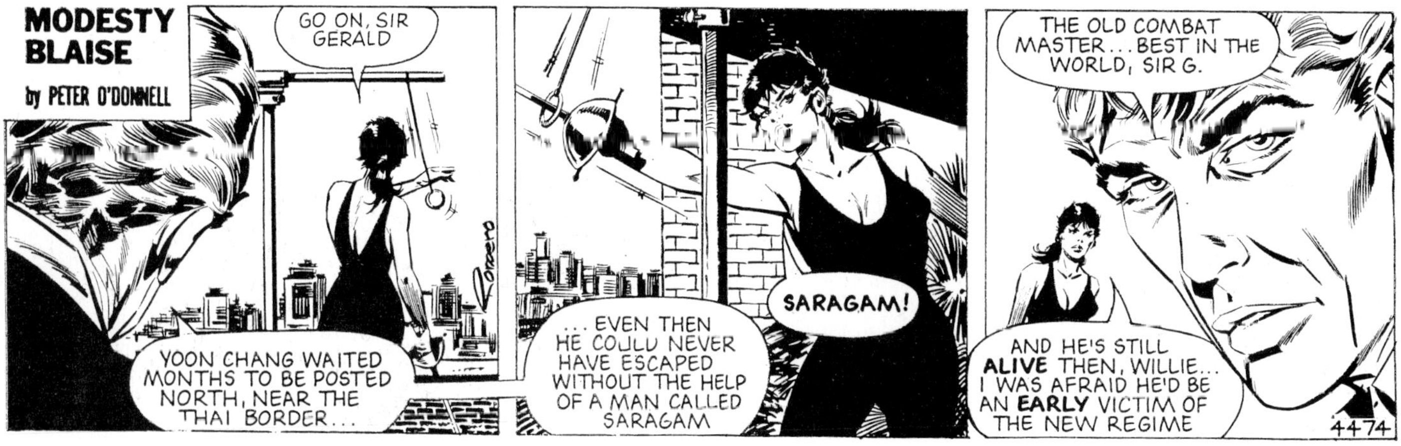
MODESTY BLAISE
by PETER O'DONNELL
GO ON, SIR GERALD
YOON CHANG WAITED MONTHS TO BE POSTED NORTH, NEAR THE THAI BORDER...
...EVEN THEN HE COULD NEVER HAVE ESCAPED WITHOUT THE HELP OF A MAN CALLED SARAGAM
SARAGAM!
THE OLD COMBAT MASTER... BEST IN THE WORLD, SIR G.
AND HE'S STILL **ALIVE** THEN, WILLIE... I WAS AFRAID HE'D BE AN **EARLY** VICTIM OF THE NEW REGIME
4474

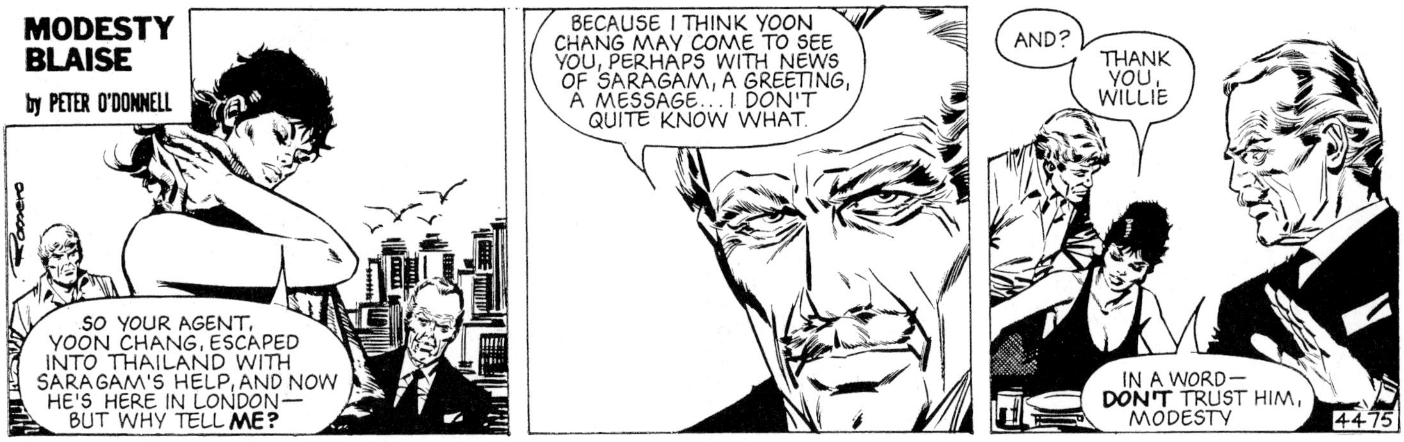
MODESTY BLAISE
by PETER O'DONNELL
SO YOUR AGENT, YOON CHANG, ESCAPED INTO THAILAND WITH SARAGAM'S HELP, AND NOW HE'S HERE IN LONDON— BUT WHY TELL **ME?**
BECAUSE I THINK YOON CHANG MAY COME TO SEE YOU, PERHAPS WITH NEWS OF SARAGAM, A GREETING, A MESSAGE... I DON'T QUITE KNOW WHAT.
AND?
THANK YOU, WILLIE
IN A WORD— **DON'T** TRUST HIM, MODESTY
4475

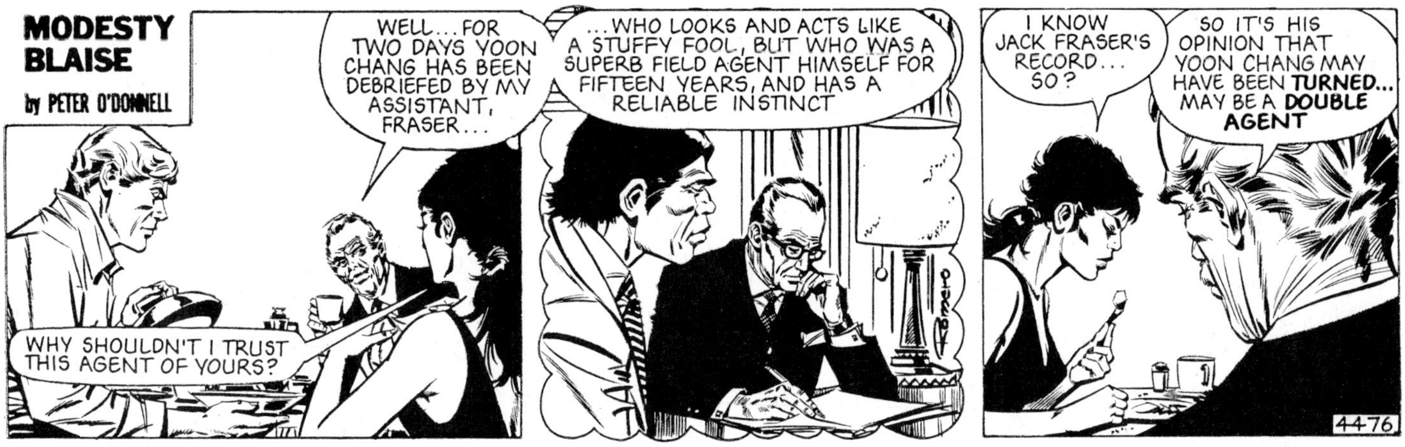
MODESTY BLAISE
by PETER O'DONNELL
WHY SHOULDN'T I TRUST THIS AGENT OF YOURS?
WELL... FOR TWO DAYS YOON CHANG HAS BEEN DEBRIEFED BY MY ASSISTANT, FRASER...
...WHO LOOKS AND ACTS LIKE A STUFFY FOOL, BUT WHO WAS A SUPERB FIELD AGENT HIMSELF FOR FIFTEEN YEARS, AND HAS A RELIABLE INSTINCT
I KNOW JACK FRASER'S RECORD... SO?
SO IT'S HIS OPINION THAT YOON CHANG MAY HAVE BEEN **TURNED...** MAY BE A **DOUBLE AGENT**
4476

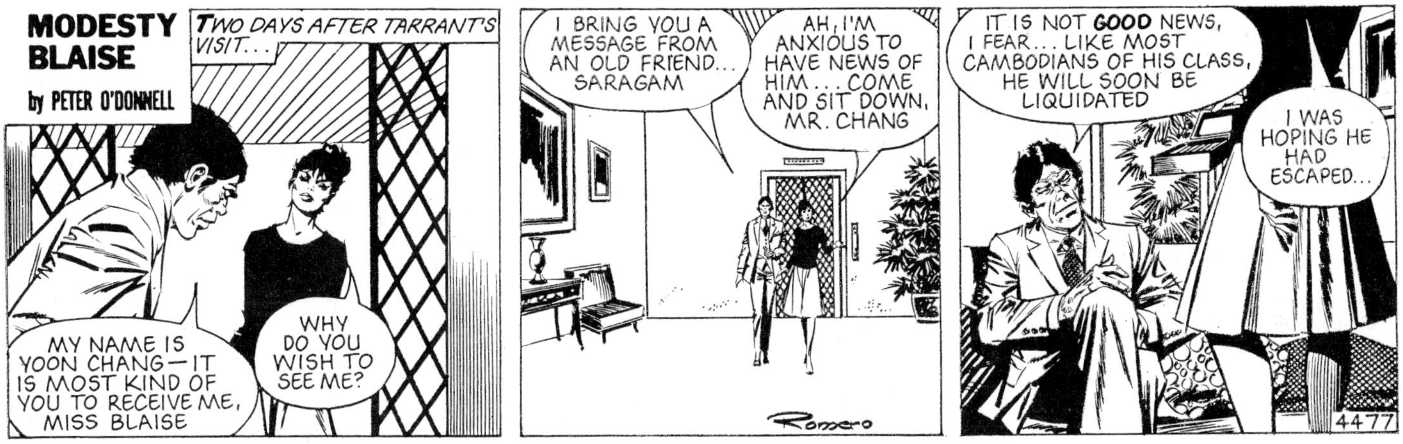
MODESTY BLAISE
by PETER O'DONNELL
TWO DAYS AFTER TARRANT'S VISIT...
MY NAME IS YOON CHANG—IT IS MOST KIND OF YOU TO RECEIVE ME, MISS BLAISE
WHY DO YOU WISH TO SEE ME?
I BRING YOU A MESSAGE FROM AN OLD FRIEND... SARAGAM
AH, I'M ANXIOUS TO HAVE NEWS OF HIM... COME AND SIT DOWN, MR. CHANG
Romero
IT IS NOT **GOOD** NEWS, I FEAR... LIKE MOST CAMBODIANS OF HIS CLASS, HE WILL SOON BE LIQUIDATED
I WAS HOPING HE HAD ESCAPED...
4477

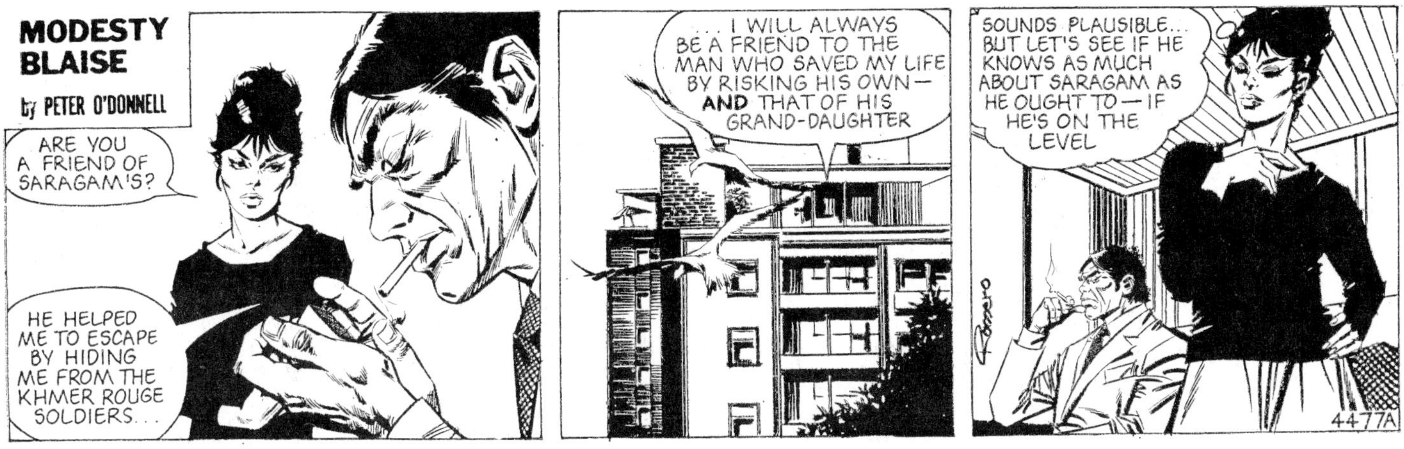
MODESTY BLAISE
by PETER O'DONNELL
ARE YOU A FRIEND OF SARAGAM'S?
HE HELPED ME TO ESCAPE BY HIDING ME FROM THE KHMER ROUGE SOLDIERS...
... I WILL ALWAYS BE A FRIEND TO THE MAN WHO SAVED MY LIFE BY RISKING HIS OWN— **AND** THAT OF HIS GRAND-DAUGHTER
SOUNDS PLAUSIBLE... BUT LET'S SEE IF HE KNOWS AS MUCH ABOUT SARAGAM AS HE OUGHT TO— IF HE'S ON THE LEVEL
4477A

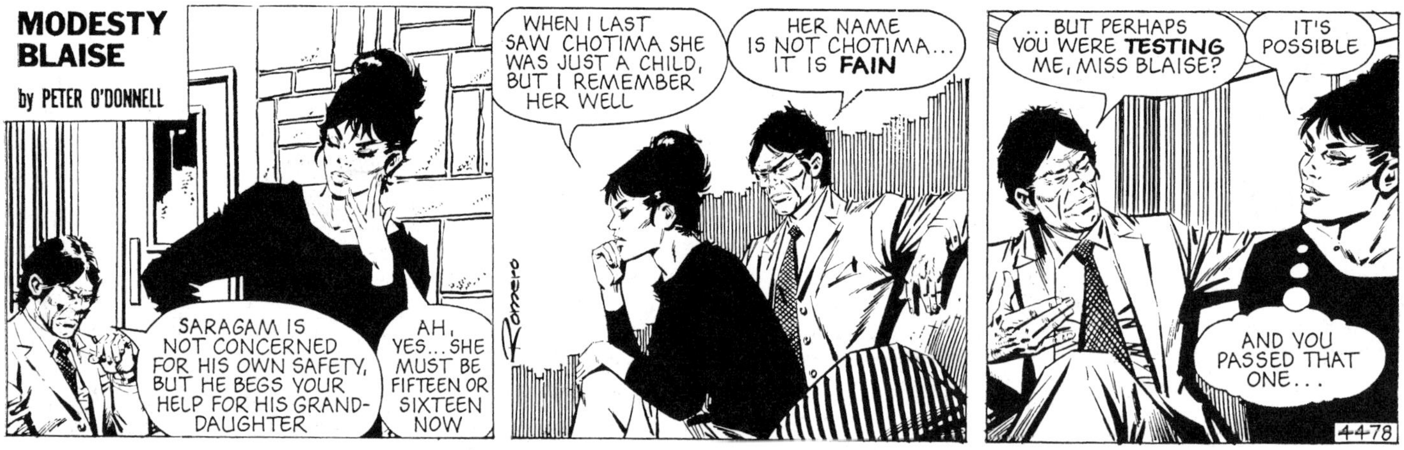
MODESTY BLAISE
by PETER O'DONNELL
SARAGAM IS NOT CONCERNED FOR HIS OWN SAFETY, BUT HE BEGS YOUR HELP FOR HIS GRAND-DAUGHTER
AH, YES... SHE MUST BE FIFTEEN OR SIXTEEN NOW
WHEN I LAST SAW CHOTIMA SHE WAS JUST A CHILD, BUT I REMEMBER HER WELL
HER NAME IS NOT CHOTIMA... IT IS **FAIN**
... BUT PERHAPS YOU WERE **TESTING** ME, MISS BLAISE?
IT'S POSSIBLE
AND YOU PASSED THAT ONE...
Romero
4478

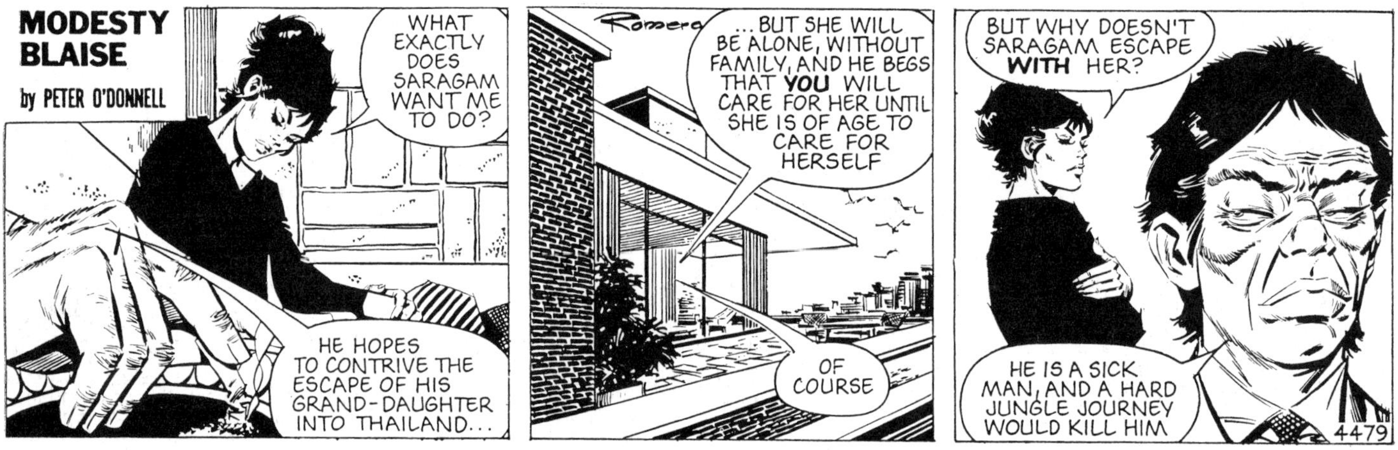
MODESTY BLAISE
by PETER O'DONNELL
WHAT EXACTLY DOES SARAGAM WANT ME TO DO?
HE HOPES TO CONTRIVE THE ESCAPE OF HIS GRAND-DAUGHTER INTO THAILAND...
Romero
... BUT SHE WILL BE ALONE, WITHOUT FAMILY, AND HE BEGS THAT **YOU** WILL CARE FOR HER UNTIL SHE IS OF AGE TO CARE FOR HERSELF
OF COURSE
BUT WHY DOESN'T SARAGAM ESCAPE **WITH** HER?
HE IS A SICK MAN, AND A HARD JUNGLE JOURNEY WOULD KILL HIM
4479

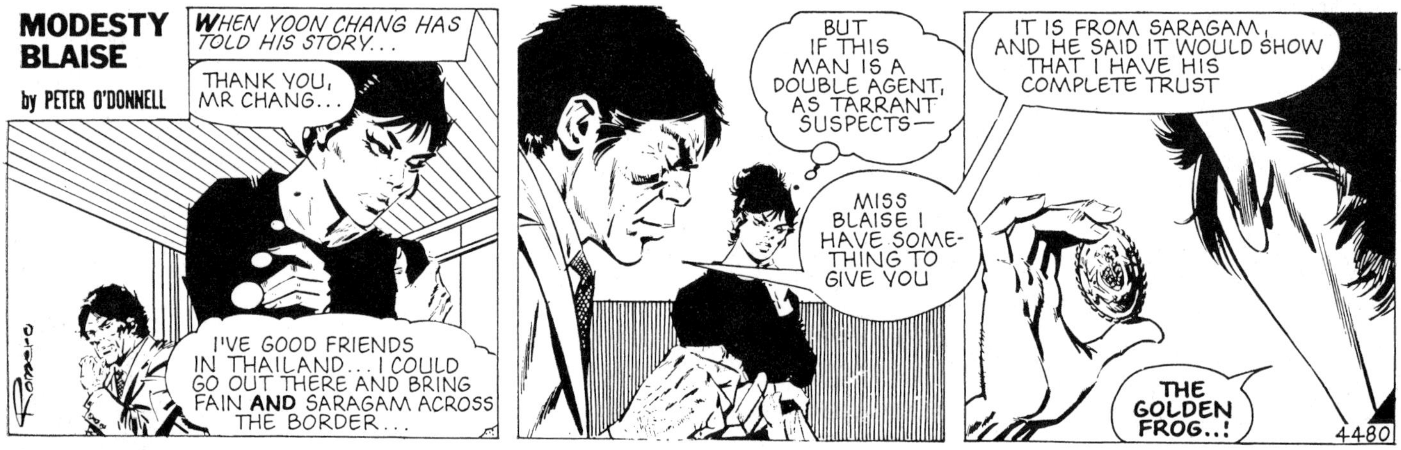
MODESTY BLAISE
by PETER O'DONNELL
WHEN YOON CHANG HAS TOLD HIS STORY...
THANK YOU, MR CHANG...
I'VE GOOD FRIENDS IN THAILAND... I COULD GO OUT THERE AND BRING FAIN **AND** SARAGAM ACROSS THE BORDER...
Romero
BUT IF THIS MAN IS A DOUBLE AGENT, AS TARRANT SUSPECTS—
MISS BLAISE I HAVE SOMETHING TO GIVE YOU
IT IS FROM SARAGAM, AND HE SAID IT WOULD SHOW THAT I HAVE HIS COMPLETE TRUST
THE GOLDEN FROG..!
4480

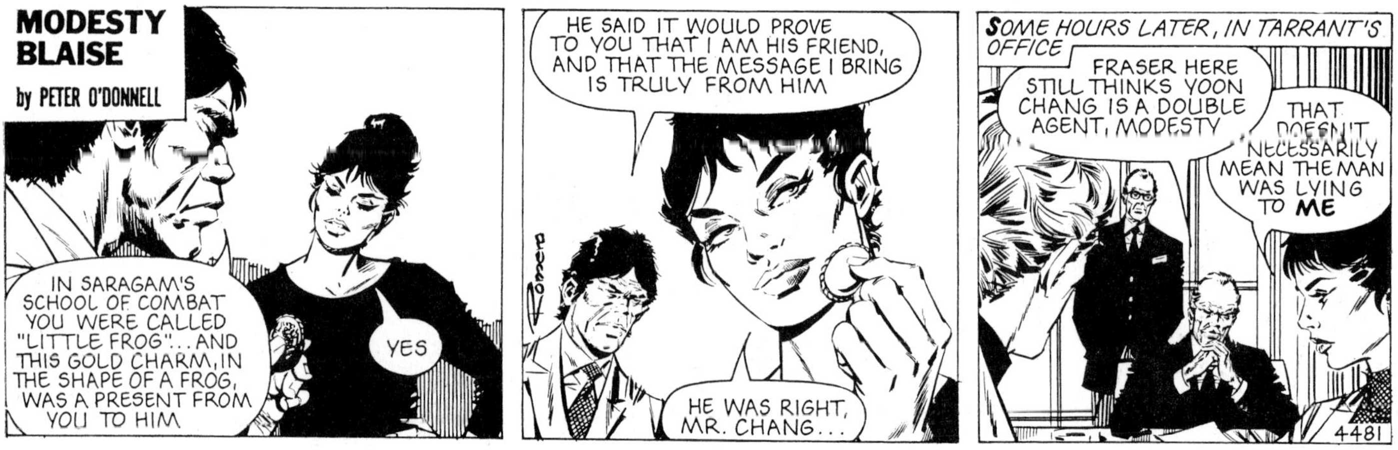
MODESTY BLAISE
by PETER O'DONNELL
IN SARAGAM'S SCHOOL OF COMBAT YOU WERE CALLED "LITTLE FROG"... AND THIS GOLD CHARM, IN THE SHAPE OF A FROG, WAS A PRESENT FROM YOU TO HIM
YES
HE SAID IT WOULD PROVE TO YOU THAT I AM HIS FRIEND, AND THAT THE MESSAGE I BRING IS TRULY FROM HIM
HE WAS RIGHT, MR. CHANG...
Romero
SOME HOURS LATER, IN TARRANT'S OFFICE
FRASER HERE STILL THINKS YOON CHANG IS A DOUBLE AGENT, MODESTY
THAT DOESN'T NECESSARILY MEAN THE MAN WAS LYING TO **ME**
4481

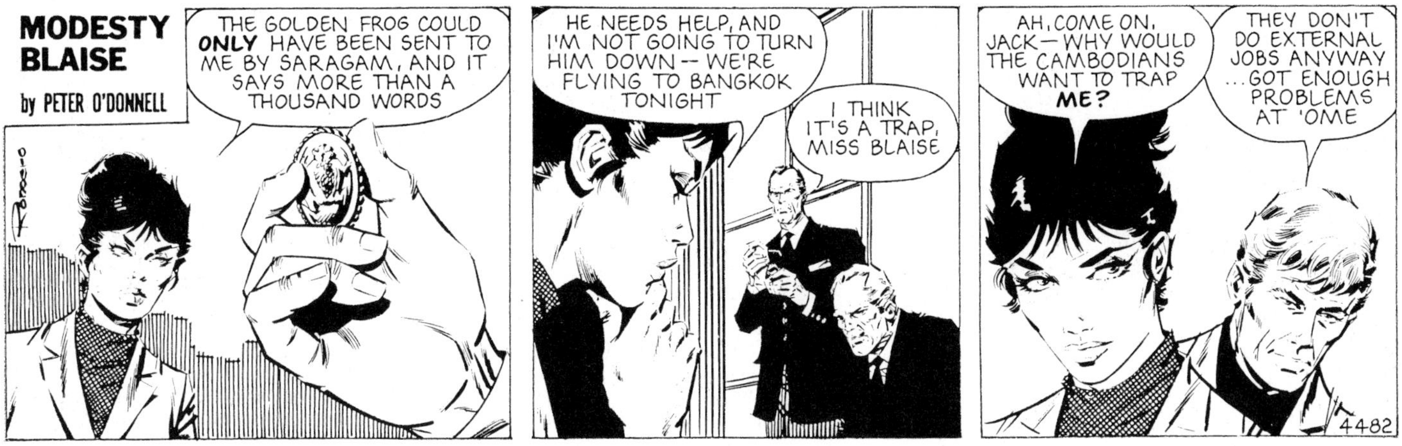
MODESTY BLAISE
by PETER O'DONNELL
THE GOLDEN FROG COULD ONLY HAVE BEEN SENT TO ME BY SARAGAM, AND IT SAYS MORE THAN A THOUSAND WORDS
HE NEEDS HELP, AND I'M NOT GOING TO TURN HIM DOWN -- WE'RE FLYING TO BANGKOK TONIGHT
I THINK IT'S A TRAP, MISS BLAISE
AH, COME ON, JACK — WHY WOULD THE CAMBODIANS WANT TO TRAP ME?
THEY DON'T DO EXTERNAL JOBS ANYWAY ...GOT ENOUGH PROBLEMS AT 'OME
4482

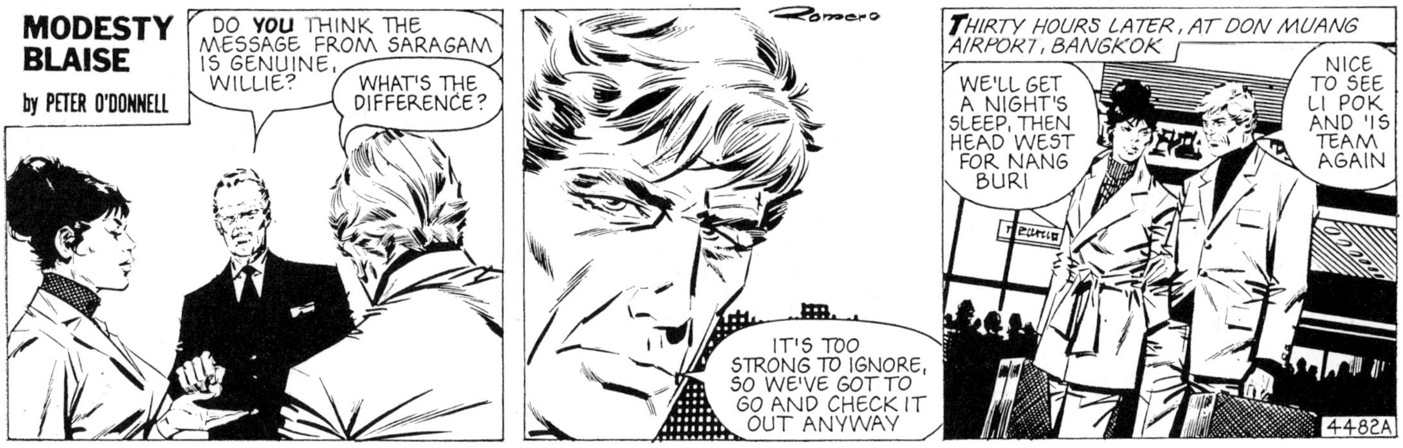
MODESTY BLAISE
by PETER O'DONNELL
DO YOU THINK THE MESSAGE FROM SARAGAM IS GENUINE, WILLIE?
WHAT'S THE DIFFERENCE?
IT'S TOO STRONG TO IGNORE, SO WE'VE GOT TO GO AND CHECK IT OUT ANYWAY
THIRTY HOURS LATER, AT DON MUANG AIRPORT, BANGKOK
WE'LL GET A NIGHT'S SLEEP, THEN HEAD WEST FOR NANG BURI
NICE TO SEE LI POK AND 'IS TEAM AGAIN
4482A

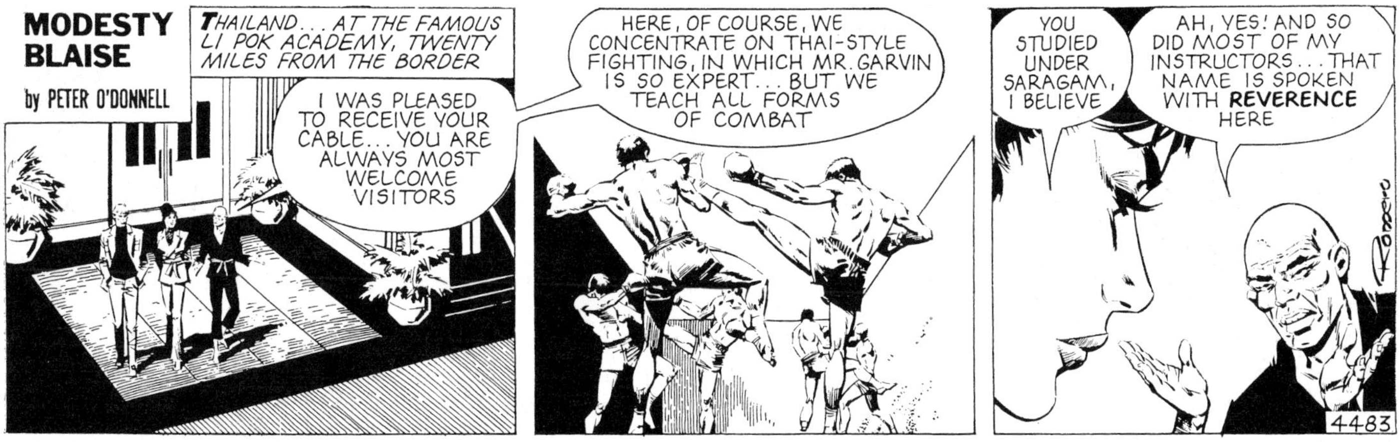
MODESTY BLAISE
by PETER O'DONNELL
THAILAND... AT THE FAMOUS LI POK ACADEMY, TWENTY MILES FROM THE BORDER
I WAS PLEASED TO RECEIVE YOUR CABLE... YOU ARE ALWAYS MOST WELCOME VISITORS
HERE, OF COURSE, WE CONCENTRATE ON THAI-STYLE FIGHTING, IN WHICH MR. GARVIN IS SO EXPERT... BUT WE TEACH ALL FORMS OF COMBAT
YOU STUDIED UNDER SARAGAM, I BELIEVE
AH, YES! AND SO DID MOST OF MY INSTRUCTORS... THAT NAME IS SPOKEN WITH REVERENCE HERE
4483

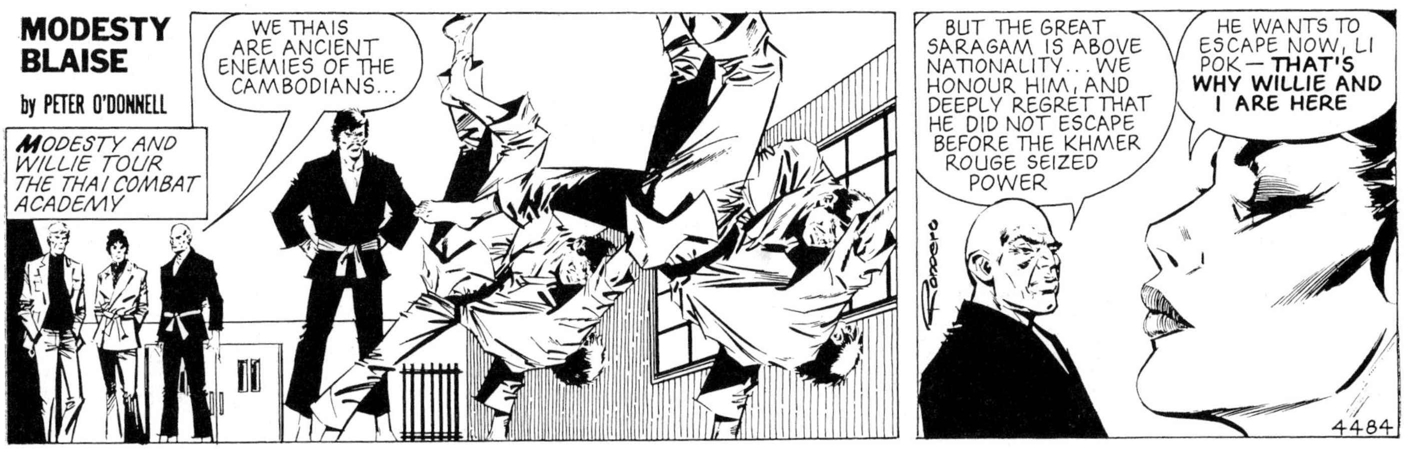
MODESTY BLAISE
by PETER O'DONNELL
MODESTY AND WILLIE TOUR THE THAI COMBAT ACADEMY
WE THAIS ARE ANCIENT ENEMIES OF THE CAMBODIANS...
BUT THE GREAT SARAGAM IS ABOVE NATIONALITY... WE HONOUR HIM, AND DEEPLY REGRET THAT HE DID NOT ESCAPE BEFORE THE KHMER ROUGE SEIZED POWER
HE WANTS TO ESCAPE NOW, LI POK — THAT'S WHY WILLIE AND I ARE HERE
4484

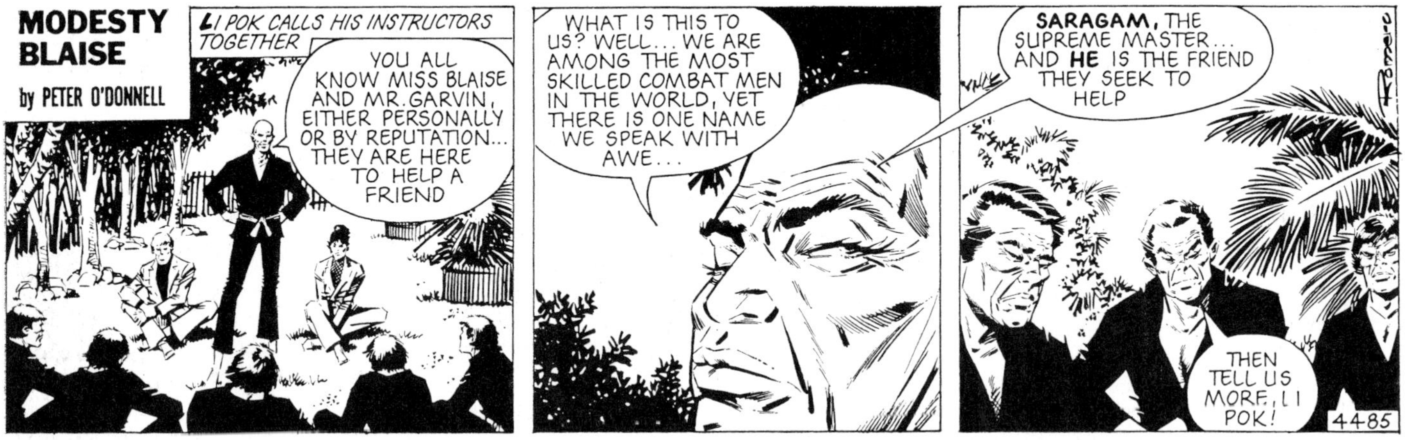
MODESTY BLAISE
by PETER O'DONNELL
LI POK CALLS HIS INSTRUCTORS TOGETHER
YOU ALL KNOW MISS BLAISE AND MR. GARVIN, EITHER PERSONALLY OR BY REPUTATION... THEY ARE HERE TO HELP A FRIEND
WHAT IS THIS TO US? WELL... WE ARE AMONG THE MOST SKILLED COMBAT MEN IN THE WORLD, YET THERE IS ONE NAME WE SPEAK WITH AWE...
SARAGAM, THE SUPREME MASTER... AND HE IS THE FRIEND THEY SEEK TO HELP
THEN TELL US MORE, LI POK!
4485

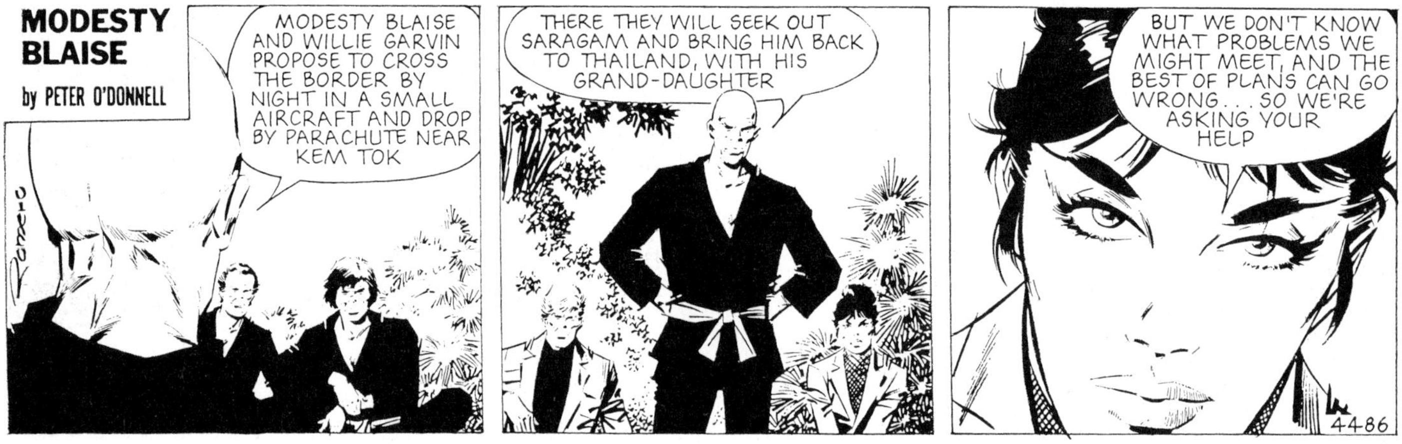
MODESTY BLAISE
by PETER O'DONNELL
MODESTY BLAISE AND WILLIE GARVIN PROPOSE TO CROSS THE BORDER BY NIGHT IN A SMALL AIRCRAFT AND DROP BY PARACHUTE NEAR KEM TOK
THERE THEY WILL SEEK OUT SARAGAM AND BRING HIM BACK TO THAILAND, WITH HIS GRAND-DAUGHTER
BUT WE DON'T KNOW WHAT PROBLEMS WE MIGHT MEET, AND THE BEST OF PLANS CAN GO WRONG... SO WE'RE ASKING YOUR HELP
4486

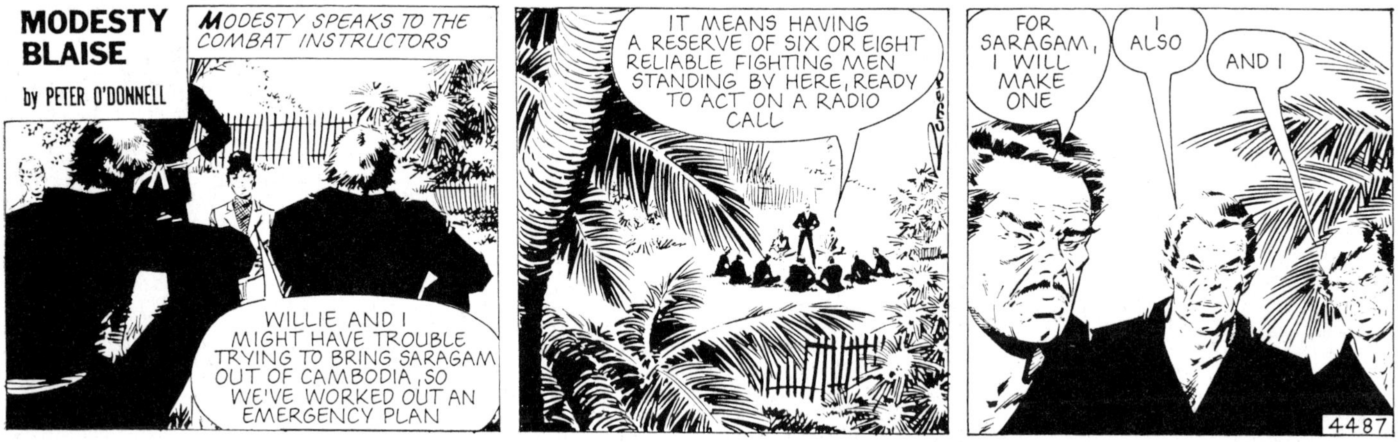
MODESTY BLAISE
by PETER O'DONNELL
MODESTY SPEAKS TO THE COMBAT INSTRUCTORS
WILLIE AND I MIGHT HAVE TROUBLE TRYING TO BRING SARAGAM OUT OF CAMBODIA, SO WE'VE WORKED OUT AN EMERGENCY PLAN
IT MEANS HAVING A RESERVE OF SIX OR EIGHT RELIABLE FIGHTING MEN STANDING BY HERE, READY TO ACT ON A RADIO CALL
FOR SARAGAM, I WILL MAKE ONE
I ALSO
AND I
4487

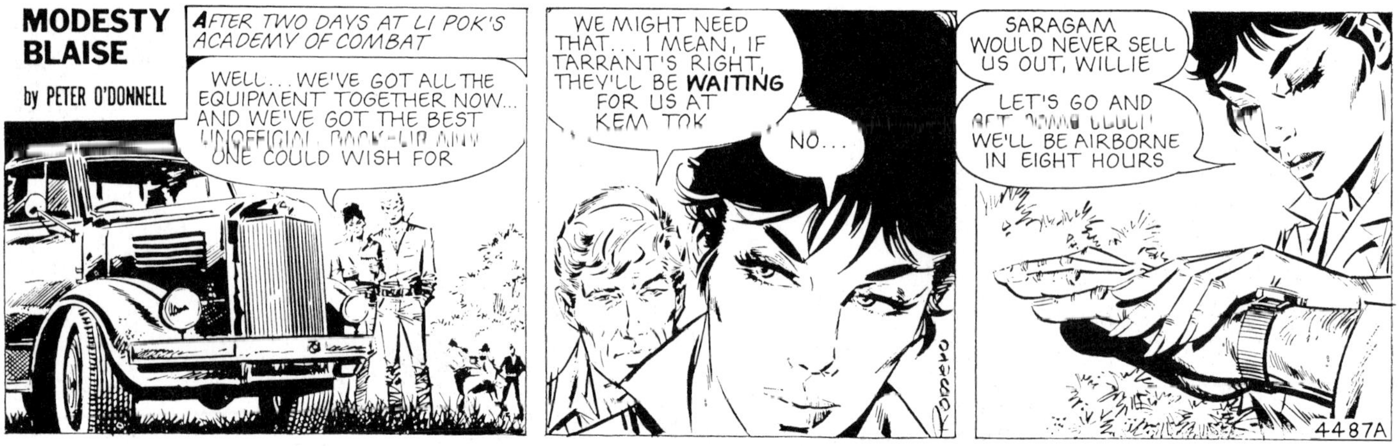
MODESTY BLAISE
by PETER O'DONNELL
AFTER TWO DAYS AT LI POK'S ACADEMY OF COMBAT
WELL... WE'VE GOT ALL THE EQUIPMENT TOGETHER NOW... AND WE'VE GOT THE BEST UNOFFICIAL BACK-UP ANY ONE COULD WISH FOR
WE MIGHT NEED THAT... I MEAN, IF TARRANT'S RIGHT, THEY'LL BE WAITING FOR US AT KEM TOK
NO...
SARAGAM WOULD NEVER SELL US OUT, WILLIE
LET'S GO AND
WE'LL BE AIRBORNE IN EIGHT HOURS
4487A

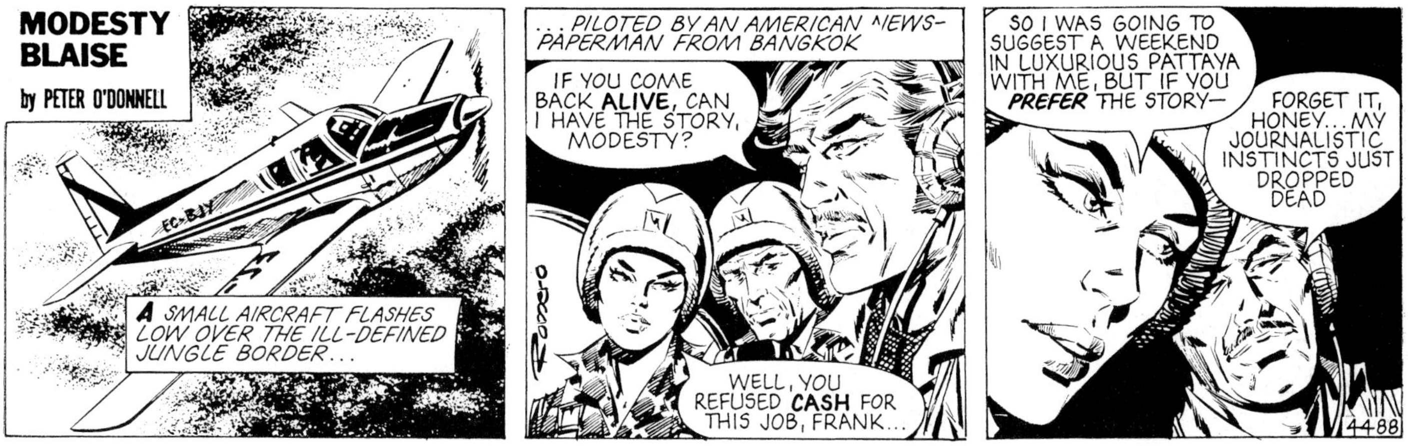
MODESTY BLAISE
by PETER O'DONNELL
A SMALL AIRCRAFT FLASHES LOW OVER THE ILL-DEFINED JUNGLE BORDER...
...PILOTED BY AN AMERICAN NEWS-PAPERMAN FROM BANGKOK
IF YOU COME BACK ALIVE, CAN I HAVE THE STORY, MODESTY?
WELL, YOU REFUSED CASH FOR THIS JOB, FRANK...
SO I WAS GOING TO SUGGEST A WEEKEND IN LUXURIOUS PATTAYA WITH ME, BUT IF YOU PREFER THE STORY—
FORGET IT, HONEY... MY JOURNALISTIC INSTINCTS JUST DROPPED DEAD
4488

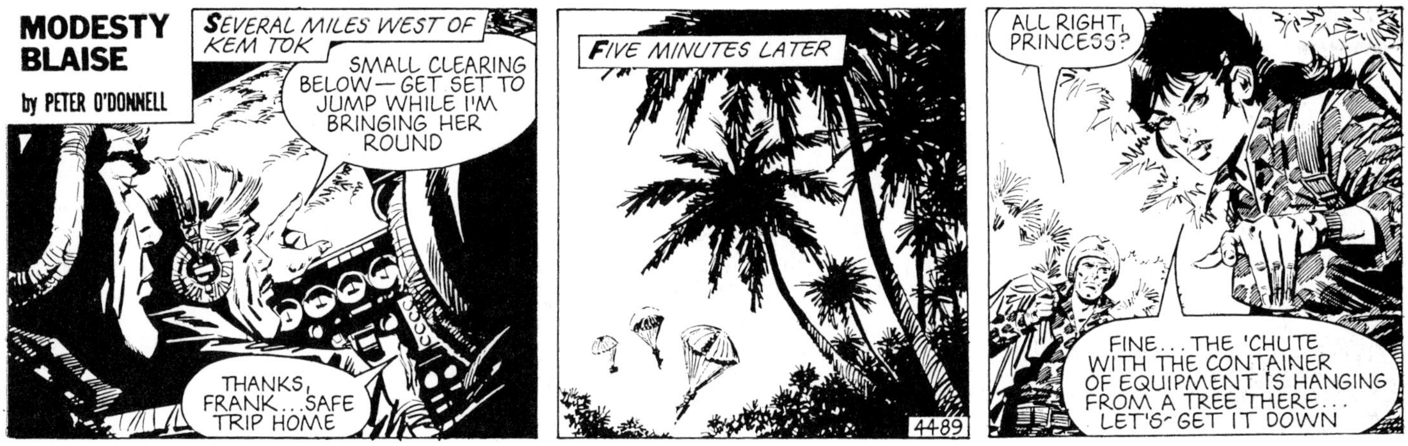
MODESTY BLAISE
by PETER O'DONNELL
SEVERAL MILES WEST OF KEM TOK
SMALL CLEARING BELOW— GET SET TO JUMP WHILE I'M BRINGING HER ROUND
THANKS, FRANK... SAFE TRIP HOME
FIVE MINUTES LATER
4489
ALL RIGHT, PRINCESS?
FINE... THE 'CHUTE WITH THE CONTAINER OF EQUIPMENT IS HANGING FROM A TREE THERE... LET'S GET IT DOWN

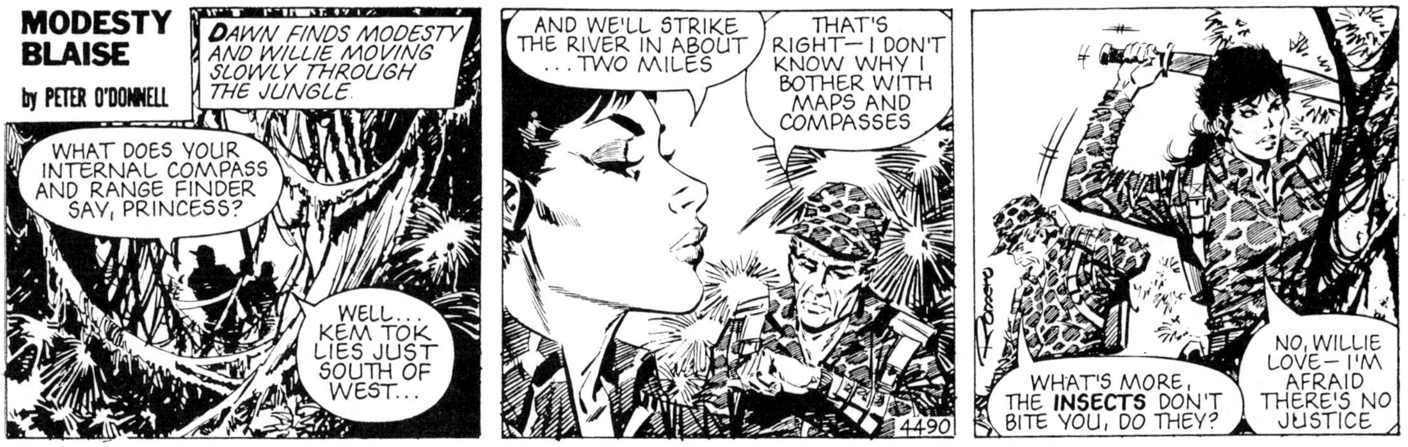
MODESTY BLAISE
by PETER O'DONNELL
DAWN FINDS MODESTY AND WILLIE MOVING SLOWLY THROUGH THE JUNGLE
WHAT DOES YOUR INTERNAL COMPASS AND RANGE FINDER SAY, PRINCESS?
WELL... KEM TOK LIES JUST SOUTH OF WEST...
AND WE'LL STRIKE THE RIVER IN ABOUT ... TWO MILES
THAT'S RIGHT— I DON'T KNOW WHY I BOTHER WITH MAPS AND COMPASSES
4490
WHAT'S MORE, THE INSECTS DON'T BITE YOU, DO THEY?
NO, WILLIE LOVE— I'M AFRAID THERE'S NO JUSTICE

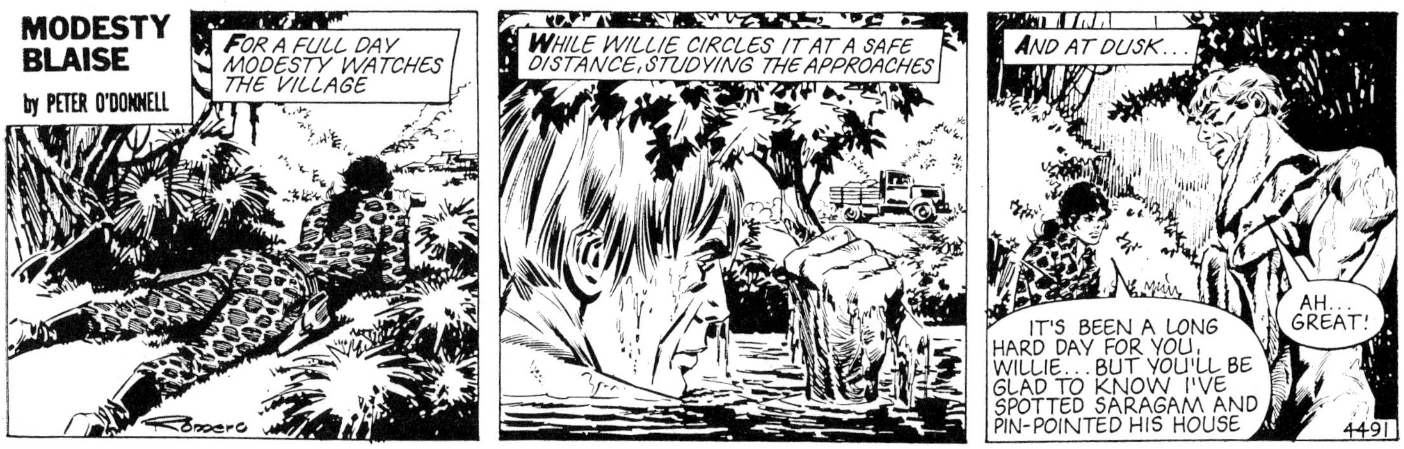
MODESTY BLAISE
by PETER O'DONNELL
FOR A FULL DAY MODESTY WATCHES THE VILLAGE
WHILE WILLIE CIRCLES IT AT A SAFE DISTANCE, STUDYING THE APPROACHES
AND AT DUSK...
IT'S BEEN A LONG HARD DAY FOR YOU, WILLIE... BUT YOU'LL BE GLAD TO KNOW I'VE SPOTTED SARAGAM AND PIN-POINTED HIS HOUSE
AH... GREAT!
4491

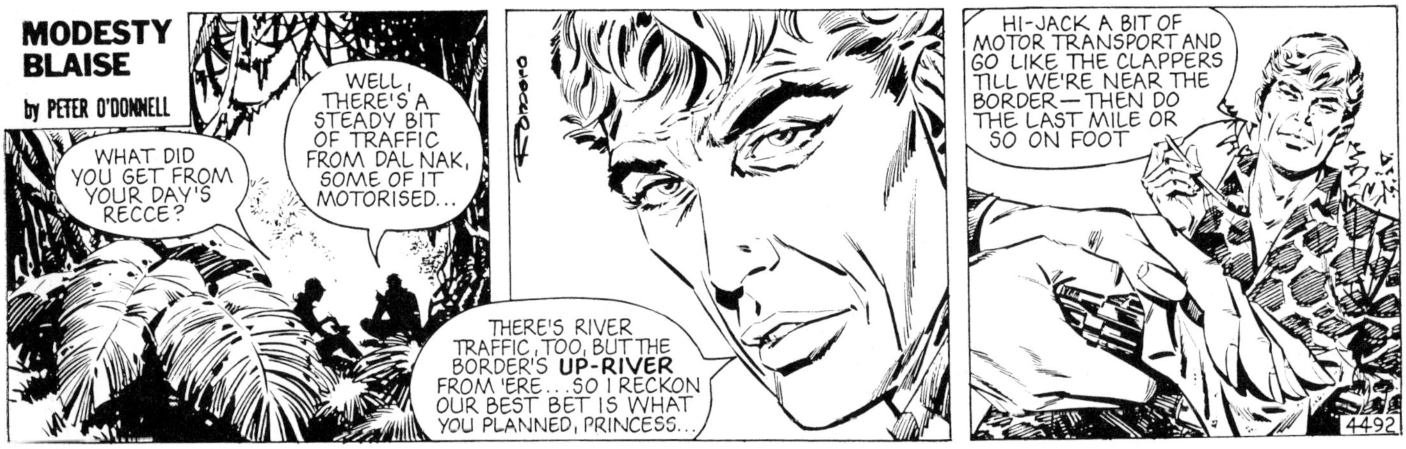
MODESTY BLAISE
by PETER O'DONNELL
WHAT DID YOU GET FROM YOUR DAY'S RECCE?
WELL, THERE'S A STEADY BIT OF TRAFFIC FROM DAL NAK, SOME OF IT MOTORISED...
THERE'S RIVER TRAFFIC, TOO, BUT THE BORDER'S **UP-RIVER** FROM 'ERE... SO I RECKON OUR BEST BET IS WHAT YOU PLANNED, PRINCESS...
HI-JACK A BIT OF MOTOR TRANSPORT AND GO LIKE THE CLAPPERS TILL WE'RE NEAR THE BORDER—THEN DO THE LAST MILE OR SO ON FOOT
4492

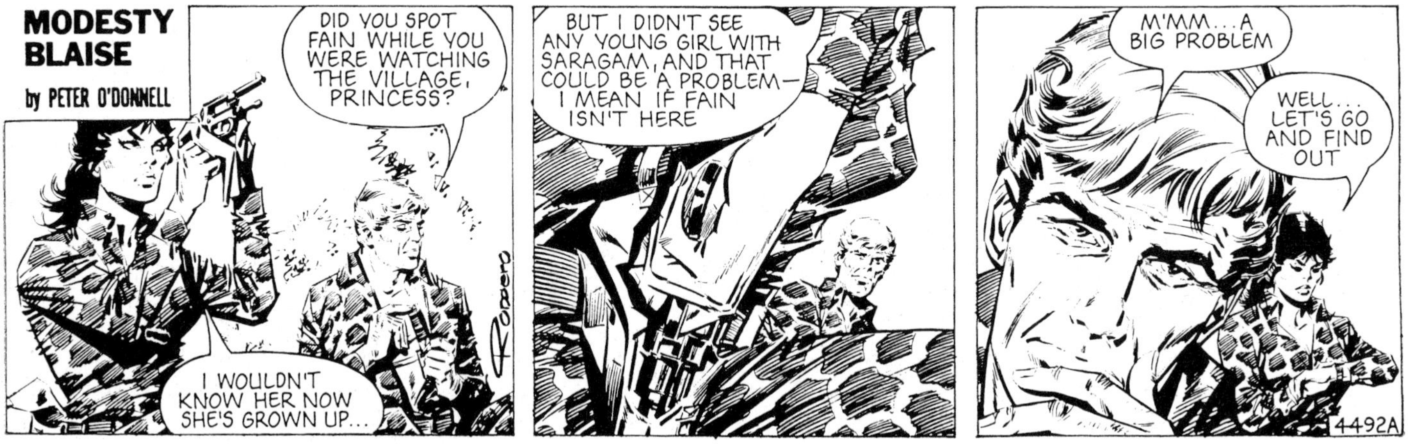
MODESTY BLAISE
by PETER O'DONNELL
DID YOU SPOT FAIN WHILE YOU WERE WATCHING THE VILLAGE, PRINCESS?
I WOULDN'T KNOW HER NOW SHE'S GROWN UP...
BUT I DIDN'T SEE ANY YOUNG GIRL WITH SARAGAM, AND THAT COULD BE A PROBLEM—I MEAN IF FAIN ISN'T HERE
M'MM... A BIG PROBLEM
WELL... LET'S GO AND FIND OUT
4492A

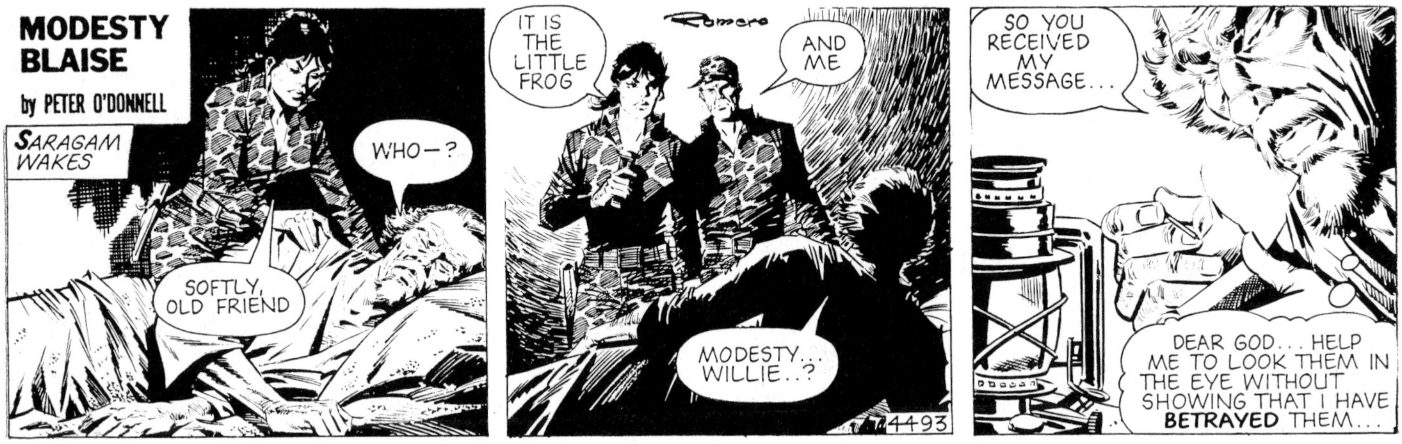
MODESTY BLAISE
by PETER O'DONNELL
SARAGAM WAKES
WHO—?
SOFTLY, OLD FRIEND
IT IS THE LITTLE FROG
AND ME
MODESTY... WILLIE..?
4493
SO YOU RECEIVED MY MESSAGE...
DEAR GOD... HELP ME TO LOOK THEM IN THE EYE WITHOUT SHOWING THAT I HAVE **BETRAYED** THEM...

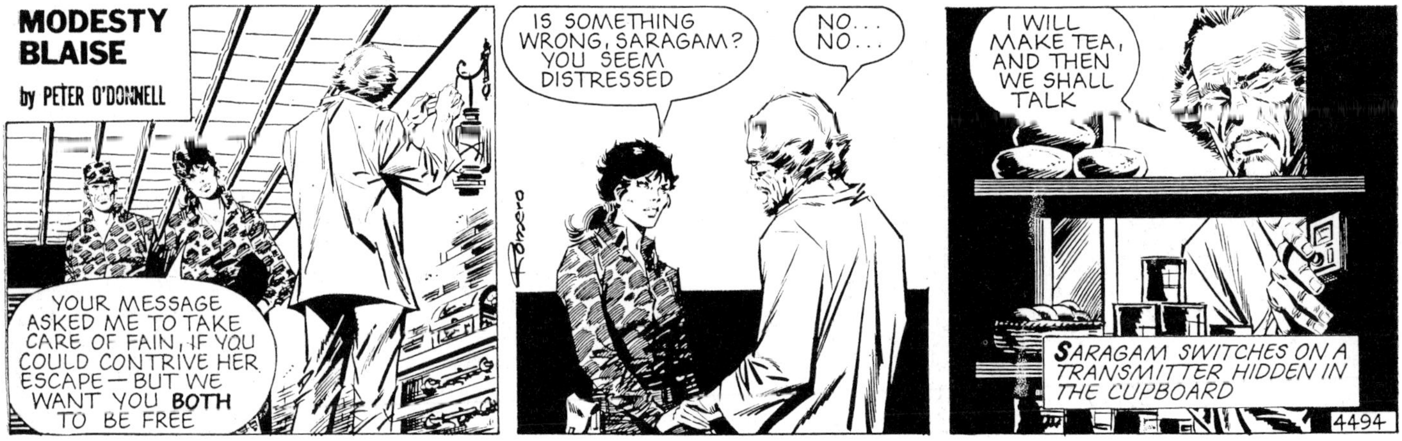
MODESTY BLAISE
by PETER O'DONNELL
YOUR MESSAGE ASKED ME TO TAKE CARE OF FAIN, IF YOU COULD CONTRIVE HER ESCAPE—BUT WE WANT YOU **BOTH** TO BE FREE
IS SOMETHING WRONG, SARAGAM? YOU SEEM DISTRESSED
NO... NO...
I WILL MAKE TEA, AND THEN WE SHALL TALK
SARAGAM SWITCHES ON A TRANSMITTER HIDDEN IN THE CUPBOARD
4494

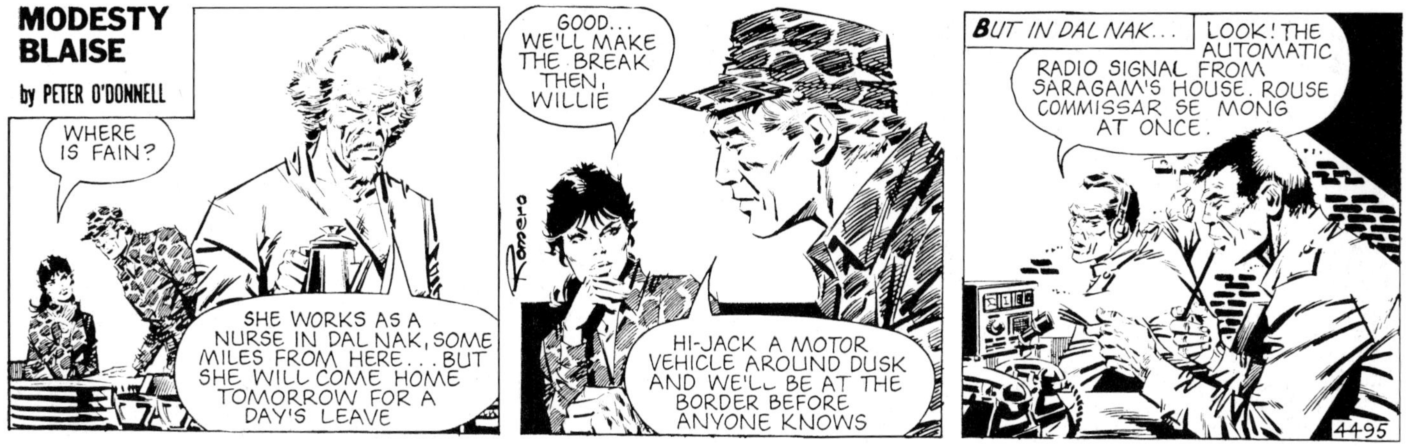
MODESTY BLAISE
by PETER O'DONNELL
WHERE IS FAIN?
SHE WORKS AS A NURSE IN DAL NAK, SOME MILES FROM HERE... BUT SHE WILL COME HOME TOMORROW FOR A DAY'S LEAVE
GOOD... WE'LL MAKE THE BREAK THEN, WILLIE
HI-JACK A MOTOR VEHICLE AROUND DUSK AND WE'LL BE AT THE BORDER BEFORE ANYONE KNOWS
BUT IN DAL NAK...
LOOK! THE AUTOMATIC RADIO SIGNAL FROM SARAGAM'S HOUSE. ROUSE COMMISSAR SE MONG AT ONCE.
4495

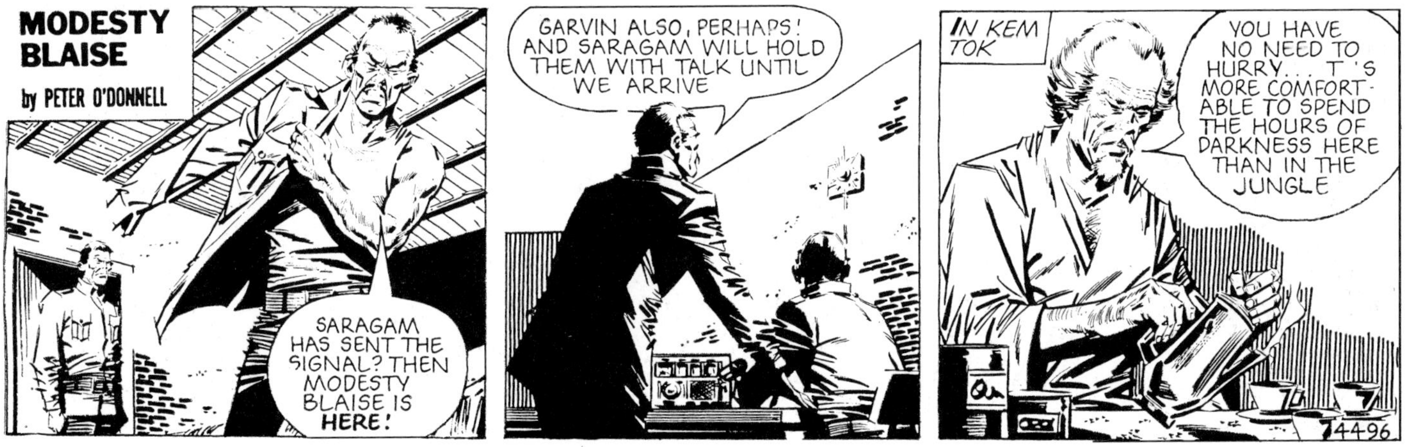
MODESTY BLAISE
by PETER O'DONNELL
SARAGAM HAS SENT THE SIGNAL? THEN MODESTY BLAISE IS **HERE**!
GARVIN ALSO, PERHAPS! AND SARAGAM WILL HOLD THEM WITH TALK UNTIL WE ARRIVE
IN KEM TOK
YOU HAVE NO NEED TO HURRY... IT'S MORE COMFORTABLE TO SPEND THE HOURS OF DARKNESS HERE THAN IN THE JUNGLE
4496

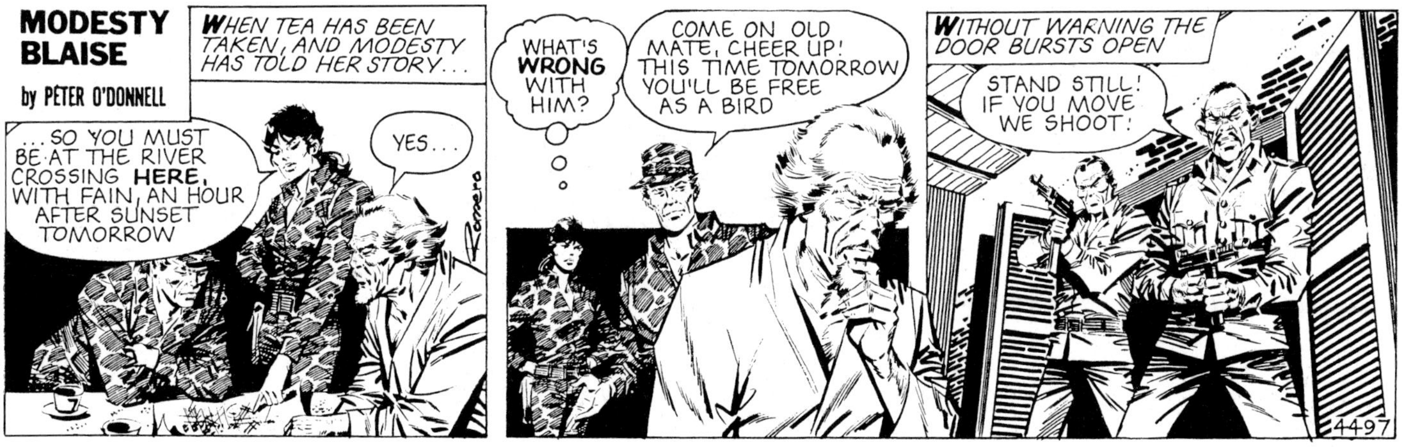
MODESTY BLAISE
by PETER O'DONNELL
WHEN TEA HAS BEEN TAKEN, AND MODESTY HAS TOLD HER STORY...
...SO YOU MUST BE AT THE RIVER CROSSING **HERE**, WITH FAIN, AN HOUR AFTER SUNSET TOMORROW
YES...
WHAT'S **WRONG** WITH HIM?
COME ON OLD MATE, CHEER UP! THIS TIME TOMORROW YOU'LL BE FREE AS A BIRD
WITHOUT WARNING THE DOOR BURSTS OPEN
STAND STILL! IF YOU MOVE WE SHOOT!
4497

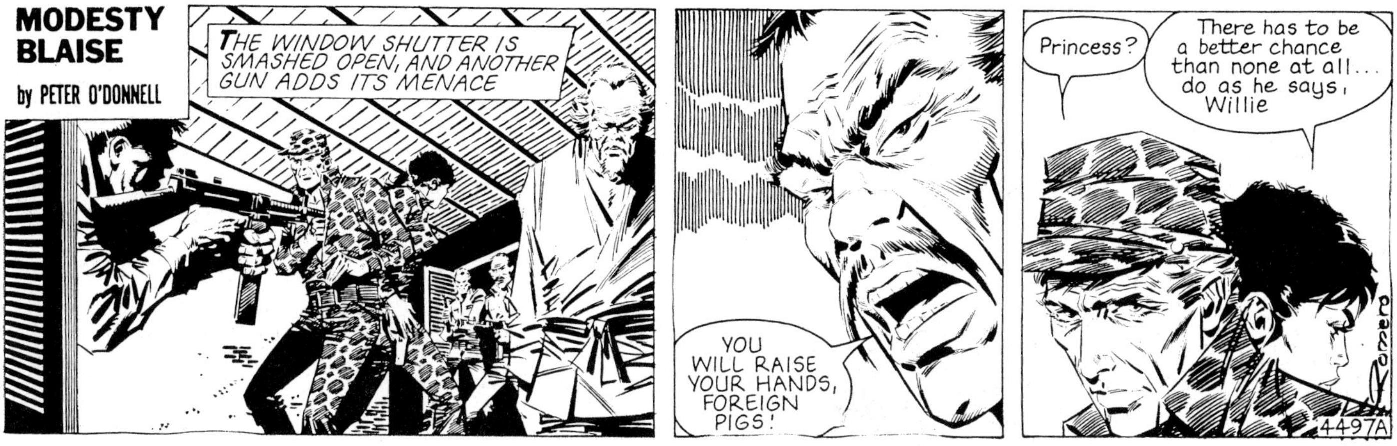
MODESTY BLAISE
by PETER O'DONNELL
THE WINDOW SHUTTER IS SMASHED OPEN, AND ANOTHER GUN ADDS ITS MENACE
YOU WILL RAISE YOUR HANDS, FOREIGN PIGS!
Princess?
There has to be a better chance than none at all... do as he says, Willie
4497A

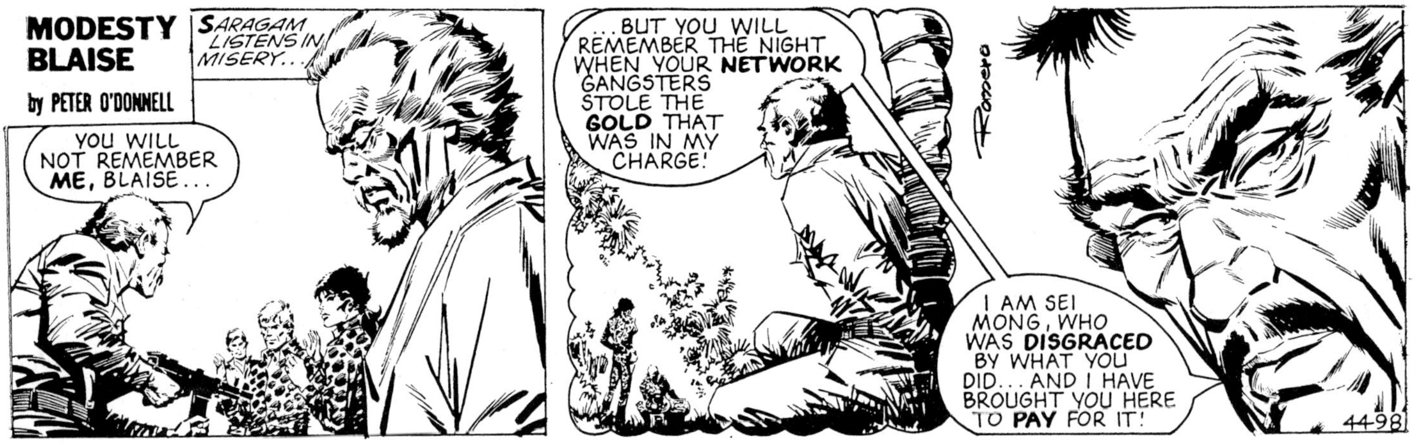
MODESTY BLAISE
by PETER O'DONNELL
SARAGAM LISTENS IN MISERY...
YOU WILL NOT REMEMBER ME, BLAISE...
...BUT YOU WILL REMEMBER THE NIGHT WHEN YOUR NETWORK GANGSTERS STOLE THE GOLD THAT WAS IN MY CHARGE!
I AM SEI MONG, WHO WAS DISGRACED BY WHAT YOU DID... AND I HAVE BROUGHT YOU HERE TO PAY FOR IT!
4498

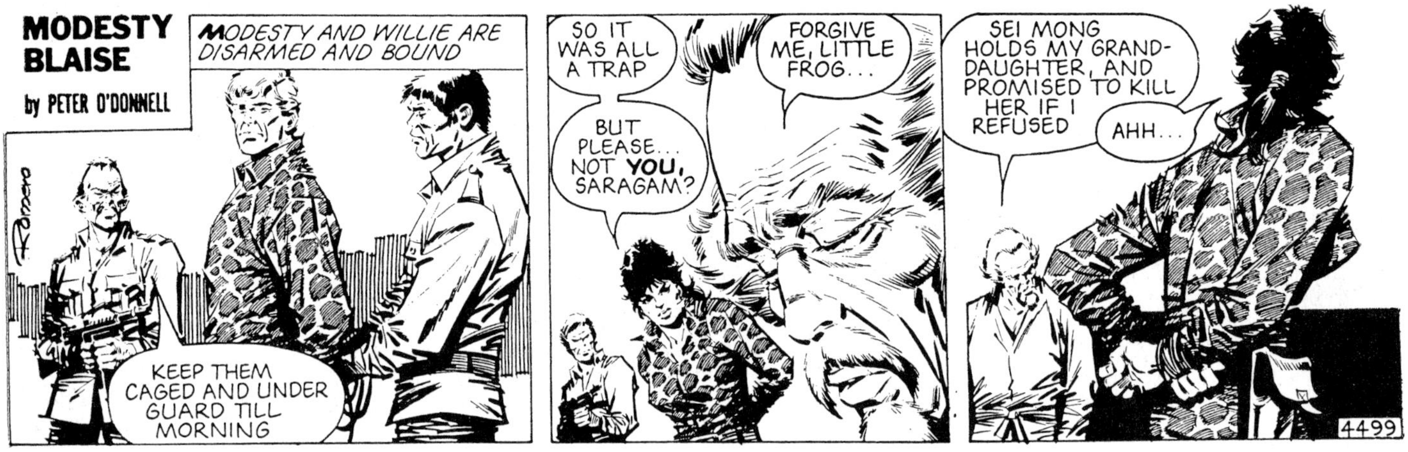
MODESTY BLAISE
by PETER O'DONNELL
MODESTY AND WILLIE ARE DISARMED AND BOUND
KEEP THEM CAGED AND UNDER GUARD TILL MORNING
SO IT WAS ALL A TRAP
BUT PLEASE... NOT YOU, SARAGAM?
FORGIVE ME, LITTLE FROG...
SEI MONG HOLDS MY GRAND-DAUGHTER, AND PROMISED TO KILL HER IF I REFUSED
AHH...
4499

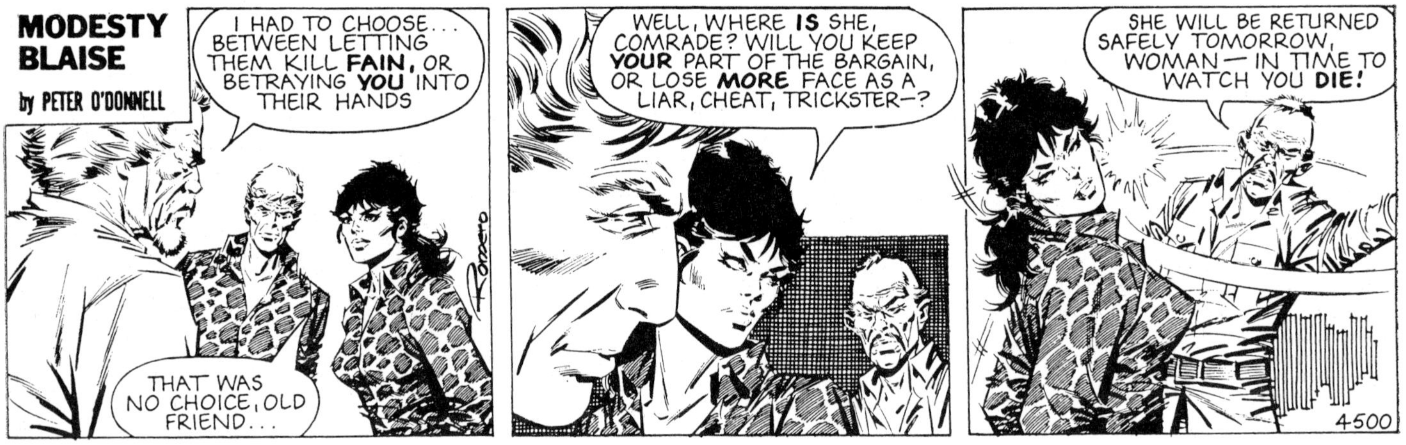
MODESTY BLAISE
by PETER O'DONNELL
I HAD TO CHOOSE... BETWEEN LETTING THEM KILL FAIN, OR BETRAYING YOU INTO THEIR HANDS
THAT WAS NO CHOICE, OLD FRIEND...
WELL, WHERE IS SHE, COMRADE? WILL YOU KEEP YOUR PART OF THE BARGAIN, OR LOSE MORE FACE AS A LIAR, CHEAT, TRICKSTER—?
SHE WILL BE RETURNED SAFELY TOMORROW, WOMAN— IN TIME TO WATCH YOU DIE!
4500

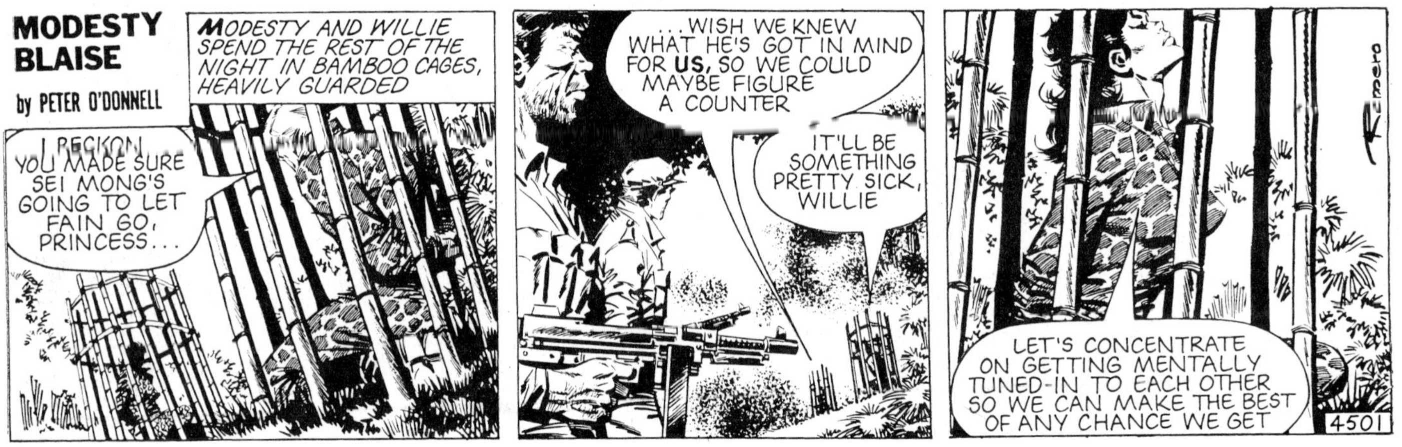
MODESTY BLAISE
by PETER O'DONNELL
MODESTY AND WILLIE SPEND THE REST OF THE NIGHT IN BAMBOO CAGES, HEAVILY GUARDED
I RECKON YOU MADE SURE SEI MONG'S GOING TO LET FAIN GO, PRINCESS...
...WISH WE KNEW WHAT HE'S GOT IN MIND FOR US, SO WE COULD MAYBE FIGURE A COUNTER
IT'LL BE SOMETHING PRETTY SICK, WILLIE
LET'S CONCENTRATE ON GETTING MENTALLY TUNED-IN TO EACH OTHER SO WE CAN MAKE THE BEST OF ANY CHANCE WE GET
4501

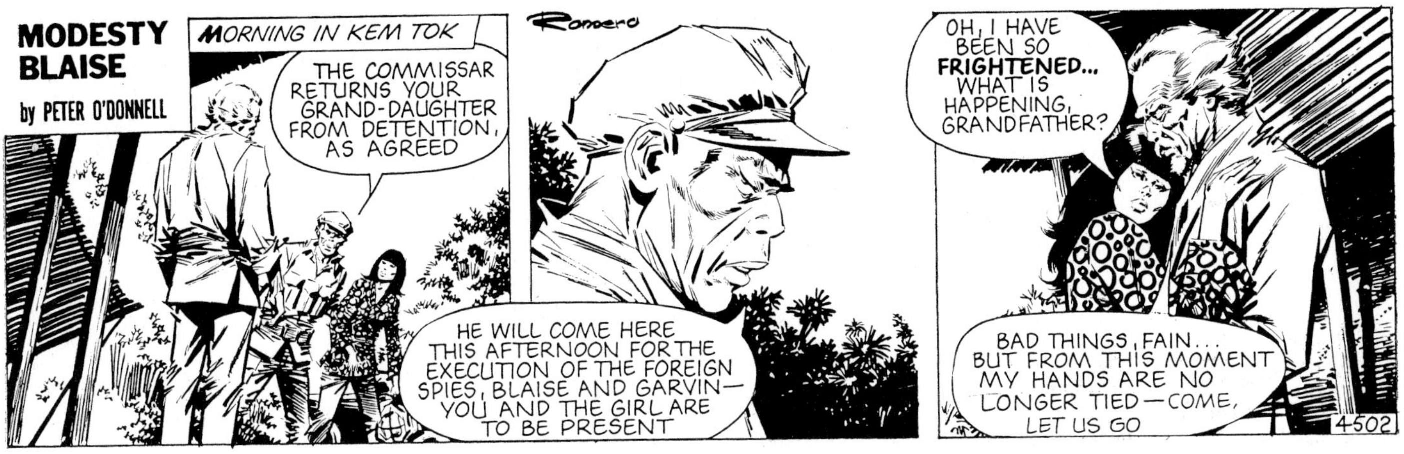
MODESTY BLAISE
by PETER O'DONNELL
MORNING IN KEM TOK
THE COMMISSAR RETURNS YOUR GRAND-DAUGHTER FROM DETENTION, AS AGREED
Romero
HE WILL COME HERE THIS AFTERNOON FOR THE EXECUTION OF THE FOREIGN SPIES, BLAISE AND GARVIN— YOU AND THE GIRL ARE TO BE PRESENT
OH, I HAVE BEEN SO FRIGHTENED... WHAT IS HAPPENING, GRANDFATHER?
BAD THINGS, FAIN... BUT FROM THIS MOMENT MY HANDS ARE NO LONGER TIED—COME, LET US GO
4502

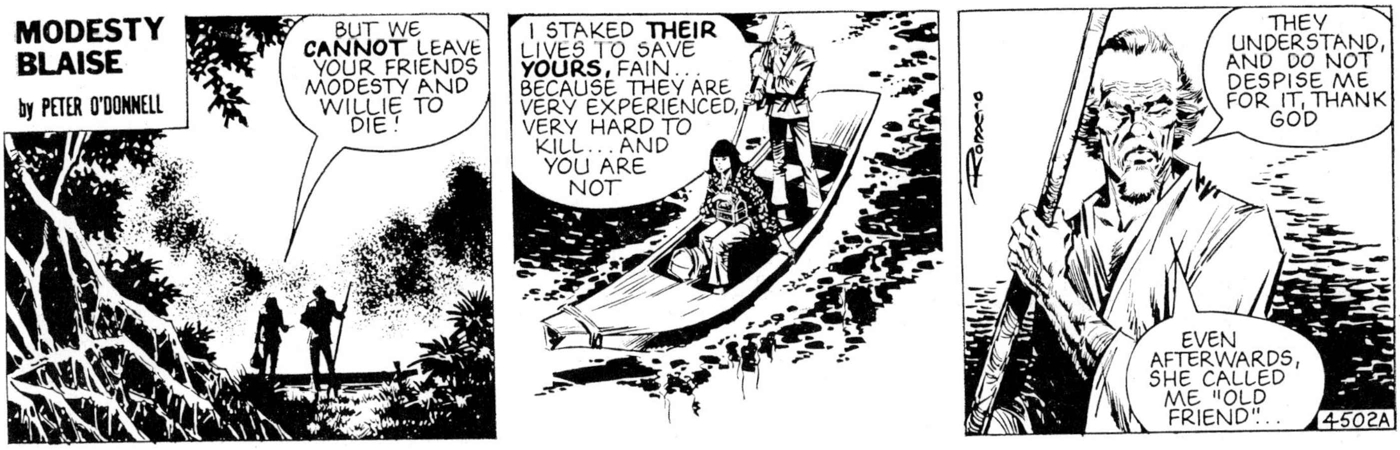
MODESTY BLAISE
by PETER O'DONNELL
BUT WE CANNOT LEAVE YOUR FRIENDS MODESTY AND WILLIE TO DIE!
I STAKED THEIR LIVES TO SAVE YOURS, FAIN... BECAUSE THEY ARE VERY EXPERIENCED, VERY HARD TO KILL... AND YOU ARE NOT
THEY UNDERSTAND, AND DO NOT DESPISE ME FOR IT, THANK GOD
EVEN AFTERWARDS, SHE CALLED ME "OLD FRIEND"...
4502A

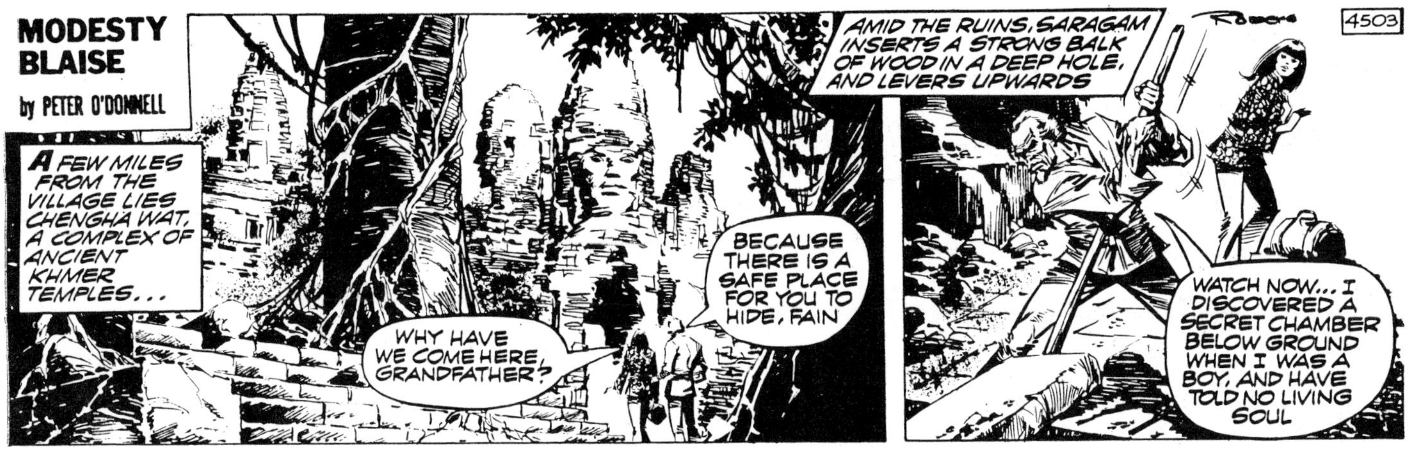
MODESTY BLAISE
by PETER O'DONNELL
A FEW MILES FROM THE VILLAGE LIES CHENGHA WAT, A COMPLEX OF ANCIENT KHMER TEMPLES...
WHY HAVE WE COME HERE, GRANDFATHER?
BECAUSE THERE IS A SAFE PLACE FOR YOU TO HIDE, FAIN
AMID THE RUINS, SARAGAM INSERTS A STRONG BALK OF WOOD IN A DEEP HOLE, AND LEVERS UPWARDS
Romero
4503
WATCH NOW... I DISCOVERED A SECRET CHAMBER BELOW GROUND WHEN I WAS A BOY, AND HAVE TOLD NO LIVING SOUL

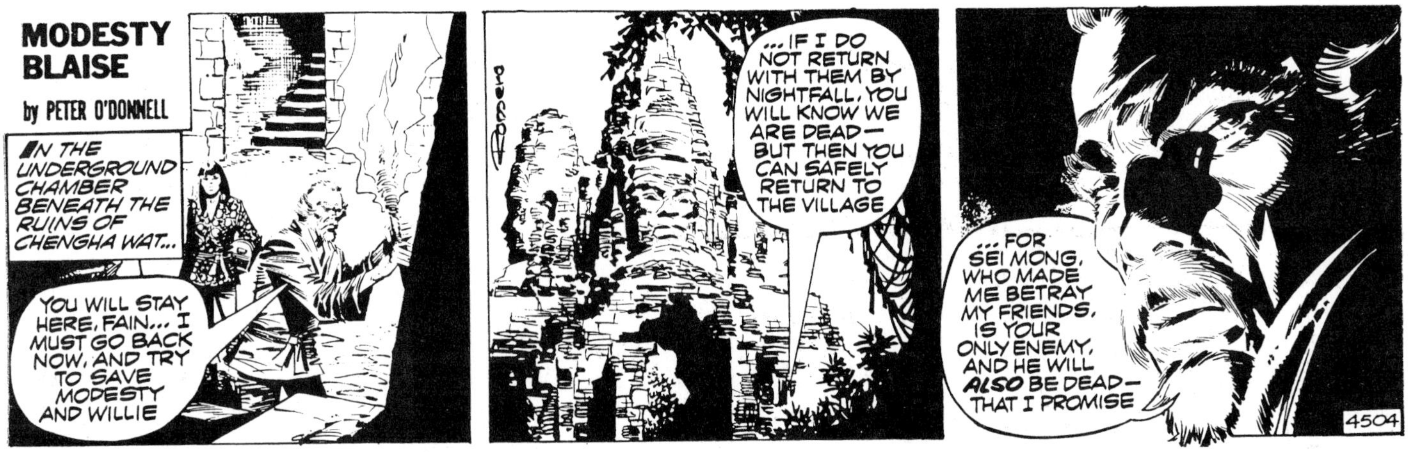
MODESTY BLAISE
by PETER O'DONNELL
IN THE UNDERGROUND CHAMBER BENEATH THE RUINS OF CHENGHA WAT...
YOU WILL STAY HERE, FAIN... I MUST GO BACK NOW, AND TRY TO SAVE MODESTY AND WILLIE
...IF I DO NOT RETURN WITH THEM BY NIGHTFALL, YOU WILL KNOW WE ARE DEAD— BUT THEN YOU CAN SAFELY RETURN TO THE VILLAGE
...FOR SEI MONG, WHO MADE ME BETRAY MY FRIENDS, IS YOUR ONLY ENEMY, AND HE WILL ALSO BE DEAD— THAT I PROMISE
4504

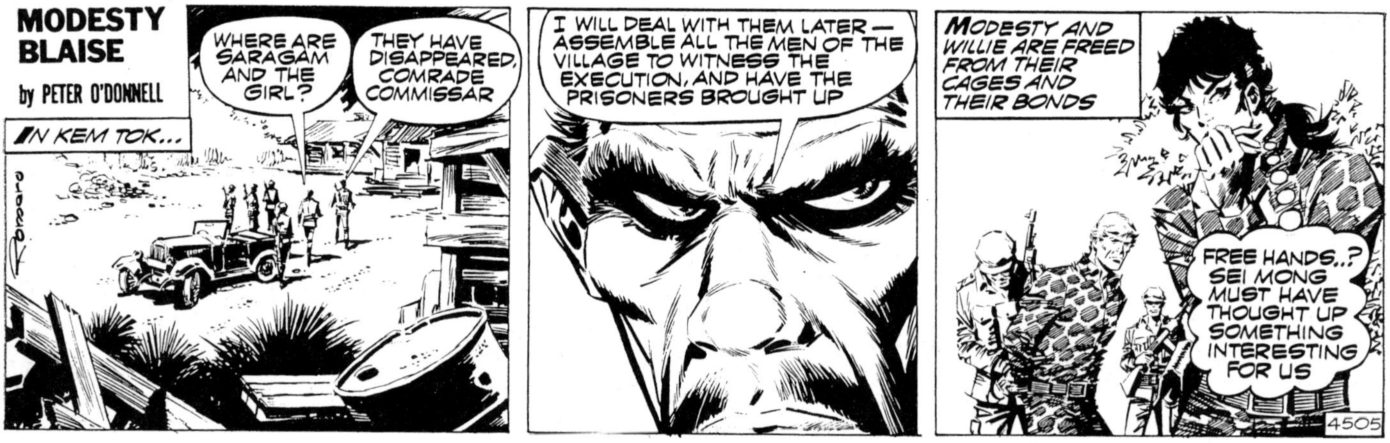
MODESTY BLAISE
by PETER O'DONNELL
IN KEM TOK...
WHERE ARE SARAGAM AND THE GIRL?
THEY HAVE DISAPPEARED, COMRADE COMMISSAR
I WILL DEAL WITH THEM LATER — ASSEMBLE ALL THE MEN OF THE VILLAGE TO WITNESS THE EXECUTION, AND HAVE THE PRISONERS BROUGHT UP
MODESTY AND WILLIE ARE FREED FROM THEIR CAGES AND THEIR BONDS
FREE HANDS..? SEI MONG MUST HAVE THOUGHT UP SOMETHING INTERESTING FOR US
4505

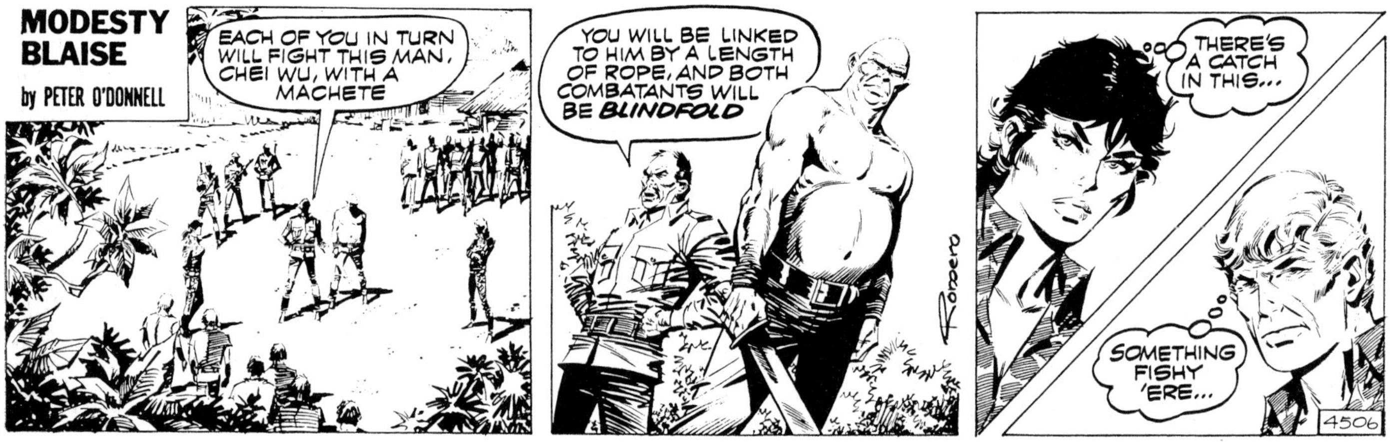
MODESTY BLAISE
by PETER O'DONNELL
EACH OF YOU IN TURN WILL FIGHT THIS MAN, CHEI WU, WITH A MACHETE
YOU WILL BE LINKED TO HIM BY A LENGTH OF ROPE, AND BOTH COMBATANTS WILL BE BLINDFOLD
THERE'S A CATCH IN THIS...
SOMETHING FISHY 'ERE...
4506

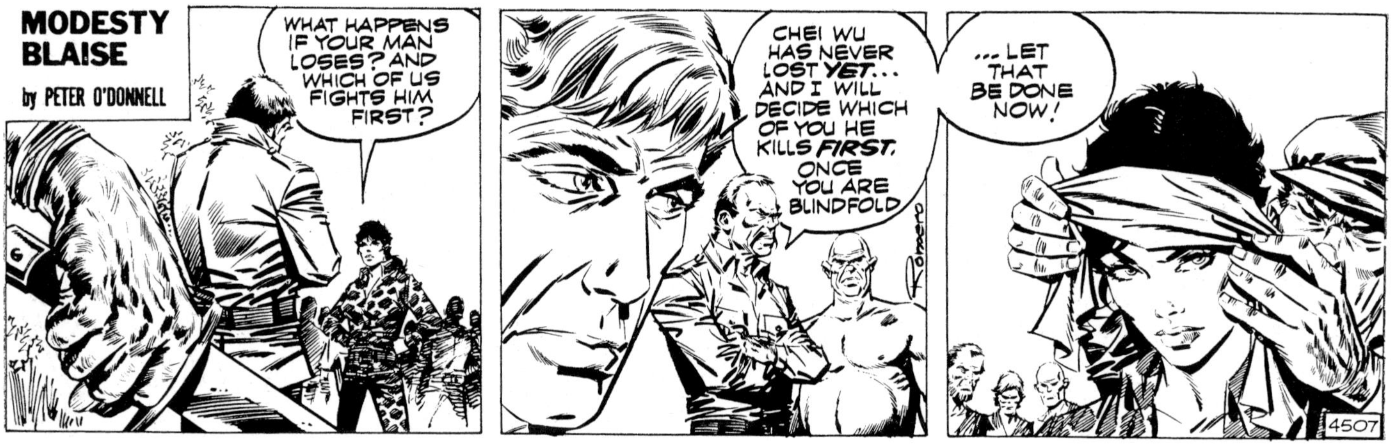
MODESTY BLAISE
by PETER O'DONNELL
WHAT HAPPENS IF YOUR MAN LOSES? AND WHICH OF US FIGHTS HIM FIRST?
CHEI WU HAS NEVER LOST YET... AND I WILL DECIDE WHICH OF YOU HE KILLS FIRST, ONCE YOU ARE BLINDFOLD
...LET THAT BE DONE NOW!
4507

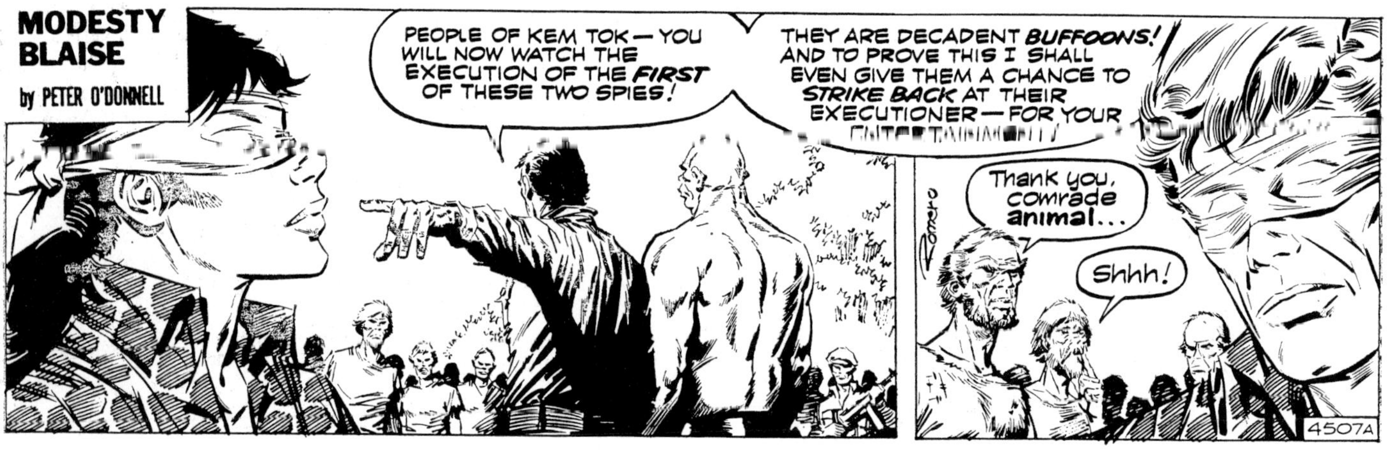
MODESTY BLAISE
by PETER O'DONNELL
PEOPLE OF KEM TOK — YOU WILL NOW WATCH THE EXECUTION OF THE FIRST OF THESE TWO SPIES!
THEY ARE DECADENT BUFFOONS! AND TO PROVE THIS I SHALL EVEN GIVE THEM A CHANCE TO STRIKE BACK AT THEIR EXECUTIONER — FOR YOUR
Thank you, comrade animal...
Shhh!
4507A

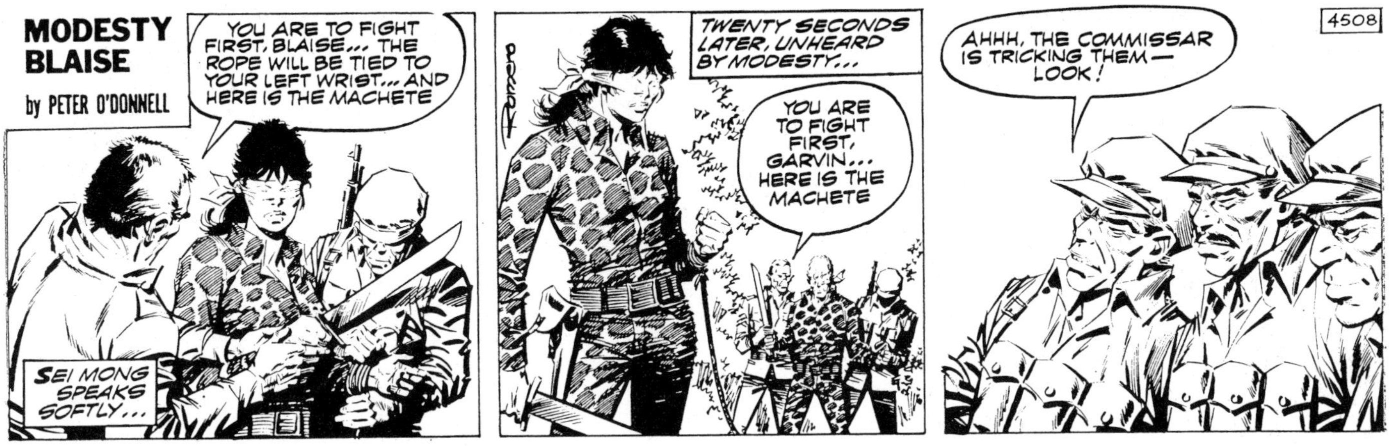
MODESTY BLAISE
by PETER O'DONNELL
4508
YOU ARE TO FIGHT FIRST, BLAISE... THE ROPE WILL BE TIED TO YOUR LEFT WRIST... AND HERE IS THE MACHETE
SEI MONG SPEAKS SOFTLY...
TWENTY SECONDS LATER, UNHEARD BY MODESTY...
YOU ARE TO FIGHT FIRST, GARVIN... HERE IS THE MACHETE
AHHH, THE COMMISSAR IS TRICKING THEM — LOOK!

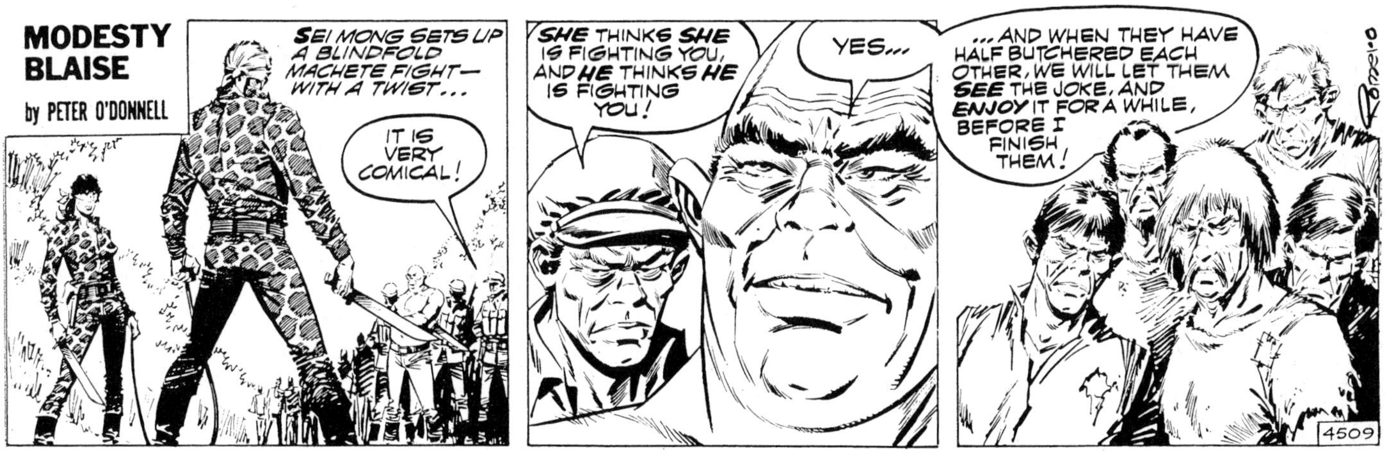
MODESTY BLAISE
by PETER O'DONNELL
SEI MONG SETS UP A BLINDFOLD MACHETE FIGHT— WITH A TWIST...
IT IS VERY COMICAL!
SHE THINKS SHE IS FIGHTING YOU, AND HE THINKS HE IS FIGHTING YOU!
YES...
...AND WHEN THEY HAVE HALF BUTCHERED EACH OTHER, WE WILL LET THEM SEE THE JOKE, AND ENJOY IT FOR A WHILE, BEFORE I FINISH THEM!
4509

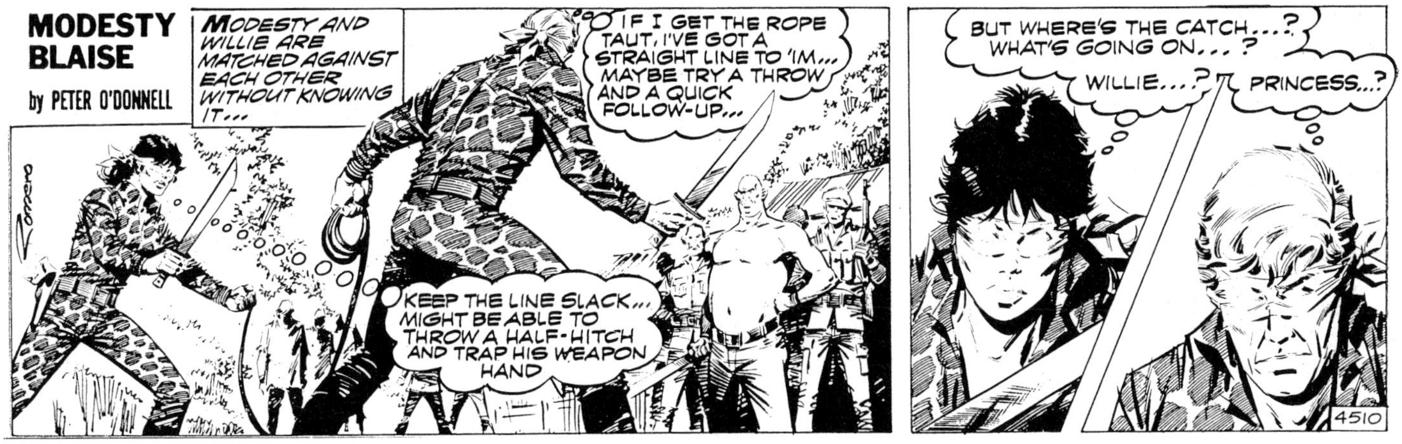
MODESTY BLAISE
by PETER O'DONNELL
MODESTY AND WILLIE ARE MATCHED AGAINST EACH OTHER WITHOUT KNOWING IT...
IF I GET THE ROPE TAUT, I'VE GOT A STRAIGHT LINE TO 'IM... MAYBE TRY A THROW AND A QUICK FOLLOW-UP...
KEEP THE LINE SLACK... MIGHT BE ABLE TO THROW A HALF-HITCH AND TRAP HIS WEAPON HAND
BUT WHERE'S THE CATCH...? WHAT'S GOING ON...?
WILLIE...?
PRINCESS...?
4510

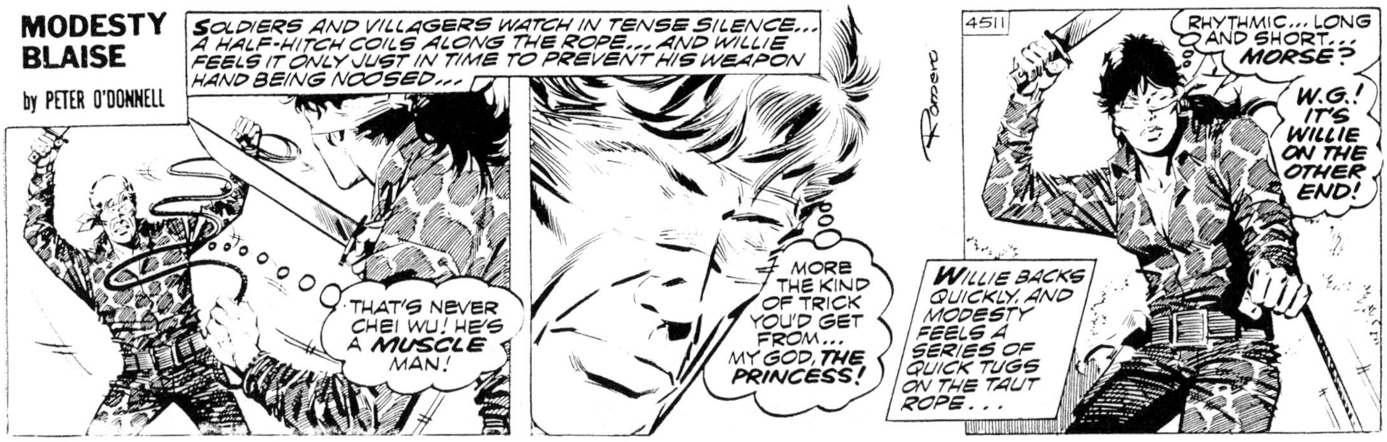
MODESTY BLAISE
by PETER O'DONNELL
SOLDIERS AND VILLAGERS WATCH IN TENSE SILENCE... A HALF-HITCH COILS ALONG THE ROPE... AND WILLIE FEELS IT ONLY JUST IN TIME TO PREVENT HIS WEAPON HAND BEING NOOSED...
THAT'S NEVER CHEI WU! HE'S A MUSCLE MAN!
MORE THE KIND OF TRICK YOU'D GET FROM... MY GOD, THE PRINCESS!
4511
RHYTHMIC... LONG AND SHORT... MORSE?
W.G.! IT'S WILLIE ON THE OTHER END!
WILLIE BACKS QUICKLY, AND MODESTY FEELS A SERIES OF QUICK TUGS ON THE TAUT ROPE...

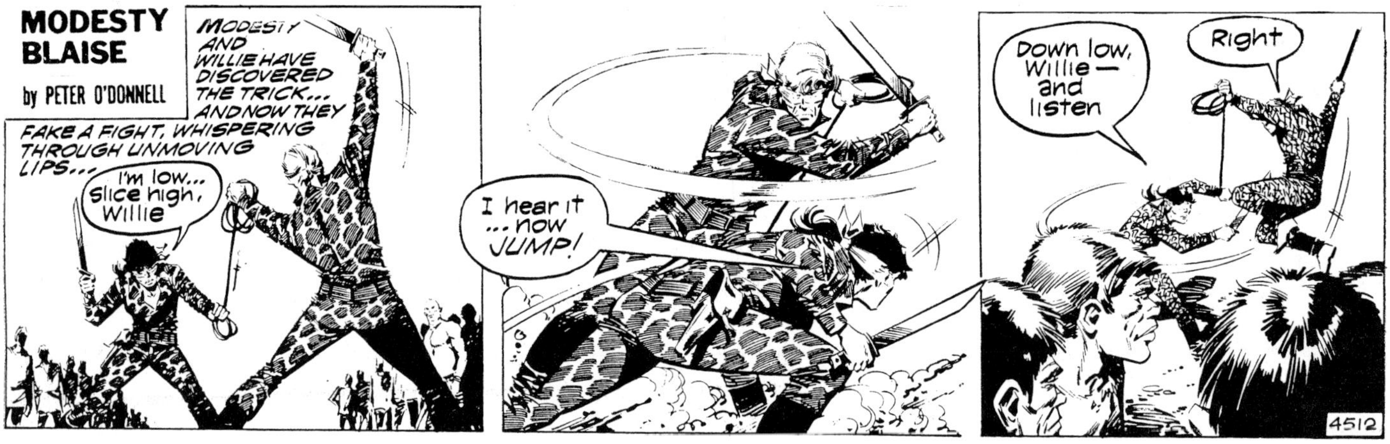
MODESTY BLAISE
by PETER O'DONNELL
MODESTY AND WILLIE HAVE DISCOVERED THE TRICK... AND NOW THEY FAKE A FIGHT, WHISPERING THROUGH UNMOVING LIPS...
I'm low... Slice high, Willie
I hear it ...now JUMP!
Down low, Willie — and listen
Right
4512

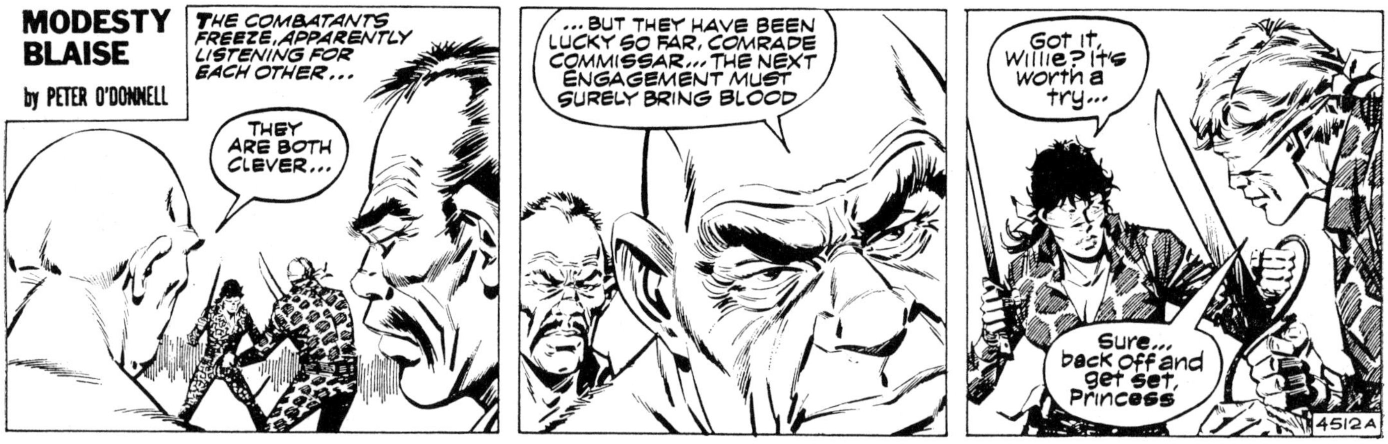
MODESTY BLAISE
by PETER O'DONNELL
THE COMBATANTS FREEZE, APPARENTLY LISTENING FOR EACH OTHER...
THEY ARE BOTH CLEVER...
...BUT THEY HAVE BEEN LUCKY SO FAR, COMRADE COMMISSAR... THE NEXT ENGAGEMENT MUST SURELY BRING BLOOD
Got it, Willie? It's worth a try...
Sure... back off and get set, Princess
4512A

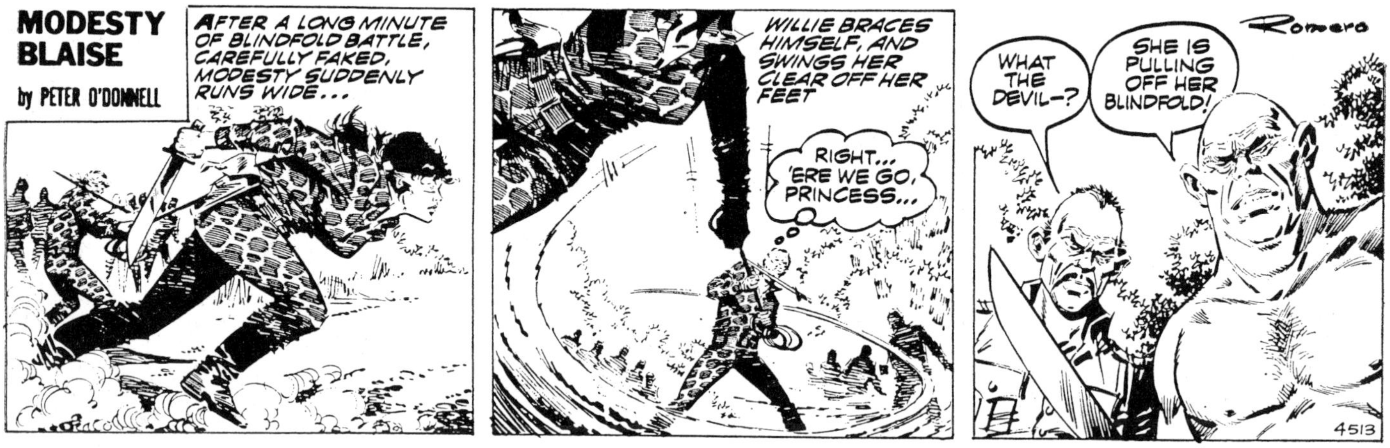
MODESTY BLAISE
by PETER O'DONNELL
AFTER A LONG MINUTE OF BLINDFOLD BATTLE, CAREFULLY FAKED, MODESTY SUDDENLY RUNS WIDE...
WILLIE BRACES HIMSELF, AND SWINGS HER CLEAR OFF HER FEET
RIGHT... 'ERE WE GO, PRINCESS...
Romero
WHAT THE DEVIL—?
SHE IS PULLING OFF HER BLINDFOLD!
4513

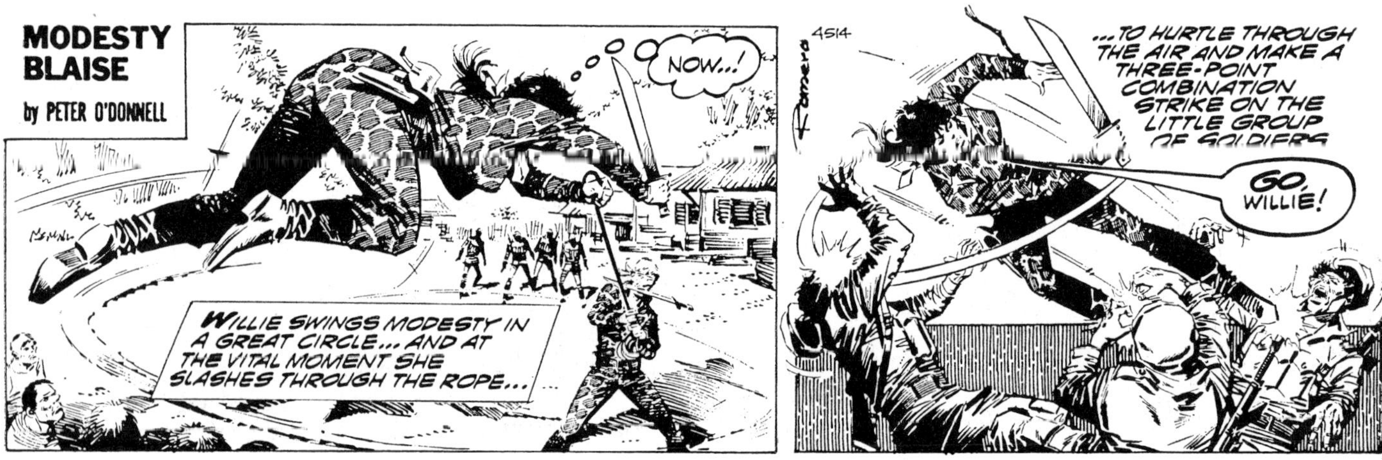
MODESTY BLAISE
by PETER O'DONNELL
NOW..!
WILLIE SWINGS MODESTY IN A GREAT CIRCLE... AND AT THE VITAL MOMENT SHE SLASHES THROUGH THE ROPE...
Romero
4514
...TO HURTLE THROUGH THE AIR AND MAKE A THREE-POINT COMBINATION STRIKE ON THE LITTLE GROUP OF SOLDIERS
GO, WILLIE!

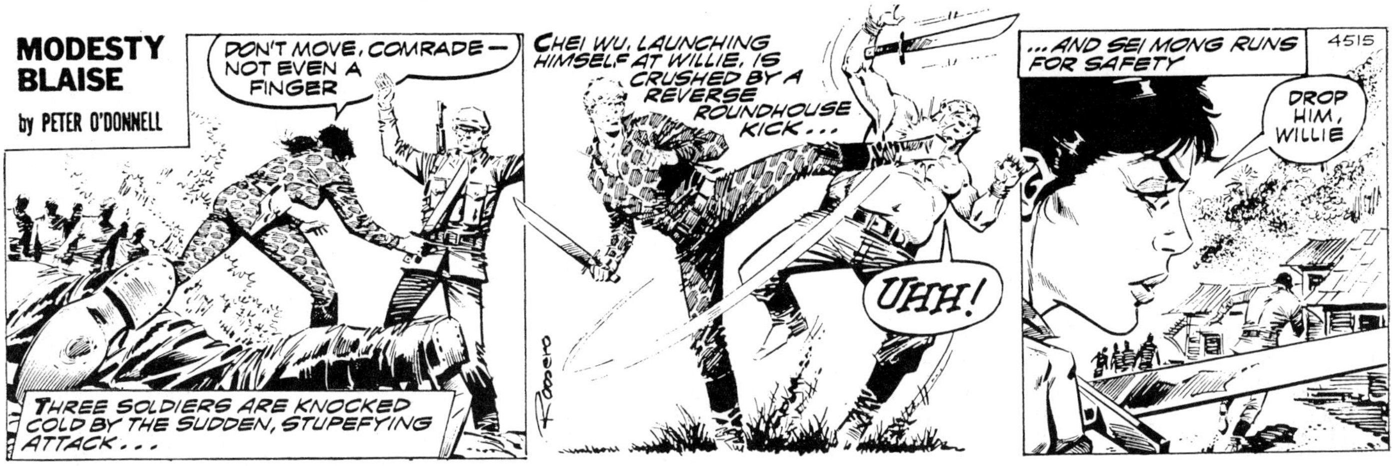
MODESTY BLAISE
by PETER O'DONNELL
DON'T MOVE, COMRADE — NOT EVEN A FINGER
THREE SOLDIERS ARE KNOCKED COLD BY THE SUDDEN, STUPEFYING ATTACK . . .
CHEI WU, LAUNCHING HIMSELF AT WILLIE, IS CRUSHED BY A REVERSE ROUNDHOUSE KICK . . .
UHH!
... AND SEI MONG RUNS FOR SAFETY
4515
DROP HIM, WILLIE

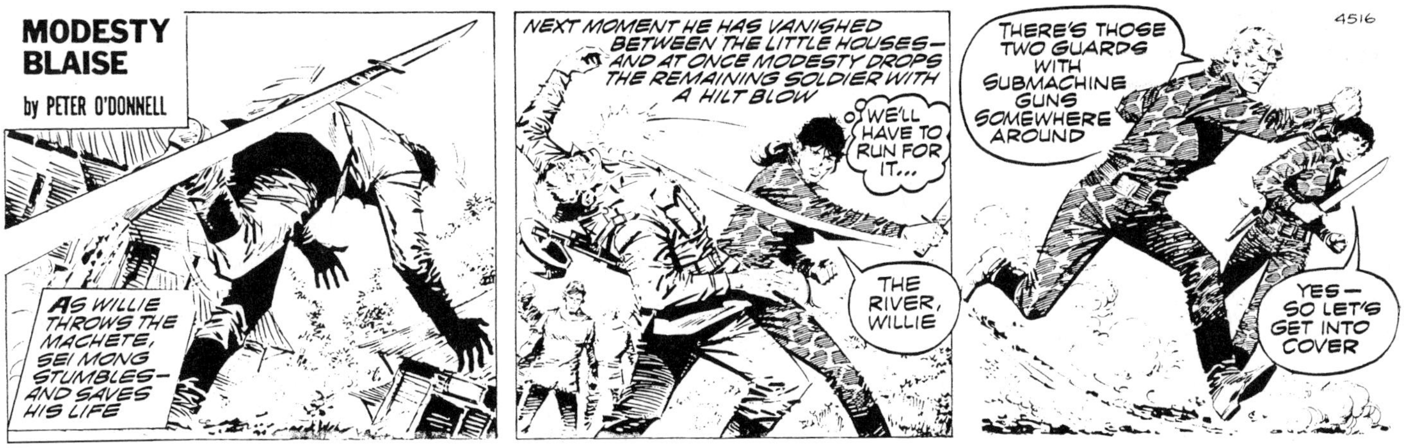
MODESTY BLAISE
by PETER O'DONNELL
AS WILLIE THROWS THE MACHETE, SEI MONG STUMBLES— AND SAVES HIS LIFE
NEXT MOMENT HE HAS VANISHED BETWEEN THE LITTLE HOUSES— AND AT ONCE MODESTY DROPS THE REMAINING SOLDIER WITH A HILT BLOW
WE'LL HAVE TO RUN FOR IT...
THE RIVER, WILLIE
4516
THERE'S THOSE TWO GUARDS WITH SUBMACHINE GUNS SOMEWHERE AROUND
YES— SO LET'S GET INTO COVER

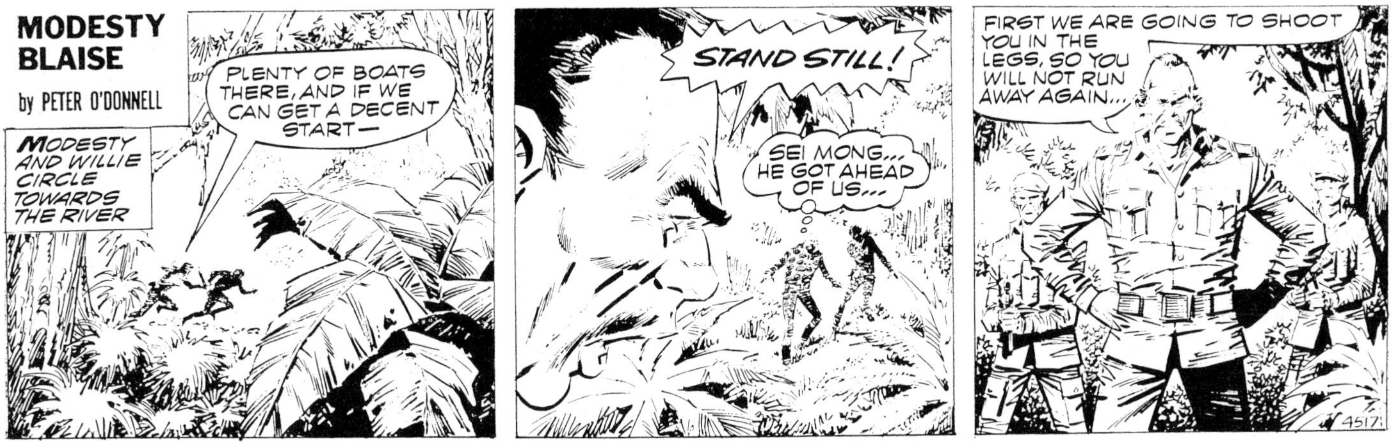
MODESTY BLAISE
by PETER O'DONNELL
MODESTY AND WILLIE CIRCLE TOWARDS THE RIVER
PLENTY OF BOATS THERE, AND IF WE CAN GET A DECENT START—
STAND STILL!
SEI MONG... HE GOT AHEAD OF US...
FIRST WE ARE GOING TO SHOOT YOU IN THE LEGS, SO YOU WILL NOT RUN AWAY AGAIN...
4517

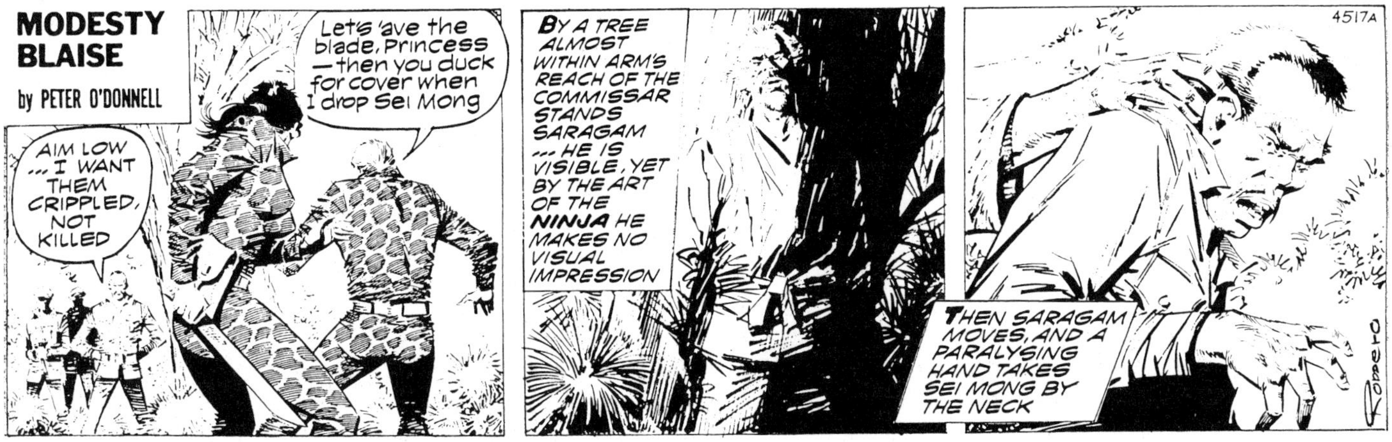
MODESTY BLAISE
by PETER O'DONNELL
Let's 'ave the blade, Princess —then you duck for cover when I drop Sei Mong
AIM LOW ... I WANT THEM CRIPPLED, NOT KILLED
BY A TREE ALMOST WITHIN ARM'S REACH OF THE COMMISSAR STANDS SARAGAM ... HE IS VISIBLE, YET BY THE ART OF THE NINJA HE MAKES NO VISUAL IMPRESSION
4517A
THEN SARAGAM MOVES, AND A PARALYSING HAND TAKES SEI MONG BY THE NECK

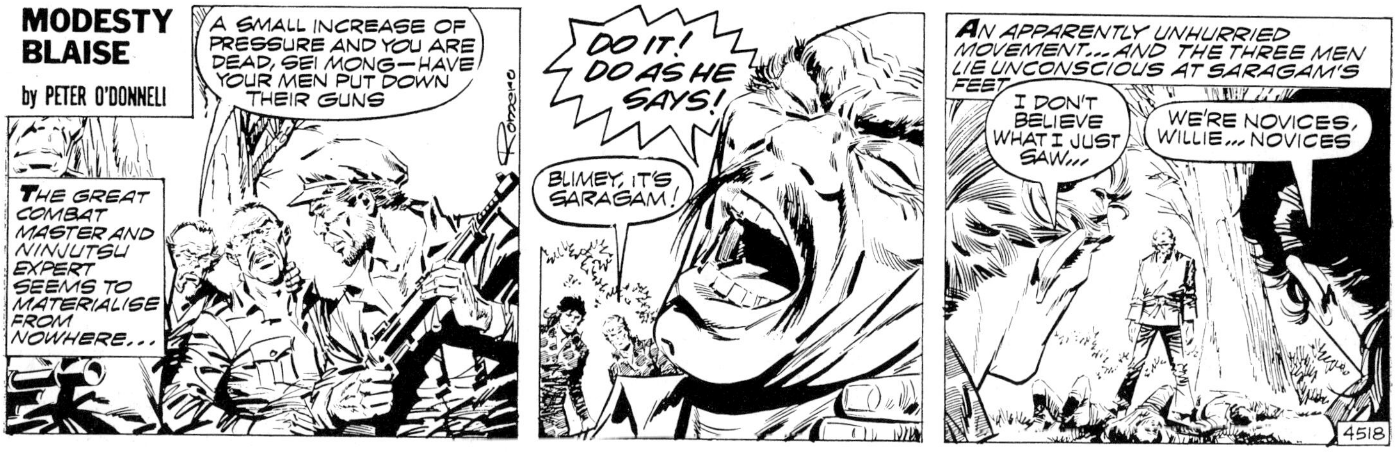
MODESTY BLAISE
by PETER O'DONNELL
THE GREAT COMBAT MASTER AND NINJUTSU EXPERT SEEMS TO MATERIALISE FROM NOWHERE...
A SMALL INCREASE OF PRESSURE AND YOU ARE DEAD, SEI MONG—HAVE YOUR MEN PUT DOWN THEIR GUNS
DO IT! DO AS HE SAYS!
BLIMEY, IT'S SARAGAM!
AN APPARENTLY UNHURRIED MOVEMENT... AND THE THREE MEN LIE UNCONSCIOUS AT SARAGAM'S FEET
I DON'T BELIEVE WHAT I JUST SAW...
WE'RE NOVICES, WILLIE... NOVICES
4518

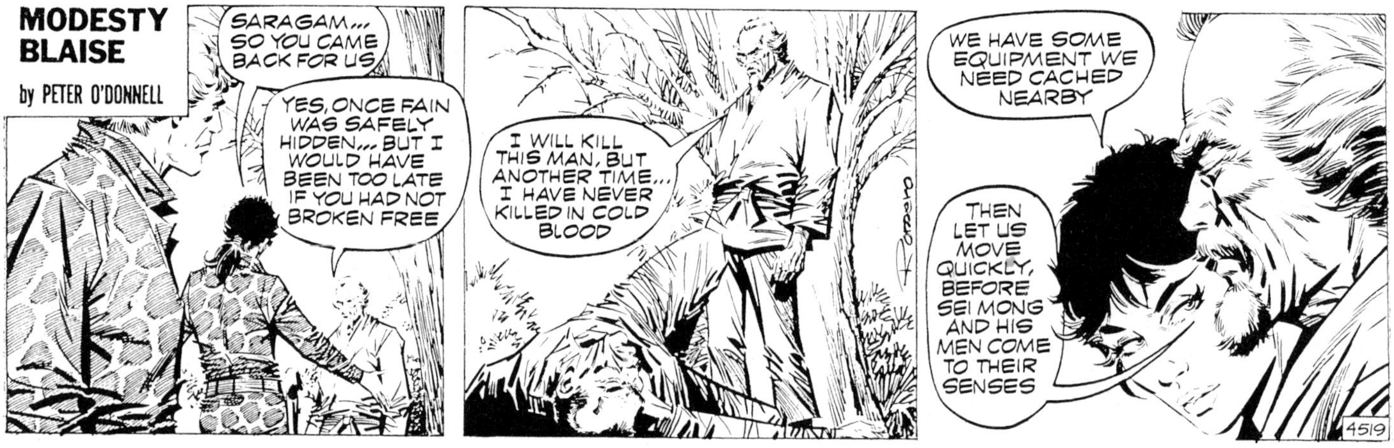
MODESTY BLAISE
by PETER O'DONNELL
SARAGAM... SO YOU CAME BACK FOR US
YES, ONCE FAIN WAS SAFELY HIDDEN... BUT I WOULD HAVE BEEN TOO LATE IF YOU HAD NOT BROKEN FREE
I WILL KILL THIS MAN, BUT ANOTHER TIME... I HAVE NEVER KILLED IN COLD BLOOD
WE HAVE SOME EQUIPMENT WE NEED CACHED NEARBY
THEN LET US MOVE QUICKLY, BEFORE SEI MONG AND HIS MEN COME TO THEIR SENSES
4519

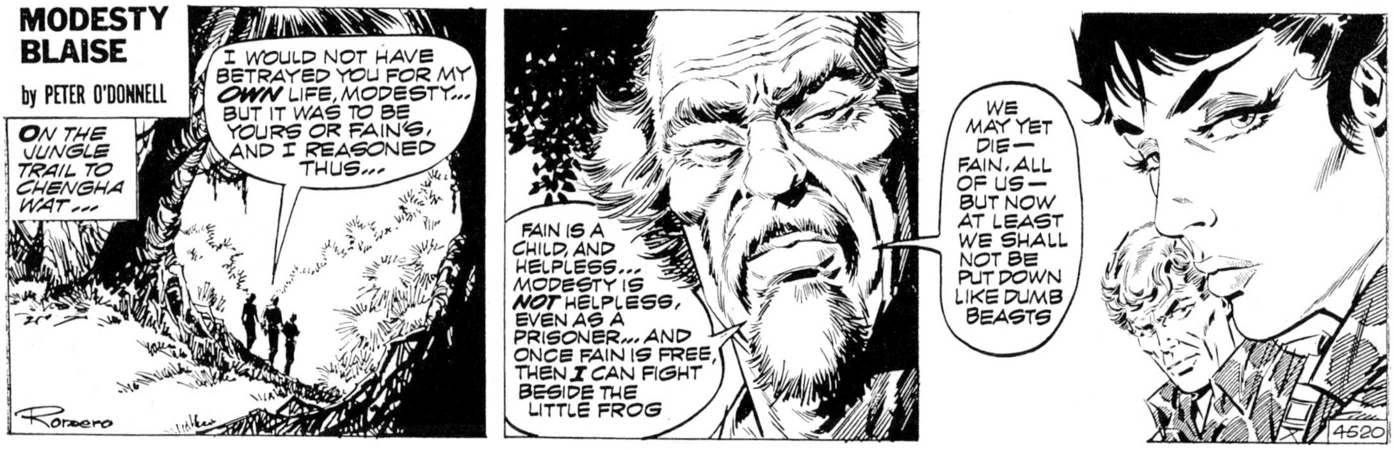
MODESTY BLAISE
by PETER O'DONNELL
ON THE JUNGLE TRAIL TO CHENGHA WAT...
I WOULD NOT HAVE BETRAYED YOU FOR MY OWN LIFE, MODESTY... BUT IT WAS TO BE YOURS OR FAIN'S, AND I REASONED THUS...
FAIN IS A CHILD, AND HELPLESS... MODESTY IS NOT HELPLESS, EVEN AS A PRISONER... AND ONCE FAIN IS FREE, THEN I CAN FIGHT BESIDE THE LITTLE FROG
WE MAY YET DIE—FAIN, ALL OF US—BUT NOW AT LEAST WE SHALL NOT BE PUT DOWN LIKE DUMB BEASTS
4520

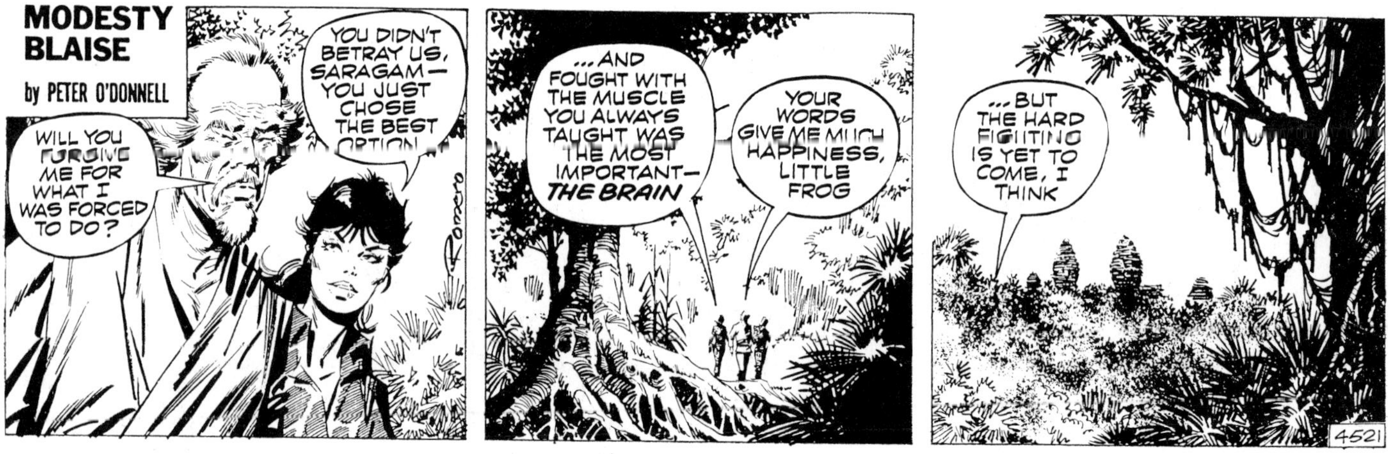
MODESTY BLAISE
by PETER O'DONNELL
WILL YOU FORGIVE ME FOR WHAT I WAS FORCED TO DO?
YOU DIDN'T BETRAY US, SARAGAM—YOU JUST CHOSE THE BEST OPTION
...AND FOUGHT WITH THE MUSCLE YOU ALWAYS TAUGHT WAS THE MOST IMPORTANT—THE BRAIN
YOUR WORDS GIVE ME MUCH HAPPINESS, LITTLE FROG
...BUT THE HARD FIGHTING IS YET TO COME, I THINK
4521

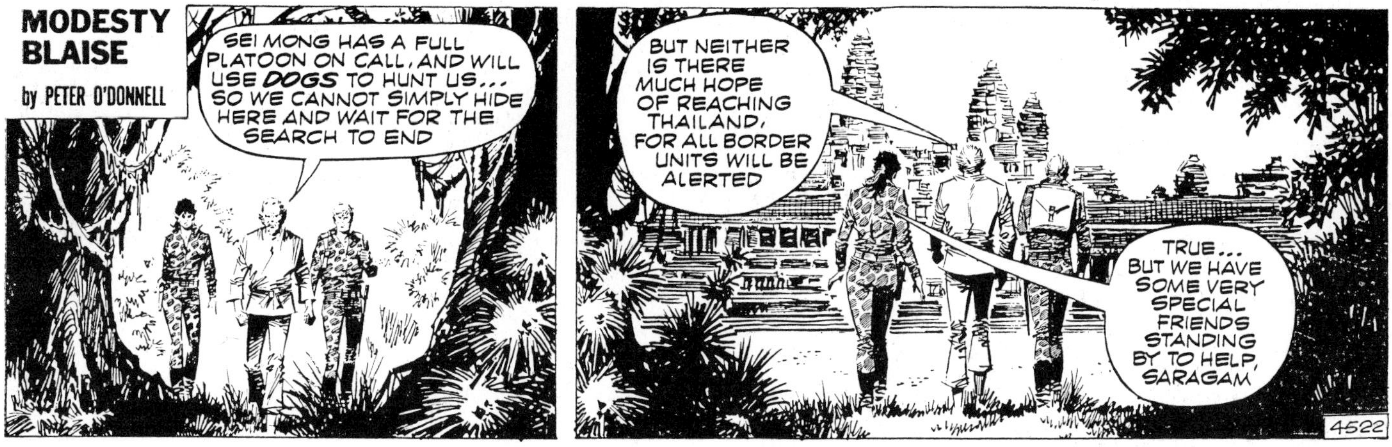
MODESTY BLAISE
by PETER O'DONNELL
SEI MONG HAS A FULL PLATOON ON CALL, AND WILL USE DOGS TO HUNT US... SO WE CANNOT SIMPLY HIDE HERE AND WAIT FOR THE SEARCH TO END
BUT NEITHER IS THERE MUCH HOPE OF REACHING THAILAND, FOR ALL BORDER UNITS WILL BE ALERTED
TRUE... BUT WE HAVE SOME VERY SPECIAL FRIENDS STANDING BY TO HELP, SARAGAM
4522

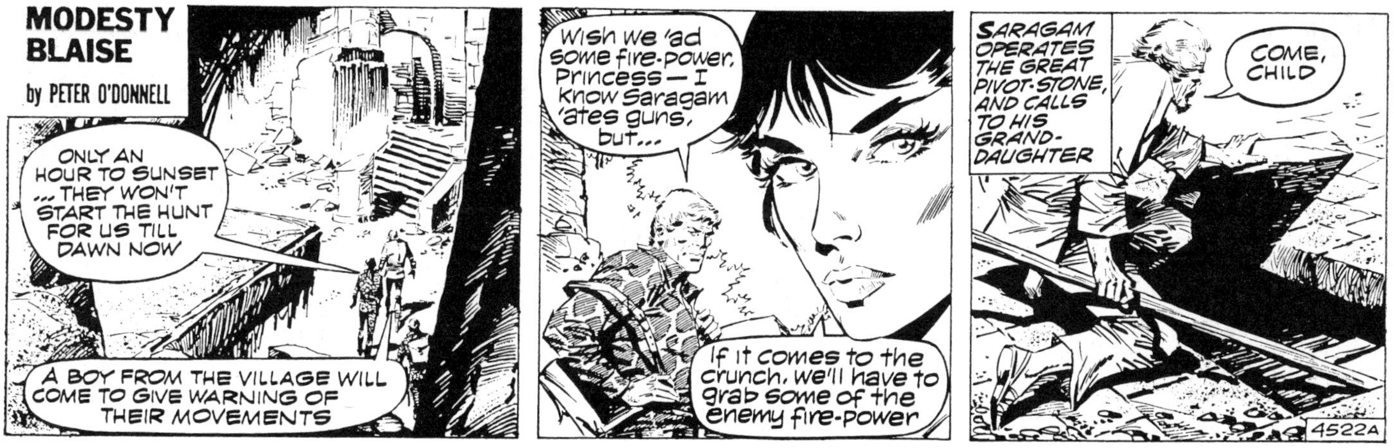
MODESTY BLAISE
by PETER O'DONNELL
ONLY AN HOUR TO SUNSET ... THEY WON'T START THE HUNT FOR US TILL DAWN NOW
A BOY FROM THE VILLAGE WILL COME TO GIVE WARNING OF THEIR MOVEMENTS
Wish we 'ad some fire-power, Princess — I know Saragam 'ates guns, but...
If it comes to the crunch, we'll have to grab some of the enemy fire-power
SARAGAM OPERATES THE GREAT PIVOT-STONE, AND CALLS TO HIS GRAND-DAUGHTER
COME, CHILD
4522A

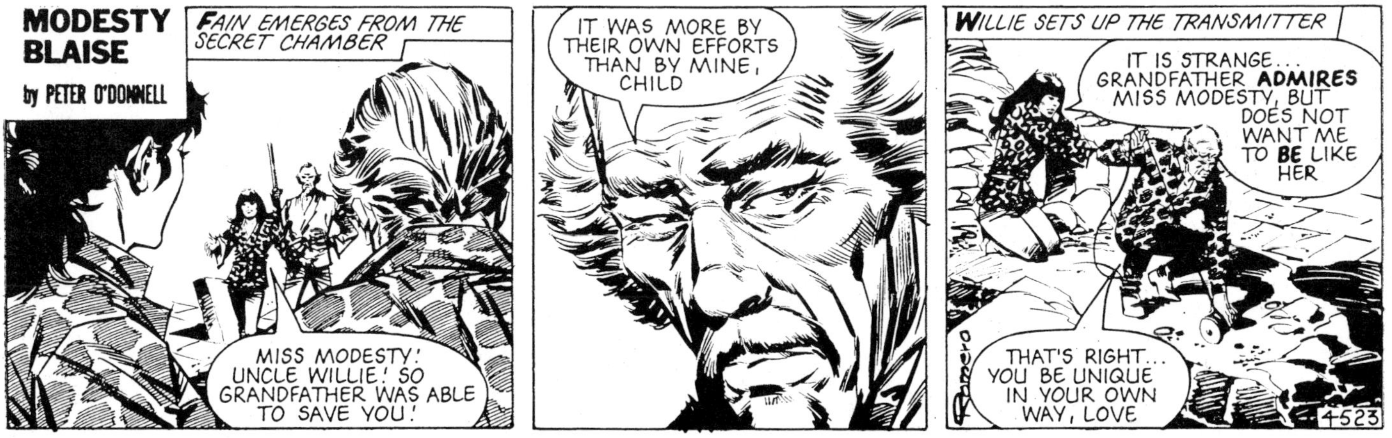
MODESTY BLAISE
by PETER O'DONNELL
FAIN EMERGES FROM THE SECRET CHAMBER
MISS MODESTY! UNCLE WILLIE! SO GRANDFATHER WAS ABLE TO SAVE YOU!
IT WAS MORE BY THEIR OWN EFFORTS THAN BY MINE, CHILD
WILLIE SETS UP THE TRANSMITTER
IT IS STRANGE... GRANDFATHER ADMIRES MISS MODESTY, BUT DOES NOT WANT ME TO BE LIKE HER
THAT'S RIGHT... YOU BE UNIQUE IN YOUR OWN WAY, LOVE
4523

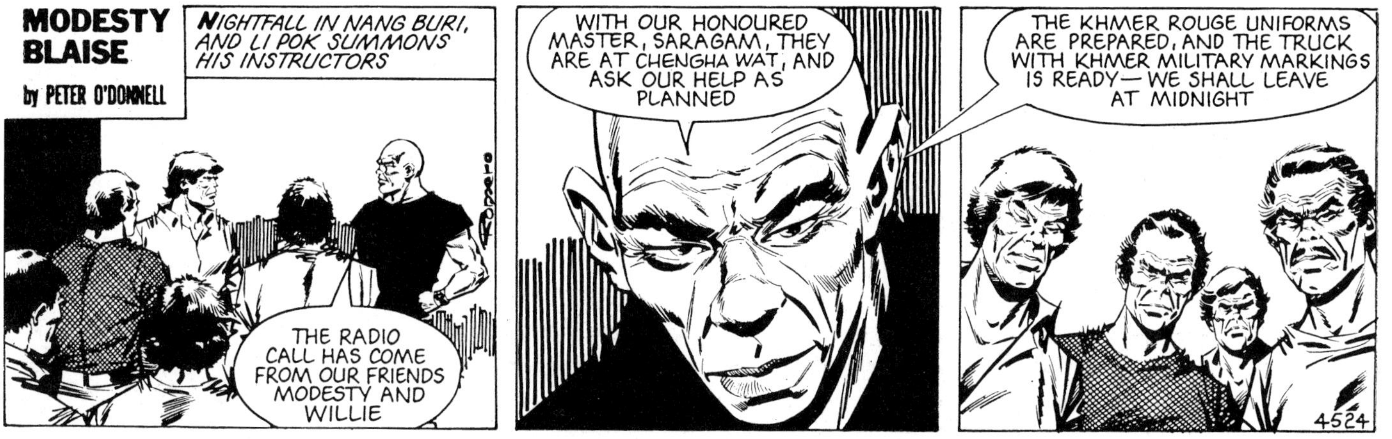
MODESTY BLAISE
by PETER O'DONNELL
NIGHTFALL IN NANG BURI, AND LI POK SUMMONS HIS INSTRUCTORS
THE RADIO CALL HAS COME FROM OUR FRIENDS MODESTY AND WILLIE
WITH OUR HONOURED MASTER, SARAGAM, THEY ARE AT CHENGHA WAT, AND ASK OUR HELP AS PLANNED
THE KHMER ROUGE UNIFORMS ARE PREPARED, AND THE TRUCK WITH KHMER MILITARY MARKINGS IS READY— WE SHALL LEAVE AT MIDNIGHT
4524

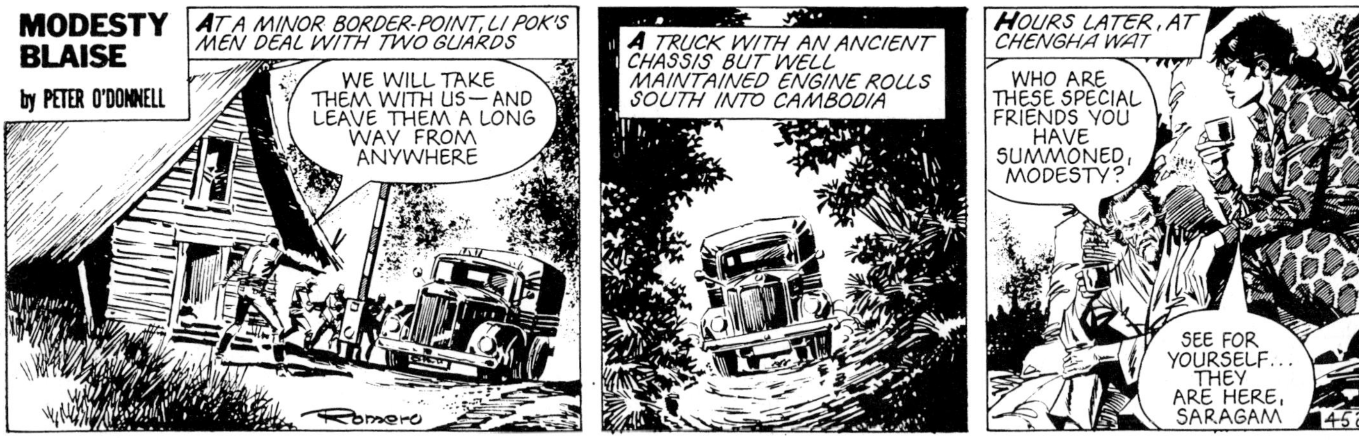
MODESTY BLAISE
by PETER O'DONNELL
AT A MINOR BORDER-POINT, LI POK'S MEN DEAL WITH TWO GUARDS
WE WILL TAKE THEM WITH US — AND LEAVE THEM A LONG WAY FROM ANYWHERE
Romero
A TRUCK WITH AN ANCIENT CHASSIS BUT WELL MAINTAINED ENGINE ROLLS SOUTH INTO CAMBODIA
HOURS LATER, AT CHENGHA WAT
WHO ARE THESE SPECIAL FRIENDS YOU HAVE SUMMONED, MODESTY?
SEE FOR YOURSELF... THEY ARE HERE, SARAGAM
4525

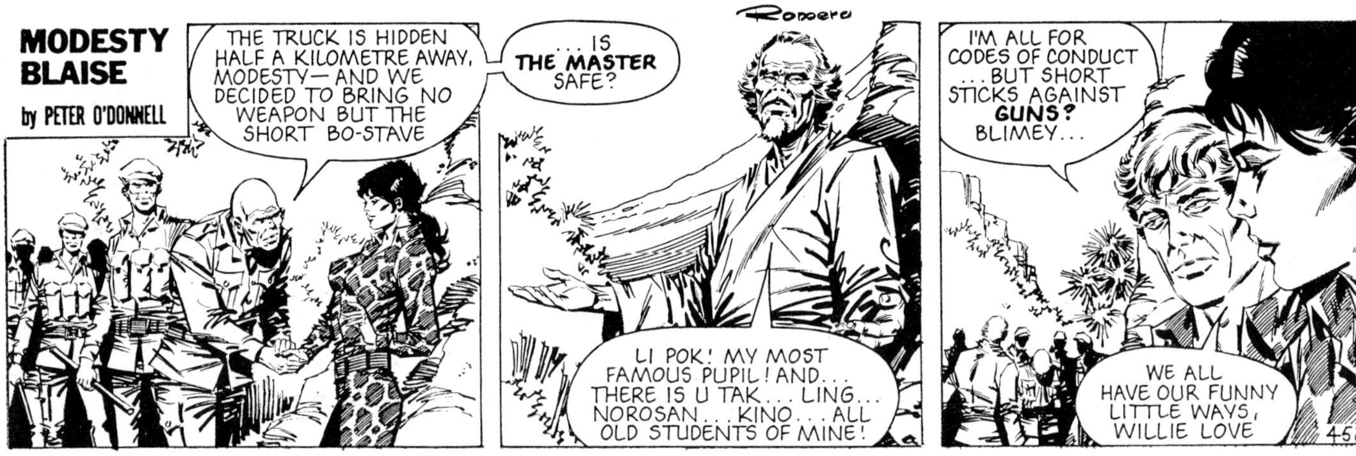
MODESTY BLAISE
by PETER O'DONNELL
THE TRUCK IS HIDDEN HALF A KILOMETRE AWAY, MODESTY — AND WE DECIDED TO BRING NO WEAPON BUT THE SHORT BO-STAVE
... IS THE MASTER SAFE?
Romero
LI POK! MY MOST FAMOUS PUPIL! AND... THERE IS U TAK... LING... NOROSAN... KINO... ALL OLD STUDENTS OF MINE!
I'M ALL FOR CODES OF CONDUCT ... BUT SHORT STICKS AGAINST GUNS? BLIMEY...
WE ALL HAVE OUR FUNNY LITTLE WAYS, WILLIE LOVE
4526

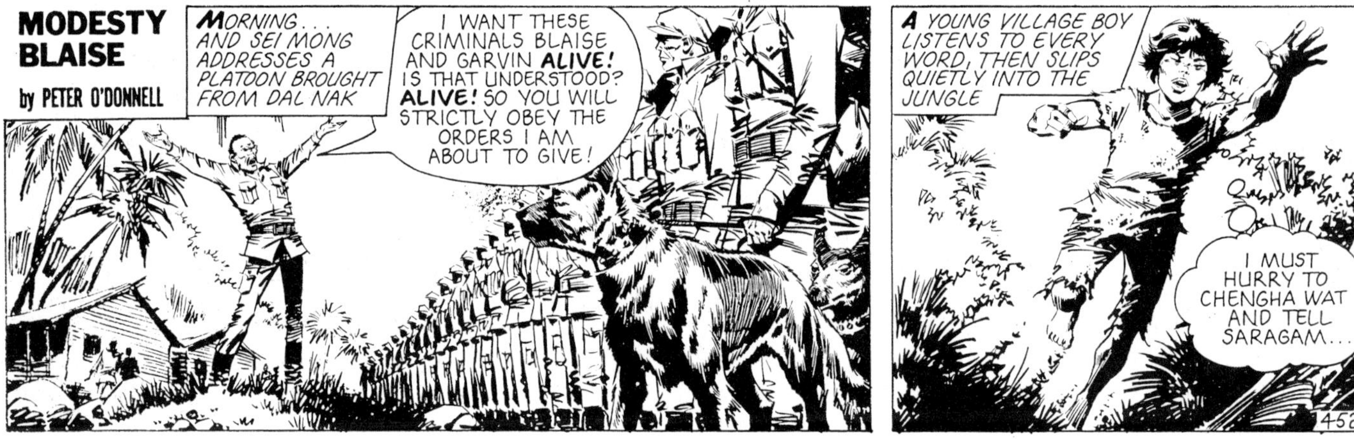
MODESTY BLAISE
by PETER O'DONNELL
MORNING... AND SEI MONG ADDRESSES A PLATOON BROUGHT FROM DAL NAK
I WANT THESE CRIMINALS BLAISE AND GARVIN ALIVE! IS THAT UNDERSTOOD? ALIVE! SO YOU WILL STRICTLY OBEY THE ORDERS I AM ABOUT TO GIVE!
A YOUNG VILLAGE BOY LISTENS TO EVERY WORD, THEN SLIPS QUIETLY INTO THE JUNGLE
Romero
I MUST HURRY TO CHENGHA WAT AND TELL SARAGAM...
4527

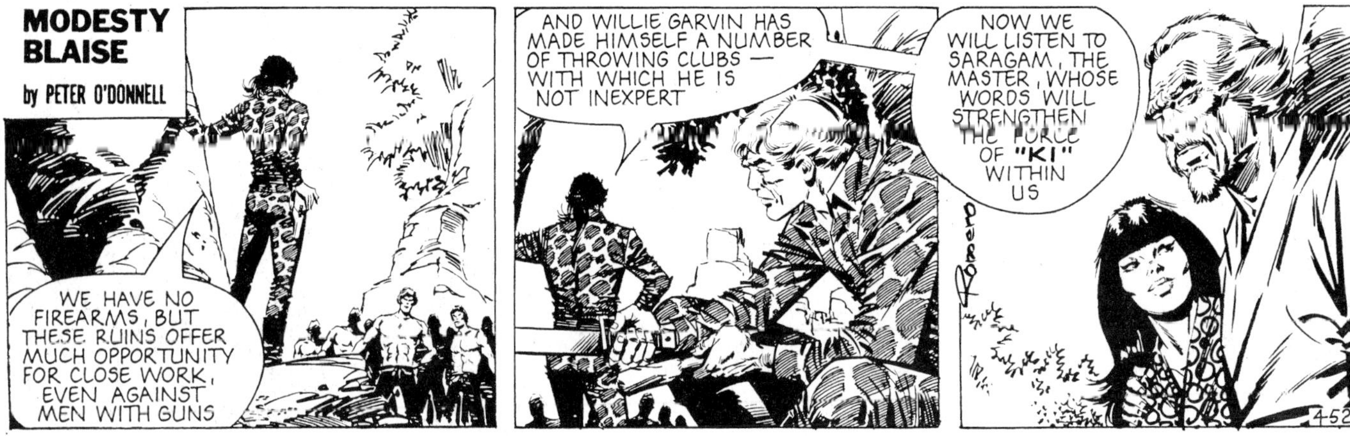
MODESTY BLAISE
by PETER O'DONNELL
WE HAVE NO FIREARMS, BUT THESE RUINS OFFER MUCH OPPORTUNITY FOR CLOSE WORK, EVEN AGAINST MEN WITH GUNS
AND WILLIE GARVIN HAS MADE HIMSELF A NUMBER OF THROWING CLUBS — WITH WHICH HE IS NOT INEXPERT
Romero
NOW WE WILL LISTEN TO SARAGAM, THE MASTER, WHOSE WORDS WILL STRENGTHEN THE FORCE OF "KI" WITHIN US
4527A

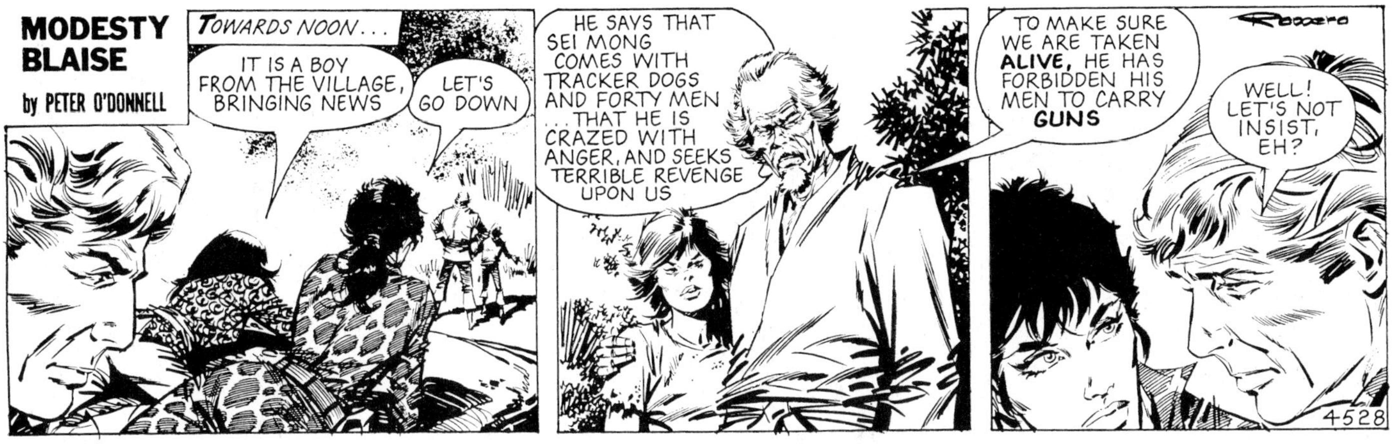
MODESTY BLAISE
by PETER O'DONNELL
TOWARDS NOON...
IT IS A BOY FROM THE VILLAGE, BRINGING NEWS
LET'S GO DOWN
HE SAYS THAT SEI MONG COMES WITH TRACKER DOGS AND FORTY MEN ...THAT HE IS CRAZED WITH ANGER, AND SEEKS TERRIBLE REVENGE UPON US
TO MAKE SURE WE ARE TAKEN ALIVE, HE HAS FORBIDDEN HIS MEN TO CARRY GUNS
WELL! LET'S NOT INSIST, EH?
4528

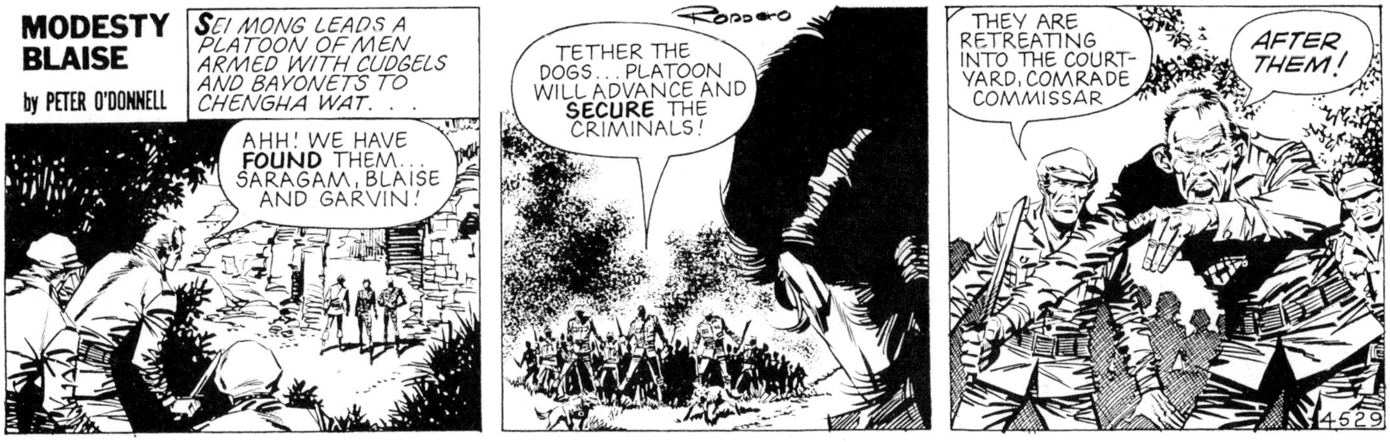
MODESTY BLAISE
by PETER O'DONNELL
SEI MONG LEADS A PLATOON OF MEN ARMED WITH CUDGELS AND BAYONETS TO CHENGHA WAT. . .
AHH! WE HAVE FOUND THEM... SARAGAM, BLAISE AND GARVIN!
TETHER THE DOGS... PLATOON WILL ADVANCE AND SECURE THE CRIMINALS!
THEY ARE RETREATING INTO THE COURT-YARD, COMRADE COMMISSAR
AFTER THEM!
4529

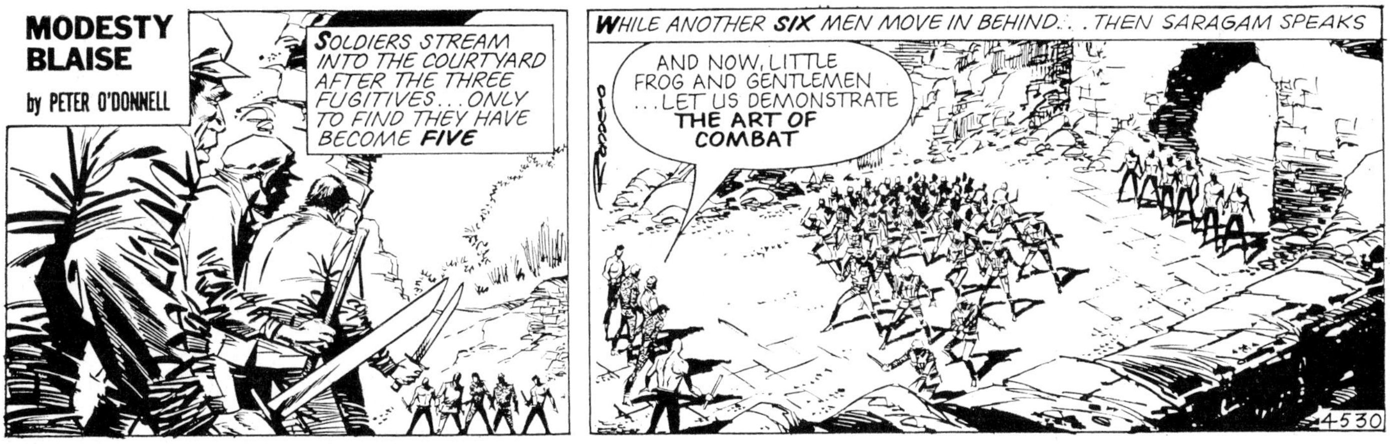
MODESTY BLAISE
by PETER O'DONNELL
SOLDIERS STREAM INTO THE COURTYARD AFTER THE THREE FUGITIVES... ONLY TO FIND THEY HAVE BECOME FIVE
WHILE ANOTHER SIX MEN MOVE IN BEHIND... THEN SARAGAM SPEAKS
AND NOW, LITTLE FROG AND GENTLEMEN ...LET US DEMONSTRATE THE ART OF COMBAT
4530

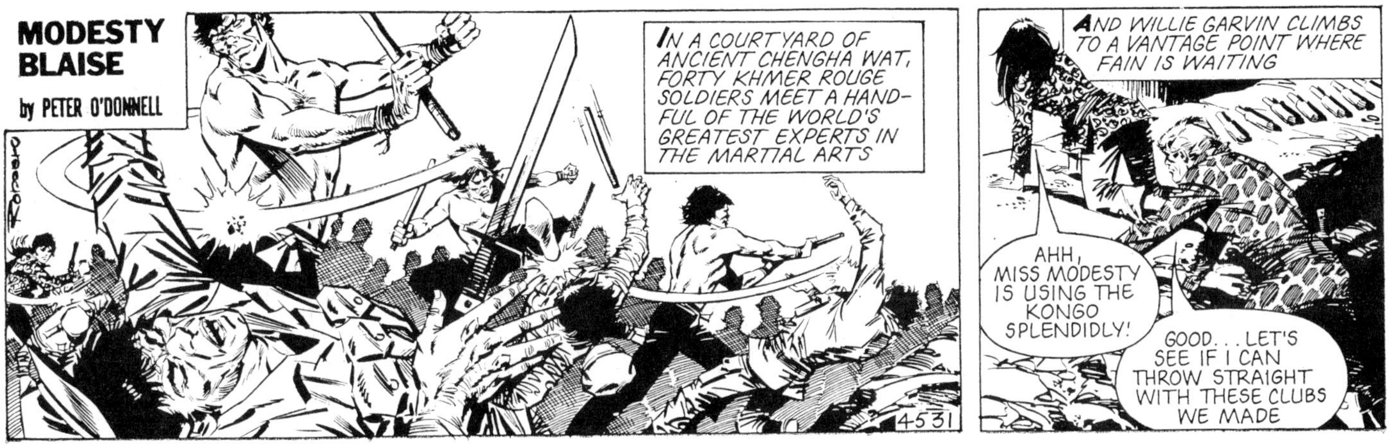
MODESTY BLAISE
by PETER O'DONNELL
IN A COURTYARD OF ANCIENT CHENGHA WAT, FORTY KHMER ROUGE SOLDIERS MEET A HAND-FUL OF THE WORLD'S GREATEST EXPERTS IN THE MARTIAL ARTS
4531
AND WILLIE GARVIN CLIMBS TO A VANTAGE POINT WHERE FAIN IS WAITING
AHH, MISS MODESTY IS USING THE KONGO SPLENDIDLY!
GOOD... LET'S SEE IF I CAN THROW STRAIGHT WITH THESE CLUBS WE MADE

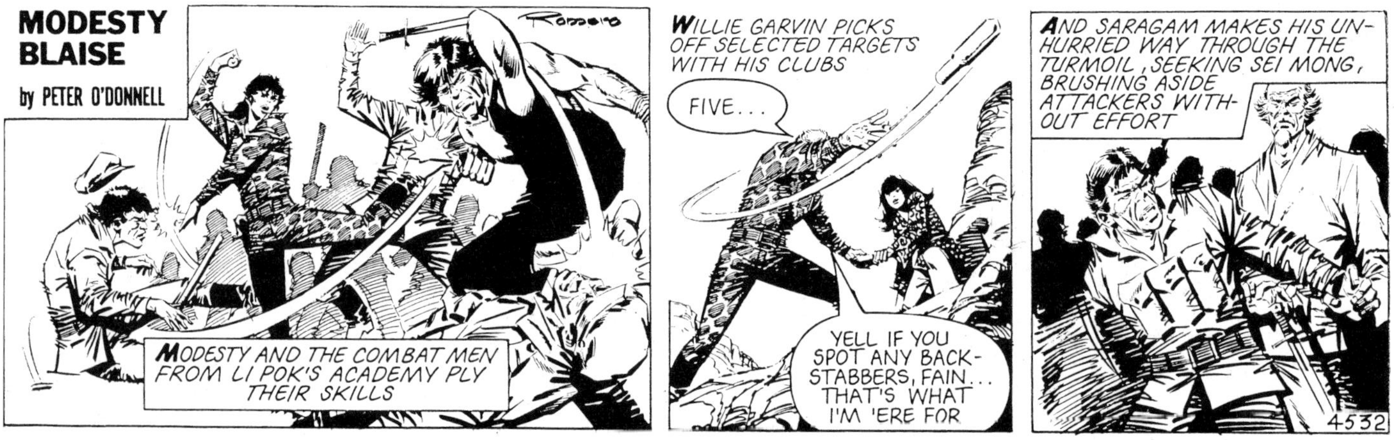
MODESTY BLAISE
by PETER O'DONNELL
Romero
MODESTY AND THE COMBAT MEN FROM LI POK'S ACADEMY PLY THEIR SKILLS
WILLIE GARVIN PICKS OFF SELECTED TARGETS WITH HIS CLUBS
FIVE...
YELL IF YOU SPOT ANY BACK-STABBERS, FAIN... THAT'S WHAT I'M 'ERE FOR
AND SARAGAM MAKES HIS UNHURRIED WAY THROUGH THE TURMOIL, SEEKING SEI MONG, BRUSHING ASIDE ATTACKERS WITHOUT EFFORT
4532

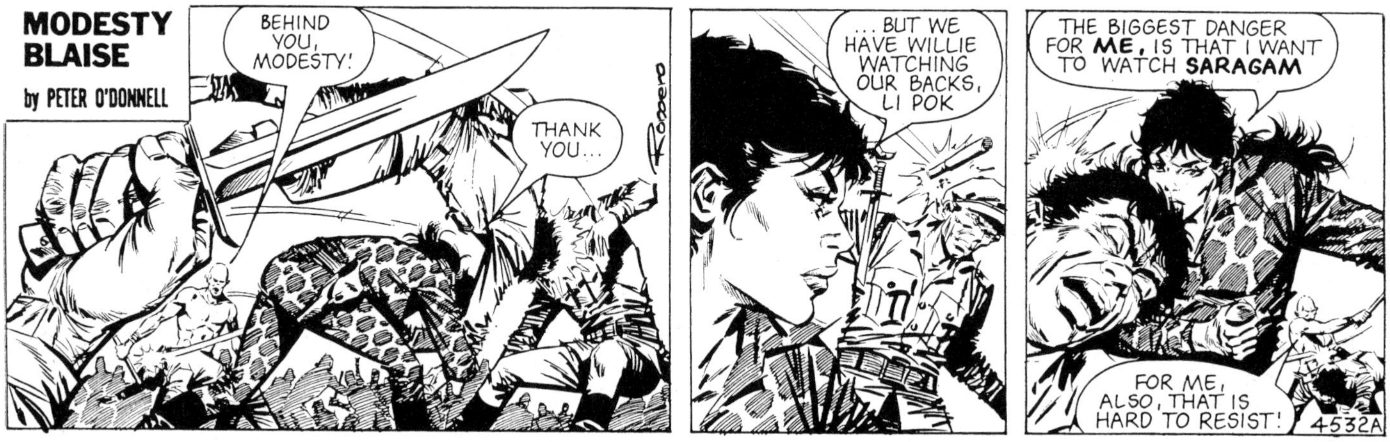
MODESTY BLAISE
by PETER O'DONNELL
BEHIND YOU, MODESTY!
THANK YOU...
Romero
...BUT WE HAVE WILLIE WATCHING OUR BACKS, LI POK
THE BIGGEST DANGER FOR ME, IS THAT I WANT TO WATCH SARAGAM
FOR ME, ALSO, THAT IS HARD TO RESIST!
4532A

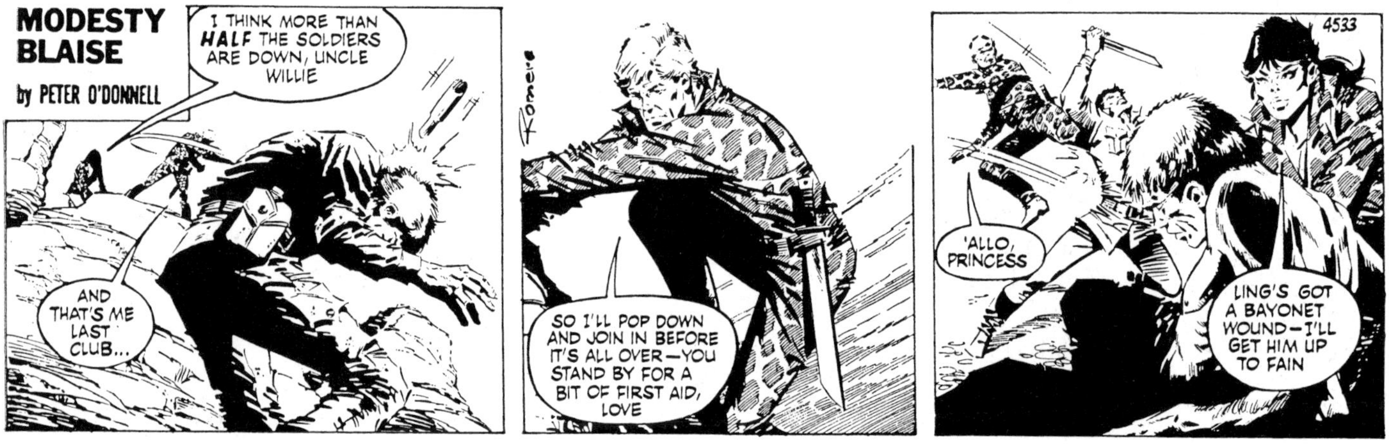
MODESTY BLAISE
by PETER O'DONNELL
I THINK MORE THAN HALF THE SOLDIERS ARE DOWN, UNCLE WILLIE
AND THAT'S ME LAST CLUB...
Romero
SO I'LL POP DOWN AND JOIN IN BEFORE IT'S ALL OVER—YOU STAND BY FOR A BIT OF FIRST AID, LOVE
4533
'ALLO, PRINCESS
LING'S GOT A BAYONET WOUND—I'LL GET HIM UP TO FAIN

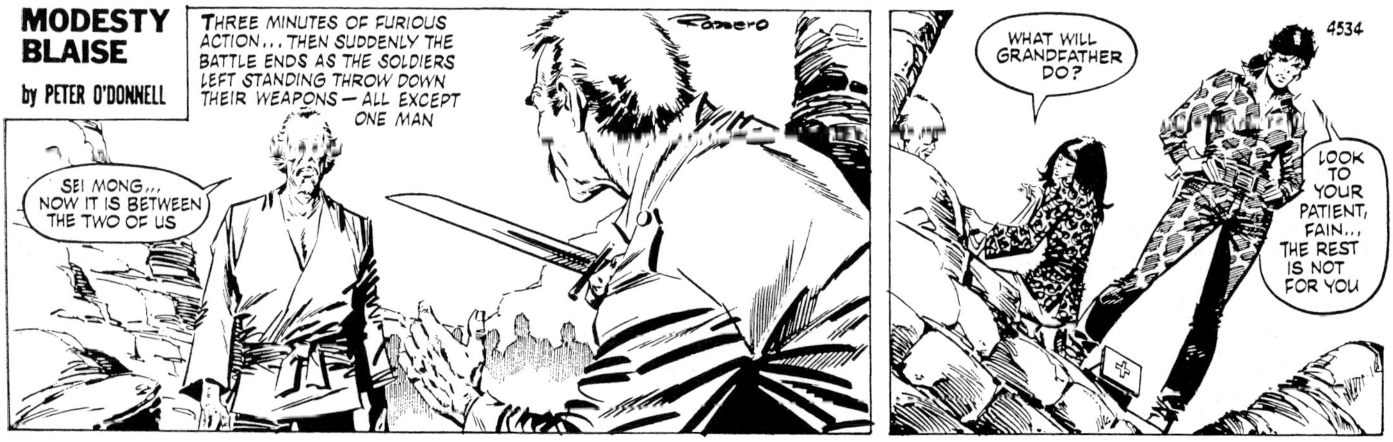
MODESTY BLAISE
by PETER O'DONNELL
THREE MINUTES OF FURIOUS ACTION... THEN SUDDENLY THE BATTLE ENDS AS THE SOLDIERS LEFT STANDING THROW DOWN THEIR WEAPONS—ALL EXCEPT ONE MAN
Romero
SEI MONG... NOW IT IS BETWEEN THE TWO OF US
4534
WHAT WILL GRANDFATHER DO?
LOOK TO YOUR PATIENT, FAIN... THE REST IS NOT FOR YOU

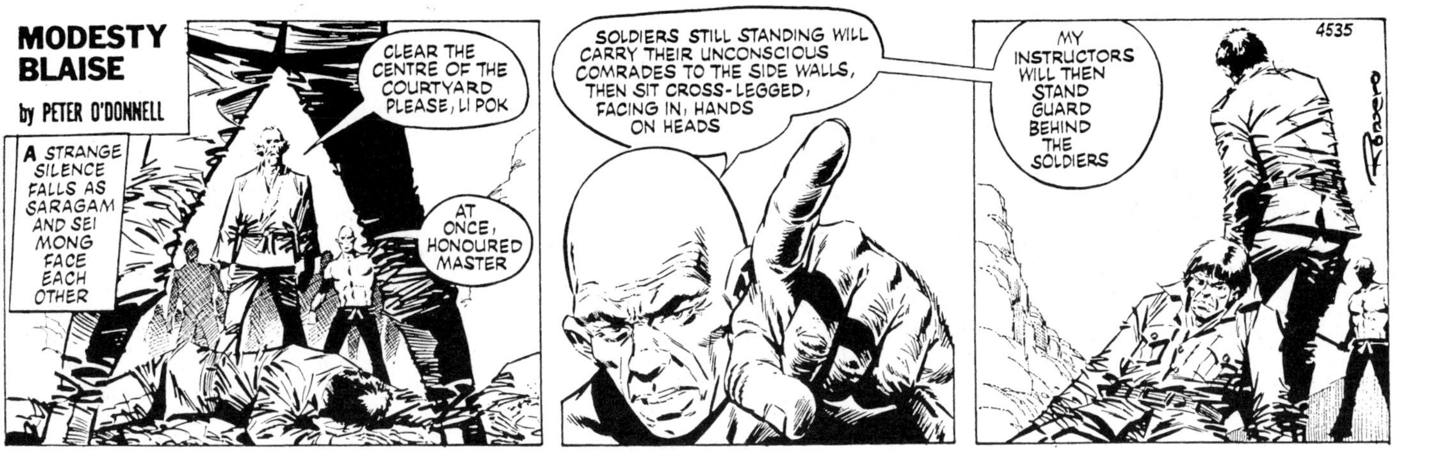
MODESTY BLAISE
by PETER O'DONNELL
A STRANGE SILENCE FALLS AS SARAGAM AND SEI MONG FACE EACH OTHER
CLEAR THE CENTRE OF THE COURTYARD PLEASE, LI POK
AT ONCE, HONOURED MASTER
SOLDIERS STILL STANDING WILL CARRY THEIR UNCONSCIOUS COMRADES TO THE SIDE WALLS, THEN SIT CROSS-LEGGED, FACING IN, HANDS ON HEADS
MY INSTRUCTORS WILL THEN STAND GUARD BEHIND THE SOLDIERS
4535
Romero

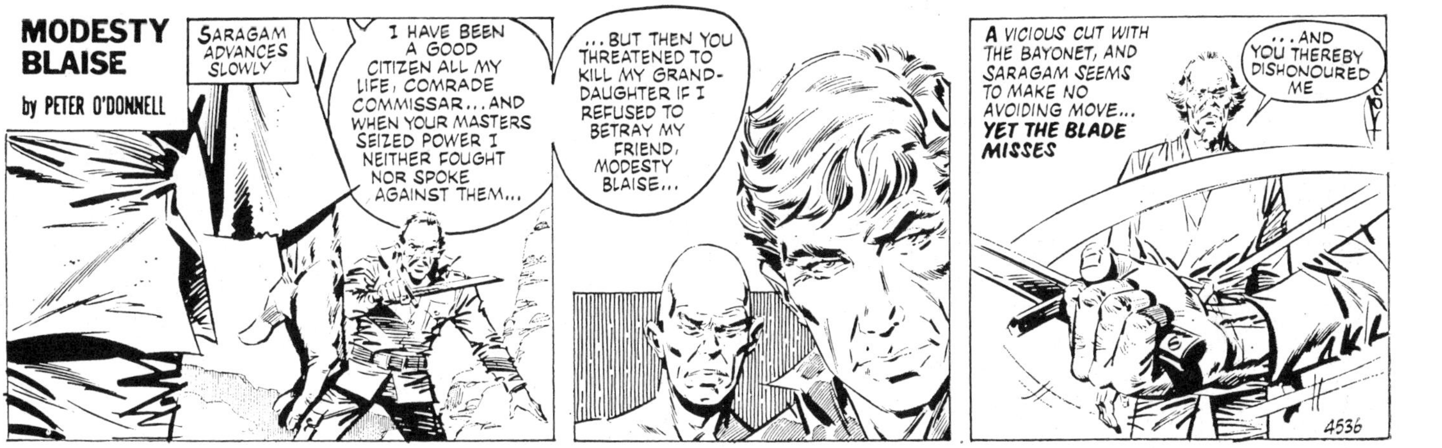
MODESTY BLAISE
by PETER O'DONNELL
SARAGAM ADVANCES SLOWLY
I HAVE BEEN A GOOD CITIZEN ALL MY LIFE, COMRADE COMMISSAR... AND WHEN YOUR MASTERS SEIZED POWER I NEITHER FOUGHT NOR SPOKE AGAINST THEM...
...BUT THEN YOU THREATENED TO KILL MY GRAND-DAUGHTER IF I REFUSED TO BETRAY MY FRIEND, MODESTY BLAISE...
A VICIOUS CUT WITH THE BAYONET, AND SARAGAM SEEMS TO MAKE NO AVOIDING MOVE... YET THE BLADE MISSES
...AND YOU THEREBY DISHONOURED ME
4536

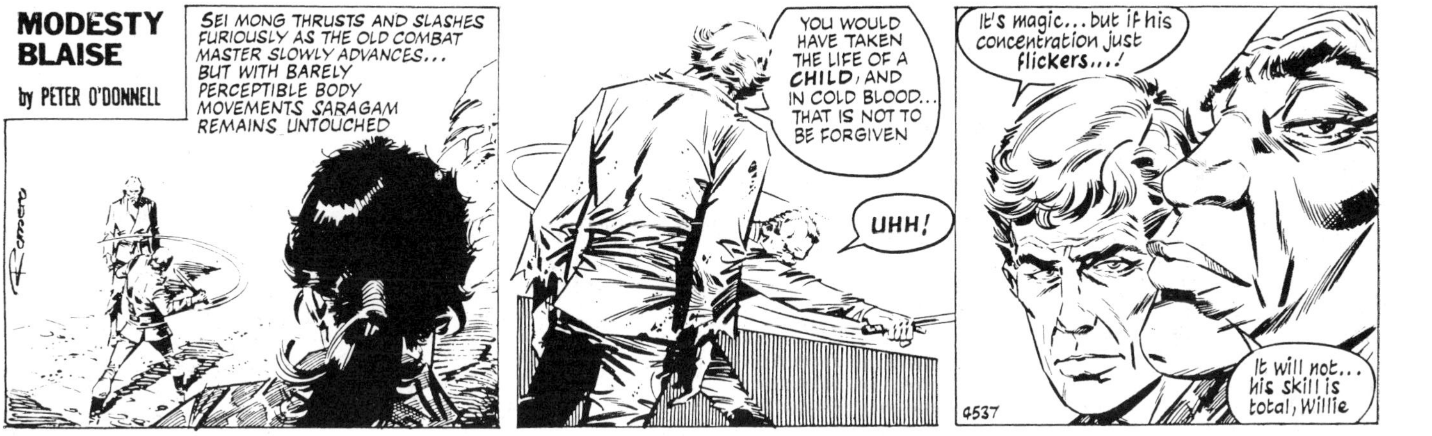
MODESTY BLAISE
by PETER O'DONNELL
SEI MONG THRUSTS AND SLASHES FURIOUSLY AS THE OLD COMBAT MASTER SLOWLY ADVANCES... BUT WITH BARELY PERCEPTIBLE BODY MOVEMENTS SARAGAM REMAINS UNTOUCHED
Romero
YOU WOULD HAVE TAKEN THE LIFE OF A CHILD, AND IN COLD BLOOD... THAT IS NOT TO BE FORGIVEN
UHH!
It's magic... but if his concentration just flickers...!
It will not... his skill is total, Willie
4537

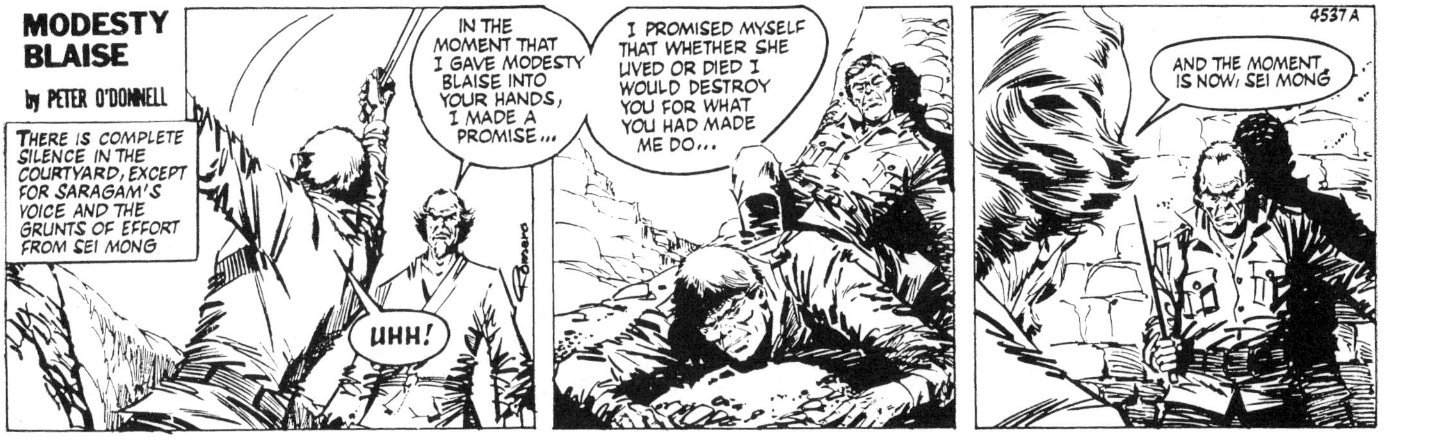
MODESTY BLAISE
by PETER O'DONNELL
THERE IS COMPLETE SILENCE IN THE COURTYARD, EXCEPT FOR SARAGAM'S VOICE AND THE GRUNTS OF EFFORT FROM SEI MONG
IN THE MOMENT THAT I GAVE MODESTY BLAISE INTO YOUR HANDS, I MADE A PROMISE...
UHH!
Romero
I PROMISED MYSELF THAT WHETHER SHE LIVED OR DIED I WOULD DESTROY YOU FOR WHAT YOU HAD MADE ME DO...
4537 A
AND THE MOMENT IS NOW, SEI MONG

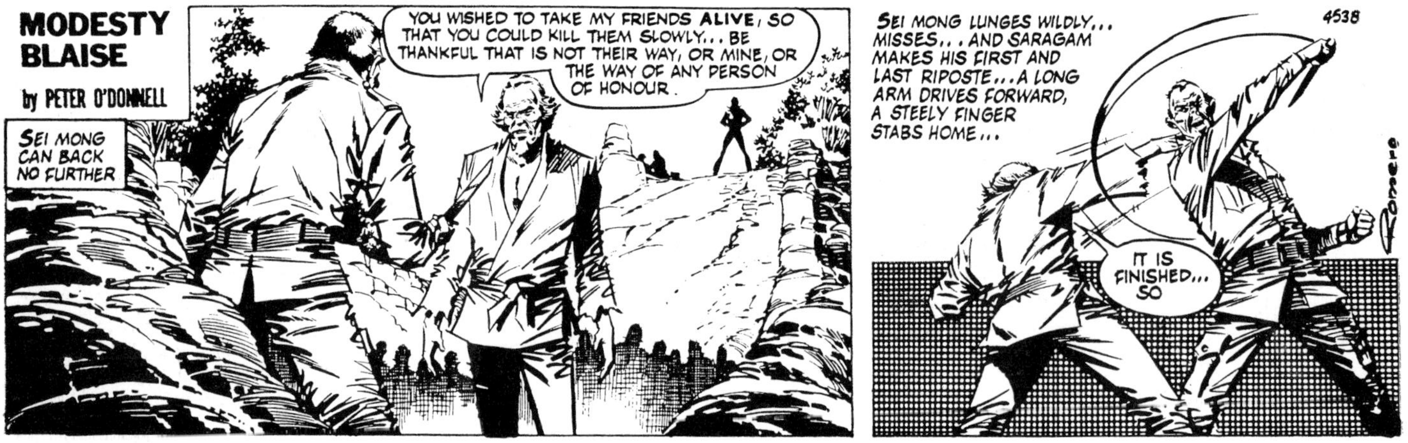
MODESTY BLAISE
by PETER O'DONNELL
SEI MONG CAN BACK NO FURTHER
YOU WISHED TO TAKE MY FRIENDS ALIVE, SO THAT YOU COULD KILL THEM SLOWLY... BE THANKFUL THAT IS NOT THEIR WAY, OR MINE, OR THE WAY OF ANY PERSON OF HONOUR.
SEI MONG LUNGES WILDLY... MISSES... AND SARAGAM MAKES HIS FIRST AND LAST RIPOSTE... A LONG ARM DRIVES FORWARD, A STEELY FINGER STABS HOME...
IT IS FINISHED... SO
4538
Romero

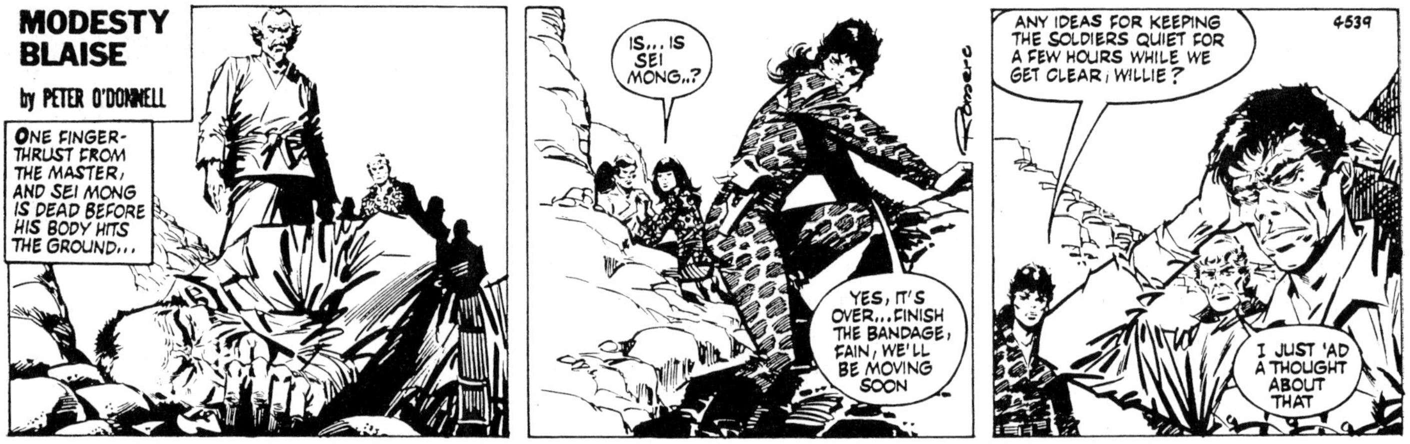
MODESTY BLAISE
by PETER O'DONNELL
ONE FINGER-THRUST FROM THE MASTER, AND SEI MONG IS DEAD BEFORE HIS BODY HITS THE GROUND...
IS... IS SEI MONG..?
YES, IT'S OVER... FINISH THE BANDAGE, FAIN, WE'LL BE MOVING SOON
Romero
ANY IDEAS FOR KEEPING THE SOLDIERS QUIET FOR A FEW HOURS WHILE WE GET CLEAR, WILLIE?
I JUST 'AD A THOUGHT ABOUT THAT
4539

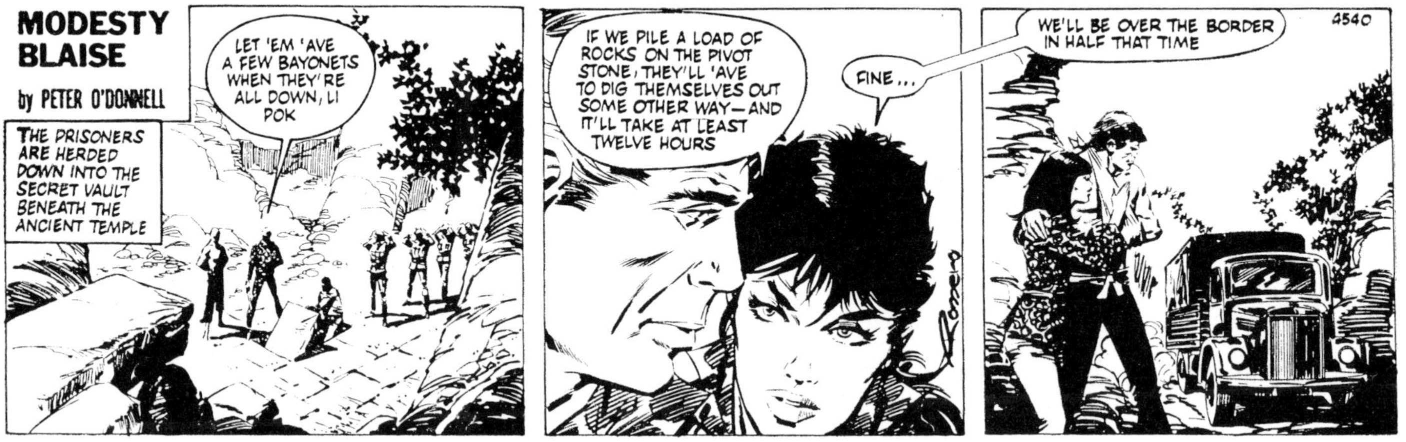
MODESTY BLAISE
by PETER O'DONNELL
THE PRISONERS ARE HERDED DOWN INTO THE SECRET VAULT BENEATH THE ANCIENT TEMPLE
LET 'EM 'AVE A FEW BAYONETS WHEN THEY'RE ALL DOWN, LI POK
IF WE PILE A LOAD OF ROCKS ON THE PIVOT STONE, THEY'LL 'AVE TO DIG THEMSELVES OUT SOME OTHER WAY—AND IT'LL TAKE AT LEAST TWELVE HOURS
FINE...
Romero
WE'LL BE OVER THE BORDER IN HALF THAT TIME
4540

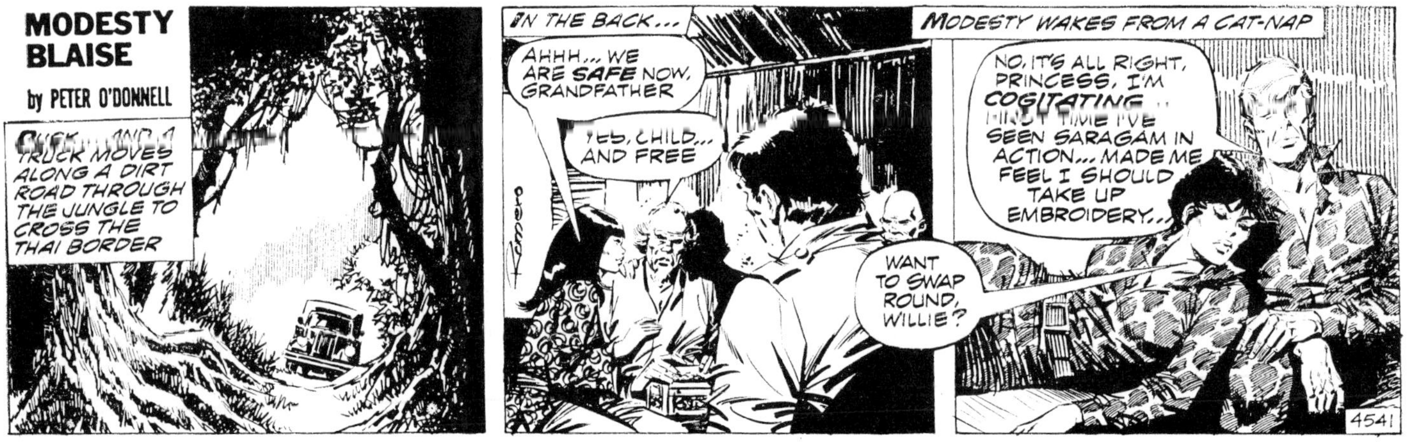
MODESTY BLAISE
by PETER O'DONNELL
TRUCK MOVES ALONG A DIRT ROAD THROUGH THE JUNGLE TO CROSS THE THAI BORDER
IN THE BACK...
AHHH... WE ARE SAFE NOW, GRANDFATHER
YES, CHILD... AND FREE
Romero
MODESTY WAKES FROM A CAT-NAP
NO, IT'S ALL RIGHT, PRINCESS, I'M COGITATING
TIME I'VE SEEN SARAGAM IN ACTION... MADE ME FEEL I SHOULD TAKE UP EMBROIDERY...
WANT TO SWAP ROUND, WILLIE?
4541

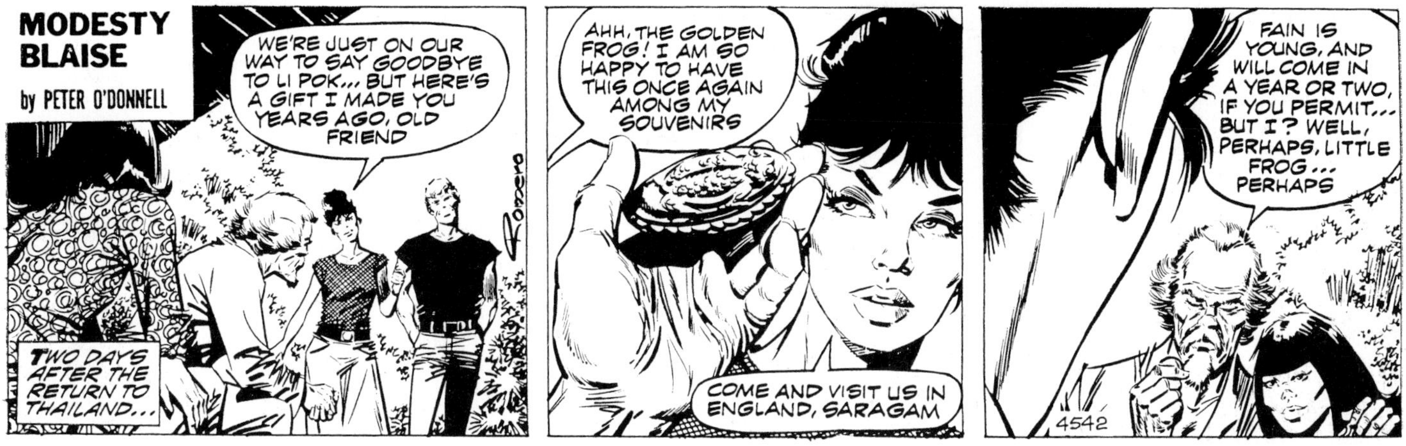
MODESTY BLAISE
by PETER O'DONNELL
TWO DAYS AFTER THE RETURN TO THAILAND...
WE'RE JUST ON OUR WAY TO SAY GOODBYE TO LI POK... BUT HERE'S A GIFT I MADE YOU YEARS AGO, OLD FRIEND
AHH, THE GOLDEN FROG! I AM SO HAPPY TO HAVE THIS ONCE AGAIN AMONG MY SOUVENIRS
COME AND VISIT US IN ENGLAND, SARAGAM
FAIN IS YOUNG, AND WILL COME IN A YEAR OR TWO, IF YOU PERMIT... BUT I? WELL, PERHAPS, LITTLE FROG... PERHAPS
4542

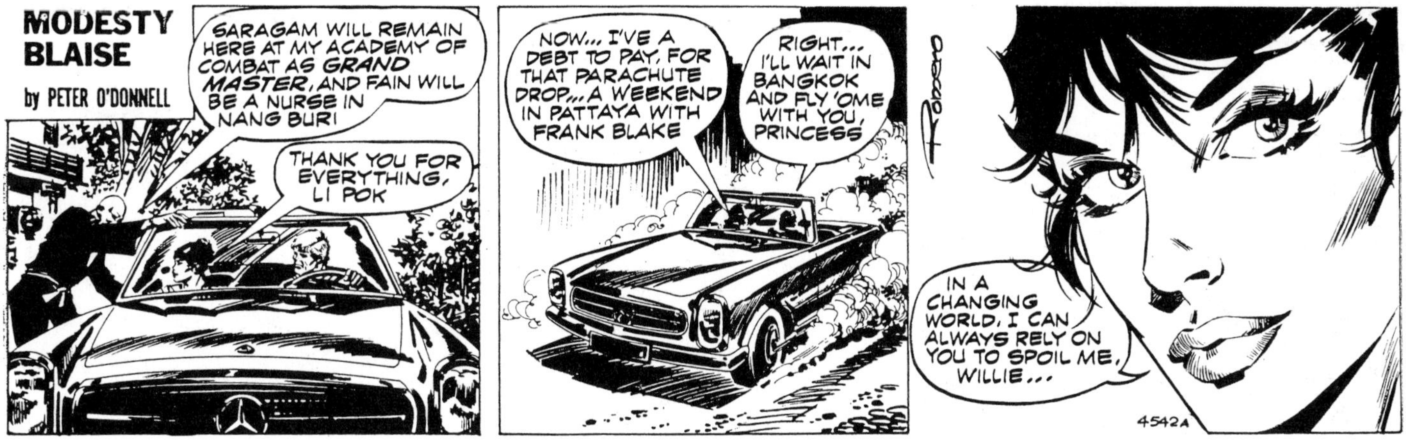
MODESTY BLAISE
by PETER O'DONNELL
SARAGAM WILL REMAIN HERE AT MY ACADEMY OF COMBAT AS GRAND MASTER, AND FAIN WILL BE A NURSE IN NANG BURI
THANK YOU FOR EVERYTHING, LI POK
NOW... I'VE A DEBT TO PAY, FOR THAT PARACHUTE DROP... A WEEKEND IN PATTAYA WITH FRANK BLAKE
RIGHT... I'LL WAIT IN BANGKOK AND FLY 'OME WITH YOU, PRINCESS
IN A CHANGING WORLD, I CAN ALWAYS RELY ON YOU TO SPOIL ME, WILLIE...
4542A

YELLOWSTONE BOOTY

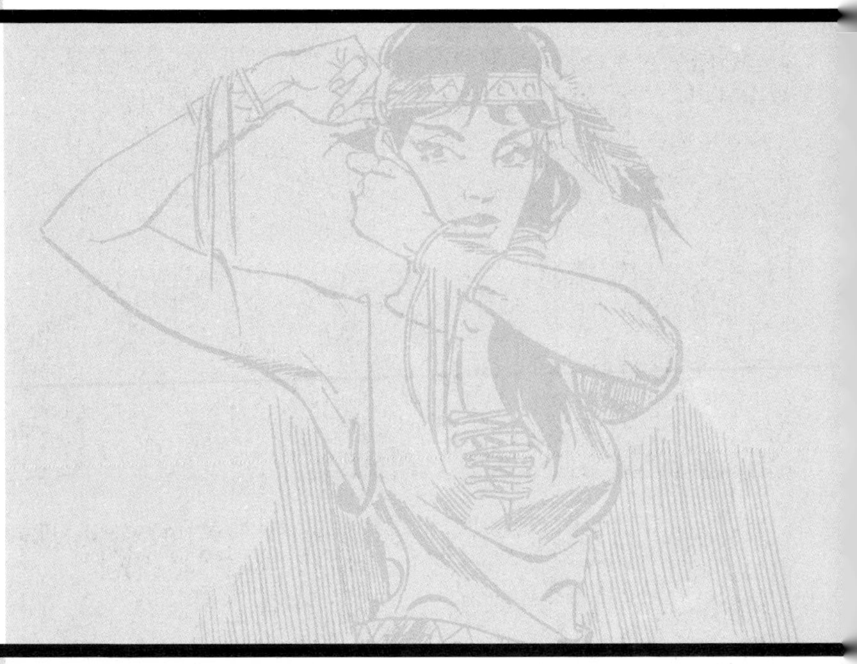

Yellowstone National Park is huge. It covers areas of Montana, Wyoming and Idaho, and it takes your breath away. I'd need pages just to list all there is to see and to do in this fabulous territory. Here wildlife large and small roams freely, and natural features (like 300-plus geysers including "Old Faithful") hold you spellbound. For me it has the added appeal of remote areas where Modesty and Willie can do battle against a bunch of bad guys without attracting unwanted attention.

The location for a story is fine. Now all I want is some bad guys and a plot. Ah yes, a plot. Well, I've found that by reversing some simple element in the opening of an old story you can create something entirely different in its development. For example, I must have written quite a few stories that open with Modesty saving somebody's life, so why not reverse that? How about opening with somebody saving Modesty's life?

So who is it going to be, man or girl? Could be both, I suppose. Young married couple perhaps. That feels all right up to a point, but how does Willie fit in? Ah yes, let's give it another twist — the girl saves Willie's life, risking her own. Make that highly visual. She's the action seeker of the couple. Husband's a gentle giant type, very dim but lovable.

All I need now are the villains. They could be after something the couple have or know about. Like what? I've no idea, but I've got enough to start scripting, and all the rest will emerge as I go along and as the characters come to life. It always does. I hope you enjoy the reading of it.

PETER O'DONNELL

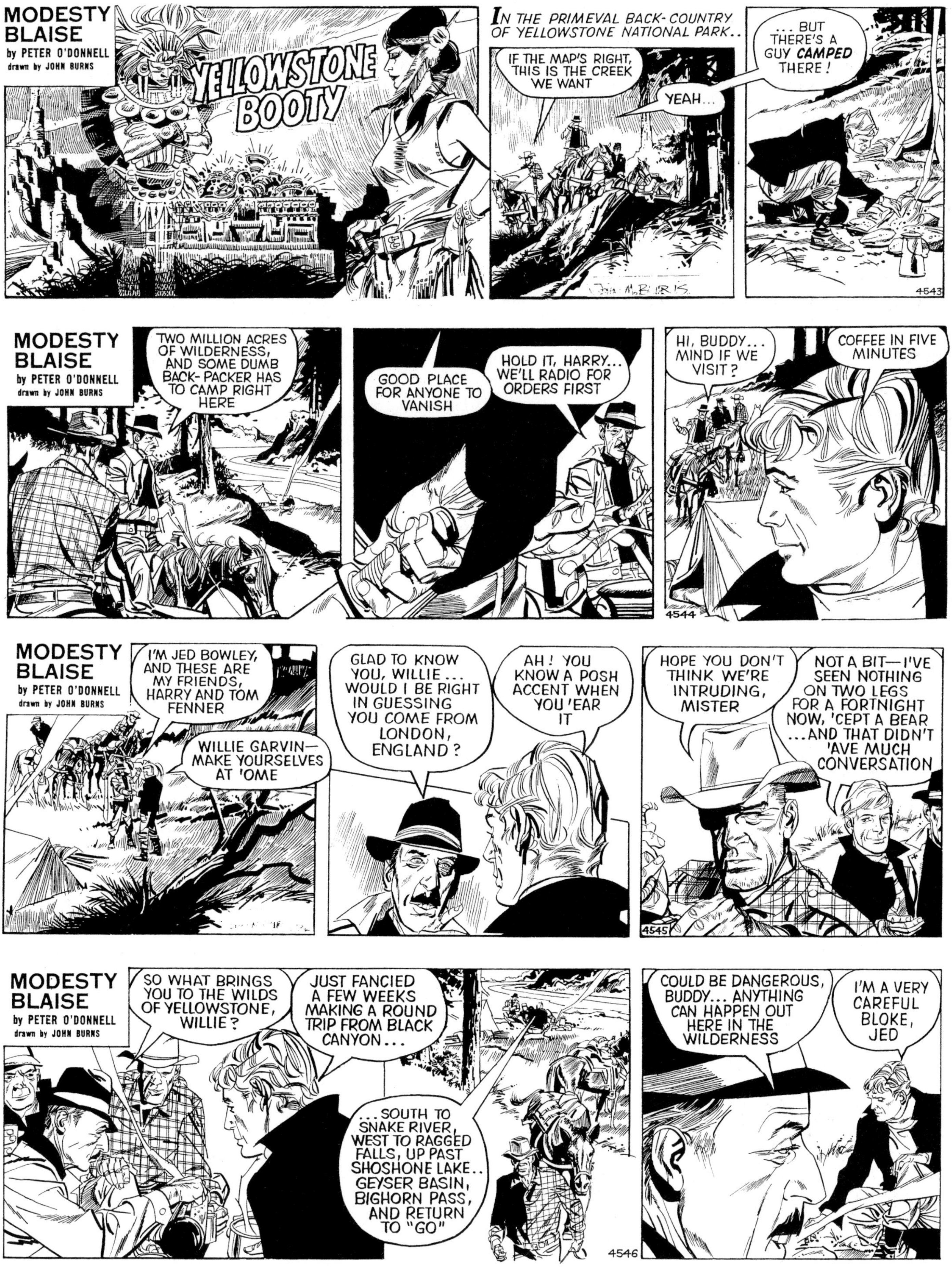
MODESTY BLAISE
by PETER O'DONNELL
drawn by JOHN BURNS
YELLOWSTONE BOOTY
IN THE PRIMEVAL BACK-COUNTRY OF YELLOWSTONE NATIONAL PARK..
IF THE MAP'S RIGHT, THIS IS THE CREEK WE WANT
YEAH...
...BUT THERE'S A GUY CAMPED THERE!
4543
MODESTY BLAISE
by PETER O'DONNELL
drawn by JOHN BURNS
TWO MILLION ACRES OF WILDERNESS, AND SOME DUMB BACK-PACKER HAS TO CAMP RIGHT HERE
GOOD PLACE FOR ANYONE TO VANISH
HOLD IT, HARRY... WE'LL RADIO FOR ORDERS FIRST
HI, BUDDY... MIND IF WE VISIT?
COFFEE IN FIVE MINUTES
4544
MODESTY BLAISE
by PETER O'DONNELL
drawn by JOHN BURNS
I'M JED BOWLEY, AND THESE ARE MY FRIENDS, HARRY AND TOM FENNER
WILLIE GARVIN—MAKE YOURSELVES AT 'OME
GLAD TO KNOW YOU, WILLIE... WOULD I BE RIGHT IN GUESSING YOU COME FROM LONDON, ENGLAND?
AH! YOU KNOW A POSH ACCENT WHEN YOU 'EAR IT
HOPE YOU DON'T THINK WE'RE INTRUDING, MISTER
NOT A BIT—I'VE SEEN NOTHING ON TWO LEGS FOR A FORTNIGHT NOW, 'CEPT A BEAR ...AND THAT DIDN'T 'AVE MUCH CONVERSATION
4545
MODESTY BLAISE
by PETER O'DONNELL
drawn by JOHN BURNS
SO WHAT BRINGS YOU TO THE WILDS OF YELLOWSTONE, WILLIE?
JUST FANCIED A FEW WEEKS MAKING A ROUND TRIP FROM BLACK CANYON...
...SOUTH TO SNAKE RIVER, WEST TO RAGGED FALLS, UP PAST SHOSHONE LAKE.. GEYSER BASIN, BIGHORN PASS, AND RETURN TO "GO"
4546
COULD BE DANGEROUS, BUDDY... ANYTHING CAN HAPPEN OUT HERE IN THE WILDERNESS
I'M A VERY CAREFUL BLOKE, JED

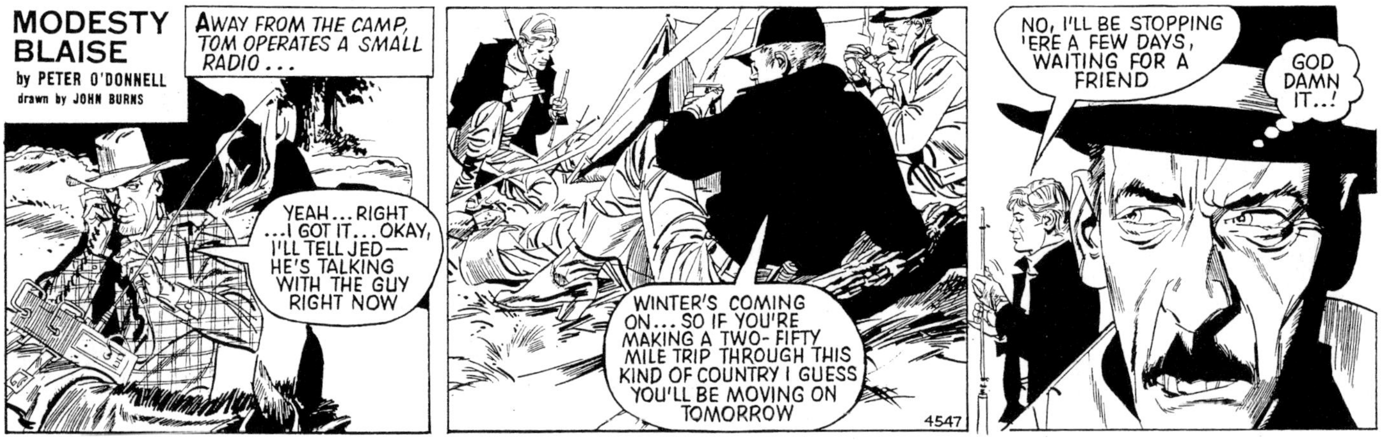
MODESTY BLAISE
by PETER O'DONNELL
drawn by JOHN BURNS
AWAY FROM THE CAMP, TOM OPERATES A SMALL RADIO . . .
YEAH . . . RIGHT . . . I GOT IT . . . OKAY, I'LL TELL JED— HE'S TALKING WITH THE GUY RIGHT NOW
WINTER'S COMING ON . . . SO IF YOU'RE MAKING A TWO-FIFTY MILE TRIP THROUGH THIS KIND OF COUNTRY I GUESS YOU'LL BE MOVING ON TOMORROW
4547
NO, I'LL BE STOPPING 'ERE A FEW DAYS, WAITING FOR A FRIEND
GOD DAMN IT . . !

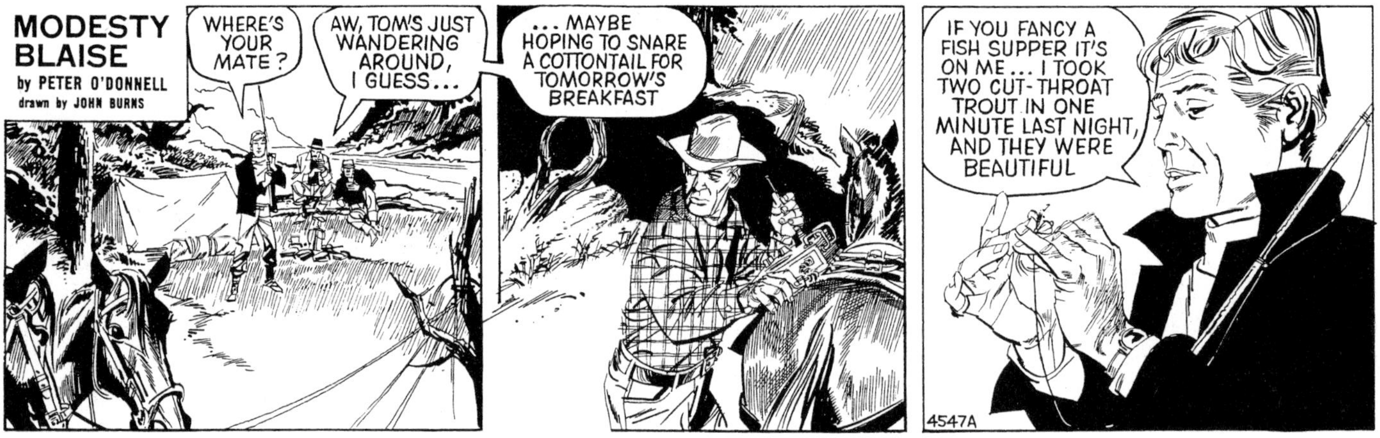
MODESTY BLAISE
by PETER O'DONNELL
drawn by JOHN BURNS
WHERE'S YOUR MATE ?
AW, TOM'S JUST WANDERING AROUND, I GUESS . . .
. . . MAYBE HOPING TO SNARE A COTTONTAIL FOR TOMORROW'S BREAKFAST
IF YOU FANCY A FISH SUPPER IT'S ON ME . . . I TOOK TWO CUT-THROAT TROUT IN ONE MINUTE LAST NIGHT, AND THEY WERE BEAUTIFUL
4547A

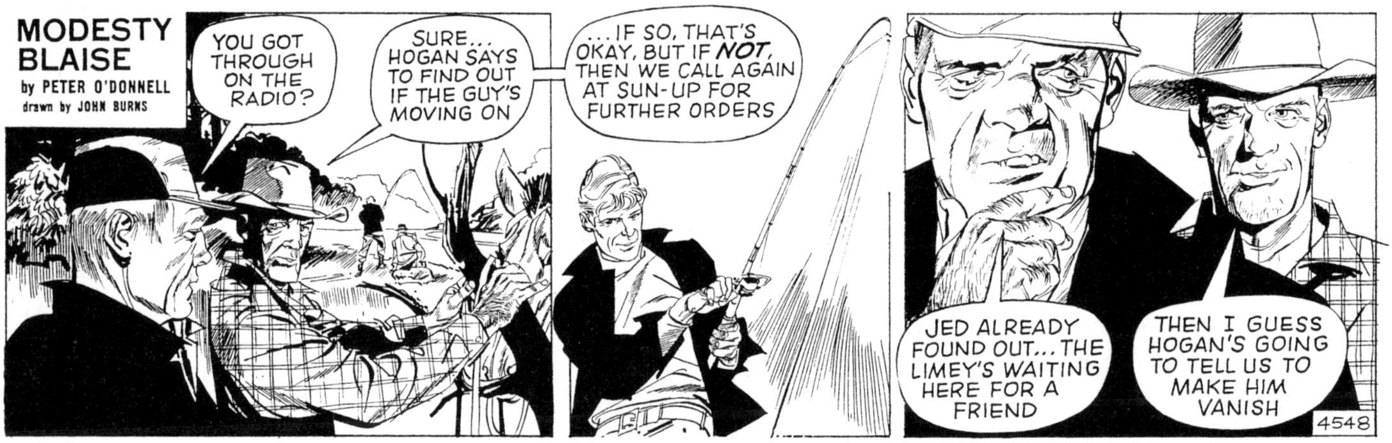
MODESTY BLAISE
by PETER O'DONNELL
drawn by JOHN BURNS
YOU GOT THROUGH ON THE RADIO ?
SURE . . . HOGAN SAYS TO FIND OUT IF THE GUY'S MOVING ON
. . . IF SO, THAT'S OKAY, BUT IF NOT, THEN WE CALL AGAIN AT SUN-UP FOR FURTHER ORDERS
JED ALREADY FOUND OUT . . . THE LIMEY'S WAITING HERE FOR A FRIEND
THEN I GUESS HOGAN'S GOING TO TELL US TO MAKE HIM VANISH
4548

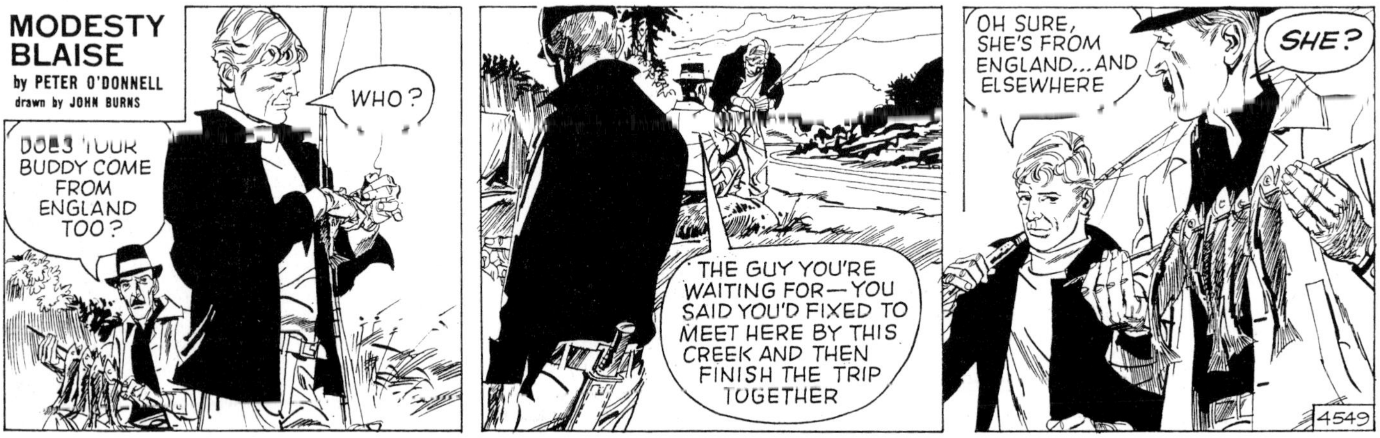
MODESTY BLAISE
by PETER O'DONNELL
drawn by JOHN BURNS
DOES YOUR BUDDY COME FROM ENGLAND TOO ?
WHO ?
THE GUY YOU'RE WAITING FOR—YOU SAID YOU'D FIXED TO MEET HERE BY THIS CREEK AND THEN FINISH THE TRIP TOGETHER
OH SURE, SHE'S FROM ENGLAND . . . AND ELSEWHERE
SHE ?
4549

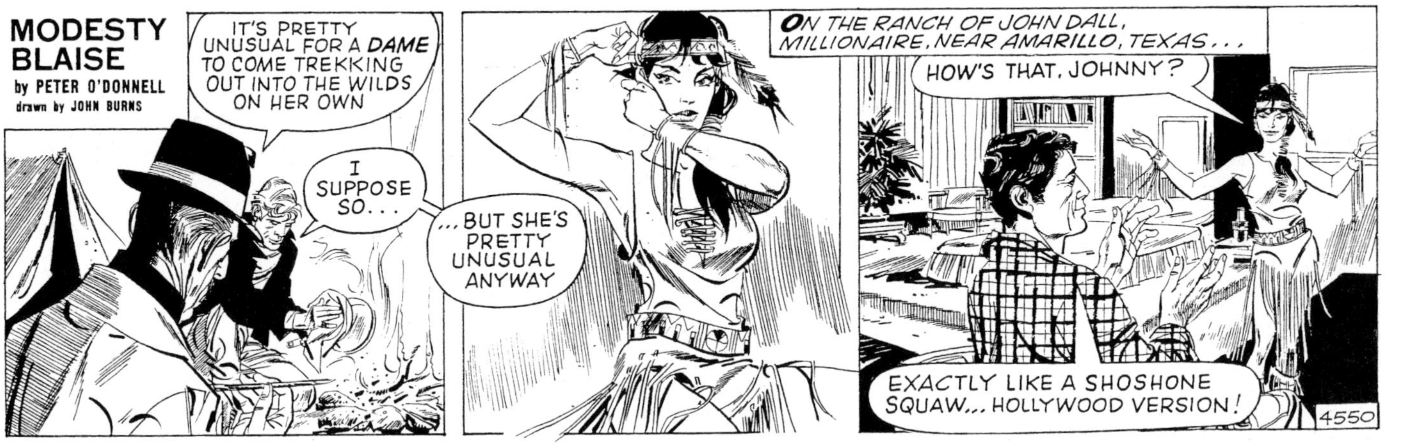
MODESTY BLAISE
by PETER O'DONNELL
drawn by JOHN BURNS
IT'S PRETTY UNUSUAL FOR A DAME TO COME TREKKING OUT INTO THE WILDS ON HER OWN
I SUPPOSE SO...
...BUT SHE'S PRETTY UNUSUAL ANYWAY
ON THE RANCH OF JOHN DALL, MILLIONAIRE, NEAR AMARILLO, TEXAS...
HOW'S THAT, JOHNNY?
EXACTLY LIKE A SHOSHONE SQUAW... HOLLYWOOD VERSION!
4550

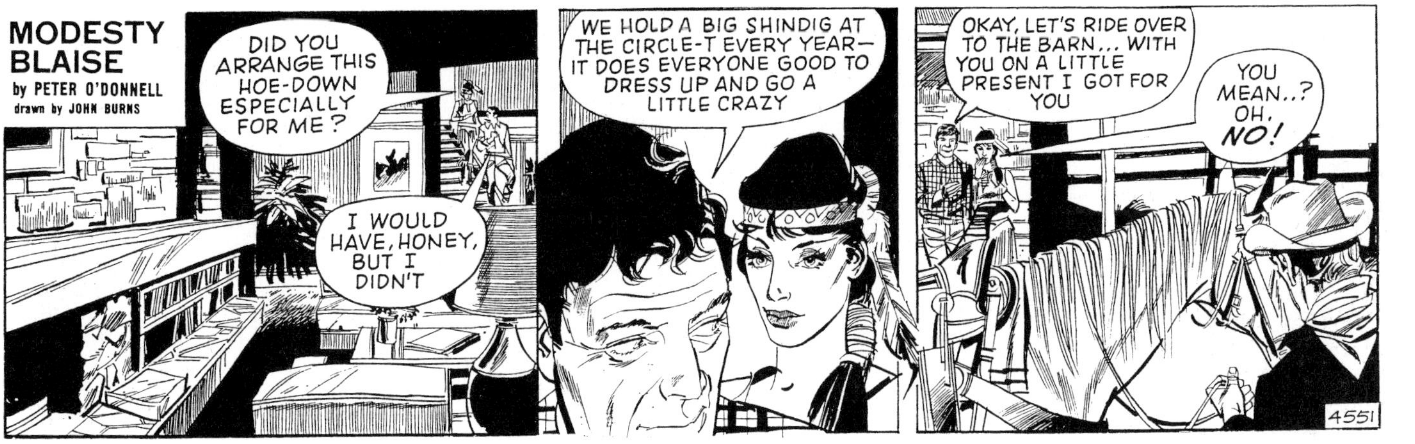
MODESTY BLAISE
by PETER O'DONNELL
drawn by JOHN BURNS
DID YOU ARRANGE THIS HOE-DOWN ESPECIALLY FOR ME?
I WOULD HAVE, HONEY, BUT I DIDN'T
WE HOLD A BIG SHINDIG AT THE CIRCLE-T EVERY YEAR– IT DOES EVERYONE GOOD TO DRESS UP AND GO A LITTLE CRAZY
OKAY, LET'S RIDE OVER TO THE BARN... WITH YOU ON A LITTLE PRESENT I GOT FOR YOU
YOU MEAN..? OH, NO!
4551

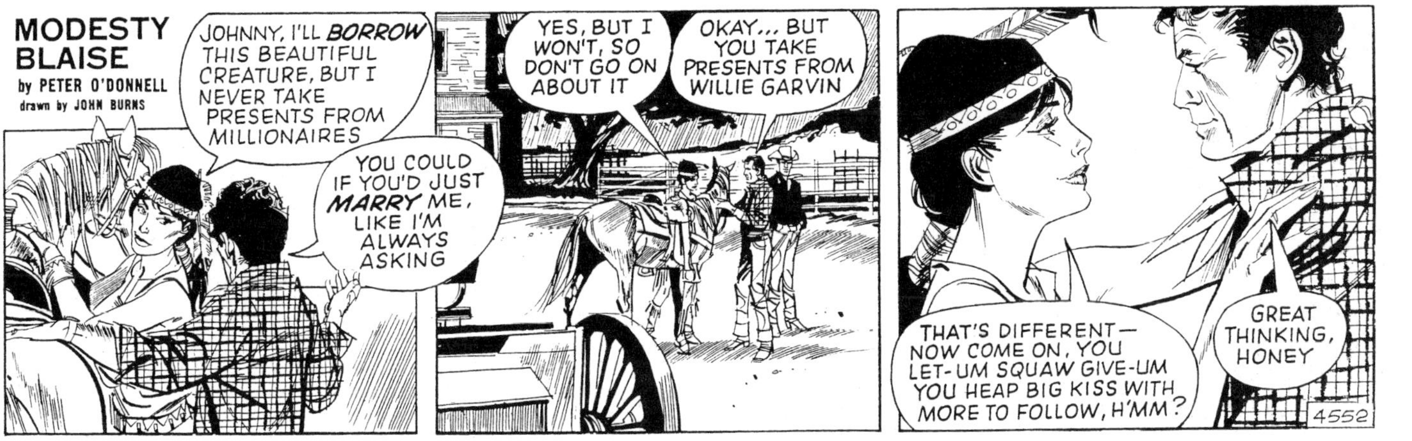
MODESTY BLAISE
by PETER O'DONNELL
drawn by JOHN BURNS
JOHNNY, I'LL BORROW THIS BEAUTIFUL CREATURE, BUT I NEVER TAKE PRESENTS FROM MILLIONAIRES
YOU COULD IF YOU'D JUST MARRY ME, LIKE I'M ALWAYS ASKING
YES, BUT I WON'T, SO DON'T GO ON ABOUT IT
OKAY... BUT YOU TAKE PRESENTS FROM WILLIE GARVIN
THAT'S DIFFERENT— NOW COME ON, YOU LET-UM SQUAW GIVE-UM YOU HEAP BIG KISS WITH MORE TO FOLLOW, H'MM?
GREAT THINKING, HONEY
4552

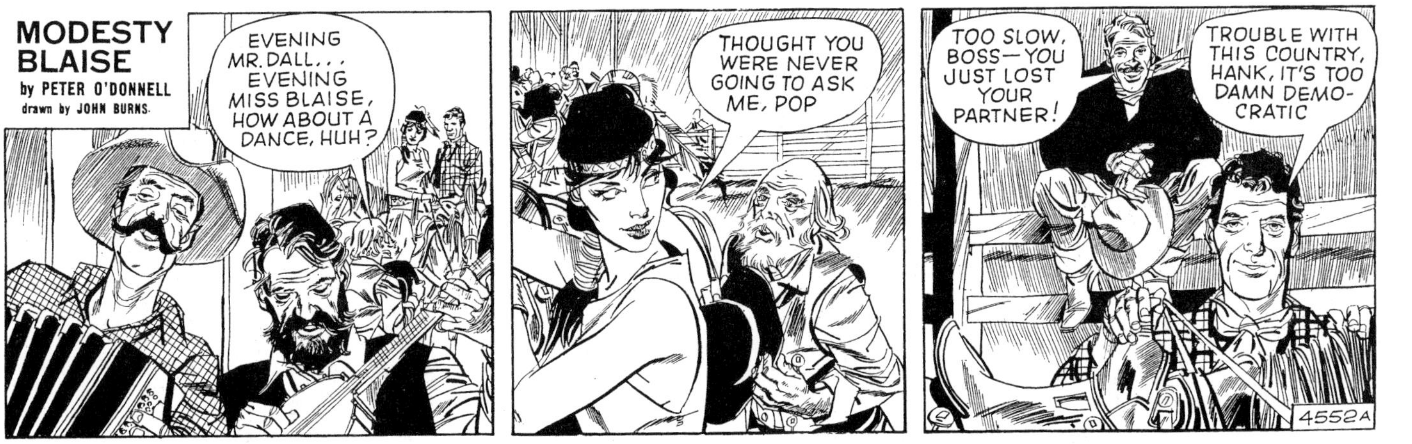
MODESTY BLAISE
by PETER O'DONNELL
drawn by JOHN BURNS
EVENING MR. DALL... EVENING MISS BLAISE, HOW ABOUT A DANCE, HUH?
THOUGHT YOU WERE NEVER GOING TO ASK ME, POP
TOO SLOW, BOSS—YOU JUST LOST YOUR PARTNER!
TROUBLE WITH THIS COUNTRY, HANK, IT'S TOO DAMN DEMO-CRATIC
4552A

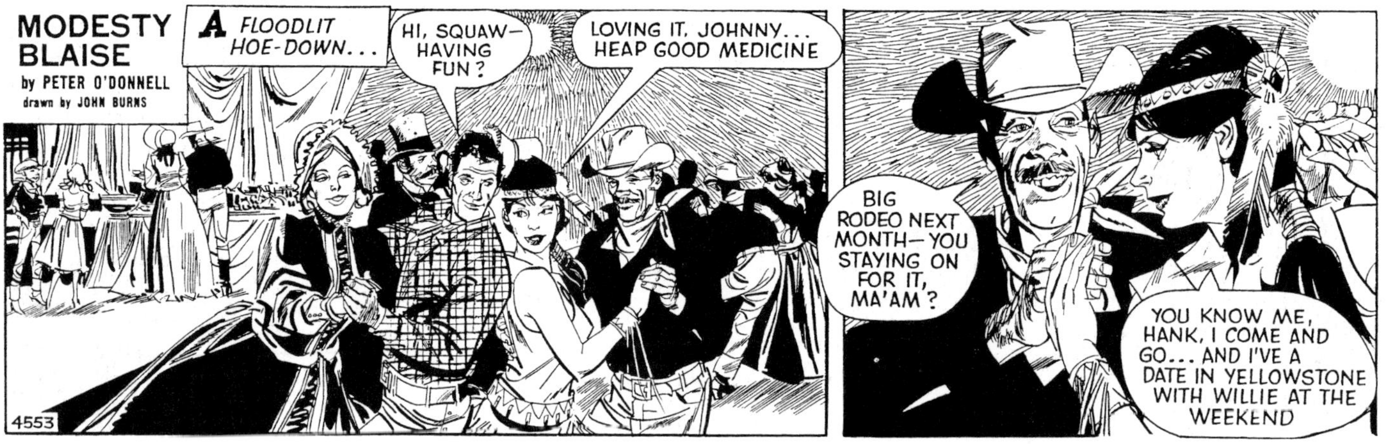
MODESTY BLAISE
by PETER O'DONNELL
drawn by JOHN BURNS
A FLOODLIT HOE-DOWN...
HI, SQUAW— HAVING FUN?
LOVING IT, JOHNNY... HEAP GOOD MEDICINE
BIG RODEO NEXT MONTH—YOU STAYING ON FOR IT, MA'AM?
YOU KNOW ME, HANK, I COME AND GO... AND I'VE A DATE IN YELLOWSTONE WITH WILLIE AT THE WEEKEND
4553

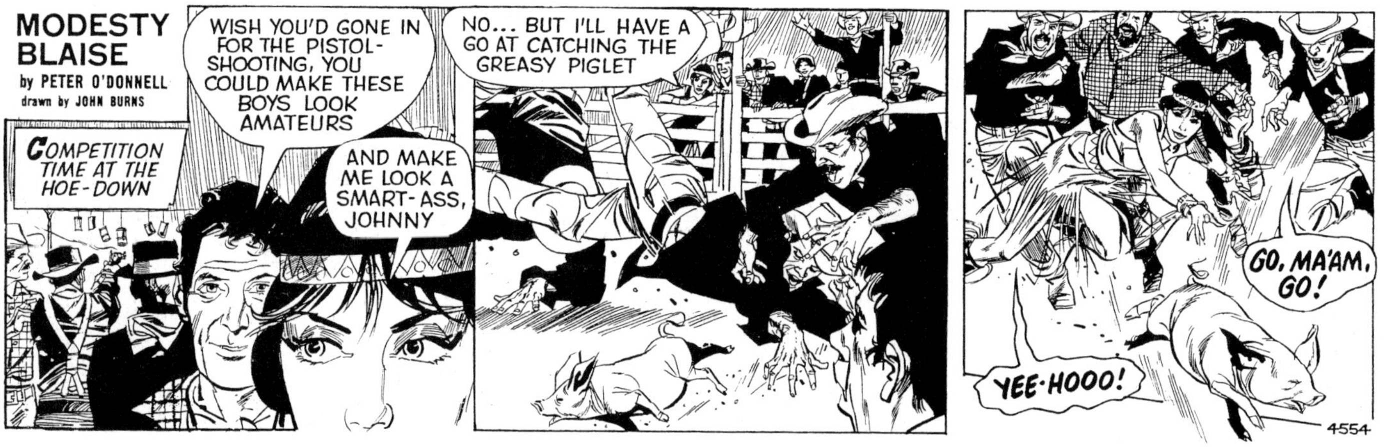
MODESTY BLAISE
by PETER O'DONNELL
drawn by JOHN BURNS
COMPETITION TIME AT THE HOE-DOWN
WISH YOU'D GONE IN FOR THE PISTOL-SHOOTING, YOU COULD MAKE THESE BOYS LOOK AMATEURS
AND MAKE ME LOOK A SMART-ASS, JOHNNY
NO... BUT I'LL HAVE A GO AT CATCHING THE GREASY PIGLET
GO, MA'AM, GO!
YEE-HOOO!
4554

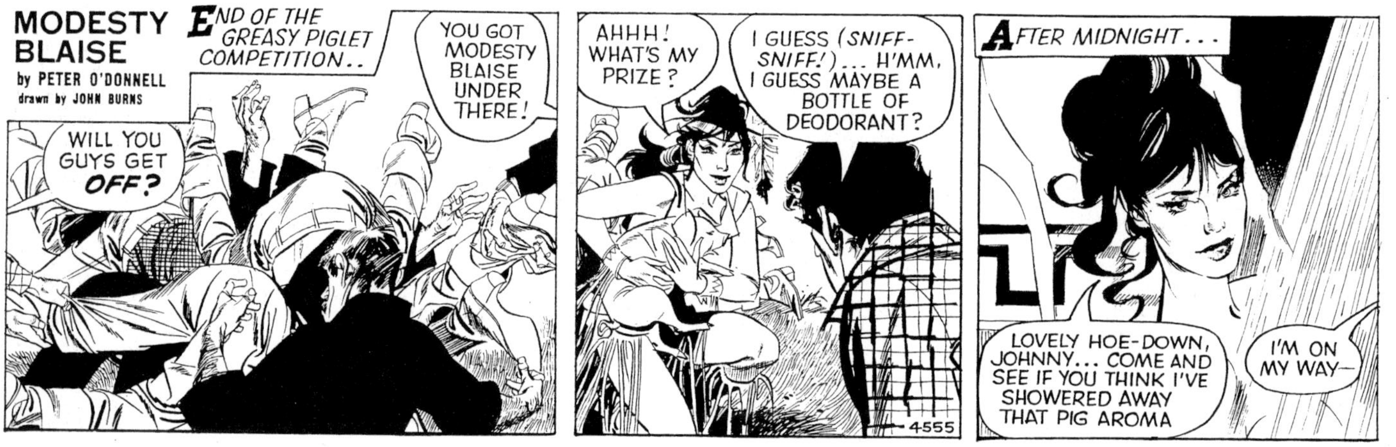
MODESTY BLAISE
by PETER O'DONNELL
drawn by JOHN BURNS
END OF THE GREASY PIGLET COMPETITION..
YOU GOT MODESTY BLAISE UNDER THERE!
WILL YOU GUYS GET OFF?
AHHH! WHAT'S MY PRIZE?
I GUESS (SNIFF-SNIFF!)... H'MM, I GUESS MAYBE A BOTTLE OF DEODORANT?
4555
AFTER MIDNIGHT...
LOVELY HOE-DOWN, JOHNNY... COME AND SEE IF YOU THINK I'VE SHOWERED AWAY THAT PIG AROMA
I'M ON MY WAY—

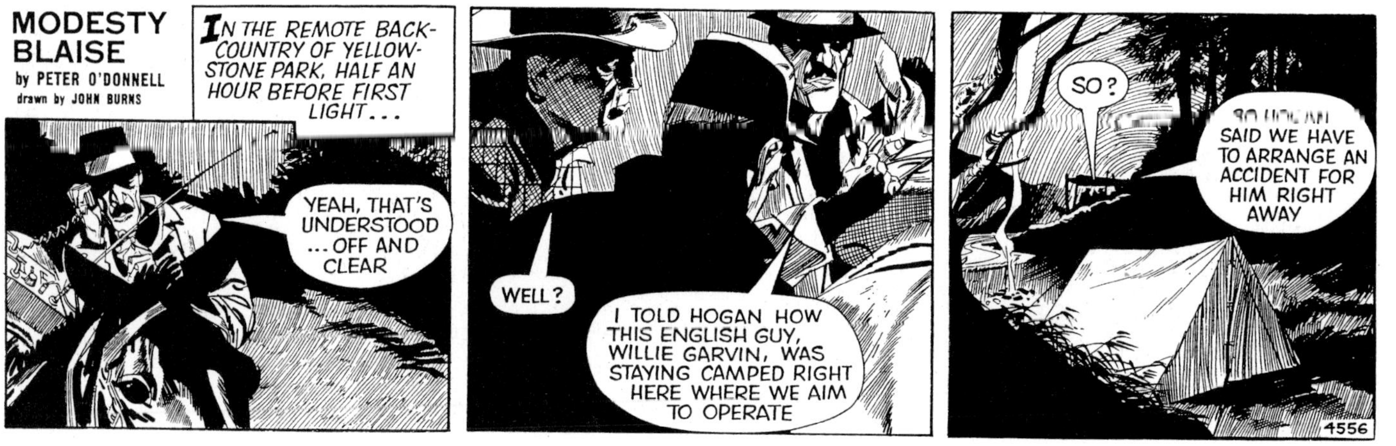
MODESTY BLAISE
by PETER O'DONNELL
drawn by JOHN BURNS
IN THE REMOTE BACK-COUNTRY OF YELLOWSTONE PARK, HALF AN HOUR BEFORE FIRST LIGHT...
YEAH, THAT'S UNDERSTOOD ...OFF AND CLEAR
WELL?
I TOLD HOGAN HOW THIS ENGLISH GUY, WILLIE GARVIN, WAS STAYING CAMPED RIGHT HERE WHERE WE AIM TO OPERATE
SO?
SAID WE HAVE TO ARRANGE AN ACCIDENT FOR HIM RIGHT AWAY
4556

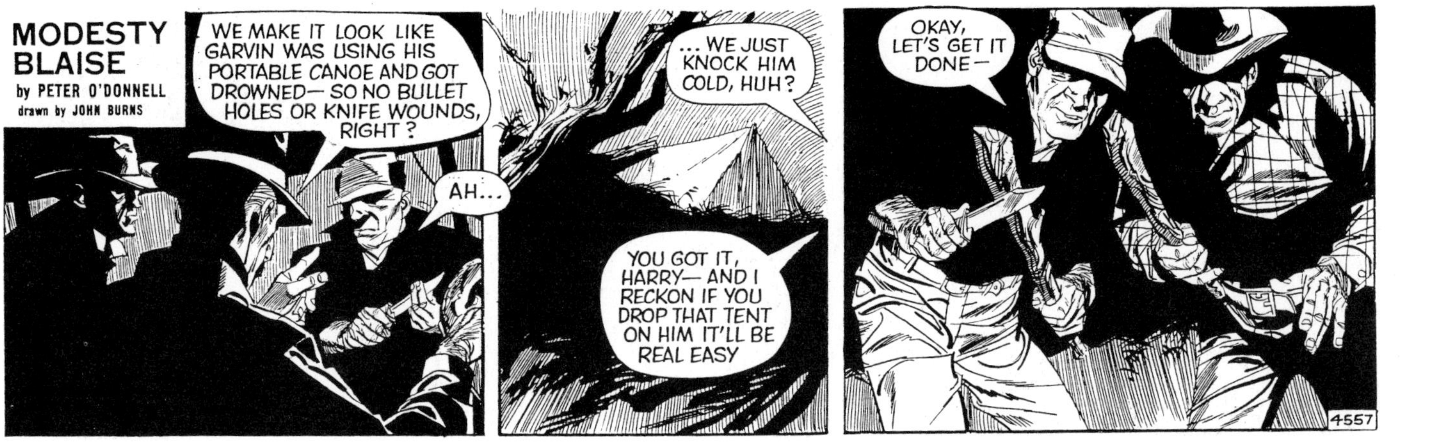
MODESTY BLAISE
by PETER O'DONNELL
drawn by JOHN BURNS
WE MAKE IT LOOK LIKE GARVIN WAS USING HIS PORTABLE CANOE AND GOT DROWNED— SO NO BULLET HOLES OR KNIFE WOUNDS, RIGHT?
AH...
...WE JUST KNOCK HIM COLD, HUH?
YOU GOT IT, HARRY— AND I RECKON IF YOU DROP THAT TENT ON HIM IT'LL BE REAL EASY
OKAY, LET'S GET IT DONE—
4557

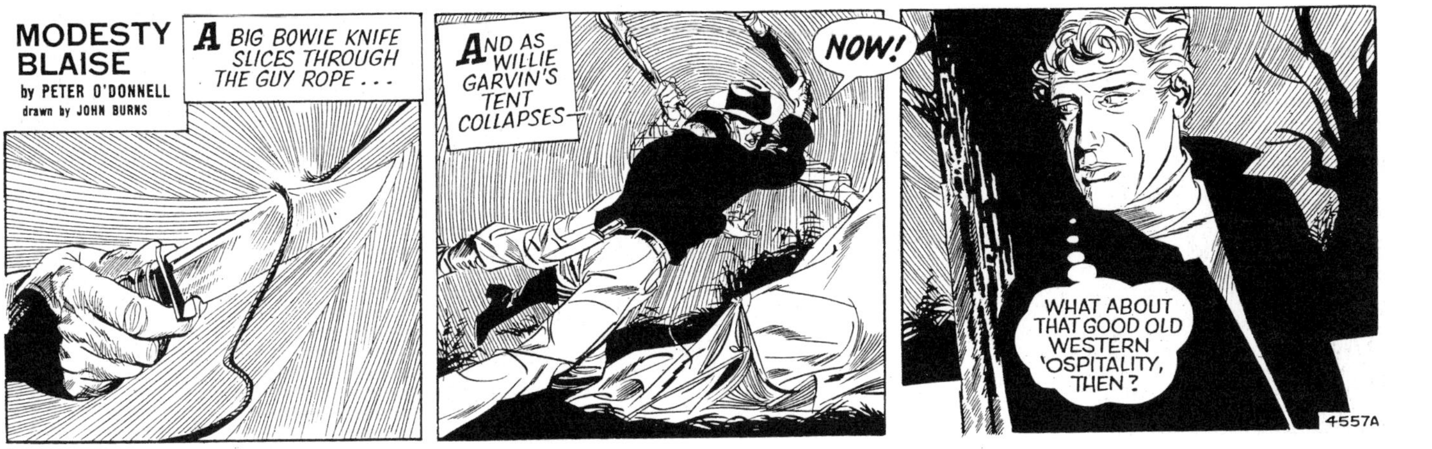
MODESTY BLAISE
by PETER O'DONNELL
drawn by JOHN BURNS
A BIG BOWIE KNIFE SLICES THROUGH THE GUY ROPE . . .
AND AS WILLIE GARVIN'S TENT COLLAPSES—
NOW!
WHAT ABOUT THAT GOOD OLD WESTERN 'OSPITALITY, THEN?
4557A

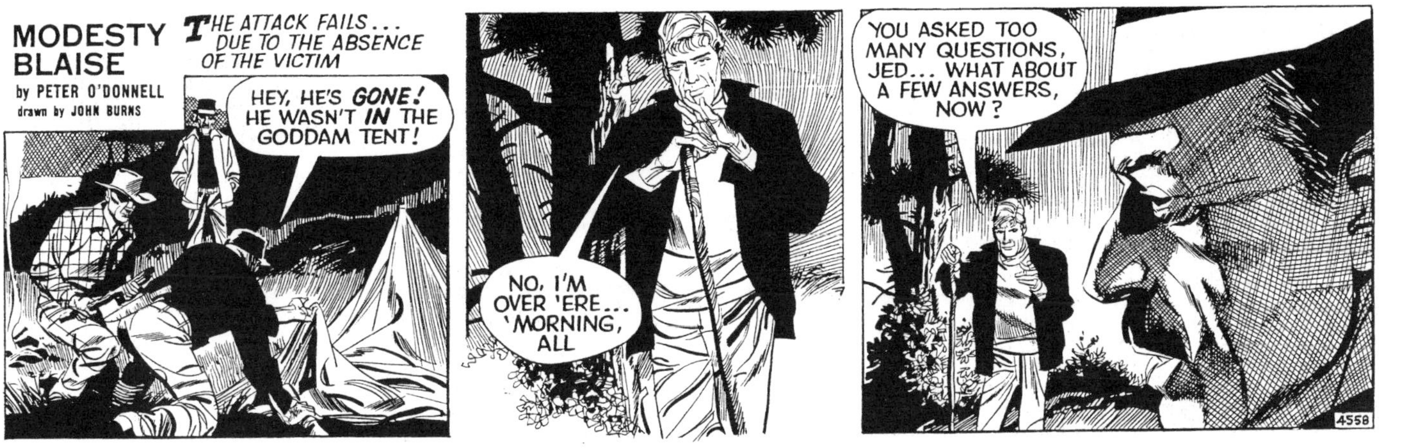
MODESTY BLAISE
by PETER O'DONNELL
drawn by JOHN BURNS
THE ATTACK FAILS... DUE TO THE ABSENCE OF THE VICTIM
HEY, HE'S GONE! HE WASN'T IN THE GODDAM TENT!
NO, I'M OVER 'ERE... 'MORNING, ALL
YOU ASKED TOO MANY QUESTIONS, JED... WHAT ABOUT A FEW ANSWERS, NOW?
4558

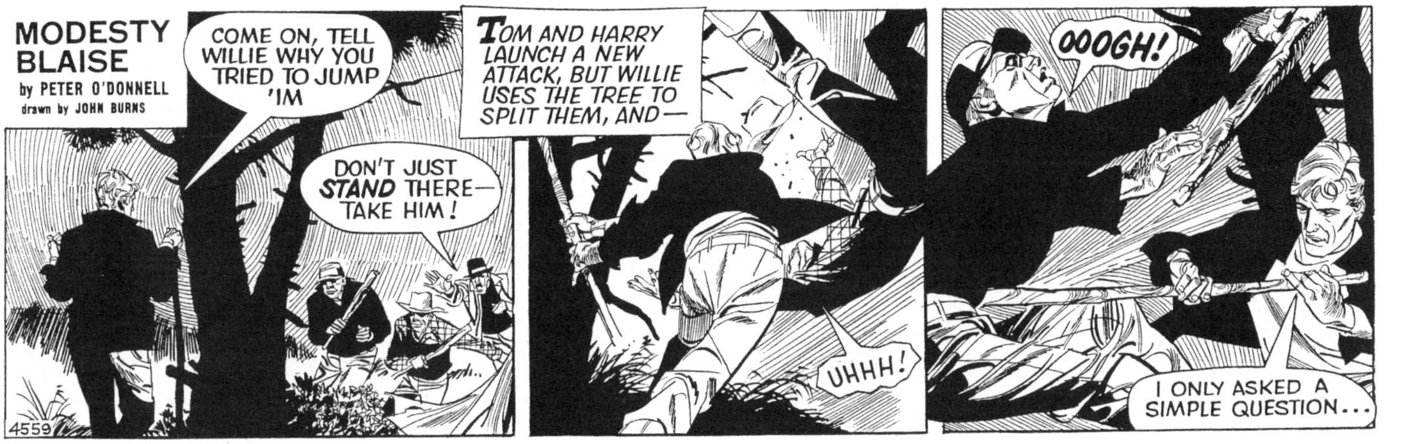
MODESTY BLAISE
by PETER O'DONNELL
drawn by JOHN BURNS
COME ON, TELL WILLIE WHY YOU TRIED TO JUMP 'IM
DON'T JUST STAND THERE— TAKE HIM!
TOM AND HARRY LAUNCH A NEW ATTACK, BUT WILLIE USES THE TREE TO SPLIT THEM, AND—
UHHH!
OOOGH!
I ONLY ASKED A SIMPLE QUESTION...
4559

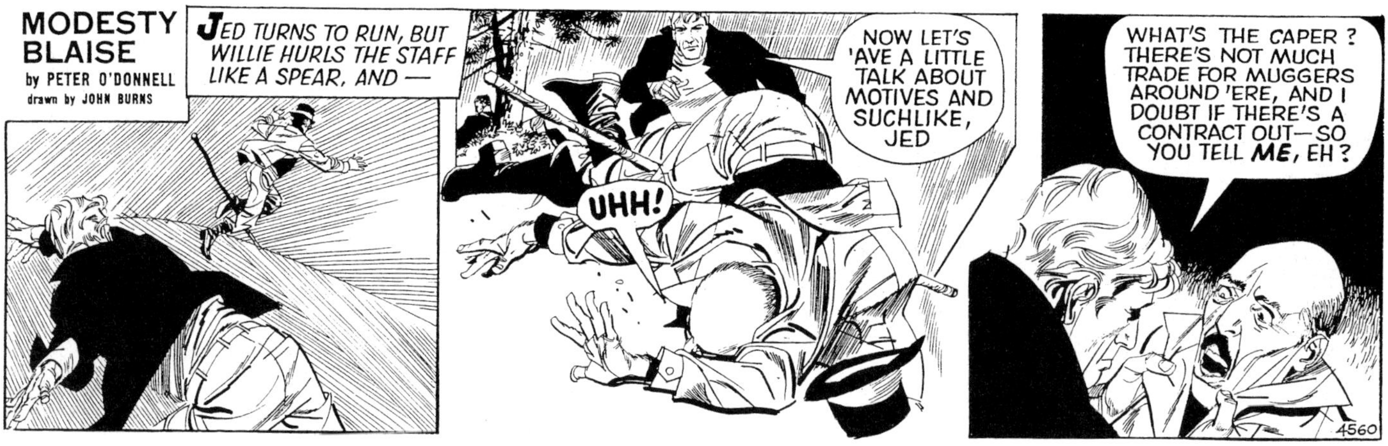
MODESTY BLAISE
by PETER O'DONNELL
drawn by JOHN BURNS
JED TURNS TO RUN, BUT WILLIE HURLS THE STAFF LIKE A SPEAR, AND —
NOW LET'S 'AVE A LITTLE TALK ABOUT MOTIVES AND SUCHLIKE, JED
UHH!
WHAT'S THE CAPER? THERE'S NOT MUCH TRADE FOR MUGGERS AROUND 'ERE, AND I DOUBT IF THERE'S A CONTRACT OUT—SO YOU TELL ME, EH?
4560

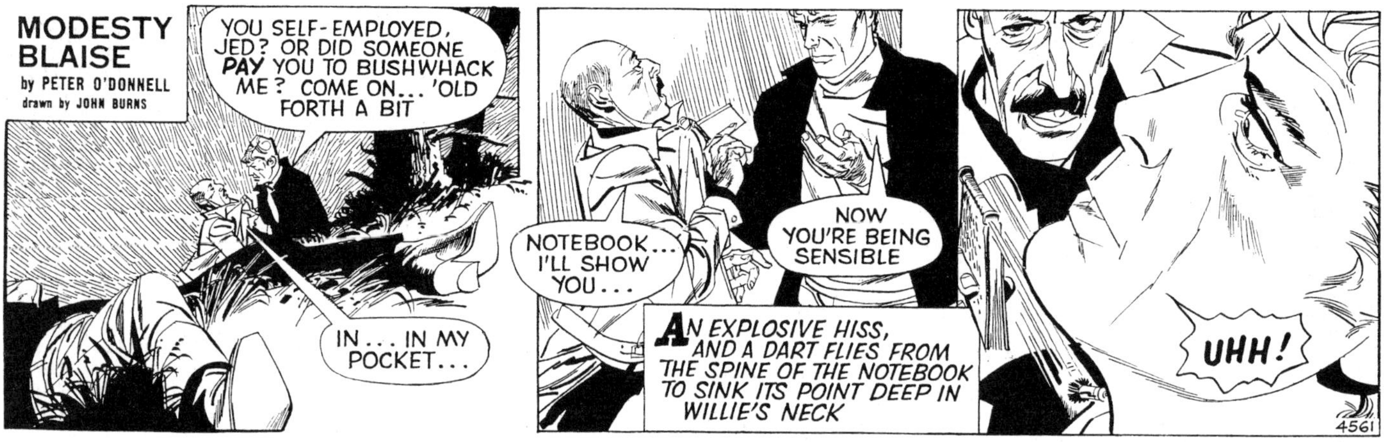
MODESTY BLAISE
by PETER O'DONNELL
drawn by JOHN BURNS
YOU SELF-EMPLOYED, JED? OR DID SOMEONE PAY YOU TO BUSHWHACK ME? COME ON... 'OLD FORTH A BIT
IN... IN MY POCKET...
NOTEBOOK... I'LL SHOW YOU...
NOW YOU'RE BEING SENSIBLE
AN EXPLOSIVE HISS, AND A DART FLIES FROM THE SPINE OF THE NOTEBOOK TO SINK ITS POINT DEEP IN WILLIE'S NECK
UHH!
4561

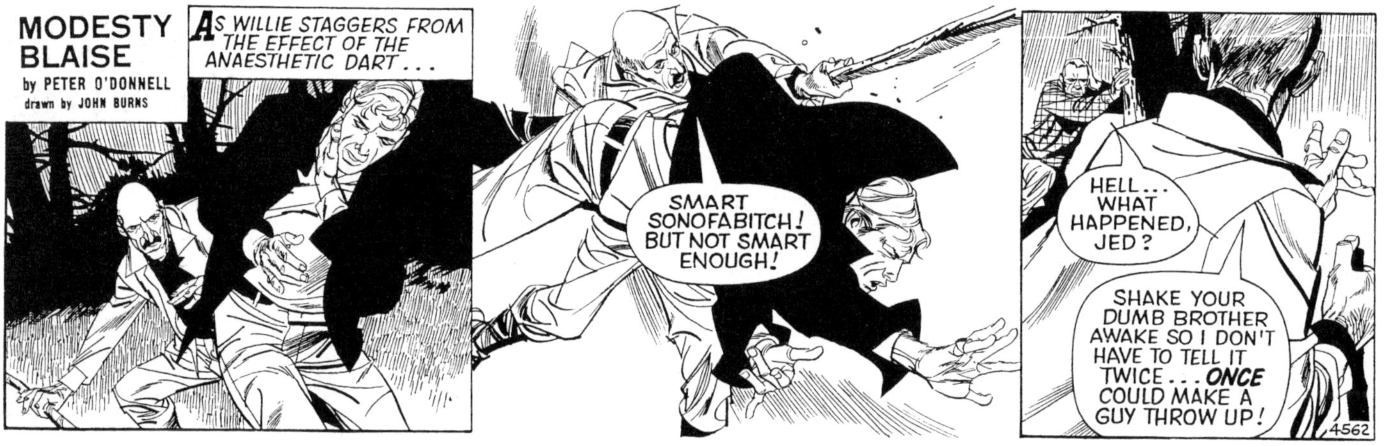
MODESTY BLAISE
by PETER O'DONNELL
drawn by JOHN BURNS
AS WILLIE STAGGERS FROM THE EFFECT OF THE ANAESTHETIC DART...
SMART SONOFABITCH! BUT NOT SMART ENOUGH!
HELL... WHAT HAPPENED, JED?
SHAKE YOUR DUMB BROTHER AWAKE SO I DON'T HAVE TO TELL IT TWICE... ONCE COULD MAKE A GUY THROW UP!
4562

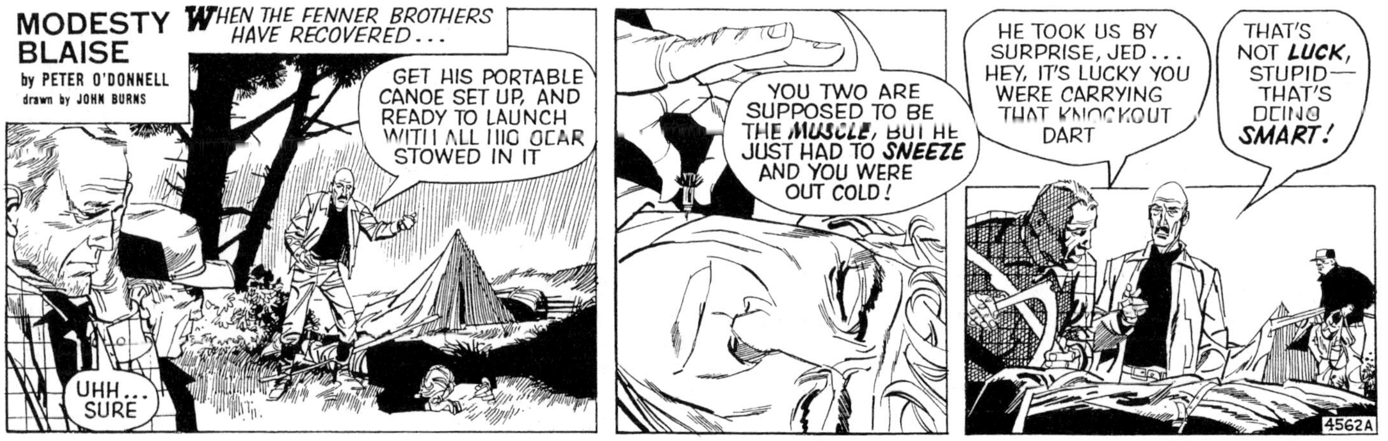
MODESTY BLAISE
by PETER O'DONNELL
drawn by JOHN BURNS
WHEN THE FENNER BROTHERS HAVE RECOVERED...
GET HIS PORTABLE CANOE SET UP, AND READY TO LAUNCH WITH ALL HIS GEAR STOWED IN IT
UHH... SURE
YOU TWO ARE SUPPOSED TO BE THE MUSCLE, BUT HE JUST HAD TO SNEEZE AND YOU WERE OUT COLD!
HE TOOK US BY SURPRISE, JED... HEY, IT'S LUCKY YOU WERE CARRYING THAT KNOCKOUT DART
THAT'S NOT LUCK, STUPID— THAT'S BEING SMART!
4562A

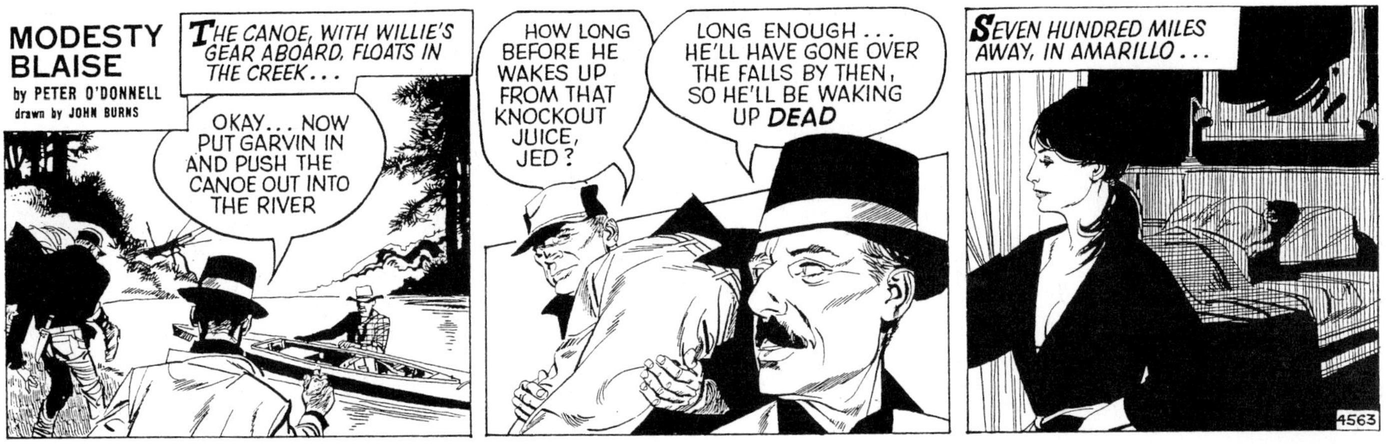
MODESTY BLAISE
by PETER O'DONNELL
drawn by JOHN BURNS
THE CANOE, WITH WILLIE'S GEAR ABOARD, FLOATS IN THE CREEK...
OKAY... NOW PUT GARVIN IN AND PUSH THE CANOE OUT INTO THE RIVER
HOW LONG BEFORE HE WAKES UP FROM THAT KNOCKOUT JUICE, JED?
LONG ENOUGH... HE'LL HAVE GONE OVER THE FALLS BY THEN, SO HE'LL BE WAKING UP DEAD
SEVEN HUNDRED MILES AWAY, IN AMARILLO...
4563

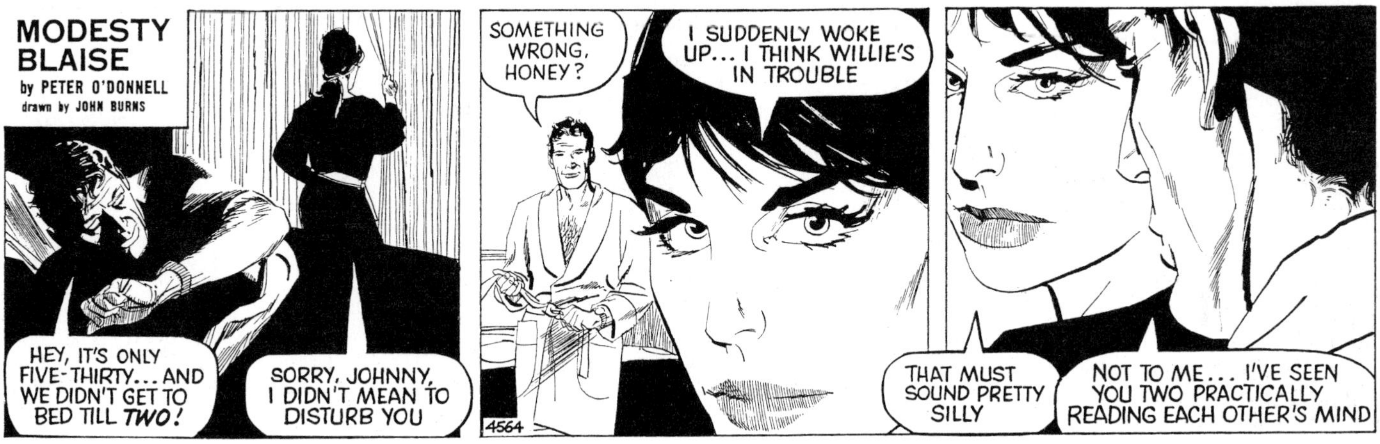
MODESTY BLAISE
by PETER O'DONNELL
drawn by JOHN BURNS
HEY, IT'S ONLY FIVE-THIRTY... AND WE DIDN'T GET TO BED TILL TWO!
SORRY, JOHNNY, I DIDN'T MEAN TO DISTURB YOU
SOMETHING WRONG, HONEY?
I SUDDENLY WOKE UP... I THINK WILLIE'S IN TROUBLE
4564
THAT MUST SOUND PRETTY SILLY
NOT TO ME... I'VE SEEN YOU TWO PRACTICALLY READING EACH OTHER'S MIND

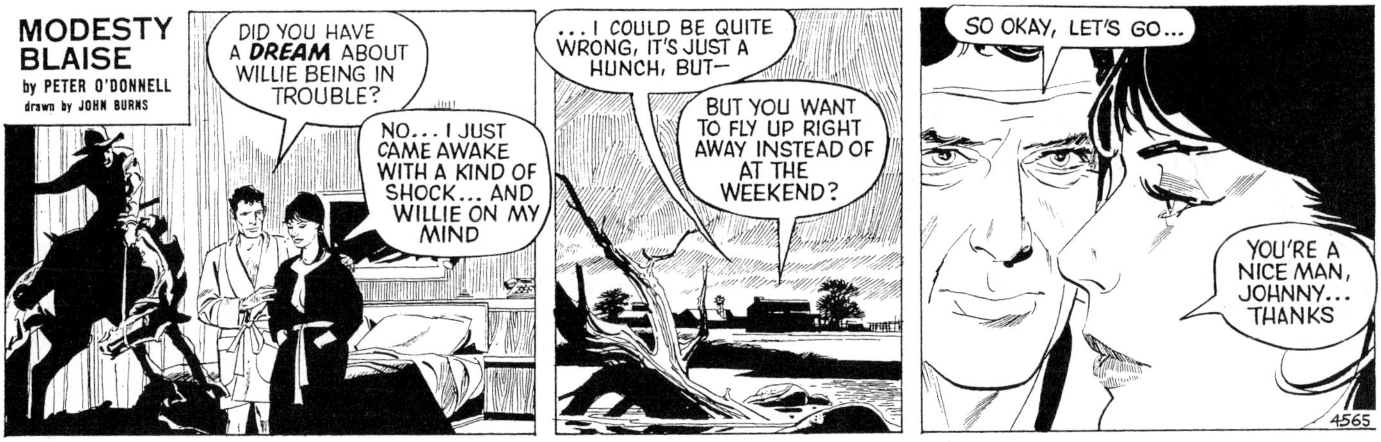
MODESTY BLAISE
by PETER O'DONNELL
drawn by JOHN BURNS
DID YOU HAVE A DREAM ABOUT WILLIE BEING IN TROUBLE?
NO... I JUST CAME AWAKE WITH A KIND OF SHOCK... AND WILLIE ON MY MIND
...I COULD BE QUITE WRONG, IT'S JUST A HUNCH, BUT—
BUT YOU WANT TO FLY UP RIGHT AWAY INSTEAD OF AT THE WEEKEND?
SO OKAY, LET'S GO...
YOU'RE A NICE MAN, JOHNNY... THANKS
4565

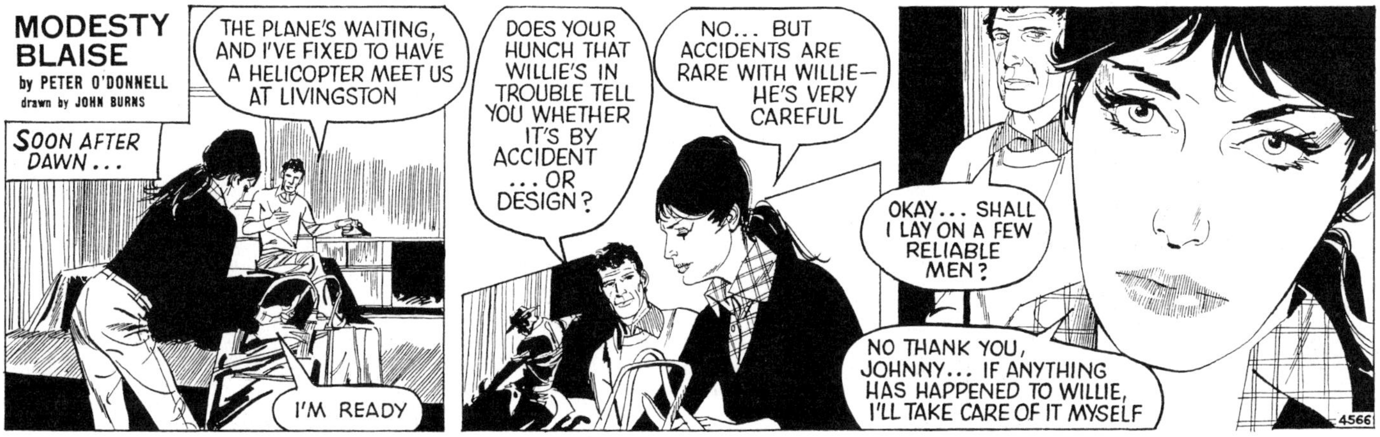
MODESTY BLAISE
by PETER O'DONNELL
drawn by JOHN BURNS
SOON AFTER DAWN...
THE PLANE'S WAITING, AND I'VE FIXED TO HAVE A HELICOPTER MEET US AT LIVINGSTON
I'M READY
DOES YOUR HUNCH THAT WILLIE'S IN TROUBLE TELL YOU WHETHER IT'S BY ACCIDENT ...OR DESIGN?
NO... BUT ACCIDENTS ARE RARE WITH WILLIE— HE'S VERY CAREFUL
OKAY... SHALL I LAY ON A FEW RELIABLE MEN?
NO THANK YOU, JOHNNY... IF ANYTHING HAS HAPPENED TO WILLIE, I'LL TAKE CARE OF IT MYSELF
4566

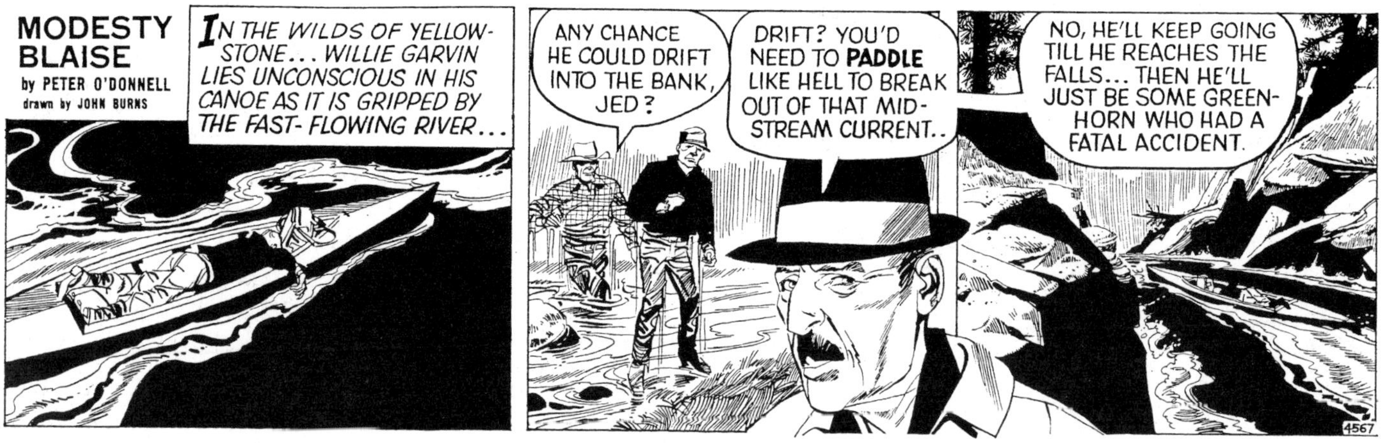
MODESTY BLAISE
by PETER O'DONNELL
drawn by JOHN BURNS
IN THE WILDS OF YELLOWSTONE... WILLIE GARVIN LIES UNCONSCIOUS IN HIS CANOE AS IT IS GRIPPED BY THE FAST-FLOWING RIVER...
ANY CHANCE HE COULD DRIFT INTO THE BANK, JED?
DRIFT? YOU'D NEED TO PADDLE LIKE HELL TO BREAK OUT OF THAT MID-STREAM CURRENT..
NO, HE'LL KEEP GOING TILL HE REACHES THE FALLS... THEN HE'LL JUST BE SOME GREENHORN WHO HAD A FATAL ACCIDENT.
4567

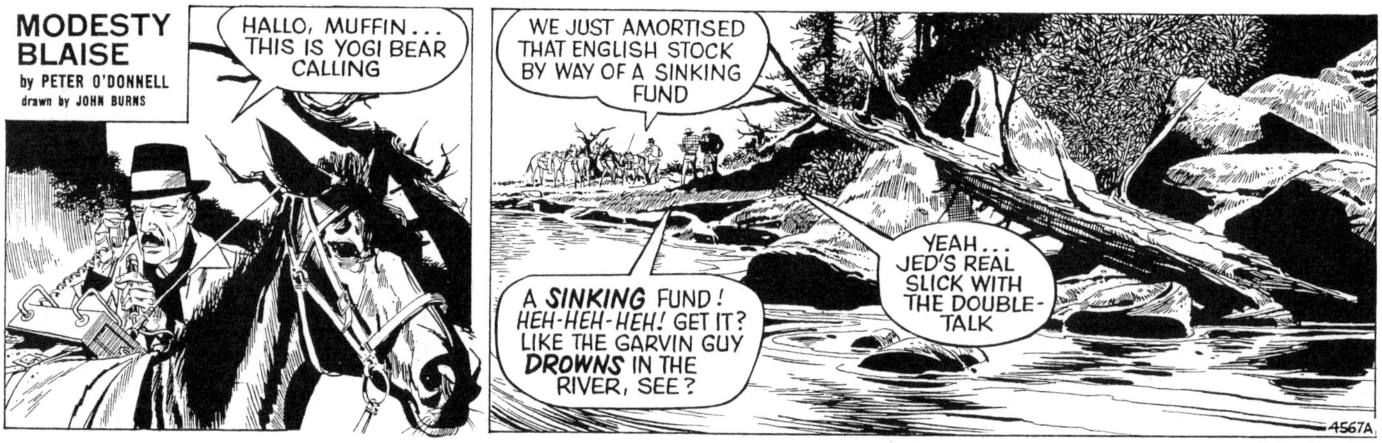
MODESTY BLAISE
by PETER O'DONNELL
drawn by JOHN BURNS
HALLO, MUFFIN... THIS IS YOGI BEAR CALLING
WE JUST AMORTISED THAT ENGLISH STOCK BY WAY OF A SINKING FUND
A SINKING FUND! HEH-HEH-HEH! GET IT? LIKE THE GARVIN GUY DROWNS IN THE RIVER, SEE?
YEAH... JED'S REAL SLICK WITH THE DOUBLE-TALK
4567A

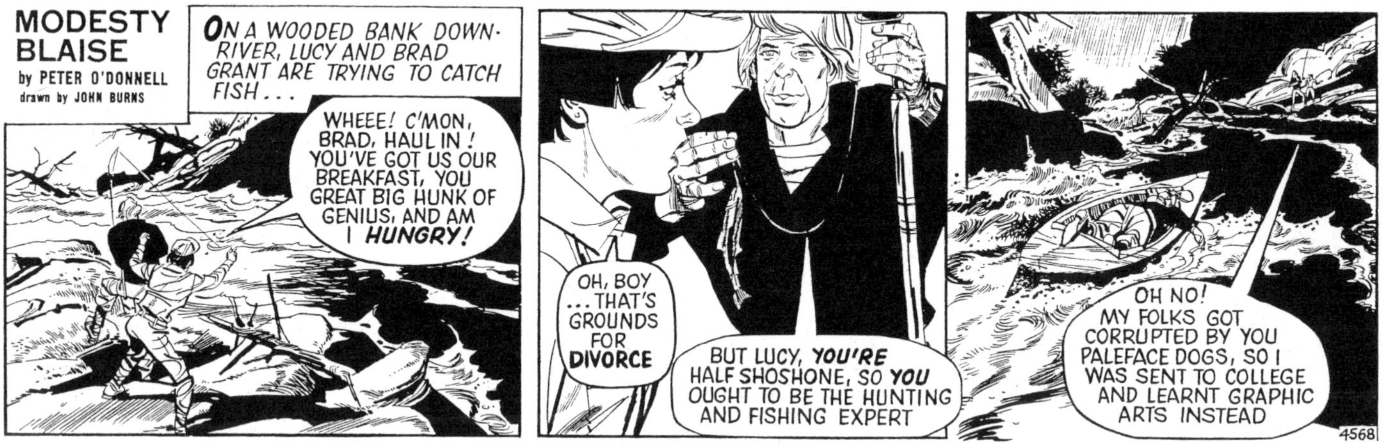
MODESTY BLAISE
by PETER O'DONNELL
drawn by JOHN BURNS
ON A WOODED BANK DOWN-RIVER, LUCY AND BRAD GRANT ARE TRYING TO CATCH FISH...
WHEEE! C'MON, BRAD, HAUL IN! YOU'VE GOT US OUR BREAKFAST, YOU GREAT BIG HUNK OF GENIUS, AND AM I HUNGRY!
OH, BOY ...THAT'S GROUNDS FOR DIVORCE
BUT LUCY, YOU'RE HALF SHOSHONE, SO YOU OUGHT TO BE THE HUNTING AND FISHING EXPERT
OH NO! MY FOLKS GOT CORRUPTED BY YOU PALEFACE DOGS, SO I WAS SENT TO COLLEGE AND LEARNT GRAPHIC ARTS INSTEAD
4568

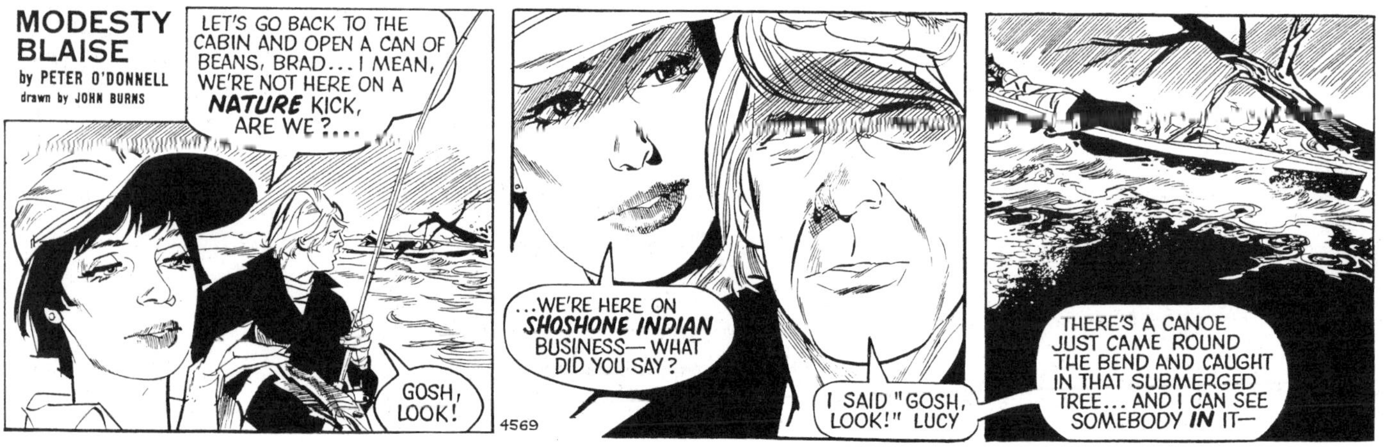
MODESTY BLAISE
by PETER O'DONNELL
drawn by JOHN BURNS
LET'S GO BACK TO THE CABIN AND OPEN A CAN OF BEANS, BRAD... I MEAN, WE'RE NOT HERE ON A NATURE KICK, ARE WE?...
GOSH, LOOK!
4569
...WE'RE HERE ON SHOSHONE INDIAN BUSINESS— WHAT DID YOU SAY?
I SAID "GOSH, LOOK!" LUCY
THERE'S A CANOE JUST CAME ROUND THE BEND AND CAUGHT IN THAT SUBMERGED TREE... AND I CAN SEE SOMEBODY IN IT—

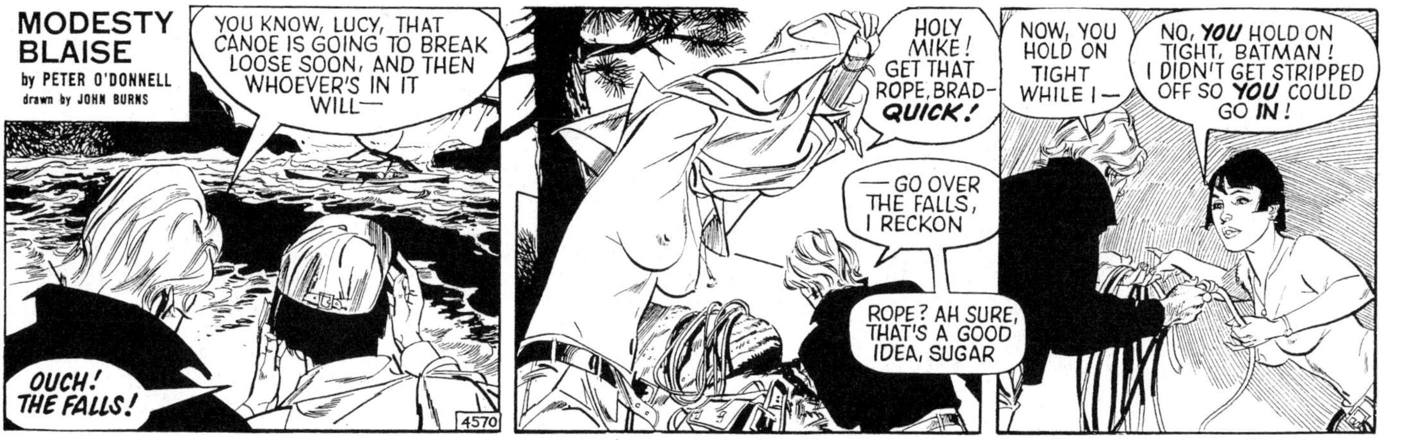
MODESTY BLAISE
by PETER O'DONNELL
drawn by JOHN BURNS
YOU KNOW, LUCY, THAT CANOE IS GOING TO BREAK LOOSE SOON, AND THEN WHOEVER'S IN IT WILL—
OUCH! THE FALLS!
4570
HOLY MIKE! GET THAT ROPE, BRAD— QUICK!
— GO OVER THE FALLS, I RECKON
ROPE? AH SURE, THAT'S A GOOD IDEA, SUGAR
NOW, YOU HOLD ON TIGHT WHILE I —
NO, YOU HOLD ON TIGHT, BATMAN! I DIDN'T GET STRIPPED OFF SO YOU COULD GO IN!

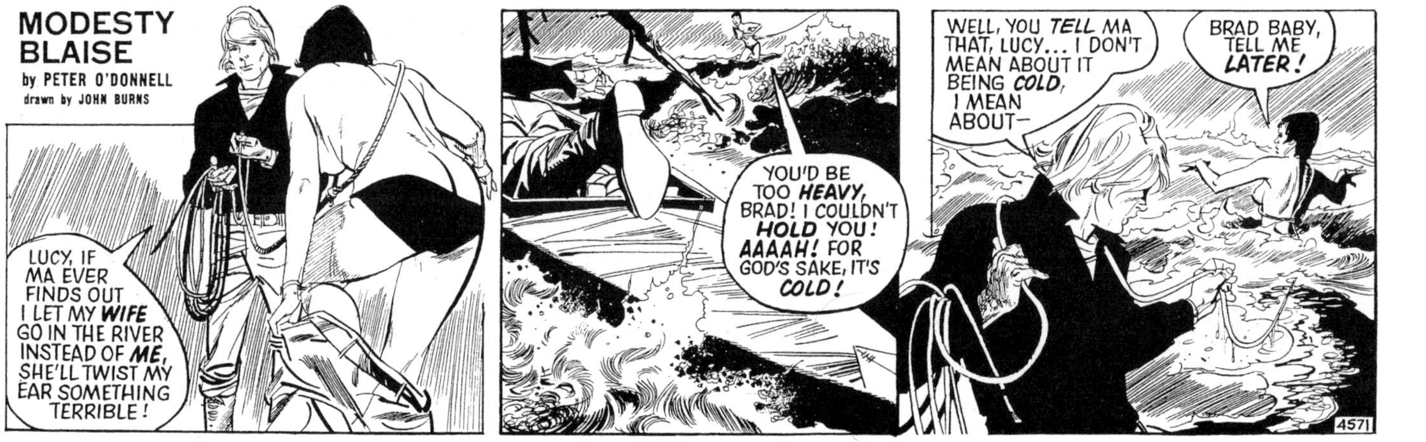
MODESTY BLAISE
by PETER O'DONNELL
drawn by JOHN BURNS
LUCY, IF MA EVER FINDS OUT I LET MY WIFE GO IN THE RIVER INSTEAD OF ME, SHE'LL TWIST MY EAR SOMETHING TERRIBLE!
YOU'D BE TOO HEAVY, BRAD! I COULDN'T HOLD YOU! AAAAH! FOR GOD'S SAKE, IT'S COLD!
WELL, YOU TELL MA THAT, LUCY... I DON'T MEAN ABOUT IT BEING COLD, I MEAN ABOUT—
BRAD BABY, TELL ME LATER!
4571

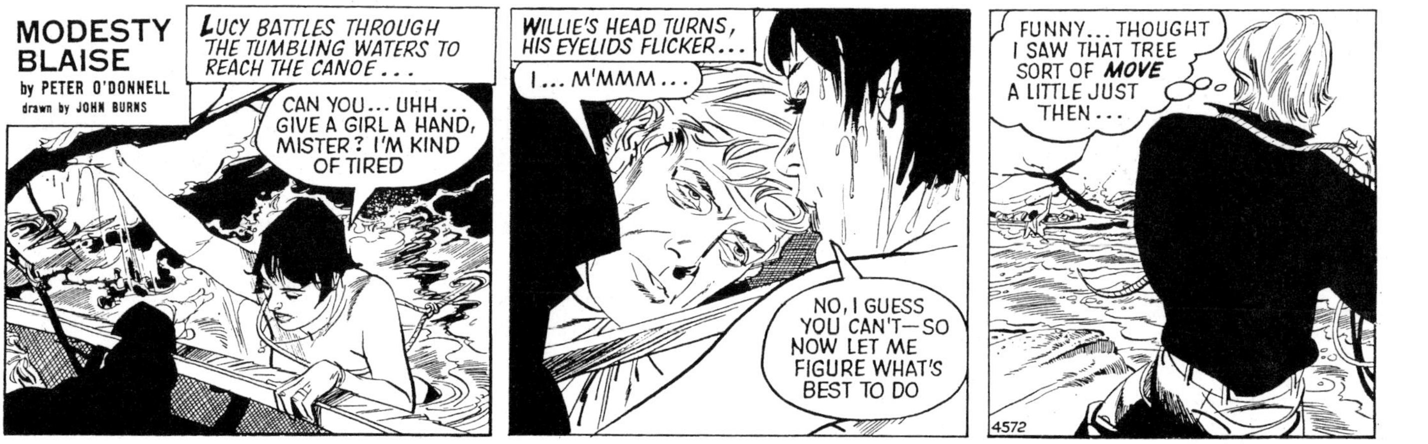
MODESTY BLAISE
by PETER O'DONNELL
drawn by JOHN BURNS
LUCY BATTLES THROUGH THE TUMBLING WATERS TO REACH THE CANOE...
CAN YOU... UHH... GIVE A GIRL A HAND, MISTER? I'M KIND OF TIRED
WILLIE'S HEAD TURNS, HIS EYELIDS FLICKER...
I... M'MMM...
NO, I GUESS YOU CAN'T—SO NOW LET ME FIGURE WHAT'S BEST TO DO
FUNNY... THOUGHT I SAW THAT TREE SORT OF MOVE A LITTLE JUST THEN...
4572

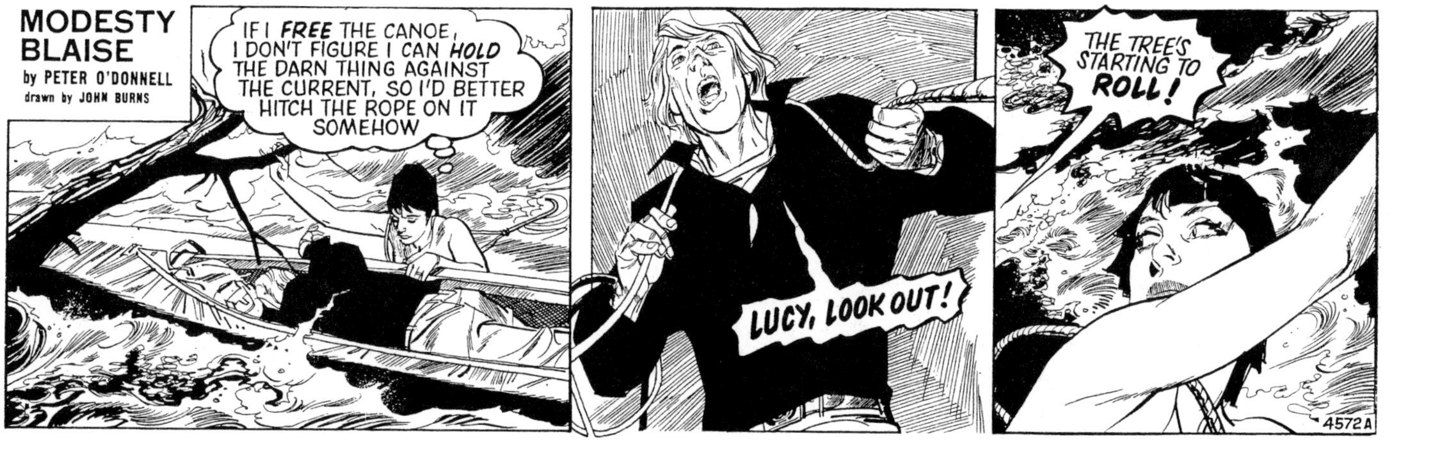
MODESTY BLAISE
by PETER O'DONNELL
drawn by JOHN BURNS
IF I FREE THE CANOE, I DON'T FIGURE I CAN HOLD THE DARN THING AGAINST THE CURRENT, SO I'D BETTER HITCH THE ROPE ON IT SOMEHOW
LUCY, LOOK OUT!
THE TREE'S STARTING TO ROLL!
4572A

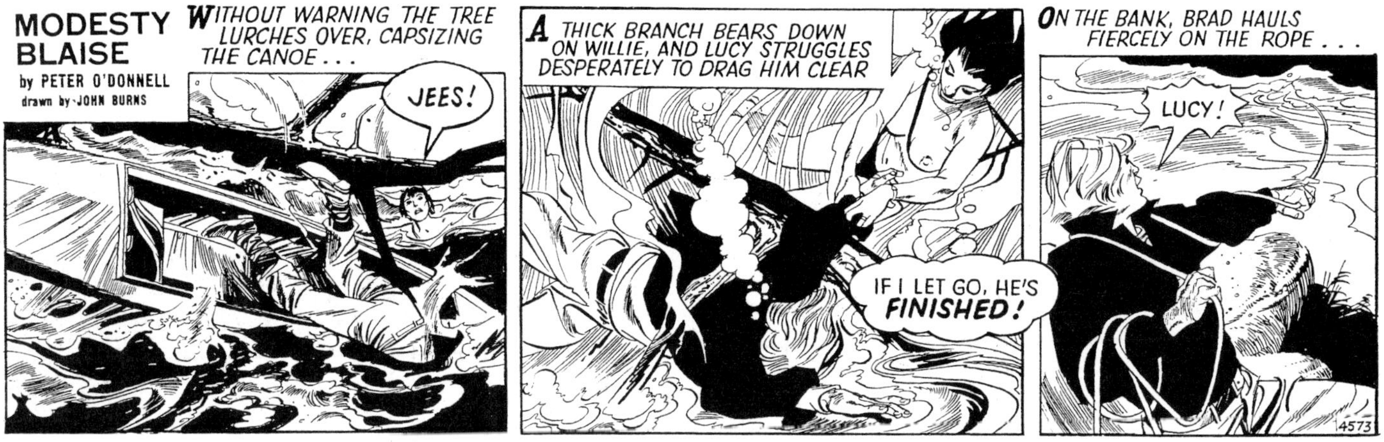
MODESTY BLAISE
by PETER O'DONNELL
drawn by JOHN BURNS
WITHOUT WARNING THE TREE LURCHES OVER, CAPSIZING THE CANOE . . .
JEES!
A THICK BRANCH BEARS DOWN ON WILLIE, AND LUCY STRUGGLES DESPERATELY TO DRAG HIM CLEAR
IF I LET GO, HE'S FINISHED!
ON THE BANK, BRAD HAULS FIERCELY ON THE ROPE . . .
LUCY!
4573

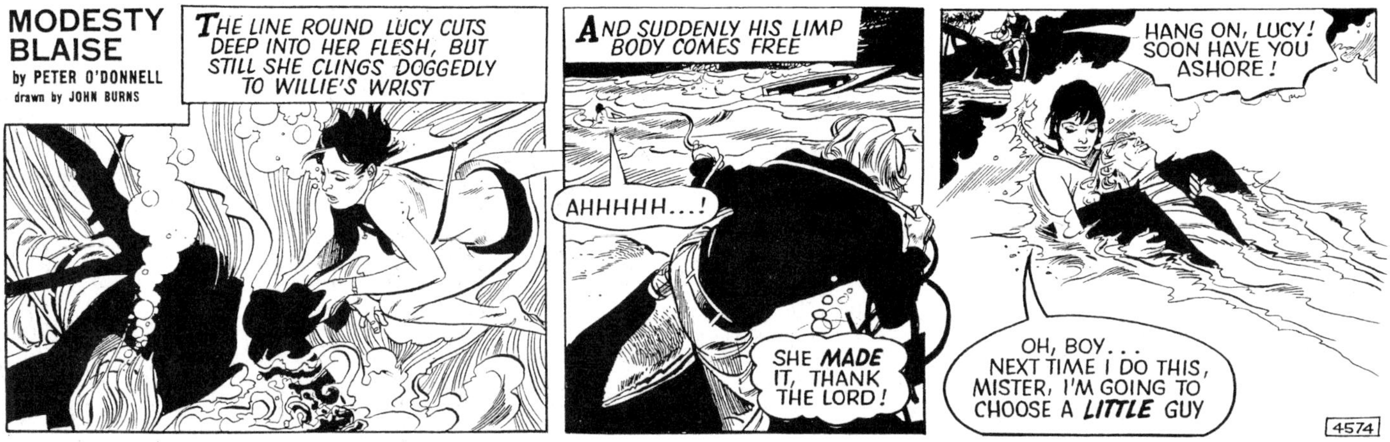
MODESTY BLAISE
by PETER O'DONNELL
drawn by JOHN BURNS
THE LINE ROUND LUCY CUTS DEEP INTO HER FLESH, BUT STILL SHE CLINGS DOGGEDLY TO WILLIE'S WRIST
AND SUDDENLY HIS LIMP BODY COMES FREE
AHHHHH...!
SHE MADE IT, THANK THE LORD!
HANG ON, LUCY! SOON HAVE YOU ASHORE!
OH, BOY... NEXT TIME I DO THIS, MISTER, I'M GOING TO CHOOSE A LITTLE GUY
4574

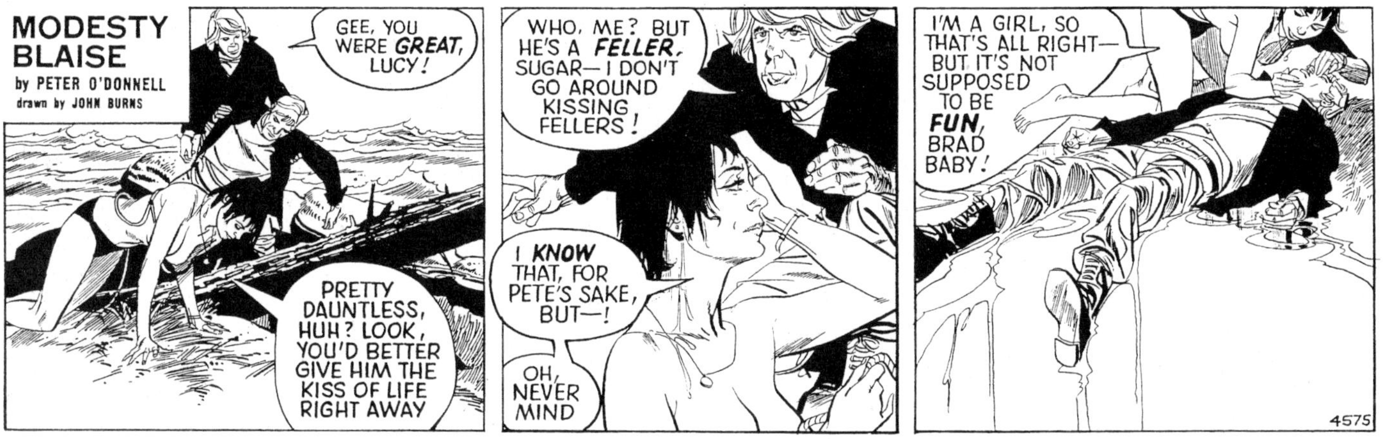
MODESTY BLAISE
by PETER O'DONNELL
drawn by JOHN BURNS
GEE, YOU WERE GREAT, LUCY!
PRETTY DAUNTLESS, HUH? LOOK, YOU'D BETTER GIVE HIM THE KISS OF LIFE RIGHT AWAY
WHO, ME? BUT HE'S A FELLER, SUGAR— I DON'T GO AROUND KISSING FELLERS!
I KNOW THAT, FOR PETE'S SAKE, BUT—!
OH, NEVER MIND
I'M A GIRL, SO THAT'S ALL RIGHT— BUT IT'S NOT SUPPOSED TO BE FUN, BRAD BABY!
4575

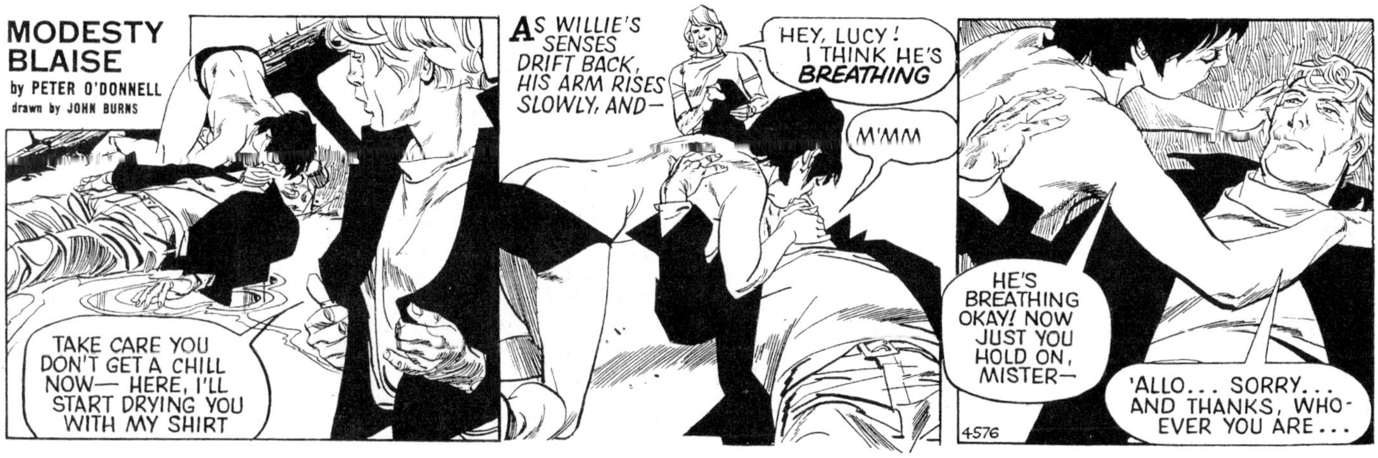
MODESTY BLAISE
by PETER O'DONNELL
drawn by JOHN BURNS
TAKE CARE YOU DON'T GET A CHILL NOW— HERE, I'LL START DRYING YOU WITH MY SHIRT
AS WILLIE'S SENSES DRIFT BACK, HIS ARM RISES SLOWLY, AND—
HEY, LUCY! I THINK HE'S BREATHING
M'MM
HE'S BREATHING OKAY! NOW JUST YOU HOLD ON, MISTER—
'ALLO... SORRY... AND THANKS, WHO-EVER YOU ARE...
4576

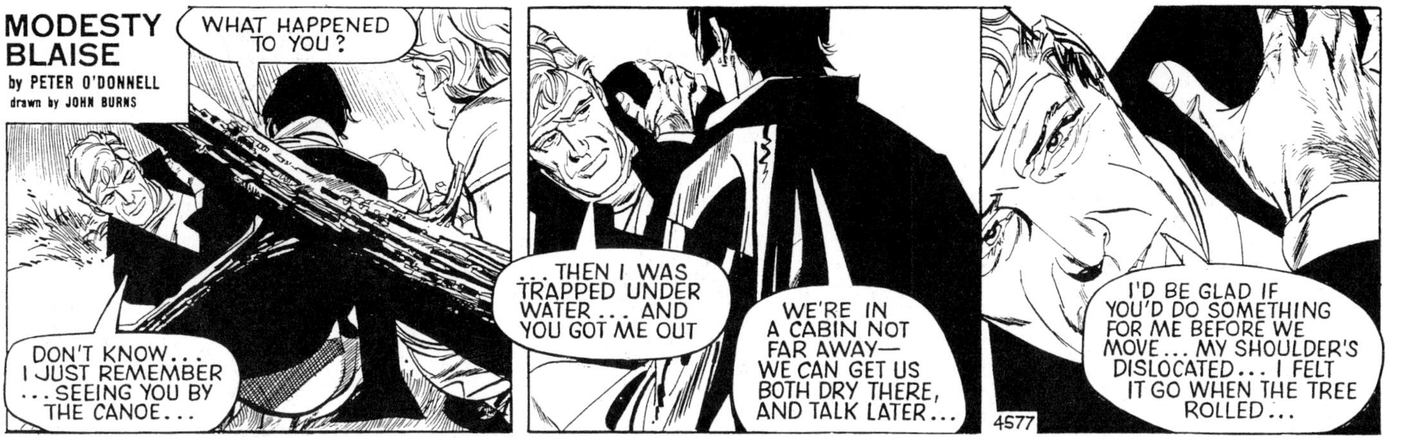
MODESTY BLAISE
by PETER O'DONNELL
drawn by JOHN BURNS
WHAT HAPPENED TO YOU?
DON'T KNOW... I JUST REMEMBER ...SEEING YOU BY THE CANOE...
...THEN I WAS TRAPPED UNDER WATER... AND YOU GOT ME OUT
WE'RE IN A CABIN NOT FAR AWAY— WE CAN GET US BOTH DRY THERE, AND TALK LATER...
I'D BE GLAD IF YOU'D DO SOMETHING FOR ME BEFORE WE MOVE... MY SHOULDER'S DISLOCATED... I FELT IT GO WHEN THE TREE ROLLED...
4577

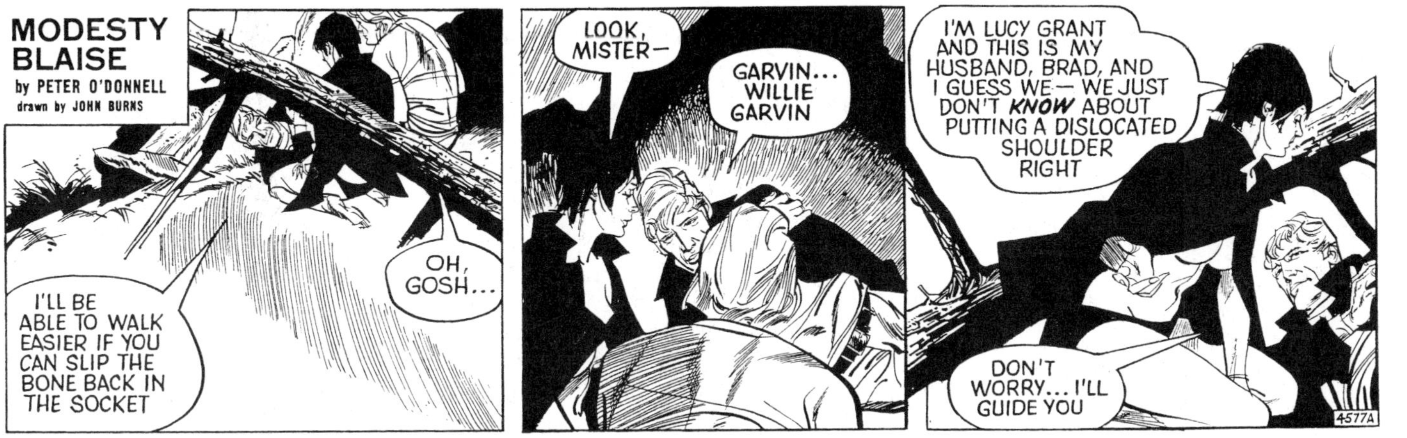
MODESTY BLAISE
by PETER O'DONNELL
drawn by JOHN BURNS
I'LL BE ABLE TO WALK EASIER IF YOU CAN SLIP THE BONE BACK IN THE SOCKET
OH, GOSH...
LOOK, MISTER—
GARVIN... WILLIE GARVIN
I'M LUCY GRANT AND THIS IS MY HUSBAND, BRAD, AND I GUESS WE— WE JUST DON'T KNOW ABOUT PUTTING A DISLOCATED SHOULDER RIGHT
DON'T WORRY... I'LL GUIDE YOU
4577A

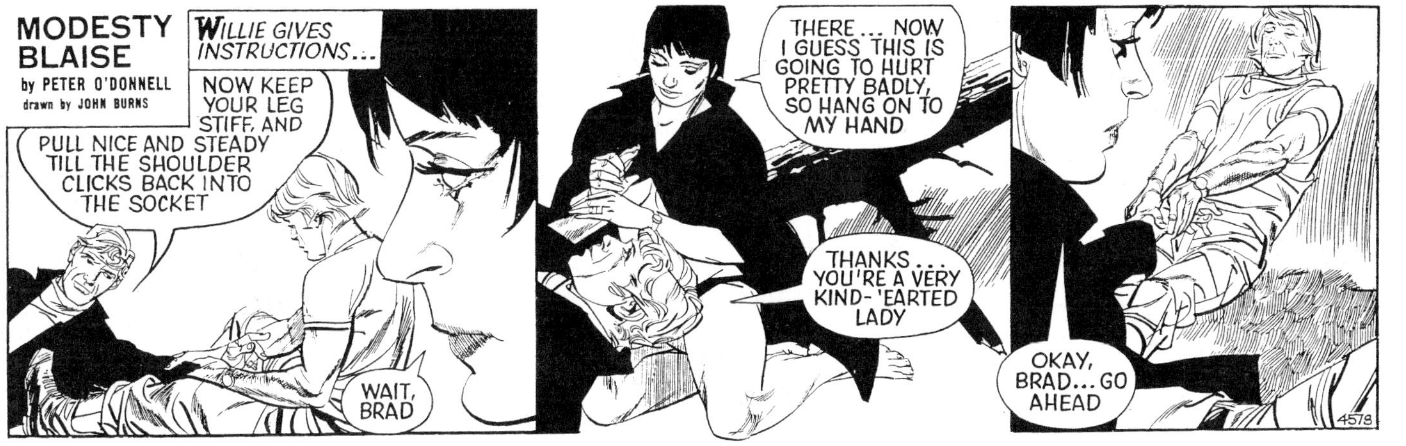
MODESTY BLAISE
by PETER O'DONNELL
drawn by JOHN BURNS
WILLIE GIVES INSTRUCTIONS...
NOW KEEP YOUR LEG STIFF, AND
PULL NICE AND STEADY TILL THE SHOULDER CLICKS BACK INTO THE SOCKET
WAIT, BRAD
THERE... NOW I GUESS THIS IS GOING TO HURT PRETTY BADLY, SO HANG ON TO MY HAND
THANKS... YOU'RE A VERY KIND-'EARTED LADY
OKAY, BRAD... GO AHEAD
4578

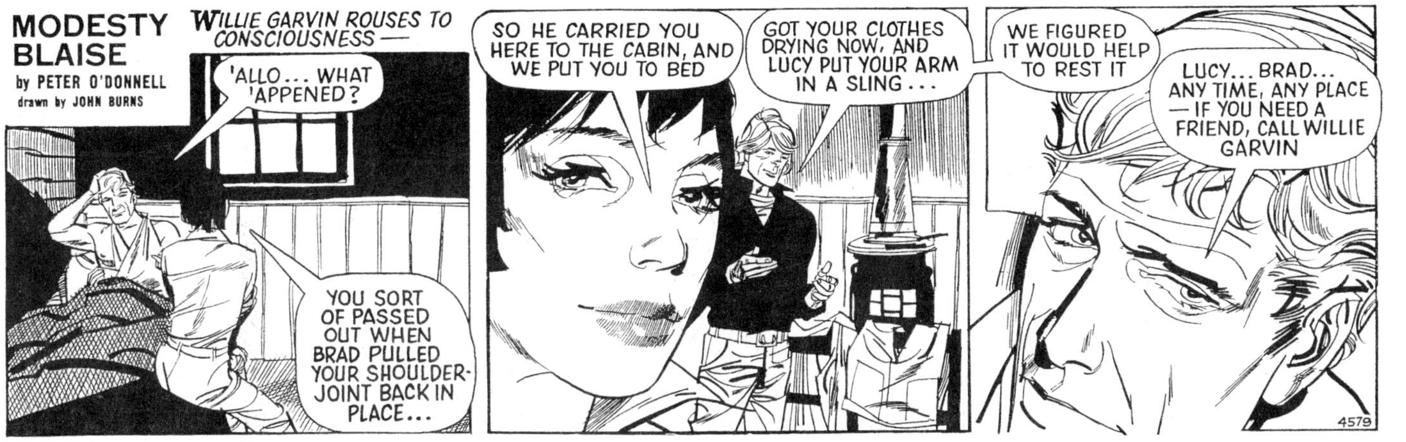
MODESTY BLAISE
by PETER O'DONNELL
drawn by JOHN BURNS
WILLIE GARVIN ROUSES TO CONSCIOUSNESS—
'ALLO... WHAT 'APPENED?
YOU SORT OF PASSED OUT WHEN BRAD PULLED YOUR SHOULDER-JOINT BACK IN PLACE...
SO HE CARRIED YOU HERE TO THE CABIN, AND WE PUT YOU TO BED
GOT YOUR CLOTHES DRYING NOW, AND LUCY PUT YOUR ARM IN A SLING...
WE FIGURED IT WOULD HELP TO REST IT
LUCY... BRAD... ANY TIME, ANY PLACE —IF YOU NEED A FRIEND, CALL WILLIE GARVIN
4579

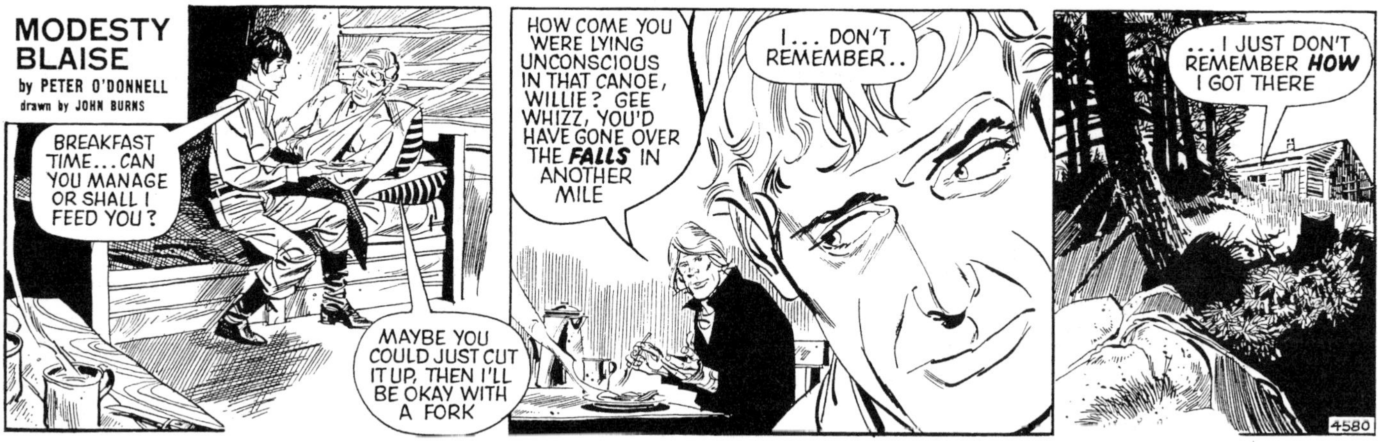
MODESTY BLAISE
by PETER O'DONNELL
drawn by JOHN BURNS
BREAKFAST TIME... CAN YOU MANAGE OR SHALL I FEED YOU?
MAYBE YOU COULD JUST CUT IT UP, THEN I'LL BE OKAY WITH A FORK
HOW COME YOU WERE LYING UNCONSCIOUS IN THAT CANOE, WILLIE? GEE WHIZZ, YOU'D HAVE GONE OVER THE **FALLS** IN ANOTHER MILE
I... DON'T REMEMBER..
...I JUST DON'T REMEMBER **HOW** I GOT THERE
4580

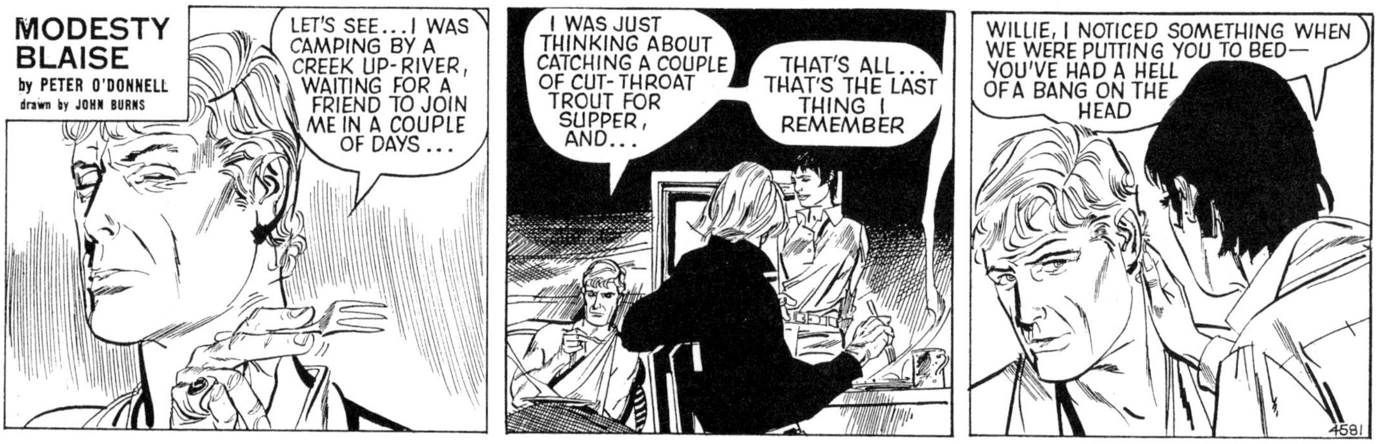
MODESTY BLAISE
by PETER O'DONNELL
drawn by JOHN BURNS
LET'S SEE... I WAS CAMPING BY A CREEK UP-RIVER, WAITING FOR A FRIEND TO JOIN ME IN A COUPLE OF DAYS...
I WAS JUST THINKING ABOUT CATCHING A COUPLE OF CUT-THROAT TROUT FOR SUPPER, AND...
THAT'S ALL... THAT'S THE LAST THING I REMEMBER
WILLIE, I NOTICED SOMETHING WHEN WE WERE PUTTING YOU TO BED— YOU'VE HAD A HELL OF A BANG ON THE HEAD
4581

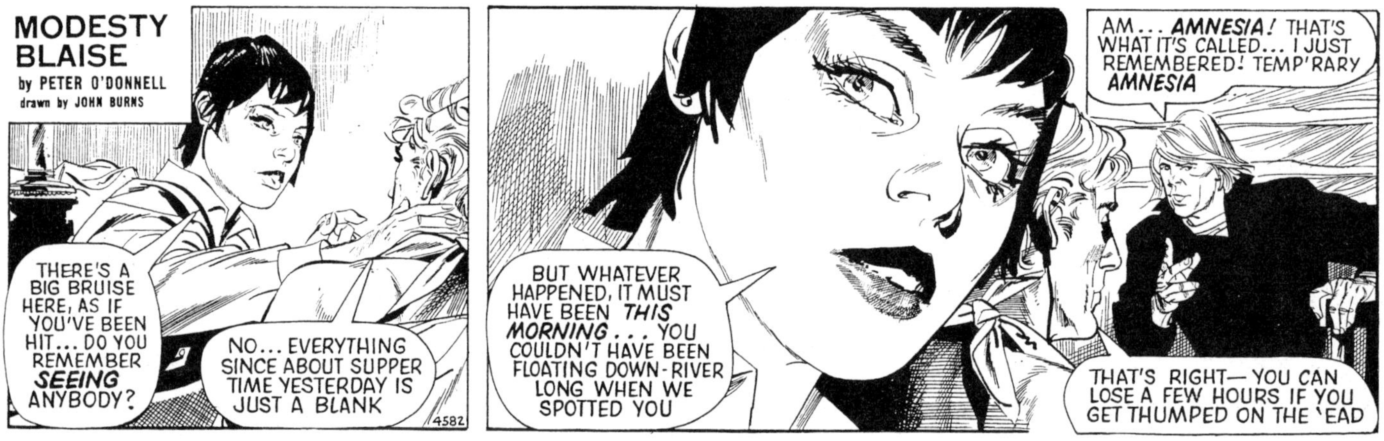
MODESTY BLAISE
by PETER O'DONNELL
drawn by JOHN BURNS
THERE'S A BIG BRUISE HERE, AS IF YOU'VE BEEN HIT... DO YOU REMEMBER **SEEING** ANYBODY?
NO... EVERYTHING SINCE ABOUT SUPPER TIME YESTERDAY IS JUST A BLANK
4582
BUT WHATEVER HAPPENED, IT MUST HAVE BEEN **THIS MORNING**... YOU COULDN'T HAVE BEEN FLOATING DOWN-RIVER LONG WHEN WE SPOTTED YOU
AM... **AMNESIA!** THAT'S WHAT IT'S CALLED... I JUST REMEMBERED! TEMP'RARY **AMNESIA**
THAT'S RIGHT— YOU CAN LOSE A FEW HOURS IF YOU GET THUMPED ON THE 'EAD

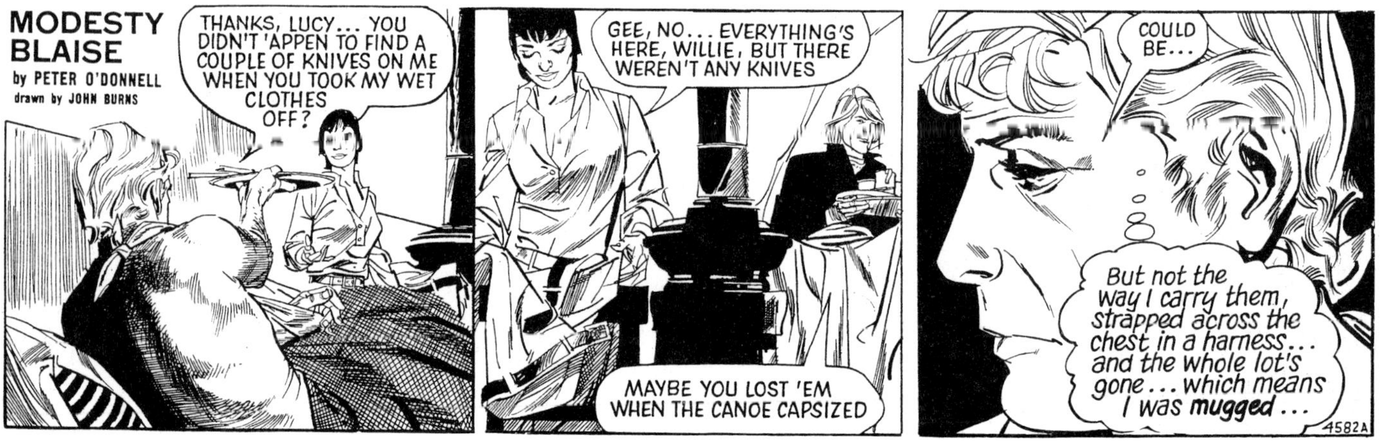
MODESTY BLAISE
by PETER O'DONNELL
drawn by JOHN BURNS
THANKS, LUCY... YOU DIDN'T 'APPEN TO FIND A COUPLE OF KNIVES ON ME WHEN YOU TOOK MY WET CLOTHES OFF?
GEE, NO... EVERYTHING'S HERE, WILLIE, BUT THERE WEREN'T ANY KNIVES
MAYBE YOU LOST 'EM WHEN THE CANOE CAPSIZED
COULD BE...
But not the way I carry them, strapped across the chest in a harness... and the whole lot's gone... which means I was ***mugged***...
4582A

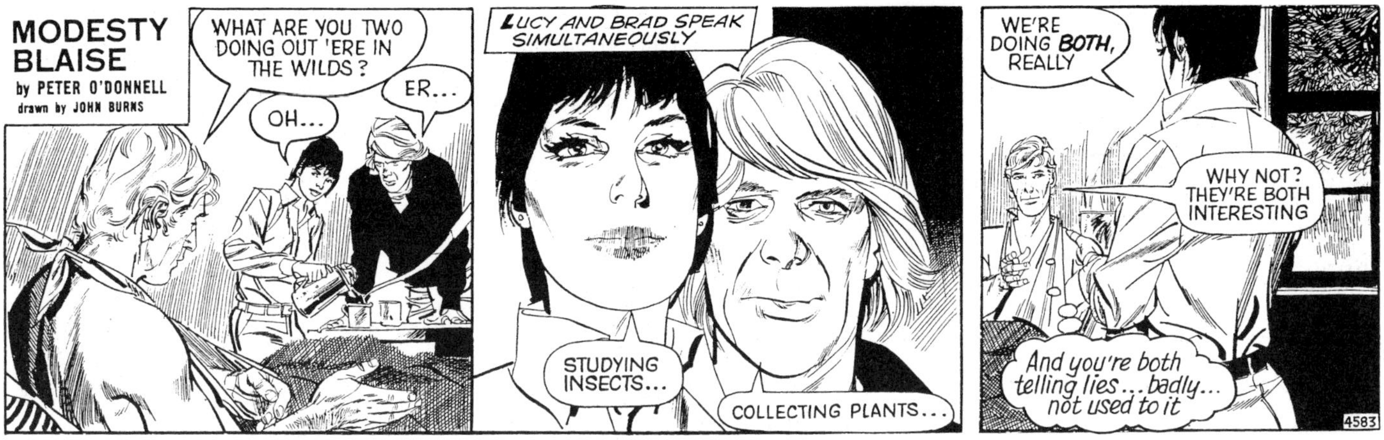
MODESTY BLAISE
by PETER O'DONNELL
drawn by JOHN BURNS
WHAT ARE YOU TWO DOING OUT 'ERE IN THE WILDS?
OH...
ER...
LUCY AND BRAD SPEAK SIMULTANEOUSLY
STUDYING INSECTS...
COLLECTING PLANTS...
WE'RE DOING BOTH, REALLY
WHY NOT? THEY'RE BOTH INTERESTING
And you're both telling lies... badly... not used to it
4583

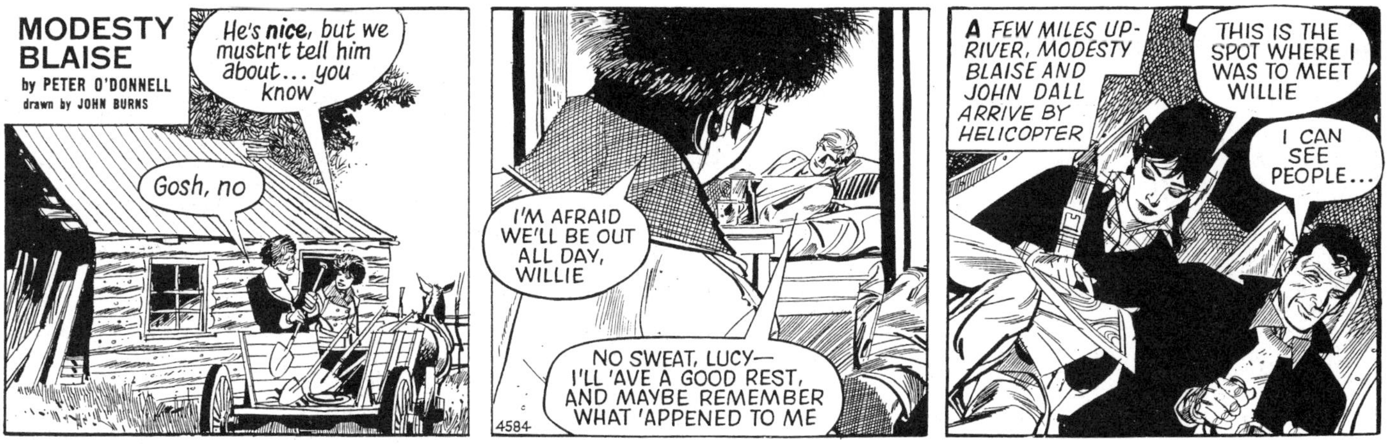
MODESTY BLAISE
by PETER O'DONNELL
drawn by JOHN BURNS
He's nice, but we mustn't tell him about... you know
Gosh, no
I'M AFRAID WE'LL BE OUT ALL DAY, WILLIE
NO SWEAT, LUCY— I'LL 'AVE A GOOD REST, AND MAYBE REMEMBER WHAT 'APPENED TO ME
4584
A FEW MILES UP-RIVER, MODESTY BLAISE AND JOHN DALL ARRIVE BY HELICOPTER
THIS IS THE SPOT WHERE I WAS TO MEET WILLIE
I CAN SEE PEOPLE...

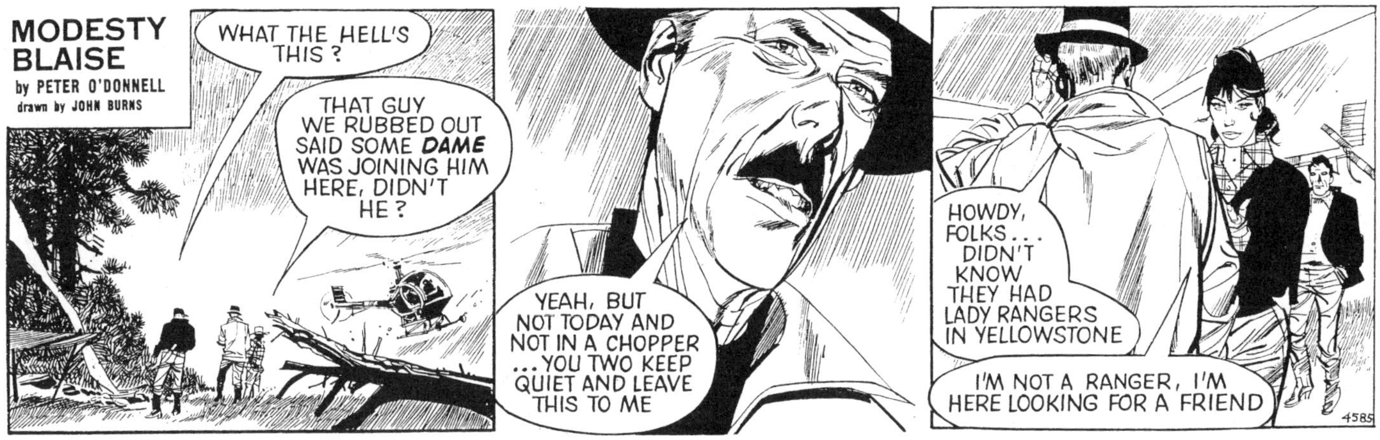
MODESTY BLAISE
by PETER O'DONNELL
drawn by JOHN BURNS
WHAT THE HELL'S THIS?
THAT GUY WE RUBBED OUT SAID SOME DAME WAS JOINING HIM HERE, DIDN'T HE?
YEAH, BUT NOT TODAY AND NOT IN A CHOPPER ...YOU TWO KEEP QUIET AND LEAVE THIS TO ME
HOWDY, FOLKS... DIDN'T KNOW THEY HAD LADY RANGERS IN YELLOWSTONE
I'M NOT A RANGER, I'M HERE LOOKING FOR A FRIEND
4585

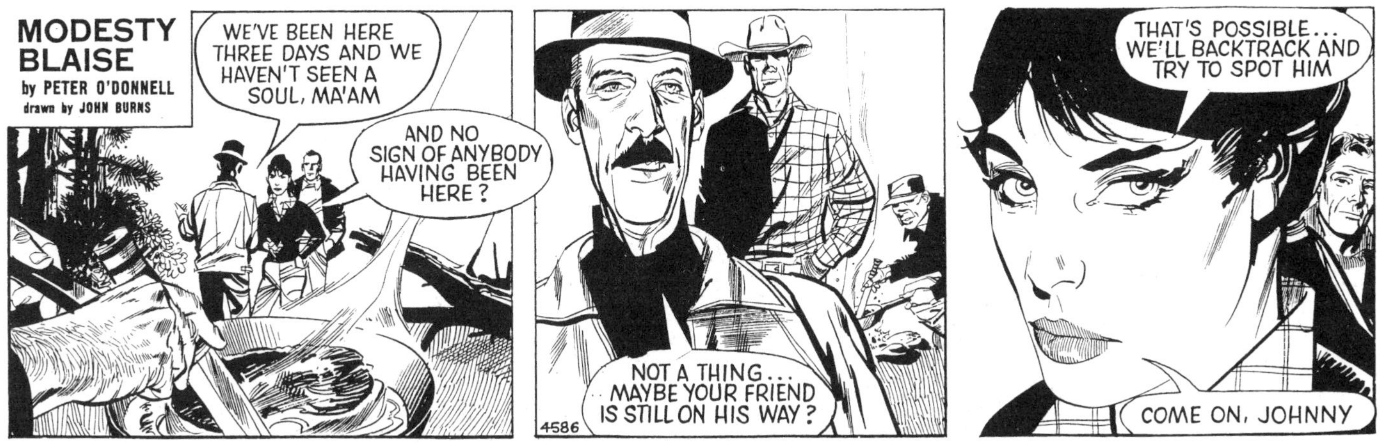
MODESTY BLAISE
by PETER O'DONNELL
drawn by JOHN BURNS
WE'VE BEEN HERE THREE DAYS AND WE HAVEN'T SEEN A SOUL, MA'AM
AND NO SIGN OF ANYBODY HAVING BEEN HERE?
NOT A THING... MAYBE YOUR FRIEND IS STILL ON HIS WAY?
4586
THAT'S POSSIBLE... WE'LL BACKTRACK AND TRY TO SPOT HIM
COME ON, JOHNNY

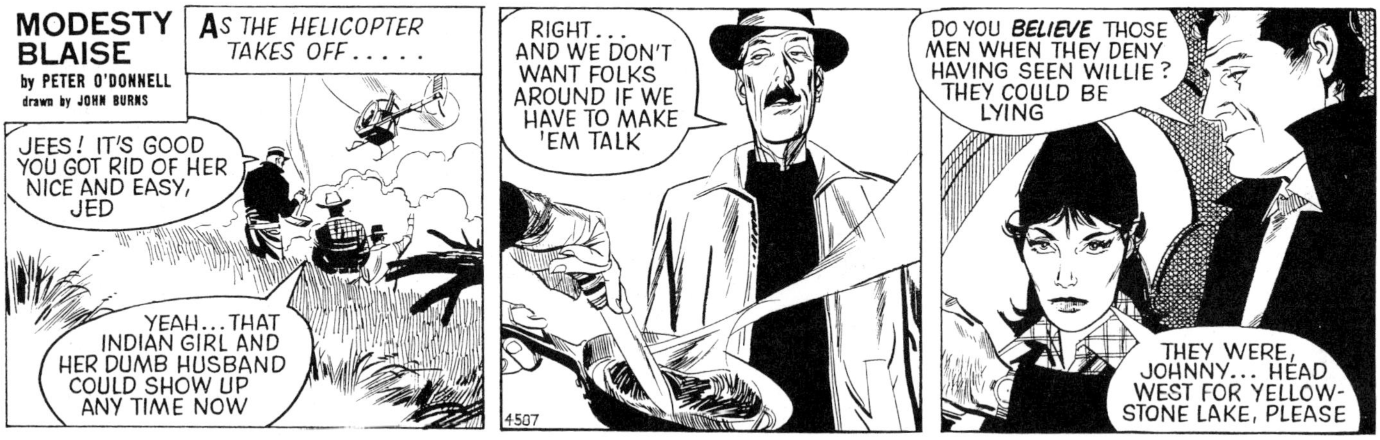
MODESTY BLAISE
by PETER O'DONNELL
drawn by JOHN BURNS
AS THE HELICOPTER TAKES OFF . . . . .
JEES! IT'S GOOD YOU GOT RID OF HER NICE AND EASY, JED
YEAH... THAT INDIAN GIRL AND HER DUMB HUSBAND COULD SHOW UP ANY TIME NOW
RIGHT... AND WE DON'T WANT FOLKS AROUND IF WE HAVE TO MAKE 'EM TALK
4587
DO YOU BELIEVE THOSE MEN WHEN THEY DENY HAVING SEEN WILLIE? THEY COULD BE LYING
THEY WERE, JOHNNY... HEAD WEST FOR YELLOWSTONE LAKE, PLEASE

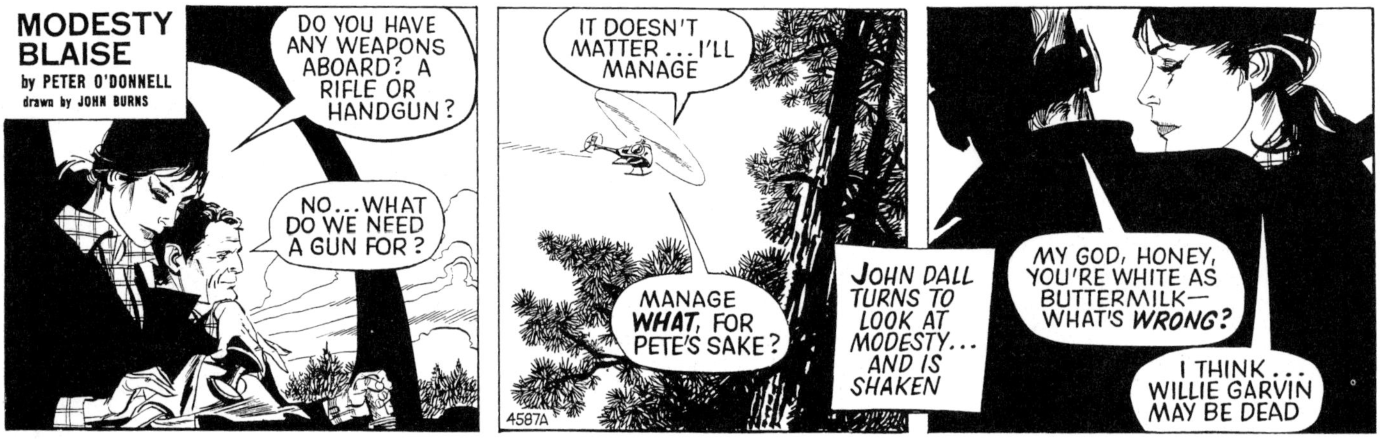
MODESTY BLAISE
by PETER O'DONNELL
drawn by JOHN BURNS
DO YOU HAVE ANY WEAPONS ABOARD? A RIFLE OR HANDGUN?
NO... WHAT DO WE NEED A GUN FOR?
IT DOESN'T MATTER... I'LL MANAGE
MANAGE WHAT, FOR PETE'S SAKE?
4587A
JOHN DALL TURNS TO LOOK AT MODESTY... AND IS SHAKEN
MY GOD, HONEY, YOU'RE WHITE AS BUTTERMILK— WHAT'S WRONG?
I THINK... WILLIE GARVIN MAY BE DEAD

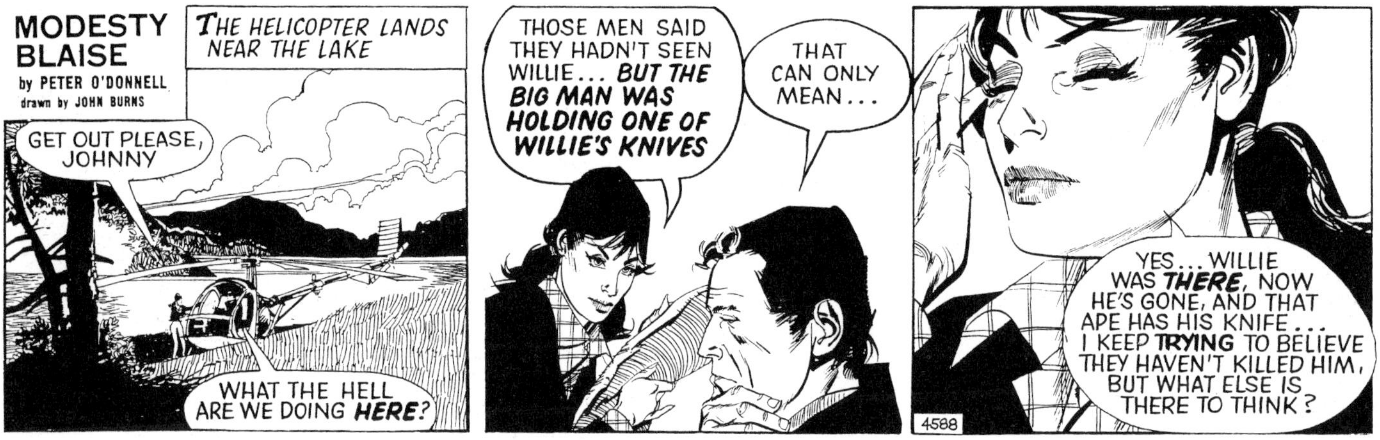
MODESTY BLAISE
by PETER O'DONNELL
drawn by JOHN BURNS
THE HELICOPTER LANDS NEAR THE LAKE
GET OUT PLEASE, JOHNNY
WHAT THE HELL ARE WE DOING HERE?
THOSE MEN SAID THEY HADN'T SEEN WILLIE... BUT THE BIG MAN WAS HOLDING ONE OF WILLIE'S KNIVES
THAT CAN ONLY MEAN...
YES... WILLIE WAS THERE, NOW HE'S GONE, AND THAT APE HAS HIS KNIFE... I KEEP TRYING TO BELIEVE THEY HAVEN'T KILLED HIM, BUT WHAT ELSE IS THERE TO THINK?
4588

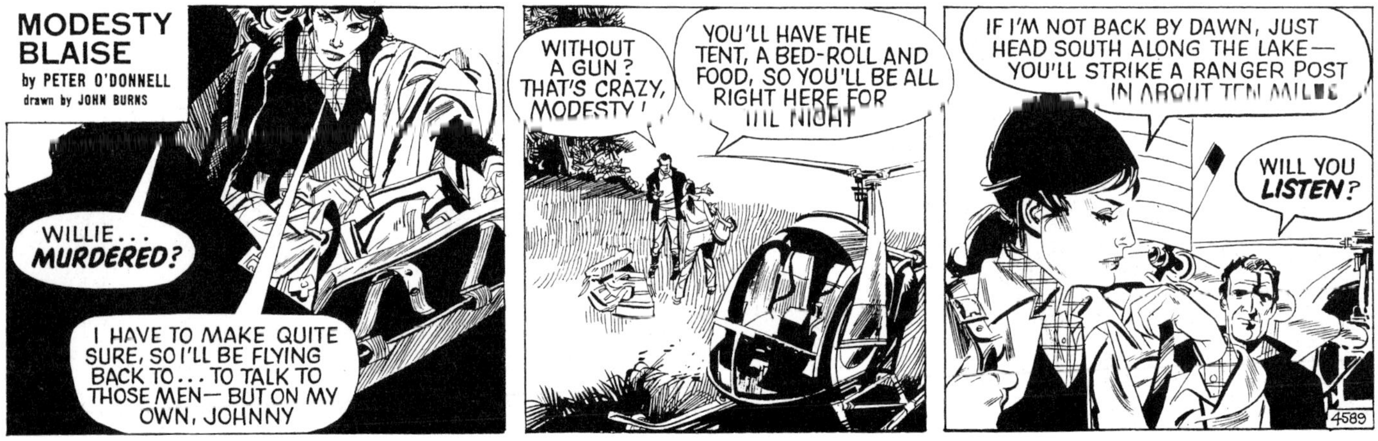
MODESTY BLAISE
by PETER O'DONNELL
drawn by JOHN BURNS
WILLIE... MURDERED?
I HAVE TO MAKE QUITE SURE, SO I'LL BE FLYING BACK TO... TO TALK TO THOSE MEN— BUT ON MY OWN, JOHNNY
WITHOUT A GUN? THAT'S CRAZY, MODESTY!
YOU'LL HAVE THE TENT, A BED-ROLL AND FOOD, SO YOU'LL BE ALL RIGHT HERE FOR
IF I'M NOT BACK BY DAWN, JUST HEAD SOUTH ALONG THE LAKE— YOU'LL STRIKE A RANGER POST
WILL YOU LISTEN?
4589

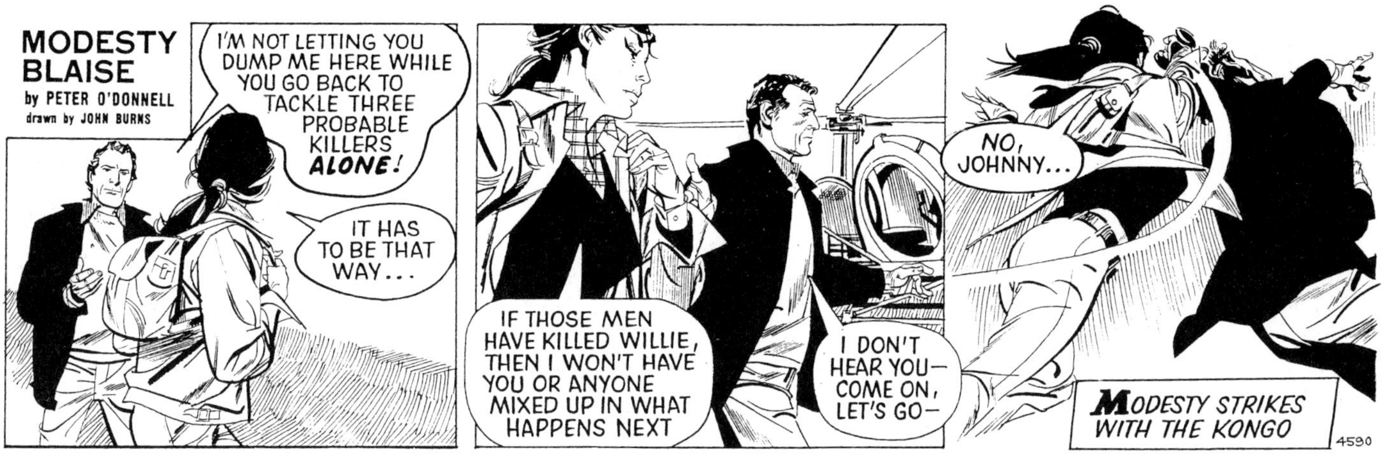
MODESTY BLAISE
by PETER O'DONNELL
drawn by JOHN BURNS
I'M NOT LETTING YOU DUMP ME HERE WHILE YOU GO BACK TO TACKLE THREE PROBABLE KILLERS ALONE!
IT HAS TO BE THAT WAY...
IF THOSE MEN HAVE KILLED WILLIE, THEN I WON'T HAVE YOU OR ANYONE MIXED UP IN WHAT HAPPENS NEXT
I DON'T HEAR YOU— COME ON, LET'S GO—
NO, JOHNNY...
MODESTY STRIKES WITH THE KONGO
4590

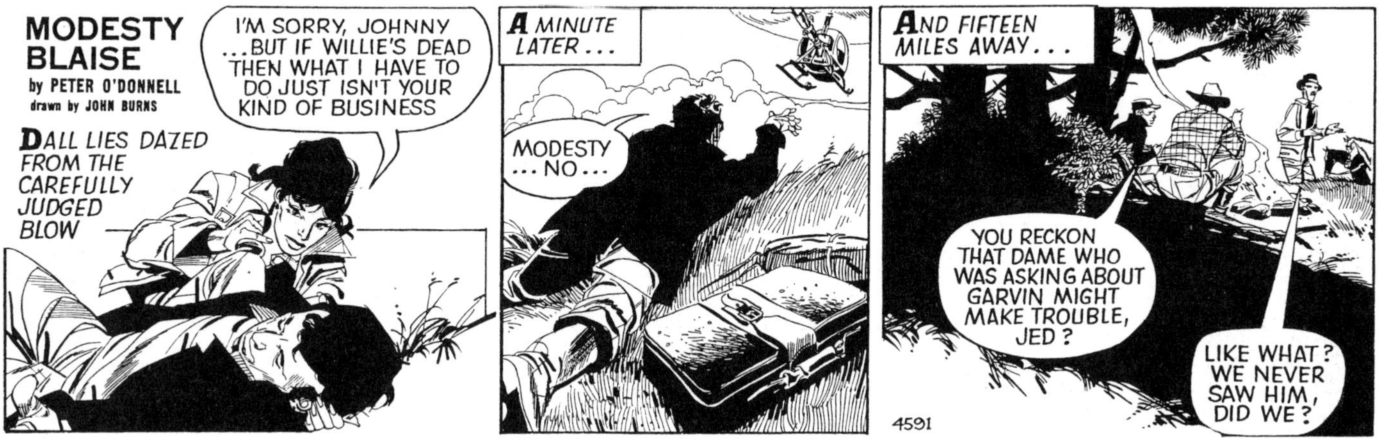
MODESTY BLAISE
by PETER O'DONNELL
drawn by JOHN BURNS
I'M SORRY, JOHNNY ...BUT IF WILLIE'S DEAD THEN WHAT I HAVE TO DO JUST ISN'T YOUR KIND OF BUSINESS
DALL LIES DAZED FROM THE CAREFULLY JUDGED BLOW
A MINUTE LATER...
MODESTY ... NO...
AND FIFTEEN MILES AWAY...
YOU RECKON THAT DAME WHO WAS ASKING ABOUT GARVIN MIGHT MAKE TROUBLE, JED?
LIKE WHAT? WE NEVER SAW HIM, DID WE?
4591

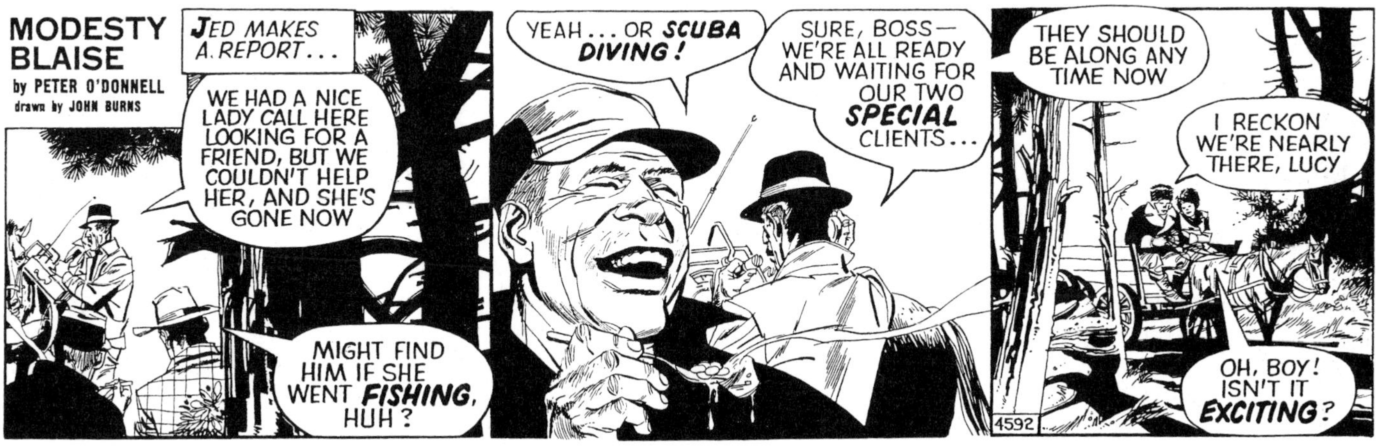
MODESTY BLAISE
by PETER O'DONNELL
drawn by JOHN BURNS
JED MAKES A REPORT...
WE HAD A NICE LADY CALL HERE LOOKING FOR A FRIEND, BUT WE COULDN'T HELP HER, AND SHE'S GONE NOW
MIGHT FIND HIM IF SHE WENT FISHING, HUH?
YEAH... OR SCUBA DIVING!
SURE, BOSS— WE'RE ALL READY AND WAITING FOR OUR TWO SPECIAL CLIENTS...
THEY SHOULD BE ALONG ANY TIME NOW
I RECKON WE'RE NEARLY THERE, LUCY
OH, BOY! ISN'T IT EXCITING?
4592

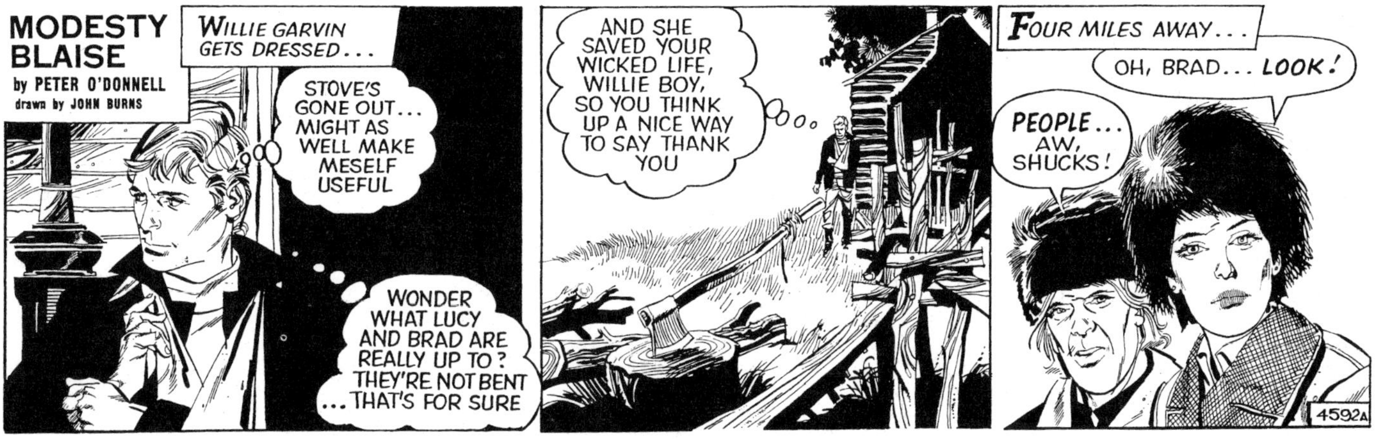
MODESTY BLAISE
by PETER O'DONNELL
drawn by JOHN BURNS
WILLIE GARVIN GETS DRESSED...
STOVE'S GONE OUT... MIGHT AS WELL MAKE MESELF USEFUL
WONDER WHAT LUCY AND BRAD ARE REALLY UP TO? THEY'RE NOT BENT ...THAT'S FOR SURE
AND SHE SAVED YOUR WICKED LIFE, WILLIE BOY, SO YOU THINK UP A NICE WAY TO SAY THANK YOU
FOUR MILES AWAY...
OH, BRAD... LOOK!
PEOPLE... AW, SHUCKS!
4592A

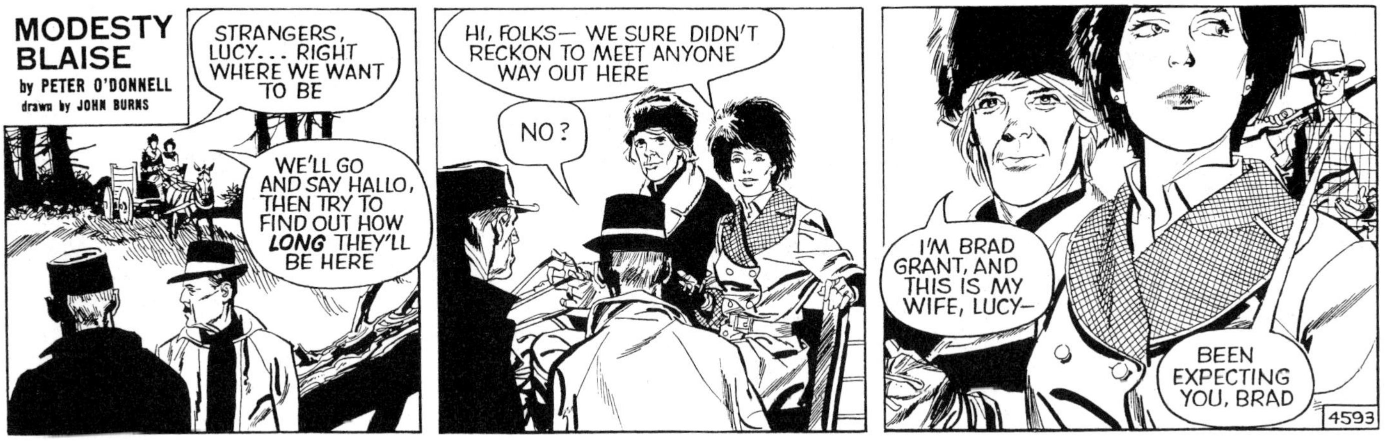
MODESTY BLAISE
by PETER O'DONNELL
drawn by JOHN BURNS
STRANGERS, LUCY... RIGHT WHERE WE WANT TO BE
WE'LL GO AND SAY HALLO, THEN TRY TO FIND OUT HOW LONG THEY'LL BE HERE
HI, FOLKS— WE SURE DIDN'T RECKON TO MEET ANYONE WAY OUT HERE
NO ?
I'M BRAD GRANT, AND THIS IS MY WIFE, LUCY—
BEEN EXPECTING YOU, BRAD
4593

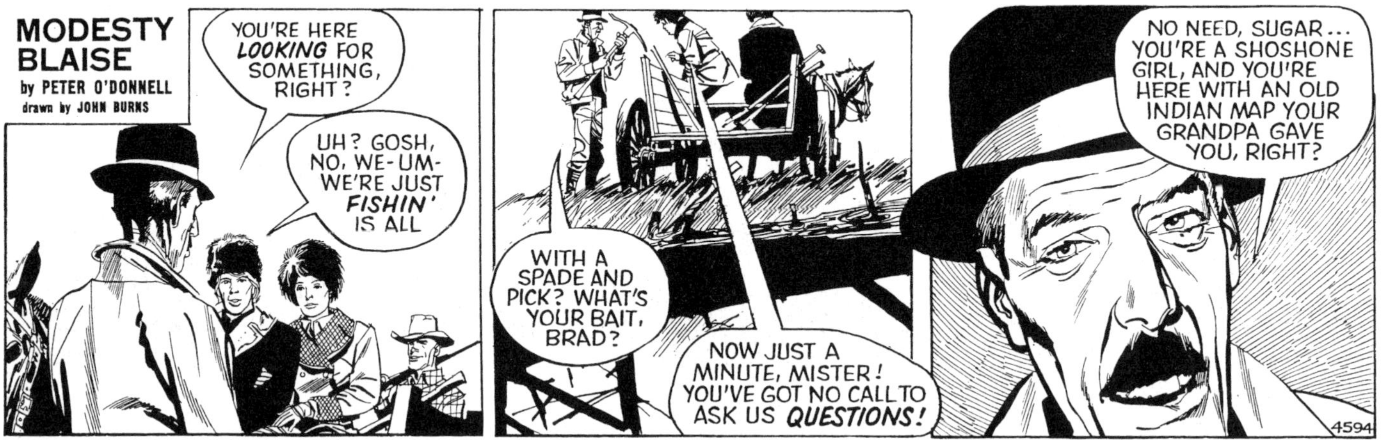
MODESTY BLAISE
by PETER O'DONNELL
drawn by JOHN BURNS
YOU'RE HERE LOOKING FOR SOMETHING, RIGHT ?
UH? GOSH, NO, WE-UM-WE'RE JUST FISHIN' IS ALL
WITH A SPADE AND PICK? WHAT'S YOUR BAIT, BRAD?
NOW JUST A MINUTE, MISTER! YOU'VE GOT NO CALL TO ASK US QUESTIONS!
NO NEED, SUGAR... YOU'RE A SHOSHONE GIRL, AND YOU'RE HERE WITH AN OLD INDIAN MAP YOUR GRANDPA GAVE YOU, RIGHT?
4594

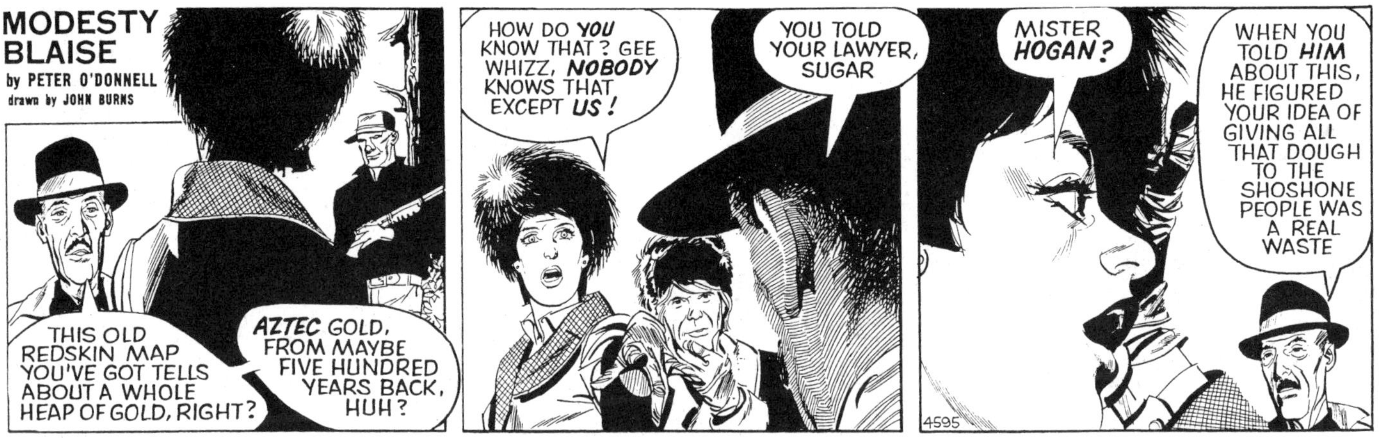
MODESTY BLAISE
by PETER O'DONNELL
drawn by JOHN BURNS
THIS OLD REDSKIN MAP YOU'VE GOT TELLS ABOUT A WHOLE HEAP OF GOLD, RIGHT?
AZTEC GOLD, FROM MAYBE FIVE HUNDRED YEARS BACK, HUH?
HOW DO YOU KNOW THAT? GEE WHIZZ, NOBODY KNOWS THAT EXCEPT US!
YOU TOLD YOUR LAWYER, SUGAR
MISTER HOGAN?
WHEN YOU TOLD HIM ABOUT THIS, HE FIGURED YOUR IDEA OF GIVING ALL THAT DOUGH TO THE SHOSHONE PEOPLE WAS A REAL WASTE
4595

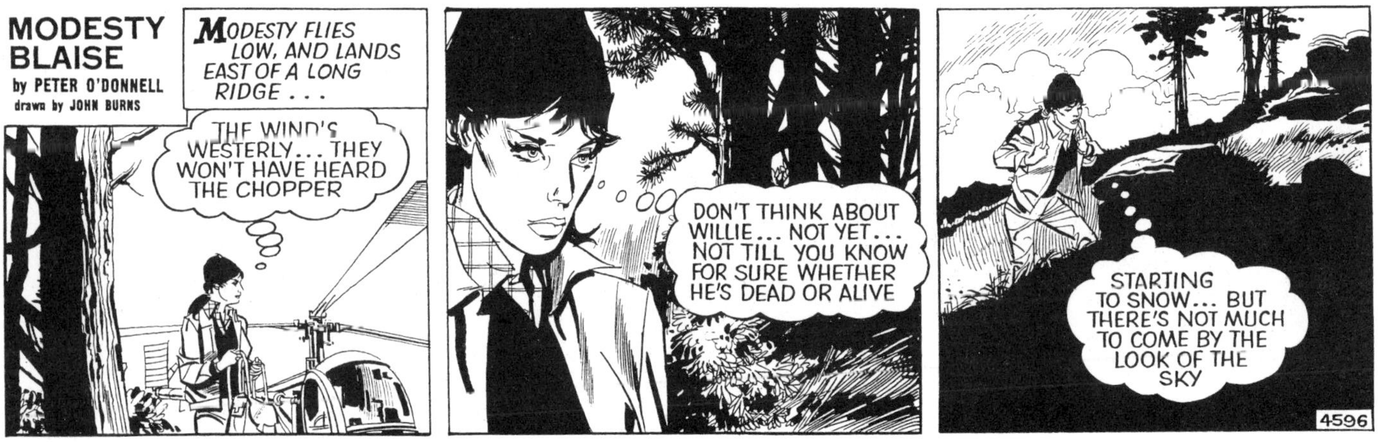
MODESTY BLAISE
by PETER O'DONNELL
drawn by JOHN BURNS
MODESTY FLIES LOW, AND LANDS EAST OF A LONG RIDGE...
THE WIND'S WESTERLY... THEY WON'T HAVE HEARD THE CHOPPER
DON'T THINK ABOUT WILLIE... NOT YET... NOT TILL YOU KNOW FOR SURE WHETHER HE'S DEAD OR ALIVE
STARTING TO SNOW... BUT THERE'S NOT MUCH TO COME BY THE LOOK OF THE SKY
4596

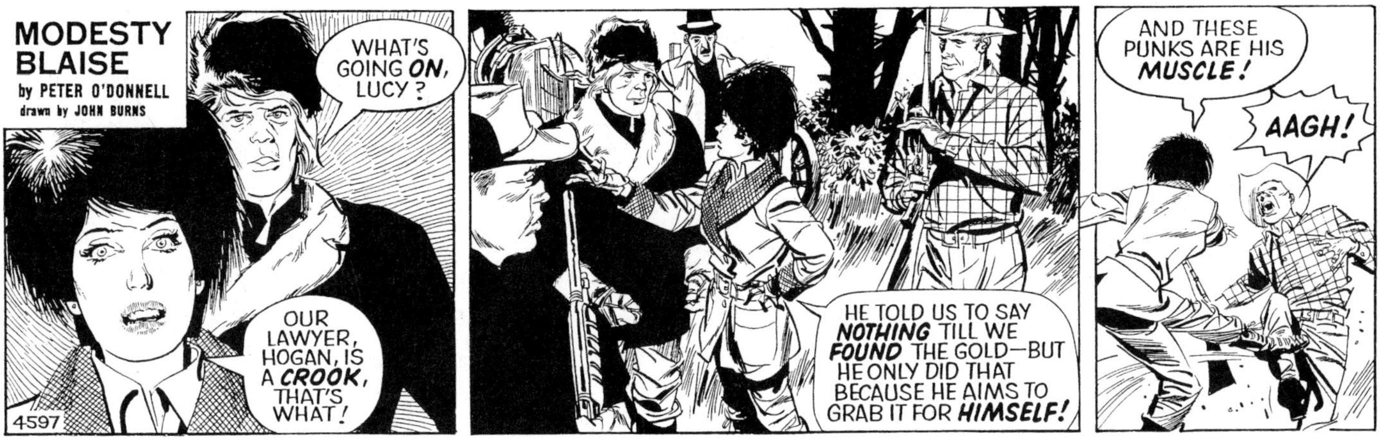
MODESTY BLAISE
by PETER O'DONNELL
drawn by JOHN BURNS
WHAT'S GOING ON, LUCY?
OUR LAWYER, HOGAN, IS A CROOK, THAT'S WHAT!
4597
HE TOLD US TO SAY NOTHING TILL WE FOUND THE GOLD—BUT HE ONLY DID THAT BECAUSE HE AIMS TO GRAB IT FOR HIMSELF!
AND THESE PUNKS ARE HIS MUSCLE!
AAGH!

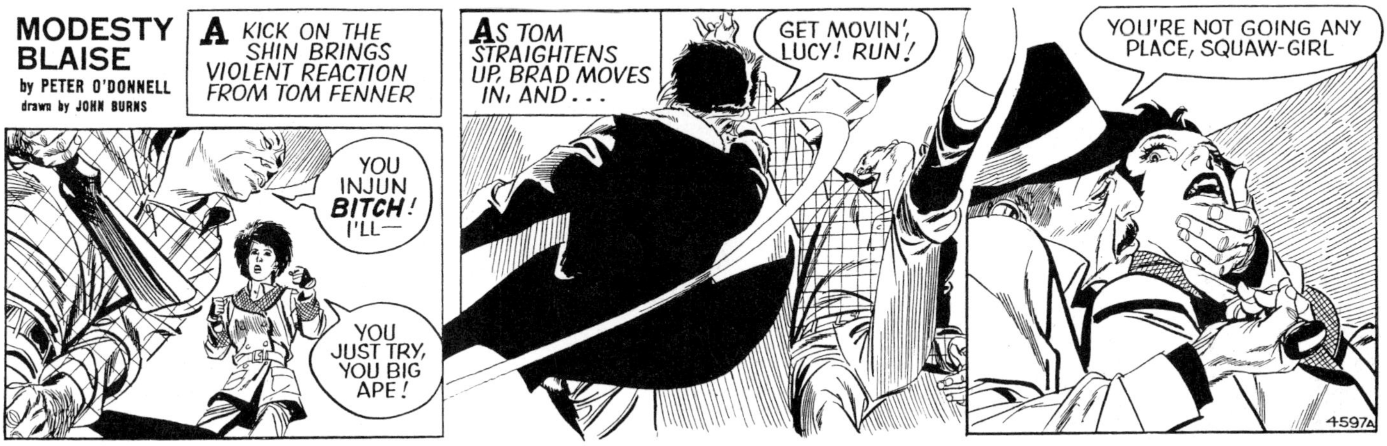
MODESTY BLAISE
by PETER O'DONNELL
drawn by JOHN BURNS
A KICK ON THE SHIN BRINGS VIOLENT REACTION FROM TOM FENNER
YOU INJUN BITCH! I'LL—
YOU JUST TRY, YOU BIG APE!
AS TOM STRAIGHTENS UP, BRAD MOVES IN, AND . . .
GET MOVIN', LUCY! RUN!
YOU'RE NOT GOING ANY PLACE, SQUAW-GIRL
4597A

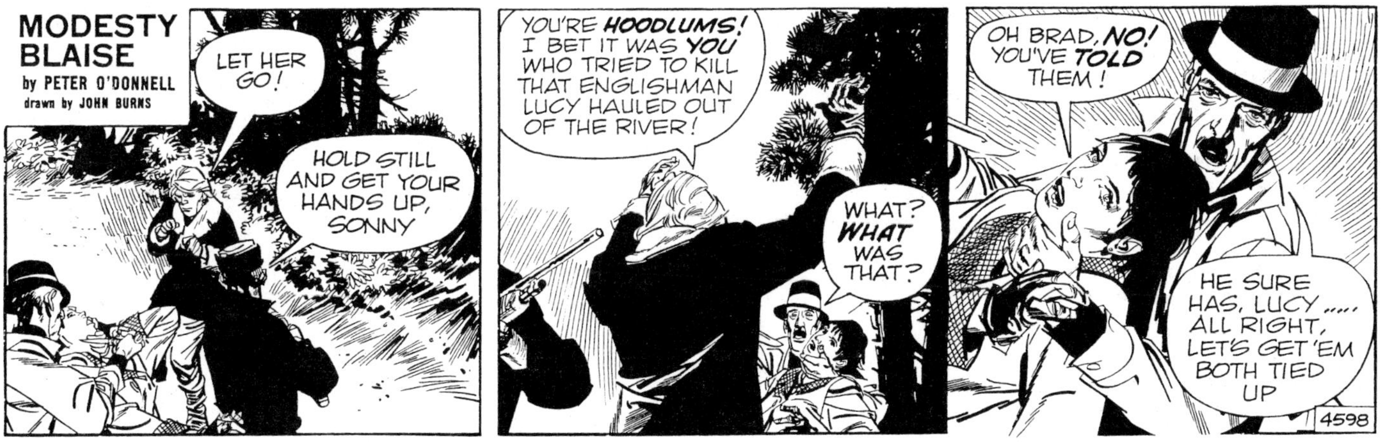
MODESTY BLAISE
by PETER O'DONNELL
drawn by JOHN BURNS
LET HER GO!
HOLD STILL AND GET YOUR HANDS UP, SONNY
YOU'RE HOODLUMS! I BET IT WAS YOU WHO TRIED TO KILL THAT ENGLISHMAN LUCY HAULED OUT OF THE RIVER!
WHAT? WHAT WAS THAT?
OH BRAD, NO! YOU'VE TOLD THEM!
HE SURE HAS, LUCY ..... ALL RIGHT, LET'S GET 'EM BOTH TIED UP
4598

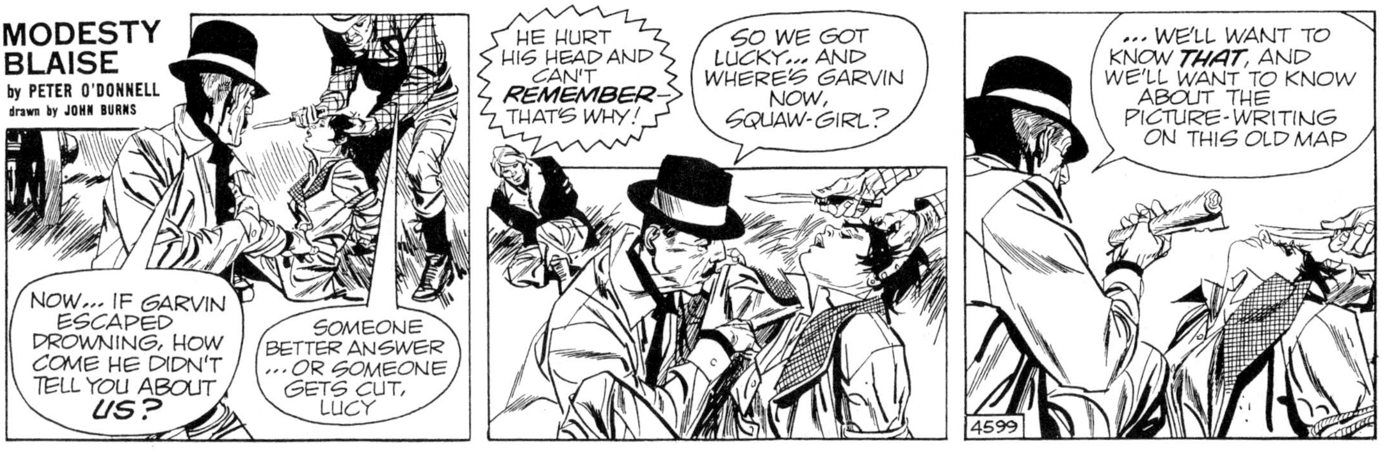
MODESTY BLAISE
by PETER O'DONNELL
drawn by JOHN BURNS
NOW... IF GARVIN ESCAPED DROWNING, HOW COME HE DIDN'T TELL YOU ABOUT US?
SOMEONE BETTER ANSWER ...OR SOMEONE GETS CUT, LUCY
HE HURT HIS HEAD AND CAN'T REMEMBER—THAT'S WHY!
SO WE GOT LUCKY... AND WHERE'S GARVIN NOW, SQUAW-GIRL?
...WE'LL WANT TO KNOW THAT, AND WE'LL WANT TO KNOW ABOUT THE PICTURE-WRITING ON THIS OLD MAP
4599

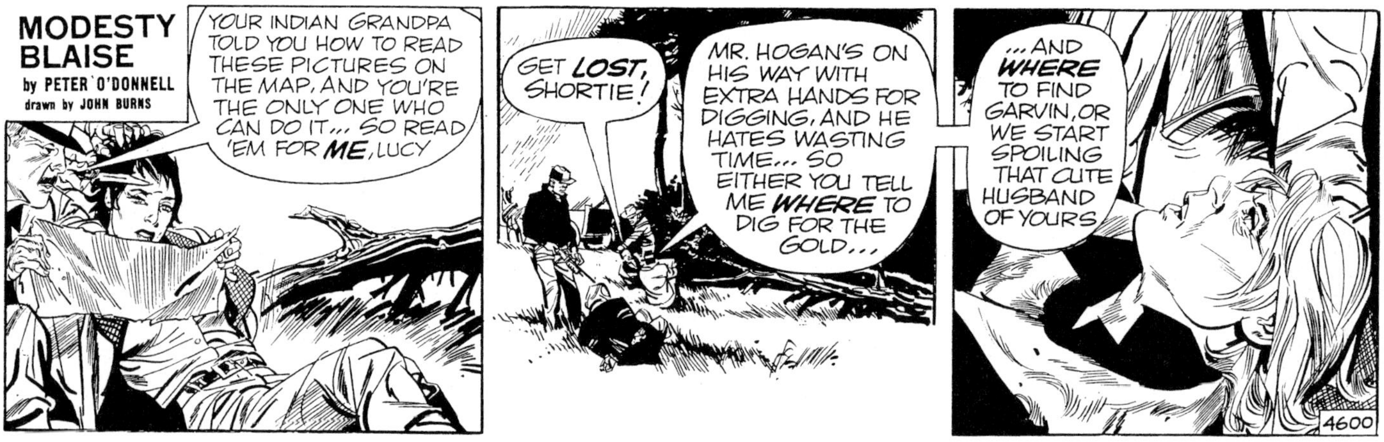
MODESTY BLAISE
by PETER O'DONNELL
drawn by JOHN BURNS
YOUR INDIAN GRANDPA TOLD YOU HOW TO READ THESE PICTURES ON THE MAP, AND YOU'RE THE ONLY ONE WHO CAN DO IT... SO READ 'EM FOR ME, LUCY
GET LOST, SHORTIE!
MR. HOGAN'S ON HIS WAY WITH EXTRA HANDS FOR DIGGING, AND HE HATES WASTING TIME... SO EITHER YOU TELL ME WHERE TO DIG FOR THE GOLD...
...AND WHERE TO FIND GARVIN, OR WE START SPOILING THAT CUTE HUSBAND OF YOURS
4600

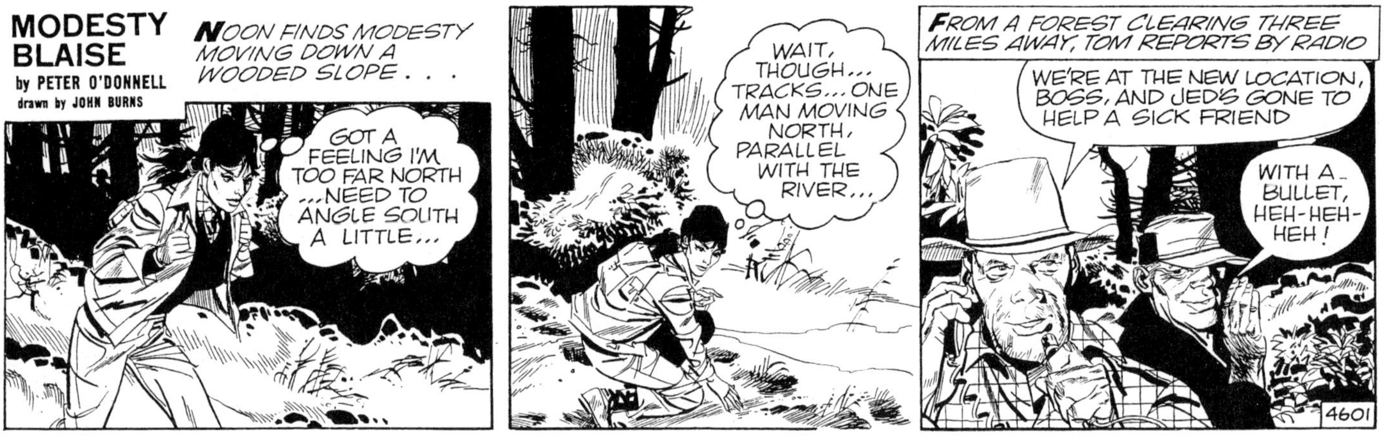
MODESTY BLAISE
by PETER O'DONNELL
drawn by JOHN BURNS
NOON FINDS MODESTY MOVING DOWN A WOODED SLOPE . . .
GOT A FEELING I'M TOO FAR NORTH ...NEED TO ANGLE SOUTH A LITTLE...
WAIT, THOUGH... TRACKS... ONE MAN MOVING NORTH, PARALLEL WITH THE RIVER...
FROM A FOREST CLEARING THREE MILES AWAY, TOM REPORTS BY RADIO
WE'RE AT THE NEW LOCATION, BOSS, AND JED'S GONE TO HELP A SICK FRIEND
WITH A BULLET, HEH-HEH-HEH!
4601

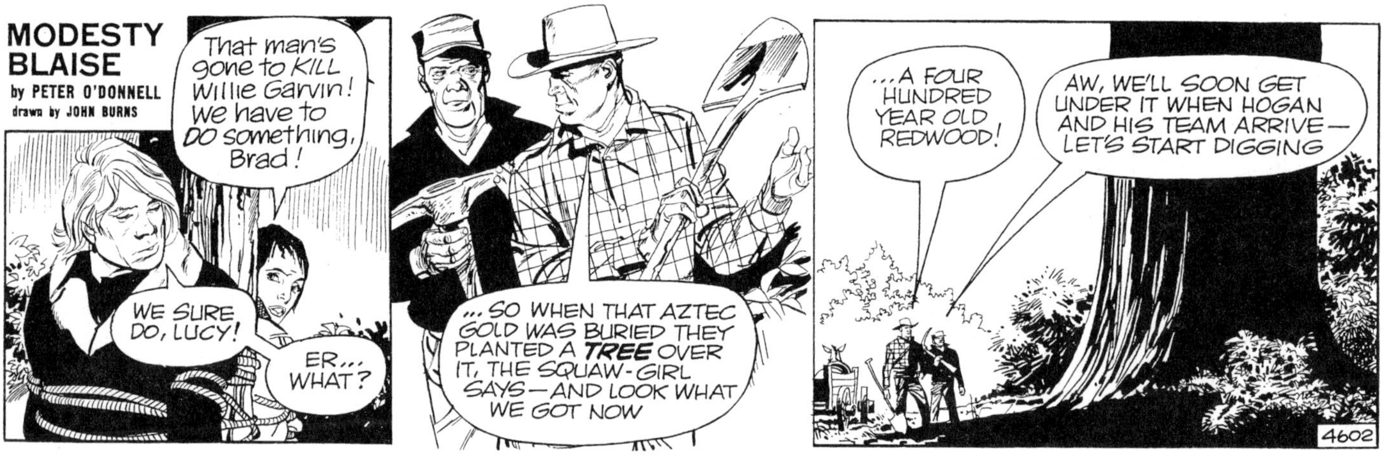
MODESTY BLAISE
by PETER O'DONNELL
drawn by JOHN BURNS
That man's gone to KILL Willie Garvin! We have to DO something, Brad!
WE SURE DO, LUCY!
ER... WHAT?
...SO WHEN THAT AZTEC GOLD WAS BURIED THEY PLANTED A TREE OVER IT, THE SQUAW-GIRL SAYS—AND LOOK WHAT WE GOT NOW
...A FOUR HUNDRED YEAR OLD REDWOOD!
AW, WE'LL SOON GET UNDER IT WHEN HOGAN AND HIS TEAM ARRIVE— LET'S START DIGGING
4602

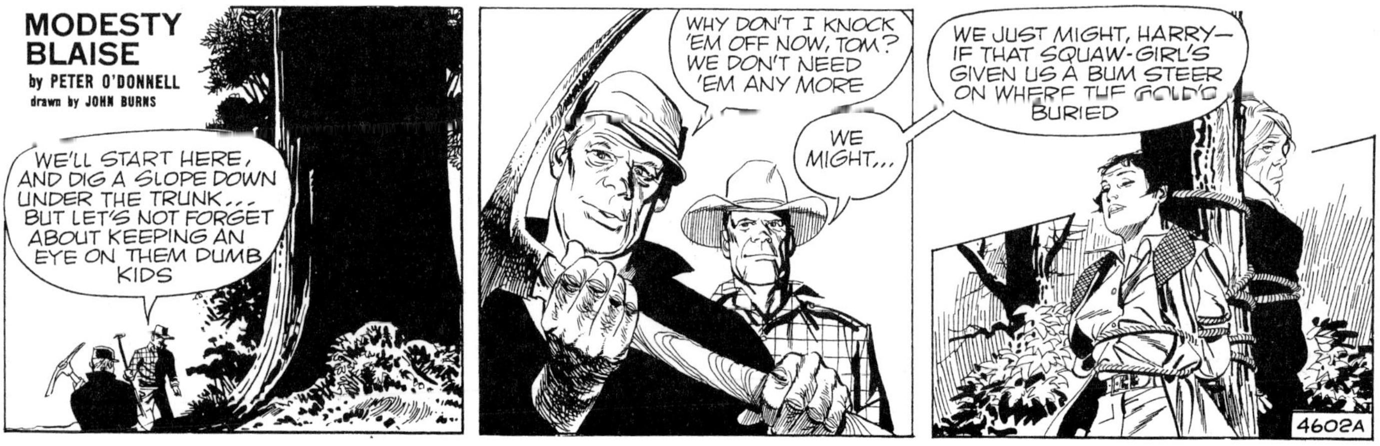
MODESTY BLAISE
by PETER O'DONNELL
drawn by JOHN BURNS
WE'LL START HERE, AND DIG A SLOPE DOWN UNDER THE TRUNK... BUT LET'S NOT FORGET ABOUT KEEPING AN EYE ON THEM DUMB KIDS
WHY DON'T I KNOCK 'EM OFF NOW, TOM? WE DON'T NEED 'EM ANY MORE
WE MIGHT...
WE JUST MIGHT, HARRY— IF THAT SQUAW-GIRL'S GIVEN US A BUM STEER ON WHERE THE GOLD'S BURIED
4602A

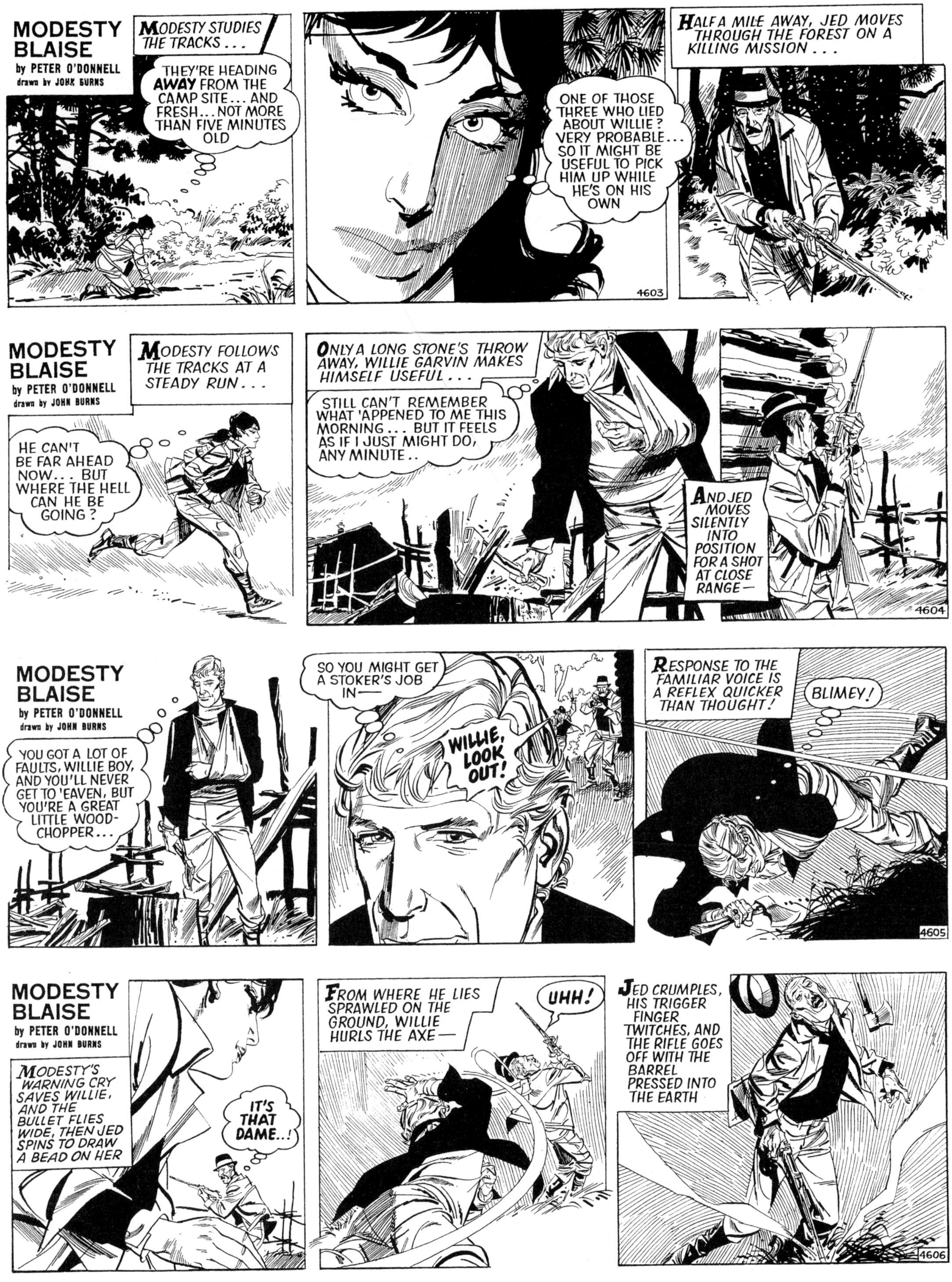
MODESTY BLAISE
by PETER O'DONNELL
drawn by JOHN BURNS
MODESTY STUDIES THE TRACKS . . .
THEY'RE HEADING AWAY FROM THE CAMP SITE . . . AND FRESH . . . NOT MORE THAN FIVE MINUTES OLD
ONE OF THOSE THREE WHO LIED ABOUT WILLIE? VERY PROBABLE . . . SO IT MIGHT BE USEFUL TO PICK HIM UP WHILE HE'S ON HIS OWN
HALF A MILE AWAY, JED MOVES THROUGH THE FOREST ON A KILLING MISSION . . .
4603
MODESTY BLAISE
by PETER O'DONNELL
drawn by JOHN BURNS
MODESTY FOLLOWS THE TRACKS AT A STEADY RUN . . .
HE CAN'T BE FAR AHEAD NOW . . . BUT WHERE THE HELL CAN HE BE GOING?
ONLY A LONG STONE'S THROW AWAY, WILLIE GARVIN MAKES HIMSELF USEFUL . . .
STILL CAN'T REMEMBER WHAT 'APPENED TO ME THIS MORNING . . . BUT IT FEELS AS IF I JUST MIGHT DO, ANY MINUTE . .
AND JED MOVES SILENTLY INTO POSITION FOR A SHOT AT CLOSE RANGE—
4604
MODESTY BLAISE
by PETER O'DONNELL
drawn by JOHN BURNS
YOU GOT A LOT OF FAULTS, WILLIE BOY, AND YOU'LL NEVER GET TO 'EAVEN, BUT YOU'RE A GREAT LITTLE WOOD-CHOPPER . . .
SO YOU MIGHT GET A STOKER'S JOB IN—
WILLIE, LOOK OUT!
RESPONSE TO THE FAMILIAR VOICE IS A REFLEX QUICKER THAN THOUGHT!
BLIMEY!
4605
MODESTY BLAISE
by PETER O'DONNELL
drawn by JOHN BURNS
MODESTY'S WARNING CRY SAVES WILLIE, AND THE BULLET FLIES WIDE, THEN JED SPINS TO DRAW A BEAD ON HER
IT'S THAT DAME . . !
FROM WHERE HE LIES SPRAWLED ON THE GROUND, WILLIE HURLS THE AXE—
UHH!
JED CRUMPLES, HIS TRIGGER FINGER TWITCHES, AND THE RIFLE GOES OFF WITH THE BARREL PRESSED INTO THE EARTH
4606

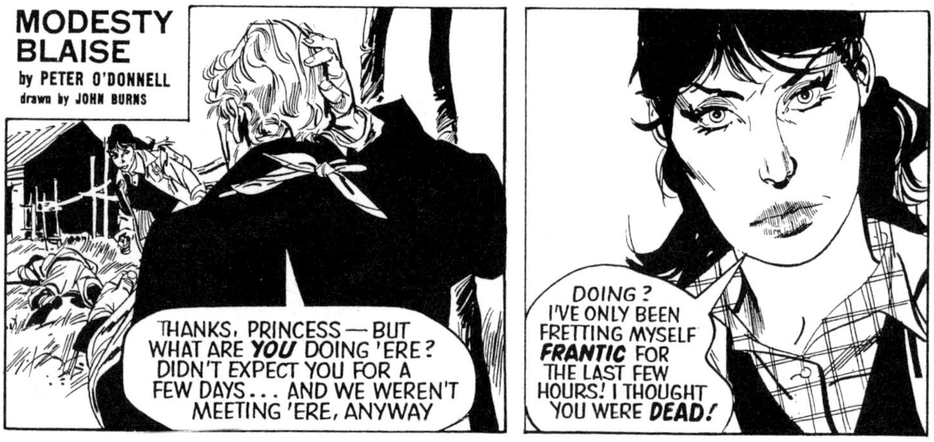
MODESTY BLAISE
by PETER O'DONNELL
drawn by JOHN BURNS
THANKS, PRINCESS — BUT WHAT ARE YOU DOING 'ERE? DIDN'T EXPECT YOU FOR A FEW DAYS... AND WE WEREN'T MEETING 'ERE, ANYWAY
DOING? I'VE ONLY BEEN FRETTING MYSELF FRANTIC FOR THE LAST FEW HOURS! I THOUGHT YOU WERE DEAD!
YOU- YOU JUST WAIT TILL I GET YOU HOME, WILLIE GARVIN!
I'LL APOLOGISE, PRINCESS... IF THAT 'ELPS?
4607

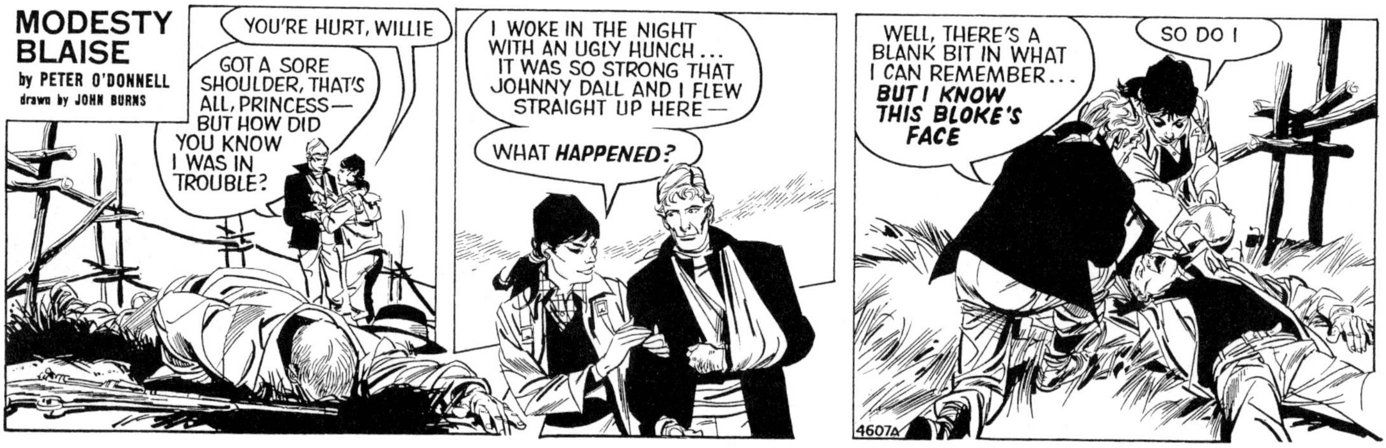
MODESTY BLAISE
by PETER O'DONNELL
drawn by JOHN BURNS
YOU'RE HURT, WILLIE
GOT A SORE SHOULDER, THAT'S ALL, PRINCESS — BUT HOW DID YOU KNOW I WAS IN TROUBLE?
I WOKE IN THE NIGHT WITH AN UGLY HUNCH... IT WAS SO STRONG THAT JOHNNY DALL AND I FLEW STRAIGHT UP HERE —
WHAT HAPPENED?
WELL, THERE'S A BLANK BIT IN WHAT I CAN REMEMBER... BUT I KNOW THIS BLOKE'S FACE
SO DO I
4607A

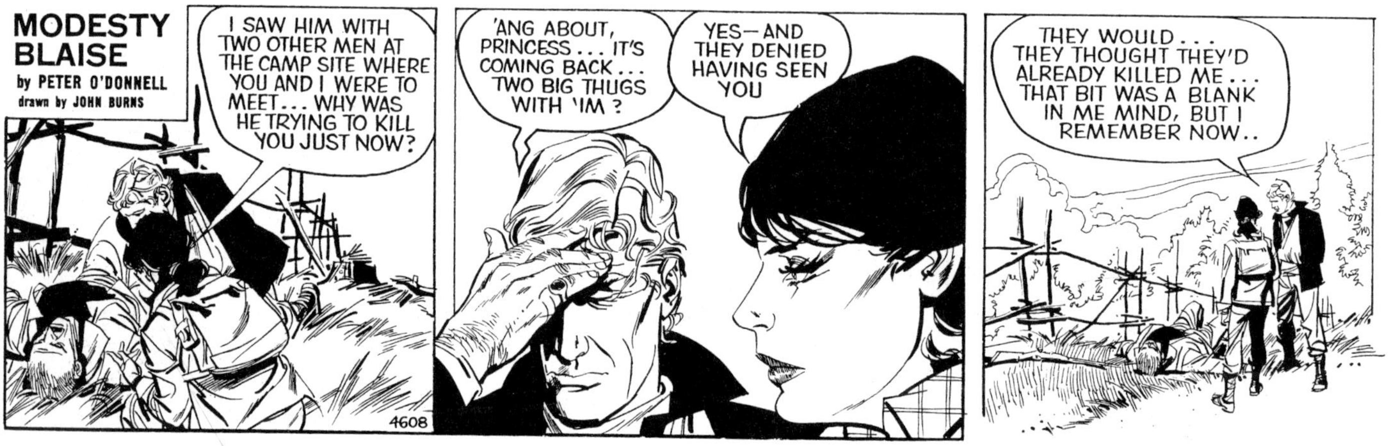
MODESTY BLAISE
by PETER O'DONNELL
drawn by JOHN BURNS
I SAW HIM WITH TWO OTHER MEN AT THE CAMP SITE WHERE YOU AND I WERE TO MEET... WHY WAS HE TRYING TO KILL YOU JUST NOW?
'ANG ABOUT, PRINCESS... IT'S COMING BACK... TWO BIG THUGS WITH 'IM?
YES— AND THEY DENIED HAVING SEEN YOU
THEY WOULD... THEY THOUGHT THEY'D ALREADY KILLED ME... THAT BIT WAS A BLANK IN ME MIND, BUT I REMEMBER NOW..
4608

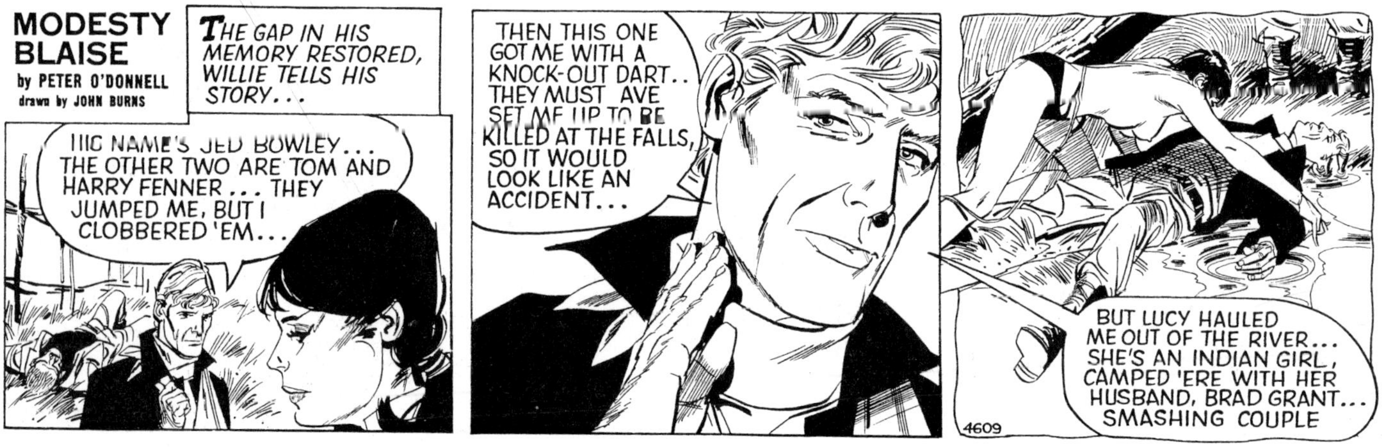
MODESTY BLAISE
by PETER O'DONNELL
drawn by JOHN BURNS
THE GAP IN HIS MEMORY RESTORED, WILLIE TELLS HIS STORY...
HIS NAME'S JED BOWLEY... THE OTHER TWO ARE TOM AND HARRY FENNER... THEY JUMPED ME, BUT I CLOBBERED 'EM...
THEN THIS ONE GOT ME WITH A KNOCK-OUT DART.. THEY MUST 'AVE SET ME UP TO BE KILLED AT THE FALLS, SO IT WOULD LOOK LIKE AN ACCIDENT...
BUT LUCY HAULED ME OUT OF THE RIVER... SHE'S AN INDIAN GIRL, CAMPED 'ERE WITH HER HUSBAND, BRAD GRANT... SMASHING COUPLE
4609

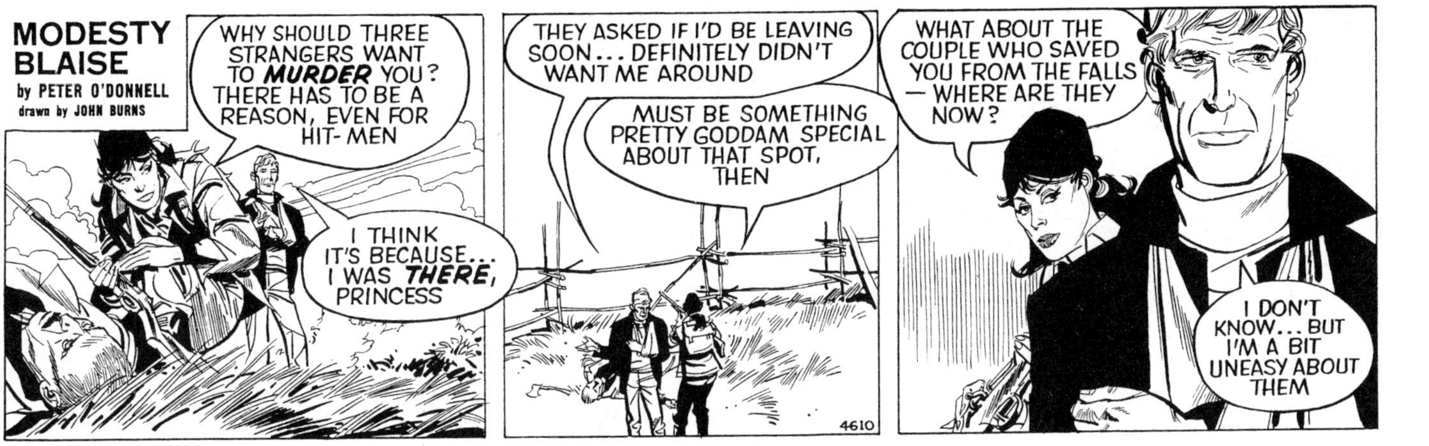
MODESTY BLAISE
by PETER O'DONNELL
drawn by JOHN BURNS
WHY SHOULD THREE STRANGERS WANT TO MURDER YOU? THERE HAS TO BE A REASON, EVEN FOR HIT-MEN
I THINK IT'S BECAUSE... I WAS THERE, PRINCESS
THEY ASKED IF I'D BE LEAVING SOON... DEFINITELY DIDN'T WANT ME AROUND
MUST BE SOMETHING PRETTY GODDAM SPECIAL ABOUT THAT SPOT, THEN
4610
WHAT ABOUT THE COUPLE WHO SAVED YOU FROM THE FALLS — WHERE ARE THEY NOW?
I DON'T KNOW... BUT I'M A BIT UNEASY ABOUT THEM

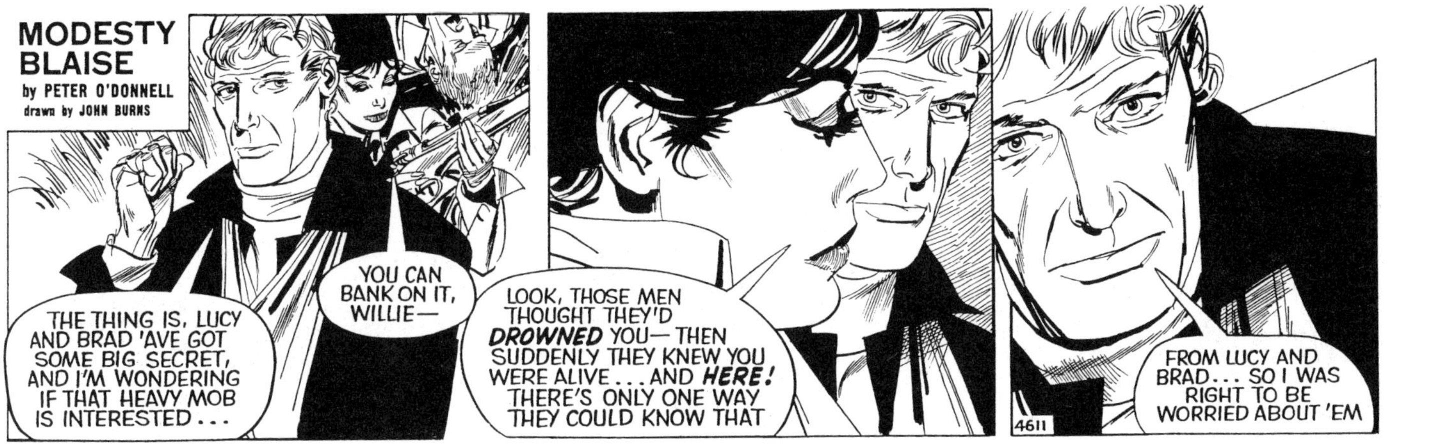
MODESTY BLAISE
by PETER O'DONNELL
drawn by JOHN BURNS
THE THING IS, LUCY AND BRAD 'AVE GOT SOME BIG SECRET, AND I'M WONDERING IF THAT HEAVY MOB IS INTERESTED...
YOU CAN BANK ON IT, WILLIE—
LOOK, THOSE MEN THOUGHT THEY'D DROWNED YOU— THEN SUDDENLY THEY KNEW YOU WERE ALIVE... AND HERE! THERE'S ONLY ONE WAY THEY COULD KNOW THAT
FROM LUCY AND BRAD... SO I WAS RIGHT TO BE WORRIED ABOUT 'EM
4611

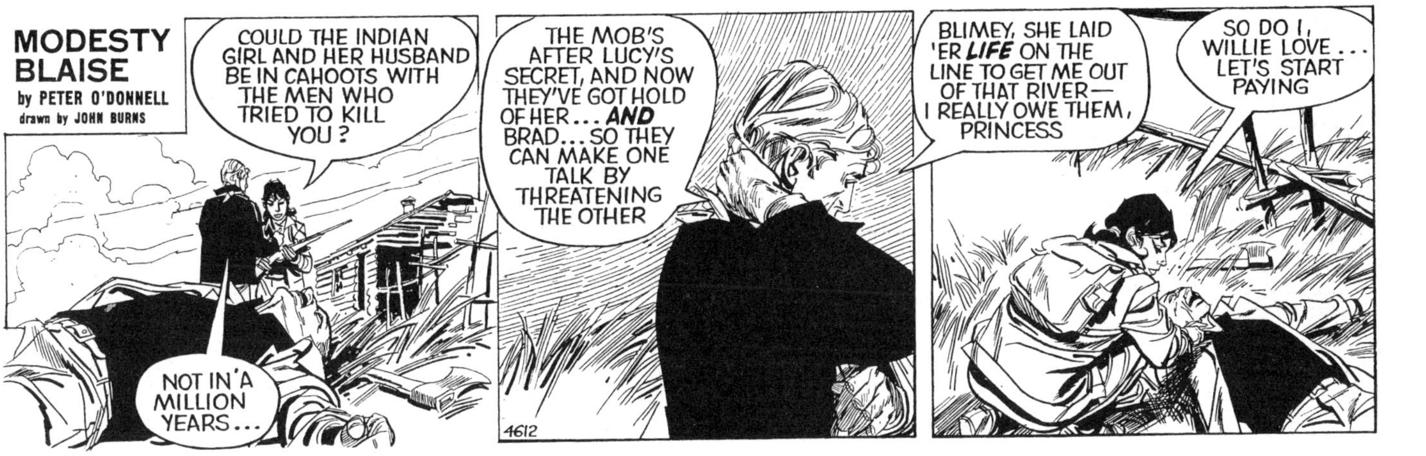
MODESTY BLAISE
by PETER O'DONNELL
drawn by JOHN BURNS
COULD THE INDIAN GIRL AND HER HUSBAND BE IN CAHOOTS WITH THE MEN WHO TRIED TO KILL YOU?
NOT IN A MILLION YEARS...
THE MOB'S AFTER LUCY'S SECRET, AND NOW THEY'VE GOT HOLD OF HER... AND BRAD... SO THEY CAN MAKE ONE TALK BY THREATENING THE OTHER
4612
BLIMEY, SHE LAID 'ER LIFE ON THE LINE TO GET ME OUT OF THAT RIVER— I REALLY OWE THEM, PRINCESS
SO DO I, WILLIE LOVE... LET'S START PAYING

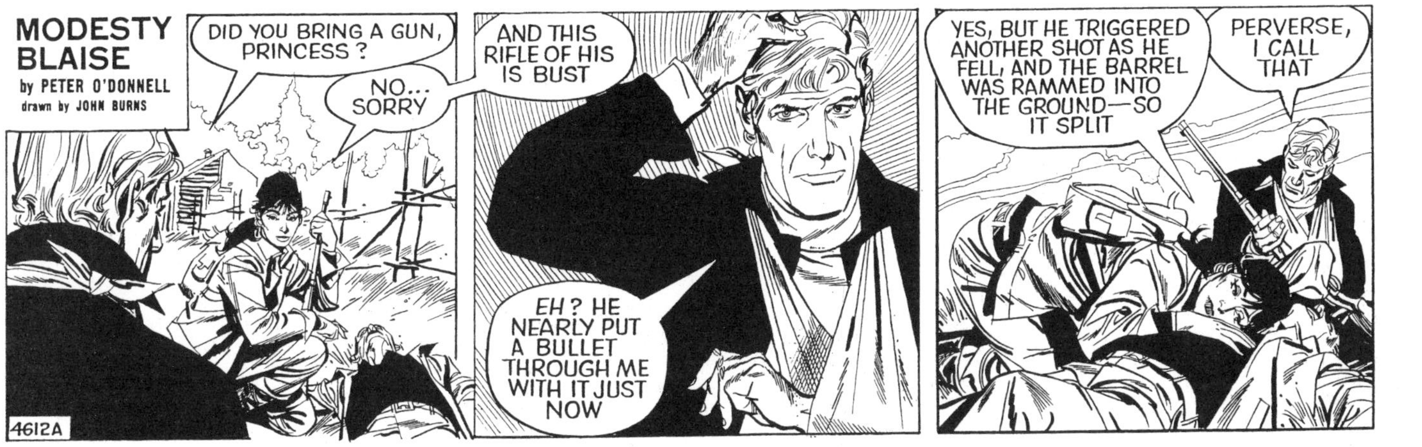
MODESTY BLAISE
by PETER O'DONNELL
drawn by JOHN BURNS
DID YOU BRING A GUN, PRINCESS?
NO... SORRY
4612A
AND THIS RIFLE OF HIS IS BUST
EH? HE NEARLY PUT A BULLET THROUGH ME WITH IT JUST NOW
YES, BUT HE TRIGGERED ANOTHER SHOT AS HE FELL, AND THE BARREL WAS RAMMED INTO THE GROUND— SO IT SPLIT
PERVERSE, I CALL THAT

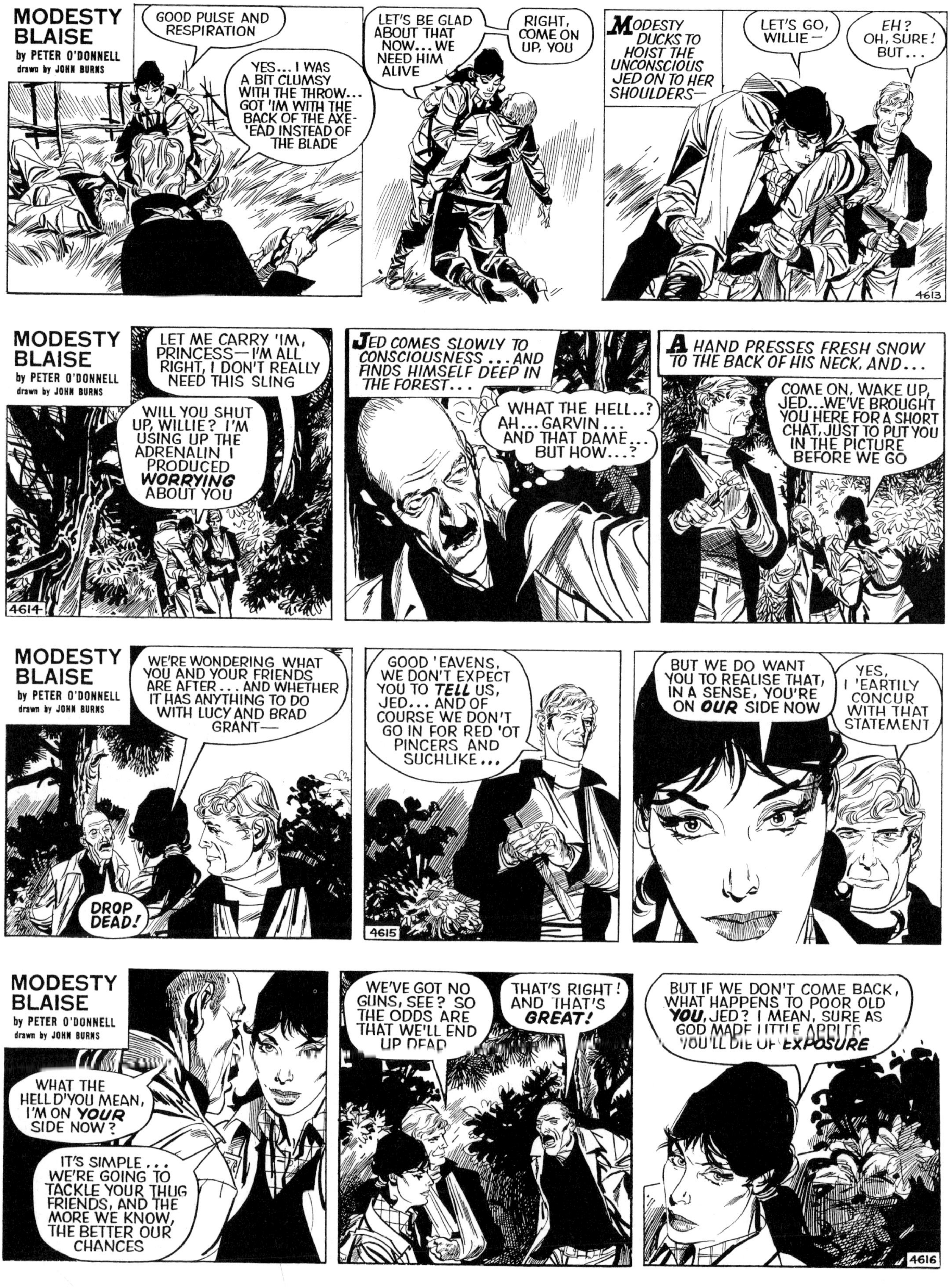

MODESTY BLAISE
by PETER O'DONNELL
drawn by JOHN BURNS
GOOD PULSE AND RESPIRATION
YES... I WAS A BIT CLUMSY WITH THE THROW... GOT 'IM WITH THE BACK OF THE AXE-'EAD INSTEAD OF THE BLADE
LET'S BE GLAD ABOUT THAT NOW... WE NEED HIM ALIVE
RIGHT, COME ON UP, YOU
MODESTY DUCKS TO HOIST THE UNCONSCIOUS JED ON TO HER SHOULDERS—
LET'S GO, WILLIE—
EH? OH, SURE! BUT...
4613
MODESTY BLAISE
by PETER O'DONNELL
drawn by JOHN BURNS
LET ME CARRY 'IM, PRINCESS—I'M ALL RIGHT, I DON'T REALLY NEED THIS SLING
WILL YOU SHUT UP, WILLIE? I'M USING UP THE ADRENALIN I PRODUCED WORRYING ABOUT YOU
4614
JED COMES SLOWLY TO CONSCIOUSNESS... AND FINDS HIMSELF DEEP IN THE FOREST...
WHAT THE HELL..? AH... GARVIN... AND THAT DAME... BUT HOW...?
A HAND PRESSES FRESH SNOW TO THE BACK OF HIS NECK, AND...
COME ON, WAKE UP, JED... WE'VE BROUGHT YOU HERE FOR A SHORT CHAT, JUST TO PUT YOU IN THE PICTURE BEFORE WE GO
MODESTY BLAISE
by PETER O'DONNELL
drawn by JOHN BURNS
WE'RE WONDERING WHAT YOU AND YOUR FRIENDS ARE AFTER... AND WHETHER IT HAS ANYTHING TO DO WITH LUCY AND BRAD GRANT—
DROP DEAD!
GOOD 'EAVENS, WE DON'T EXPECT YOU TO TELL US, JED... AND OF COURSE WE DON'T GO IN FOR RED 'OT PINCERS AND SUCHLIKE...
4615
BUT WE DO WANT YOU TO REALISE THAT, IN A SENSE, YOU'RE ON OUR SIDE NOW
YES, I 'EARTILY CONCUR WITH THAT STATEMENT
MODESTY BLAISE
by PETER O'DONNELL
drawn by JOHN BURNS
WHAT THE HELL D'YOU MEAN, I'M ON YOUR SIDE NOW?
IT'S SIMPLE... WE'RE GOING TO TACKLE YOUR THUG FRIENDS, AND THE MORE WE KNOW, THE BETTER OUR CHANCES
WE'VE GOT NO GUNS, SEE? SO THE ODDS ARE THAT WE'LL END UP DEAD
THAT'S RIGHT! AND THAT'S GREAT!
BUT IF WE DON'T COME BACK, WHAT HAPPENS TO POOR OLD YOU, JED? I MEAN, SURE AS GOD MADE LITTLE APPLES YOU'LL DIE OF EXPOSURE
4616

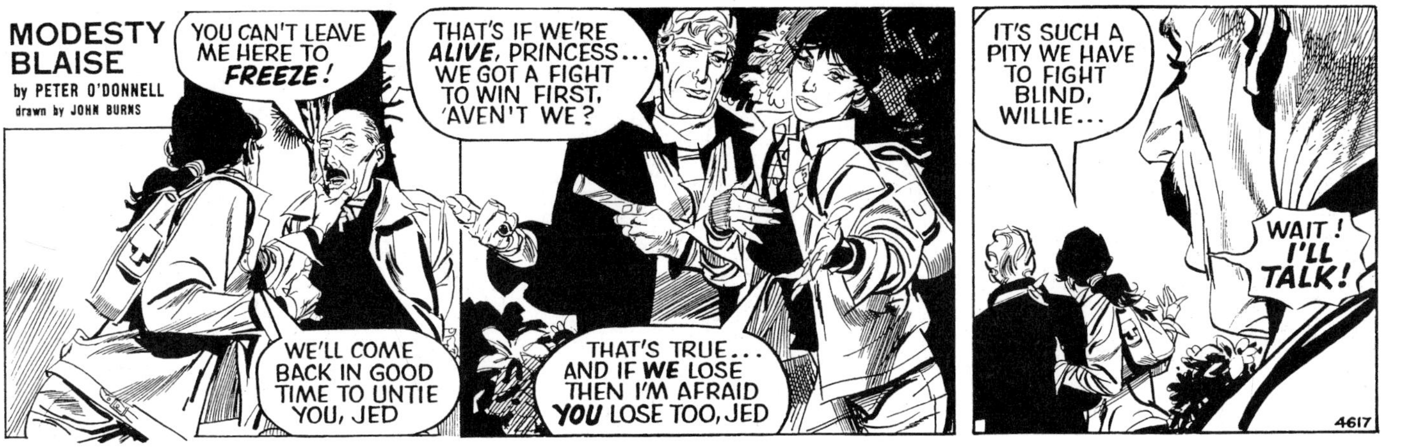
MODESTY BLAISE
by PETER O'DONNELL
drawn by JOHN BURNS
YOU CAN'T LEAVE ME HERE TO FREEZE!
WE'LL COME BACK IN GOOD TIME TO UNTIE YOU, JED
THAT'S IF WE'RE ALIVE, PRINCESS... WE GOT A FIGHT TO WIN FIRST, 'AVEN'T WE?
THAT'S TRUE... AND IF WE LOSE THEN I'M AFRAID YOU LOSE TOO, JED
IT'S SUCH A PITY WE HAVE TO FIGHT BLIND, WILLIE...
WAIT! I'LL TALK!
4617

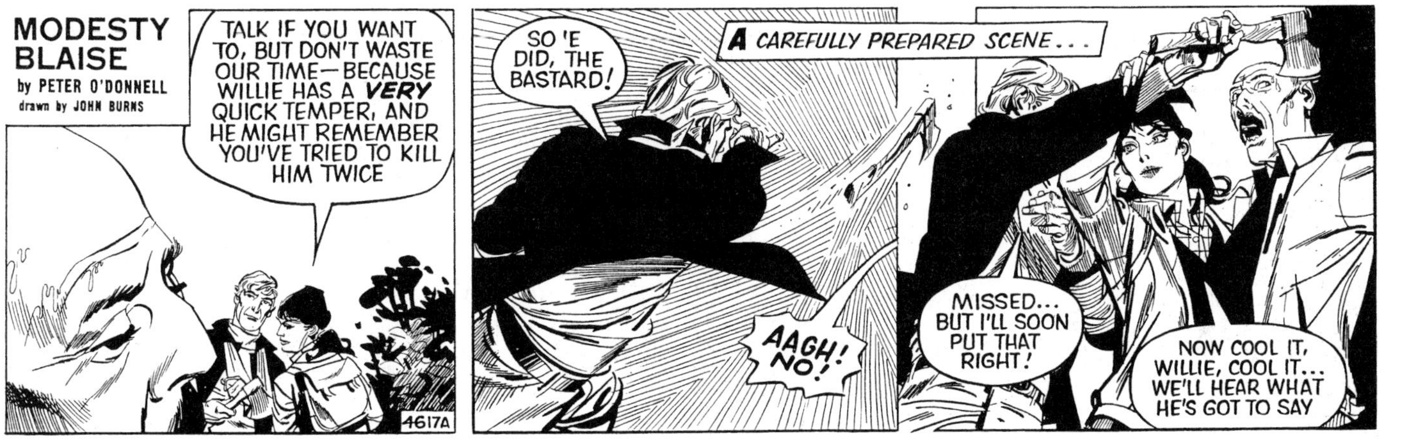
MODESTY BLAISE
by PETER O'DONNELL
drawn by JOHN BURNS
TALK IF YOU WANT TO, BUT DON'T WASTE OUR TIME—BECAUSE WILLIE HAS A VERY QUICK TEMPER, AND HE MIGHT REMEMBER YOU'VE TRIED TO KILL HIM TWICE
4617A
SO 'E DID, THE BASTARD!
AAGH! NO!
A CAREFULLY PREPARED SCENE...
MISSED... BUT I'LL SOON PUT THAT RIGHT!
NOW COOL IT, WILLIE, COOL IT... WE'LL HEAR WHAT HE'S GOT TO SAY

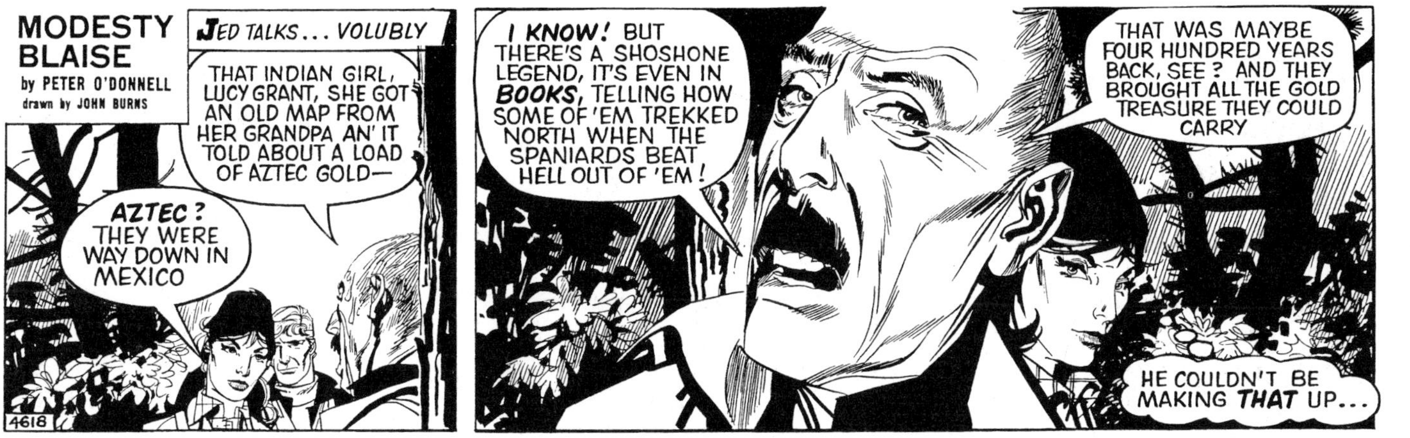
MODESTY BLAISE
by PETER O'DONNELL
drawn by JOHN BURNS
JED TALKS... VOLUBLY
THAT INDIAN GIRL, LUCY GRANT, SHE GOT AN OLD MAP FROM HER GRANDPA AN' IT TOLD ABOUT A LOAD OF AZTEC GOLD—
AZTEC? THEY WERE WAY DOWN IN MEXICO
4618
I KNOW! BUT THERE'S A SHOSHONE LEGEND, IT'S EVEN IN BOOKS, TELLING HOW SOME OF 'EM TREKKED NORTH WHEN THE SPANIARDS BEAT HELL OUT OF 'EM!
THAT WAS MAYBE FOUR HUNDRED YEARS BACK, SEE? AND THEY BROUGHT ALL THE GOLD TREASURE THEY COULD CARRY
HE COULDN'T BE MAKING THAT UP...

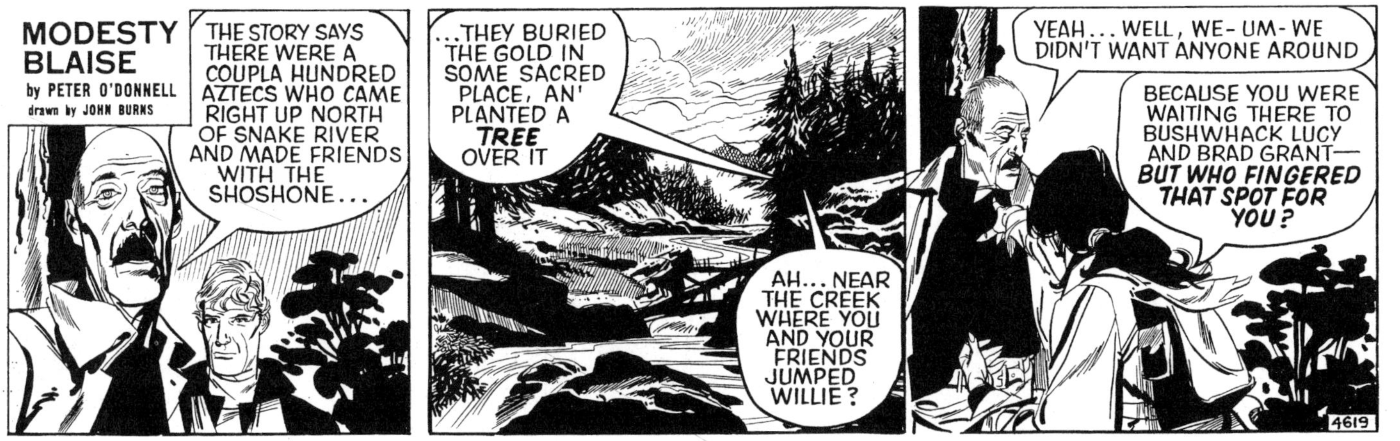
MODESTY BLAISE
by PETER O'DONNELL
drawn by JOHN BURNS
THE STORY SAYS THERE WERE A COUPLA HUNDRED AZTECS WHO CAME RIGHT UP NORTH OF SNAKE RIVER AND MADE FRIENDS WITH THE SHOSHONE...
...THEY BURIED THE GOLD IN SOME SACRED PLACE, AN' PLANTED A TREE OVER IT
AH... NEAR THE CREEK WHERE YOU AND YOUR FRIENDS JUMPED WILLIE?
YEAH... WELL, WE-UM-WE DIDN'T WANT ANYONE AROUND
BECAUSE YOU WERE WAITING THERE TO BUSHWHACK LUCY AND BRAD GRANT— BUT WHO FINGERED THAT SPOT FOR YOU?
4619

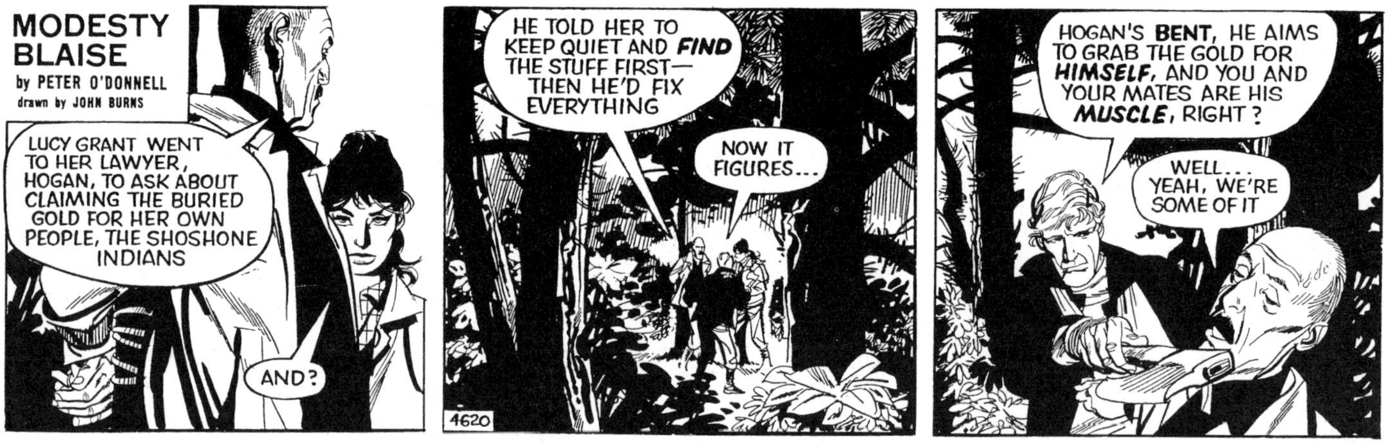
MODESTY BLAISE
by PETER O'DONNELL
drawn by JOHN BURNS
LUCY GRANT WENT TO HER LAWYER, HOGAN, TO ASK ABOUT CLAIMING THE BURIED GOLD FOR HER OWN PEOPLE, THE SHOSHONE INDIANS
AND?
HE TOLD HER TO KEEP QUIET AND FIND THE STUFF FIRST— THEN HE'D FIX EVERYTHING
NOW IT FIGURES...
4620
HOGAN'S BENT, HE AIMS TO GRAB THE GOLD FOR HIMSELF, AND YOU AND YOUR MATES ARE HIS MUSCLE, RIGHT?
WELL... YEAH, WE'RE SOME OF IT

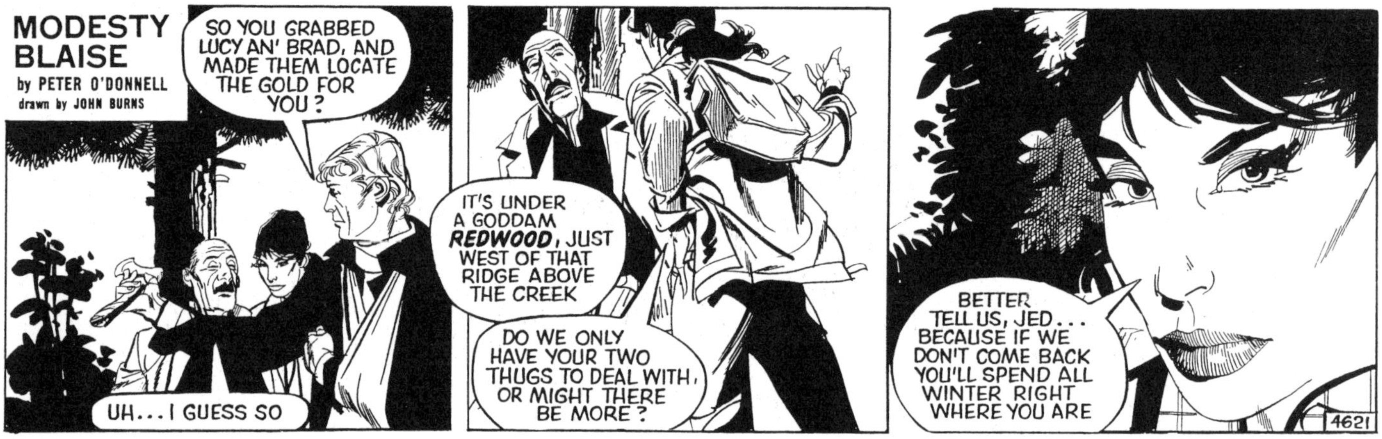
MODESTY BLAISE
by PETER O'DONNELL
drawn by JOHN BURNS
SO YOU GRABBED LUCY AN' BRAD, AND MADE THEM LOCATE THE GOLD FOR YOU?
UH... I GUESS SO
IT'S UNDER A GODDAM REDWOOD, JUST WEST OF THAT RIDGE ABOVE THE CREEK
DO WE ONLY HAVE YOUR TWO THUGS TO DEAL WITH, OR MIGHT THERE BE MORE?
BETTER TELL US, JED... BECAUSE IF WE DON'T COME BACK YOU'LL SPEND ALL WINTER RIGHT WHERE YOU ARE
4621

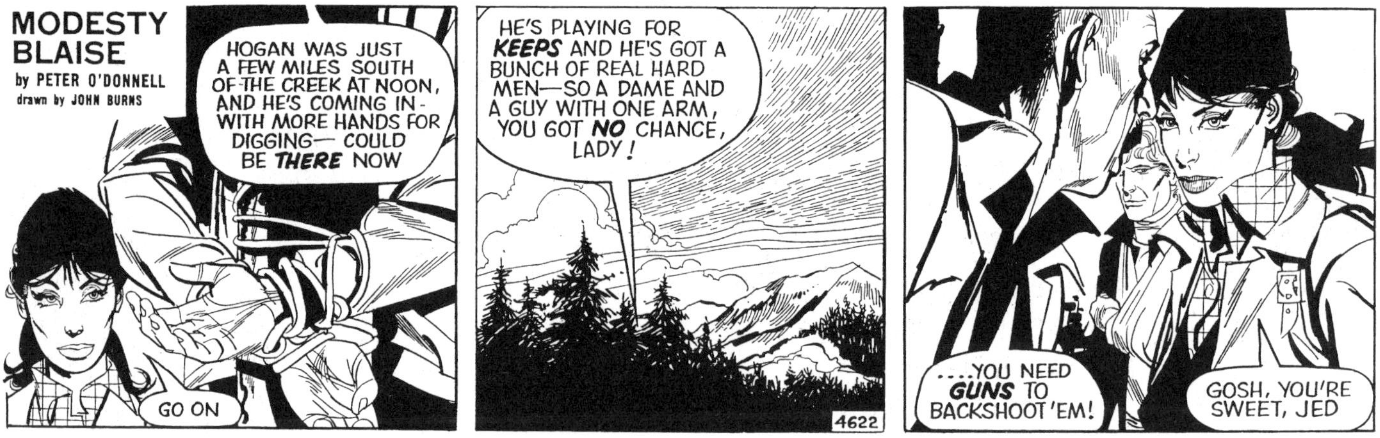
MODESTY BLAISE
by PETER O'DONNELL
drawn by JOHN BURNS
HOGAN WAS JUST A FEW MILES SOUTH OF THE CREEK AT NOON, AND HE'S COMING IN - WITH MORE HANDS FOR DIGGING— COULD BE THERE NOW
GO ON
HE'S PLAYING FOR KEEPS AND HE'S GOT A BUNCH OF REAL HARD MEN—SO A DAME AND A GUY WITH ONE ARM, YOU GOT NO CHANCE, LADY!
4622
....YOU NEED GUNS TO BACKSHOOT 'EM!
GOSH, YOU'RE SWEET, JED

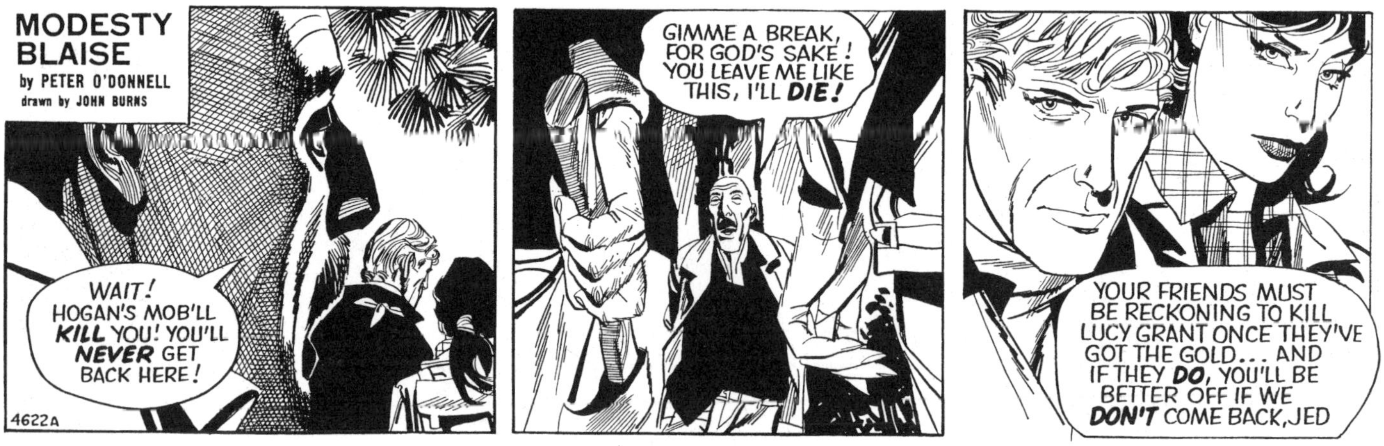
MODESTY BLAISE
by PETER O'DONNELL
drawn by JOHN BURNS
WAIT! HOGAN'S MOB'LL KILL YOU! YOU'LL NEVER GET BACK HERE!
4622A
GIMME A BREAK, FOR GOD'S SAKE! YOU LEAVE ME LIKE THIS, I'LL DIE!
YOUR FRIENDS MUST BE RECKONING TO KILL LUCY GRANT ONCE THEY'VE GOT THE GOLD... AND IF THEY DO, YOU'LL BE BETTER OFF IF WE DON'T COME BACK, JED

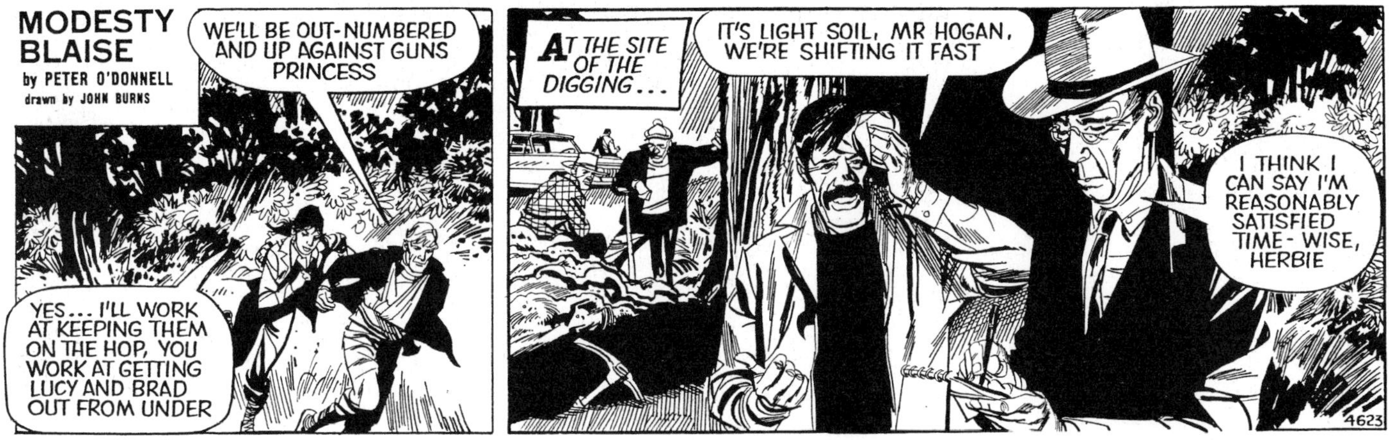
MODESTY BLAISE
by PETER O'DONNELL
drawn by JOHN BURNS
WE'LL BE OUT-NUMBERED AND UP AGAINST GUNS PRINCESS
YES... I'LL WORK AT KEEPING THEM ON THE HOP, YOU WORK AT GETTING LUCY AND BRAD OUT FROM UNDER
AT THE SITE OF THE DIGGING...
IT'S LIGHT SOIL, MR HOGAN, WE'RE SHIFTING IT FAST
I THINK I CAN SAY I'M REASONABLY SATISFIED TIME-WISE, HERBIE
4623

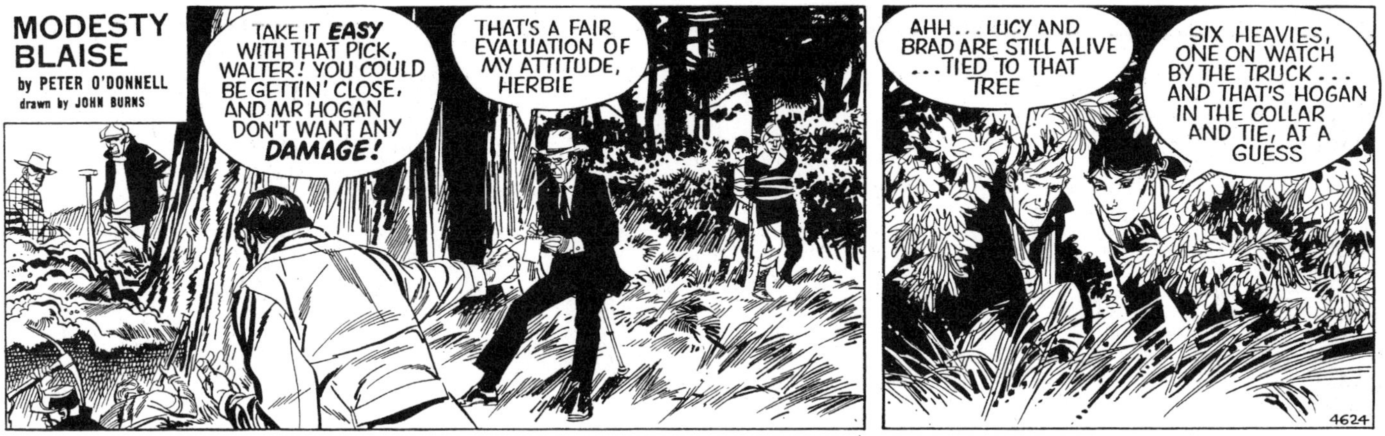
MODESTY BLAISE
by PETER O'DONNELL
drawn by JOHN BURNS
TAKE IT EASY WITH THAT PICK, WALTER! YOU COULD BE GETTIN' CLOSE, AND MR HOGAN DON'T WANT ANY DAMAGE!
THAT'S A FAIR EVALUATION OF MY ATTITUDE, HERBIE
AHH... LUCY AND BRAD ARE STILL ALIVE ...TIED TO THAT TREE
SIX HEAVIES, ONE ON WATCH BY THE TRUCK... AND THAT'S HOGAN IN THE COLLAR AND TIE, AT A GUESS
4624

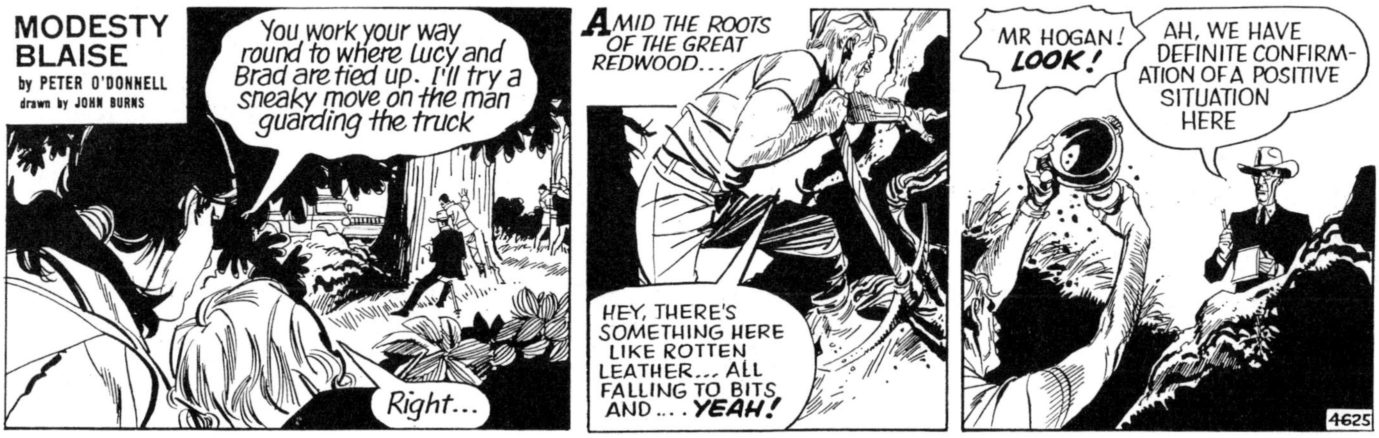
MODESTY BLAISE
by PETER O'DONNELL
drawn by JOHN BURNS
You work your way round to where Lucy and Brad are tied up. I'll try a sneaky move on the man guarding the truck
Right...
AMID THE ROOTS OF THE GREAT REDWOOD...
HEY, THERE'S SOMETHING HERE LIKE ROTTEN LEATHER... ALL FALLING TO BITS AND.... YEAH!
MR HOGAN! LOOK!
AH, WE HAVE DEFINITE CONFIRMATION OF A POSITIVE SITUATION HERE
4625

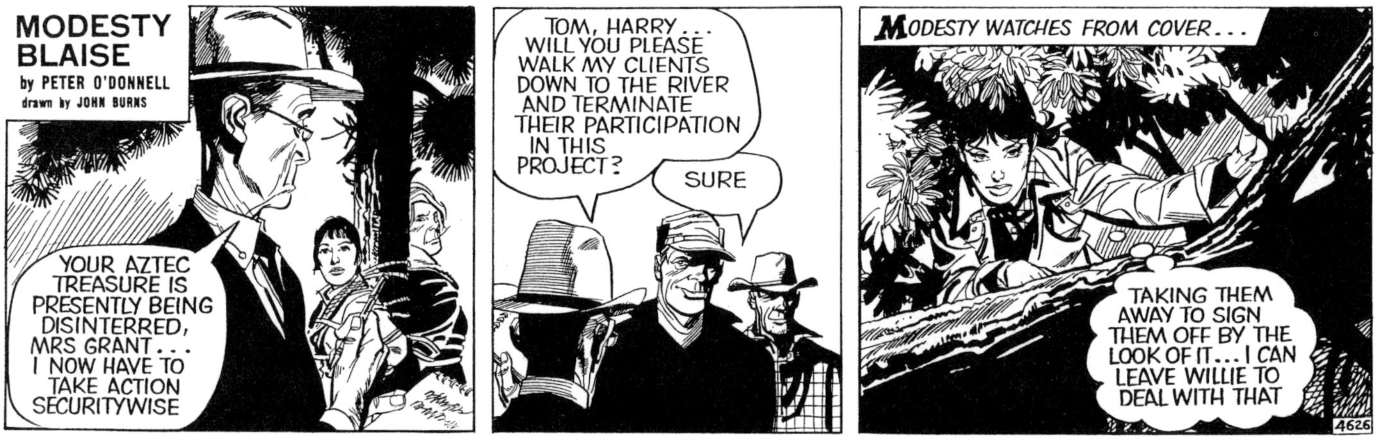
MODESTY BLAISE
by PETER O'DONNELL
drawn by JOHN BURNS
YOUR AZTEC TREASURE IS PRESENTLY BEING DISINTERRED, MRS GRANT... I NOW HAVE TO TAKE ACTION SECURITYWISE
TOM, HARRY... WILL YOU PLEASE WALK MY CLIENTS DOWN TO THE RIVER AND TERMINATE THEIR PARTICIPATION IN THIS PROJECT?
SURE
MODESTY WATCHES FROM COVER...
TAKING THEM AWAY TO SIGN THEM OFF BY THE LOOK OF IT... I CAN LEAVE WILLIE TO DEAL WITH THAT
4626

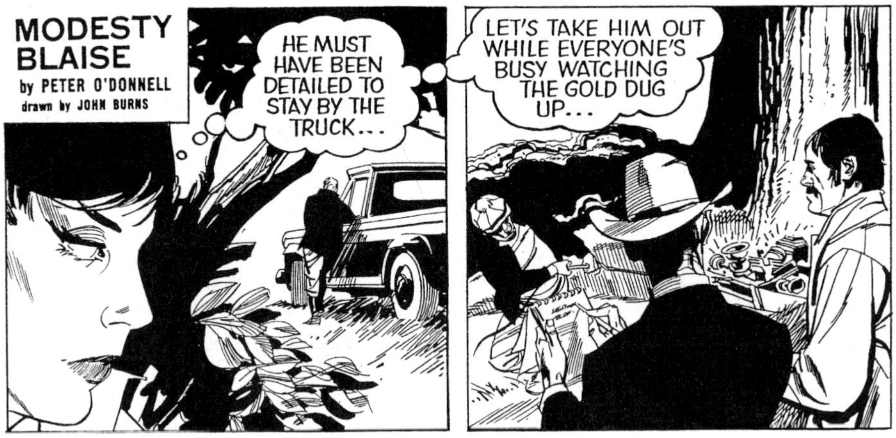
MODESTY BLAISE
by PETER O'DONNELL
drawn by JOHN BURNS
HE MUST HAVE BEEN DETAILED TO STAY BY THE TRUCK...
LET'S TAKE HIM OUT WHILE EVERYONE'S BUSY WATCHING THE GOLD DUG UP...
NEARER THE RIVER...
LISTEN, ARE YOU GOING TO KILL US?
WHAT ELSE? CAN'T LEAVE YOU AROUND TO TALK, CAN WE? BE REASONABLE, BABE
4627

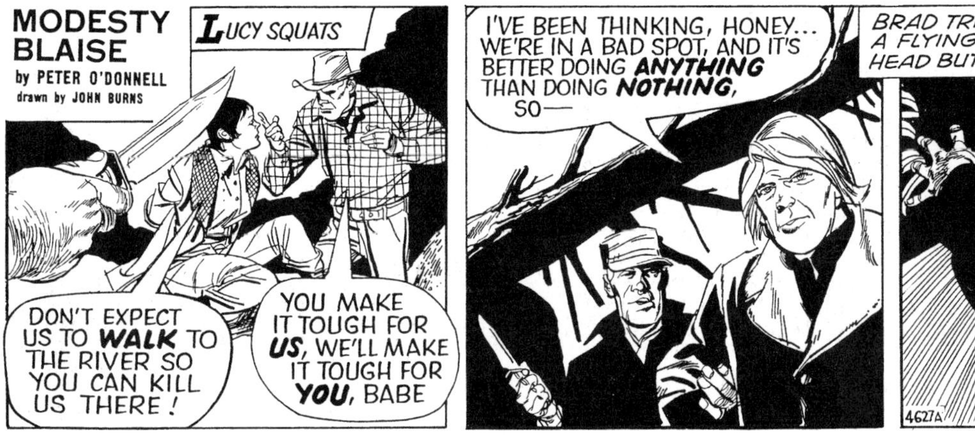
MODESTY BLAISE
by PETER O'DONNELL
drawn by JOHN BURNS
LUCY SQUATS
DON'T EXPECT US TO WALK TO THE RIVER SO YOU CAN KILL US THERE!
YOU MAKE IT TOUGH FOR US, WE'LL MAKE IT TOUGH FOR YOU, BABE
I'VE BEEN THINKING, HONEY... WE'RE IN A BAD SPOT, AND IT'S BETTER DOING ANYTHING THAN DOING NOTHING, SO—
BRAD TRIES A FLYING HEAD BUTT.
RUN, LUCY!
4627A

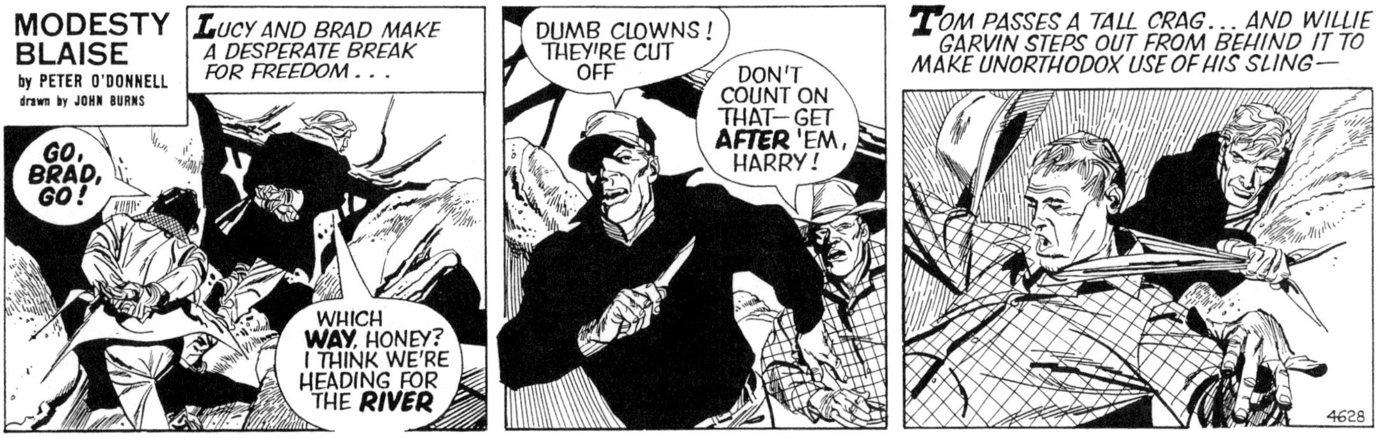
MODESTY BLAISE
by PETER O'DONNELL
drawn by JOHN BURNS
LUCY AND BRAD MAKE A DESPERATE BREAK FOR FREEDOM...
GO, BRAD, GO!
WHICH WAY, HONEY? I THINK WE'RE HEADING FOR THE RIVER
DUMB CLOWNS! THEY'RE CUT OFF
DON'T COUNT ON THAT— GET AFTER 'EM, HARRY!
TOM PASSES A TALL CRAG... AND WILLIE GARVIN STEPS OUT FROM BEHIND IT TO MAKE UNORTHODOX USE OF HIS SLING—
4628

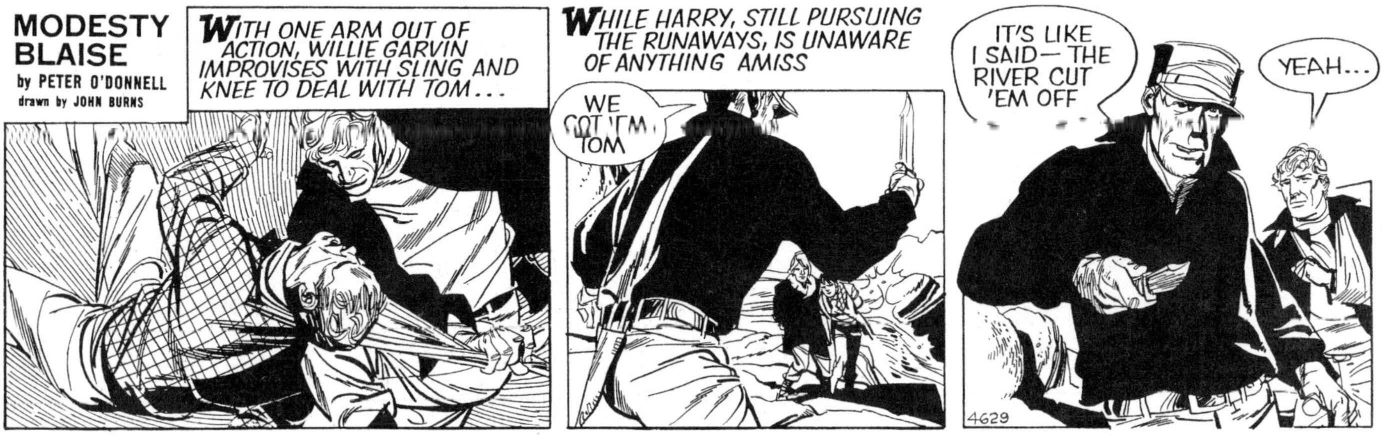
MODESTY BLAISE
by PETER O'DONNELL
drawn by JOHN BURNS
WITH ONE ARM OUT OF ACTION, WILLIE GARVIN IMPROVISES WITH SLING AND KNEE TO DEAL WITH TOM...
WHILE HARRY, STILL PURSUING THE RUNAWAYS, IS UNAWARE OF ANYTHING AMISS
WE GOT 'EM, TOM
IT'S LIKE I SAID— THE RIVER CUT 'EM OFF
YEAH...
4629

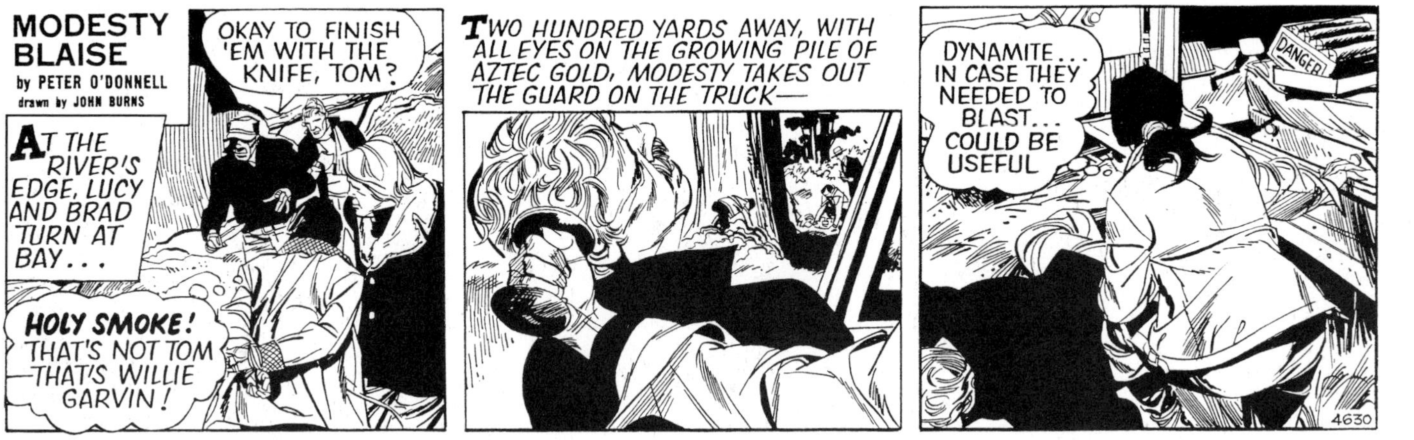
MODESTY BLAISE
by PETER O'DONNELL
drawn by JOHN BURNS
OKAY TO FINISH 'EM WITH THE KNIFE, TOM?
AT THE RIVER'S EDGE, LUCY AND BRAD TURN AT BAY...
HOLY SMOKE! THAT'S NOT TOM —THAT'S WILLIE GARVIN!
TWO HUNDRED YARDS AWAY, WITH ALL EYES ON THE GROWING PILE OF AZTEC GOLD, MODESTY TAKES OUT THE GUARD ON THE TRUCK—
DYNAMITE... IN CASE THEY NEEDED TO BLAST... COULD BE USEFUL
DANGER
4630

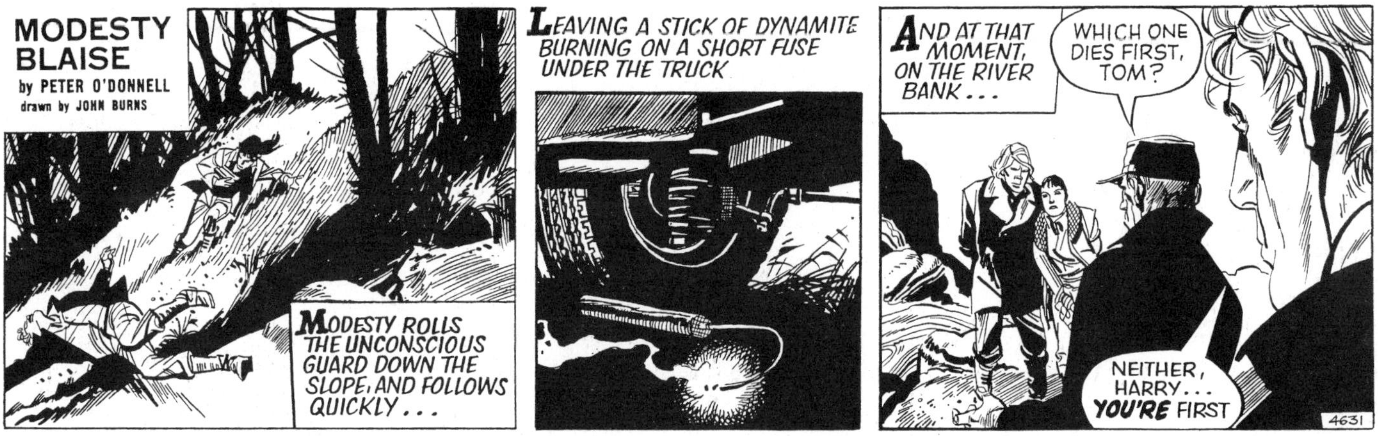
MODESTY BLAISE
by PETER O'DONNELL
drawn by JOHN BURNS
MODESTY ROLLS THE UNCONSCIOUS GUARD DOWN THE SLOPE, AND FOLLOWS QUICKLY...
LEAVING A STICK OF DYNAMITE BURNING ON A SHORT FUSE UNDER THE TRUCK
AND AT THAT MOMENT, ON THE RIVER BANK...
WHICH ONE DIES FIRST, TOM?
NEITHER, HARRY... YOU'RE FIRST
4631

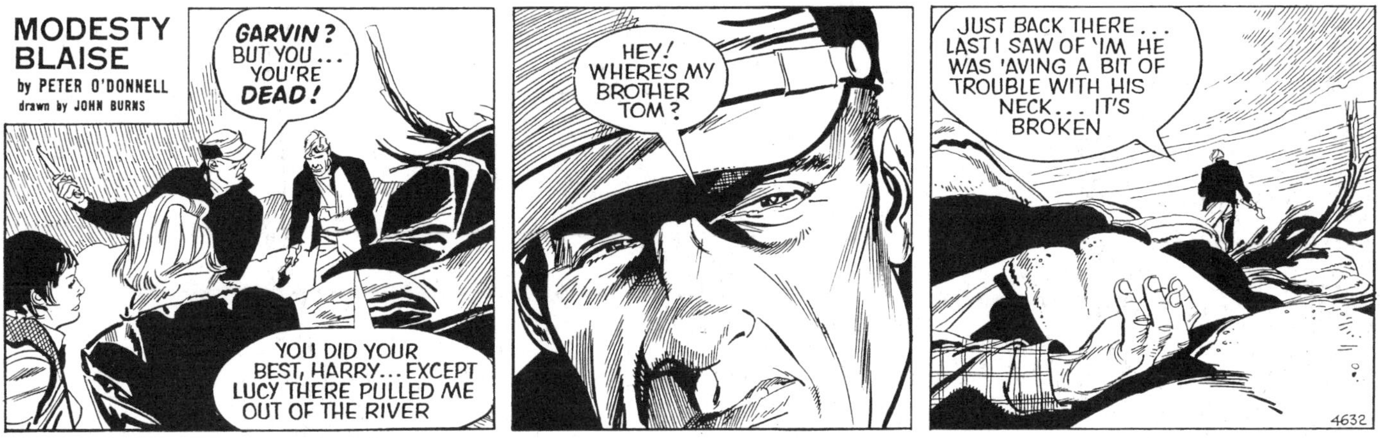
MODESTY BLAISE
by PETER O'DONNELL
drawn by JOHN BURNS
GARVIN? BUT YOU... YOU'RE DEAD!
YOU DID YOUR BEST, HARRY... EXCEPT LUCY THERE PULLED ME OUT OF THE RIVER
HEY! WHERE'S MY BROTHER TOM?
JUST BACK THERE... LAST I SAW OF 'IM HE WAS 'AVING A BIT OF TROUBLE WITH HIS NECK... IT'S BROKEN
4632

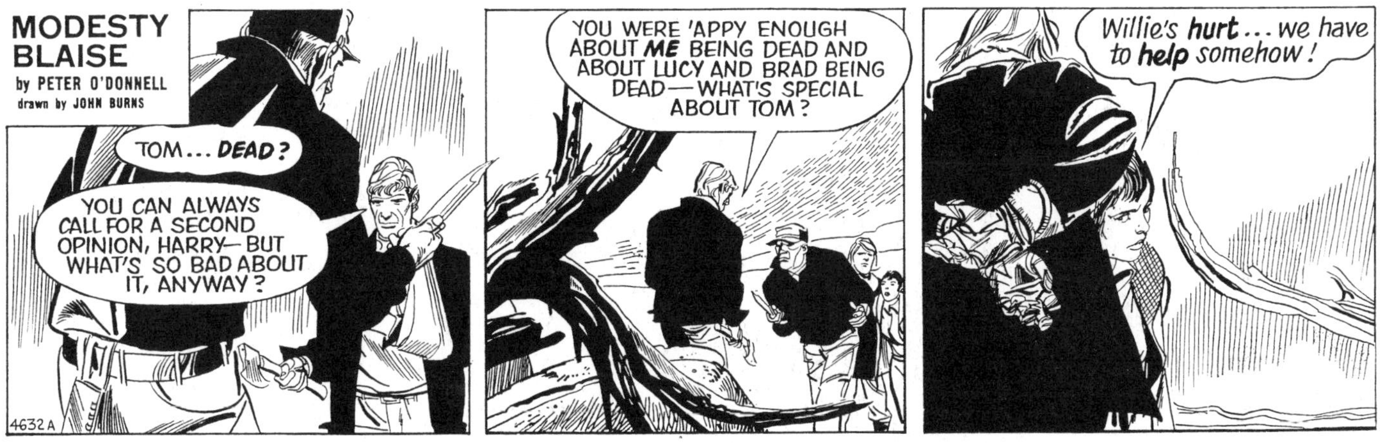
MODESTY BLAISE
by PETER O'DONNELL
drawn by JOHN BURNS
TOM... DEAD?
YOU CAN ALWAYS CALL FOR A SECOND OPINION, HARRY— BUT WHAT'S SO BAD ABOUT IT, ANYWAY?
4632 A
YOU WERE 'APPY ENOUGH ABOUT ME BEING DEAD AND ABOUT LUCY AND BRAD BEING DEAD — WHAT'S SPECIAL ABOUT TOM?
Willie's hurt... we have to help somehow!

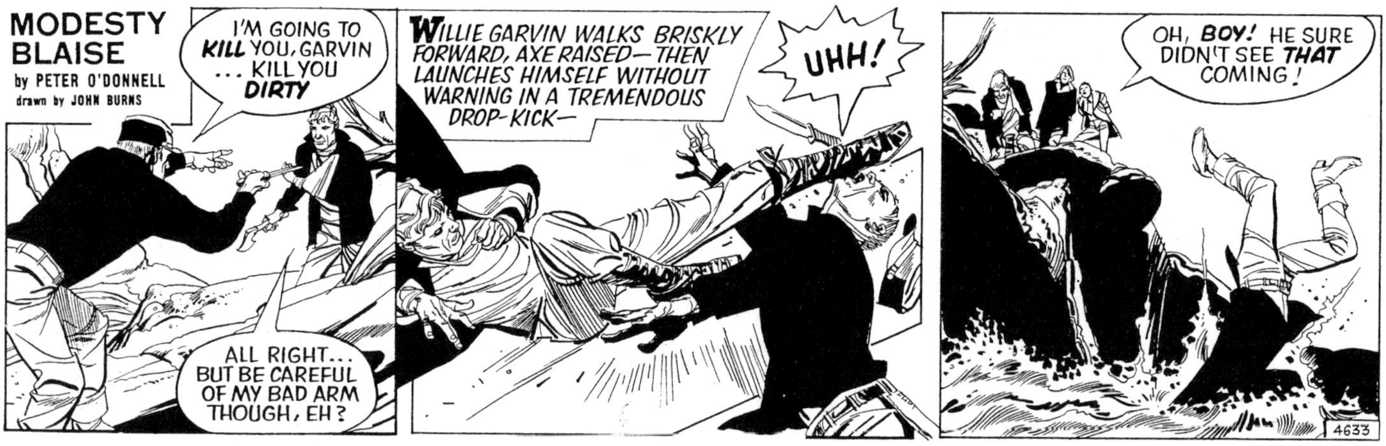
MODESTY BLAISE
by PETER O'DONNELL
drawn by JOHN BURNS
I'M GOING TO KILL YOU, GARVIN ... KILL YOU DIRTY
ALL RIGHT... BUT BE CAREFUL OF MY BAD ARM THOUGH, EH?
WILLIE GARVIN WALKS BRISKLY FORWARD, AXE RAISED—THEN LAUNCHES HIMSELF WITHOUT WARNING IN A TREMENDOUS DROP-KICK—
UHH!
OH, BOY! HE SURE DIDN'T SEE THAT COMING!
4633

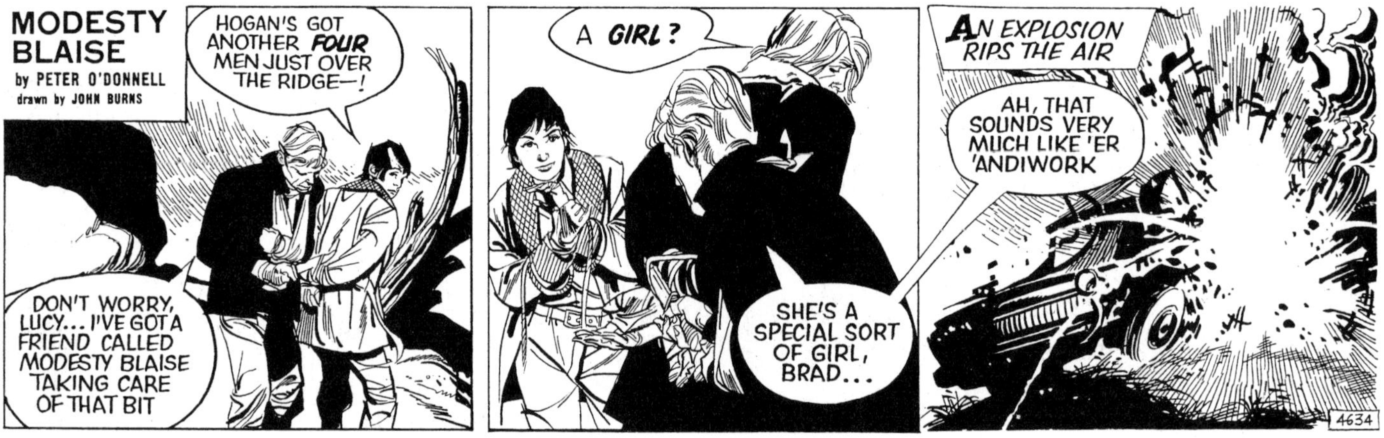
MODESTY BLAISE
by PETER O'DONNELL
drawn by JOHN BURNS
HOGAN'S GOT ANOTHER FOUR MEN JUST OVER THE RIDGE—!
DON'T WORRY, LUCY... I'VE GOT A FRIEND CALLED MODESTY BLAISE TAKING CARE OF THAT BIT
A GIRL?
SHE'S A SPECIAL SORT OF GIRL, BRAD...
AN EXPLOSION RIPS THE AIR
AH, THAT SOUNDS VERY MUCH LIKE 'ER 'ANDIWORK
4634

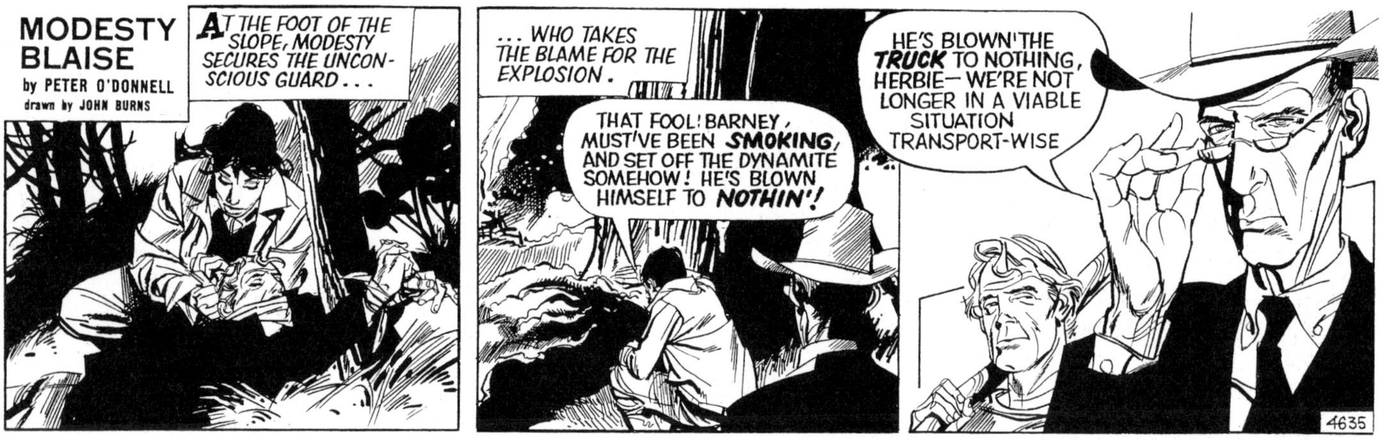
MODESTY BLAISE
by PETER O'DONNELL
drawn by JOHN BURNS
AT THE FOOT OF THE SLOPE, MODESTY SECURES THE UNCONSCIOUS GUARD...
... WHO TAKES THE BLAME FOR THE EXPLOSION.
THAT FOOL! BARNEY MUST'VE BEEN SMOKING, AND SET OFF THE DYNAMITE SOMEHOW! HE'S BLOWN HIMSELF TO NOTHIN'!
HE'S BLOWN THE TRUCK TO NOTHING, HERBIE— WE'RE NOT LONGER IN A VIABLE SITUATION TRANSPORT-WISE
4635

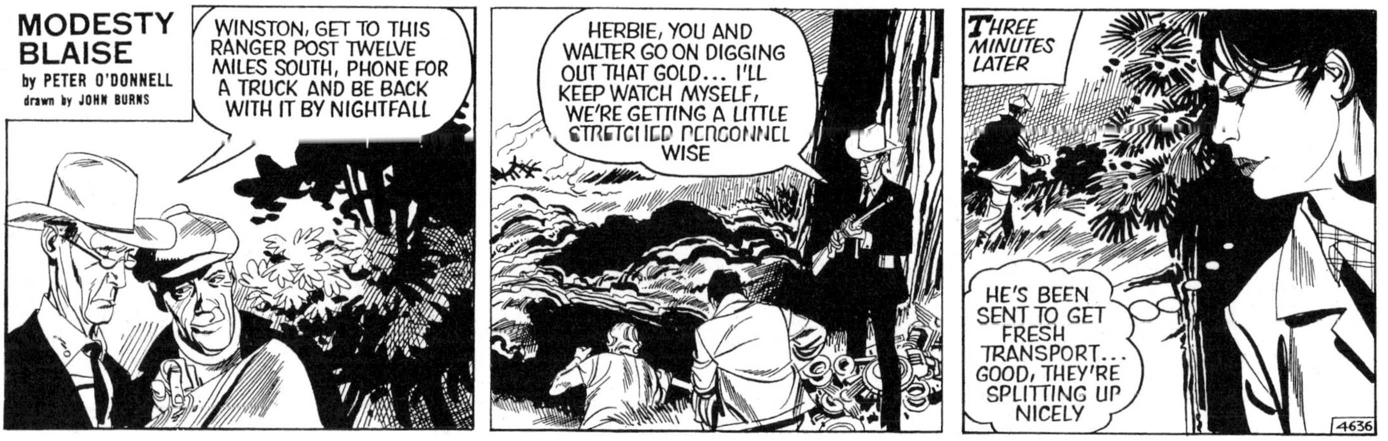
MODESTY BLAISE
by PETER O'DONNELL
drawn by JOHN BURNS
WINSTON, GET TO THIS RANGER POST TWELVE MILES SOUTH, PHONE FOR A TRUCK AND BE BACK WITH IT BY NIGHTFALL
HERBIE, YOU AND WALTER GO ON DIGGING OUT THAT GOLD... I'LL KEEP WATCH MYSELF, WE'RE GETTING A LITTLE STRETCHED PERSONNEL WISE
THREE MINUTES LATER
HE'S BEEN SENT TO GET FRESH TRANSPORT... GOOD, THEY'RE SPLITTING UP NICELY
4636

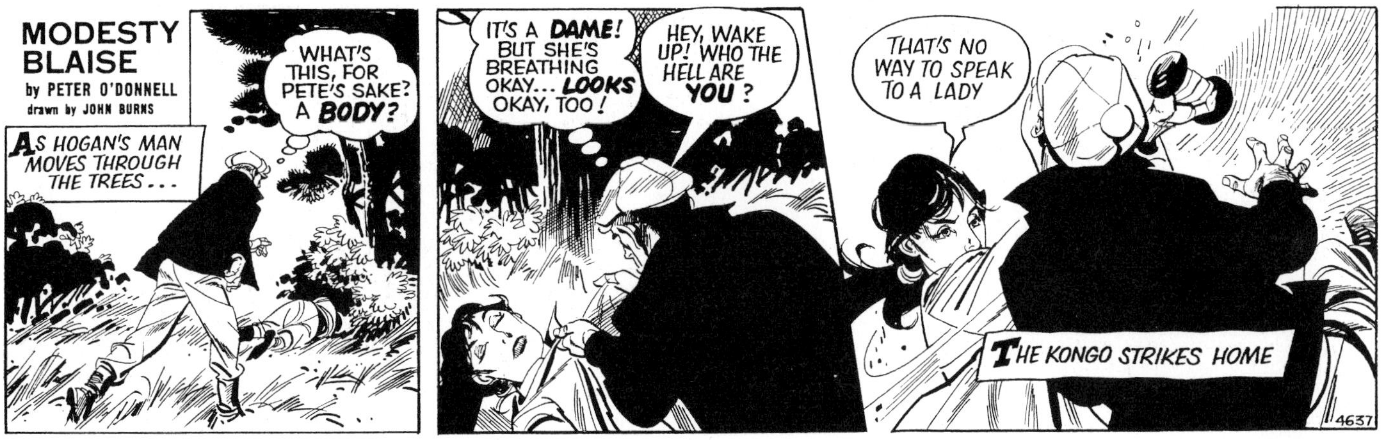
MODESTY BLAISE
by PETER O'DONNELL
drawn by JOHN BURNS
AS HOGAN'S MAN MOVES THROUGH THE TREES...
WHAT'S THIS, FOR PETE'S SAKE? A BODY?
IT'S A DAME! BUT SHE'S BREATHING OKAY... LOOKS OKAY, TOO!
HEY, WAKE UP! WHO THE HELL ARE YOU?
THAT'S NO WAY TO SPEAK TO A LADY
THE KONGO STRIKES HOME
4637

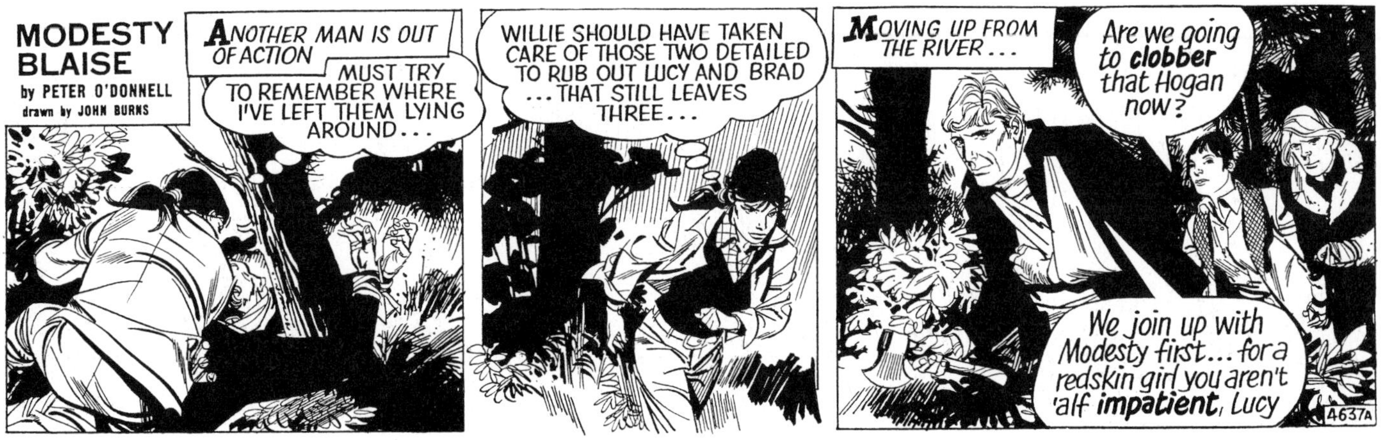
MODESTY BLAISE
by PETER O'DONNELL
drawn by JOHN BURNS
ANOTHER MAN IS OUT OF ACTION
MUST TRY TO REMEMBER WHERE I'VE LEFT THEM LYING AROUND...
WILLIE SHOULD HAVE TAKEN CARE OF THOSE TWO DETAILED TO RUB OUT LUCY AND BRAD ... THAT STILL LEAVES THREE...
MOVING UP FROM THE RIVER...
Are we going to clobber that Hogan now?
We join up with Modesty first... for a redskin girl you aren't 'alf impatient, Lucy
4637A

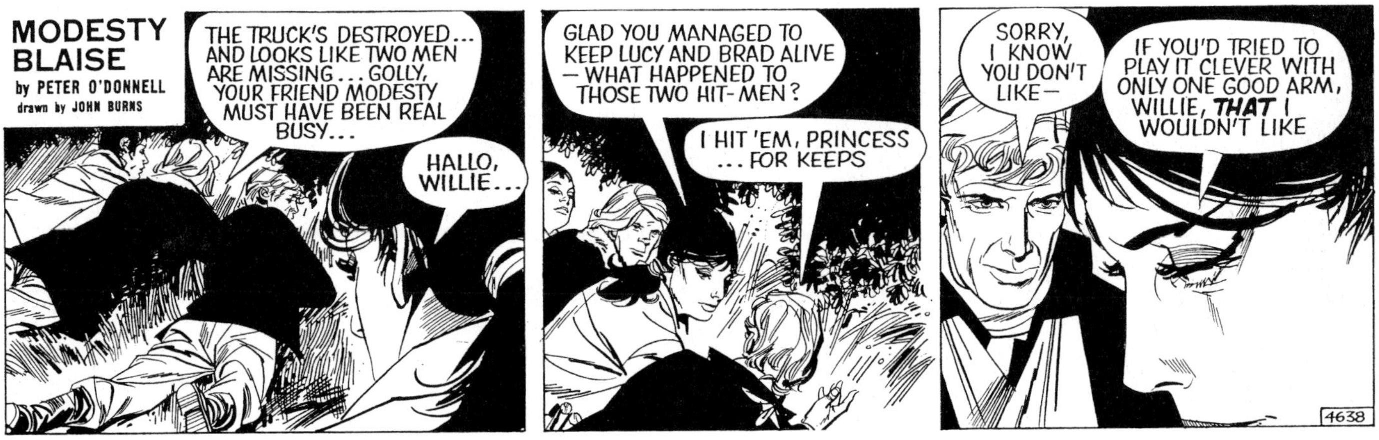
MODESTY BLAISE
by PETER O'DONNELL
drawn by JOHN BURNS
THE TRUCK'S DESTROYED... AND LOOKS LIKE TWO MEN ARE MISSING... GOLLY, YOUR FRIEND MODESTY MUST HAVE BEEN REAL BUSY...
HALLO, WILLIE...
GLAD YOU MANAGED TO KEEP LUCY AND BRAD ALIVE — WHAT HAPPENED TO THOSE TWO HIT-MEN?
I HIT 'EM, PRINCESS ... FOR KEEPS
SORRY, I KNOW YOU DON'T LIKE—
IF YOU'D TRIED TO PLAY IT CLEVER WITH ONLY ONE GOOD ARM, WILLIE, THAT I WOULDN'T LIKE
4638

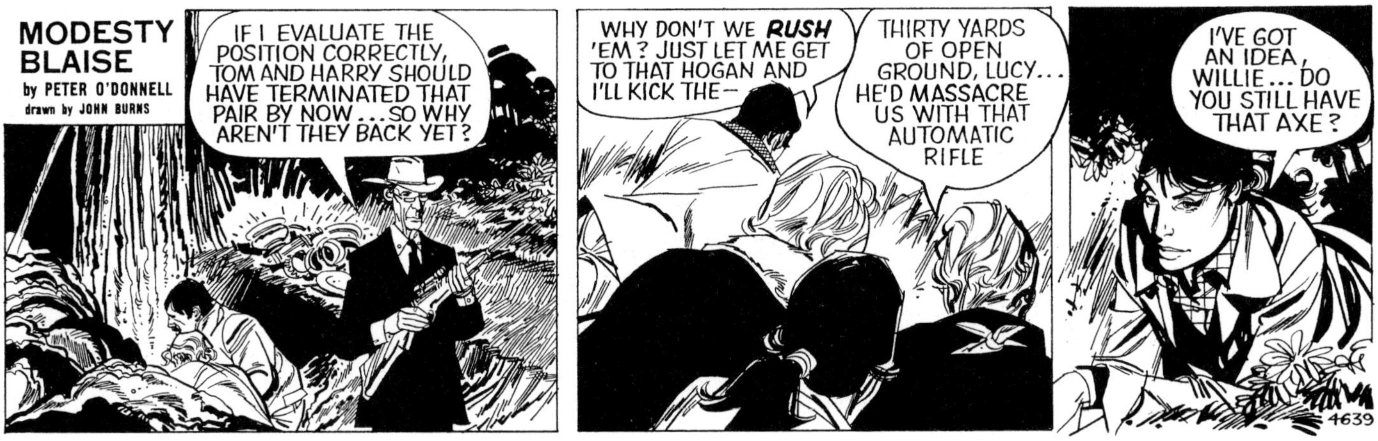
MODESTY BLAISE
by PETER O'DONNELL
drawn by JOHN BURNS
IF I EVALUATE THE POSITION CORRECTLY, TOM AND HARRY SHOULD HAVE TERMINATED THAT PAIR BY NOW... SO WHY AREN'T THEY BACK YET?
WHY DON'T WE RUSH 'EM? JUST LET ME GET TO THAT HOGAN AND I'LL KICK THE—
THIRTY YARDS OF OPEN GROUND, LUCY... HE'D MASSACRE US WITH THAT AUTOMATIC RIFLE
I'VE GOT AN IDEA, WILLIE... DO YOU STILL HAVE THAT AXE?
4639

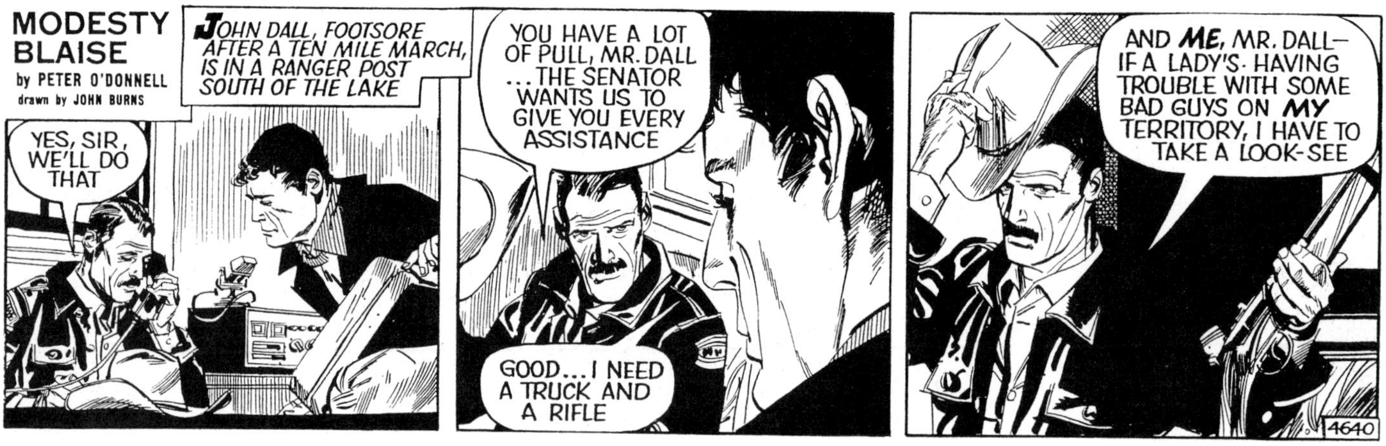
MODESTY BLAISE
by PETER O'DONNELL
drawn by JOHN BURNS
JOHN DALL, FOOTSORE AFTER A TEN MILE MARCH, IS IN A RANGER POST SOUTH OF THE LAKE
YES, SIR, WE'LL DO THAT
YOU HAVE A LOT OF PULL, MR. DALL ... THE SENATOR WANTS US TO GIVE YOU EVERY ASSISTANCE
GOOD... I NEED A TRUCK AND A RIFLE
AND ME, MR. DALL— IF A LADY'S HAVING TROUBLE WITH SOME BAD GUYS ON MY TERRITORY, I HAVE TO TAKE A LOOK-SEE
4640

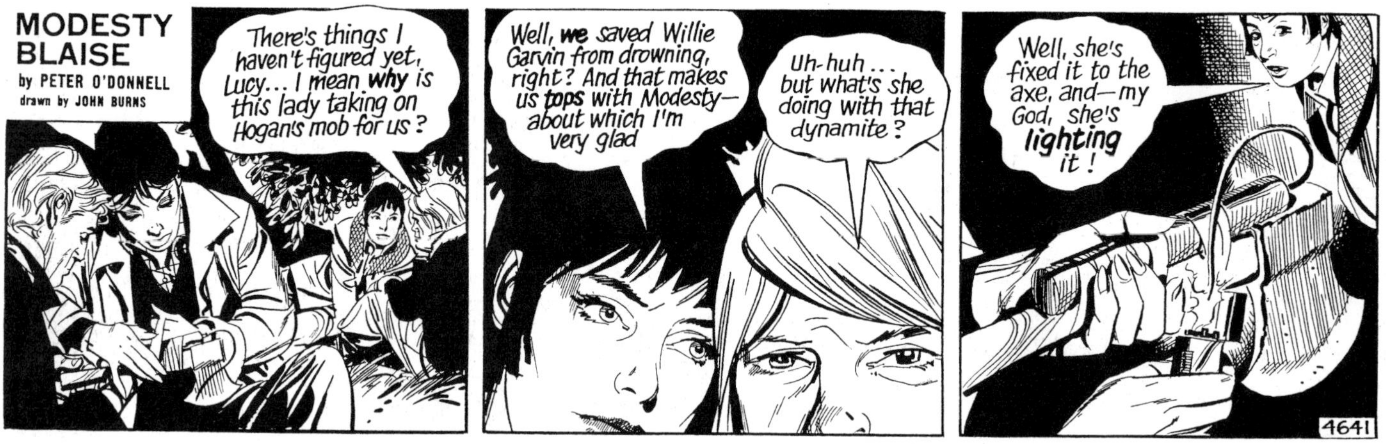
MODESTY BLAISE
by PETER O'DONNELL
drawn by JOHN BURNS
There's things I haven't figured yet, Lucy... I mean why is this lady taking on Hogan's mob for us?
Well, we saved Willie Garvin from drowning, right? And that makes us tops with Modesty— about which I'm very glad
Uh-huh... but what's she doing with that dynamite?
Well, she's fixed it to the axe, and—my God, she's lighting it!
4641

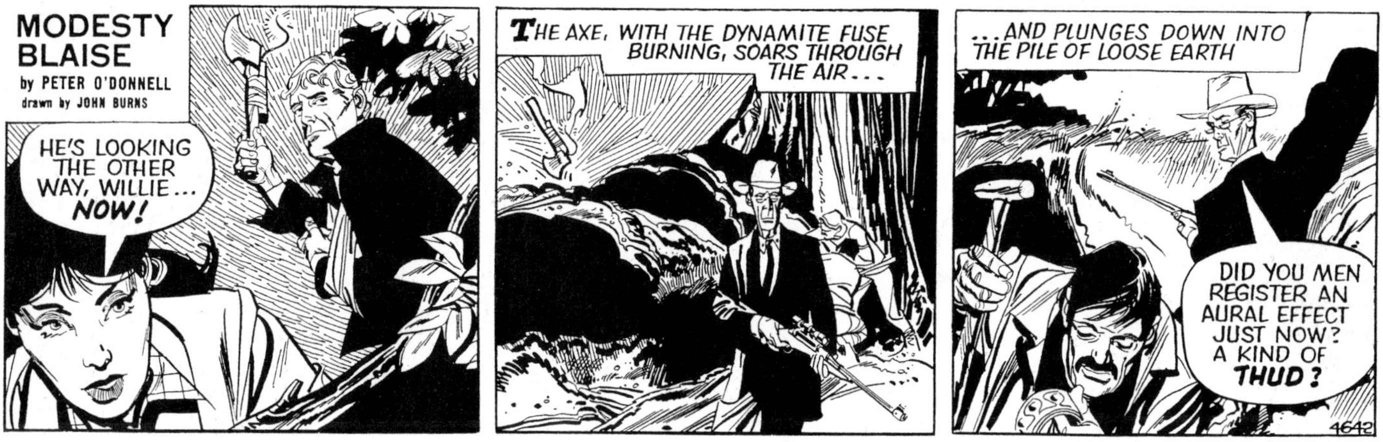
MODESTY BLAISE
by PETER O'DONNELL
drawn by JOHN BURNS
HE'S LOOKING THE OTHER WAY, WILLIE... NOW!
THE AXE, WITH THE DYNAMITE FUSE BURNING, SOARS THROUGH THE AIR...
...AND PLUNGES DOWN INTO THE PILE OF LOOSE EARTH
DID YOU MEN REGISTER AN AURAL EFFECT JUST NOW? A KIND OF THUD?
4642

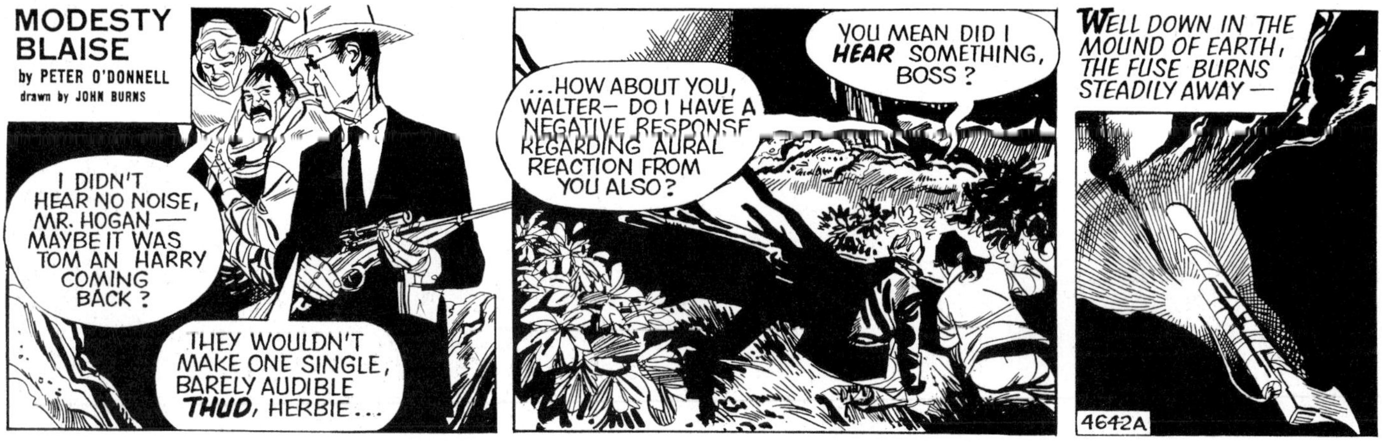
MODESTY BLAISE
by PETER O'DONNELL
drawn by JOHN BURNS
I DIDN'T HEAR NO NOISE, MR. HOGAN — MAYBE IT WAS TOM AN HARRY COMING BACK?
THEY WOULDN'T MAKE ONE SINGLE, BARELY AUDIBLE THUD, HERBIE...
...HOW ABOUT YOU, WALTER— DO I HAVE A NEGATIVE RESPONSE REGARDING AURAL REACTION FROM YOU ALSO?
YOU MEAN DID I HEAR SOMETHING, BOSS?
WELL DOWN IN THE MOUND OF EARTH, THE FUSE BURNS STEADILY AWAY—
4642A

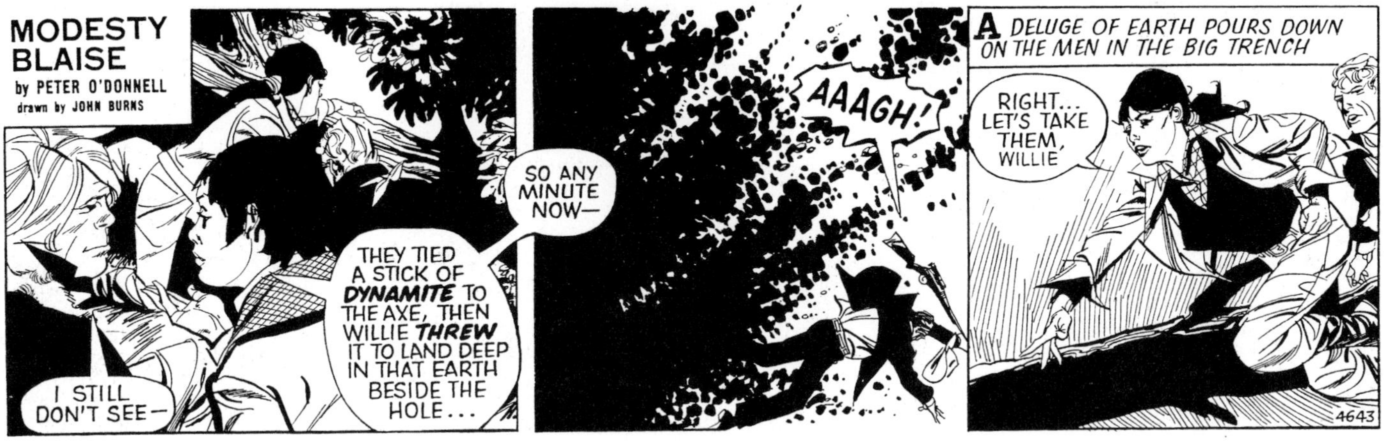
MODESTY BLAISE
by PETER O'DONNELL
drawn by JOHN BURNS
I STILL DON'T SEE—
THEY TIED A STICK OF **DYNAMITE** TO THE AXE, THEN WILLIE **THREW** IT TO LAND DEEP IN THAT EARTH BESIDE THE HOLE . . .
SO ANY MINUTE NOW—
AAAGH!
A DELUGE OF EARTH POURS DOWN ON THE MEN IN THE BIG TRENCH
RIGHT... LET'S TAKE THEM, WILLIE
4643

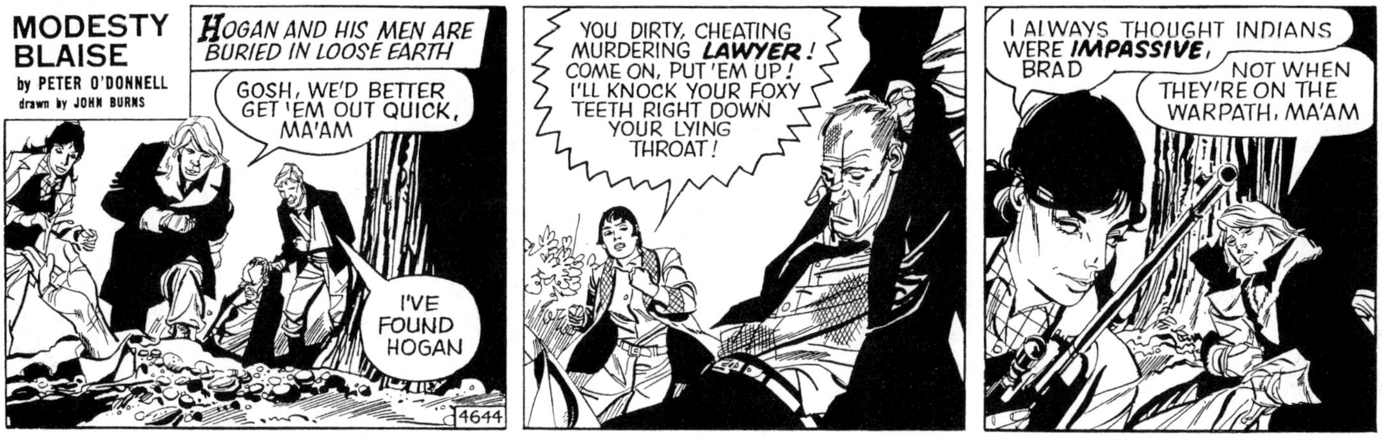
MODESTY BLAISE
by PETER O'DONNELL
drawn by JOHN BURNS
HOGAN AND HIS MEN ARE BURIED IN LOOSE EARTH
GOSH, WE'D BETTER GET 'EM OUT QUICK, MA'AM
I'VE FOUND HOGAN
4644
YOU DIRTY, CHEATING MURDERING **LAWYER**! COME ON, PUT 'EM UP! I'LL KNOCK YOUR FOXY TEETH RIGHT DOWN YOUR LYING THROAT!
I ALWAYS THOUGHT INDIANS WERE **IMPASSIVE**, BRAD
NOT WHEN THEY'RE ON THE WARPATH, MA'AM

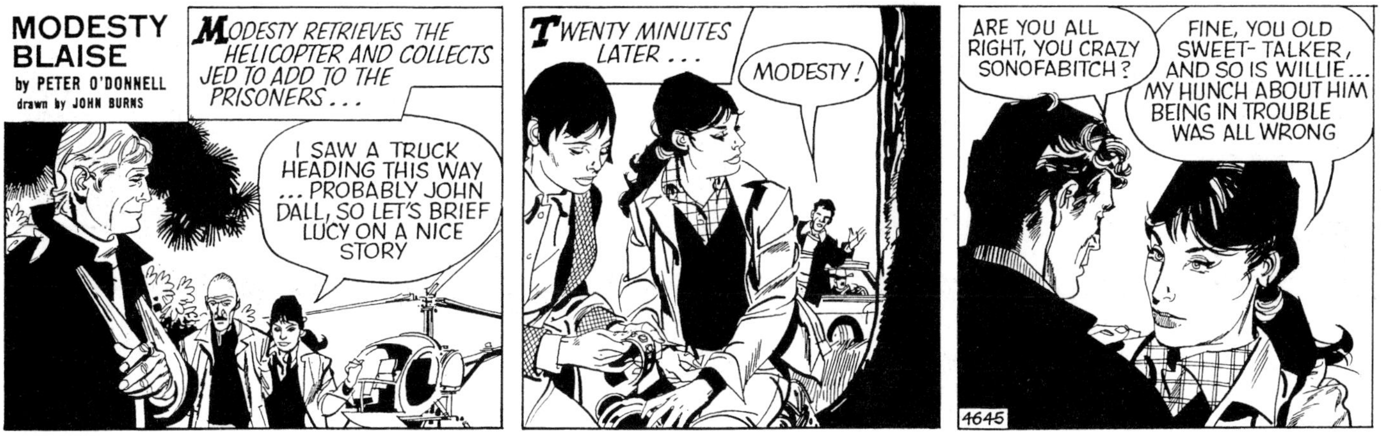
MODESTY BLAISE
by PETER O'DONNELL
drawn by JOHN BURNS
MODESTY RETRIEVES THE HELICOPTER AND COLLECTS JED TO ADD TO THE PRISONERS . . .
I SAW A TRUCK HEADING THIS WAY ... PROBABLY JOHN DALL, SO LET'S BRIEF LUCY ON A NICE STORY
TWENTY MINUTES LATER . . .
MODESTY!
ARE YOU ALL RIGHT, YOU CRAZY SONOFABITCH?
FINE, YOU OLD SWEET- TALKER, AND SO IS WILLIE... MY HUNCH ABOUT HIM BEING IN TROUBLE WAS ALL WRONG
4645

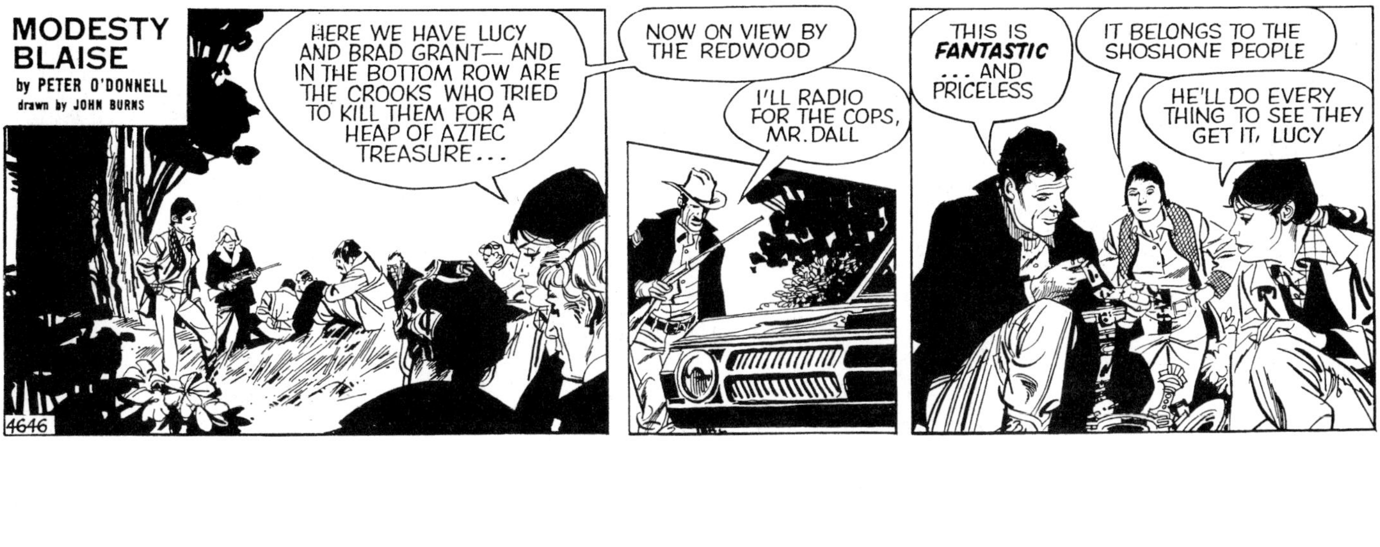
MODESTY BLAISE
by PETER O'DONNELL
drawn by JOHN BURNS
HERE WE HAVE LUCY AND BRAD GRANT— AND IN THE BOTTOM ROW ARE THE CROOKS WHO TRIED TO KILL THEM FOR A HEAP OF AZTEC TREASURE . . .
NOW ON VIEW BY THE REDWOOD
4646
I'LL RADIO FOR THE COPS, MR. DALL
THIS IS **FANTASTIC** . . . AND PRICELESS
IT BELONGS TO THE SHOSHONE PEOPLE
HE'LL DO EVERY THING TO SEE THEY GET IT, LUCY

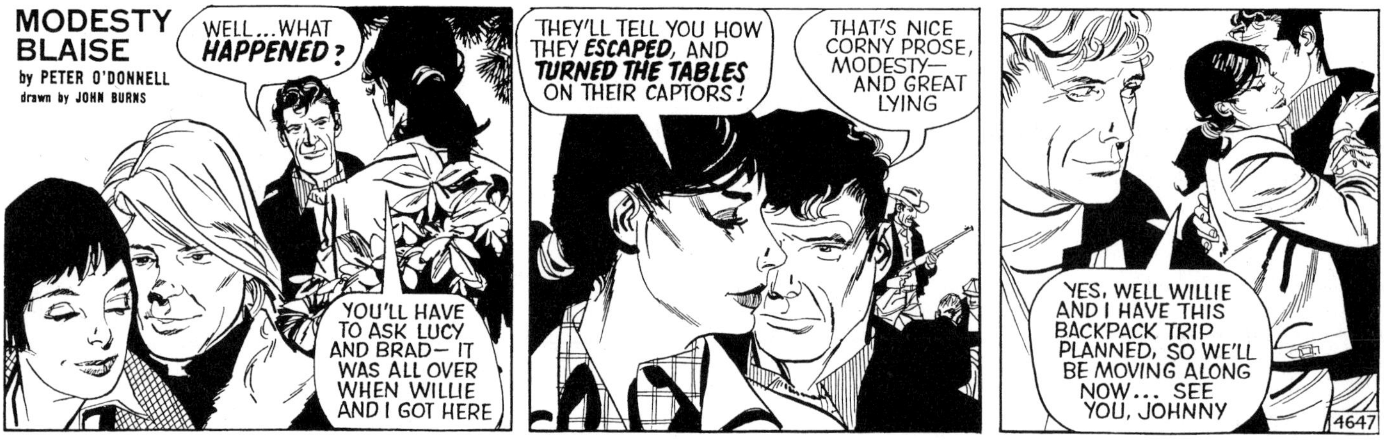
MODESTY BLAISE
by PETER O'DONNELL
drawn by JOHN BURNS
WELL... WHAT *HAPPENED*?
YOU'LL HAVE TO ASK LUCY AND BRAD— IT WAS ALL OVER WHEN WILLIE AND I GOT HERE
THEY'LL TELL YOU HOW THEY *ESCAPED*, AND *TURNED THE TABLES* ON THEIR CAPTORS!
THAT'S NICE CORNY PROSE, MODESTY— AND GREAT LYING
YES, WELL WILLIE AND I HAVE THIS BACKPACK TRIP PLANNED, SO WE'LL BE MOVING ALONG NOW... SEE YOU, JOHNNY
4647

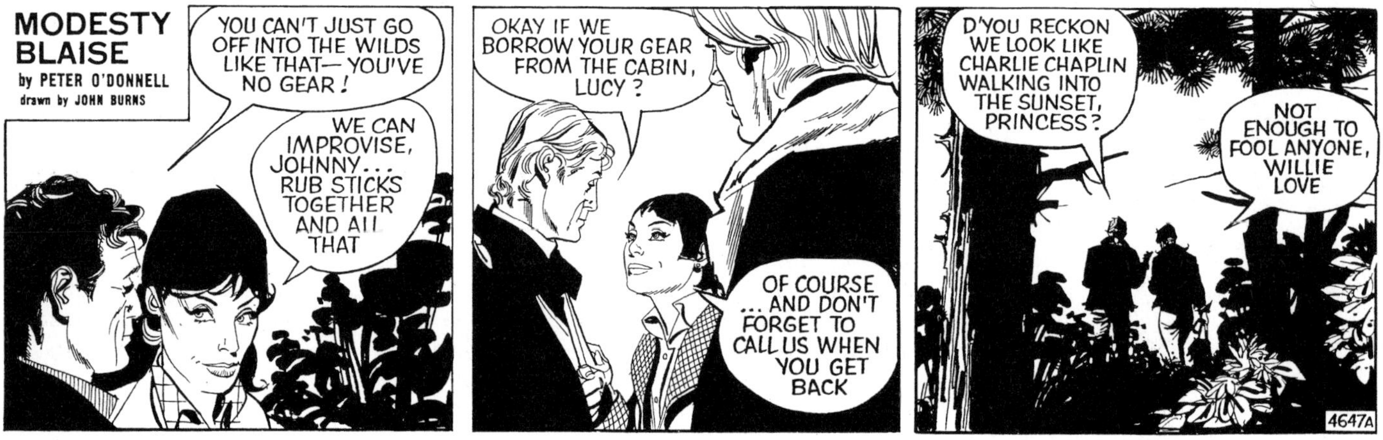
MODESTY BLAISE
by PETER O'DONNELL
drawn by JOHN BURNS
YOU CAN'T JUST GO OFF INTO THE WILDS LIKE THAT— YOU'VE NO GEAR!
WE CAN IMPROVISE, JOHNNY... RUB STICKS TOGETHER AND ALL THAT
OKAY IF WE BORROW YOUR GEAR FROM THE CABIN, LUCY?
OF COURSE ... AND DON'T FORGET TO CALL US WHEN YOU GET BACK
D'YOU RECKON WE LOOK LIKE CHARLIE CHAPLIN WALKING INTO THE SUNSET, PRINCESS?
NOT ENOUGH TO FOOL ANYONE, WILLIE LOVE
4647A

MODESTY BLAISE CHECKLIST

The following is a complete checklist of Modesty Blaise stories that have appeared in the London Evening Standard. All stories were written by Peter O'Donnell.

GLOSSARY

KEY TO ARTISTS

JH = Jim Holdaway

ER = Enric Badia Romero

JB = John Burns

PW = Pat Wright

NC = Neville Colvin

DATES

13/5/63 = 13th May 1963

SERIAL NUMBERS

Each serial number represents a day. When the Evening Standard stopped publishing on Saturdays the suffix 'a' (e.g. 3638a) was introduced for those papers in syndication that wanted a Saturday Modesty Blaise; the Standard did not run these strips.

*This story was written and drawn in 66 for syndication only to introduce the character to its new audience.

**This story was written for the *Glasgow Evening Citizen*, an associated newspaper of the *Evening Standard*, to cover a break in publication of Story 14 in the *Evening Standard* due to an industrial dispute in London.

Many thanks to Trevor York and Lawrence Blackmore for their help in compiling this list.

STORY	ARTIST	DATE	SERIAL No.
1. La Machine	JH	13/05/63 - 21/09/63	1-114
2. The Long Lever	JH	23/09/63 - 02/01/64	115-211
3. The Gabriel Set-Up	JH	03/01/64 - 18/06/64	212-354
4. Mister Sun	JH	19/06/64 - 05/12/64	355-500
5. The Mind of Mrs Drake	JH	07/12/64 - 19/04/65	501-612
6. Uncle Happy	JH	20/04/65 - 18/09/65	613-743
7. Top Traitor	JH	20/09/65 - 19/02/66	744-873
8. The Vikings	JH	21/02/66 - 9/07/66	874-992
8A. In The Beginning	JH	1966	(1-12) *
9. The Head Girls	JH	11/07/66 - 10/12/66	993-1124
10. The Black Pearl	JH	12/12/66 - 22/04/67	1125-1235
11. The Magnified Man	JH	24/04/67 - 02/09/67	1236-1349
12. The Jericho Caper	JH	04/09/67 - 13/01/68	1350-1461
13. Bad Suki	JH	15/01/68 - 25/05/68	1462-1574
14. The Galley Slaves (Part 1)	JH	27/05/68 - 06/08/68	1575-1630
14A. The Killing Ground	JH	11/09/68 - 16/11/68	(A1-A36) **
14B. The Galley Slaves (Part 2)	JH	11/09/68 - 16/11/68	1630a-1688
15. The Red Gryphon	JH	18/11/68 - 22/03/69	1689-1794
16. The Hell-Makers	JH	24/03/69 - 16/08/69	1795-1919
17. Take-Over	JH	18/08/69 - 10/01/70	1920-2043
18. The War-Lords of Phoenix	JH/ER	12/01/70 - 30/05/70	2044-2162
19. Willie the Djinn	ER	01/06/70 - 17/10/70	2163-2282
20. The Green-Eyed Monster	ER	19/10/70 - 20/02/71	2283-2388
21. Death of a Jester	ER	22/02/71 - 10/07/71	2389-2507
22. The Stone Age Caper	ER	12/07/71 - 27/11/71	2508-2627
23. The Puppet Master	ER	29/11/71 - 08/04/72	2628-2738
24. With Love From Rufus	ER	10/04/72 - 12/08/72	2739-2846
25. The Bluebeard Affair	ER	14/08/72 - 06/01/73	2847-2970
26. The Gallows Bird	ER	08/01/73 - 12/05/73	2971-3077
27. The Wicked Gnomes	ER	14/05/73 - 29/09/73	3078-3197
28. The Iron God	ER	01/10/73 - 09/02/74	3198-3309
29. "Take Me To Your Leader…"	ER	11/02/74 - 01/07/74	3310-3428
30. Highland Witch	ER	02/07/74 - 16/11/74	3429-3548
31. Cry Wolf	ER	18/11/74 - 25/03/75	3549-3638 a
32. The Reluctant Chaperon	ER	26/03/75 - 14/08/75	3639-3737 a
33. The Greenwood Maid	ER	15/08/75 - 02/01/76	3738-3829 a
34. Those About To Die	ER	05/01/76 - 28/05/76	3830-3931 a
35. The Inca Trail	ER	01/06/76 - 20/10/76	3932-4031 a
36. The Vanishing Dollybirds	ER	21/10/76 - 28/03/77	4032-4141 a
37. The Junk Men	ER	29/03/77 - 19/08/77	4142-4241 a
38. Death Trap	ER	22/08/77 - 20/10/78	4242-4341 a
39. Idaho George	ER	23/01/78 - 16/06/78	4342-4447 a
40. The Golden Frog	ER	19/06/78 - 31/10/78	4448-4542 a
41. Yellowstone Booty	JB	01/11/78 - 30/03/79	4543-4647 a
42. Green Cobra	JB	02/04/79 - 10/08/79	4648-4737 a
43. Eve and Adam	JB/PW	13/08/79 - 04/01/80	4738-4837 a
44. Brethren of Blaise	PW	07/01/80 - 23/05/80	4838-4932 a
45. Dossier on Pluto	NC	27/05/80 - 14/10/80	4933-5032 a
46. The Lady Killers	NC	15/10/80 - 03/03/81	5033-5127 a
47. Garvin's Travels	NC	04/03/81 - 27/07/81	5128-5229 a
48. The Scarlet Maiden	NC	28/07/81 - 16/12/81	5230-5329 a
49. The Moonman	NC	17/12/81 - 07/05/82	5330-5424 a
50. A Few Flowers for the Colonel	NC	10/05/82 - 24/09/82	5425-5519 a
51. The Ballonatic	NC	27/09/82 - 18/02/83	5520-5619 a
52. Death in Slow Motion	NC	21/02/83 - 15/07/83	5620-5719 a
53. The Alternative Man	NC	18/07/83 - 28/11/83	5720-5814 a
54. Sweet Caroline	NC	29/11/83 - 19/04/84	5815-5914 a
55. The Return of the Mammoth	NC	24/04/84 - 14/09/84	5915-6014 a
56. Plato's Republic	NC	17/09/84 - 06/02/85	6015-6114 a
57. The Sword of the Bruce	NC	07/02/85 - 02/07/85	6115-6214 a
58. The Wild Boar	NC	03/07/85 - 20/11/85	6215-6314 a
59. Kali's Disciples	NC	21/11/85 - 16/04/86	6315-6414 a
60. The Double Agent	NC	17/04/86 - 15/09/86	6415-6519 a
61. Butch Cassidy Rides Again	ER	16/09/86 - 12/02/87	6520-6624 a
62. Million Dollar Game	ER	13/02/87 - 08/07/87	6625-6724 a
63. The Vampire of Malvescu	ER	09/07/87 - 03/12/87	6725-6829 a
64. Samantha and the Cherub	ER	04/12/87 - 06/05/88	6830-6934 a
65. Milord	ER	09/05/88 - 27/09/88	6935-7034 a
66. Live Bait	ER	28/09/88 - 17/02/89	7035-7134 a
67. The Girl from the Future	ER	20/02/89 - 21/07/89	7135-7239 a
68. The Big Mole	ER	24/07/89 - 11/12/89	7240-7339 a
69. Lady in the Dark	ER	12/12/89 - 08/05/90	7340-7439 a
70. Fiona	ER	09/05/90 - 09/10/90	7440-7544 a
71. Walkabout	ER	10/10/90 - 11/03/91	7545-7649 a
72. The Girl in the Iron Mask	ER	12/03/91 - 02/08/91	7650-7749 a
73. The Young Mistress	ER	05/08/91 - 06/01/92	7750-7854 a
74. Ivory Dancer	ER	07/01/92 - 05/06/92	7855-7959 a
75. Our Friend Maude	ER	08/06/92 - 02/11/92	7960-8064 a
76. A Present for the Princess	ER	03/11/92 - 08/04/93	8065-8174 a
77. Black Queen's Pawn	ER	13/04/93 - 10/09/93	8175-8279 a
78. The Grim Joker	ER	13/09/93 - 09/02/94	8280-8384 a
79. Guido the Jinx	ER	10/02/94 - 05/07/94	8385-8484 a
80. The Killing Distance	ER	06/07/94 - 30/11/94	8485-8589 a
81. The Aristo	ER	01/12/94 - 03/05/95	8590-8694 a
82. Ripper Jax	ER	04/05/95 - 02/10/95	8695-8799 a
83. The Maori Contract	ER	03/10/95 - 01/03/96	8800-8904 a
84. Honeygun	ER	04/03/96 - 02/08/96	8905-9009 a
85. Durango	ER	05/08/96 - 03/01/97	9010-9114 a
86. The Murder Frame	ER	06/01/97 - 06/06/97	9115-9219 a
87. Fraser's Story	ER	09/06/97 - 03/11/97	9220-9324 a
88. Tribute of the Pharaoh	ER	04/11/97 - 03/04/98	9325-9429 a
89. The Special Orders	ER	06/04/98 - 04/09/98	9430-9534 a
90. The Hanging Judge	ER	07/09/98 - 10/02/99	9535-9644 a
91. Children of Lucifer	ER	11/02/99 - 13/07/99	9645-9749 a
92. Death Symbol	ER	14/07/99 - 15/12/99	9750-9859 a
93. The Last Aristocrat	ER	16/12/99 - 19/05/00	9860-9964 a
94. The Killing Game	ER	22/05/00 - 17/10/00	9965-10069 a
95. The Zombie	ER	18/10/00 - 11/04/01	10070-10183

The Dark Angels (with art by Enric Badia Romero): This story first appeared in *Comics Revue* #200 in a longer comic strip form and is not included in this checklist as it is not a true strip story.

MODESTY IS THE BEST POLICY!

MODESTY
Blaise
THE GABRIEL SET-UP
PETER O'DONNELL
JIM HOLDAWAY

The Gabriel Set-Up
Also features *La Machine, The Long Lever & In The Beginning*
ISBN-13: 9781840236583

MISTER SUN
MODESTY
Blaise
PETER O'DONNELL
JIM HOLDAWAY

Mister Sun
Also features *The Mind of Mrs Drake & Uncle Happy*
ISBN-13: 9781840237214

TOP TRAITOR
MODESTY
Blaise
PETER O'DONNELL
JIM HOLDAWAY

Top Traitor
Also features *The Vikings & The Head Girls*
ISBN-13: 9781840236842

THE BLACK PEARL
MODESTY
Blaise
PETER O'DONNELL
JIM HOLDAWAY

The Black Pearl
Also features *The Magnified Man, The Jericho Caper & The Killing Ground*
ISBN-13: 9781840238426

BAD SUKI
MODESTY
Blaise
PETER O'DONNELL
JIM HOLDAWAY

Bad Suki
Also features *The Galley Slaves & The Red Gryphon*
ISBN-13: 978184023864

MODESTY
Blaise
PETER O'DONNELL
JIM HOLDAWAY
ENRIC BADIA ROMERO
THE HELL MAKERS

The Hell-Makers
Also features *Take-Over & The War-Lords of Phoenix*
ISBN-13: 978184023865

THE GREEN-EYED MONSTER
MODESTY
Blaise
PETER O'DONNELL
ENRIC BADIA ROMERO

The Green-Eyed Monster
Also features *Willie the Djinn & Death of a Jester*
ISBN-13: 9781840238662

THE PUPPET MASTER
MODESTY
Blaise
PETER O'DONNELL
ENRIC BADIA ROMERO

The Puppet Master
Also features *The Stone Age Caper & With Love From Rufus*
ISBN-13: 9781840238679

MODESTY
Blaise
THE GALLOWS BIRD
PETER O'DONNELL
ENRIC BADIA ROMERO

The Gallows Bird
Also features *The Bluebeard Affair, The Wicked Gnomes & The Iron God*
ISBN-13: 9781840238686

CRY WOLF
MODESTY
Blaise
PETER O'DONNELL
ENRIC BADIA ROMERO

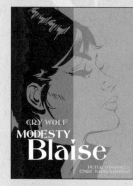

Cry Wolf
Also features *Take Me To Your Leader & Highland Witch*
ISBN-13: 9781840238693

THE INCA TRAIL
MODESTY
Blaise
PETER O'DONNELL
ENRIC BADIA ROMERO

The Inca Trail
Also features *The Reluctant Chaperon, The Greenwood Maid & Those About To Die*
ISBN-13 9781845764180

DEATH TRAP
MODESTY
Blaise
PETER O'DONNELL
ENRIC BADIA ROMERO

Death Trap
Also features *The Vanishing Dollybirds & The Junk Men*
ISBN-13: 9781845764180

GREEN COBRA
MODESTY
Blaise

Green Cobra
COMING SEPTEMBER 2008
ISBN-13: 9781845764203